WORLD OF WARCRAFT

TABLE OF CONTENTS

BACK INTO THE BREACH

The first Dungeon Companion for World of Warcraft did a very good job of covering the vast majority of the dungeon and raid content of its day. Due to the publishing date of the first book, Naxxramas could not be included. With the release of The Burning Crusade, there is now time and content to warrant a heroic return, with 15 new dungeons covered, Naxxramas in all its glory, and the new raid dungeons/encounters of the expansion all explained. The template has been improved for even more ease of use and visual style, and the level of detail is better than ever.

Heroic Mode tips, more thorough boss strategies, and complete walkthroughs for everywhere you want to go are crammed inside this book. Now you don't have to look up information from ten different sources before going into a new dungeon. We'll tell you what your class and character can bring, how to make it through with a variety of crowd control and damage options, and what you'll earn as each boss falls.

Whether you are clearing Karazhan, frustrated by Gruul, or just stepping into Hellfire Ramparts for the first time, this book is a powerful weapon that you won't need to farm. It's here now.

PART OF THE TEAM

The guide covers the instances and raids in World of Warcraft, giving players the maps, walkthroughs, strategy, item information, and tips to make it through the many encounters. We won't take much time before driving right into the heart of things, but there are several general strategies and roles within this guide's context that are useful to explain. Read through this primer on dungeon and raid skills and roles, then get to the fun stuff!

This section contains some of the tried-and-true tips that have been accurate as long as the game has gone live. In addition, new aspects of gameplay and items in The Burning Crusade are discussed here to give you further means of advancing your characters.

GROUP DYNAMICS

ROLES

Unlike soloing, group roles demand fewer things from a character yet more from what they excel in doing. Out in the field, alone, even a tanking character needs to be able to deal damage, mitigate damage, and restore their health (with First Aid, Food, and so forth). That isn't the way of things in a group. There, a tank NEEDS to be able to mitigate damage while generating as much Threat as possible. Bandaging, dealing maximum damage, and other concerns fall to the back of the list when compared with the power of intercepting the deadliest foes and keeping them off of healers and softer damage dealers.

The first issue of group roles is to determine who will be doing what. The following list explains the slots of a group.

Main Tank (MT): A Primary damage mitigater with high health, armor, and abilities to reduce incoming damage or extend survivability. Equipment and Talents that add to a Main Tank's Defense and Resilience are also vital, as these points reduce the chance of the person being critically hit (a major problem in late Instances and Heroic

Mode where criticals deal so much damage that healers must rush to catch up). Warriors, Bear Druids, and Paladins are very good at this role.

Secondary Tank or Off Tank: This is a character that grabs adds and monsters that peel onto casters and other softer targets. While the Main Tank is busy keeping multiple enemies engaged, a Secondary Tank focuses on any that slip through the cracks. Again, damage mitigation is a major role here, though higher DPS than a Main Tank is useful (for grabbing more aggro and possibly even killing the offending monster). Arms/Fury Warriors, Druids, and Paladins are the best for this task, though there are times when Hunter Pets, Rogues (using their timers), and other classes can accomplish this. In high level areas, often only another protection specced Warrior can OT.

Main Assist (MA): Someone in the group needs to decide what creature to attack. In low-level groups, many people choose the Main Tank for this, but that sours over time. The Main Tank needs to do many things to maintain aggro against many foes, and that sometimes involves switching targets frequently. The Main Assist should be a melee character that has the freedom to grab a single enemy and stick with it. Almost anyone can do this, but a melee character with high damage output is excellent. Be sure to have all group members form an /assist macro on the MA before the fighting starts. Arms/Fury Warriors and Rogues are amazing character to serve as the MA, though any person in the party can do this. In fact, high intelligence and quick thinking (from the player) are even more important than having the "best" character for the job.

Marker: Any class can fill this role as it's far more important that a fast and decisive player manage this. Having someone as Marker takes some of the responsibility from the Assist and Crowd Control characters. Use the Raid Icons to mark each mob to be controlled and have a planned killing order.

ICON	KILL ORDER	PURPOSE
Skull	1	First Target for DPS
Blue Square	2	Frost Trap Target and second kill target as Frost Trap doesn't last long
Circle	3	Sap Target and third kill target as Sap isn't renewable
Moon	4	Hibernate Target and last kill target as Hibernate is long lasting and can be renewed

Rezzer: Priests, Shamans, and Paladins are very good Rezzers. These are people who get Soulstoned if there is a Warlock around, and they are chosen because they can pull the rest of the group back from the brink (sometimes even after a full wipe). Paladins also have the ability to use Divine Intervention on another player; this puts the person out of combat, but it clears all of the aggro from them. If the group is doomed to lose, the Paladin can use this option to have one person survive the encounter while the monsters strike home. Make sure the person saved is a Rezzer for the most effect!

If there aren't Warlocks around, it is very good to have characters in a group that can self-rez (be sure to have Ankhs for your Shamans). These characters are prepared so that a group can return from a wipeout without having to travel through the entire dungeon again, possibly facing respawns. This can be the same person as the Primary Healer.

Note that Druids can Rez in battle (Rebirth, on a 30 minute timer), but this does not make a Druid a Rezzer for a group. Rather, they are able to mitigate the loss of a single important character during a longer pull. For example, a group's Primary Healer is Intercepted and one-shotted by a Heroic mob. It can happen. Because the group is deep inside an Instance, the Druid decides to do an in-battle Rez of the Primary Healer while the group tries to survive.

Primary Healer or Main Healer: Primary Healers should be characters that are dedicated to keeping the group going and almost ignoring damage output. Priests are perceived as the shining light of this role, but equipment specialization and Talent choices make even more of a different. Shamans and Druids that focus on Restoration builds can serve very well as Primary Healers. Priests with Shadow builds instead are far better at healing in a secondary fashion (by keeping everyone topped off as they rip enemies to shreds).

Secondary Healer: Secondary Healers switch between offense and healing as the group needs. Shamans, Paladins, Shadow Priests, and Druids are all able to move between these roles fluidly, making them ideal for healing the Primary Healer or for jumping in to heal when the Primary Healer is out of mana or has too much to do at once.

Support: Support characters add various levels of protection of functionality to a group. Warlocks are able to deal damage, use Soulstones for wipe insurance, summon wayward characters, and so forth. Hunters can be dealing heavy damage, use their pets to act as a Secondary Tank, detect and defeat stealth, find monsters or enemy players with their Tracking, and hit troublesome targets at great range WITH staying power.

Crowd Control: Crowd Control abilities are used to keep enemies out of battle for a substantial duration. This involves using abilities that Stun, Fear, Snare, Root, or otherwise disable the target. In-combat Crowd Control offers the most tactical advantage, as it can be used repeatedly throughout an engagement (sometimes on the same target and sometimes on new targets as needs permit). Out-of-combat Crowd Control (such as Sap), must be prepared ahead of time and cannot be renewed during a skirmish.

Raid dynamics are build so that Crowd Control is often impossible (there are very few enemies and all are supposed to be dealt with simultaneously through complex strategies). Groups, however, are challenged by facing proportionately more targets! Crowd Control is life in higher dungeons.

Many classes have some form of Crowd Control. You duty is to understand what you class is capable of doing to stop enemies from hurting the group. Then, you must master the timing and effectiveness of these abilities. Consult the table below to learn more

CROWD CONTROL ABILITIES

ABILITY	CLASS	UTILITY
Polymorph	Mage	Useful on Many Types of Enemies, Can be Renewed In-Combat, Amazingly Useful
Frost Nova	Mage	Dangerous to use as it's short range, but can root several enemies at once
Mind Control	Priest	Used Against Humanoids, Risky, Sometimes Makes Brutal Fights Quite Easy
Shackle Undead	Priest	Used Against Undead, Very Powerful Against Elite Undead
Psychic Scream	Priest	AoE Fear, Useful Against Most Monsters, Situational (Must Have Cleared Area)
Sap	Rogue	Out-of-Combat, Long Duration, Requires Setup Time, Some Risk
Chain Stuns	Rogue	Stunlocking Can be Amazing Against Non-Bosses (Especially Elite Casters)
Blind	Rogue	Short Range, Instant, but on a timer
Howl of Terror	Warlock	AoE Fear (Must Have Cleared Area)
Fear	Warlock	Single-Target Fear for Moderate Duration
Banish	Warlock	Long Duration Control Against Elementals and Demons, Obviously Situational But Powerful
Enslave Demon	Warlock	Carries Immense Risk if Used Carelessly, But Promises Great Power
Seduce	Warlock	Succubus Pet Control Against Humanoids, Supplementary
Freezing Trap	Hunter	Easier to Use Than in the Old Days, Short Duration, Still Very Powerful
Wyvern Sting	Hunter	Survival Talent Required, Moderate Duration, Supplementary
Scare Beast	Hunter	Fear Effect Vs. Beasts Only, Situational
Frost Trap	Hunter	Slows large groups of enemies, helps with kiting or fleeing a bad situation
Hibernate	Druid	Sleep Vs. Beasts and Dragonkin (One of the Only Crowd Control Forms Against Dragonkin)
Turn Undead	Paladin	Fear Vs. Undead, Moderate Duration, Situational
Seal of Judgement	Paladin	Stuns the target occasionally and can be Judged to keep a target from fleeing
Intimidating Shout	Warrior	AoE Fear, Useful Against Most Monsters (Must Have Cleared Area)

Not every group has to have people taking care of every role. At the same time, some characters are likely to fill multiple roles at the same time or be able to switch comfortably between roles. Rogues are going to act as Crowd Control characters before some fights begin, then switch into a DPS or Assist role after the good Sapping is done. A Holy/Disc Priest would likely be the Rezzer for the group AND the Primary Healer; that same Priest could also serve as additional Crowd Control during pulls with Undead or when an AoE Fear is needed.

Some of these roles won't even be defined by a party leader or a conversation. People are somewhat expected to understand their place in a group and act accordingly. If you are the only tanking class in a party, it is expected that you will be a damage mitigater. Unless someone says otherwise, step up and declare that you are going to be the Main Tank. Put on your high Defense, Resilience, and general survivability gear and get ready for fun.

If it seems like someone is off from their role (e.g. a Priest without healing backup is nuking all the time and spending 50% of their mana of damage), consider whether this is a problem. If a group is blowing through targets and there aren't deaths or near-deaths, let things slide. Better to kill quickly and have a good time. However, if deaths are occurring and it seems like there is a weakness in the group's dynamic, ask people to take on more of a needed role.

To Warrior: The healers are getting a lot of aggro from keeping you alive; could you put away your two-hander and switch to your tanking gear?

To a Priest: Could you save more mana for healing? We've got the DPS handled and our healers are going OOM (out of mana) a bit often.

Once people in a group know all of their potential for Crowd Control, it is easier to come up with strategies that use these abilities to their fullest. Very few fights are designed so that the monsters cannot be controlled at all. There is usually some type of Fear, or Polymorph, or Banishment that can be done to make things much easier. With fewer incoming enemies to worry about, healing doesn't need to be as frantic and mistakes in targeting are fewer.

DPS: Damage Per Second characters are purely intended to get involved in the battle and use their skills, mana, etc. to destroy enemies. Once the necessary roles for a group are filled out, DPS characters are chosen to fill the remaining slots. Rogues, Hunters, Mages, Warlocks, and Arms/Fury Warriors are very good for this.

SAMPLE GROUPS

Do not let your group decisions be guided purely by standards; there are many successful parties that form with an odd combination of abilities (skill and fun are still far more important than format)! That said, the standard party layout can be quite effective, and it's good to know where to start if you have no idea what to put together.

SAMPLE DPS GROUP

Protection Warrior (Main Tank)

Assassination/Subtlety Rogue (Assist, Crowd Control Before Battle)

Marksmanship Hunter (DPS, Secondary Crowd Control)

Arcane Mage (DPS, Crowd Control In-Battle)

Holy Priest (Healer, Rezzer)

The group above is almost out of a textbook for a DPS group. There is a very solid tank who will only contribute some damage, and the Priest is going to be too busy to add much, but there are three good DPS classes in the mix. There is potential for Sap, Polymorph, Freezing Traps, and Mind Control all in the same pulls, so there is plenty of crowd control to enjoy. DPS groups are good to blowing through Instances of equal or lower level at high speed (great for farming, great for having fun). The biggest weakness of DPS groups comes when they hit new content, as having a single healer means that one mistake can easily lead to a wipe when it involved losing your only healer.

SAMPLE HEALING GROUP

Feral Druid (Main Tank)

Beast Mastery Hunter (DPS, Pet as Offtank)

Frost Mage (DPS, Crowd Control In-Battle)

Retribution Paladin (Some DPS/Secondary Healer)

Restoration Shaman (Primary Healer)

This group stacks on survivability from every angle; it's probably more than they need for most challenges. There is a major healer in the mix, and there are two backup healers as well (the main tank won't usually be able to do much healing, but if something goes wrong they can try to get aggro back by healing while saving the character that is taking damage).

By having redundant levels of survivability, a group can take on an Instance that is new to them without as many risks of frequent wipes. As long as there aren't bosses with DPS races, this is probably going to work (it'll be slow, and this group would not be fun for farming items).

CAN I BE......?

Not every character in a group has to be specced for their role. Protection Warriors are the most survivable. It's true. They get a great deal of aggro against their targets, and their ability to continue accruing high Threat with one-handed weapons and shield abilities places them far above Arms and Fury Warriors for the main tank position.

But any Warrior with a +Stamina and +Defense set of gear and a decent shield can still tank an Instance outside of Heroic Mode. Even in Heroic Mode a very good Warrior can tank without speccing in a specific way.

The same is true for healers who don't have their Holy, Restoration speccs "just right."

For these characters, it's most advisable to have a backup set of equipment that has all of the stats that you need. Your Arms Warrior is walking around with a 106 DPS 2h Axe, a 32% critical chance, and enough Attack Power to frighten a Rogue. It's great, isn't it? Now take the gear off and put one your Stamina, Defense, Resilience gear, and your best shield and one-hander. Now you're a tank. You can't Shield Block as well, you don't have Last Stand (a somewhat major loss), and you don't have Defiance (a very frustrating loss). But you can still get the job done!

Proper specializations give groups leeway, but they aren't required unless you group can barely handle an Instance in the first place. To find leeway in other areas, spend the time and farm for consumables (nice Elixirs, Sharpening Stones, etc.), gear up, and practice the Instance. Specialization is 25% of the puzzle, gear is 25%, but skill handles the other 50%. Be sure to have the right gear for your secondary job; that way you can guarantee 75% of what you need, and that is enough to pass for a 5-character group.

RAID ENVIRONMENTS

CATEGORY	HOW TO GET	PURPOSE
Potions	Alchemists	Health, Mana, Protection From Various Damage Types
Elixirs	Alchemists	Long-Duration Buffs
Flasks	Alchemists	Super Buffs (Last After Deaths)
Poisons	Rogue-Only	Rogue Weapon Buffs
Weapon/Armor Items	Blacksmith Craftables	Raise Weapon Damage and Add Armor Absorption
Secondary Cooldown (Night Dragon's Breath, Whipper Root Tubers)	World Drops	Use without Tripping Potion Cooldown

ITEM ENHANCEMENT

CATEGORY	HOW TO GET	PURPOSE
Cloak, Chest, Wrist, Hand, Feet, Weapon, and Shield Improvements	Enchanters	Variety of Major Improvements to Stats
Rings Improvements	Enchanter Only	Enchanters Learn Self-Enchants for Rings
Leg Improvements	Leatherworkers	Wonderful New Recipes Exist for Leg Armor Patches
Head Improvements	Raise Faction	Several Factions Have Purchasable Head Enchantments (Cenarion Expedition, Lower City, etc.)
Shoulder Improvements	Raise Scryer/Aldor Faction	At Honored and Exalted Scryer/Aldor Have Major Enchantments (Turn in Arcane Tomes and Fel Armaments for These)
Ranged Weapon Scopes	Engineers	Add Damage or Critical Rating to Ranged Weapons

Group roles and tactics are shared by raids, but the depth of skills and roles for a given character shrinks even further. Because so many people are involved in the fighting, people seldom need to take on multiple roles. Tanks are there to mitigate damage as much as possible, and sacrificing their damage output is a trivial loss to the raid. Healers are there to heal and/or resurrect the fallen; their damage is also trivial in a major engagement compared to their ability to save lives. DPS characters often have less visible and exciting roles in raids, compared to their glory days in earlier dungeons; the goal is to find a place where you can do something for the raid better than just about anyone else, and do ONLY THAT.

NEVER LEAVE HOME WITHOUT IT

Raids have even more demands on Food, Water, Ammo, Reagents (Ankhs, Candles, etc.), Potions, and Buffs than even the toughest groups in the lower dungeons. Be absolutely sure to repair, restock, and equip yourself for raids ahead of time.

It takes long enough for a good raid to get moving, and having as much of the work done as possible ahead of time is going to keep you up to speed! By the same token, it's best to arrive at the area for the raid on-time without begging for a summon. Doing these things properly say "I'm a team player" loud and clear. If it makes you earlier than other people in the raid, feel free to check in every few minutes while reading email, doing chores, etc. There is no need to waste your time while waiting.

Meeting Stones negate this issue to a moderate extent in The Burning Crusade; characters can summon each other without the time and effort of having Warlocks farm enemies. Still, the sooner you are ready to go, the better it is for all concerned.

RAID LEADERSHIP

Leading a raid takes a great deal of organization, personality, and experience. If you are the leader, be sure to have macros that let people know when to attack and when to shift their focus. Be clear and concise, and don't add flavor or fun to raid text until the fighting is over. None of this makes for a casual experience, but that is the way of things as a raid leader; you don't do it to make friends or relax. That is why very few people make great leaders or enjoy being leaders in the first place!

Try to establish a level of command that is sensible. Have a single raid leader, then a group leader within each group that handles the local calls, the general chatter, and communicates the group's needs if there are any. General raid members should not be spamming a lot of text on the /raid channel. This makes things absolutely nuts for the raid commander and for everyone else. If it's important, let the group leader know.

Commands for the raid should be very simple (e.g. Open Fire, Hold Back). Whether you agree with what the raid leader is commanding, do it. Your life isn't on the line in a real sense, and if the raid leader isn't any good, choose a better raid leader for your future efforts. But don't rock the boat during the actual raid. Dissent and confusion are the bane of good raid work, and a mediocre raid leader who is being heeded is still a league better than 20 "great" raid leaders who are vying for control.

PROPER ETIQUETTE OF A GROUP/RAID

MASTER LOOTER

With roles established for the characters, it's important to finalize elements of etiquette. More than a few fights have occurred because loot rules and leadership were not clearly identified ahead of time. It's FAR better to have any arguments over loot distribution BEFORE THERE IS ANY LOOT to worry about. Once there are actual goodies on the table, people have more potential to lose their heads, and that can be disastrous for continuing in a dungeon.

There are several loot rules that are favored by groups of people who are not real-life, personal friends. Most of the time, even guild groups can be composed to players who don't know each other and may not even be particularly close. Thus, a system that is fair for all of the players is necessary.

Some groups stick with a Master Looter for grabbing all Bind-on-Equip items. In these cases, the items are distributed at the end of the dungeon or raid, to keep from breaking the flow of the action. Bind-on-Pickup items are still dealt with on the spot, through rolling on the items. This requires a Master Looter who is known to be honest, consistent, and who can deal with all sorts of people. Make sure that the person has a great deal of bag space for keeping all of the nice items around. It might also be useful for the person to be an Enchanter (they can break worthless items into stackable goods that can later be rolled on).

One of the downsides of Master Looter is that people who leave early lose their chance for anything; sometimes, there are legitimate reasons to leave, if a dungeon run is going into the wee hours of the morning and has had several failures, for example. In those cases, it is fair to bow out, and that should not preclude players from having a chance at established loot. Between failed runs, the Master Looter should be aware of this danger and try to accommodate players who reasonably have put in their time and express the issue clearly.

In later dungeons, when things become more formal, many groups decide on a number of Ups. Everyone in the group/raid has a set number of Ups (determined before the group leaves town). Players who want an item as an upgrade declare their Up and only roll against other people who are also using an Up. Only the person who wins has expended their Up on that item. This keeps one lucky roller from raking in all of the goodies.

50 DKP Minus!

A number of guilds are going to have their own, internal point systems. This ensures that luck of the roll is not what determines loot (when people spend weeks waiting for that one special drop, you can understand that they want the distribution to be fair).

Talk to you guild officers when joining a raiding guild, read the websites or other materials that they provide for you, and make sure that you ask any questions if you are confused about the specifics of loot distribution within your guild.

GROUP LOOT

When items above a certain threshold drop, everyone gets a box for Need, Greed, or Pass. It is up to the group and each person ahead of time to figure out what constitutes fair Greed (some people want to roll Greed on everything while others Pass unless the item is something that they have mild interest in). Make sure that you understand what is proper etiquette for a given group.

A very common baseline would be that Bind on Equip items get a Greed roll from everyone, while Bind-on-Pickup items are only chosen as Need if a person can and will use the item as an upgrade. Even that is never an absolute. There may be groups where class priorities take place.

Example: A ring drops with Agility, Stamina, and Attack Power. A Fury Warrior wants to roll Need for it, but other members of the group say that the ring should only be rolled on by a Hunter or Rogue, as those classes benefit even more from Agility improvements.

There is no pure "right" or "wrong" on this matter. Decide what you are comfortable with before going into the Instance and stick with the loot rules that you accepted.

LOOTING MISTAKES

Mistakes can and do happen. Many are avoided by not rolling or looting during battle, when there is urge to do something quickly! Wait until things are calm and settled before worrying about any treasure. Next, be prepared to apologize VERY soundly if you are responsible for any mistakes, and figure out exactly what led you to click Need when you meant Greed or Pass.

Everyone makes a small slip at some time in their character's careers; "Doh, I didn't realize that was a Main Hand Axe instead of an Off Hand." That type of thing must be dealt with nicely by the person who made the mistake. Apologize, find out if you need to make things right with anyone, and move on with it. Don't try to defend an action when you are in the wrong. Accept what happened and strive to do better; if everyone does that, the entire realm gets better every day!

OTHER MISTAKES

There is only one person who is the best player on your server. This is an obvious thing to say, but understanding it reveals a great depth of empathy for everyone beneath that standard. Few players are great, no matter how much time they put into the game. Having a Level 70 character, logging 50 /played days, and wielding incredible equipment does not guarantee a master. Thus, many of the groups that you choose are going to have people making some mistakes here and there. Pick-up-Groups are obviously the most notorious for this because the people in them don't know each other and don't know how to work as a team at first. Even good team players can't develop an instant understanding of how everyone in the group uses their class.

So, be careful when dealing with mistakes. Don't assume that the person who made the mistake is an idiot or a jerk. Don't ignore the mistake either, else it's more likely to be repeated. Instead, take the fair ground and point out the problem comfortably and rationally. Only escalate if there is an absolute need. Let us present an example of worst case so that the point is clear.

EXAMPLE OF A MISTAKE

A Warrior keeps targeting Polymorphed enemies and smacking them out of CC. After a couple incidents of this, the Mage speaks the next time the Priest sits down for mana.

Mage: "One second everyone. Warrior, doing damage to anything that is sheeped ends the spell. I'm making sure to sheep one of the adds each time. Please try not to hit them until the other targets are down. :)"

If the Warrior was a cool person either way, that comment would go over without a problem. It sticks to the point but does not accuse, insult, or condescend. If said Warrior is interested in being part of a good group, they are certainly going to try and do better in the future, but let us continue this example as if the Warrior completely ignored the Mage. The offending action continues.

Mage: "We still have a problem with CC here. My sheep keep getting hit, and we're getting deep enough into the Instance that it's getting dangerous. We almost lost the Priest that fight because of healing aggro. Warrior, is there anything that I can do to sheep targets in a better way for you?"

At this point, the whole group knows that it isn't the Mage who is making the mistake here, but offering to work with the Warrior is still a good idea just for getting through the dungeon. If the Warrior is played by a very young person or someone with poor language skills, it may be that they just don't understand what you are talking about. Opening a conversation about what to actually DO about crowd control may greatly help that person (and save your sanity). If they still ignore you entirely, don't group with that person again. But, there is still a level of escalation that happens in very rare cases. See the worst possible response from the Warrior.

Warrior: "Shut up, I didn't break it."

Mage: "I'm certain about it; this has happened a few times already. It wasn't the Rogue or the Shaman."

Warrior: "Whatever."

Here comes the biggest problem. Inept players can improve. Nasty ones are going to be nasty whatever they learn. Be open to future apologies if that person was just having a horribly bad day, but as a rule it's very wise to avoid players who are unskilled and are outright rude about working as part of a team. If a person gets too belligerent, the party leader may need to kick them from the group outright and pull in a new player.

DUNGEON PROGRESSION

RAIDING PROGRESSION

You couldn't take characters terribly far with just five characters in the old game. Without raiding or extremely-devoted PvP, a person could only hope to upgrade their dungeon set and have a mix of high blues and tier 1-equivalent epics. That is no longer the case.

After gearing up in the end-game 5-character dungeons for a time, a skilled group can enter Heroic Mode dungeons and work on getting a strong assortment of epic gear. Not only are there epic drops from the bosses of these dungeons; there are Badges that drop and allow characters to turn them in for epics from the Sha'tar faction. Thus, a non-raider has many more opportunities to collect the type of gear that will keep them competitive.

To enter Heroic Mode dungeons, each person in a 5-character group has to key a Key for that dungeon. See the table below.

HEROIC MODE KEYS

GROUP OF DUNGEONS	WHERE TO RAISE FACTION/BUY KEY
Hellfire Citadel	Shattered Halls/Either Honor Hold or Thrallmar Quartermaster
Coilfang Reservoir	The Steamvault/The Cenarion Expedition Quartermaster
Auchindoun	Shadow Labyrinth/Lower City Quartermaster
Caverns of Time	Any Caverns of Time Instance/Quartermaster for the Keepers of Time
Tempest Keep	Any Tempest Keep Instance/Sha'tar Quartermaster

Each person who wants to get into a Heroic Dungeon should strive to reach Revered with the appropriate faction for said dungeon then purchase the Key they need from the Quartermaster. These Keys cost a trivial amount, so that is fortunately not a factor (and most of the factions have other rewards along the way that make it worth your efforts).

In fact, there are epic items at the Exalted end of almost all Outland factions! Patterns for suits of craftable armor with very high Resists are included in this rewards as well, making it easier to beat the roadblock encounters found inside the Heroic Mode versions of each dungeon.

Raiders get their love too. Though the tiers of armor are closer together in power now, raiders can still get an edge if they are able to conquer the new perils of Outland. There are three known tiers of raiding armor that are available. Instead of dropping an individual pieces, these armor now fall as Tokens that are handed in. The Tokens fall for groups of classes (e.g. there are three types of Tokens, so more people have a chance to be involved in a given loot drop). The Tokens are handed in at Shattrath City.

RAIDING TIERS FOR OUTLAND

TIER	WHERE THE TOKENS ARE FOUND
Four	Karazhan (Deadwind Pass), Gruul's Lair (Blade's Edge Mountains), Magtheridon (Hellfire Citadel Raid)
Five	The Eye (Raiding Zone of Tempest Keep), Serpentshrine Cavern (Coilfang Reservoir Raid)
Six	Black Temple (Shadowmoon Valley), CoT: Mount Hyjal

HELLFIRE RAMPARTS

DUNGEON INFORMATION

Name	Hellfire Ramparts
Location	Hellfire Peninsula, Hellfire Citadel
Suggested Levels	Group of 5, Levels 59-63
Reputation	Thrallmar/Honor Hold
Primary Enemies	Humanoids, Beasts
Damage Types	Physical, Shadow, Fire
Time to Complete	60 to 90 Minutes

WHO TO BRING

JOBS

CLASS	ABILITIES
Druid	Non-Elite destruction, Hibernate Against Wolves, Remove Curse vs. Omor the Unscarred
Hunter	Non-Elite destruction, Freezing Trap, Off-Tanking (Pet) vs. Omor the Unscarred, Silencing Shot in Most Pulls
Mage	Polymorph in Most Pulls, Remove Curse on Omor the Unscarred, Counterspell
Paladin	Mana Recovery, Cleanse, Resistance Buffs in Omor the Unscarred and Final Boss Fights
Priest	Shadow Protection, Mind Control, Psychic Scream vs. Bleeding Hollow Scryers
Rogue	Non-Elite destruction, Sap, Blind
Shaman	Fire Resistance Totem, Tremor Totem, Earth Shock
Warlock	Devour Magic (Felhunter), Seduce (Succubus)
Warrior	Intimidating Shout vs. Bleeding Hollow Scryers

Hellfire Ramparts has a number of opportunities for specific classes to shine. With many pulls of five or more enemies, crowd control makes the fights much simpler and more survivable. All of the trash enemies are either Humanoids or Beasts. This gives quite a few classes the ability to aid in simplifying the pulls.

The Beasts of the instance are not elite, but deal very high damage. Having someone who can destroy these quickly reduces the damage the party takes tremendously. Any high DPS character is good for this.

GETTING TO HELLFIRE RAMPARTS

Hellfire Ramparts is one wing of Hellfire Citadel. Situated nicely in the center of Hellfire Peninsula, it's close to both Horde and Alliance flight points and graveyards.

Alliance parties can climb the wall on the southern side of the ravine and drop down to the Instance entrance. Horde parties should climb the wall on the northern side of the ravine and take the ramp down to the Instance entrance.

A QUICK IN AND OUT!

One of the greatest parts of the Hellfire Ramparts is the shortness of the instance. It can be done multiple times in a day or during a shorter window of play for the more casual players.

REPUTATION GAINS

ACTION	FACTION	REPUTATION GAIN	END POINT
Kill Elite	Thrallmar/Honor Hold	5	Honored
Kill Non-Elite	Thrallmar/Honor Hold	2-3	Honored
Kill Boss	Thrallmar/Honor Hold	50	Honored
Quest: Weaken the Ramparts	Thrallmar/Honor Hold	350	N/A

THE ENEMY GARRISON

BOSSES

NAZAN

OMOR THE UNSCARRED

VAZRUDEN

WATCHKEEPER GARGOLMAR

TROOPS

BLEEDING HOLLOW ARCHER
Notes: Ranged Attacks, High DPS

BLEEDING HOLLOW DARKCASTER
Notes: Shadow bolt, Lower Health

BLEEDING HOLLOW SCRYER
Notes: Shadow bolt, Fear

BONECHEWER BEASTMASTER
Notes: Summons 3 Shattered Hand Warhounds, Stealth Detection

BONECHEWER DESTROYER
Notes: Cleave, Mortal Strike, Knockback

BONECHEWER HUNGERER
Notes: Demoralizing Shout, Disarm, Strike

BONECHEWER RAVENER
Notes: Kidney Shot

BONECHEWER RIPPER
Notes: Enrage

FIENDISH HOUND
Notes: Drain Life, Spell Lock

HELLFIRE SENTRY
Notes: Kidney Shot, Stealth Detection

HELLFIRE WATCHER
Notes: Heal Watchkeeper Gargolmar

SHATTERED HAND WARHOUNDS
Notes: Stealth Detection

WEAKEN THE RAMPARTS

Quest Level	59 to obtain
Quest Giver	Caza'Rez (Horde) or Gunny (Alliance)
Goal	Collect Watchkeeper Gargolmar's Hand, Omor the Unscarred's Hoof, and Nazan's Head
Experience Gained	12,600
Reward	Handguards of Precision (Mail Hands, 307 Armor, +28 STA, +20 AGI, +38 Attack Power), Jade Warrior Pauldrons (Plate Shoulder, 655 Armor, +20 STR, +28 STA, +19 AGI), Mantle of Magical Might (Cloth Shoulder, 88 Armor, +17 INT, +16 STA, +10 SPI, Increases damage and healing done by spells and effects by up to 19, +16 spell critical strike rating), or Sure Step Boots (Leather Feet, 155 Armor, +20 AGI, +28 STA, +38 Attack Power)

With the attention of the Burning Legion focused on the Dark Portal, now is the time to strike a blow against the forces of Hellfire Citadel. The Ramparts must be weakened before any greater assault can be mounted. Slay the leaders to throw the troops into confusion.

DARK TIDINGS

Quest Level	59 to obtain
Quest Giver	Ominous Letter
Goal	Take the Ominous Letter to Force Commander Danath Trollbane at Honor Hold (Alliance) or Nazgrel at Thrallmar (Horde)
Experience Gained	10,500
Reward	None

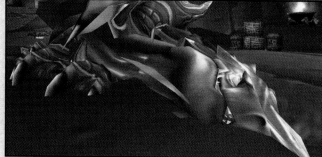

Found on the body of Vazruden the Herald, you find a letter letter of most disturbing origin. Signed by Illidan himself, your commander will want to know about it.

ATOP THE WALLS

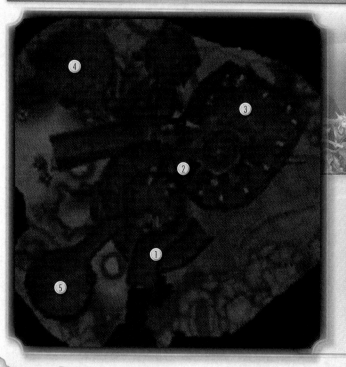

MAP LEGEND	
1	Entrance from Hellfire Peninsula
2	Bonechewer Beastmaster
3	Watchkeeper Gargolmar
4	Omor the Unscarred
5	Vazruden the Herald, Nazan

THE RAMPARTS

While the trip in was uneventful and unhindered, that ends at the instance portal. The rest of the trip is a hard fight through legions of enemies.

Guarding the first bridge is a pair of Bonechewer Hungerers. Wait for the patrolling Bonechewer Ravener to be on the other side of the bridge before pulling the first two. The fight is fairly straight-forward.

Take this opportunity to practice the group's crowd control. The fight is small enough that failed crowd control isn't a death sentence and the instance portal is right behind you if anything goes wrong. The party leader should designate a symbol for each type of target and explain the attack order.

SAMPLE EXPLANATION

SYMBOL	DESIGNATION	ATTACK ORDER
Star	Sap	2
Skull	Tank & DPS	1
Moon	Polymorph	3

This example assumes three enemies and a group with a Rogue and Mage. Your group may be different, so take the time to find what everyone is comfortable with.

With the first two guards out of the way, grab the Bonechewer Ravener next time he wanders to this side of the bridge. Destroy him and dispatch the far two Bonechewer Hungerers in the same way you did the first two.

Cross the bridge and prepare for slightly more difficult fights. There are now three enemies in each group and all of them are elite. The Bleeding Hollow Darkcasters and Archers attack from range, so they are good candidates for Polymorph or Seduce. The Bonechewer Destroyer has a number of melee attacks that make him quite dangerous. Kill him first to keep him from making the life of a caster very difficult.

Should you be without sufficient crowd control, pull the enemies and duck around a corner to break line of sight. This forces the Archers and Darkcasters to approach you. Tank the Destroyer while your party kills the Darkcasters and Archers first; they have lower Health and die much faster.

WATCH YOUR BACK

Keep your backs facing the bridge (or other areas you've cleared) while fighting the Bonechewer Destroyer. He can knock you off the ramparts if you are unlucky. A fall from the ramparts is death no matter who you are. Keep the Destroyer facing away from melee DPS characters and away from softer party members as he also has a cleave attack.

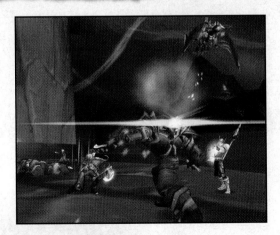

The Bleeding Hollow Darkcaster should be your next target as he can be interrupted with a variety of abilities and pulled to the group. Silencing Shot, Earth Shock, Counterspell, Kick, Shield Bash, and Pummel are all examples of interrupts. Without the use of his spells, he's little more than a glorified bookworm. With only one enemy left, the Bleeding Hollow Archer won't last long.

THE LESSER OF TWO EVILS

If you are short on crowd control, but your Priest is equal or higher level than the enemies, you have another option.

Mind Control the most damaging enemy in a pull. It's important to warn your party this is going to happen as it greatly changes the tactics of the fight. Once you have an enemy under your sway, allow its friends to kill it before your party joins the fight. This starts the fight with one enemy already dead and possibly another wounded.

If your party joins early, you run into two problems. The first problem is that your Priest is busy and will not be able to heal anyone. The other is that the controlled mob may survive long enough to break the Mind Control (or have another enemy hit the Priest and break it). This spells disaster as the previously controlled enemy will not allow itself to be taunted off the Priest. You'll have to kill it to save your cloth-wearing friend.

Move to the next group and handle it with the same technique. Continue along the rampart until you reach the group of two Bonechewer Hungerers and two Shattered Hand Warhounds. The Warhounds are not elite and can be killed quickly. Crowd control the Hungerers with Polymorph, Freezing Trap, or Seduce until the Warhounds have been dispatched. Avoid using AoE attacks as the Warhounds deal high damage and breaking the crowd control on either or both of the Hungerers will prove to be deadly to the group.

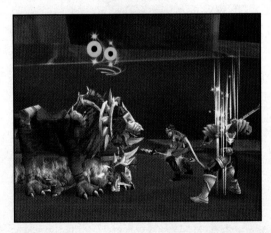

THE WOLVES CAN SMELL STEALTHERS

Do not attempt to use Sap on enemies near the Warhounds. The Warhounds can smell through stealth and will alert others to the presence of a Rogue. If the only in-combat CC you have in the party is Hibernate, the tactics should change slightly. Hibernate one of the Warhounds; kill the other Warhound, then the two Hungerers. Kill the final Warhound last.

Once again, the enemies have upped the ante. There is a group of three Bleeding Hollow Scryers surrounding a Bonechewer Ripper. This fight is going to test your crowd control capabilities as well as your pulling. All four enemies are elite.

Crowd control as many of the Scryers as possible and pull the fight back, because your enemies can fear. You don't want to fight near another group. One unlucky fear and you'll be fighting far more than you can handle. If you're using a Freezing trap, be sure to pull the Ripper away from the trap. He is immune to all crowd control and will spring your trap with no effect on his way to you.

Kill the active Scryers first as they have a long fear. If you have an off-tank, they should hold the Ripper away from the rest of the party until all active Scryers are dead. Focus on the Ripper next, then the remaining Scryers as they break out of crowd control or are intentionally broken out when your party is done with other targets.

THE CORRIDOR

A Bonechewer Beastmaster and two Bonechewer Destroyers stand before you. Don't pull this group yet. Wait for the patrolling Bonechewer Hungerer with his two Shattered Hand Warhounds. When they're closest to you, pull them away from the Destroyers and Beastmaster. Pulling these prior to the Beastmaster fight will keep them from joining when you least want them to.

Use crowd control on the Hungerer when he is well away from the Beastmaster then kill the two Warhounds. Once the Warhounds are dead, finish the Hungerer.

The next fight looks much easier than it is. Two Bonechewer Destroyers stand near a Bonechewer Beastmaster. If you intend to use Sap, wait for the Beastmaster to walk far to the right before Sapping the left of the Destroyers. The Beastmaster can smell through stealth and will uncover you if he's too close to your target. Polymorph, Seduce, or Trap one of the Destroyers as soon as the fight starts.

If you have spare crowd control, use it on the Beastmaster while you kill the remaining Destroyer. Keep the first Destroyer ineffective by using repeatable crowd control as you move to the Beastmaster. During the fight, he will summon several Shattered Hand Warhounds.

Hold the Beastmaster while you destroy all the Warhounds he summoned. They aren't elite, but will do incredible damage if allowed to chew on a caster. With all his friends dead, finish off the Beastmaster and the last Destroyer.

An alternate strategy is to crowd control the Destroyers and throw all your DPS on the Beastmaster. Kill him as quickly as you can without pulling agro off the tank. Killing him quickly prevents him from summoning his Warhounds and makes the fight much simpler. This tactic can still be used if you are short on crowd control abilities, but gets more difficult as your tank has to hold the attention of all three enemies and your healer will have a lot of damage to heal.

LEARNING THE ROPES

This is one of the 'wipe' fights for players new to the instance. The run from the graveyard is short so don't despair and don't destroy a group by blaming the wipe on a specific person. Examine what you could have done better and note it for future runs as you make your way back to the instance.

The next fight is against another group of four elite enemies. One Bonechewer Hungerer and a Bonechewer Destroyer are guarding two Bleeding Hollow Darkcasters. If you have enough in-combat crowd control, keep the Darkcasters from participating in the fight while you kill the Hungerer and Destroyer. Or you may choose to CC the Hungerer and one Darkcaster, tank the Destroyer, and DPS the other Darkcaster

Many of the next fights involve both elite enemies and the Shattered Hand Warhounds. Polymorph, Seduce, or Trap the elite enemies and kill the Warhounds. This tactic is extremely useful and keeps you safe until you see Watchkeeper Gargolmar and his Hellfire Watchers patrolling.

This is the first boss and not to be taken lightly. Wait for him to patrol away and pull the enemy groups on each side of the corridor. The fights are similar to what you've done already, and the enemies need to be cleared before you engage Gargolmar to prevent adds. When the way is clear, take a moment to regain Health and Mana before pulling Gargolmar's group.

WATCHKEEPER GARGOLMAR

HP	33381/103320 (Heroic)	Damage	603-838/1882-2661 (Heroic)
Abilities	**Surge:** 40 yards, Charge inflicting 90 to 110 damage, as well as knocking them all back.		
	Overpower: After the target dodges causes weapon damage plus 93. Cannot be blocked, dodged, or parried.		
	Mortal Wound: Inflicts 150% weapon damage and leaves it wounded, reduces healing by 5% for 20 seconds. Stacks multiple times. **Heroic:** 10% per application.		
	Retaliation: At low health, counterattack any melee attack for 15 seconds.		

THE WATCHKEEPER'S STASH

Bracers of Finesse (Leather Wrist, 99 Armor, +18 AGI, +16 STA, +28 Attack Power)

Light Touched Breastplate (Plate Chest, 873, +26 STR, +25 STA, +25 INT, 1 Red Socket, 1 Yellow Socket, 1 Blue Socket, Socket Bonus: +5 Spell Damage, Restores 5 Mana per 5 sec.)

Pauldrons of Arcane Rage (Cloth Shoulder, 88 Armor, +18 STA, +18 INT, +12 SPI, Increases damage and healing done by magical spells and effects by up to 27)

Shadowrend Longblade (Main Hand Sword, 52.9 DPS, +12 STA, +12 Critical Strike Rating, +22 Attack Power)

Scale Leggings of the Skirmisher (Mail Legs, +22 AGI, +24 STA, +15 INT, 1 Red Socket, 1 Blue Socket, 1 Yellow Socket, Socket Bonus: 2 Mana per 5 sec., +32 Attack Power)

Gargolmar inflicts high melee damage and can Surge the party member furthest from him. The tank should hold Gargolmar while the rest of the group kills the two Hellfire Watchers. The Watchers heal Gargolmar if allowed to live. CC one if you have in-combat CC and kill the other. If you don't have any in-combat CC, have someone with interrupts keep the second Hellfire Watcher ineffective while the party kills the first.

Pet classes can leave their pet at range to take the brunt of Gargolmar's Surges. This keeps the more fragile party members safe from his attention. When both of the Watchers are dead, show Gargolmar the power of Azeroth!

Heroic Mode

Things change slightly when in Heroic Mode. Watchkeeper Gargolmar's Mortal Wound ability decreases healing by 10% per stack instead of 5%. Even just a few of these make keeping the tank alive much more difficult. This puts more pressure on the rest of the party to kill his healers quickly and bring their attention to Gargolmar.

Falling behind on healing the main tank doesn't spell absolute doom for your party if you have a secondary tank. Switch agro from one to the other and keep the secondary tank alive while the main tank's healing debuff wears off.

ADVANCING TOWARD THE SECOND FLOOR

JUMPING AHEAD

If your party is experienced with Hellfire Ramparts and in a hurry, the groups on the right side of the corridor can be skipped by sticking to the left. This should only be done by experienced parties as most characters can benefit from the practice, the reputation gains from combat, and the item drops.

On the right are two more groups very similar to what you've already fought. With all the patrollers removed, these are straightforward fights. Crowd control the casters, kill any non-elites, then kill the elites one at a time.

The doorway at the end of the corridor is guarded by two Bonechewer Hungerers. You've fought these before and they aren't a threat if your party has made it this far. Kill them and enter the staircase. Approach the top of the staircase carefully as a large and challenging fight awaits you in the next corridor.

Four Bleeding Hollow Scryers surround one Bonechewer Ripper in the next hallway. The Scryers cast Shadow bolt and can be quite dangerous with so many of them. The Ripper can enrage and all of the enemies can cast fear.

Pull them with a ranged attack and wait for the Scryers to start casting. As soon as they begin casting, duck around the corner and back onto the stairs. This line-of-sight pull (LOS) gives you time as they will try to complete their castings before they realize you are out of line of sight. Once they realize this, they will run to the stairs then begin casting again.

If you are using a Freezing Trap, have someone who isn't the puller grab the Ripper and keep him away from the trap. He is immune to all crowd control abilities and will destroy the usefulness of your trap.

Jump on the Ripper and kill him quickly. Use AoE crowd control abilities to keep the Scryers from doing anything useful. Psychic Scream and Intimidating Shout are good examples of these. If you are without AoE crowd control, use what crowd control you can and burn through the enemies at maximum speed. The fewer crowd control abilities you have the more damage you have, so use it.

Once the Ripper and a couple of the Scryers are down, the battle becomes much easier. It's far harder to die in a couple seconds when there are only two enemies, although some groups still manage the task. Once the encounter is done, rest.

The doorway at the end of the corridor is guarded by two Bonechewer Destroyers. When your party is ready, pull and kill these two rather pathetic guards. The open area beyond is of much more concern.

THE PLATFORMS

There are groups on the left, on the right, in the center, and patrolling the area. Wait for the roaming group to be away before pulling the group to the right back into the hallway.

If you fight them at the edge of the open area, the patrolling group will join. Have someone who isn't the tank pull this group and run back to the staircase and around the corner. This forces the two Bleeding Hollow Archers to run down the hallway to their doom, and allows any Warriors in the group to use Charge. Use in-combat crowd control to hold the Archers while you dispatch the Destroyer then the Archers.

The roaming Bonechewer Ravener and two Shattered Hand Warhounds are your next targets. Wait for them to patrol away from the other groups and pull them into the hallway. Kill the dogs first and the Ravener won't stand a chance.

The area is much clearer now. The group to the left consists of a Bleeding Hollow Darkcaster, a Bonechewer Hungerer, and two Bonechewer Destroyers. Polymorph, Sap, or Seduce the Destroyers and rush the group. Kill the Darkcaster first as it won't have time to be effective before you're finished with it. The Hungerer is your second target and finish with the Destroyers.

The final group on the platform should be very scared. Charge them and kill the Darkcaster, then the Warhound before engaging the melee enemies. Both the Darkcaster and Warhound have lower Health and neither lasts long. Using a Voidwalker, Hunter pet, or Freezing Trap to hold as many of the melee enemies as possible reduces the damage your party takes and makes the fight much smoother.

Take the entrance guarded by two Bonechewer Hungerers. This is to the right if you just came out onto the platform. Kill the Hungerers and proceed to Omor the Unscarred.

Two Darkcasters guard the edge of the platform. These can be killed without angering Omor, but don't charge them. Have ranged interrupts and crowd control ready. Pull one, CC the other, and interrupt the first to

force it to come to you. Repeat with the other to clear the way to Omor.

OMOR THE UNSCARRED

HP	59836/82642 (Heroic)	Damage	1110-1549/1939-2740 (Heroic)
Abilities	**Shadow Bolt:** Dark magic bolt, dealing approximately 1500-2000 shadow damage.		
	Treacherous Aura: 60 yard range, dealing 360 to 440 Shadow damage every 1 sec. to nearby friends. Lasts 15 sec.		
	Summon Fiendish Hound: Uses Spell Lock ability, Drains Life for 400 health over 5 seconds. Heroic: Mana Burn spell.		
	Demonic Shield: At 20% health, use Demonic Shield, decreases physical and magical damage by 75% for 10 seconds.		
	Orbital Strike: Launches a player into the air.		
	Shadow Whip: Pulls the player targeted by Orbital Strike back down to the ground.		

OMOR'S COLLECTION

Bloodstained Ravager Gauntlets (Mail Hands, 307 Armor, +13 AGI, +19 STA, +14 INT, 2 Red Sockets, Socket Bonus: +3 INT, +26 Attack Power)

Tenacious Defender (Plate Waist, 491 Armor, +15 STR, +14 AGI, +19 STA, 2 Red Sockets, Socket Bonus: +3 Resilience Rating)

Heartblood Prayer Beads (Neck, +15 STA, +15 INT, Restores 4 Mana per 5 sec., Increases healing done by spells and effects by up to 31)

Crystalfire Staff (Two-Hand Staff, 57.3 DPS, +34 STA, +34 INT, +16 Spell Critical Strike Rating, Increases damage and healing done by magical spells and effects by up to 46)

Garotte-String Necklace (Neck, +16 STA, +14 Critical Strike Rating, +36 Attack Power)

Heart Fire Warhammer (Two-Hand Mace, 68.9 DPS, +19 STR, +23 STA, +19 INT, Increases damage and healing done by magical spells and effects by up to 12, Restores 4 Mana per 5 sec.)

THE CURSE OF OMOR

Omor has an ability called Treacherous Aura. Anyone able to remove curses should be prepared to do so. The aura causes massive Shadow damage to all members near the afflicted.

Equipping items that increase your Shadow Resistance can make this less painful, but nothing beats removal.

Omor isn't someone to be taken lightly. He has reasonable Health, summons friends, and casts a curse that can affect an entire party if you aren't careful. Your tank should charge in and hold Omor as close to the center of the platform as possible. Ranged DPS should spread out while still being in healing range.

This keeps your party out of range of the curse without reducing their effectiveness. If anyone gets cursed near you, move away from them to avoid taking damage. The Shadow damage will cause a wipe if you don't keep track of it and reduce it when you can.

Several times throughout the fight, Omor will summon Felhounds to aid him. Burst DPS classes should destroy these before they can cause a problem for your healer. They have a Spell Lock ability that prevents casters from using any spells.

With all of this in mind, the fight will go smoothly. Keep your party healed and Omor will fall. Collect your booty.

Heroic Mode

Omor has a new ability called Bane of Treachery. It functions similar to Treacherous Aura. It cannot be removed. This makes it even more important to have your party as spread out as healing allows. Should any party member be affected by Omor, it is their duty to move away from other party members.

A Rogue, Hunter pet, Warlock pet, or second Warrior should be ready to deal with the Felhounds. Omor calls them more often and they deal a great amount of damage. They also have a Mana Burn ability that is the bane of any Mana-using class. Keep these off your healer at all costs.

Reverse course to the central platform. Vazruden the Herald flies over the final platform. There is a small group of enemies guarding the bridge, but they are of little consequence. Kill them, but don't pull the Hellfire Sentries. Rest to full Health and Mana and prepare for a frantic fight.

VAZRUDEN AND NAZAN

VAZRUDEN

HP	33381/62730 (Heroic)	Damage	1085-1510/3764-5323 (Heroic)
Abilities	**Revenge**: Counterattacks for 115 to 125 damage. Revenge must follow a dodge, block, or parry.		
	Shield Slam: Inflicts 144 damage, stunning it for 2 seconds.		

NAZAN

HP	88560 (Heroic)	Damage	904-1258/3136-4435 (Heroic)
Abilities	**Fireball**: 800 points of fire damage.		
	Cone of Fire: 10 yard range. Inflicts 1388 to 1612 fire damage.		
	Liquid Fire: Nazan's fireballs leave fire on the ground dealing 200-400 points of fire damage per second.		
	Bellowing Roar: Area of effect fear, Heroic Mode only.		

A DRAGON-RIDER'S HORDE

Mok'Nathal Clan Ring (Finger, 180 Armor, +16 STA, +14 Resilience Rating)

Mok'Nathal Wildercloak (Back, 59 Armor, +21, +21 Resilience Rating)

Sorcerer's Band (Finger, +16 STA, +14 INT, Increases damage and healing done by magical spells and effects by up to 21)

Lifegiver Britches (Cloth Legs, 103 Armor, +16 STA, +25 INT, +12 SPI, 1 Red Socket, 2 Blue Sockets, Socket Bonus: 2 Mana per 5 sec., Increases healing done by spells and effects by up to 44), Ursol's Claw (Two-Hand Staff, 57.3 DPS, +28 STR, +27 AGI, +27 STA, Increases attack power by 160 in Cat, Bear, Dire Bear, and Moonkin forms only)

Hellreaver (Two-Hand Polearm, 68.8 DPS, +30 STR, +27 STA, +25 Critical Strike Rating)

THE FIRES FROM ABOVE

Vazruden the Herald employs a number of fire attacks throughout the fight. Consider using Fire Protection Potions and equipping items that increase your Fire Resistance to make the fight less stressful.

The tank needs to keep Nazan facing away from the party without standing in a circle of fire. Use all your Mana on your fastest damaging spells. Use any timers you have that increase your damage output. Keep the tank up as best you can with rapid fire healing. This is a race to see who can kill who first.

If your party stays out of the circles of fire, the healer will have enough Mana to keep the tank alive long enough for the party to kill the dragon. If the tank goes down, abandon all hope of healing people and switch to all out DPS. The only way to win is to kill the beast before it kills you.

Pulling the Hellfire Sentries begins the final fight. While they aren't of consequence, Vazruden jumps off his dragon and engages you as soon as you kill the Sentries. Vazruden does high physical damage, but he's not your primary concern. Nazan breathes fire from the sky and small areas will burn with dragonfire for a short time. Do not stand in these flaming circles. The damage they do is immense.

Slowly kill Vazruden while dodging the breath attacks of Nazan. Hold as much of your Mana as you can as things get much worse later. When Vazruden

gets low on Health, he'll summon his dragon to land and fight with him. Finish Vazruden quickly and turn your attention to Nazan.

Even on the ground, Nazan is terribly dangerous. His physical attacks aren't that strong, but he still uses his Liquid Fire in addition to a cone of fire attack and a single target fire attack.

Heroic Mode

The strategies for fighting the Hellfire Sentries and Vazruden remain the same. Nazan however is much more powerful in Heroic Mode.

All the damage done by his fire abilities is much greater. The initial damage of his fire circles as well as the reoccurring damage has been increased.

During the fight, he will also use Bellowing Roar to fear all party members around him before charging an individual. Use abilities that prevent or dispel fear on your main tank to avoid Nazan killing your healer during the AoE fear.

Fear Ward and Tremor Totem are excellent examples of these. Having a Beast Mastery Hunter use Bestial Wrath and Intimidation can hold Nazan for the few seconds it may take for the tank to recover. This almost ensures the death of the pet, but it's far more recommended than a group wipe.

Resurrect any party members that died in the engagement before collecting your loot. Check the bodies for the Ominous Letter and search inside the large chest.

THE BLOOD FURNACE

DUNGEON INFORMATION

Name	The Blood Furnace
Location	Hellfire Citadel, Hellfire Peninsula
Suggested Levels	Group of 5, Level 60-64
Reputation	Thrallmar/Honor Hold
Primary Enemies	Humanoids, Demons
Damage Types	Physical, Shadow, Nature
Time to Complete	60 to 80 Minutes

WHO TO BRING

JOBS

CLASS	ABILITIES
Druid	Abolish Poison, Remove Curse, Innervate
Hunter	Freezing Trap, Aspect of the Wild vs. the Second Boss
Mage	Polymorph, Frost Nova, Counterspell, Remove Curse vs. the Final Boss
Paladin	Blessing of Wisdom, Cleanse, Shadow Resistance Aura vs. the Final Boss
Priest	Shadow Protection, Mind Control, Dispel Magic, Psychic Scream vs. the Second and Final Bosses
Rogue	Sap, Blind, Stuns, Disarm Trap vs. Shadowmoon Technicians
Shaman	Poison Cleansing Totem and Nature Resistance Totem vs. the Second Boss, Earth Shock
Warlock	Devour Magic (Felhunter), Seduce (Succubus), Banish, Enslave Demon
Warrior	Intimidating Shout vs. the Second and Final Bosses, Challenging Shout, Whirlwind, Cleave

As there are a great many demons in the Blood Furnace, bringing a Warlock makes your pulls much more controlled. Grabbing one of the Imps (via Enslave) at the beginning also gives the Warlock a powerful servant to use during the run. Later on, there are Felguards that can also be Enslaved by a happy Warlock.

Two of the boss fights involve large numbers of enemies. Having classes with AoE crowd control abilities will be invaluable in these fights. Many of the encounters are long and involve curses. Grab a person or two that can help regenerate mana and remove curses.

GETTING TO THE BLOOD FURNACE

As part of Hellfire Citadel, The Blood Furnace stands almost equidistant from either flight point. This is misleading however. The Blood Furnace can only be entered by the highest part of the wall and must be reached from the southern ramparts. These stairs are farther west than the steps players use to reach Hellfire Ramparts.

Alliance parties can climb the wall on the southern side of the ravine and enter the instance. Horde parties need to travel across the Path of Glory to the southern part of the wall and make their way to the instance.

REPUTATION GAINS

ACTION	FACTION	REPUTATION GAIN	END POINT
Kill Non-Elite	Thrallmar/Honor Hold	1	Honored
Kill Elite	Thrallmar/Honor Hold	5	Honored
Kill Boss	Thrallmar/Honor Hold	50	Honored
Quest: Heart of Rage	Thrallmar/Honor Hold	350	None
Quest: The Blood is Life	Thrallmar/Honor Hold	350	None

THE ENEMY GARRISON

BOSSES

BROGGOK

KELI'DAN THE BREAKER

THE MAKER

TROOPS

FEL ORC NEOPHYTE
Notes: Intercept, Enrage (physical damage increased by 122, attack speed increased by 60%)

FELGUARD BRUTE
Notes: Knockback

FELGUARD ANNIHILATOR
Notes: Intercept, Knockback

HELLFIRE IMP
Notes: Fire Bolt

LAUGHING SKULL ENFORCER
Notes: Shield Bash, Heroic Strike

LAUGHING SKULL LEGIONNAIRE
Notes: Enrages at 25% health

LAUGHING SKULL ROGUE
Notes: Poison, Stealth, Kidney Shot, Backstab

LAUGHING SKULL WARDEN
Notes: Fast attack speed

NASCENT FEL ORC
Notes: Thunderclap

SHADOWMOON ADEPT
Notes: Shadow Bolt

SHADOWMOON SUMMONER
Notes: Shadow Bolt, Inferno, Summons Succubus

SHADOWMOON TECHNICIAN
Notes: Proximity Bombs (1800 damage to all in range), Silence

SHADOWMOON WARLOCK
Notes: Shadow Bolt, Corruption, Curse of Tongues

SHADOWMOON CHANNELER
Notes: Shadow Bolt, Mark of Shadow (Magic, All Shadow damage taken is increased by 1,100. 2 minute duration)

QUEST LISTING

HEART OF RAGE

Quest Level	61 to obtain
Quest Giver	Nazgrel (Horde) or Force Commander Danath Trollbane (Alliance)
Goal	Explore the Blood Furnace
Experience Gained	12,950
Reward	Crimson Pendant of Clarity (Neck, +15 INT, Restores 6 mana every 5 sec., Increases damage and healing done by magical spells and effects by up to 18), Holy Healing Band (Finger, +15 INT, Increases healing done by spells and effects by up to 33, Restores 6 mana per 5 sec.), or Perfectly Balanced Cape (Back, 61 Armor, +15 AGI, +22 STA, +30 Attack Power)

Something is going on in the Blood Furnace and arcane scrying is being blocked. The information is important enough that you have been asked to gather a group and investigate the furnace. Take care as a great deal has been invested to obscure the site from magical observation.

THE BLOOD IS LIFE

Quest Level	61 to obtain
Quest Giver	Caza'rez (Horde) or Gunny (Alliance)
Goal	Collect 10 Fel Orc Blood Vials
Experience Gained	7,750
Reward	Breastplate of Retribution (Plate Chest, 902 Armor, +33 STA, +23 STR, +22 INT, Increases damage and healing done by magical spells and effects by up to 27), Deadly Borer Leggings (Cloth Legs, 106 Armor, +23 INT, +21 STA, +15 SPI, Increases damage and healing done by magical spells and effects by up to 27, +22 Spell Critical Strike Rating), Moonkin Headdress (Leather Head, 188 Armor, +30 STA, +20 INT, +20 SPI, Increases damage and healing done by magical spells and effects by up to 23, +19 Spell Critical Strike Rating), or Scaled Leggings of Ruination (Mail Legs, 444 Armor, +33 STA, +23 INT, Increases damage and healing done by magical spells and effects by up to 27, +22 Spell Critical Strike Rating)

A new batch of Fel Orcs is being created. This can't be allowed. While you're inside the Blood Furnace damaging the enemy's production, gather samples of the Fel Orc Blood. If there's a way to reverse the process, we'll find it.

OUT OF THE FIRE AND INTO THE FURNACE

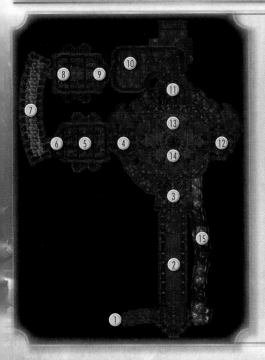

MAP LEGEND	
1	Instance Entrance
2	The Stairs
3	Southern Viewing Room
4	Western Viewing Room
5	The Prison
6	The Maker
7	The Pods
8	The Lab
9	Boggock
10	Barracks
11	Northern Viewing Room
12	Guardpost
13	The Channeling Room
14	Keli'dan the Breaker
15	Shortcut Home

THE STAIRS

The Fel Orcs of Hellfire Citadel have been warped and corrupted. They are far stronger and more resilient than normal Orcs and they are multiplying like they're being made at a factory. Intelligence indicates that the Blood Furnace is an essential part of this operation.

Two Laughing Skull Enforcers guard the entrance. While this fight is very simple, take the opportunity to discuss battle plans with the party. Use the party symbols to indicate who is targeting what to avoid confusion. Also discuss the attack order so you can keep your party's attacks focused and avoid breaking CC early.

SAMPLE EXPLANATION

SYMBOL	DESIGNATION	ATTACK ORDER
Skull	Tank & DPS	1
Star	Seduce	2
Moon	Polymorph	3

The above example assumes three enemies and a party with a Warlock and Mage. Your party may be different, so take the time to work out the battle strategy before you need it.

There are several groups guarding the bottom of the stairs. Each group consists of two Shadowmoon Adepts and a Hellfire Imp. The Adepts are elite and seem to be the real threat, but they are not. The Imp does immense damage, will not advance on you, and has relatively low health.

If you have a Warlock, keep the Imp banished until the Adepts are killed. Use Interrupts to keep the Adepts from using their more powerful attacks. Another option is to have your Warlock enslave the first Imp. This gives your party a rather powerful ally. Be sure the Warlock warns you before he or she releases the Imp though.

If you are without a Warlock, Polymorph or Sap as many of the Adepts as you can and kill the Imp quickly. At 1,000 Fire damage a cast, you can't leave it alive and kicking long. Remember that a tank of low level can't Charge forward without pulling a second group. As such, they should get aggro on the group from range and use the hallway to block line-of-sight and force the Imp's group forward.

Another pair of Laughing Skull Enforcers guards the stairs. Pull them away from the stairs and kill them as you did the first pair. Ascend the stairs slowly and together. Stealthing enemies wander the stairs and can do a good bit of damage to a caster before the party can react. Have Hunters Flare to assist with spotting the troublesome Orcs, or have any soft targets follow at distance while more heavily armored targets scour the stairway.

THE SOUTH VIEWING ROOM

The enemy groups at the top of the stairs are packed fairly close together and have a wanderer with them. Each group has three Shadowmoon Adepts and a Hellfire Imp. Wait until the Shadowmoon Summoner wanders to the left side before pulling the right group.

Use a ranged attack and line-of-sight pull (LOS). By hiding behind a wall you break their line-of-sight and force them to come to you. Have Polymorph, Seduce, or Freezing Trap ready when the enemies join you. As with the battles at the bottom of the stairs, if you have a Warlock, banish the Imp and kill the Adepts. If you are without a Warlock, crowd control the Adepts and kill the Imp first.

Wait for the Summoner to wander to the right side once the group is clear. When he is clear, pull the front left group into the previous room. Dispatch them as you did the first group. The Summoner is your next target. Use a ranged attack to get his attention and interrupts such as Earth Shock, Silencing Shot, or Counterspell to keep him from casting. When he joins you, kill him.

The final group should feel very alone and scared. Descend on them and show them the power of Azeroth. Proceed down the hall on your left.

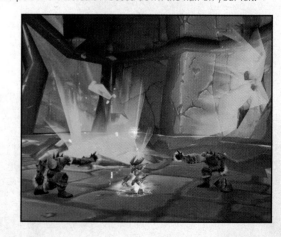

There are two groups of guards. Each has a Laughing Skull Enforcer and Laughing Skull Legionnaire. Kill the Enforcer first as the Legionnaire enrages at low health. Be ready for the increase in enemy damage and blow the Legionnaire down.

The next set of guards can be dealt with in exactly the same manner. Proceed along the hallway until it connects with a larger room. As with the previous room, there are several groups and a wandering Shadowmoon Warlock. The groups here are much more dangerous than the previous room however.

THE WEST VIEWING ROOM

Each group consists of Shadowmoon Adepts and Summoners. The Adepts aren't nearly as dangerous as the Summoners. In pulls with more than one Summoner, Polymorph or Seduce one and interrupt the other until it's dead. If allowed time, the Summoners will call various minions to their aid, including a Succubus. This may not seem like much, but, if allowed, the Succubus will Seduce your healer. If a Summoner calls a Succubus, kill the pet first. You can't afford to have 20% of your party Seduced by a demon. Hunters pulling with Silencing Shot is a good way to force the Summoners forward early on. Otherwise, have someone with a ranged Interrupt prepare to pull the Summoner forward when they stop to cast.

Avoid using Sap in this room as a Laughing Skull Rogue can wander around it. Pull the fights into the hallway when possible. If the Rogue adds during a fight, tank it immediately. Cloth-wearing friends won't last long against his attacks.

Pull the first group when the Shadowmoon Warlock is away. Have crowd control and Interrupts ready. The fighting is simple as long as the Summoner is locked down or killed quickly.

The wandering Warlock is your next target. Wait for him to wander away from the far group and pull it around a wall. Kill it and engage the far group like you did the first group of this room. It's more likely that this group will have two Summoners. If you don't have enough crowd control for both, kill one quickly while the other is crowd controlled.

With the room cleared, only the two guards at the next doorway block your way forward. The Laughing Skull Enforcers aren't anything you haven't fought before. Dispatch them and rest to full as the next area requires more finesse.

THE PRISON

While there are fewer enemies in each group here, the targets are much more dangerous. Shadowmoon Summoners and Technicians are in pairs throughout the room. A Laughing Skull Warden and Shadowmoon Technician patrol. The Technicians are present throughout the next several areas, so you need to learn how to deal with them.

SHADOWMOON TECHNICIANS HATE EVERYONE

The Shadowmoon Technicians can cast Silence. This lasts for several seconds and will make your life much more difficult as tanks can't taunt, healers can't heal, and casters can't cast while Silenced. Kill the Technicians quickly to avoid a much more troubling fight.

Technicians also drop Proximity Bombs. Once armed, these will explode and do 1,800 Fire damage to any party members nearby. These bombs are very visible, and should be avoided at all costs. Once the immediate fight is finished, have a Rogue disarm them or have a high-health party member set them off (after being healed to full). This keeps the bombs from hindering anyone in the next fight.

If you don't have any ranged Interrupts, or if the Summoner resisted the Interrupt, the fight is more challenging. Crowd control the Technician as soon as it gets to the doorway. Kill the Succubus first! This leaves the Summoner free to cast, but you need the Succubus down before you engage the Summoner. Once the pet is dead, focus on the Summoner then the Technician.

Pull the first group on the left when the patrollers are away and duck around the doorway. Have an Interrupt such as Silencing Shot, Counterspell, or Earth Shock ready to force the Shadowmoon Summoner to come to you. When the enemies reach the doorway, Polymorph, Seduce, or Freezing Trap the Shadowmoon Technician and kill the Summoner.

THE MAKER

HP	38722/100534 (Heroic)	Damage	1255-1746/4492-6353 (Heroic)
Abilities	**Domination**: Mind controls a humanoid up to level 70 for 10 sec.		
	Throw Beaker: Deals approximately 1000-1200 nature damage and knocks the party member in the air. **Heroic**: 2500 damage.		

THE MASTERWORKS OF A CRAFTSMAN

Diamond Core Sledgemace (Main Hand Mace, 41.2 DPS, +12 STA, +14 INT, Increases damage and healing done by magical spells and effects by up to 51, Restores 5 mana per 5 sec.)

Girdle of the Gale Storm (Mail Waist, 285 Armor, +13 STA, +19 INT, 1 [Red Socket], 1 [Blue Socket], Socket Bonus: +3 INT, Restores 6 mana per 5 sec., Increases healing and damage done by magical spells and effects by up to 18)

Ironblade Gauntlets (Plate Hands, 564 Armor, +20 STR, +14 AGI, +19 STA, 1 [Red Socket], 1 [Yellow Socket], Socket Bonus: +3 Parry Rating, +6 Hit Rating)

Libram of Saints Departed (Libram, Causes your Judgements to heal you for 41-49)

Pendant of Battle-Lust (Neck, +19 STR, +14 AGI, +19 STA)

The Maker has high health, deals impressive damage, and has a couple tricks up his sleeve just to make your life more difficult (and possibly shorter as well). He can throw party members into the air; this effectively crowd controls the character for a couple seconds, and Interrupts any spellcasts. If the tank is thrown into the air, stop attacks until the tank can regain aggro. Have a pet or backup tank pull aggro until the primary tank lands.

The second ability is just as devastating. The Maker can force a party member to join him for several seconds. This means the fight changes from five-on-one to four-on-two. Ignore the controlled character and keep focusing on the Maker. Using Polymorph, Seduce, or Freezing Trap will keep the afflicted party member from harming others.

As long as your group mitigates the problems caused by these two abilities, the boss fight here is a simple tank and trash skirmish.

Heroic Mode

The primary difference is his Exploding Breaker hits for about 2500 damage making it impossible to ignore.

The group on the right is your next target. Wait for the patrol to wander away before pulling the same way you did before. Continue this until the room is clear of all enemies except the Maker.

There are two doors on each side of the room with captured Orcs within, but they are too far gone for you to help. Rest to full and prepare for a fast and frantic fight.

Kill the Maker and the door behind him opens. More of the Blood Furnace's function is revealed by a peak inside the next area. Shadowmoon Technicians stand around pods of some sort where Nascent Fel Orcs are being corrupted.

THE PODS

Pull the group of two Technicians and one Fel Orc into the previous room when the patrolling Laughing Skull Enforcers are away. As the Nascent Fel Orcs are not elite, they should be killed first while the Technicians are crowd

controlled or kept busy. If you are without crowd control, tank the Technicians with two different party members and keep them away from each other. Having two bombs blow up simultaneously inflicts terrible damage. Once the Fel Orc is killed, dispatch the Technicians one at a time. Be watchful of the Proximity Bombs during the fight.

Wait for the Laughing Skull Enforcers to patrol back near the doorway and pull them into the previous room. This is another fight that is more to slow you down than to kill you. Slay the Enforcers as you have before.

Send your tank into the hallway towards the left side. It's a dead end, but a Laughing Skull Rogue often waits here to ambush an unsuspecting caster. Destroy this Orc. Don't be alarmed if you can't find this Rogue; there are several possible points for this foe along the corridor, so sometimes the way is clear.

Now that it's safe for the softer party members, move into the hallway. The groups lining the hallway vary in composition, but you've fought all of them before. Watch the two patrolling Laughing Skull Enforcers further down. Don't let these join an existing fight.

Shadowmoon Technicians, Nascent Fel Orcs, and various Shadowmoon casters will comprise the groups. The Fel Orcs can be slain quickly and should be your first targets. The Technicians should be crowd controlled until you're ready to deal with them. The casters should be interrupted when possible. To pull the casters to you, hide behind the jagged parts of the walls to break line of sight or have Earth Shock, Silencing Shot, or Counterspell ready.

Move through the corridor slowly and rest to regain health and mana after each fight. You'll want to be at your best if something goes wrong. Be sure to uncover and kill the Laughing Skull Rogue at the very end of the hallway before he can jump one of your casters. Again, if he isn't there, don't worry.

THE LAB

Another large room with prison doors on both sides greets you. A great many groups of Shadowmoon Summoners and Technicians fill the room. The entire room needs to be cleared before you can advance, so start pulling the groups.

Pull the groups into the previous hallway. Use Counterspell, Silencing Shot, or Earth Shock to keep the Summoners from calling their pets. Polymorph, Seduce, or Freezing Trap the Technicians as soon as they get to the hallway, then kill the Summoner. The Technicians are easy prey when taken one at a time.

If you do not have a ranged Interrupt, pull the group around the corner. Crowd control the Technicians as soon as they get there and kill any pets the Summoners have called.

When the Summoners and Technicians are cleared from the room, Fel Orc Neophytes comprise the final groups.

The Fel Orc Neophytes are fully corrupted and very dangerous. Unlike their Nascent cousins, they are Elite. They also Enrage themselves on occasion. This burning hatred increases their attack power and attack speed immensely. They can also Intercept to stun and damage casters in your party without warning!

Polymorph, Seduce, or Freezing Trap the Neophytes and kill the other enemy first. These fights are more to give you a taste of what you're about to face then to kill you. Don't let anyone touch the lever on the floor until you've rested fully and are ready for a very difficult fight.

When all of the pulls are completed, look through the far gate. Even through an obstructed view, Broggok isn't pretty and you'll be fighting him before long. It's now time to figure out how to get that gate open!

Pulling the lever begins an event that will test your group's ability to survive against the odds. Rather than opening the door to Broggok, the lever opens one of the prison doors. These prisoners are much more aware than the previous ones, but they aren't your friends.

The enemies will engage you and fight to the death. When they fall, the next door opens and another group charges you. The fights get progressively more difficult as more elite enemies are in each batch. Only after all four of the groups are dead with Broggok come forward. The order for the doors is back-left, back-right, front-left, front-right. Thus, the two initial encounters start very close to the party.

You will not have any time to rest between the Orc battles, so any class that can restore mana or health during the fighting will be worth its weight in gold.

ORC GROUPS

ORDER	NASCENT FEL ORCS	FEL ORC NEOPHYTES
1	3	0
2	2	1
3	2	2
4	1	3

Take stock and make sure you're using all your characters to their fullest. Mages should Conjure Mana Rubies for themselves. Warlocks should provide a Healthstone to each party member. Blessing of Wisdom and Mana Spring Totem are going to be essential in keeping your casters in the fight. Innervate and Evocation are important to use if you have them. Consider passing out potions as well to keep some of the strain from the healers.

The first fight is against three Nascent Fel Orcs. While none of them are elite, avoid using AoE attacks as you need to conserve your mana. Polymorph, Seduce, or Freezing Trap some to lessen damage taken by the party, but let melee and efficient ranged attacks do the bulk of the damage.

When the last Orc falls, the second fight begins. This fight has an Elite enemy and two non-elites. Crowd control the Fel Orc Neophyte above all else. If you have extra in-combat crowd control abilities available, use them against the Nascent Fel Orcs, but the Neophyte needs to be kept ineffective until the party is ready. Kill the weaker Orcs, then the Neophyte.

The third group is more dangerous then the second. With two Fel Orc Neophytes, two Nascent Fel Orcs, and no rest since the last two fights, the fighting is getting a bit chaotic. Watch your mana and use any timed abilities that will regenerate it if you get low. Mana Tide Totem, Innervate, and Evocation are all abilities that can make a huge difference in this event. Using mana potions is another option to keep you casting.

Crowd control both the Fel Orc Neophytes with Seduce, Polymorph, or Freezing Trap if you can. Because there are no enemy groups to aggro, use Fear spells if they are needed or available. Kill both the Nascent Fel Orcs then focus on the Neophytes one-at-a-time.

The final fight is treacherous. You're low on mana, low on health, and the enemy has three Fel Orc Neophytes and a Nascent Fel Orc. Use any AoE crowd control you have to keep the enemies from dealing any substantial damage. This is a good time for Intimidating Shout or Psychic Scream. Kill the Nascent Fel Orc and take the Neophytes one-at-a-time. A good tactic is to CC the final Orc while casters and healers restore some of their precious mana. Melee characters should take this opportunity to bandage. Once you engage the final enemy, pull the fight to the previous hallway. Killing the last Orc releases Broggok and he's not happy. By staying near the hallway, you give your group a few precious moments to get their bearings.

THE PRICE OF FAILURE

This is one of the 'wipe' fights for players new to the Instance. The run from the graveyard is short so don't despair and don't destroy a group by blaming the wipe on a specific person.

Wiping on any of the Orc battles resets the entire event. Discuss what you can do better this time and come at it with a fresh mind and a little bit of petty vengeance!

Dying against Broggok does not reset the Orc encounters however. Once you kill the final Orc, they stay dead (until you come back for another run).

BROGGOK

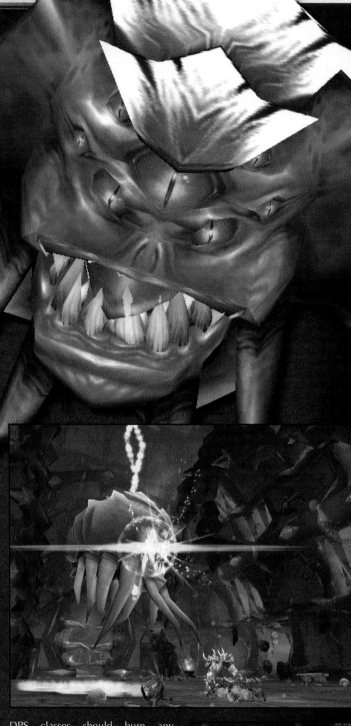

HP	30960/82656 (Heroic)	Damage	651-937/2846-4129 (Heroic)
Abilities	**Slime Spray**: Deals 700-800 nature damage to all targets in a cone in front of Broggok.		
	Poison Bolt: Deals about 600-700 nature damage **Heroic**: 891 to 1003 nature damage every 3 seconds for 12 seconds		
	Poison Cloud: Deals about 600-700 nature damage every second. **Heroic**: 2400 damage per second.		

THE SLIMY LEFTOVERS

Kilt of the Night Strider (Leather Legs, 203 Armor, +21 STA, +26 INT, +8 SPI, 2 [Red Socket]s, 1 [Blue Socket], Socket Bonus: +4 SPI, Restores 6 mana every 5 sec., Increases healing done by spells and effects by up to 33)

Arcing Bracers (Cloth Wrist, 53 Armor, +15 STA, +15 INT, +10 SPI, Increases damage and healing done by magical spells and effects by up to 18)

Auslesse's Light Channeler (Trinket, Increases healing done by spells and effects by up to 59, Use: Reduces the cost of your next spell within 10 seconds by up to 215 mana)

Legion Blunderbus (Gun, 52.5 DPS, +9 AGI, +24 Ranged Attack Power)

Bloody Surgeon's Mitts (Cloth Hands, +10 STA, +20 INT, +12 SPI, 1 [Red Socket], 1 [Blue Socket], Socket Bonus: +3 SPI, Increases healing done by spells and effects by up to 31)

Broggok engages the party immediately and you won't have time to eat or drink. He uses Slime Spray as well as a Poison Cloud (seen as rings of sickly green energy). Avoid standing in the green rings and keep Broggok as far from ranged group members as possible. This limits the damage his AoE poison attacks do.

The tank should grab Broggok early and keep him facing away from the party. Move whenever Broggok uses Poison Cloud, but keep Broggok away from the softer party members. Anything that can Cure Poison will be used heavily in this fight. Use Aspect of the Wild and Nature Resistance Totem if you have them to reduce the damage each attack does. Keep poison off as many party members as possible.

DPS classes should burn any cooldowns they have that increase damage. This is a make-or-break fight. Throw everything you have at this disgusting creature. When Broggok crashes to the ground, collect your loot, pat yourselves on the back, and regain health and mana…you're not done yet.

Avoid standing near the body until the mist of poison clears. Broggok spews the foul stuff even after death, and it's quite easy for a character who is focused on looting to get killed off needlessly.

THE BARRACKS

The room beyond is fairly large. Shadowmoon Warlocks with Felguard Brutes patrol. To the left is a large group of three Hellfire Imps and three Shadowmoon Warlocks. When the patrols are away, pull the group and duck around the corner. This forces them to approach you. Seduce, Polymorph, Banish, and Freezing Trap as many as you can when they come around the corner. Kill any Imps that aren't crowd controlled first. They aren't as damaging as the Imps near the entrance, but they are still very weak and can be taken out without much effort.

Once the active Imps are dead, kill any active Warlocks before breaking crowd control and dealing with the remaining enemies in a less chaotic fashion.

Wait for a patrol to wander near the door and pull it toward you. Kill the Shadowmoon Warlock first as it will buff the Felguard Brute if you don't. Move the party to where the Hellfire Imps were and look for the Laughing Skull Rogue. It's better to kill this treacherous snake on your terms.

The remaining patrol should be getting to your party soon. Engage and destroy it much the way you did the first patrol. Only two Felguard Brutes guarding the door remain of the room. Banish one if you have a Warlock and kill the other. If you are without a Warlock, use ranged snares or a Freezing Trap to keep it ineffective while you kill the other. Finish the final enemy and get your AoEs ready.

It's always a gamble to Enslave something as powerful as a Felguard, but it can be done. If your group is comfortable with the idea and a Warlock is ready and willing, try this to make the upcoming fights easier. Just don't carry a Brute all the way into the boss fight (that is just asking for trouble).

THE NORTHERN VIEWING ROOM

The next room has only one group of enemies in it, but it's a large group. One Shadowmoon Warlock is surrounded by six Hellfire Imps. These aren't nearly as dangerous as the Imps before. They do less damage and have lower health, but there are more of them. Pull the group around the corner to clump them all together and use AoE attacks to destroy the Imps. With his helpers dead, the Warlock is doomed.

If you are without sufficient AoE attacks, charge into the room and use burst DPS to kill the Imps as quickly as possible. Once the tank takes the first blast from all the enemies, the healer should use his or her largest heal and duck around the corner. Using a large heal like that will pull aggro from all the enemies that aren't engaged. This is good as they have to run around the corner to attack the healer. The time they spend running is time they don't spend casting.

Once the enemies close with the healer, he or she should run around the corner again (into the room with the party). This will disrupt the enemies again and bring them back to the party. Many of the Imps should be dead at this point and the tank needs to grab the remaining aggro before this little game of tag turns deadly. Handle the remainders as a standard fight.

THE GUARDPOST

Take the ramp to the right and start down to the main level. Two Felguard Annihilators guard the ramp. These are stronger than Felguard Brutes, but can be dealt with in the same fashion. Crowd control one and kill the other. Having a Warlock to Banish is ideal, but Frost Nova, Freezing Trap or other rooting effects work as well. Having the primary tank hold one while the rest of the party kills the other is the least ideal option, but it is still effective.

The bottom of the ramp reveals tougher enemies. Groups of one Shadowmoon Warlock and two Felguard Annihilators stand guard. If you can Banish or Freezing Trap an Annihilator do so and kill the Warlock first followed by the active Annihilator second. The Warlocks can buff the Annihilators just as they could buff the Brutes.

You can also use humanoid based crowd control on the Warlock and kill the Annihilators first. Seduce and Polymorph are ideal for this. Be extremely careful using Sap as the second group is very close and you don't want to fight both at once.

A LITTLE PRIEST FUN

If you are without any ability to crowd control the enemies, but have a Priest you can use Mind Control. Start the fight by Mind Controlling the Warlock and watch as his servants pound him into a bloody pulp.

Avoid laughing too hard as the Annihilators will be charging the party as soon as the Warlock is dead. Don't engage the Annihilators in any way until the Warlock dies as your Priest won't be able to heal you until the Mind Control ends.

With the first group dead, pull the second in the same fashion and rest to full health and mana. Through the doorway you can see the goal of your quest here. Keli'dan the Breaker stands in the center of five Shadowmoon Channelers.

THE CHANNELING CHAMBER

SO FAR FROM THE LIGHT

Consider equipping any items that increase your Shadow Protection. Both the Shadowmoon Channelers and Keli'dan use Shadow-based attacks. Any abilities that increase Shadow Protection should be cast or renewed if their duration is getting short. Shadow Protection and Shadow Resistance Aura are great for this.

The Channelers will also cast Mark of Shadow. This magic debuff increases Shadow damage taken by 1,100 and lasts for two minutes. Characters with Cleanse, Dispel Magic, or Devour Magic (Felhunter) should be ready to keep this debuff from destroying your party.

KELI'DAN THE BREAKER

HP	34930/103320 (Heroic)	**Damage**	805-1158/2439-3539 (Heroic)
Abilities	**Shadow Bolt Volley:** 30 yard range. Deals 950-1150 Shadow damage. **Heroic:** 2000 Shadow damage.		
	Corruption: 30 yard range. Deals 542 shadow damage every 3 seconds for 24 seconds. **Heroic:** 700 damage every 3 seconds.		
	Burning Nova: Invulnerable for 5 seconds while channeling. A wave of fire that deals 2000 Fire damage. **Heroic:** Deals about 9000 – 11000 Fire damage.		

WHAT'S LEFT OF THOSE WHO WENT BEFORE

Mantle of the Dusk-Dweller (Leather Shoulder, 174 Armor, +20 AGI, +21 STA, +13 Hit Rating, +40 Attack Power)

Mindfire Waistband (Cloth Waist, 68 Armor, +10 STA, +14 INT, +8 SPI, 1 [Yellow Socket], 1 [Blue Socket], Socket Bonus: +3 Spell Hit Rating, +11 Spell Critical Strike Rating, Increases damage and healing done by magical spells and effects by up to 21)

Raiments of Divine Authority (Cloth Chest, 122 Armor, +16 STA, +21 INT, +18 SPI, 1 [Red Socket], 1 [Yellow Socket], 1 [Blue Socket], Socket Bonus: +6 STA, Increases healing done by spells and effects by up to 46)

Vest of Vengeance (Leather Chest, 232 Armor, +27 AGI, +18 STA, 1 [Red Socket], 1 [Yellow Socket], 1 [Blue Socket], Socket Bonus: +4 Dodge Rating, +11 Hit Rating, +42 Attack Power)

Warsong Howling Axe (Two-Hand Axe, 70.3 DPS, +37 STA, +80 Attack Power)

Take the time to restore buffs, pass out Shadow Protection Potions, Healthstones, etc. while you discuss the plan ahead. With five elite enemies, you'll need to use every ounce of crowd control you have.

The Shadowmoon Channelers attack at the same time and cannot be pulled singly. Start the fight with Sap or Mind Control. If your Rogue has Improved Sap, let him or her Sap one before you Mind Control. Let the Mind-Controlled enemy die before the rest of the party engages. You don't get experience or loot from that enemy, but victory is more important.

Polymorph any you can and have interrupts ready for the enemies that still active. If a caster or healer gains aggro, they should duck into the previous room to break line of sight. This gives the rest of the party time to pull the enemy off the endangered.

While Frost Nova won't do much to crowd control the enemies when used in the large room, pulling the enemies into the previous room before using it is much more useful. This roots the enemies where they can't cast on the party. Other abilities that work well are Intimidating Shout, Psychic Scream, and other fear attacks. Keli'dan won't attack until all the Channelers are dead, so fear away!

Use any abilities that regenerate mana or health once you get down to the final Channeler. If Innervate, Evocation, or Mana Tide Totem has recycled since you last used them, now is a good time to use it again. Having full health and mana when you engage Keli'dan makes the fight much easier.

As soon as the last Shadowmoon Channeler dies, Keli'dan the Breaker attacks. Don't stand near him unless you have to. His primary attack is a Shadow Bolt Volley, but he uses Burning Nova. If you have Mark of Shadow on more than a couple party members, this fight will quickly devolve into a mad dash to kill before being killed.

Several times during the fight, Keli'dan will stop attack for a moment and taunt you to "Come closer!" Get out of melee range as quickly as you can. Keli'dan casts Burning Nova. Any characters hit by this takes a great deal of damage and may be killed before the healer can restore their health.

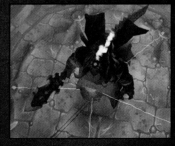

This is the final fight of the instance. Any timed abilities or trinkets that increase damage or reduce the damage taken should be used. Don't hold anything back as Keli'dan surely isn't.

When his corpse is finally beneath your feet, collect your loot and follow the door that opened for a shortcut to the entrance and daylight.

THE SHATTERED HALLS

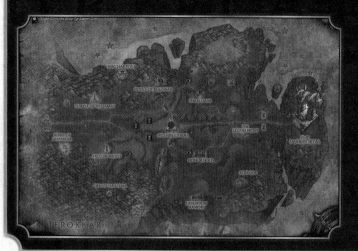

DUNGEON INFORMATION

Name	The Shattered Halls
Location	Hellfire Peninsula, Hellfire Citadel
Suggested Levels	Group of 5, Level 70
Primary Enemies	Humanoids
Damage Types	Physical, Fire, Some Shadow
Time to Complete	90 to 120 Minutes

WHO TO BRING

As The Shattered Halls is a rather difficult Instance, there are several things you need to bring with you. Failure to bring these will result in a more difficult run, added risk of party wipes, and, very likely, a failed run.

Almost every non-Boss encounter in The Shattered Halls involves many Elite enemies. Having recastable crowd control is an absolute must. Polymorph, Fear, Freezing Trap, and Seduce are good single-target crowd control abilities while Howl of Terror, Psychic Scream, and Intimidating Shout are obvious multi-target abilities.

Less standard multi-target crowd control abilities are Frost Trap, Earthbind Totem, Piercing Howl, Blast Wave, and Frost Nova. These can Snare/Root an entire enemy force while the puller is safe to retreat. The enemies will continue to follow the puller while the remainder of your party destroys the targets individually. This tactic is broken if anyone else in the party pulls aggro by damaging or healing more than the puller.

One healer can keep a group alive through The Shattered Halls, but having a second person that can heal in emergencies will take a lot of stress off your primary healer. Shadow Priests, Enhancement or Elemental Shamans, Retribution Paladins, and Feral or Balance Druids can all take up the burden of healing while still contributing to DPS during most pulls.

As far as group composition is concerned, shoot for having two characters with in-combat crowd control; optionally bring a person with a third method of control for the especially evil pulls. Always have an exceptional tank. They need to be smart and quick; there will be many targets to choose from, and often more than a couple uncontrolled monsters in the mix. Though gear is important, the intelligence for playing the tank's class is even more vital.

Shoot for a healer with a large mana pool. Large pulls and a couple of longer boss fights mean that The Shattered Halls has both endurance and burst challenges to worry about. Intellect gear should be favored, if the healer has a few choices, and a pool of extra mana potions never hurt.

JOBS

CLASS	ABILITIES
Druid	Great Instance for Offtanking Due to Large Enemy Groups, Backup Healing Also a Huge Boon
Hunter	Trap Crowd Control, Long-Distance Pulls with Feign Death
Mage	Polymorph, Counterspell, Frost Nova, Ice Block Pulls (If Spec Allows)
Paladin	High Health and Mitigation Needed for All Boss Fights, Blessing of Freedom, Aura of Shadow Protection
Priest	Power Word: Shield Saves Lives (Pre-Battle "Healing" is Very Helpful), Psychic Scream, Mind Control, Shadow Protection
Rogue	Burst DPS on Non-Elites, Sap, Crippling Poison, Stuns
Shaman	Emergency Tanking w/ Earth Elemental, Earthbind Totem for Kiting Pulls, Earth Shield (If Spec Allows), Tremor Totem
Warlock	Sustained DPS Through DOTs, Fear, Death Coil, Seduce (Succubus), Offtanking (Voidwalker), Howl of Terror
Warrior	High Health and Mitigation Needed for All Boss Fights, Intimidating Shout

GETTING TO THE SHATTERED HALLS

The Shattered Halls is a part of Hellfire Citadel. As such, it sits almost equidistant from either Alliance or Horde flight points. The Instance portal is just above the Summoning Stone, but there is a locked gate blocking your way. To enter, one person in the group needs to have the key, or your party can wait for a high-level Rogue to come and pick the lock (350 Lockpicking is required).  Also, you can wait for other groups to open the gate, then hurry through.

Obtaining the Key to The Shattered Halls involves beginning a quest chain by killing Smith Gorlunk on the Ata'mal Terrace of the Black Temple. This causes an item to drop that sends your character to either Thrallmar or Honor Hold (depending on your faction). Ultimately, this quest chain requires only about an hour or so of work, a group of 3-5 characters around level 70 to complete the last step, and several items (4 Fel Iron Bars, 2 Arcane Dust, and 4 Motes of Fire). All of the items that you need can be purchased from the Auction House for a sum that is still less than the gold rewards for completing this chain!

REPUTATION GAINS

ACTION	FACTION	REPUTATION GAIN	END POINT
Kill Trash Mobs	Honor Hold/Thrallmar	3-24 Points	N/A
Kill Bosses	Honor Hold/Thrallmar	150 Points	N/A
Quest: The Will of the Warchief	Thrallmar	500	N/A
Quest: Turning the Tide	Honor Hold	500	N/A
Quest: Pride of the Fel Horde	Honor Hold/Thrallmar	250 Points	N/A

THE SEAT OF THE FEL HORDE

BOSSES

GRAND WARLOCK NETHEKURSE

BLOOD GUARD PORUNG (HEROIC MODE)

WARBRINGER O'MROGG

WARCHIEF KARGATH BLADEFIST

MINIONS

CREEPING OOZE
Notes: Elite, Nature Damage, Sticky Ooze (Debuff to Movement/Attack, Stacks to 10)

CREEPING OOZELING
Notes: Non-Elite, Nature Damage, Sticky Ooze (Debuff to Movement/Attack, Stacks to 10), Low Health

FEL ORC CONVERT
Notes: Non-Elite, Hemorrhage, Can Be Called by Legionaries, Low Health

HEATHEN GUARD
Notes: Generic Target, Not Worth Reputation

RABID WARHOUND
Notes: Non-Elite, Patrollers, See Through Stealth, Heavily Upgraded in Heroic Mode, Furious Howl, Carnivorous Bite

REAVER GUARD
Notes: Cleave, High Melee Damage, High Health

SHADOWMOON ACOLYTE
Notes: Power Word: Shield, Resist Shadow, Prayer of Healing

SHADOWMOON DARKCASTER
Notes: Shadowbolt, Fear, Rain of Fire Damage

SHARPSHOOTER GUARD
Notes: High Ranged Damage, Low Melee Damage

SHATTERED HAND ARCHER
Notes: AoE Ranged Fire Attack, Shout, Multi-Shot

SHATTERED HAND ASSASSIN
Notes: Stealth, Sap, Cheapshot, Kidney Shot, Backstab

SHATTERED HAND BLOOD GUARD
Notes: High Health/Armor

SHATTERED HAND BRAWLER
Notes: Kick, Thrash

SHATTERED HAND CENTURION
Notes: Immune to Crowd Control, Directs Gladiators to Attack Targets, Battle Shout, Sunder Armor

SHATTERED HAND CHAMPION
Notes: Immune to Crowd Control, High Health, Concussion Blow, Shield Block

SHATTERED HAND GLADIATOR
Notes: Fights Other Gladiators When Not Engaged (Pull Their Groups When They Are Wounded), Mortal Strike Warriors

SHATTERED HAND HEATHEN
Notes: Melee DPS Class, Enrage, Bloodlust

MINIONS

SHATTERED HAND HOUNDMASTER
Notes: Ranged DPS, Volley, Break CC on Hounds (Heroic Only), Shoot, Impaling Bolt

SHATTERED HAND LEGIONNAIRE
Notes: High Health, Summon Allies, Must Be Killed First in Any Group That Has One, Pummel, Aura of Discipline

SHATTERED HAND REAVER
Notes: Cleave, High Melee Damage, Enrage, Uppercut

SHATTERED HAND SAVAGE
Notes: Slice and Dice, Enrage

SHATTERED HAND SCOUT

SHATTERED HAND SENTRY
Notes: Hamstring, Charge

SHATTERED HAND SHARPSHOOTER
Notes: Scatter Shot, High Damage, Shout, Incendiary Shout

SHATTERED HAND ZEALOT
Notes: Non-Elite, Hamstring

QUEST LISTING

PRIDE OF THE FEL HORDE

Level Requirement	70
Quest Giver	Field Commander Romus (Alliance) or Shadow Hunter Ty'jin (Horde)
Quest Goal	Slay 8 Shattered Hand Legionnaires, 4 Shattered Hand Centurions, and 4 Shattered Hand Champions
Experience Reward	12,650

Kargath Bladefist's Fel Horde is one of the major powers in Hellfire Peninsula. Many have died simply trying to get this information. Beyond the bloodthirsty and battle-hardened Fel Orc regulars, there is an elite force that serves as officers.

The Shattered Hand Legionnaires, Champions, and Centurions command through fear. Take your group into The Shattered Halls and kill all of these officers of the Fel Horde. A single run of Shattered Halls is enough to get the kills for all of these enemies, and non of them are hidden or are off the beaten path.

TEAR OF THE EARTHMOTHER

Level Requirement	70
Quest Giver	David Wayne
Quest Goal	Collect the Tear of the Earthmother
Experience Reward	12,650
Additional Rewards	Continues the Quest Chain

Though secluded at his refuge, David Wayne is still willing to work with you to create a powerful weapon. The next item he needs is the Tear of the Earth. It's held by Warbringer O'mrogg. Kill this boss and loot him to collect the item you need, then return to David Wayne (this is part of a long chain that begins when you loot an item off of the Mo'arg Weaponsmiths in Shadowmoon Valley).

THE WILL OF THE WARCHIEF (HORDE ONLY)

Level Requirement	70
Quest Giver	Nazgrel
Quest Goal	Take Warchief Kargath's Fist by force
Experience Reward	12,650
Additional Rewards	Rod of Dire Shadows (Wand, 121.1 DPS, +10 INT, Increases damage and healing done by magical spells and effects by up to 11, +10 Spell Critical Rating), Vicar's Cloak (Back, 74 Armor, +18 INT, Restores 7 mana per 5 sec., Increases healing done by spells and effects by up to 40), Conqueror's Band (Finger, +27 STA, +34 Attack Power, +18 Critical Strike Rating), or Maimfist's Choker (Neck, +27 STA, +17 STR, +18 Defense Rating)

Once a mighty Orcish hero, Kargath Bladesfist has proclaimed himself 'Warchief' of the Fel Horde. He has vowed to destroy Thrallmar and he has an army of Fel Orcs with which to accomplish this.

Thrall has commanded that Kargath and his forces must be defeated. Your task is to fight your way into Kargath's stronghold, The Shattered Halls, and slay him. Proof of your success garners quite the reward.

Kargath is the third and final boss of the Instance, and the linear progression of this dungeon means that there are no tricks or hidden ways to make it to the end. Read the full walkthrough for the best strategies to get your group to the end of the dungeon and defeat this fallen Orc. Once Kargath is dead, remind all group members with the quest to loot his corpse for the Fist.

TURNING THE TIDE (ALLIANCE ONLY)

Level Requirement	70
Quest Giver	Force Commander Danath Trollbane
Quest Goal	Collect Warchief Kargath's Fist
Experience Reward	12,650
Additional Rewards	Nethekurse's Rod of Torment (Wand, 121.1 DPS, +10 INT, Increases damage and healing done by magical spells and effects by up to 11, +10 Spell Critical Rating), Mantle of Vivification (Back, 74 Armor, +18 INT, Restores 7 mana per 5 sec., Increases healing done by spells and effects by up to 40), Naliko's Revenge (Finger, +27 STA, +34 Attack Power, +18 Critical Strike Rating), or Medallion of the Valiant Guardian (Neck, +27 STA, +17 STR, +18 Defense Rating)

The history of Honor Hold is a bloody one. The Alliance soldiers there have carved their survival out of a hostile land with blood, sweat, and tears. They will not allow it to be taken by anyone, especially the Fel Horde!

Your job is to seek out and destroy Warchief Kargath and return with proof of his destruction. Read through the strategies in the walkthrough to make a clean run of the dungeon. At the end, kill Kargath and have everyone loot the Orc's Fist as proof of victory.

STORMING THE CASTLE

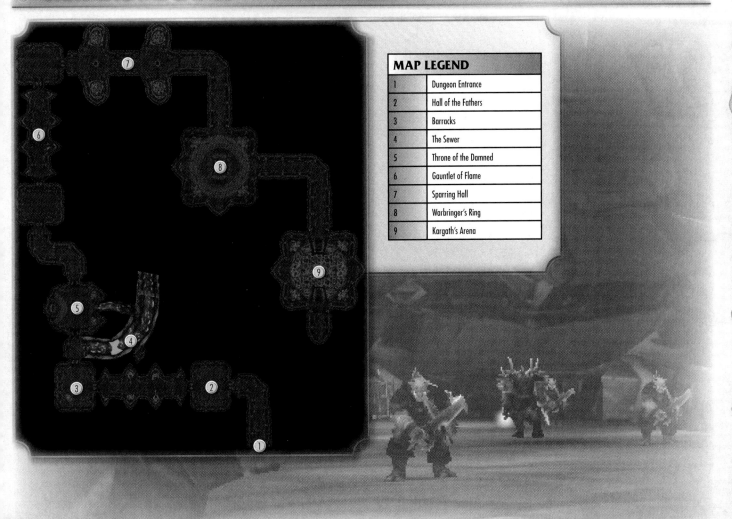

MAP LEGEND	
1	Dungeon Entrance
2	Hall of the Fathers
3	Barracks
4	The Sewer
5	Throne of the Damned
6	Gauntlet of Flame
7	Sparring Hall
8	Warbringer's Ring
9	Kargath's Arena

THE ENTRANCE HALL

Enter The Shattered Halls and hold your ground during the buffing and trading period. Let your group know that the hall ahead won't stay clear for long so that nobody wanders too much, then look on as a Shattered Hall Legionnaire marches into position with Savages and Heathens in tow.

Once everyone is ready to start pulling, target the Legionnaire. Though you can freely pull the forward targets without getting their officer, there is no reason to do so. Heathens and Savages in this corridor aren't worth any Reputation, and the Legionnaire will immediately replace any of his troops that you kill.

Thus, take the Legionnaire out when he is as far forward as possible. This brings him with only one of his troops (two if you pull too late or early, but that still makes for an easy fight). Use any crowd control against the adding troops and focus all damage onto the Legionnaire directly.

THE THREAT OF LEGIONNAIRES

Legionnaires are a very unusual enemy. These officers must always be the first target in a group that has one. If you kill one of the Legionnaires' soldiers beforehand, the Legionnaire will simply replace them with a fresh troop. This can easily mean that your group won't be able to survive the already challenging pull. There are sometimes six Elites to face in the first place, or five Elites and a couple of non-Elites. Adds are NOT what you want.

Thus, crowd control is never used on a Legionnaire. It is used on their higher DPS companions while all fire is brought to bear on their leader.

The other Fel Orcs in the hall can be pulled separately and dispatched without trouble. Nothing comes to replace them once their Legionnaire is dead, so your group won't have any problems at all.

Turn west at the end of the hallway and look for the two Shattered Hand Sentries by the next room. These enemies are linked, but they aren't terribly difficult targets. Sentries are Warriors, with Hamstring and moderate damage. They can easily be tanked and brought down in a variety of methods.

HALL OF THE FATHERS

The next serious pulls are inside the room itself. There are nine Elites holding the chamber, with a Legionnaire patrolling from left to right in front of his soldiers. The troops themselves are arrayed in pairs. This looks like a very scary place, but well-informed pulling makes it much easier to handle.

Wait until the Legionnaire is on the far left side of the room, then pull the RIGHT pair of enemies. These come by themselves, without any of the other Elites adding and without the Legionnaire.

For an especially smooth pull, use crowd control on the higher-threat target of the pair. Dark Casters and Acolytes are certainly the most frustrating ones in this area, so they are the targets for crowd control.

Thus, pull the right group and have the tank and DPS hit the melee troop that comes forward (usually a Savage). While the group kills this target, the Acolyte will approach. Use ranged Interrupts/Silence to keep the Acolyte coming forward, then use crowd control when it gets close to your group. This avoids having the Legionnaire patrol over to the enemy while it is under the effect of crowd control.

Let your tank know that non-Elite adds will appear during the fight. What happens is that the Legionnaire calls for troops to attack your group once he realizes that some of his Elites are dying. Thus, you'll have one non-Elite Fel Orc Convert attack as soon as you kill the first target. Then, a second comes when your other primary target dies.

Pull quickly, kill the melee Elite, kill the Convert that adds. Break crowd control on the second Elite, kill it, then kill the other Convert. Done! Rest and repeat the process on the left pair of enemies.

To be especially mean, you can now pull the Legionnaire when he is alone. Target the officer when he is at the far edge of his patrol, on either side. This gets him without a single add, and he is a piece of cake! Grab the remaining two pairs on their own for more easy kills. You won't even have Converts to worry about.

Two Shattered Hand Sentries protect the western hallway. Pull those, but don't move forward for a few moments. The deaths of the Sentries alert the Legionnaires in the next hallway; they will start to move into position.

Once the enemies settle, you should see a set party of five Elites ahead of you (one Legionnaire, Brawler, Sharpshooter, Heathen, and Reaver). Brawler and Heathens are the lowest order of threat in such groups. Sharpshooters and Reavers are far worse. The Sharpshooters have Scatter Shot and high DPS, while the Reavers have a foul Cleave that spells doom if you let them get into your rear lines.

LONG PULLS

One strategy that works for the large Elite pulls in this dungeon is a long pull. To do this, have a speedy ranged character start the battle then flee down the corridors, taking most of the enemies with him. Hunters are ideal for this, with ranged, Feign Death, and traps. However, Mages with Blink and possibly Ice Block are very good as well.

Your group's remaining four characters are free to engage the Legionnaire and one or two targets with relative safety. When those enemies fall, let the puller know to stop the long pull and return the surviving enemies to the group.

THE TERRIBLE TABLE OF FEL ORCS

ORC NAME	DANGER LEVEL	NOTES
Legionnaire	Special	Not Terribly Bad on Their Own, But Must Be Killed First Due to Adds
Dark Caster	Very High	Warlock, Fear, AoEs, High DPS
Acolyte	Very High	Priest, Mind Blast, Shield Allies
Sharpshooter	Very High	Hunter, Scatter Shot, Weaker at Melee Range
Reaver	High	Warrior, High Melee DPS, Cleave
Savage	Moderate	Pummel
Brawler	Moderate	Curse (Raises Damage Taken)
Heathen	Moderate	Pummel
Convert	Rogue	Low Health, Hemorrhage

All of the pulls in this hallway are meant to be done with some distance. You never want to risk adds while Fearing or using other crowd control methods. In addition, kiting enemies is important, and the more room you have the better!

Use the cleared room behind your party for the first pull. Place traps along the walls and let the puller know which side of the corridor to use while breaking line-of-sight (this ensures that an enemy winds up in the trap). Freezing Traps are a good choice, though any group using a long pull with a Hunter can rely on Explosive Traps to keep enemy aggro on the Hunter; note that Hunters can redeploy traps periodically on the way if more time is needed.

Getting back to the group at hand, the first group in the hallway has five Elite enemies. A Legionnaire walks there with a Sharpshooter, Reaver, Heathen, and Brawler. Use crowd control against the Sharpshooter and Reaver if possible, while your group kills the Legionnaire and tanks the Heathen/ Brawler combo.

Fear abilities are wonderful in this and other major pulls; the dungeon is filled with many such groups, and Intimidating Shout, Psychic Scream, and Howl of Terror adds to your survivability. Lacking those, group Snare abilities slow the enemies' progress, ensuring that the rear of the party has time to retreat if some of the enemies start to peel off of the tank. Piercing Howl, Frost Trap, Blast Wave/Frost Nova (as a last resort), and similar abilities work for this.

Organize the group so that everyone knows what to do ahead of time. There should be an order for Fears and other important abilities so that they are not used simultaneously and wasted. Being on a voice-communication program aids this, but solid text communication does the trick too. Example: Fear 1 (Warrior uses Intimidating Shout), Fear 2 (Priest hits Psychic Scream).

When this first group dies, two more Legionnaires arrive. Each brings a similar group of enemies. The new groups have a nastier concentration of DPS troops, but the strategies for beating them are similar.

When there are more Sharpshooters and Dark Casters in the mix, you can sacrifice a pet for tanking those at long range while the group is busy with the Legionnaire. This is doubly effective against the Dark Casters because it keeps them out of range for Rain of Fire.

HEALERS WITH AGGRO

If you are a healer and get aggro from the ranged enemies in The Shattered Halls, be ready to break line-of-sight. Your group can't afford to lose healing for long, but neither can they afford to lose you to death! There are many corners in these hallways, and slipping around them breaks line-of-sight against Sharpshooters. Sometimes you can still see and heal the party while doing this!

Hopefully, drawing the ranged enemies forward is going to make it even easier for the tank to see what is going on. They can then slap the Sharpshooters and get the foes back where they should be.

At the far end of the hallway is the Barracks. A fourth group guards that room, and there are four sleeping enemies in that room as well. You always want to pull this fourth group way back to avoid the dangers of awakened Elites!

That group of Elites has a Legionnaire with two non-Elite Converts, one Reaver, a Savage, an Acolyte, and a Dark Caster. This is not a simple fight!

Hit the Acolyte and hopefully the Dark Caster too with crowd control. Kill the Legionnaire and use any Fears to keep the enemy group off of your back as long as possible. Otherwise, have a character organize a long pull to get the melee enemies charging away while the Legionnaire and casters are killed.

To leave the Barracks, one more pull must be made. The Shattered Hand Houndmaster with two Rabid Warhounds guard the northern exit. On Normal Mode, this is a simple fight. Use crowd control on the Houndmaster and destroy his non-Elite Warhounds quickly. Pull the group back into the eastern hallway so that the Houndmaster can run around and wake up the sleeping Elites while he is trying to get range on the party.

Heroic Mode

In Heroic Mode, this "simple" fight gets ugly. The Rabid Hounds become MAJOR DPS dealers. They won't let you use crowd control on their master either, so you are forced to use crowd control against them instead. This is fleeting, because the Houndmaster periodically breaks control against the Rabid Hounds (just not as often as they can break it when he is controlled).

Pull the group back into the eastern hallway, as usual, and use heavy DPS on one Hound while characters keep the other Hound under crowd control. Be certain to re-apply control when the second Hound breaks free, and hurry to burst down the main target. As soon as that Hound dies, take on Houndmaster. When the initial method of crowd control grows stale due to diminishing returns, have a different character us their abilities on the spare Hound; this keeps things from getting too frantic!

THE SEWER

The entrance to the Throne of the Damned is closed, but your group has access to the Sewer on the right side of the new hallway. Jump down there as a group, with the tank(s) going down first.

Inside the Sewer, there are two types of enemies. Creeping Oozes are the Elite slimes of the area, and each of them has five Creeping Oozlings. Beyond that, Creeping Oozlings spawn periodically and patrol through the hallway to attack your group.

Always have the tanks start the fights in here, as there is no room to kite. Use area-of-effect abilities to accrue Threat against as many enemies as possible (Thunderclap is always nice, with Challenging Shout reserved for emergencies).

Keep Nature Resistance active during these fights; Hunters and Shamans are both good for this, and should be using (Aspect of the Wild and Nature Resistance Totems respectively).

Once aggro is firmly on the tanks and the Creeping Ooze is taking major damage, the area-of-effect abilities from other characters can be used to destroy the Oozlings. Get some rest between such encounters, and have the tanks watch for Oozling adds so that the softer members of the party don't get aggroed while drinking.

This time is also necessary for letting Stick Ooze fall; the debuff used by all of the enemies lowers Movement and Attack Speed, and it stacks up to ten times. You certainly want that to go away before you engage the next packet of Slimes.

Look on the left side of the passage after clearing the major groups of Oozes (you can skip clearing the last Ooze at the far north end of the hall). Climb out of the muck and approach the Throne of the Damned from that position.

THRONE OF THE DAMNED

The first boss of The Shattered Halls sits on the Throne of the Damned. This lower entrance to the room gives your party a clear view of the mighty Warlock, and he is hard at work torturing some of his newest Converts. There are four non-Elite Orcs, and Nethekurse really doesn't care whether they live or die.

Rest now and read about the boss fight, then explain the various aspects of the encounter to everyone. Once your group starts pulling the Converts, there won't be an infinite amount of time before Nethekurse gets bored and wants to have some fun himself.

Without fear or worry of retribution, pull a Convert and kill him. Nethekurse watches you do it and practically cheers you on. Kill two more of the Converts, then get any rest you need. Pull the last Convert when ready and expect Nethekurse to aggro soon afterward.

GRAND WARLOCK NETHEKURSE

HP	107700/149420 (Heroic)	**Damage**	1433-2025/3637-5138 (Heroic)
Abilities	**Shadow Cleave**: Inflicts melee damage plus 275 to the target and near allies, affecting up to 3 targets. **Heroic (Shadow Slam)**: Inflicts weapon damage plus 350		
	Death Coil: 30 yard range, run in horror for 4 sec and causes 1260 Shadow damage. The caster gains 100% of the damage caused in health.		
	Lesser Shadow Fissure: Summons a void zone dealing 878 to 1072 Shadow damage every second. **Heroic**: Deals approximately 3400 to 3700 Shadow damage per second.		
	Dark Spin: Launches a shadow bolt at a nearby target every second for about 1200-1500 Shadow damage, also deals weapon damage to all targets within melee range.		

FEL GIFTS

Greathelm of the Unbreakable (Plate Head 922 Armor, +36 Str, +48 Stam, +30 Defense)

Ivory Idol of the Moongoddess (Idol +55 to Starfire Damage)

Cloak of Malice (Back 76 Armor, +21 Agi, +18 Stam, +38 Attack Power)

Telaari Hunting Girdle (Mail Waist 333 Armor, +24 Agi, +17 Int, +50 Attack Power, 6 Mana/5 Seconds)

Bands of Nethekurse (Cloth Wrist 67 Armor, +18 Int, +13 Spi, +21 Damage/Healing, +15 Spell Penetration)

The bulk of the Nethekurse fight is a simple one if your party is well informed of the dangers. While your tank is engaged with Nethekurse, have a secondary character or a pet prepared to grab the boss, as he has Death Coil to Fear off his enemies, and sometimes it gets used on the main tank.

All characters in the group must stay vigilant during the engagement. If a red light starts to appear near your person, move immediately. This is the herald for a Void Zone; the pink pillars of light that shine after a short time deal Shadow damage to anyone standing in them, and this damage adds up quickly!

Avoid the Void Zones and use any possible Shadow Resistance buffs for your party. Doing so makes the fight relatively safe until the later stage.

When Nethekurse is brought below one-quarter of his health, the Warlock enters a permanent Whirlwind. Melee characters should back off, at least at first. Ranged DPS must stay on the leader to bring him down, and all the while Nethekurse launches Shadowbolts at the party.

If your team has enough ranged DPS for a quick finish to this phase, then just keep doing what you are doing and let the tank take a break (they can use some ranged attacks or spells to contribute, depending on your class).

However, if your group is melee heavy, use burst attacks to bring down Nethekurse. Wait for full Energy or for timers to collapse as a Warrior. Then, rush in and use your best attacks on Nethekurse for a moment then retreat. Bandage as needed.

Heroic Mode

The primary change in Heroic difficulty is his Lesser Shadow Fissure spell deals 3x more damage.

GAUNTLET OF FLAME

The northern doorway out of Nethekurse's room leads toward the Gauntlet of Flame. Consider the next leg to be more of an event, because the entire run is almost a single series of fights. Though there is some time to rest in the middle, it won't be clean or orderly. Your group is going to be under fire for most of the process, and spawning enemies come at regular intervals, so it's wise to read about the Gauntlet now.

The northern halls are filled with non-Elite Zealots and an odd Assassin or two (you'll see many of these later on in the dungeon). While advancing, a group of Elite Archers fires down the hall with area-of-effect Fire shots. These leave a burning area on the ground that continues to do damage when characters pass through it.

Your goal is to run north, fight both the set groups of Zealots and the spawning groups that come at you. Oh...and you have to do it without taking so much time that the waves wear you down. Use either side of the hallway for shelter. The fire won't reach into the tiny nooks, and breaking line-of-sight with the Elite Archers makes it possible to get out of combat unless there are Zealots nearby.

Don't worry about taking on a couple of Zealot groups simultaneously; these Orcs aren't very tough, and facing 4-5 of them isn't a big deal for a group that can comfortably clear this far into the Instance.

The cubby holes near the end of the hall are the best for catching a breather. Do this when you are close to the group of four Zealots, and wait to pull those until you have just defeated a spawn of incoming Zealots (so you won't get adds during the fight).

Use ranged attacks to bring the Zealots into your cubby, thus avoiding the risk of aggroing the Archers. Kill these Zealots, take out one more incoming spawn group, then rest a final time. If this is a Normal Mode run on The Shattered Halls, the next fight is easy. There are two Elite Archers and a single Blood Guard to fight. Use crowd control on the Archers, burn down the Blood Guard, then finish off the Archers at your leisure. The Gauntlet is defeated!

BLOOD GUARD PORUNG (HEROIC MODE ONLY)

HP	139482 (Heroic)	Damage	6398-9049 (Heroic)
Abilities	Heroic: Only exists on Heroic difficulty.		
	Cleave: Deals 110% weapon damage to the target and its nearest ally.		

EXTRA LOOT

Nimble-Foot Treads (Leather Feet 201 Armor, +32 Agi, +24 Stam, +25 Dodge Rating)

Shoulders of the Slaughter (Plate Shoulder 873 Armor, +30 Str, +22 Stam, +27 Critical Rating)

Pantaloons of Flaming Wrath (Cloth Legs 136 Armor, +28 Int, +33 Damage/Healing, +42 Spell Critical Rating)

Blood Guard's Necklace of Ferocity (Neck +54 Attack Power, +17 Critical Rating)

Porung and his two Archers are very difficult if your group doesn't position themselves correctly. Porung's Cleave hits like the end of the world, and his range is absurd!

To limit this, have your tank engage Porung and take him back to the northern wall of the room. Use crowd control against one Archer and destroy the other, then keep the initial Archer under crowd control throughout the fight.

Place all ranged DPS on Porung at this time, and have melee DPSers go in after the next Cleave and use any abilities that they have to mitigate these physical attacks (Evasion, etc.). If a second Warrior is in the mix, they should be ready to retreat and allow the healers to catch up if the incoming damage is too high. Even if this means losing DPS from that character, it's far better than a death.

Once the Blood Guard falls, only a single major hallway stands between your group and the final two bosses of the Instance! Turn east and face the Sparring Hall.

SPARRING HALL

Wait at the entrance to the Sparring Hall and pull the Warhound patrol when it gets to the front of the area. Use the same tactics as before with this group to dispatch them. That is the only patrolling entity in the area, so the rest of the pulls are fixed.

If your group is running the quest to kill the officers of the dungeon, there are four extra pulls to do in this part of the dungeon; they are hidden in the side-notches of the area, and all of the skirmishes are challenging.

Each of pull involves four Gladiators and their single Centurion leader. Centurions are Immune to crowd control, and the Gladiators are all Mortal Strike Warriors with a great deal of stopping power. Even worse, the Centurions are smart enough to order the Gladiators around; sometimes the entire group will choose a target to attack without regard to aggro.

The saving grace of these encounters is that all five of the melee targets can be kited decently and that only the Centurion will have full health. Here is the trick; have a good puller (preferably a Hunter, due to their Instant attacks at range) target the Centurion. While doing this, highlight the health bar of one Gladiator and wait for the group to start fighting. When the Gladiators begin to fight and take each other down near one-third of their health total, pull the Centurion. This makes it very fast to dispatch the Gladiators!

When the group comes, have the main tank snag the Centurion and tank him while getting as much group aggro as possible. Have the character who is handling the main targeting choose one Gladiator and kill it. Repeat this for all of the Gladiators, then finish with the Centurion. By pulling far enough back, Intimidating Shout/Psychic Scream/Howl of Terror gives you enough room to slaughter these groups before they have a chance to do much.

As mentioned before, these groups are optional. If you aren't trying to complete the quest to kill the officers of the Fel Orcs, skip them. Your group can clear the center of the hallway ahead and move carefully to avoid aggroing anything from the side cubbies. This saves a great deal of time and avoids four fights that are rather tricky if you get unlucky.

Unfortunately, you can't avoid the large fights in the center, and these too are quite difficult. You face six Elites, and one of them is a Legionnaire. If you pull when the Legionnaire is on the side of his patrol, he can even aggro a seventh Orc...mean!

If your group doesn't have major crowd control through Fears AND Polymorph, Traps, etc., use a long pull so that the Legionnaire and ranged enemies can be killed without the melee troops being involved in the fight. A Hunter can kite for a VERY long time at this point in the Instance, so long pulls are fairly safe (they are just time consuming).

Try to get the Legionnaire killed while the Acolyte and Dark Caster are under crowd control. Take out the Dark Caster next, then the Acolyte. When the melees are engaged, focus on the Reaver, then the Brawler, and finally the Savage.

After a well-earned rest, clean the middle of the hall of the three remaining Elites (two Brawlers and a Savage). It's an odd pull, because it looks like these guys are not linked, but they are. The fact is that the three aren't hard-linked, but pulling one of them gets the others eventually. An odd dynamic, but your group will understand it once you see it happen.

Clear the next set of cubbies if you like. Otherwise, pull the second Legionnaire group all the way back to the entrance of the Sparring Hall to avoid adds. Use similar tactics against the second set of foes. Take out the practicing melee foes afterward, then bid your time while watching the end of the corridor.

There are two Champions at the end of the passage, but you can't afford to pull them until the Warhound patrol is well out of the way. If you have a Hunter, let them track the patrol to give you an even better idea when to pull the Champions. Bring these foes far enough back to stay quite safe and clear of the Hounds.

Champions are Immune to standard crowd control, but they can be Stunned and Disarmed (and should be whenever possible). If you have a character with major stunlock potential, use their abilities to the fullest to keep damage off of the party. In Heroic Mode, these guys slap on damage like...well, Champions.

Pull the Hound patrol after a good rest and beat them in the tried and true fashion that your group has been perfecting. Then, repeat the Champion fight as well, as there are two more before you reach the next room.

WARBRINGER'S RING

You won't have to face adds and other troubles during the fight in his room, but it's still wise to Flare the eastern side of the arena before the fight begins, just to make sure there aren't any Assassins close by. They aren't always in the same place, and sometimes they can be near the Warbringer's Ring.

WARBRINGER O'MROGG

HP	153135/206732 (Heroic)	**Damage**	1610-2277/3450-4879 (Heroic)
Abilities	**Thunderclap:** Inflicts 938 to 1062 Nature damage, reducing their attack speed by 35% and slowing their movement speed by 35% for 10 sec.		
	Blast Wave: Deals approximately 2550-2850 Fire damage.		
	Fear: Causing them to flee for 3 sec.		
	Burning Maul: Chance on hit to add approximately 1000 Fire damage.		
	Beatdown: Randomly chooses a new player to attack and wipes threat list. **Heroic:** Adds approximately 3000-3400 Fire damage.		

FASHION TIPS FROM AN OGRE MAGI

Jeweled Boots of Sanctification (Cloth Feet 105 Armor, +22 Stam, +25 Int, +55 Healing, 6 Mana/5 Seconds)

Firemaul of Destruction (2h Mace 90.3 DPS, +31 Str, +50 Stam, +40 Resilience Rating)

Skyfire Hawk-Bow (Bow 64.6 DPS, +14 Hit Rating, +26 Attack Power)

Tidefury Shoulderguards (Mail Shoulders 489 Armor, +18 Stam, +23 Int, 1 [red socket], 1 [blue socket], Socket Bonus: +4 Spell Damage, +19 Damage/Healing, 6 Mana/5 Seconds)

World's End Bracers (Mail Wrist 253 Armor, +18 Stam, +19 Int, +17 Spell Critical Rating, +21 Damage/Healing)

Runesong Dagger (Mh Dagger 39.4 DPS, +12 Stam, +11 Int, +20 Spell Critical Rating, +121 Damage/Healing)

Obviously, the main tank needs to rely on abilities with added Threat even more than usual. There is no safety net through Mocking Blow, Challenging Shout, Taunt, and other such abilities, so you must be ahead on the Threat list at all times. O'mrogg's damage isn't high enough to discourage you from using Deathwish (if you are a Warrior who has it); this avoids the Fear issue for a fair portion of the encounter and gives you a considerable increase to Threat without too much extra damage taken.

If you are Feared or Dazed by O'mrogg as a main tank and lose aggro, rely on Intercept-type abilities to get back to the Ogre and start grabbing aggro back as soon as possible. Again, if you are a Warrior, this is a good time to hit Berserk Rage as you are in Berserk Stance already. Then you can drop back into Defensive Stance for its added Threat generation.

O'mrogg is a very fun boss. Give your party boosts to Nature or Fire damage before starting the engagement against him (Fire Resistance armor is a fair choice for your tank if they have any), then go forward and be ready for a laugh. This Ogre spends most of the fight talking back and forth between his heads, so don't let that distract you too much from what must be done.

O'mrogg has Taunt Immunity, can dump aggro a couple of times during the fight using his Beatdown ability, has an immensely effective attack in Burning Maul, and he uses Blast Wave to Daze/damage enemies and AoE Fear to throw people off outright.

Just in hearing that, you probably have realized that this is an aggro-sensitive fight. Your DPS characters must be very careful not to throw an extra spell or shoot at the wrong time, otherwise aggro can go their way very quickly when your tank has little they can do about it.

O'mrogg has two modes of attack—normal and fire. Normal O'mrogg lasts 45 seconds. His Fire mode lasts for 18 seconds during which he uses Burning Maul and Blast Nova.

Because O'mrogg uses his magic at close range, there is a small amount of kiting that can be done by a ranged class if they get aggro during a Fear. Try to stay at range as best you can until the tank gets O'mrogg back into position.

O'mrogg's Blast Wave is heralded by a weapon glow. If your melee characters have any abilities to avoid AoE damage (e.g. Cloak of Shadows) or to get away from the area (e.g. Intervene) use those immediately.

Note that Disarm does work against O'mrogg. Save these for times when aggro is going nutty, which happens pretty much every time you fight him; use Disarm to lower the damage against a non-tank while O'mrogg is rampaging around.

Heroic Mode

Most of the fight is the same. The primary difference is the Burning Maul ability deals significantly more damage.

The last hallway toward the final boss only has a single visible patrol (a standard Hound patrol, as you've been dealing with throughout the dungeon). Yet, things aren't as they appear; there are Assassins EVERYWHERE. Advance very slowly, use Flare if possible, and clear the area comfortably to avoid getting multiple foes simultaneously.

Assassins start their fights with Sap, then they Cheap Shot the next person in line. Their weapons have Crippling Poison, and their DPS is high even in Normal Mode. Healers should be ready, tanks should stay near the front of the group even during rest, and all should be on the lookout.

Get the patrol pulled at the very front of its route and lure it back a fair distance for a safer encounter. Then, take out the rest of the Assassins on the way to Kargath's room.

END OF THE SIEGE

Kargath Bladefist is the leader of the Fel Horde, and he'll take on your party in the middle of his arena. Though it's dangerous for all of your people to be inside the arena with such a skilled Orc Warrior, you won't have much of a choice. Though you don't know it yet, more Assassins will soon fill the corridor that you just cleared (this happens as soon as you engage Kargath).

If you leave characters outside of the arena for this encounter, those poor suckers are going to get cut to ribbons. Everyone inside the arena will be somewhat safe. Kind of...sort of...well, not really. Rest and buff.

KARGATH BLADEFIST

HP	167895/206640 (Heroic)	Damage	1387-1962/2823-3992 (Heroic)
Abilities	Blade Dance: Deals weapon damage to all enemy targets within 15 yards.		

ARTIFACTS OF THE FEL HORDE

Beast Lord Handguards (Mail Hands 407 Armor, +25 Agi, +12 Stam, +17 Int, 1 [red socket], 1 [blue socket], Socket Bonus: +3 Hit Rating, +34 Attack Power)

Demonblood Eviserator (Mh Fist Weapon 71.7 DPS, +16 Stam, +28 Attack Power, +17 Unarmed Skill Rating)

Figuring of the Colossus (Trinket +32 Shield Block Rating, Use to Add +120 Health Per Shield Block, 20 Second Duration)

Gauntlets of Desolation (Mail Hands 407 Armor, +25 Stam, +16 Int, 2 [red socket], Socket Bonus: +3 Resilience Rating, +17 Critical Rating, +32 Attack Power)

Gauntlets of the Righteous (Plate Hands 728 Armor, +22 Stam, +20 Int, +21 Damage/Healing, 7 Mana/5 Seconds, +19 Defense Rating)

Gloves of Oblivion (Cloth Hands 97 Armor, +33 Stam, +21 Int, +20 Spell Hit Rating, +26 Damage/Healing)

Greaves of the Shatterer (Plate Legs 1019 Armor, +25 Str, +37 Stam, 1 [red socket], 1 [yellow socket], 1 [blue socket], Socket Bonus: +6 Block Value, +25 Defense)

Hallowed Handwraps (Cloth Hands 89 Armor, +19 Stam, +20 Int, +26 Spi, +51 Healing)

Hortus' Seal of Brilliance (Off-Hand +18 Stam, +20 Int, +23 Damage/Healing)

Lightsworn Hammer (Mh Mace 41.4 DPS, +12 Stam, +11 Int, +227 Healing, 8 Mana/5 Seconds)

Nexus Torch (129.4 DPS, +9 Stam, +10 Int, +11 Spell Critical Rating, +8 Damage/Healing)

Wastewalker Gloves (Leather Hands 183 Armor, +32 Agi, +33 Stam, 1 [red socket], 1 [yellow socket], Socket Bonus: +3 Dodge Rating, +16 Attack Power)

Physical damage is the mainstay of this fight, and staying spread out and away from melee is the way to get things done. When the fight starts, your main tank is going to hurry to the center of the ring and start to fight Kargath there. Your healer should enter the ring and take one nearby corner. Ranged DPS characters should take another of the two corners, such that neither are out of the healer's range.

Then, one character should stay by the opening to the ring (where you just entered). If that person is also a ranged DPS class, they can fire from there to hit Kargath, for now. If that person is a melee class, they should engage Kargath for about 20 seconds, then return to this position. The first of the Elite adds to the encounter is coming from the hallway you cleared. Be ready for them!

At the 30-second mark, Kargath starts his first Blade Dance. If everyone is close together, he'll slice and dice in such a way that everyone is taking damage constantly, and it's way too much for the healer to compensate for. Even if you live, it'll deplete your healer's reserves too much during this long fight.

If you use the positions that were described above, Kargath must waste a great deal of his Blade Dance rushing between characters, losing the potential to do most of his damage. Almost everyone will take hits, but it won't be more than a few thousand damage on any single person.

Bandage unless you are a healer or main tank, then continue the fight. The healer only needs to heal the main tank normally, then top off anyone who is in trouble from a Blade Dance or from a tougher encounter with the adds. Let your DPS people know if an add escapes and gets to you, and they will destroy it (not the main tank).

The adds don't come in very quickly, but unless you have a wonderful person to deal with these Orcs, it's good to have one of the Ranged characters back them up whenever possible (throwing DOTs on the target, shooting them a few times, landing spells or debuffs, etc.).

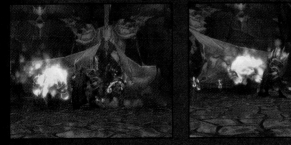

Kargath isn't a hard hitter most of the time, but he has mastered a Blade Dance that is his key to victory against large groups of opponents. His other great skill is his ability to lead; the Fel Orcs aren't going to turn on Kargath or let him die just so they can have a chance of advancement. Rather, the remaining Orcs of Hellfire Citadel are going to charge the arena throughout the fight in any hope of stopping your party from slaying their beloved leader.

Heroic Mode

In Heroic Mode, Kargath hits like a truck. This means his Blade Dance hits like a fleet of trucks...landing on your head...over and over... until you die.

Loot the slain Kargath once the fight is yours, and take his Fist back to your faction for the appropriate cheers and rewards. You know now how to defeat this very enjoyable dungeon, and this is where you can return to get Thrallmar/Honor Hold Reputation (both have some very important rewards for characters).

THE SLAVE PENS

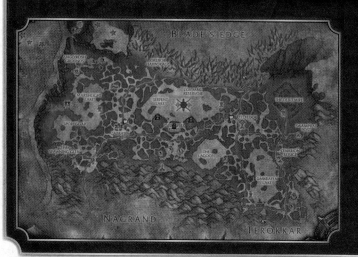

DUNGEON INFORMATION

Name	Slave Pens
Location	Coilfang Reservoir, Zangarmarsh
Suggested Levels	Group of 5, Level 61-65
Reputation	Cenarion Expedition
Primary Enemies	Humanoids
Damage Types	Physical, Frost, Nature
Time to Complete	60 to 90 Minutes

WHO TO BRING

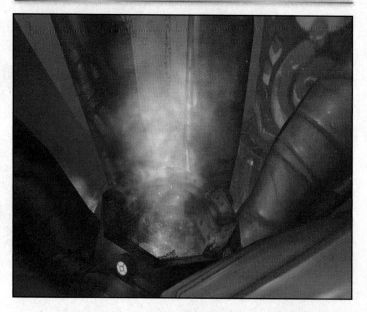

Poison is only a factor in a single fight, but you don't want to get stopped at the final boss simply because you don't have anyone who can Cure Poison. Any class that can remove this life-threatening effect will make a huge difference against the final boss.

JOBS	
CLASS	**ABILITIES**
Druid	Abolish Poison for Quagmirran, Gift of the Wild for All Bosses, Hibernate for Coilfang Rays
Hunter	Freezing Trap in most pulls, Aspect of the Wild for Quagmirran, Scare Beast for Coilfang Rays
Mage	Polymorph for most pulls
Paladin	Cleanse for Final Boss, Frost Resistance Aura for Rokmar
Priest	Mind Control for most pulls, Power Word: Shield for All Bosses
Rogue	Sap in most pulls
Shaman	Frost Resistance Totem for Rokmar, Nature Resistance Totem for Quagmirran, Poison Cleansing Totem for Quagmirran
Warlock	Seduce for most pulls, Healthstones for Boss Fights
Warrior	Intercept

Crowd control is both important and easy in Slave Pens. The enemies you face are almost entirely Humanoid. This opens the door for a great many classes to be of use. Rogues, Hunters, Mages, Warlocks, and Priests all bring a great deal to a party. Have someone willing to use the Raid Icons to mark targets as the leader. Don't let your party break crowd control early; there are some rather large fights later in the instance.

Bring a tank that is ready for everything. Many fights have several enemies, so high Armor Rating and health are important. The boss encounters require even more from your tank as the bosses hit very hard and use different elemental attacks. Do not bring a tank that is unwilling to put away their DPS weapons and use a shield for the boss fights. A tank with high Frost and Nature Resistance is a plus, but there are many classes that can increase Resistances for the entire party. Druids, Hunters, Shamans, and Paladins pay for themselves just by raising the party's Resistance to either Frost or Nature damage.

GETTING TO THE SLAVE PENS

Slave Pens is one of the many wings of Coilfang Reservoir. Horde parties can fly into Zabra'jin while Alliance parties fly into Telredor.

At the center of Serpent Lake is the Coilfang Reservoir. Dive beneath the water at the center of the pumping station and look for the drain. Swim through the drain and surface within the Reservoir. The Slave Pens are the western-most Instance portal.

REPUTATION GAINS

ACTION	FACTION	REPUTATION GAIN	END POINT
Kill Trash	Cenarion Expedition	5	Honored
Kill Boss	Cenarion Expedition	70	Honored
Quest: Lost in Action	Cenarion Expedition	500	N/A

THE SLAVES AND THEIR KEEPERS

BOSSES

MENNU THE BETRAYER

ROKMAR THE CRACKLER

QUAGMIRRAN

MINIONS

BOGSTROK

Notes: Piercing Jab (Reduces armor by 15% for 20 sec.)

COILFANG CHAMPION

Notes: Intimidating Shout, Cleave

COILFANG COLLABORATOR

Notes: Cripple (Reduces movement speed by 50%, increases swing time by 100%), Enrage

COILFANG DEFENDER

Notes: Spell Shield (reflects magic attacks when active)

COILFANG ENCHANTRESS

Notes: Frost Bolt, Entangling Roots, Lightning Storm

COILFANG OBSERVER

Notes: Immolate, Accompanied by Coilfang Ray

COILFANG RAY

Notes: Psychic Horror (6 second Horror)

COILFANG SCALE-HEALER

Notes: Heal, Holy Nova

COILFANG SLAVEHANDLER

Notes: Rend, Hamstring

COILFANG SOOTHSAYER

Notes: Decayed Intelligence (Magic, Intellect reduced by 25%, Area of Effect, Lasts 15 seconds), Mind Control

COILFANG TECHNICIAN

Notes: Rain of Fire

GREATER BOGSTROK

Notes: Decayed Strength (Disease, Strength reduced by 25)

WASTEWALKER SLAVE

Notes: Amplify Magic, Fireball, Frost Bolt

WASTEWALKER TASKMASTER

Notes: Cripple (Reduces movement speed by 50%, increases swing time by 100%)

WASTEWALKER WORKER

QUEST LISTING

LOST IN ACTION

Level Requirement	62
Quest Giver	Watcher Jhang
Quest Goal	Find Earthbinder Rayge, Naturalist Bite, Weeder Greenthumb, and Windcaller Claw
Experience Reward	16,500

Additional Rewards: Cenarion Ring of Casting (Ring, +16 INT, +24 STA, Increases damage and healing done by magical spells and effects by up to 18), Goldenvine Wraps (Cloth Wrist, 56 Armor, +19 STA, +13 INT, +13 SPI, Increases damage and healing done by magical spells and effects by up to 29), or Dark Cloak of the Marsh (Back, 64 Armor, +16 AGI, +24 STA, +30 Attack Power)

Watcher Jhang's friends have done something very stupid. The group was sent to investigate Coilfang Reservoir by Ysiel. The other four, confident in their abilities, split up and went in without Jhang. They have not returned and Jhang fears the worst.

She's fairly certain her companions only went into the Slave Pens and Underbog. This quest requires both these Instances to complete, so don't be upset about it sitting in your quest log.

DOWN THE DRAIN

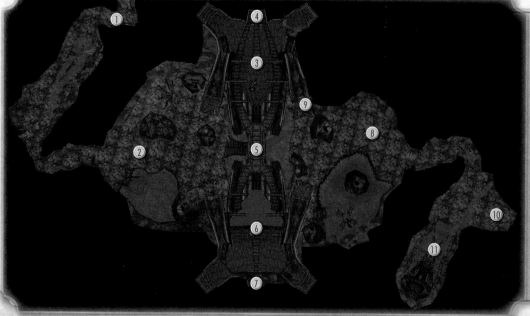

MAP LEGEND	
1	Instance Entrance
2	The Slaves
3	Northern Fortress
4	Mennu the Betrayer
5	The Bridges
6	Southern Fortress
7	Weeder Greenthumb
8	The Deeper Tunnel
9	Rokmar the Crackler
10	Naturalist Bite
11	Quagmirran

THE SLAVES

At first, there is little sign of a Naga presence in the Slave Pens. Bogstrok and Greater Bogstrok patrol the area in groups of three. There are two of these groups just in front; they move very quickly and cannot be safely bypassed.

Though quite monstrous looking, the Bogstrok are considered Humanoid. This opens a variety of crowd control options including Polymorph, Freezing Trap, Blind, and Fear. Avoid using Fear as you don't need the fight to be any larger.

Gather aggro on the tank and slug away at the chitin-covered foes one at a time. While they aren't terribly dangerous, they present ideal practice for your party's ability to control the fracas.

DON'T HIT THE SHEEP!

As there are many fights that involve multiple forms of crowd control, have the party leader use the Raid Symbols before each large pull. These can be found by right clicking on the party leader's portrait.

Use the raid symbols to let everyone know what order to kill the enemies in. No enemy will last long with your entire party firing at them. This allows your party to engage the fewest enemies possible to maximize killing speed.

SAMPLE EXPLANATION

SYMBOL	DESIGNATION	ATTACK ORDER
Star	Sap	2
Skull	Tank & DPS	1
Moon	Polymorph	3

The first group was probably a little rough. The second group has the same composition and presents another try at perfection. Keep your tank's health high and all aggro on the tank as the Bogstroks do a good bit of damage if they get onto someone with lower armor.

Continue down the tunnel until it widens. Several Naga guard are watching over Broken slaves. They can be used to your advantage. The slaves will only fight you while their Naga master stands. Concentrate all your fire on the Coilfang Slavehandler and kill him quickly. When the Naga falls, the Wastewalker Workers will thank you for their freedom and run away.

Use a ranged attack to pull the enemies to you. This keeps you from fighting both groups at once. The first group consists of one Coilfang Slavehandler and three Wastewalker Workers.

As the Slavehandler is Elite and well-armored, he won't drop fast. Use crowd control to keep the Workers from dealing significant damage or have your tank hold the attention of all four enemies. Area-of-effect debuffs (such as Demoralizing Shout and Thunderclap) help to mitigate some of the incoming damage while keeping aggro on the main tank.

The next group is similar to the first. Instead of three Wastewalker Workers, there are two Wastewalker Slaves. The Slaves cast spells from range. This can be a problem as they do not realize their freedom if the Slavehandler dies too far away. Drag the fight to the Slaves and kill the Naga first. Should the Slaves continue attacking you when the Naga falls; you have no choice but to kill them.

A pair of Coilfang Champions patrol ahead. Pull these back to your party as you don't want to fight them near the room ahead. Use crowd control on one and pull the other to you. The tank should hold the target away from as much of the party as possible as Coilfang Champions use Intimidating Shout. This single ability can cause your entire party to run if used close enough. Fear Ward and Tremor Totem help mitigate the damage of this ability.

Should you be in a group with little or no crowd control, use a secondary tank to pull the second Champion away from the first. Keep as much of your party out of melee range of either one as possible. Kill the Champions one-at-a-time before proceeding. If your secondary tank is a Warrior, have them stay in Berserk Stance and ready to use Fear-breaking abilities.

Further down, the tunnel opens into a large cavern. Several groups of Naga and Bogstrok patrol the cave. The enemy has established forces in the entire cavern, but you only have a few objectives; you can skip many of the enemies without endangering your mission. Should you want the additional experience or treasure, kill them.

Hold your party at the entrance of the cavern for the time being. To the right are four Naga and a pet: a Coilfang Observer, two Coilfang Champions, a Coilfang Scale-Healer, and a Coilfang Ray. Remember that the Champions can Fear several members of your party at once.

Pull the group and remove as many of the Champions from the fight as possible. Use the tunnel wall to break line of sight and force the enemies to close the distance. The Scale-Healer uses Holy Nova to do damage to any of your party in range and heals its companions. Keep it away from the bulk of the party and kill it first. The Coilfang Ray can Fear one person at a time, but only uses it on a party member that doesn't have aggro. This means that the Ray won't Fear your tank.

JUMPING AHEAD

Many of the enemies within Slave Pens can be avoided. If your party is in need of practice, experience, or loot, take the time to clear more.

With the bridge clear of patrols, it's time to make your way to the passage on the left. Several groups of Coilfang Slavehandlers, Wastewalker Workers, and Wastewalker Slaves are between you and the doorway. Pull and destroy each group as you have been doing. Only the two Coilfang Defenders guard the passage directly.

Once the Scale-Healer is dead, turn your focus to the Coilfang Ray. Renew the crowd control on the Champions as needed. If either breaks free, an off-tank or pet should grab them and keep them away from the party. This ensures they can't Fear everyone. Kill the Observer next and the Champions last.

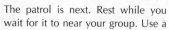

The patrol is next. Rest while you wait for it to near your group. Use a ranged attack to pull the Coilfang Enchantresses and Champion. As before, crowd control the Champion until the softer targets are dealt with. The Enchantresses use area of effect attacks and should be kept away from as many party members as possible. If you have extra crowd control, keep one of the Enchantresses held while the party kills the other. Clean the mobs up one-at-a-time and prepare to pull the Bogstrok on the bridge.

You've fought groups of Bogstrok before and these are no different. Use the same tactics of control and focused fire that you used at the beginning of the Instance.

NORTHERN STRONGHOLD

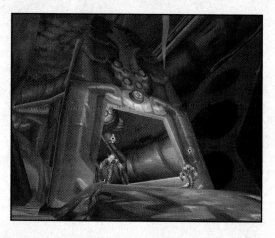

The Coilfang Defenders are fairly sturdy, but don't deal much damage unless you cast at them while they have a spell shield up. When the shield is up, all spells are reflected back at the caster. Stop casting when the shield goes up and kill the two annoyances (there is a white visual effect that starts when the Spell Reflect goes up, and that is a caster's cue to stop their spells immediately).

Move into the passage and engage the two wandering Coilfang Technicians. Have Interrupts such as Kick, Shield Bash, and Silencing Shot ready as the Technicians can cast AoE fire spells. These are channeled spells, so any Interruption stops the rest of the spell.

To the right, Mennu the Betrayer paces up and down a ramp. There are groups of Coilfang Collaborators and Technicians at the bottom of the ramp. When Mennu is at the top of the ramp, pull the first group into the corridor. The Broken here are different. These have chosen to join forces with the Naga and fight to the death. Deal with the Technician first while keeping the Collaborators controlled. The Collaborators Enrage at low health, so keep your attacks focused. Healers must be ready for somewhat higher burst damage when the Elite Broken Enrage.

Wait in the corridor once more and wait for Mennu to path up the ramp again. Grab the group of three Coilfang Collaborators and one Technician on the other side of the ramp and pull them back to the corridor. As before, control the Collaborators until the Technician is dead. Keep your tank's health high and kill them one at a time to avoid two Enraged enemies.

When all enemies have been killed, rest to full health and mana and prepare to fight Mennu the Betrayer.

MENNU THE BETRAYER

HP	77724/135474 (Heroic)	**Damage**	619-864/1745-2466 (Heroic)
Abilities	**Lightning Bolt**: 40 yard range. Dealing 1900 points of nature damage. **Heroic**: 3500 Nature damage.		
	Healing Ward: Heals Mennu for 2500 health. **Heroic**: 3500 health on Heroic difficulty.		

A MENU OF DELIGHTS

Princely Reign Leggings (Cloth Legs, 110 Armor, +18 STA, +28 INT, +12 SPI, +18 Spell Hit Rating, Increases damage and healing done by magical spells and effects by up to 33)

Spellfire Longsword (Main Hand Sword, 41.5 DPS, +15 STA, +14 INT, +10 Spell Hit Rating, Increases damage and healing by magical spells and effects by up to 56)

Tracker's Belt (Mail Waist, 294 Armor, +21 STA, +14 Hit Rating, +21 Critical Strike Rating, +42 Attack Power)

Vest of Living Lightning (Mail Chest, 523 Armor, +12 STA, +15 INT, 1 [Red Socket], 1 [Blue Socket], 1 [Yellow Socket], Socket Bonus: +9 Healing, Increases damage and healing done by magical spells and effects by up to 18, Restores 6 mana per 5 sec.)

Wastewalker Shiv (Main Hand Dagger, 55.3 DPS, +12 STA, +12 Hit Rating, +28 Attack Power)

MENNU THE BETRAYER'S TOTEMS

TOTEM	EFFECT	TARGET PRIORITY
Tainted Earthgrab Totem	Lasts for 30 sec. Immobilizes all players in range.	2
Tainted Healing Ward	Restores 1% of Mennu's health every second	1
Corrupted Nova Totem	Explodes for 2700 Fire damage when the duration expires or when it is destroyed by damage. Heroic: 6500 Fire damage.	4
Tainted Stoneskin Totem	Decreases melee damage received by Mennu by 50.	3

Hold your Interrupts for his heals unless you have several in your party. When green energy surrounds his hands, use your Interrupts. With his heals disabled and his totems destroyed, Mennu doesn't have much to rely on and won't survive your group's coordinated attacks.

Keep your casters at maximum range at all times. This keeps them outside the range of Tainted Earthgrab and Nova Totems.

Mennu has done far more than any Coilfang Collaborator. He has not only worked with the Naga willingly, but he has betrayed his own people to further his power. The Naga recognized him as both an ally and a power to be trusted.

Slug it out with Mennu until he falls. Regroup and prepare to ascent the ramp to the bridges.

DESTROY THE TOTEMS

The Betrayer is a Shaman of extreme prowess; his own attacks and defenses aren't terribly powerful, but his totems have ended the lives of many. Fight him at the bottom of the ramp where you'll have plenty of room to move around.

Assign someone of substantial burst damage to 'totem-duty.' The player on totem-duty should target and destroy as quickly as possible all totems save one — the Corrupted Nova Totem. Rather than damage the totem the tank should move the fight as soon as he drops the Corrupted Nova Totem.

Heroic Mode

While Mennu has substantially more health and mana in Heroic Mode, the strategy is the same. The primary increase in difficulty is the effects of his totems. This is especially important with the Corrupted Nova Totems as it's explosion causes about 6500 fire damage. The strategy is the same, but the price for failure is far higher.

THE BRIDGES

A pair of Coilfang Technicians patrol along each bridge above. There are only two so the fights are fairly easy. Immediately rest after the first fight and prepare for the second. Though you only need to clear one bridge, clearing both will save you headache and a possible wipe ahead.

Follow a bridge to the center of the area and several more groups of enemies. Where the bridges connect, there is a group of two Coilfang Defenders and one Coilfang Collaborator.

Pull the fight to you as another group patrols on the other side of the walkway. Control the Defenders and kill the Collaborator first. With their spell shield, the Defenders take longer to kill while the Collaborator deals more damage.

Charge the next group now that the path is clear. The Coilfang Technician is flanked by two Coilfang Collaborators. Control the Collaborators first and kill the Technician. Have Interrupts ready to keep the Technician from using its Rain of Fire. Once the Naga is dead, focus on the Collaborators.

Both of the bridges have been destroyed and there is no way to proceed except jumping into the water below; it's deep enough that you won't take damage from the fall. Do not jump toward the ledges below. Jump toward the center of the water, and the Southern Stronghold, instead.

SOUTHERN STRONGHOLD

Keep most of your party in the water and have your highest level member creep onto the broken portion of wall. There are three patrols nearby; one on each side and one on the ramp ahead. When all three are away, signal the party to ascend the broken wall and climb onto the wall to the left. Follow the wall as far as you can and wait. This gives the entire party a chance to see the Coilfang Enchantress and two Coilfang Technicians patrolling below. Decide on crowd control duties and attack order before dropping down and engaging the enemy group.

The Enchantress is a high priority target. Her spells deal higher damage and she has lower health. Keep her spells Interrupted and destroy her quickly while keeping the Technicians controlled or otherwise occupied. Once the Enchantress is dead, kill the Technicians and look around. There is a passage to the left.

If you are trying to complete the quest, **Lost in Action**, your group needs to clear the way to the ramp. Otherwise, you can take the small passage around the left corner now.

Assuming that you are doing the quest, turn back to the ramp. One Coilfang Technician and two Collaborators patrol there. When your party is ready, pull the enemies into the passage. Breaking line-of-sight forces the enemy to come to you and keeps them from getting help from the other patrol. Control the Collaborators and kill the Technician first. Watch the last patrol and make your way up the ramp when it's clear.

Weeder Greenthumb isn't in the best shape, but now you know. Examine the body if you have the quest. With one Druid found, it's time to exit the Naga Stronghold and head into the deepest part of the dungeon. Take the passage out. Only two Coilfang Champions are guarding it.

Keep in mind the type of Fear the Coilfang Champions use when you engage them. Control one and kill the other to keep them from Fearing your entire group for long periods. When both enemies are dead, rest to full health and mana while you look around.

THE DEEPER TUNNELS

Don't get too used to the expansive cavern. You'll be back in cramped quarters soon. For now, there is a group of four Bogstrok that need to be killed. This is a simple and straight-forward fight. Avoid using AoE attacks as your tank may not be able to keep the entire group from eating your casters or healer.

A fight that will truly test your party's crowd control and focus fire capabilities is ahead. A Coilfang Tempest, a Scale-Healer, an Observer, and a Ray stand guard near the center of the area. As before, the Scale-Healer should be your first target. Control as many of the others as you can starting with the Coilfang Ray; its Fear can send a party member into other nearby groups.

Keep the fight away from as many party members as possible. The Scale-Healer uses Holy Nova and the Ray uses Psychic Horror. These abilities can make a fight very chaotic. Once the Scale-Healer is dead, turn to the Ray and destroy it. Kill the Observer and Tempest last as they are melee enemies and much easier for the tank to deal with.

When the bodies of your enemies litter the floor around you, rest to full health and mana before engaging Rokmar.

ROKMAR THE CRACKLER

HP	97155/169371 (Heroic)	Damage	1264-1767/4705-6653 (Heroic)
Abilities	**Grievous Wound**: Deals 685 to 815 damage every 2 seconds until healed. **Heroic**: 1096 to 1304 damage every 2 seconds.		
	Ensnaring Moss: 30 yard range. Slows attack and casting speed by 50%.		
	Water Spit: 45 yard range, Dealing about 1800-2000 points of Frost damage.		

PRIED OFF A GIANT CRUSTACEAN

Bogstrok Scale Cloak (Back, 223 Armor, +22 STA, +16 Defense Rating)

Calming Spore Reed (Wand, 96.9 DPS, +8 INT, +9 SPI, Increases healing done by spells and effects by up to 20)

Coilfang Needler (Crossbow, 53.6 DPS, +12 AGI, +22 Attack Power)

Runed Fungalcap (Trinket, +30 Resilience Rating, Use: Absorbs 440 damage. Lasts 20 seconds)

Coilfang Hammer of Renewal (Main Hand Mace, 41.4 DPS, +10 STA, +13 INT, +12 SPI, Increases healing done by spells and effects by up to 106)

Rokmar's Water Spit isn't a cone effect. It doesn't matter which way Rokmar is facing. As long as you are within range and line of sight, you will get hit. Be ready to use Potions, Bandages, or Healthstones if your healer falls behind. He or she will have enough work to do just keeping the tank alive against this monstrous beast.

Rokmar isn't likely to be lost in a crowd. He's a towering lobster and it's anyone's guess as to how the Naga got him in here. He patrols the dead-end to the left. Engage him at the most forward point of his patrol. This gives you more room to move around and makes it easier for the casters to avoid some of his attacks.

The Crackler doesn't have any abilities that incapacitate your tank, so aggro shouldn't be a problem. Give the tank a few seconds to build aggro, and then start doing damage. Keep Ensnaring Moss dispelled from your tank. It doesn't crowd control your tank, but makes it more difficult to hold aggro.

Rokmar's other ability of note is Grievous Wound. Rokmar hits the tank with this fairly early and will use it again if it's removed. As a Bleed effect, it can't be removed by most classes. The tank needs to sit and eat food as soon as the fight ends. Heal your tank to full during the fight and immediately afterward to remove the effect.

This fight will give your healer a taste of what's in store. Use more mana-efficient heals on the tank when he or she needs it. Cast faster heals on each party member after a Water Spit.

AS COLD AS ICE

Rokmar is physically impressive. He deals high physical damage and has high health. He also casts spells that can't be interrupted!

Rokmar uses a Water Spit ability. This attack hits your entire party for moderate damage. Consider using any Frost Resistance abilities or gear you have and keep your member's health high during the engagement.

Heroic Mode

There are very few changes to Rokmar in Heroic mode. His health and damage are vastly increased, but he is only granted one new ability.

At 20% health, Rokmar becomes enraged and increases his damage output substantially. To counter this, conserve mana after he hits 50% health. This gives you quite a reserve when he enrages. When he goes insane, do the same. Level your most damaging attacks against him in a mad race that leaves one side dead and the other nearly so.

When the Crackler falls, resurrect any fallen members, collect your loot and continue your journey. The next group of Naga is similar to the previous; one Coilfang Scale-Healer, one Observer, one Ray, and two Tempests.

Wait for the two patrolling Coilfang Defenders to move away before using a ranged attack to pull the larger group. As before, control the Tempests and focus all fire on the Scale-Healer. If you are short on crowd control, have an off-tank or pet hold the two Tempests away from the party. Or, turn the tables on these darn Naga and Fear them! AoE Fear spells (Psychic Scream/ Intimidating Shout) give you a number of extra seconds to kill a full target before having to worry about the others in a pull. When the Scale-Healer falls, engage the Ray and Observer. Leave the Tempests for last.

Engage the Defenders when they patrol back toward you. There are only two and you've fought them before. Keep your fire focused and eliminate the Naga. The group on the left side of the ramp is your next real target.

Two Coilfang Champions stand with an Enchantress and a Soothsayer. Control the Champions to keep them from Fearing your group around and kill the Soothsayer first. The Enchantress is a quick kill, but the Soothsayer can turn a party member against you. Pull the fight back if the Champions break control early as you don't want to be Feared into the next group.

Another large group stands on the right side of the ramp. Two Coilfang Tempests, an Observer, a Ray, and a Scale-Healer comprise the group. Start the fight by controlling as many enemies as possible. The Ray should be your number one target for control, followed by the Scale-Healer. The Tempests and Observer are much easier for the tank to hold and survive as they are melee enemies. Kill the Scale-Healer first as it can draw the fight out significantly. If you are short on crowd control, have a pet or off-tank hold the two Tempests

away from the party while you kill the first three. When the enemies are dead, rest while waiting for the patrol to come to the top of the ramp.

When the patrol stops at the top of the ramp, pull them. As before, control the Champions and kill the casters first. This fight is marginally safer than the previous, but don't relax too much as the Soothsayer can make your life much more difficult if she is allowed to live very long; if she gets a hold of either your tank or your healer, you may not live long at all.

With the patrol dead, the passage is much safer for a short while. Ahead are two pair of Wastewalkers. Ignore these entirely as they will not attack unless you strike first.

There are four Bogstrok in the group ahead and all look very similar. When you begin the fight, pull the active enemies away from the controlled enemies. This keeps focusing fire simple and avoids accidentally breaking crowd control with AoE abilities. Avoid using AoE attacks near the Wastewalkers. They will attack you if they feel you are a threat. Use this same tactic on the next group of three Bogstrok.

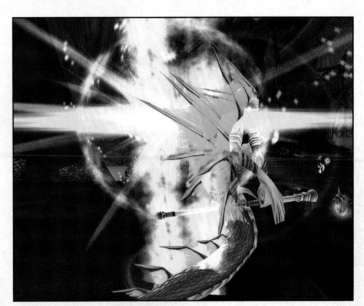

Take a moment to rest. You want full health and mana for the next fight. Two Coilfang Defenders and two Coilfang Observers guard a cage. The Defenders take a lot of punishment before going down, so crowd control these first. Have an off-tank or pet hold the second Observer while the party kills the first. Use Interrupts to keep the damage your party takes to a minimum. Kill the second Observer once the first is dead. Finish the fight by killing the Defenders. *Do not* let anyone speak with Naturalist Bite in the cage until the party has a chance to rest.

Speak with the Druid when your party is ready. This triggers a fight against a Coilfang Enchantress, a Soothsayer and a Champion.

As the enemy forces you into combat, Sap isn't an option. Control the Champion immediately as it can use its AoE fear to disrupt your party. With the Champion dealt with for now, turn your entire party against the Soothsayer as it can turn party members against you!

Once the Soothsayer is dealt with, turn your damage to the Enchantress. Keep the Champion controlled until both casters are dead. Once he is alone, kill the Champion and speak with Naturalist Bite once again. The grateful Druid gives you the Mark of Bite which increases your Nature Resist immensely as well as all your statistics. Rest to full health and mana before triggering the fight with Quagmirran.

QUAGMIRRAN

HP	102870/179334 (Heroic)	Damage	2334-3263/6398-9049 (Heroic)

Abilities	**Poison Bolt Volley**: Deals 1500 points of initial Nature damage plus 400 Nature damage every 2 seconds for 6 seconds. **Heroic**: 2300 initial Nature damage, plus 800-800 periodic nature damage every 2 seconds for 6 seconds
	Cleave: Inflicts 110% melee damage to a target and up to 2 other targets in front of Quagmirran.
	Uppercut: Inflicts normal damage plus 200, knock-back.
	Acid Spray: Deals approximately 300-350 nature damage. **Heroic**: Deals 900-1000 Nature damage

BOGGED DOWN NO MORE!

Deft Handguards (Leather Hands, 149 Armor, +18 STA, 1 [Blue Socket], 1 [Yellow Socket], Socket Bonus: +3 Hit Rating, +12 Critical Strike Rating, +52 Attack Power)

Scorpid-Sting Mantle (Mail Shoulder, 392 Armor, +21 AGI, +12 STA, 1 [Red Socket], 1 [Blue Socket], Socket Bonus: +3 INT, +30 Attack Power, Restores 6 mana every 5 sec.)

Azureplate Greaves (Plate Legs, 815 Armor, +27 STR, +27 STA, +26 INT, Restores 6 mana per 5 sec., Increases damage and healing done by magical spells and effects by up to 16)

Spore-Soaked Vaneer (Back, +15 STA, +15 INT, +11 Spell Critical Rating, Increases damage and healing done by magical spells and effects by up to 19)

Unscarred Breastplate (Plate Chest, 932 Armor, +26 STR, +21 AGI, +23 STA, 2 [Red Socket], 1 [Blue Socket], Socket Bonus: +4 Defense Rating)

Walking near the deep pool to the south gets Quagmirran's attention, but doesn't start the fight. Quagmirran slowly walks out of the pool and reveals himself to be a heaping mass of mold and other...stuff. Wait for him to stop on the ledge before engaging him as the fight is difficult enough without worrying about breathing.

Before beginning the fight, pass out potions and Healthstones (if you have a Warlock), and recast any buffs that are near to falling. Spread out your casters and begin the DPS race when you're ready.

Quagmirran is a mountain of mold that submerges itself in slime. Perhaps it's no wonder that his most damaging attacks are Nature-based.

Several times during the fight, Quagmirran uses an AoE Poison Bolt. This does significant Nature damage immediately and even more Nature damage over time. Be ready to use Cleanse, Cure Poison, Abolish Poison, or Poison Cleansing Totem to counter this.

Equipping items and trinkets that increase your Nature Resistance is highly recommended. Abilities such as Nature Resist Totem and Aspect of the Wild make the fight much easier.

Once the tank engages Quagmirran, turn him away from the group. He has an Acid Geyser attack that is a cone-effect nature attack as well as a Cleave. Melee DPS should stand behind Quagmirran to reduce the damage taken by Cleave.

Heroic Mode

As if Quagmirran wasn't a difficult fight before, he gets more health and damage in Heroic Mode. The tactics are identical, but be ready for a wipe or two when your party first finds the pile of sludge in a Heroic dungeon.

The tank should have high Nature Resistance, but avoid giving up Stamina or Armor Rating for it. Other party members will need to raise their health to avoid being killed before the healer can save them.

Using Trinkets that absorb or reduce damage from Nature-based attacks are going to be worth their weight in Arcanite. Nature Resistance Potions and items that remove Poison effects are also highly recommended. If you don't have a Warlock in your party, consider buying some Healthstones from one before entering the dungeon.

Quagmirran often turns to another party member when he uses his Acid Geyser. Your tank needs to be ready to immediately pull Quagmirran's attention away from the rest of the party. If your tank is having difficulty doing this, stop all DPS until Quagmirran is facing only the tank.

Keep the Nature DoT portion of Poison Bolt cured at all costs. It does remarkable damage and will over-tax your healer. Ranged DPS can retreat slightly and use bandages once the DoT has run its course to take some of the strain off the party healer.

Quagmirran is the final fight of the Instance. If you have timed abilities or trinkets that you haven't used, now is the time! With Quagmirran's damage output, your healer *will* run out of mana so use anything you have that can reduce the damage you take, reduce the damage others take, or increase the damage Quagmirran takes.

Lay everything you have into Quagmirran and kill him as quickly as possible. If your tank or healer goes down, keep blasting away.

With the hulking mass of Quagmirran decaying, resurrect the fallen, collect your loot and make your way out of the instance. If you want to walk out, follow the tunnel back to Rokmar's room and jump into the water on the left. There is a ramp across the water that leads you to the front of the dungeon.

THE UNDERBOG

DUNGEON INFORMATION

Name	Underbog
Location	Zangarmarsh, Coilfang Reservoir
Suggested Levels	Group of 5, Levels 63-65
Primary Enemies	Humanoids, Beasts, Elementals
Damage Types	Physical, Nature
Time to Complete	90 to 120 Minutes

WHO TO BRING

JOBS

CLASS	ABILITIES
Druid	Abolish Disease, Mark of the Wild, Dire Bear Form, Hibernate
Hunter	Freezing Trap, Aspect of the Wild, Silencing Shot, Wyvern Sting, Scare Beast
Mage	Polymorph, Counterspell
Paladin	Blessing of Wisdom, Cleanse, Tanking
Priest	Mind Control, Psychic Scream, Power Word: Shield, Power Word: Fortitude
Rogue	Sap, Blind, Burst DPS
Shaman	Nature Resistance Totem, Poison Cleansing Totem, Earth Elemental Totem
Warlock	Seduce (Succubus), Banish Plant Elementals
Warrior	Tanking, Hamstring, Shield Wall

Though the Naga control Underbog, there aren't as many of these vile Humanoids as there are in the Slave Pens. Rather, there are a great many Beasts and Elementals. This narrows your options for crowd control. Because the less controllable pulls are smaller, this puts a lower emphasis on crowd control. Having a Rogue, Priest, or Mage to control during the Naga pulls balanced with a Hunter or Druid to control during Beast pulls is more than sufficient if your party can focus fire.

With the crowd control taken care of, there is something else to consider; bring at least one person who can increase the party's Nature Resistance. Many of the enemies and three of the bosses use Nature-based attacks. Druids, Hunters, and Shamans all have abilities that can increase the Nature Resistance of others.

It pays to have a secondary tank during several fights and one boss encounter. While not as well-armored as a primary tank, this person needs to survive and hold aggro from an uncontrolled enemy or two. Druids in Dire Bear Form (provided they aren't your only healer), Hunter Pets, Voidwalkers, Paladins, and Warriors can all serve this function.

GETTING TO UNDERBOG

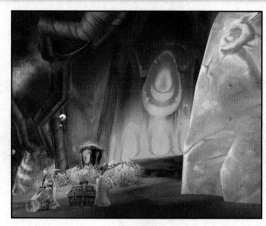

Underbog is one of the many wings of Coilfang Reservoir. Horde parties can fly into Zabra'jin while Alliance parties fly into Telredor.

At the center of Serpent Lake is the Coilfang Reservoir. Dive beneath the water at the center of the pumping station and look for the drain. Swim through the drain and surface within the Reservoir. Underbog is the eastern most instance portal.

REPUTATION GAINS

ACTION	FACTION	REPUTATION GAIN	END POINT
Kill Trash	Cenarion Expedition	8	Honored
Kill Bosses	Cenarion Expedition	80	Honored
Quest: Bring Me a Shubbery	Sporeggar	750	N/A
Quest: Oh, It's On	Sporeggar	1,050	N/A
Quest: Stalk the Stalker	Sporeggar	1,050	N/A

WHAT'S BENEATH THE SINK?

BOSSES

HUNGARFEN

GHAZ'AN

SWAMPLORD MUSEL'EK AND CLAW

THE BLACK STALKER

MINIONS

BOG GIANT
Notes: Enrage, Fungal Decay (Disease. Nature damage every 3 seconds. Movement speed reduced by 40%)

FEN RAY
Notes: Horror

LYKUL STINGER
Notes: Frenzy

LYKUL WASP
Notes: Ranged poison attack

MURKBLOOD HEALER
Notes: Healer

MURKBLOOD ORACLE
Notes: Fireball

MURKBLOOD TRIBESMAN
Notes: Enrages

UNDERBAT
Notes: Knockdown

UNDERBOG FRENZY
Notes: Aquatic, Pierce Armor (75% for 20 seconds)

UNDERBOG LORD
Notes: Fungal Rot

UNDERBOG LURKER
Notes: Fungal Decay (Disease. Nature damage every 3 seconds. Movement speed reduced by 40%)

UNDERBOG SHAMBLER
Notes: Fungal Decay (Disease. Nature damage every 3 seconds. Movement speed reduced by 40%)

WRATHFIN MYRMIDON
Notes: Coral Cut (Physical Damage every 3 seconds for 15 seconds)

WRATHFIN SENTRY
Notes: Stealth Detection

WRATHFIN WARRIOR
Notes: Enrages at low health, Heroic Strike, Shield Bash

LOST IN ACTION

Level Requirement	62
Quest Giver	Watcher Jhang
Quest Goal	Find Earthbinder Rayge, Naturalist Bite, Weeder Greenthumb, and Windcaller Claw
Experience Reward	16,500
Additional Rewards	Cenarion Ring of Casting (Ring, +16 INT, +24 STA, Increases damage and healing done by magical spells and effects by up to 18), Goldenvine Wraps (Cloth Wrist, 56 Armor, +19 STA, +13 INT, +13 SPI, Increases damage and healing done by magical spells and effects by up to 29), or Dark Cloak of the Marsh (Back, 64 Armor, +16 AGI, +24 STA, +30 Attack Power)

Watcher Jhang's friends have done something very stupid. The group was sent to investigate Coilfang Reservoir by Ysiel. The other four, confident in their abilities, split up and went in without Jhang. They haven't returned and Jhang fears the worst.

She's fairly certain her companions only went into the Slave Pens and Underbog. This quest requires both these Instances to complete, so don't be upset about it sitting in your quest log.

BRING ME A SHRUBBERY!

Level Requirement	63
Quest Giver	Gzhun'tt
Quest Goal	Collect five Sanguine Hibiscus
Experience Reward	11,000
Additional Rewards	Becomes a repeatable quest (without the experience reward)

The Naga have been draining the water from all of Zangarmarsh. The Sporeggar have been hard hit as some of the herbs they use have all but died out. Sanguine Hibiscus is used for a variety of things and only grows in Underbog now. Gzhun'tt would really appreciate it if you brought him some to restock the Sporeggar supplies.

OH, IT'S ON!

Level Requirement	63
Quest Giver	T'shu
Quest Goal	Collect the Underspore Frond
Experience Reward	13,750
Additional Rewards	Everlasting Underspore Frond (Use: Creates 10 Edible Underspore Pods, 12 hour cooldown)

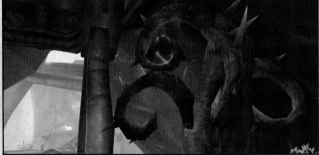

Much of the Fungal Giants food has been destroyed by the lowering of the water levels. This has forced them to find a new food source… the Sporeggar.

Though not a war-like people, the Sporeggar know that war has been forced upon them and are unwilling to wilt before the might of the Fungal Giants. One of the larger giants has been cultivating a plant in the Underbog for more than a millennia. T'shu wants you to steal the plant to break the spirit of Hungarfen.

The Edible Underspore Pods restore 4,410 health and mana over 30 seconds. While not the greatest food or water, you can create as many as 20 per day for no charge. Classes that can't summon their own food or water are sure to find these useful when not in a group.

STALK THE STALKER

Level Requirement	63
Quest Giver	Khn'nix
Quest Goal	Collect the Brain of the Black Stalker
Experience Reward	13,750
Additional Rewards	Essence Infused Mushroom (Trinket, Restores 200 health when you kill a target worth experience or honor. This effect cannot occur more often than every 10 seconds), Power Infused Mushroom (Trinket, Restores 200 mana when you kill a target worth experience or honor. This effect cannot occur more often than every 10 seconds)

With the new threat of the Fungal Giants, the Sporeggar can't afford to be attacked by the Marshwalkers again. A two front war is more than these little people can handle.

Khn'nix wants you to travel into the Underbog and slay the great mother of all Marshwalkers. If you bring him the Brain of the Black Stalker as proof of your heroism, he'll reward you well.

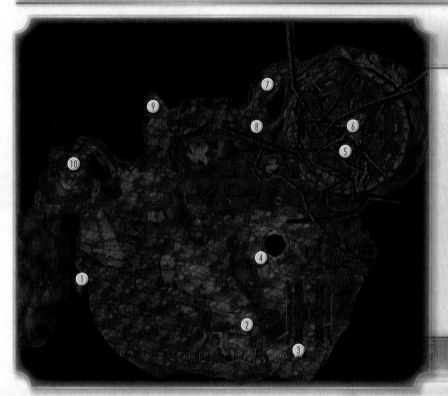

MAP LEGEND	
1	The Instance Entrance
2	The Ramps
3	Hungarfen
4	The Bridges
5	The Tank
6	Ghaz'an
7	The Tunnels
8	Earthbinder Rayge
9	Swamplord Musel'ek and Claw
10	The Black Stalker

CLIMBING THE RAMPS

Leave the light behind for damp and slick walls. You start in a tunnel with enemies patrolling nearby. The Underbats can be pulled singly or as a group. The first couple fights are very easy. The Underbats have only an AoE Knockdown as a special ability. If your group includes a Warlock, grab a couple easy Soul Shards.

The easy fights don't last long. As the passage opens into an immense cavern, a group of Underbog Lurkers and an Underbog Shambler patrol ahead. These creatures are immune to many forms of crowd control. Only Freezing Trap, Fear, and Banish are effective, and using Fear with other enemies close by is begging for problems.

I DON'T FEEL SO WELL

Many of the enemies within Underbog have Poisons or Diseases. These ailments can affect a character's performance greatly. Any class that can remove Diseases or Poisons should do so to keep everyone fighting at their fullest.

Use the raid symbols to designate which enemies to control and in what order to kill them. This keeps your party from breaking crowd control and allows you to kill each enemy quicker.

SAMPLE EXPLANATION

SYMBOL	DESIGNATION	ATTACK ORDER
Skull	Tank & DPS	1
Blue Box	Freezing Trap	2
Moon	Banish	3

The example above assumes three enemies and a group with both a Hunter and a Warlock. Your group will be different so take the time to get comfortable with the raid symbols. Time spent now will more than make up for itself by the end of the instance.

Follow the wall to the left as you move ahead. To the right is a group very similar in makeup to the previous fight. If your party had trouble with the previous fight, pull the group to the right for a little more practice before you get to the tougher opponents.

Pull the group of three Underbats ahead. While Underbats only have a knockdown ability and do little damage, having three Underbats on your tank will become very frustrating very quickly. A tank that is knocked down can't hold aggro, so use Polymorph, Freezing Trap, or Hibernate to deal with what you can. If you are short on crowd control, use other Warriors, Paladins, Hunter Pets, or Warlock Pets to hold aggro from the other Underbats until the first is dead. If you are using a secondary tank, have them pull an Underbat away from its friends. There is no point in tanking several Underbats if they can still knock everyone in melee down.

Near the water and to the left is a group of three Underbog Lurkers. Deal with these just as you did earlier. If you are short on crowd control, have your tank hold all the active enemies and bring them down one-at-a-time. Don't use AoE's unless your tank feels comfortable holding aggro against AoE's.

IT GROWS EVERYWHERE DOWN HERE!

Watch for Sanguine Hibiscus as you move through Underbog. It grows in many places and there will be enough for every party member to complete the quest by the end of the instance.

The red, flowering plant grows almost anywhere it won't get stepped on in here. Watch for it along the sides of waterways and passages. Herbalists can use Find Herbs to make the Hibiscus even harder to miss!

With the path clear, move to the edge of the water. Don't enter the water as Underbog Frenzies are waiting for a taste of your flesh. Watch the patrolling Underbats and Bog Giant. Pull the Bog Giant when the Underbats are away. The Bog Giant hits extremely hard and can Disease your party. Have abilities to Cure Disease ready and watch the tank's health. These mammoths only dent plate, but they tear through cloth pretty quickly if the tank falls.

The patrolling Underbats are your next target. Pull them to you and kill them. Remember that they have a Knockdown ability and the tank will have a harder time holding aggro. Focusing your fire makes the tank's job much easier.

PRACTICE MAKES PERFECT

The groups of enemies along the right walls can be skipped entirely if you follow the waterline. If your party needs the practice using crowd control or is in the mood to kill everything, take these groups down. If people are still low on Cenarion Expedition Rep, this is also a way to get more with each run.

The enemy groups are mixed. Two Underbats and one Underbog Lurker comprise each group. These mixed groups make crowd control easier. Warlocks or Hunters can control the Underbog Lurker, while Mages, Druids, or Hunters can control the Underbats.

Follow the waterline until you get to the ramp up. Underbog Lurkers and Shamblers guard the bottom of the ramp while several enemies patrol the length of the ramp. When the patrols are away, pull the Underbogs to you and destroy them one at a time. Avoid falling into the water nearby as the Underbog Frenzies are still looking to take a nibble out of you.

Wait for the patrollers to come down the ramp before you pull them. Take the Bog Giant first. Keep your tank's health high as the Giant can inflict some troubling hits and you don't want to lose your tank due to an untimely critical.

Pull the group of Underbats next. You've fought them before so use the techniques that have worked for you. Control them if you have the classes to do so. Use off-tanks if you don't have the abilities to control them. Ascend the ramp when the way is clear.

Two Bog Giants stand in front of Hungarfen. The good news is that these two can be pulled before you engage Hungarfen. The bad news is that you will get both and neither is vulnerable to many forms of crowd control. If you have a Hunter, use Freezing Trap for one while the party focuses on the other. Using an off-tank for the second Bog Giant is also feasible if you have a really attentive healer.

Keep your damage focused on one Giant. Their high health means they won't go down fast and your healer will run out of Mana keeping two tanks at high health for long. When both Giants are dead, rest to full mana and health. Hungarfen will the first true test of your party.

ALL MUCKED UP

This is one of the 'wipe' fights for players new to the instance. The run from the graveyard is short so don't despair and don't destroy a group by blaming the wipe on a specific person. Examine what you could have done better and note it for future runs as you make your way back to the instance.

HUNGARFEN

HP	65054/109593 (Heroic)	Damage	2004-2808/4705-6653 (Heroic)
Abilities	**Summon Underbog Mushroom**: After about 10 seconds, the mushroom explodes, creating a Spore Cloud. Spore Cloud deals 360-540 Nature damage every 2 seconds per application, and can stack up to five times (1800 to 2700 damage every 2 sec). **Heroic**: Deals 423-603 Nature damage per application		
	Foul Spores: At 20% health, Hungarfen drains health from all nearby players. Foul Spores deals about 450-550 Shadow damage per second and heals Hungarfen for about four times the amount of damage dealt.		
	Acid Geyser: Deals 2188 to 2812 Nature damage to a target within 35 yards and all other nearby targets. (Heroic Mode)		

FUNGAL REWARDS

Lykul Bloodbands (Mail Wrist, 236 Armor, +18 AGI, +18 STA, +30 Attack Power)

Manaspark Gloves (Cloth Hands, 81 Armor, +14 STA, +14 INT, +10 SPI, 1 [Red Socket], 1 [Yellow Socket], Socket Bonus: +3 Spell Crit Rating, +15 Spell Hit Rating, Increases damage and healing done by magical spells and effects by up to 16)

Marshlight Gloves (Leather Hands, 153.Armor, +10 STA, +21 INT, +8 SPI, 2 [Blue Socket], Socket Bonus: +5 Healing and Spell Damage, Increases damage and healing done by magical spells and effects by up to 25)

Needle Strike (Thrown, 54.6 DPS, +11 Hit Rating, +24 Attack Power)

Totem of the Thunderhead (Totem, Increases the mana gained from Water Shield by 12 per charge)

Hungarfen has immense Health and does incredible physical damage in melee. These are troubling but they are not the true power of this beast. Throughout much of the fight, Hungarfen will drop mushrooms on the group. They will increase in size until they pop and infect any party members near them with a Nature DoT that cannot be cured. They make a distinct sound as they grow larger that is louder when they are close to you.

This means that the encounter is a moving battle. Everyone in the party must be constantly aware of their surroundings and move away from any mushrooms growing near them. Keeping Hungarfen's attention on the tank won't be difficult as long as the tank is kept alive.

The radius of the mushrooms' DoT is quite large. Move away from them as soon as you seem them near you. Warn other party members if a mushroom is growing behind them and they aren't moving. All ranged party members need watch for mushrooms growing near the melee members. If a mushroom pops on your tank, the fight is likely over.

While losing your tank makes the battle much more difficult, it isn't over until it's over. Have a secondary tank grab Hungarfen and keep trying. Hunter Pets, Voidwalkers, or Earth Elemental Totems can give your party the time it needs to recover. If you have a Druid with you, now's a good time for an in-combat rez.

When Hungarfen reaches 20% health, he surrounds himself in vines. This is your cue to stop all melee damage and move away from him. The vines absorb any attack and heal Hungarfen by damaging nearby party members. Take this time to bandage any wounded party members. Avoid healing if possible to conserve mana.

This phase won't last long and Hungarfen will soon reengage you. Use your most damaging attacks against him to finish the fight.

Heroic Mode

Hungarfen deals more damage in melee and has more health in Heroic Mode. This isn't a surprise and neither should him dropping mushrooms faster. He tends to drop mushrooms in bursts. Up to one per-second can be dropped for 15 seconds before he'll slow down. What might be a surprise is the Acid Geyser which is as nasty as it gets. Players should space out to avoid collateral damage.

Nearby is a large thorny vine holding a red crystal. This wonder of Herbology is the **Underspore Frond**. Collect it for the quest and to send a message to the Fungal Giants. Rest at the next bridge and prepare for the pulls to resume.

A group of four Underbats patrols on the next rise. Pull them across the bridge when the patrolling Bog Giant is away. As all of the Underbats can knock your tank down, be very careful to focus fire. Polymorph, Hibernate, and Freezing Trap all work against the Underbats. As you're pulling them across the bridge, Fear is a relatively safe option as well so have Intimdating Shout or Psychic Scream ready.

When the Underbats are dead, pull the Bog Giant. Being alone, he won't pose any significant threat. Keep your tank's health high and the enemy away from the softer party members and you'll be fine. Repeat this several times as you move across the bridge and left around the pillar.

Watch for the Sanquine Hibiscus as you move. These groundspawns appear heavily in this area. There are only two more Bog Giants before the enemies change greatly. Pull the final Bog Giant when the Wrathfin Myrmidons are at the top of the ramp to avoid a much larger engagement.

THE TANK

With the Bog Giant out of the way, move your party to the bottom of the ramp and against the wall. The enemies in this section are primarily Humanoid. Polymorph, Mind Control, Seduce, Sap, and Freezing Trap are all valid forms of crowd control.

When the two Wrathfin Myrmidons are at the bottom of the ramp, pull them. This engages only the two and leaves the Naga at the top of the ramp for next pull. The Myrmidons are melee enemies and will engage your tank directly. Kill them, but don't move up the ramp yet.

Have your puller move to the top of the ramp and watch for the patrol in the corridor ahead. When you see the patrol move away from the doorway, pull the two Wrathfin Sentries to the bottom of the ramp. Don't attempt to Sap either as they can see through Stealth. Once they get to the bottom of the ramp, control one and kill the other. These are also melee enemies, so not having any crowd control isn't as large a problem.

Ascend the bridge and prepare for a much larger fight. Wait for the patrol to move away again before pulling the group to the right, just inside the doorway. There are four enemies in this group so crowd control and raid symbols will make your lives much easier. Have a higher health and armor party member pull the Naga fights. The Spearmen can inflict massive damage at range to softer targets and no one wants to be killed before a single heal can land. For the next couple fights, the puller should run down the ramp to force the Spearmen to leave the comfort of the hallway.

MURKBLOOD HEALERS ARE TOO GOOD TO LIVE

The Murkblood Healers are very powerful. They have both a single target heal and an AoE heal. Both are far more powerful than anything you have access to. They are so powerful that your entire attack plan must hinge on how to deal with them.

If you have a Priest, use Mind Control. You can either let the other enemies kill the Healer for you, or use the Healer to keep your party alive while the other enemies are dispatched.

If you do not have a Priest in your party, kill the Murkblood Healer first. Do not attempt any other form of crowd control. If it breaks early, the Healer can restore the Health of all other enemies very quickly.

The group consists of two Murkblood Spearmen, one Murkblood Healer, and one Wrathfin Warrior. Use the wall to break line of sight and force the enemies to come out of the corridor. Allow them to join you on the platform before you control any. This is important as you don't want the patrol to join the fight and letting the Spearmen stay at range can cause just that.

Control the Spearmen and deal with the Healer and Warrior first. Once the Healer and Warrior are dead (or controlled), kill the Spearmen one at a time and watch the patrol again. As the patrol moves down the corridor, pull the group just inside and to the left of the doorway and have the puller run down the ramp again.

There are only three enemies in this group; one Murkblood Healer and two Murkblood Spearmen. Deal with this group much the same way you did with the previous group. Control or engage the Spearmen as they join you on the platform and deal with the Healer first. When the Healer is taken care of, kill the Spearmen one at a time. Pull the patrol next time you see it.

Kill the Myrmidons and move your party into the corridor and to the right. This is a dead end, but gives you a better view of the next few pulls. The hallway continues west and there are several groups of enemies along the walls.

Rest and prepare for the next couple fights. Wait for the larger patrol to move away before pulling the group of three. One is a Murkblood Oracle and will cast at you from range. Use a ranged Interrupt or duck out the door to force it to close with you. If you leave it at range, the patrol will add and overwhelm your party.

Deal with the Healer first, then the Oracle, then the Tribesman. This drops the enemies very quickly and opens your party to the least amount of damage. Grab the patrol as it comes back your direction. As the group is very large, crowd control will be important.

The Murkblood Healer must be dealt with first. Control the Murkblood Tribesman and Spearman. The Wrathfin Warrior can be controlled until the Healer is dead if you have extra crowd control. Kill the Warrior, then Spearman, then Tribesman. Avoid using Fear as there are many enemies close by.

When the group is dead, move down the hall and to the bottom of the ramp. Rest here while your puller ascends the ramp to get the next group. The enemies are very close to the ramp, so avoid letting lower level members ascend. There are four enemies in this group just as there were in the last. Deal with them in the same fashion.

Move up the ramp and take a moment to look around. Groups of Naga stand along the path to the right and Ghaz'an swims in the water below.

Pull the groups along the walkway to the right. You've fought them all before and ducking down the stairs will force them to close with you. This keeps them well away from the other groups and avoids potential wipe situations.

Deal with the Healers first, then the casters, then the melee enemies. Watch the center of the room as you kill the groups. Ghaz'an climbs the pipes and perches atop the central platform.

GHAZ'AN

HP	59140/99630 (Heroic)	**Damage**	981-1375/4182-5914(Heroic)
Abilities	**Tail Sweep**: 30 yard range. Inflicts 600 to 1000 damage, knocking them back. **Heroic**: Deals 1265 to 2015 damage.		
	Acid Spit: 40 yard range. Deals approximately 2000 initial Nature damage, plus 155 Nature damage every 3 seconds for 20 seconds per application. Stacks up to 10 times.		
	Thrash: Occasionally gains two extra melee attacks immediately after an attack.		

TREASURES OF THE DEEP

Cloak of Healing Rays (Back, 64 Armor, +12 STA, +13 INT, +15 SPI, Increases healing done by spells and effects by up to 33)

Hatebringer (Two-Hand Mace, 73.6 DPS, +25 STR, +21 STA, 1 [Red Socket], 1 [Yellow Socket], 1 [Blue Socket], Socket Bonus: +4 STR, +22 Critical Strike Rating)

Studded Girdle of Virtue (Plate Waist, 540 Armor, +14 STR, +18 STA, +14 INT, 1 [Red Socket], 1 [Yellow Socket], Socket Bonus: +4 Critical Strike Rating, Increases damage and healing done by magical spells and effects by up to 13, Restores 4 mana per 5 sec.)

Luminous Pearls of Insight (Neck, +15 INT, Increases damage and healing done by magical spells and effects by up to 25, +15 Spell Critical Strike Rating)

Talisman of Tenacity (Neck, +30 STA, +20 Resilience)

Kayal

You've faced much worse than Ghaz'an before. This overgrown Hydra isn't anything special. Before engaging Ghaz'an, take notice of two things: the vertical pipes on the edge of the platform and the pipes leading up from the water.

The vertical pipes are where the tank will pull Ghaz'an. This puts Ghaz'an's side facing the area where most of the party will be standing. Positioning is the most important part of this fight. Anyone not positioned correctly will incur unnecessary damage, be tossed into the water, or just simply kill everyone in the party.

Ghaz'an spits a cone of acid at anyone in front of him. This acid does damage initially and again every three seconds. If that weren't enough, it can stack up to 10 times on a single target. For this reason, any Nature Resistance buffs need to be used as the DoT cannot be cured.

Avoid standing behind Ghaz'an as his tail is massive and he'll swat aggressors into the water below. The initial swipe deals damage and characters then end up in eel-infested waters (and not for a pleasure cruise). This is where the pipe leading up from the water comes in handy. If you get knocked off the platform, make your way up the pipe as quickly as possible and rejoin the fight.

The proper position for anyone who isn't the tank is beside Ghaz'an. This keeps you away from both his acid spit and tail swipe. Once everyone is in position, you can start blasting away. With steady healing, the tank will last far longer than Ghaz'an.

Heroic Mode

Heroic Mode Ghaz'an has no new abilities. Rather, his acid breath is more damaging and thus Nature Resistance is more important. Make sure you have at least one form of Resistance buff provided by Hunters, Shamans, or Druids before coming in here. Nature Resistance Potions can get you by in a pinch, but be sure to bring some extra.

With the water calm again, jump into the water on the north side and climb out the hole in the side of the tank. Rest to full health and mana before continuing.

THE DRUIDS AND GETTING OUT

Follow the tunnel until it forks. On the left path is Earthbinder Rayge. He's hiding, so you'll have to get closer before he identifies you as friends. Speak with him briefly for **Lost in Action** before moving your party back to the fork. Only the puller should descend the right path for now. The next two pulls have three Fen Rays in each.

Each Fen Ray has a Horror effect that is used against someone in melee range who isn't the tank. It lasts only a couple seconds, but cannot be broken and they can use it several times in the fight. Focus fire and destroy the Rays.

Polymorph, Freezing Trap, and Hibernate can make these fights much easier. Fear and Scare Beast are safe to use with added room. If you have none of these, keep aggro on the tank and pull the Rays far enough back that you won't get a second group.

Control as many as you can to keep the fight from becoming a nightmare and kill them. When the first group is dead, grab the second. The party should remain at the fork until both Fen Ray groups have been dispatched.

Move your group to the bottom of the ramp and engage the flying bugs. One Lykul Wasp and two Lykul Stingers make up the group. Destroy the Wasp first as its ranged Poison attack can make the life of a caster more difficult. Be ready to use a Power Word: Shield, HOT (heal over time) from a secondary healer, or throw heals a bit faster when the Stingers glow red. This signals a Frenzy and an increase in attack speed and overall damage. Keep a close eye on your tank's health during this.

Hold your party at the bottom of the ramp and send your puller forward. There is another group of Fen Rays that needs to be pulled back. Destroy these as you have the others but don't move forward yet. Once again, send your puller ahead.

Bring the group of two Fen Rays and one Lykul Wasp back to the group. Kill the Rays first as they interfere with standard group procedure by fearing your members around. Once the Rays are dealt with, kill the Wasp.

A group of two Fen Rays is next. It's a smaller group, so you can handle it without worry if you've gotten this far. Once this group is dead, move forward until you can see the last group of Fen Rays.

Two Fen Rays and a Lykul Wasp hover just before a boss encounter. Pull the fight well back as you don't want to be feared into either of the bosses or the patrolling Bog Giant. As before, kill the Rays first and the Wasp last.

Have your party rest while your puller hugs the left wall. Do not engage Swamplord Musel'ek or Claw yet. A Bog Giant patrols on the left and will make the boss fight much more difficult if it's allowed to join. Wait for it to patrol close to you and pull it back to the group. Kill it as you have in the past and rest to full in preparation of the next encounter.

MUSEL'EK AND CLAW

SWAMPLORD MUSEL'EK

HP	53224/89652 (Heroic)	Damage	1507-2109/3055-4318 (Heroic)
Abilities	**Raptor Strike:** Deals increased damage on the next successful melee attack.		
	Multi-Shot: Deals normal Arcane damage plus 2000 to up to 3 targets. **Heroic:** Increases damage by 2280.		
	Deterrence: Increases dodge and parry by 25% for 10 sec.		
	Hunter's Mark: Increases the attack power of all attackers against the target by 1500.		
	Freezing Trap: Traps a player in a block of ice for 4 seconds.		
	Knock Away: Deals about 1200 damage to a target, knocking the target back. **Heroic:** Deals approximately 1800 damage on Heroic difficulty.		
	Bear Command: Forces Claw to charge a player, stunning the target.		
	Aimed Shot: Deals normal damage plus 600.		

CLAW

HP	53226/135474 (Heroic)	Damage	400-561/1306-1848 (Heroic)
Abilities	**Echoing Roar:** Decreases armor by 75% for 20 seconds. **Heroic:** Decreases armor by 82%.		
	Maul: Adds 150 damage to the next attack.		
	Enrage: Temporarily increases damage by 192 and attack speed by 60%.		
	Feral Charge: Charges a target, dealing about 800 to 1600 damage.		

TITHES OF A SWAMPLORD

Cloak of Enduring Swiftness (Back, 64 Armor, +12 AGI, +13 STA, +23 Dodge Rating)

Greaves of the Iron Guardian (Plate Legs, 841 Armor, +32 STR, +33 STA, 2 [Yellow Socket], 1 [Blue Socket], Socket Bonus: +4 Hit Rating, +7 Hit Rating)

Truth Bearer Shoulderguards (Plate Shoulder, 721 Armor, +14 STR, +21 STA, +22 INT, 2 [Red Socket], Socket Bonus: +3 Spell Crit Rating, Increases damage and healing done by magical spells and effects by up to 8)

Zangartooth Shortblade (Main Hand Dagger, 41.3 DPS, +13 STA, +14 INT, +12 Spell Hit Rating, Increases damage and healing done by magical spells and effects by up to 61)

Tunic of the Nightwatcher (Leather Chest, 244 Armor, +27 STA, +21 INT, +18 SPI, 1 [Red Socket], 1 [Yellow Socket], 1 [Blue Socket], Socket Bonus: Restores 2 mana every 5 sec., Increases healing and damage done by magical spells and effects by up to 26)

Musel'ek and Claw attack as a pair. Claw has immense health while Musel'ek deals amazing damage. This means that Musel'ek needs to die first.

If you have a secondary-tank as well as your primary tank, have the secondary-tank hold Claw away from the party. This keeps the primary tank out of range of Claw's armor-reducing shout (-75% Armor!). Remember to stay within healing range.

The primary tank will need to hold Musel'ek; he deals massive damage. Voidwalkers and Hunter Pets can off-tank Claw if you need, but Warriors and Paladins are better suited for it.

Use your most powerful attacks to bring Musel'ek down quickly, but don't use abilities that have substantial timers as there is a more difficult encounter shortly. Your healer will be strained at the start of the fight keeping two tanks alive. DPS Casters shouldn't worry about conserving mana in the beginning. Blow everything your have to kill Musel'ek. All party members that aren't Hunters need to move into close range with Musel'ek. This will keep him from using Multi-Shot against any softer targets.

Multiple times during the fight, Musel'ek will use a Freezing Trap that Hunters could only dream of. This Freezes everyone in range. Musel'ek uses this time to retreat to range and start using his more powerful attacks. Simply wait until you can break free of the trap and again rush to close range with him. Keep the damage flowing and this guy will fall.

Once Musel'ek is dead, the fight gets much simpler. Keep you tank above half health in case Claw gets a couple critical strikes in a row. Lay into him with everything you have left. When Claw is defeated, he reverts to Windcaller Claw. Speak with him before continuing.

Move along the path to the south. An Underbog Lord stands guard over the way forward. While not a full boss, the Underbog Lord is quite damaging. He can instantly stack five Fungal Rots on a target, so keep him looking at the same targets as much as possible. If you have someone who can remove the Disease who isn't your healer, have them keep the tank clean. Bring the Lord down as quickly as you can without using your timed abilities. Rest to full health before venturing further.

When you see the bodies of the Fen Rays littering the floor, you're close. Around the corner, the passage opens into a large room. Engage the Black Stalker when you party is ready.

THE BLACK STALKER

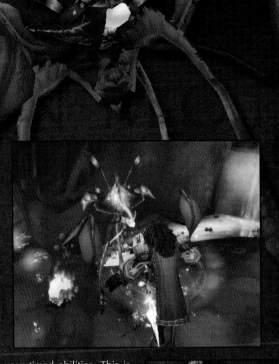

HP	75696/127505 (Heroic)	Damage	1822-2549/2909-4111 (Heroic)
Abilities			

Static Charge: Inflicts 4500 Nature damage over 12 sec. and sends the target into a state of panic. While affected, the static periodically shocks nearby allies for 750 Nature damage.

Chain Lightning: Spell affects up to 5 targets, and deals successively greater Nature damage to each affected target. Chain Lightning deals about 1800-2200 Nature damage to the first target. **Heroic:** Deals about 2800-3200 Nature damage to the first target on Heroic mode.

Levitate: Tosses an enemy into the air.

Magnetic Pulse: Moves a player that is under the effect of the Levitate spell.

Summon Spore Strider: Summons three Spore Strider adds, each of which has about 5500 health. They can cast a Lightning Bolt for about 800-1000 Nature damage with a 3 second casting time. (Heroic Mode)

LET'S LOOT THIS MOTHER STALKER

Pauldrons of Brute Force (Plate Shoulder, 721 Armor, +16 STR, +22 STA, 1 [Yellow Socket], 1 [Blue Socket], Socket Bonus: +3 Dodge Rating, +18 Defense Rating)

Robes of the Augurer (Cloth Chest, 129 Armor, +18 STA, +18 INT, +11 SPI, 1 [Red Socket], 1 [Yellow Socket], 1 [Blue Socket], Socket Bonus: +4 Spell Crit Rating, Increases damage and healing done by magical spells and effects by up to 28)

Shamblehide Chestguard (Mail Chest, 539 Armor, +16 STA, +19 INT, 1 [Red Socket], 1 [Yellow Socket], 1 [Blue Socket], Socket Bonus: +4 AGI, +21 Critical Strike Rating, +44 Attack Power)

Skulldugger's Leggings (Leather Legs, 214 Armor, +24 STA, 2 [Red Socket], 1 [Blue Socket], Socket Bonus: +4 Dodge Rating, +21 Dodge Rating, +16 Hit Rating, +40 Attack Power)

The Stalker's Fangs (One-Hand Dagger, 56.7 DPS, +16 STA, +15 Critical Strike Rating, +20 Attack Power)

The Black Stalker uses a great many Nature-based attacks. Refresh any buffs and use any potions that increase your Nature Resistance before beginning this fight. Have your tank charge in when you're ready.

Spread ranged attackers about the room so none are close to each other, but all are within healing range. The tank should hold the Stalker at the southern portion to the room. Dismiss any pets before the fight begins as they are a liability to your survival.

This boss deals Physical damage and has Chain Lightning (multiple target Nature damage), Static Field (debuff that damages all party members near the afflicted), and can Levitate and Suspend your party members in the air. As the Chain Lightning can bounce from your tank, to a pet, back to your tank, it's important that no pets join the tank in melee.

Keeping your party spread out will reduce the damage done by Static Field. This debuff can not by dispelled, so reducing the damage is the best you can do. The Black Stalker can also throw members into the air and hold them there. This is devastating to melee characters, but casters can still use spells when held in the air. Don't panic and keep being as useful as possible. Melee party members should switch to a ranged weapon until they fall back to the ground. Suspend can by removed by Dispel Magic.

Use all your timed abilities. This is the final fight of the dungeon and The Black Stalker is quite lethal. There is little rhyme or reason to which attack it uses when. Positioning is the best defense you have so blast away with everything you've got.

An unlucky Levitate can throw the tank or healer out of the fight. If this happens, a secondary tank should grab the Black Stalker's attention and drag the fight closer to the airborne healer or tank if you can't Dispel the Suspend.

Heroic Mode

The Black Stalker wasn't a pushover before and is even more dangerous in Heroic Mode. He has far more health, but doesn't deal much more damage. The damage increase comes from the multiple Spore Striders which the Black Stalker summons every 10 to 15 seconds.

Three are summoned at a time and they deal Nature damage with every attack. Your Nature Resistance is even more important now! Focus fire directly on the Black Stalker and the Black Stalker will fall just as she does in normal mode.

Your tank truly benefits from having a Nature Resistance armor set if you want to defeat Heroic Mode of Underbog without major frustrations.

When the smoldering corpse of the Stalker falls, take its brain if you have the quest. Resurrect any members who fell and take the path further to leave the dungeon. A short fall brings you back to the entrance and that much closer to drier socks.

THE STEAMVAULT

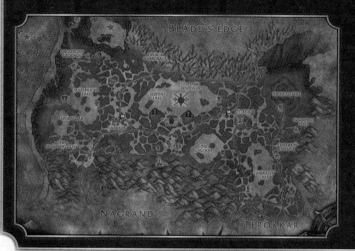

DUNGEON INFORMATION

Name	The Steamvault
Location	Zangarmarsh, Coilfang Reservoir
Suggested Levels	Group of 5, Levels 68-70
Primary Enemies	Humanoids, Elementals
Damage Types	Physical, Nature
Time to Complete	35 to 50 Minutes

WHO TO BRING

The Steamvault is the best place for a new party of level 70 characters to explore; this Instance is far shorter and easier than many of the others in its range, and even characters with slightly weaker gear can make a substantial contribution. With barely over 20 pulls needed to clear all three bosses, your group can grab quite a bit of loot as well.

Most pulls in The Steamvault are small, so crowd control is important but not needed in huge supply. Having one out-of-combat and one in-combat form of control will suffice, and having two in-combat forms is just glorious. Bring a Mage and a Rogue or Hunter for an easy slide through the dungeon.

Nature Resistance is only important in a couple places, but when it's needed it is VERY useful to have. Shamans and Hunters both help here. For that matter, Shamans bring a great deal as healers or DPS to this dungeon (depending on their spec). Shamans can buff Nature Resistance, help with Cleansing Poison/Disease, Interrupt Casters at range, and still help with the fighting or healing. It's a lot to bring to the table. Priests, on the other hand, have one of their few poor dungeons; super healing is rarely needed if Resistances are properly

placed, Mind Control is a gamble, and Psychic Scream is ill-advised (as the corridors are tight and Fear is not safe usually). That said, nobody hates having Priests around even in The Steamvault.

If you can snag a person to offtank, go ahead and do so. Though not necessary, it helps in the first boss fight (where there will be two mean Elementals that should be dispatched before the Boss is fully engaged). In a pinch, with good healing or high DPS, a beefy Hunter pet or Mail-wearer can handle this task.

Using the proper strategies for this Instance, almost any good tank should be fine. Bear Druids, Warriors, and Paladins can each handle their own. With small pulls and mostly simple enemies, there are few times when extraordinary measures are required. Decent crowd control means that you often only have two enemies to worry about, and if you can't keep their aggro . . . well, practice!

JOBS

CLASS	ABILITIES
Druid	Mark of the Wild, Backup Healing, HOTs While Keeping DPS on Targets
Hunter	Freezing Traps, Ranged DPS is Safer vs. Thespia
Mage	Polymorph, Counterspell
Paladin	Tank or Offtank vs. Thespia, Consecration
Priest	Healing and Buffing
Rogue	Sap in Larger Naga Fights, Burst DPS Versus Peripheral Targets in All Boss Fights
Shaman	Tremor Totems, Nature Resistance and Remove Poison/Disease vs. Bog Overlords
Warlock	Banish in Thespia, Dots
Warrior	Primary Tank or Offtank, Thunder Claps

GETTING TO THE STEAMVAULT

Underbog is one of the many wings of Coilfang Reservoir. Horde parties can fly into Zabra'jin while Alliance parties fly into Telredor. From there, ride or fly out to Serpent Lake, at the northern end of Zangarmarsh.

At the center of Serpent Lake is the Coilfang Reservoir. Dive beneath the water at the center of the massive pumping station there and look for a drain. Swim through the drain and surface within the Reservoir (there are pockets of air to keep your characters from drowning along the way).

The small tunnel to the northwest leads to The Steamvault. You can use the Meeting Stone at the front of the area to gather more party members if a couple of you arrive ahead of the others (this often happens in Coilfang because of the extensive time getting to the lake then swimming into the drain).

REPUTATION GAINS

ACTION	FACTION	REPUTATION GAIN	END POINT
Kill Trash Mobs	Cenarion Expedition	12 Points	Exalted
Kill Bosses	Cenarion Expedition	120 Points	Exalted
Quest: The Warlord's Hideout	Cenarion Expedition	500 Points	N/A
Quest: Orders From Lady Vashj	Cenarion Expedition	500 Points	N/A
Collect: Coilfang Armaments (Repeatable)	Cenarion Expedition	75 Points	N/A

MOST DREADED OF NAGA

BOSSES

HYDROMANCER THESPIA

MEKGINEER STEAMRIGGER

WARLORD KALITHRESH

MINIONS

BOG OVERLORD
Notes: Massive Health and Damage Output, Disease Cloud, Fungal Decay, Detect Stealthers, Trample

COILFANG ENGINEER
Notes: Net (Immobilize), Throws AoE Explosives

COILFANG LEPER
Notes: Non-Elite, Large Pulls, Use Melee or Ranged Attacks

COILFANG MYRMIDON
Notes: High Health, High Armor, Cleave, Execute

COILFANG ORACLE
Notes: Healer, Sonic Burst (Long-Duration Silence), Frost Shock

COILFANG SIREN
Notes: Arcane Flare, Lightning Bolt, Fear

COILFANG SLAVEMASTER
Notes: High Health, High Armor, Knockback

COILFANG SORCERESS
Notes: Frostbolt, Blizzard, Frost Nova

COILFANG WARRIOR
Notes: High Health, Low DPS Output, Mortal Blow, Defensive Stance, Battle Shout

DREGHOOD SLAVE
Notes: Aggro With Coilfang Slavemasters, De-aggro on Death of Slavemasters

STEAM SUGER
Notes: Water Bolt

TIDAL SURGER
Notes: Come with Four Smaller Shards, Can Be Banished, Use AoE Frost, Immune to Frost, Ranged Knockback, Water Spout, Frost Nova

THE WARLORD'S HIDEOUT

Level Requirement	68
Quest Giver	Watcher Jhang (Outside Instance Area)
Quest Goal	Kill Warlord Kalithresh
Experience Reward	19,000
Additional Rewards	Hydromancer's Headwrap (Cloth Head 127 Armor, +21 Stam, +27 Int, 1 [blue socket], 1 [meta socket], Socket Bonus: +5 Spell Damage, +33 Damage/Healing), Helm of the Claw (Leather Head 237 Armor, +25 Agi, +21 Stam, 1 [yellow socket], 1 [meta socket], Socket Bonus: +4 Resilience Rating, +66 Attack Power, +14 Hit Rating), Earthwarden's Coif (Mail Head 530 Armor, +25 Agi, +25 Stam, +18 Int, 1 [red socket], 1 [meta socket], Socket Bonus: +4 Agi, +34 Attack Power, 7 Mana/5 Seconds), Myrmidon's Headdress (Plate Head 946 Armor, +17 Str, +37 Stam, 1 [red socket], 1 [meta socket], Socket Bonus: +4 Str, +33 Defense Rating)

Any full run of The Steamvault will take care of this quest, as the final boss is your target for killing. Collect The Warlord's Hideout by talking to Watcher Jhang, near the Meeting Stone of Coilfang Reservoir. As long as you are high enough level, the quest should be available. Then, head into The Steamvault and kick some Naga tail! It's that easy.

ORDERS FROM LADY VASHJ

Level Requirement	68
Quest Giver	Drop Item
Quest Goal	Deliver the Orders From Lady Vashj to Ysiel Windsinger at the Cenarion Refuge (in Zangarmarsh)
Experience Reward	12,650
Additional Rewards	Repeatable Quest to turn in Coilfang Armaments

The Orders From Lady Vashj drop for everyone in a group while fighting through The Steamvault. Any of the Naga in the Instance can drop this, so a single run through the dungeon is often more than enough to see this item. Right-click on the Orders to start the quest, then travel to the Cenarion Refuge after the run is over.

Ysiel Windsinger is at the back of the Inn at the Cenarion Refuge. She'll not only give you the experience/gold for completing the quest; she'll also tell you that she is now looking for Coilfang Armaments. These are gained as random drops from monsters in The Steamvault, and each turn-in of the Armaments nets your character +75 Cenarion Expedition Reputation, all the way through to Exalted!

THE SECOND AND THIRD FRAGMENTS

Level Requirement	70
Quest Giver	Khadgar (Shattrath City, Terrace of Light)
Quest Goal	Obtain the Second Key Fragment
Experience Reward	N/A
Additional Rewards	Leads to The Master's Touch (Chain to Unlock Karazhan)

This part of the quest is completed in The Steamvault. When your characters are on the bridge that leads toward the Warlord's area, look over the side. There is water below, and beneath that clear surface is the Shard you need. The Third Fragment is found in The Arcatraz and is not covered here.

UNDERWORLD LOAM

Level Requirement	70
Quest Giver	David Wayne (Wayne's Ridge, Eastern Terokkar Forest)
Quest Goal	Kill at Loot Hydromancer Thespia and Return to David Wayne
Experience Reward	N/A
Additional Rewards	Continues Quest Chain for Demon-Bane Weapon

The Demon-Bane Weapons are created by David Wayne. This chain starts in Shadowmoon Valley but soon leads to David Wayne, a crafter who lives in a small building eastern of Firewing Point (in Terokkar Forest). Underworld Loam is the fifth step in this phase of the chain. All that you need to do is make it to Hydromancer Thespia and kill her; she is the first boss of the Instance, and a group can reach her in 10 minutes if things run well. Of course, you might as well run the whole Instance unless nobody in the group is interested in the other bosses.

TRIAL OF THE NAARU: STRENGTH

Level Requirement	70
Quest Giver	A'dal (Shattrath City, Terrace of Light)
Quest Goal	Defeat and Loot Warlord Kalithresh and Murmur in Heroic Mode
Experience Reward	N/A
Additional Rewards	Part of Multiple Quests to Earn the Tempest Key

After completing the Cipher of Damnation quest chain in Shadowmoon Valley, your character will receive a letter in your mailbox. This is from A'dal, the Naaru in the center of Shattrath City, asking that you come to the Terrace of Light. Several quests are granted at that time (all of them quite difficult), and this quest specifically is the Trial of Strength.

Your character must enter The Steamvault in Heroic Mode and defeat Warlord Kalithresh. You also must defeat Murmur on Heroic Mode (Murmur is the final boss of the Shadow Labyrinth).

To access Heroic Mode, gain Revered status with the Cenarion Expedition, purchase the Key to Coilfang Reservoir from their Quartermaster, then set your group's difficulty to Heroic before entering The Steamvault. Good luck!

And in case you were wondering, the final Trial of the Naaru is to defeat Magtheridon in a 25-man raid. Nifty!

UNDER PRESSURE

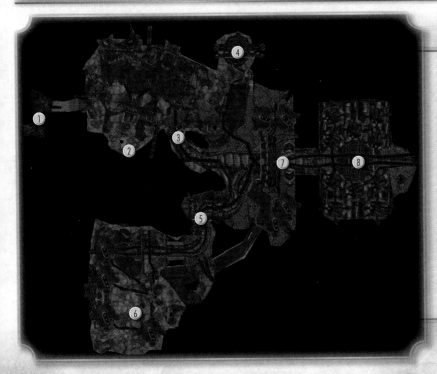

	MAP LEGEND
1	Dungeon Entrance
2	Hidden Path Through Bushes
3	Passage Toward Steamrigger and Kalithresh's Areas
4	Hydromancer Thespia (First Access Panel)
5	Slaves' Work Area
6	Mekgineer Steamrigger (Second Access Panel)
7	Entrance to Main Chambers
8	Warlord Kalithresh

A QUIET ENTRANCE

The Steamvault isn't an Instance that tries to crowd your group at the beginning. There is plenty of room to zone in and get the usual chores done (pass around food/water, buff, and talk about crowd control duties). Once that is done, look ahead toward the end of the entrance hallway; there are two Coilfang Warriors guarding the passage. These Naga are the weakest of the foes that you find in The Steamvault, and as long as the Coilfang Warrior/Siren patrol isn't nearby, you can pull the initial Warriors at your leisure. That patrol doesn't get too close, so you shouldn't have many problems.

After dispatching these soft targets, wait for the aforementioned patrol and eliminate them. Use crowd control to keep the Siren out of action until the Warrior is down, then pull the Siren back to your group's position using ranged Interrupts on her if she stops at any time.

FIGHT SIRENS ON YOUR TURF

Coilfang Sirens use AoE Fears with relative frequency, and that can easily spell trouble for your group. The enemies are packed rather tightly into The Steamvault, and bumping into another set of enemies is rather likely if you've approached the Siren's original position during a fight.

Instead, use normal line-of-sight tricks and Interrupts to ensure that the Sirens come quickly to your group's position after crowd control has been broken. Dispatch the Sirens quickly, and move on.

Though your group is free to clear the entire cavern by the entrance, it is easy to skip MANY fights by going around and hugging the right wall of the area. Instead of fighting a couple-dozen monsters, you can slip by with only two fights!

Sadly, both of these are against Bog Overlords; these Giants see through Stealth, deal AoE damage through Poison, Disease, and their trample, and don't play nicely in melee either. Take each Overlord on its own, using as much ranged damage as possible. Nature Resistance is a huge plus (Hunters, Shamans, and Druids help for this). Also, if you have an offtank or Rogue, remind them to back off and bandage if there is only one healer; they may very well be too busy to save secondary melee characters.

Walk through the bushes and fight the next Overlord by the corner. There is plenty of room, and the Overlords don't throw anyone around. That said, make sure that your ranged characters have line-of-sight for the area before starting the pull (you don't want anyone to be too close, and neither do you want your DPS and healers characters to have to re-position during the skirmish).

With the second Overlord down you are almost to the main door. That will be on the right side when you come out from the bushes, but there is a pull to the left that must be made to get through. Though you can't see all of the enemies clearly, there are four Naga waiting for a tussle: two Coilfang Engineers, one Warrior, and a nasty Siren.

Prepare any crowd control that will be used, and plan for it to hit the Coilfang Siren first, then use secondary methods on the Engineers (if possible). Don't worry about the trivial Warrior; he can easily be tanked while any active Engineers are dispatched. Obviously, without crowd control the kill order is Siren, Engineers, Warrior.

Stay near the wall again, and use proximity aggro to grab the two Coilfang Myrmidons by the door. If you have a Hunter, have them Track Humanoids so that your group knows when to aggro the monsters. You DON'T want to do it when the patrol of three Naga is wandering down the ramp.

The Myrmidons are best tanked by a single person, but if you have more melee characters it will still be alright; Myrmidons use Sweeping Strikes all the time. Luckily, they aren't Immune to crowd control, so your group is only going to face one of them at any given time.

Next, grab that patrol that you avoided a moment ago. A Coilfang Sorceress is slithering around with two Warriors are her escorts. Use crowd control on the caster and fight the two Warriors before attacking the female Sorceress. She is an Ice-caster, using Frostbolts and Blizzards to beat on your party. Interrupts are quite successful and useful against the Sorceress, and her health is quite poor for an Elite.

MOVING UP TOWARD THESPIA

Though the hallway at map point three is now clear, ignore it. You've effectively protected your back from aggro, but the first boss is ahead of your party (not up the hall). Pass the corridor and keep hugging the wall as you look ahead.

There is a Tidal Surger patrol, and it's one of the nastier things in this Instance. In front of it is a group with two Coilfang Sirens, and Oracle, and a Warrior. There is a similar group behind the Tidal Surger.

You are going to pull the first Siren group, defeat them, then position your group on the rocks to your right for the second pull. Done correctly, the Tidal Surger doesn't have to be fought at all. Done poorly, it'll join in the fight and possibly wipe your party.

For the first pull, avoid Sap (it might break at the wrong time and bring adds). Instead, pull from range and retreat to the hallway that you cleared earlier. Use crowd control on at least one of the two Sirens, and kill the enemy group from the safe shelter of the corridor. It's just too risky to have Fear hit your group in the thick, open chambers. The pulling technique mentioned above is slower, but it saves many headaches.

If you want to keep playing it safe, pull the Tidal Surger's group after the Siren group is dead. Banish the large Tidal Surger if you have a Warlock, and focus on killing the smaller Elementals first regardless. Keep the tank ahead of the group so that AoEs from the monsters don't tear everyone to ribbons. Losing control of a Tidal Surger group is horrific to watch (and somewhat amusing if you don't mind repair bills).

ORACLES ARE SCREAMERS

Coilfang Oracles have a 10-second Silence that they place on groups when using Sonic Burst. This means that Oracles are very good to hit first while the Sirens are under the effect of crowd control. Otherwise, you are going to spend too much of the fight with Silence on your casters/healers, and risking the healing spells that the Oracles love to cast on themselves and others.

Pull the second large Naga group up to the boulders on the right side of the cavern (wait for the patrol on the far ramp to clear off). Fight them there, and remember to use anti-Fear abilities if they are available (Fear Ward, Tremor Totem, Berserk Rage, etc.

The final pull before the first boss has only three enemies. These patrol down their ramp and close to the other Siren group. There is a single Warrior with two Sirens. It's clear that crowd control must go on the Sirens. Kill the spare Siren if you have one form of control, or the Warrior then the Sirens if you have two consistent means of crowd control. It's a simple fight now that you have some space without the threat of adds!

In the small cave at the top of the ramp is Hydromancer Thespia, flanked by two Coilfang Water Elementals. Rest and prepare to take her on!

HYDROMANCER THESPIA

HP	100351/141672 (Heroic)	Damage	1576-2226/2968-4193 (Heroic)
Abilities	**Enveloping Winds**: Surrounds an enemy in a cyclone for up to 6 seconds.		
	Lightning Cloud: 30 yard range, Lasts for 14 sec., dealing targets in selected area for 1575 to 2025 Nature damage and inflicting 1838 to 2362 additional Nature damage every 2 sec.		
	Lung Burst: 40 yard range, deals 602-698 Physical damage every 2 seconds for 10 seconds; can be dispelled.		

THESPIA'S BAUBLES

Chestguard of No Remorse (Leather Chest 285 Armor, +35 Stam, +21 Critical Rating, +92 Attack Power)

Cloak of Whispering Shells (Back 76 Armor, +15 Stam, +16 Int, 4 Mana/5 Seconds, +40 Healing)

Incanter's Gloves (Cloth Hands 97 Armor, +21 Stam, +24 Int, +12 Spi, +14 Spell Critical Rating, +29 Damage/Healing)

Moonrage Girdle (Leather Waist 160 Armor, +22 Int, +21 Spi, +20 Spell Critical Rating, +25 Damage/Healing)

Scintillating Coral Band (Finger +14 Stam, +15 Int, +17 Spell Critical Rating, +21 Damage/Healing)

Hydromancer Thespia is clearly a caster, and her two Elementals are there to supplement her damage. Luckily, those two creatures are easy to destroy and can be taken out of the battle early on. That should certainly be part of your battleplan.

The standard method for victory here is to have the main tank enter the room and go after Thespia directly. While this is happening, the rest of the group (except for the healers) pull and attack the Water Elementals. Focus on the left Elemental first, to keep it simple, then blow down the right one. As long as the group is fast on DPS, it doesn't even require a solid tank to pull this off.

If your group has a Warlock, kill one of the Elementals and just Banish the other one to get DPS onto Thespia even earlier in the fight.

Hydromancer Thespia likes to use a random Stun against opponents. The effect from Enveloping Winds lasts for five seconds, and it can be Dispelled. If Thespia uses her Stun when a Lightning Cloud is nearby, Dispel the effect immediately.

Thespia's Lung Burst deals 500 damage per tick. This too is magical and Dispellable. To do her real damage though, this caster likes to summon Lightning Clouds; these Nature storms deal around 2,000 damage per tick if you don't have Nature Resistance gear/buffs. If a Cloud appears where the tank is standing, have the tank quickly move Thespia to a safer area. When other characters are caught in the Cloud, their duty is to move immediately and consider self bandaging to keep the load off of the healer.

As long as your group understands that initial DPS must go heavily on the Elementals and that the Cloud must be quickly avoided, this fight is fairly easy. Thespia is tough but fair, and a five-on-three battle is in your favor!

When the excitement is over, loot Hydromancer Thespia and pull the lever on the nearby Access Panel. This is the first part of unlocking the final boss. To fully open the door, your group must use the other Access Panel as well.

Hydromancer Thespia carries the **Underworld Loam** for a quest. Only those on the quest can loot this.

GOING SOUTH

Heroic Mode

Heroic Steamvault battles are similar to the normal fighting. Thespia's Water Elementals can volley for over twice their original damage, but they still hit lightly in melee. Do what you can to Interrupt or Stun them, and remind people ahead of time that aggro isn't a big deal with the Water Elementals. Enter blowdown mode and use heavy burst DPS so that the Elementals die before they can do much damage.

Thespia has the same tricks, but her buff is that she summons two Clouds at the same time. Characters who are running from one AoE must be very cautious not to rush into the area of another!

Return to map point three and enter that hallway. The first new group of monsters to be see is a fight with a single Warrior and two Sorceresses. Control one or both of the Sorceresses and defeat the loner as needed. This fight rarely has any complications, and there is plenty of room.

Advance slightly and wait for the hallway patrollers to come near: a Sorceress and two Myrmidons. Control the Sorceress and fight both of the Myrmidons without fear of spellcraft.

Though there are many enemies on the left side of the passage, you don't need to clear a single group over there. Instead, take only the fights on the right side so that your group can move into the southern hallway.

Note that groups looking for the **Second Shard** are going to jump off into the water underneath this bridge area. The Shard in down in the water there and can be collected without major difficulty.

The next group has four foes (two Myrmidons, a Siren, and a Sorceress). Sap/Polymorph/etc. to keep the Siren from entering the early battle, and blow down the Sorceress with speed. After this, whittle away at the Myrmidons and re-apply crowd control to the Siren if you group is taking a bit too long. This prevents our green beauty from suddenly breaking free and using her Instant AoE Fear!

Now that your group is fully in the southern hallway there is even more room to fight, so Fear becomes an option as long as your people are willing to pull back slightly. The next group has two more Myrmidons, a Sorceress, and the new Coilfang Slavemaster. Slavemasters take more damage to defeat, and they have a somewhat heavy Knockback.

Take out the Sorceress with crowd control, beat down the Slavemaster second, then work on the Myrmidons. Afterward, look into the extended hallway and wait for the lone Slavemaster to patrol toward your group. Pulling him at the end of his route means that only two of the nearby Dreghood Slaves add to the fight. Kill the Slavemaster and the Slaves will de-aggro automatically, so your best move is to keep those guys crowd controlled as best you can.

The next patrolling Slavemaster goes all the way to the end of the hall on the other side. Fight him in the small covered area there and have your characters keep their backs to each wall; nobody can be knocked back into the area with the Slaves or knocked ahead into the next group of Naga! If you rush in to fight this Slavemaster there, none of the Slaves will be in range to add (good deal)!

The final Slavemaster fight is the only one with two Slavemasters! You have to fight both of them to stop the Dreghood Slave. For a simple fight, use crowd control on the second Slavemaster, kill the first, then break crowd control and kill the second Slavemaster. Sometimes this Slave will go a bit odd and stay aggressive to your group, but he can be quickly put out of his misery.

Across the next bridge are two encounters then the next boss. Both of the non-Elite encounters ahead involve AoE pulls against Leper Gnomes (joy)! You get to plow through eight of the little fiends per fight.

Stop for a moment and inform any new players to the Instance about the difficulties of this AoE grouping. The Coilfang Lepers can go into melee- or ranged-attack mode, and that can make it harder to consolidate them for good AoEs!

Let your best tank get the initial aggro and bring the Gnomes onto the bridge in as fight a group as possible (don't worry if one or two stay outside of the bridge and use Shadowbolts or Frost Nova; they won't do too much damage). When the enemies are consolidated, blast them with everything the group has. If you have a Warrior, Challenging Shout is a superb last-resort if anything goes wrong with aggro during either pull. They can only use this once during the period, but it's unlikely that your group will have trouble both times.

It may seem tricky to handle the AoE pulls on the small bridge, but it isn't. There are no Knockback attacks in these fights, and neither are there Fear abilities to worry about. Everyone should be just fine.

Lasts, there is a Gnome with a team of technicians idling at the other end of the cave. Those guys sure look cocky. That gearhead is about to get tooled!

MEKGINEER STEAMRIGGER

	HP	103320/ 125460 (Heroic)	Damage	2091-2957/ 4265-6032 (Heroic)
Abilities	**Electrified Net**: Immobilizes and enemy for 6 sec., dealing about 600-750 Nature damage every 2 sec.			
	Super Shrink Ray: Decreases the damage output of nearby targets by 35% for 15 seconds.			
	Saw Blade: Deals approximately 1500-2000 Physical damage to the target and all nearby targets.			
	Summon Gnomes: Summons several gnomes with the Repair ability, which will restore Mekgineer Steamrigger's health.			

INSIDE THE TOOLBOX, YOU FIND . . .

Earth Mantle Handwraps (Mail Hands 397 Armor, +21 Stam, +18 Int, 1 [red socket], 1 [yellow socket], Socket Bonus: +3 Int, +17 Spell Critical Rating, +20 Damage/Healing)

Recoilless Rocket Ripper X-54 (Gun 64.7 DPS, +13 Stam, +16 Critical Rating)

Mask of Penance (Plate Head 922 Armor, +27 Stam, +30 Int, +66 Healing, 10 Mana/5 Seconds)

Serpentcrest Life-Staff (Staff 59.9 DPS, +27 Stam, +27 Int, +46 Spi, +227 Healing)

Steam-Hinge Chain of Valor (Neck +26 Stam, +19 Shield Block Rating, +29 Shield Block Value)

Mekgineer Steamrigger starts with three Steamrigger Mechanics around his mech; each of these non-Elites has the ability to repair the mech at a substantial rate. For this reason alone, the little fellows need to bite the dust early and hard (and often as it turns out).

At several points (75%/50%/25% health), Mekgineer Steamrigger will yell "Tune 'em up good boys!" This summons three more Mechanics, though it takes them a short time to arrive.

Your party needs to be able to beat the four waves of Mechanics without losing aggro or stumbling in the process. The good news is that the repairs done by the Mechanics are disrupted by area-of-effect abilities. Even a single Warrior using Thunder Clap can delay the group for a short time.

Assign a main tank to deal with Steamrigger, and have three other characters assigned to one-each of the initial Mechanics. As soon as those are blown down, everyone focuses on Steamrigger until the next wave arrives. At that time, the DPSers switch, kill the non-Elites, then return their damage to the boss.

Alternatively, a good AoE class can handle all of the Mechanics without help. A Mage with a fair plus to spell damage can use Arcane Explosion to disrupt any and all healing that the Mechanics would hope to accomplish. This won't work as cleanly in Heroic Mode, as explained below, but it's quite easy in Normal Mode.

As for the boss himself, Mekgineer Steamrigger isn't so bad if you have a tank with fair armor. His Shrink Ray debuffs damage done, but it can be Reflected if you are lucky with the timing!

The Sawblade that Steamrigger throws does almost 2,000 to anyone in its range. As with many bosses, have your ranged DPS characters and healers stay spread out in the area. This minimizes the danger from Sawblade throws.

Aggro must stay on the main tank because of the Electrified Net that Steamrigger uses. This net Immobilizes the target for 10 seconds and deals modest damage. If the main tank loses aggro during this time, Intercept out of the net, Shapeshift to get out of it, etc. All tanks have something that they can do to avoid letting this break the party.

Use your knowledge of the adds and their timing to its fullest. Disrupt repairs quickly and keep damage on Steamrigger throughout the fight. Until you try him on Heroic Mode, this boss isn't so bad at all!

Heroic Mode

And when it comes time to beat Steamrigger in this more challenging mode, it will take some entirely new tricks. Mechanics are summoned at the same times throughout the encounter, but additional Gnomes arrives from time-to-time as well. This added chaos makes things harder to deal with, and to make it worse the adds have major health!

You won't be able to clear out the no-Elites with any speed, and the encounter is on a timer. If your group can't down Steamrigger in five minutes, the game is up. Painfully.

Thus, most strategies revolved around disrupted the Mechanics without taking the time to actually kill them. Paladin Consecration is wonderful, as it keeps the aggro on a tank while continuously throwing off the Mechanics' work.

Warrior Thunder Clap is great too, but it only hits four targets and doesn't come out of cooldown quite as quickly as you need. It won't be enough. Instead of using this as the primary means of disruption, use it to keep aggro on the Warrior and let a Mage or other AoE class do the disrupting.

The trick for such a caster is to use their weakest possible AoE. A Mage with Rank 1 Arcane Explosion does trivial damage, but it is fast, effective, and won't rip aggro off of the Thunder Clap that the Warrior is running. Perfect!

Use the Main Chambers Access Panel here to finish the second step of opening the doors at map point seven. Warlord Kalithresh is now exposed, and your group only has to return to the central hallway to start advancing against him.

THE BELL TOLLS FOR KALITHRESH

Take the central hallway east toward the Warlord's room. Though each of the remaining pulls is rather large, they are still easily defeated when your reward is so close at hand!

Your first fight is near the doorway itself. There are two Myrmidons guarding an Oracle and a Sorceress. Use crowd control against the Oracle to avoid her Silence and blast down the Sorceress. Wipe up the Myrmidons, then break control and finish off the Oracle.

Inside the room itself, there are three pulls. The front fight has two Myrmidons, an Oracle, and a Siren. Control the Siren (and the Oracle if you can). If the Oracle is out of crowd control, kill that first, then move on to fight the Myrmidons.

If you are having trouble and need to use Fear to win the fight, pull the enemies farther back into the hallway to avoid getting adds while the enemies are running around.

Then final two pulls are against equivalent groups; each with a Myrmidon, a Siren, an Oracle, and a Sorceress. Control the Siren, slay the Oracle, turn on the Sorceress, then dispatch the Myrmidons when the deadlier targets are out of the way.

Enough with the warm ups. Catch your breath, explain any new tactics, then rush Kalithresh directly. Kill him a lot!

WARLORD KALITHRESH

HP	147600/236160 (Heroic)	**Damage**	1699-2402/4265-6032 (Heroic)
Abilities	**Spell Reflection**: Reflects all spells for 8 seconds.		
	Head Crack: Reduces the target's stamina by 72 for 20 seconds.		
	Impale: 8-35 yard range, deals 415 Physical damage every 3 seconds for 12 seconds.		
	Warlord's Rage: Increases attack speed by 70% and the physical damage by 75 for 10 min. Stack up to 10 times.		

LOOK IN THIS CONTAINER!

Beast Lord Leggings (Mail Legs 570 Armor, +30 Agi, +25 Stam, +19 Int, +52 Attack Power, 7 Mana/5 Seconds)

Beast Lord Mantle (Mail Shoulder 489 Armor, +25 Agi, +12 Int, 1 [yellow socket], 1 [red socket], Socket Bonus: +4 Stam, +34 Attack Power, 5 Mana/5 Seconds)

Devilshark Cape (Back 78 Armor, +22 Stam, +20 Defense Rating, +18 Dodge Rating, +29 Block Value)

Gauntlets of Vindication (Plate Hands 728 Armor, +24 Stam, +25 Int, 2 [red socket], Socket Bonus: +3 Resilience Rating, 7 Mana/5 Seconds, +11 Damage/Healing)

Incanter's Pauldrons (Cloth Shoulder 117 Armor, +24 Stam, +17 Int, +16 Spi, 1 [yellow socket], 1 [red socket], Socket Bonus: +3 Spell Critical Rating, +20 Damage/Healing)

Wastewalker Shoulderpads (Leather Shoulder 219 Armor, +25 Agi, +13 Stam, 1 [red socket], 1 [blue socket], Socket Bonus: +3 Critical Rating, +16 Hit Rating, +34 Attack Power)

Ring of the Silver Hand (Finger +18 Stam, +18 Int, +19 Defense Rating, 5 Mana/5 Seconds)

Sash of Serpentra (Cloth Waist 88 Armor, +31 Stam, +21 Int, +17 Spell Hit Rating, +25 Damage/Healing)

Gauntlets of the Bold (Plate Hands 728 Armor, +17 Str, +16 Agi, +31 Stam, 1 [red socket], 1 [yellow socket], Socket Bonus: +3 Parry Rating, +14 Defense Rating)

Tidefury Gauntlets (Mail Hands 407 Armor, +22 Stam, +26 Int, +29 Damage/Healing, 7 Mana/5 Seconds)

Vermillion Robes of the Dominant (Cloth Chest 156 Armor, +37 Stam, +33 Int, +12 Spell Hit Rating, +42 Damage/Healing)

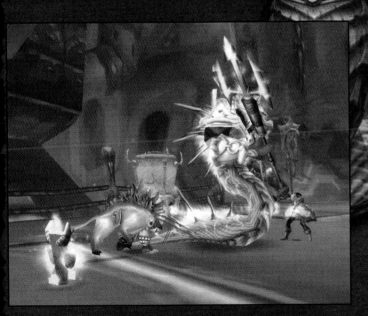

Warlord Kalithresh is fought by himself, without any Naga, Gnomes, or Elementals to come to his aid. He'll seem easy at first, and indeed he is a very simple boss if you keep him from getting his amazing buffs.

Normally, Kalithresh has a Spell Reflect (with a standard white glow to let you know not to cast). He also has a Physical DOT Impale. This only does about 500 a tick, so it's not a show stopper.

Otherwise, Kalithresh happily melees away and stays onto the main tank without trying to dump aggro or do anything strange. "This sounds too good to be true" you are saying. Well, yes and no.

Kalithresh has a plan, you see. He tries to crack open the containers in his room to get a buff from them. This buff is called Warlord's Rage, and it raises his Damage by 75% and his Attack Speed by 100%. If he gets this once, you've probably lost the fight. If he gets it twice, you've REALLY lost the fight (yes, it does stack).

To keep Kalithresh honest, have your tank pull him over toward one of his containers during the early part of the fight. Kalithresh always tries to break open the nearest container; by tanking the Warlord near one of them, you always know which container he'll choose.

As soon as the text message informs you that Kalithresh "begins to channel from the nearby distiller," all of your party members must switch damage to the container and destroy it. You have almost 15 seconds to do this, so it should be easy. Even it's going to be close, even the healer can jump in.

Tanks and offtanks can feel free to use area-of-effect attacks to handle this. Sweeping Strikes is wonderful for keeping damage on the Warlord while taking out his lovely fluids.

As soon as the container is destroyed, have your main tank lead Kalithresh over to another vat. Repeat the process for the rest of the encounter!

Heroic Mode

The primary difference is Kalithresh hits significantly harder and the channeled containers have increased health.

The Coilfang Reservoir is now mostly safe! Your group has defeated the best and brightest that the area has to offer. Well, except for Serpentshrine Cavern. That 25-man raid area is extremely challenging, but it waits for those interested in plumbing the depths of Coilfang even farther.

MANA TOMBS

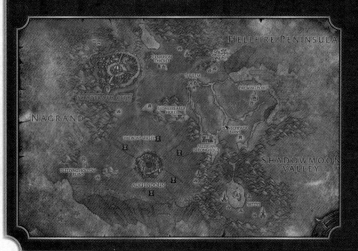

DUNGEON INFORMATION

Name	Mana Tombs
Location	Terokkar Forest, Auchindoun
Suggested Levels	Group of 5, Levels 64-67
Primary Enemies	Ethereals, Voidwalkers
Damage Types	Physical, Shadow
Time to Complete	60 to 90 Minutes

WHO TO BRING

JOBS

CLASS	ABILITIES
Druid	Shapeshifting to break/be immune to Polymorph, DPS for adds in Final Fight
Hunter	Great for Adds in Final Fights, Safe DPS Vs. First Two Bosses, Freezing Trap for many pulls, Silencing Shot
Mage	Polymorph of Casters, Counterspell
Paladin	Shadow Protection, Self-Heals During Pandemonius Reflect
Priest	Mind Control, Shadow Protection
Rogue	Stunlock for Many Caster Mobs, DPS Burst on Final Boss Adds, Sap
Shaman	Ranged Interrupts vs. Dark Casters/Theurgists/Etc. (Earth Shock)
Warlock	Fel Hunter and Succubus Pets Are Strong, Strong Anti-Caster Potential
Warrior	Less Tanking Than Usual, More DPS Duties, Bring HP Gear Instead of +DEF Gear

Because of the heavy caster population within Mana Tombs, it's extremely useful to have extra crowd control. The mix of a Mage and either a Hunter or Rogue can be especially nice here. If you have a Priest along as a healer, they can double as crowd control during many Ethereal pulls by using Mind Control on some of the nastier healers or DPS classes in the enemy population.

Tanks have a less standard role than usual inside Mana Tombs; many of the monsters deal less physical than you are used to, but the incoming Shadow damage can be mean (in trash and boss encounters). Thus, tanks should stack as much Stamina gear on as they can find, and use buffs, potions, or armor pieces to increase Shadow Resistance as well. That said, a two-handed weapon or dual-wield configuration is quite useful except during the fights against Tavarok and Shaffar. If your enemies aren't hitting you hard in melee, give up armor for increased damage/threat!

GETTING TO MANA TOMBS

The Mana Tombs are found in the center of Terokkar Forest's Bone Wastes. This area is known as Auchindoun, and there are four instances to be discovered within its depths (Mana Tombs, Auchenai Crypts, Sethekk Halls, and the Shadow Labyrinth). The Mana Tombs is easier to complete than the other Instances, which are of higher level.

Look on the northern side of Auchindoun to find Mana Tombs. Talk with the NPCs outside to get the two quests that you need inside the Instance, then head on in when you have your group ready.

REPUTATION GAINS

ACTION	FACTION	REPUTATION GAIN	END POINT
Kill Trash Mobs	Consortium	2-12 Points	Honored
Kill Bosses	Consortium	91 Points	Honored
Quest: Safety is Job One	Consortium	350	N/A
Quest: Someone Else's Hard Work Pays Off	Consortium	500	N/A
Quest: Undercutting the Competition	Consortium	500	N/A

BOSSES

NEXUS-PRINCE SHAFFAR

PANDEMONIUS

TAVAROK

WHAT STIRS WITHIN THE TOMBS

MINIONS

ETHEREAL CRYPT RAIDER
Notes: Soul Strike Acts as a Mortal Strike, Charge, Battle Shout

ETHEREAL DARKCASTER
Notes: Very Nasty Shadow Word: Pain, Ranged Mana Burn for Extremely High Damage, Shadowform

ETHEREAL PRIEST
Notes: Holy Nova, Heal, Power Word: Shield

ETHEREAL SCAVENGER
Notes: Singe, Strike, Shield Bash

ETHEREAL SORCERER
Notes: Arcane Missile, Low HPs, Summon Arcane Fiends (2); Arcane Fiends have Low Health, Arcane Explosion, Slow

ETHEREAL SPELLBINDER
Notes: Summon Ethereal Wraiths (2, which have Shadow Volley), Immolate (18-Second Fire DOT), Counterspell

ETHEREAL THEURGIST
Notes: Polymorph (20 seconds), Strike, Blast Wave

MANA LEECH
Notes: Arcane Explosion, Faerie Fire (Standard Armor Debuff), Mana Burn

NEXUS STALKER
Notes: Gouge, Rend, Phantom Strike (Increases Casting, Ranged, and Melee time by 50%) + Nature Damage every 3 seconds

NEXUS TERROR
Notes: High Health, Shadowy Embrace (2850 to 3150 Over 6 seconds and a Debuff Silence + -50% to Physical Damage Dealt), Curse of Impotence (-316 to all Magic Damage for 1 min), Psychic Scream

SHADOW LORD XIRAXIS
Notes: Very Simple Quest Target

SAFETY IS JOB ONE

Level Requirement	64
Quest Giver	Artificier Morphalius (Outside of Mana Tombs)
Quest Goal	Kill 10 Ethereal Crypt Raiders, 5 Nexus Stalkers, 5 Ethereal Sorcerers, and 5 Ethereal Spellbinders
Experience Reward	14,150
Additional Rewards	Chains to Someone Else's Hard Work Pays Off

The quest giver for this important quest is just outside of Mana Tombs. Talk to Artificier Morphalius on the way in, then kill all of the targets that are on the way toward the final boss. There are always enough spawns to complete your goals.

In the second Reactor Room, turn in the quest on the right side of the room (there is a floating cube to access). Make sure that EVERYONE in the group turns in the quest but does not start the next step.

The first person who starts the next step triggers Someone Else's Hard Work Pays Off. It's an escort (so others would miss the quest if they weren't done turning in Safety is Job One). Beyond that, it's wiser to finish off the nearby boss of the dungeon before running the escort.

So, move on and kill Shaffar, then return to the second Reactor Room and start the escort.

SOMEONE ELSE'S HARD WORK PAYS OFF

Level Requirement	64
Quest Giver	Cryo-Engineer Sha'heen
Quest Goal	Escort Sha'heen to the Exit
Experience Reward	14,150
Additional Rewards	Consortium Prince's Wrap (Cloth Waist 75 Armor, +22 Spell Critical Rating, +30 to Damage/Healing, +20 Spell Penetration), Cryo-Mitts (Leather Hands 156 Armor, +22 Int, +16 Spi, +57 Healing), Consortium Mantle of Phasing (Mail Shoulder 416 Armor, +21 Critical Strike Rating, +46 Attack Power, +9 Mana/5 Seconds), Flesh Beast's Metal Greaves (Plate Feet 680 Armor, +25 Stam, +18 Defense, +28 Dodge Rating)

The escort quest out of Mana Tombs is challenging for a lower-level group, especially if the group lacks in-combat crowd control. There are four fights that you run into on the way out of the dungeon.

Fight one: when Sha'heen reaches the first Reactor Room, he'll trigger four elites. Two come from each side, so it's a tank's worst nightmare. Do what you can to start crowd control against the higher DPS enemies that spawn (Polymorph, Hunter Traps, etc.), and have everyone assist off of their lead DPS character to blow down single targets instead of attacking everything in sight.

Fight two: this also has four elites, and they come in Tavarok's area, when Sha'heen reaches another power system. This fight is almost exactly the same as the first, so survival in one likely means that you can survive the second. The really good news is that the rest of the escort is easy.

Fight three: two Nexus Terrors spawn in the Great Hall. Pull the first by having one person run somewhat ahead of the party (not too far). This gives you some time to beat down the first Terror before the second patrols into your group or the advancing Sha'heen. This fight is way easier than the previous two!

Final fight: Shadow Lord Xiraxis attacks your party on the way out of Mana Tombs. You would think this would be the make or break fight of the quest, but it's really just a free beat down for Xiraxis. Give your tank a few moments to cement aggro before going all out, then have fun.

UNDERCUTTING THE COMPETITION

Level Requirement	64
Quest Giver	Nexus-Prince Haramad
Quest Goal	Kill Nexus-Prince Shaffar and Loot His Wrappings
Experience Reward	17,000
Additional Rewards	Haramad's Leggings of the Third Coin (Leather Legs 219 Armor, +29 INT, 2 [yellow socket], 1 [red socket], Socket Bonus: +5 Spell Damage, +16 Spell Critical Rating, +27 Damage/Healing), Consortium Plated Legguards (Plate Legs 866 Armor +23 INT, 1 [red socket], 1 [yellow socket], 1 [blue socket], Socket Bonus: +9 Healing, +51 Healing, +9 Mana/5 Seconds), Haramad's Leg Wraps (Cloth Legs 116 Armor +29 Spi, 3 [red socket], Socket Bonus: +4 Spi, +24 Healing, +11 Mana/5 Seconds), Haramad's Linked Chain Pantaloons (Mail Legs 485 Armor, 3 [yellow socket], Socket Bonus: +4 Int, +10 Spell Critical Rating, +34 Damage/Healing, +12 Mana/5 Seconds)

Get this quest from Haramad before heading inside Mana Tombs; let the other starting quest, this is found just outside the entrance of the Instance.

Your goal is to beat the final boss of Mana Tombs: Nexus-Prince Shaffar. Read through the full walkthrough to get a detailed guide of how to beat the dungeon and its bosses. Shaffar himself is not overly brutal as long as you know how to prevent his adds from joining the fight. Once Shaffar falls, make sure that everyone loots his corpse to get the necessary Wrappings. Turn these in outside the dungeon for a very nice group of rewards.

TAKING BACK THE TOMBS

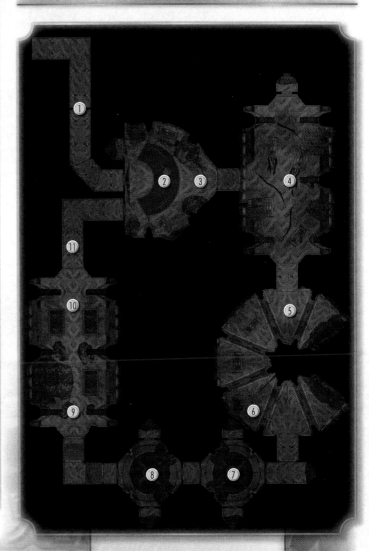

MAP LEGEND	
1	Tomb Entrance
2	Ravaged Crypt
3	Pandemonius (Boss)
4	The Great Hall
5	The Crescent Hall
6	Tavarok (Boss)
7	First Reactor Room
8	Second Reactor Room (Quest Location)
9	Hall of Twilight
10	Nexus-Prince Shaffar
11	Passage to Balcony (Fast Exit)

ENTERING THE DUNGEON

Walk through the Instance portal into the Mana Tombs and stop immediately. There is no danger of aggro from the patrollers or set group at the front of the Instance, but you can't advance very far without getting their attention. Wait for all of your group members to arrive, buff, and trade around food/water/potions and such.

Then, discuss the standard loot rules (as needed), and figure out how crowd control is going to be run in this Instance. Because Ethereal Humanoids dominate the entire Instance, most of your targets are going to be exposed to crowd control (Freezing Trap, Polymorph, Fear, Sap, etc.). Thus, there are many options for how you want to deal with the fights ahead.

As a rule, there are no more than four Elites per fight in Mana Tombs; these aren't large encounters. Instead, the composition of enemy groups and their high reliance on DPS/casters is what creates the challenge.

Your first pull is the set group south of your position. There are two foes, an Ethereal Scavenger and an Ethereal Raider. The Scavenger is a great interrupter, so he is the better person to use crowd control against. Pull this group back to your position before fighting them; this avoids complications from the patrolling Scavenger and Raider. Once the set group is done, attack the patrollers in this hallway or at the corner.

SCAVENGERS LOVE YOUR HEALERS

Scavengers are Rogues, and they love to jump onto your healers. Once that happens, expect the occasional interrupt. In small fights that is nothing of great concern, but in larger fights it might prove lethal. If you are the main tank or an off-tanking class, watch those Scavengers and keep them away from your healing class. The healer doesn't even need to have aggro to be interrupted by these villains.

Turn the corner and look at the archway beyond. There are two more foes there, and they can be pulled back to your corner without trouble. Now, the path is clear to start pulling from the Ravaged Crypt.

THE RAVAGED CRYPT

The room ahead has several pulls and a boss encounter. For the first few fights, it's best to stay in the initial hallway where the possibility of adds is at a minimum. Watch for the room's one patrol group (an Ethereal Sorcerer and an Ethereal Raider), then pull the first fight when they are not close by.

The first fight is your first group of three enemies in Mana Tombs. Your first Sorcerer is in there as well, so now you get a look at the Instance's casters. Sorcerers rely mostly on channeled Arcane Missiles, so they are quite interruptible. None-the-less, they are the best target in this group for crowd control. Deal with the melee enemies as long as the Sorcerer is out of combat, then slam the Sorcerer when it is by itself.

If you are lacking in crowd control, or want to ensure that the Sorcerer does not get to break out of shorter effects (such as a Hunter Trap), deal with the Sorcerer first. These casters are low on health, so they make for fast victories when the group focuses fire.

Pull the patrolling Sorcerer/Raider duo back into the hallway and deal with them. This makes the room nice and clean for continued pulls.

The remaining three groups in the room are on the left (usually a couple Scavengers and a Sorcerer), the right (Raider, Scavenger, Sorcerer), and at the far right side of the room (just a Sorcerer and a Raider).

If you are comfortable with this fighting, clear the enemies from the doorway instead of back in the hall (this makes for shorter pulls and less wasted time). However, if your group is still a tad shaky, stay in the hall and use the structure and cover that it provides to keep these pulls clean.

RANGED INTERRUPTS AND USE OF COVER

For these encounters and for future ones in Mana Tombs, it's good to practice interrupting casters at range. There are many different types of casting monsters in the dungeon, and you want to be very good at bringing them back to the group (sometimes in a hurry). To do this, interrupt them if they stop to cast spells before you have them where you want.

Silencing Shot, Counterspell, and Earthshock are all good choices because of their speed and use from range. If you don't have a Hunter, Mage, or Shaman hanging around, use the cover of walls to force casters to you. If they cannot keep line of sight on their target, they have to stop casting and move forward eventually.

Now that the room is clear, look back and above you. There is a ledge; this is the rear way to the exit. That is used after defeating the boss of the dungeon. Next, stare ahead and into the shifting blackness that is Pandemonius! Don't worry, he won't aggro until you get rather close to him, so there is quite a bit of time to rest and prepare.

PANDEMONIUS

HP	73392/119556 (Heroic)	**Damage**	734-1031/2823-3992 (Heroic)
Abilities	**Dark Shell:** Reflects all spells for 5 seconds. Melee attackers who strike Pandemonius suffer 750 Shadow damage. **Heroic:** Reflects 1500 damage to melee.		
	Void Blast: Three bolts of shadow strike random targets for about 1800-2100 Shadow damage and knock the target back. **Heroic:** Deals approximately 2700-3000 Shadow damage per bolt.		

TREASURES OF THE ABYSS

Creepjacker (Main Hand Fist 58.3 DPS, +13 Stam, +13 Critical Strike Rating, +28 Attack Power)

Faith Bearer's Gauntlets (Plate Hands 619 Armor +18 Str, +18 Stam, +19 Int, 1 [red socket], 1 [blue socket], Socket Bonus: +3 Hit Rating, +14 Damage/Healing, +3 Mana/5 Seconds)

Idol of the Claw (Idol 20% Chance per combo point to heal yourself for 90 to 110 each time you land a finishing move)

Shield of the Void (Shield 3234 Armor, +24 Stam, +16 Defense Rating, +24 Block Value)

Voidfire Wand (Wand 103.9 DPS +9 Stam, +9 Int, +7 Spell Hit Rating, +11 Damage/Healing)

Boots of the Outlander (Mail Feet 381 Armor, +22 Agi, +21 Stam, +15 Int, +44 Attack Power)

When the battle commences, have the tank grab attention from Pandemonius and back toward the nearby wall. Your tank should keep their back near the wall during the engagement so that Pandemonius can't throw them around. This way, any Knockbacks are going to be mitigated and prevent the tank from losing time getting back to their target.

Pandemonius' Void Blast fires three bolts at random targets. Potentially all three bolts could hit the same player. To minimize this, have ranged DPS stay back in the heart of the room. Many ranged classes can stay far enough back to avoid the Void Blast!

The real party wiper for those players who haven't faced Pandemonius before happens when he raises his Shadow Shield. Pandemonius glows green during this phase, and he'll punish anyone who attacks with melee or magical damage. Spells are reflected back to their casters, and melee dealers take 750 Shadow damage in normal mode and 1500 iin Heroic.

Though ranged attacks are not reflected, it is important to focus on health before damage dealing; you don't want to accrue too much aggro from Pandemonius while your tank is disengaged anyway.

Rather, use this time to bandage if the fight is a close one. Even your healer may want to bandage, conserving mana for the rest of the encounter!

With a party that understands this shield, Pandemonius shouldn't be a problem for long. If you have too many melee attackers the fight is harder because more people will be in range for the Void Blast. Remind the offtanks/melee DPS people to back off periodically to bandage themselves while outside the range of Void Blast. A group with high melee and low healing can't demand everything from a lone healer; they have to do some of the work themselves in a fight like this.

Pandemonius is a large Voidwalker with a bad attitude. Before engaging Pandemonius, use any buffs for Shadow Protection that your party has. Especially focus these on the main tank, as Pandemonius even does melee damage that counts as Shadow based.

HEADING TOWARD THE GREAT HALL

Loot Pandemonius after he falls, then walk east toward the Great Hall. There are two fights to control the hallway. The first is a two-enemy pull, but the second fight has four Elites! Look over the group and spot all of your targets before the fight begins. It's a mixed group, with a Scavenger, a Sorcerer, a Raider, and a Priest.

Priests have Holy Nova, and deal a moderate amount of damage. You won't want one of those to rampage through your group while the other enemies are active, so your best crowd control should go onto the Priest. After that, it's a matter of fast killing against the Sorcerer, the Scavenger, and finally the Raider.

MIND CONTROLLING THE PRIESTS

It's ironic, but the Ethereal Priests are great targets to Mind Control. Not only are these good enemies to take out before an engagement, but they are useful even once your party goes into a battle. Ethereal Priests have effective Heals, and their Power Word: Shield is nothing to sneeze at either.

Additionally, Priests aren't very hard targets to bring down, so a failed Mind Control does not mean that your own Priest is doomed. Have the group jump on the Ethereal Priest with DPS and Stuns, and watch the foe evaporate before they can do anything.

As with many pulls of this type, you won't want to move forward to engage the group of four. A Fear when your party is so close to the Great Hall would risk a wipe from adds. Instead, pull the fighting back to the Ravaged Crypt.

Now the pulls start to focus even more on casters. Look for the nearby group of three as your first target. There should be two Sorcerers and a Priest. Control the Priest and blow down the Sorcerers; do this back in the hallway to the Crypt.

Clear the patrol that comes close to the front; it's a duo with a Sorcerer and a Priest. Another patrol on the right is next. It involves a lone foe (but not a soft target). This is a Nexus Terror, and you never want to have one of those add to an encounter. Nexus Terrors have a boatload of abilities, high health, and the potential to wipe parties if you get one that you don't expect.

Pull the Nexus Terror when he is near the right side (the western wall). There aren't any enemy groups there, and you can easily get him by himself even using ranged weapons without instants.

THE HORROR OF THE NEXUS

Nexus Terrors load damage onto their targets. They have debuffs to weaken people. Using Curse of Corruption, they also put a solid DOT onto their target. They couple this with frequent Shadowy Embraces, which can be used even at the very start of a fight. Shadow Embrace deals 2850 to 3150 over only six seconds, and its debuff Silences and lowers Physical damage by 50%.

Nexus Terrors are ferocious against casters as well, using Curse of Impotence to lower Magic damage by 316 for a full minute.

You can certainly see why these foes must be taken by themselves. A full group of enemies dealing damage with a Nexus Terror on top is too much for your group's healing to keep up with unless everyone is well overleveled for Mana Tombs.

Pull Nexus Terrors when their patrol route is away from other groups. Then, keep aggro on the main tank and use your best efforts to brute force the Terrors into submission. You can always rest afterward, so don't try to take out the Nexus Terrors in an elegant way. Waste mana, use big heals if you think they are needed, toss around the damage, and blow shorter timers. There are five of you and only one Terror!

One of the truly horrible attacks of the Nexus Terrors is their Psychic Scream. This fear only lasts four seconds, but can be quite damaging to your party. Use any abilities that increase resistance to Fear (Fear Ward) or remove Fear (Tremor Totem) to reduce the damage this effect does. This is another reason to pull the Terrors well away from other enemies before engaging them.

The left side of the Great Hall (north on your map) is filled with Mana Leeches and a few extra Ethereals. Don't clear these unless people in your group are planning on doing the escort later. The fights are safely skipable otherwise.

If you are doing the quests in Mana Tombs, clear the northern part of the room now to avoid complications later. There are three fights involved; the first is against two Sorcerers and a Priest. Then other two are against groups of Mana Leeches, with three in the first group and five in the rear group.

Use the fight against three Mana Leeches to get a feel for what they are capable of doing. These are not a standard non-Elite target you blast away with caster AoEs to defeat. Instead, have your tank agro all of the Mana Leeches and use abilities to build threat from as many targets as possible. Keep the group's DPS on a single target at a time.

If you try a standard AoE fight, the Mana Leeches get to explode all over your casters. You see, they are the ones with the area-of-effect powers in these scuffles! Your tank may survive this, but your casters can't. A flood of incoming damage might overwhelm the healer(s) in your group if several Mana Leeches die at once.

When your group starts pushing south, there are three more fights in the Crypt. Wait for the Sorcerer/Priest patrol first, and kill them when they are as far forward as they come.

Then, jump the full caster group on the right side and the final casters group by the hallway. Both of those fights are against a mere three Elites, but the high prevalence of casting ensures that you have your work cut out if crowd control isn't properly used.

Another simple caster fight with three foes starts the next hallway, and is not a great concern. Instead, it is the far fight that your group needs to worry about. This is one of the four Elite pulls, and you face a new enemy during the encounter. The normal configuration is with a Priest, Scavenger, Sorcerer, and a Darkcaster.

Ethereal Darkcasters are your new priority target for this section of the dungeon. Even meaner than Priests, these targets put the D back into DPS. They use Shadow Word: Pain on their primary target quite frequently. That delivers 1,000 damage per tick, but it's only the start. Darkcasters love to use Mana Burn against casters and healers, and this attack can deal several thousand damage. It's mean, it's scary, and it will rip your party to shreds if you don't treat the Darkcasters with respect.

For this first group, use crowd control on the Darkcaster, DPS with focused fire on the Priest, then take out the Sorcerer and Scavenger. Only when all targets are down should you break control and hit the Darkcaster with everything your party has.

If you lack lengthy in-combat crowd control as well as Sap, you are going to be forced into killing the Darkcaster immediately. When that is the case, pull the group of four back around a corner and hit them with an area-of-effect Fear (Psychic Scream/Intimidating Shout). By the time these wear off, the Darkcaster should be dead.

There, you have now gained access to the Crescent Hall!

THE CRESCENT HALL

The first pull in the Crescent Hall is one of the trickiest, not for the combat itself, but for the skill of the puller. There are two patrollers, and it's almost a certain wipe if you get both of them at the same time. There is a Nexus Terror, and two Darkcasters walk closely behind him.

There is also a stable group at the front of the room (Sorcerer, Priest, Darkcaster).

If you pull very quickly, and can get out of casting range, the stable group is good to grab first. Run back and around the corner to force the enemies to you before they can agro the patrols.

Optionally, you can pull the Nexus Terror when it's on the left side of the hall. Have the puller run back to the group, but you won't have to worry about interrupting the Terror, as they don't stop for anything.

There really isn't a specific order in how to defeat these three groups. The key issue is in precise pulling of whichever group you decide to take first. If you don't have ranged interrupts, the Nexus Terror is probably the easiest choice. If you do have ranged interrupts, the stable group is the best (just note that you don't have a big window to pull those guys after the Darkcaster patrol leaves).

Now with some breathing room, walk to the west and look around the side of the rubble there for a Sorcerer and a Dark Caster. They are by themselves, so it's a trivial pull. Just don't wander into them; it's always harder to control a fight when you agro with proximity as opposed to purpose.

Around the bend is a series of encounters. It looks like some tricky pulling, as the groups are close together, but the groups aren't as dangerous to grab as it seems. Stay on the west wall and pull the three Mana Leeches that are in the center. Once they are dealt with the pulls for the other two groups can be made very safely.

There is a mean fight on the left with two Darkcasters and an Ethereal Priest. Pull them far back and around the corner to avoid Fear issues, and use the best crowd control you can.

The pair on the right is a double Darkcaster group, but they don't have a Priest to help out, so it should be easy.

On the southern side of the Crescent is a patrolling Nexus Terror. You have tons of room to grab him. Afterward, kill the two Darkcasters on the inside of the curve and get some rest.

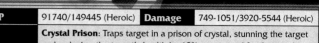

HP	91740/149445 (Heroic)	Damage	749-1051/3920-5544 (Heroic)
Abilities	**Crystal Prison**: Traps target in a prison of crystal, stunning the target and reducing the target's health by 10% per second for 6 seconds.		
	Earthquake: Inflicts 919 to 1181 physical damage to nearby enemies, stunning them for 3 sec.		
	Arcing Smash: Arc attack deals damage in a cone.		

MINING FOR LOOT!

Cloak of Revival (Back 66 Armor, +15 Stam, +16 Int, +4 Mana/5 Seconds, +35 Healing)

Lightning-Rod Pauldrons (Mail Shoulders 416 Armor, +18 Str, +18 Stam, +19 Int, +5 Mana/5 Seconds, +22 Damage/Healing)

Hethershade Boots (Leather Feet 172 Armor, +22 Agi, +21 Stam, +15 Parry Rating, +44 Attack Power)

Scimitar of the Nexus-Stalkers (1h Sword 58.3 DPS +14 Agi, +16 Stam, +12 Hit Rating)

Shaarde the Greater (2h Sword 75.6 DPS +34 Str, +33 Stam, +29 Critical Strike Rating)

Staff of Polarities (Staff 59.0 DPS +34 Stam, +33 Int, +67 Damage/Healing, +28 Spell Hit Rating)

Tavarok is usually the easiest boss of Mana Tombs. His somewhat light melee damage is supplemented by a great DOT and an area-of-effect Stun that deals damage as well. But, this Giant can only do so much when a group is prepared for these things, and the fight is controllable.

First off, have the tank engage Tavarok and stay very defensive throughout the fight. This isn't a DPS race, and keeping solid aggro is the way to avoid the only dire complication here. As long as your tank has tons of threat build against Tavarok, all will go well.

All non-melee characters must stay at fair range to avoid the Earthquake that Tavarok uses, which has about a 30-yard radius. This attack keeps affected characters Stunned for a brief period, but it does not take them off of the agro list. Thus, even with your main tank being within the area, they should be able to maintain agro just by being far enough ahead in the agro list. Ranged DPS/casters should slow down for a moment to make sure that the tank doesn't lose Tavarok's attention, but damage can soon return to normal as the tank comes out of the Stun.

Occasionally, Tavarok chooses a random target for his Crystal Prison DOT. This attack does 60% over a person's health over six seconds. If the fight is going smoothly, the healer can certainly take care of that without exposing the tank. With a low-level group, the character who gets hit might consider using a Bandage instead to keep the healer's attention on the main battle.

Tavarok won't last for too long against a knowledgeable group. Once all looting is done, have any Miners in the group roll to see who gets to Mine the corpse of Tavarok. He always has a fair reward, with many pieces of Adamantite, some Eternium Ore, and Lesser Planar Essences!

Heroic Mode

In Heroic Mode, Tavarok adds no new abilities. His Arcing Smash is more potent so it is vitally important to face Tavarok away from the party. Arcing Smash deals high damage, making it even more important for the healer to stay attentive to the main tank.

With two bosses down, your group can walk into the southern hallway and start fighting toward the end of the dungeon. Quests completion is only a few steps away!

MOVING INTO THE REACTOR ROOMS

The two Reactor Rooms along the southern hallway are filled with enemies. Kill the four Mana Leeches kill after the patrol has moved safely away. Then, take on the patrol when there is proper room for the fight.

The patrol itself is comprised of an Ethereal Priest (your crowd control target), and two Nexus Stalkers. These upgraded Rogue-like foes deal fairly high damage and control fights more comfortably than the earlier Ethereal Scavengers. Your tank is going to get Gouged from time-to-time, so having an offtank ready is useful. Otherwise, just keep the DPS burning against a single Stalker. Gouge will break soon enough and the tank can steal aggro from the second Stalker right back.

Wait and watch from the hallway as you approach the first Reactor Room. There are two Stalkers who walk the circumference of the chamber, and you don't want to try any pulls before they are dead. When the Stalkers are near the doorway, grab them and slap them around.

The pulls on the left and right side after are very easy. Each has a Darkcaster and a Sorcerer. Keep any low level folks at the back of the room to avoid aggroing the Nexus Terror on the far side, but otherwise this is a simple place to fight. When the groups are downed and you are ready, focus fire on the Nexus Terror.

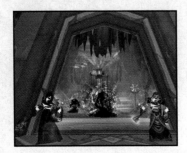

The hallway into the second Reactor Room has a new foe type: Ethereal Spellbinders. These casters use Immolate, Counterspell, have high DPS, and summon Mana Wraiths if you take too long to defeat them. In essence, you are facing upgraded Sorcerers. Use crowd control against one Spellbinder and beat down the other before it can bring its buddies into the fight.

If the Mana Wraiths do arrive, have the main tank use any area-of-effect aggro generator to get their attention (Demoralizing Shout works just fine). DPS characters should finish off the Spellbinder, who is probably almost down by now. The tank can start on the Mana Wraiths, and the group will shift to them as soon as the Spellbinder falls.

The next Reactor Room has a Nexus Terror in front. Pull it back and fight in the hallway for safety. Creep out and pull the group on the right; this one has three Elites (two Spellbinders and a Nexus Stalker). Use crowd control on one of the Spellbinders, or two of them if you are lucky! Then, clear the left, which has a trio of Elites as well.

Yet another Nexus Terror waits in the back, and he is safe to destroy once the other Elites are gone. **Safety is Job One** can be turned in here, on the northern side of the room. Use the cube there and have each person with the quest turn in the first step. Do not start the second stage yet, as that is better to do after the final boss has been defeated. If anyone starts the escort phase you have to do that now. To learn more, read about **Someone Else's Hard Work Pays Off** in the quest listing.

Use the western hallway to approach the Hall of Twilight. The first fight in there is a tricky one, with two melee targets, a Spellbinder, and a Priest. Get that Spellbinder controlled and focus fire on the Priest.

Dispatch another Nexus Terror at the northern turn in the passage, then enter the next room.

HALL OF TWILIGHT

Though the Hall of Twilight is quite large, there are only a few fights in here. Stay calm, get a good look at the patrols, then be ready for fighting!

Pull the patrolling Theurgist and Spellbinder first. Use crowd control on the Theurgist. Even though the Spellbinder will get to summon his Mana Wraiths, it's still better than having a loose Theurgist; these casters use Instant spells like Blast Wave, and they can Polymorph. Did that last one get your attention? It should, as this is a 20-second spell that wreaks havoc when used on your main tank.

Fight the Nexus Terror on the left side of the room to stop its patrol, then line up for the caster group on the right. There are two Theurgists and a Spellbinder there. Control one of the Theurgists and focus fire on the other.

The best test of your group's fire and crowd control comes afterward. As one of the best trash fights in the dungeon (or worst depending on your view), there are two Spellbinders and two Theurgists standing in the center of the Hall. If you pull these back, it avoids any add problems. You can combine this with area-of-effect Fears and such to keep the casters from having any clean attacks on your group until the early, frantic phase of the battle is done.

Everything else in the room is easy. There is one more Nexus Terror, then there are two pulls with five Mana Leeches in each. You've faced all of that already, so there is little chance of a problem.

Rest and start explaining the strategy against Shaffar to your group. There are specific assignments to go over, so don't rush ahead!

NEXUS-PRINCE SHAFFAR

HP	88056/143443 (Heroic)	Damage	1136-1625/3462-4892 (Heroic)
Abilities	**Fireball:** 40 yard range. Deals approximately 1500-1800 Fire damage. **Heroic:** Deals approximately 1800 to 2100 Fire damage.		
	Frostbolt: Deals approximately 1400-1700 Frost Damage and slows movement speed for 4 seconds. **Heroic:** Deals approximately 1700 to 2000 Frost damage.		
	Frost Nova: Deals approximately 800 Frost damage to all nearby targets and immobilizes them for 5 seconds.		
	Blink: Teleports the caster forward 20 yards.		
	Summon Ethereal Beacon: Summons an Ethereal Beacon that casts Arcane Bolts. If the Ethereal Beacon is not killed within about 10 seconds, it will transform into an Ethereal Apprentice.		

A PRINCE'S RANSOM

Ethereal Boots of the Skystrider (Cloth Feet 91 Armor, +19 Stam, +19 Int, +12 Spi, +17 Spell Critical Rating, +26 Damage/Healing)

Ethereal Warp-Bow (Bow 55.7 DPS +13 Stam, +14 Critical Strike Rating)

Longstrider's Loop (Finger +16 Agi, +15 Stam, +11 Hit Rating, +32 Attack Power)

Mask of the Howling Storm (Mail Head 451 Armor +20 Str, +28 Stam, +21 Int, 2 [red socket], 1 [yellow socket], Socket Bonus: 2 Mana/5 Seconds, +18 Damage/Healing)

Nexus-Bracers of Vigor (Plate Wrist 433 Armor, +23 Str, +13 Agi, +13 Stam)

Sigil of Shaffar (Neck +18 Stam, +16 Int, +21 Damage/Healing)

The idea here is to have the main tank start the engagement by going after Shaffar directly. Not terribly much healing will be required, especially if your tank is a Warrior who is good at using Spell Reflect.

While the tank does some damage to Shaffar and keeps his attention, the other characters destroy all of the Beacons. Not only do these Beacons deal damage on their own; they turn into Ethereal Apprentices if the players take too long.

When one DPS character finishes a Beacon, their job is to switch and help with the other Beacons. Only when all Beacons are down should the others switch to hurting Shaffar. Even then it is essential to keep an eye out for newly-created Beacons, as they will continue to arrive during the fight. Any DPS must switch to these as they appear.

The main tank is free to stay only on Shaffar. If the tank has a Trinket for escaping from root, that is always nice. Druids do especially well here, as Shaffar's Frost Novas mean very little to a Shapeshifting Druid tank.

Shaffar's repertoire consists of Blink, Frost Nova, and Frost/Fire spells. Without adds, he is a nice little fight. Control the Beacons and you win. Let the Beacons start to summon add and you are fighting a losing battle.

Shaffar floats at the back of the Hall of Twilight. He keeps three Beacons around him, and these are clearly important to his defense. Before beginning the fight, assign a character to each of the Beacons (DPS characters are clearly ideal, though you can have someone make due even if they aren't normally a DPS build).

If DPS lets control of the Beacons slip when the Prince is at very low health, you can turn on full damage and have everyone beat him into oblivion. The adds remain, but once you've won, you've won. Under this circumstance, even the tank should probably switch into a more aggressive role and do everything possible to kill Shaffar. Once the adds build up, it's a total DPS race. Try to avoid that scenario.

Mine any Adamantite Veins that remain in the dungeon, return to the second Reactor Room and run the escort quest if you need to, and take a fun look around. To hurry out of Mana Tombs, take the hallway behind Shaffar's body to jump back out into the first room from the balcony you saw earlier.

Turn in your quests outside and congratulate yourself on another great Instance run. Fine work!

AUCHENAI CRYPTS

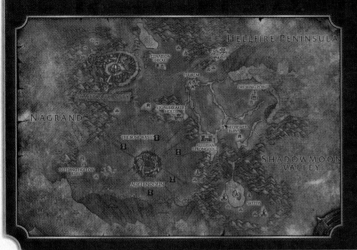

DUNGEON INFORMATION

Name	Auchenai Crypts
Location	Terokkar Forest, Auchindoun
Suggested Levels	Group of 5, Levels 65-68
Primary Enemies	Undead, Humanoids
Reputation	Lower City
Damage Types	Physical, Shadow
Time to Complete	50 to 80 Minutes

WHO TO BRING

Auchenai Crypts is a more challenging Instance than its level implies. Although the pulls are often quite small when you look at them on paper, what develops from them is harder to control. Practically all of the Elite Humanoids in the Instance come with non-Elite spawns that only appear once the fight is initiated. This makes effective crowd control a much tougher task than usual. Moreover, the non-Elites can spawn as many different classes, meaning that you might shrug and say "who cares" about an add, or you might lose your lunch as a Possessor takes over your only healer or your main tank.

It's important to bring a flexible tank into Crypts. Don't bring someone who gets flustered easily; they have to be able to communicate well, switch targets when needed, and slug it out with the best of them. Warriors, Bear Druids, and Pallies are all effective choices for most of the fighting; it's mostly about player skill in here.

When it comes to healing, Priests are slightly preferable. This isn't because other healers are poor. Rather, the Shackle Undead ability that a Priest brings to a party is a godsend in the Crypts. There are fights with up to five Elite

skeletons, some of whom can Enrage! With incoming damage like that, it's very nice to have some extra crowd control.

When it comes to DPS, many of the classes have something special to add. Rogues are able to burst down non-Elites (very important). Hunters bring traps, and there are fights when traps do a great deal (Explosive Traps in the final room's AoE encounters, Freezing Trap for many control situations, and so forth).

JOBS

CLASS	ABILITIES
Druid	Great Instance for Offtanking Due to Unexpected Adds, Heal Over Times for First Boss
Hunter	Traps Are Great for Crowd Control in Crypts, Kiting
Mage	Polymorph Versus Humanoid Elites, Kiting
Paladin	Cleanse for Mana Stings/Poisons from Non-Elites, Turn Undead
Priest	Shackle Can Be a Life-Saver in Crypt of the Restless
Rogue	Burst DPS on Non-Elites (Especially Possessors), Also Good in Final Boss Fight (to Kill the Shadows)
Shaman	Poison Cleansing, Emergency Tanking w/ Earth Elemental (if Level 66+)
Warlock	Sustained DPS Through DOTs is Very Useful in Final Boss Fight
Warrior	High Health and Mitigation Needed for Both Boss Fights, Crypt of the Restless Also Benefits From a Warrior Tank

GETTING TO AUCHENAI CRYPTS

Auchenai Crypts is on the western side of Auchindoun, in Terokkar Forest. Fly into the nearest town in Terokkar and ride down into the south. There, in the Bone Wastes, is your goal. Get the single quest from outside the Instance (Everything Will Be Alright), then walk inside when you are ready to start the fun.

REPUTATION GAINS

ACTION	FACTION	REPUTATION GAIN	END POINT
Kill Trash Mobs	Lower City	8-10 Points	Honored
Kill Bosses	Lower City	80 Points	Honored
Quest: Auchindoun	Sha'tar/Mag'har	350/700 Points	N/A
Quest: Everything Will Be Alright	Sha'tar	500 Points	N/A

THEY LIVE!

BOSSES

AVATAR OF THE MARTYRED

EXARCH MALADAAR

SHIRRAK THE DEAD WATCHER

MINIONS

ANGERED SKELETON
Notes: Enrage at Low Health

AUCHENAI MONK
Notes: Counter Kick, Overpower, Cyclone Strike, Spiritual Sight

AUCHENAI NECROMANCER
Notes: Drain Soul, Seed of Corruption (250 Damage/Second for 10 Seconds, Then Causes Explosion That Hurts Enemies), Shadow Mend

AUCHENAI SOULPRIEST
Notes: Ranged Shadowbolt, Touch of the Forgotten (Curse that Debuffs Healing), Falter (AoE Immobilize)

AUCHENAI VINDICATOR
Notes: High Health/Armor, Shadowguard (Deals Shadow Damage), Shadowbolt

PHANTASMAL POSSESSOR
Notes: Non-Elite, Low Health, Very Long Duration Mind Control (Once Successful Cannot Be Interrupted)

PHASING ENEMIES
Notes: Same abilities as their Unliving counterparts

RAGING SKELETON
Notes: High Damage

REANIMATED BONES
Notes: Low Health, Moderate Damage, Comes in Large Groups

UNLIVING CLERIC
Notes: Heal, Renew

UNLIVING SOLDIER
Notes: Protection Aura, Shield Bash

UNLIVING SORCERER
Notes: Fireball, Frost Bolt, Blast Wave

UNLIVING STALKER
Notes: Shoot, Serpent Sting, Viper Sting, Spirit Vengeance

QUEST LISTING

EVERYTHING WILL BE ALRIGHT

Level Requirement	65
Quest Giver	Greatfather Aldrimus
Quest Goal	Slay Exarch Maladaar
Experience Reward	17,450
Additional Rewards	Auchenai Anchorite's Robe (Cloth Chest 136 Armor, +24 Int, 2 [yellow socket], 1 [red socket], Socket Bonus: +4 Spell Critical Rating, +23 Spell Hit Rating, +28 Damage/Healing), Auchenai Monk's Tunic (Leather Chest 255 Armor, +24 Agi, 2 [red socket], 1 [yellow socket], Socket Bonus: +6 Attack Power, +24 Dodge Rating, +19 Hit Rating, +18 Attack Power), Auchenai Tracker's Hauberk (Mail Chest 570 Armor, +29 Int, 3 [blue socket], Socket Bonus: +4 Critical Rating, +60 Attack Power, +5 Mana/5 Seconds), or The Exarch's Protector (Plate Chest 1018 Armor, +30 Str, 3 [yellow socket], Socket Bonus: +6 Stam, +23 Defense Rating, +18 Critical Rating)

Greatfather Aldrimus is outside of the Auchenai Crypts Instance area, in Auchindoun. Six quests, starting with "I See Dead Draenei", must be done before Aldrimus offers this quest.

The goal is to kill Exarch Maladaar, the leader of Auchenai Crypts, so it takes a full and successful run to earn your reward. Once the Exarch has fallen, return to the Greatfather and choose the chest piece you wish!

AUCHINDOUN… (HORDE ONLY)

Level Requirement	65
Quest Giver	A'dal
Quest Goal	Slay Exarch Maladaar and Speak with D'ore
Experience Reward	14,950
Additional Rewards	Continues Chain to Bring Thrall to Outland

A rarity in Outland is to find a major dungeon quest that is only for one faction, but this is such a quest. Auchindoun… is a quest to slay Exarch Maladaar, and it can be completed while running Everything Is Going To Be Alright as well. Slay Exarch Maladaar just as you would normally, then speak with D'ore (one of the Sha'tar), who appears once the Exarch and his avatar are down.

If you haven't found this quest chain yet, complete all of the major Mag'har quest lines in Nagrand and speak with Greatmother Geyah. This begins a long chain to bring Thrall into Outland. Not only are the rewards impressive, but the money, experience, and sheer joy of this line makes it a must-complete for any Horde player in Outland.

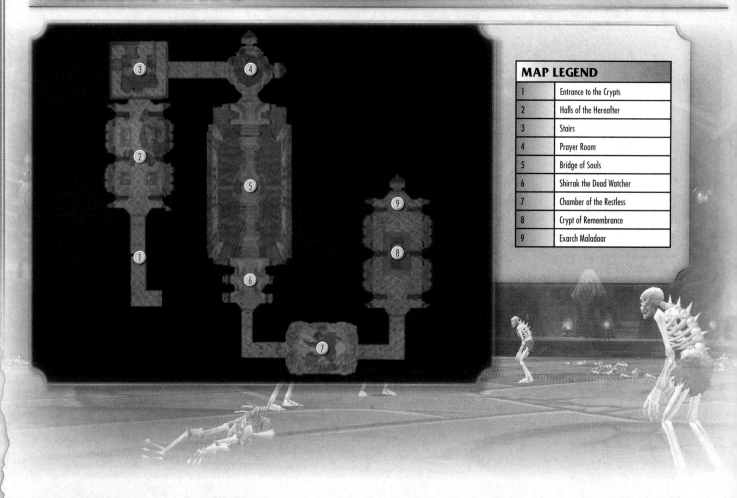

MAP LEGEND	
1	Entrance to the Crypts
2	Halls of the Hereafter
3	Stairs
4	Prayer Room
5	Bridge of Souls
6	Shirrak the Dead Watcher
7	Chamber of the Restless
8	Crypt of Remembrance
9	Exarch Maladaar

HALLS OF THE HEREAFTER

The initial hall of the Auchenai Crypts is deceptively clear, as with so much of this Instance. While others are buffing and preparing themselves, take a look around and spot the patrols in the region. There are two Soulpriests wandering through (they aren't grouped).

Those two are the first two pulls of the dungeon, and they sure are useful to let you see what happens when an Elite is attacked here.

DOUBLE EVERYTHING

Double the size of every creature you see when estimating the difficulty of a fight. Crypt enemies are far more than what they appear. Thus, the Humanoids you see in this area are linked with Undead. Each Elite that is aggroed will spawn a Non-Elite foe of a random type. The following list gives you an idea of what to expect, and it is ordered from the most dangerous to the least.

- Phantasmal Possessor
- Unliving Sorcerer
- Unliving Cleric
- Unliving Stalker
- Unliving Soldier

With many pulls, your people need to have someone to assist off of, and that person must be able to switch targets cleanly and decisively. Once the Elites are engaged, the person who is calling the targets must make critical decisions.

Look for which Non-Elites are spawning. If there are any Possessors, switch to target them immediately. Possessors have a form of Mind Control that is far more deadly than a Priest's.

Possessors need several seconds to fully take over a victim. During this time, a red line appears between the Possessor and the target. This is your cue to batter the Possessor out of this world. Once a person is under control, the Possessor has a full minute to destroy your party with them. Bringing that victim to 50% of their normal health is the only way to end the Possession after that point.

Sorcerers have a number of Instant and castable spells, so they are also worthy of re-targeting. Clerics heal, and that makes the Elites even more of a pain. Thus, they should be killed before the Elites are dealt with.

Stalkers and Soldiers should be tanked but ignored by the DPS until the Elites and more important Non-Elites are all gone or under crowd control.

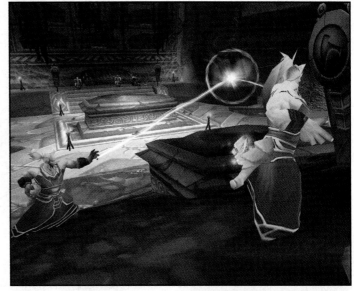

Use the two patrollers to get your feet wet. Get used to watching for the blue, ghostly sign of a Non-Elite spawning. Not only are these enemies going to attack when you pull Elite Humanoids; they also have Phasing versions that pop into and out of reality from time-to-time. You might clear an area entirely only to have a Phasing Stalker jump onto your healer's back when people are resting. Don't let your group string out and always be wary of everyone's health bars. If someone starts taking damage suddenly, be ready to fight!

With the patrollers gone, you are free to make the first two group pulls. The right and left sides of the aisle have pairs of Elites, with Auchenai Vindicators and Soulpriests. If possible, use Sap/Polymorph/Freezing Traps to control the Soulpriests and keep them out of battle for as much time as possible. Destroy the two Non-Elites that come in each fight and the lower-DPS Vindicator, then turn on the Soulpriest at the end of the encounter.

If you have both a Priest and a Mage for this run (joy), then recognize your potential to have crowd control against both groups. Have the Mage Polymorph one of the Elites and use the Priest to Shackle Undead any time there is a problem. Did a Phasing enemy just pop out on your group? Shackle it!

The far sides of the room have more Elite enemies, but they are absorbed in prayer. You don't need to clear these, even if you have a lower-level person in the party. The only good reason to fight these targets is if everyone in the group badly needs some extra Lower City Reputation from the kills.

Toward the center of the passage is the next group. This time there are three Elites. One of them is a Monk, and the other two are likely to be Soulpriests. Don't try to use crowd control on the Monk; they are immune to just about everything. Thus, use one or two abilities to put control on the Soul Priests and keep them out of the coming battle. Pull this fight back to your cleared area; there are more enemies on the ruined boulders along the right wall, and you sure don't want adds.

Though Monks are never going to be hit with crowd control, they are a slow target to kill and end up surviving for most of the battle. Target them early on if both of the Soulpriests are under control, but switch to just about any Non-Elite before bringing down the Monk. Almost all of the Non-Elites are faster to destroy than Monks and pose more of a risk to your party.

Pull the two Elites from rocks on the right to ensure safe passage, then advance along the corridor. Again, there is a group on the left side in prayer. They can be skipped, and unless they have a chest stay away.

The last pull in this room is that of an Auchenai Monk and a Vindicator. Control the Vindicator, kill the Non-Elites that come, then fight the Monk before breaking the Vindicator out of control.

The patrols by the stairs don't come all the way out to where your party is now; they stay on and around the stairs themselves. Thus, you have quite a bit of room to do the fighting during the next two battles.

Bash the next Vindicator/Monk duet, then try it again with the Soulpriest and Monk on the right side. When the way is clear, watch the steps and wait to ambush any Phasing enemies that appear. Jump onto them for quick clearing, and eliminate the two Elites that come up and down the way too.

Climb the stairs and expect another patrol in the hallway up top; this leads toward the Prayer Room, and two more patrolling Elites. These aren't dangerous fights unless you fail to see the enemies approaching and lose opportunities for crowd control. Thus, have Paladins or Hunters Track Undead to assist with warning others.

PRAYER ROOM

There is only one fight in the Prayer Room, but it's quite worthy of mention. You'll be facing two Soulpriests and an Auchenai Monk. With three Non-Elite targets adding in, it's more than likely that you will see a Phantasmal Possessor or at least an Unliving Sorcerer in the mix. Jump onto these deadly foes immediately.

For your group's tank, do everything possible to get lots of aggro from the incoming wave of foes early on; it helps with keeping any Rage that your class might use, and it keeps you from falling behind by having your healers get attacked.

To get the most agro, back the fight away from any crowd controlled enemies early on. This gives you more room to see the Non-Elites that are spawning, and it allows the tanks to use area-of-effect abilities to mitigate damage and/or collect aggro. Thunder Clap, for example, is a great way to get the attention on Non-Elites that are inbound.

If you can handle this encounter, only the two boss fights of the Instance are going to be in question. These triple Elite + triple Non-Elite pulls are about as hard as they come. After a short rest, step onto the Bridge of Souls, to the south.

PASSING THE BRIDGE OF SOULS

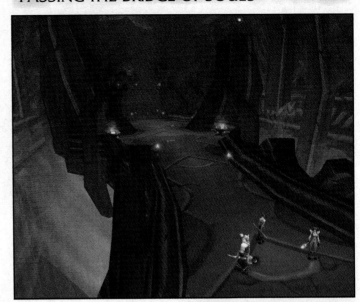

There are only two more fights before the first boss gives you a proper welcome. The first on the bridge is a patrol of three Elites. There is a Vindicator, a Soulpriest, and a Monk. Get the Soulpriest under control, and consider using area-of-effect Fear if it is available to your group. Fearing away the Vindicator and Soulpriest during a stressful time in the battle can be a lifesaver, and the bridge doesn't have any nearby enemies to bump into.

DON'T LOOK OVER THE SIDES

Both during and outside of battle, you may see Raging Souls along the length of the bridge. Stay near the center of the structure, because Raging Souls aggro onto your characters and explode. This doesn't directly deal damage (thankfully), but it throws your people around quite a bit.

Thus, if you are already close to the side of the bridge things can end up very badly. It's not as easy to fall to your death here as it used to be, but it's not fun if it does happen. Besides, your rezzer won't be able to bring you back, so the whole group ends up waiting just as long as if there had been a wipe.

Note that Raging Souls respawn frequently. When you pass the bridge in the future, don't assume that the way is totally safe. Again, stay in the center and stay on the path!

At the far end of the bridge is a pair of Auchenai Monks. It's a simple fight unless a Possessor, Sorcerer, or Cleric appears and gets away from you. Use DPS to bring down the adds, then worry about the two frustrating Monks!

SHIRRAK THE DEAD WATCHER

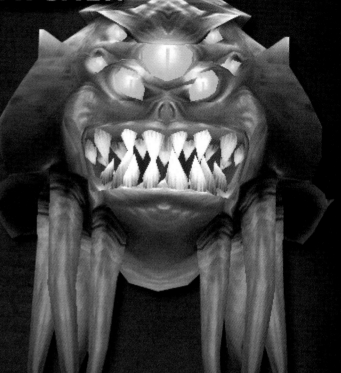

HP	77049/122132 (Heroic)	**Damage**	1136-1593/1388-1961 (Heroic)

Abilities	
	Carnivorous Bite: Inflicts 497 physical damage every 3 seconds for 20 seconds. Stack up to 5 times. Heroic: Deals 628 damage every 3 seconds per application.
	Inhibit Magic: Increases the casting time based on their distance from the caster up to 200%.
	Attract Magic: Pulls a target with mana toward the caster.
	Focus Fire: Launches 3 Fiery Blasts. Deal approximately 1600 Fire damage each. **Heroic**: Deals approximately 3800 Fire damage per Fiery Blast.

WHERE WAS HE HIDING THESE?

Collar of Command (Cloth Head 111 Armor, +22 Stam, +23 Int, +29 Spi, +66 Healing)

Hope Bearer Helm (Plate Head 827 Armor, +30 Str, +23 Agi, +19 Stam, 1 [red socket], 1 [yellow socket], 1 [blue socket], Socket Bonus: 2 Mana/5 Seconds, +13 Hit Rating)

Oculus of the Hidden Eye (Trinket +33 Damage/Healing, Use: The next opponent killed within 10 seconds that yields experience/honor restores 900 mana)

Raven-Heart Headdress (Leather Head 208 Armor, +22 Str, +24 Stam, +23 Int, +16 Spi, 1 [red socket], 2 [blue socket], Socket Bonus: 2 Mana/5 Seconds, +35 Healing)

Shaarde the Lesser (Mh Sword 60.3 DPS +25 Stam, +14 Sword Skill)

Bracers of Shirrak (Mail Wrist 285 Armor, +17 Stam, +14 Int, +48 Attack Power, +5 Mana/5 Seconds)

Shirrak is a very weak target with an extremely wonderful debuff that keeps him from being a cakewalk! This Undead monstrosity Inhibits Magic, causing all spells cast near him to take far longer to complete. At maximum range for healing and combative spells, this is "only" a 50% increase in casting time. However, the debuff stacks up to four times as you get closer to him, meaning that characters close to Shirrak experience a 200% increase in casting time. Ouch!

This makes magical DPS far more tricky, and healers are forced to plan way ahead of time. Tanks should boost their health and armor before going into the fight, just in case there are problems with the flow of healing. This is double true when there is only one character healing.

The melee aspect of the battle is simple. Your tank can engage Shirrak at the top of the stairs at the southern end of the bridge. Holding aggro is very easy, so stay in place and deal your damage. For once, you have the easiest task in the engagement!

Physical DPS is also fairly straight forward. Engage, keep up the damage, and only back off if you are having health problems or are the target of Focus Fire (more on this soon). Don't be afraid to self-bandage, as your healer may be having all kinds of issues.

Healers must stay as far back as possible. Use Instant heal-over-time abilities or shields when they are available, as these are not hampered by the debuff. When going for standard heals, assume that each heal will need to be bigger than what you'd normally plan for, so cast early and often. As you are often the target of Focus Fire, be ready to interrupt a heal and move around. It's far more important to keep yourself alive than for the heal to land.

Magical DPS can mitigate some of their problems against Shirrak by relying on Instant and Channeled spells. Though less efficient on mana, on sometimes controlled by cooldowns, these are still good ways to supplement your hampered DPS in this fight.

As for Shirrak, he'll do two things to your people at range while sticking to your tank. Somewhat often, Shirrak likes to pull a ranged target close to him and slap them with a Carnivorous Bite. Retreat outside of his debuff range if you are a healer or DPS caster, let the stacked debuff fall, then you can return to your normal combat position. When the group's only healer has this happen, use any Instant healing or heal-over-time spells before leaving range to let the debuff fall.

The other attack is Shirrak's Focus. During this phase, a text message appears to let characters know who is the target of an upcoming spell. That person needs to flee at high speed away from the spot where they were standing. Shortly thereafter, a triple Fire spell impacts the spot they were standing. Other characters, if they are close by, would be wise to evacuate before this occurs (those Fireballs deal area-of-effect damage).

The three fire attacks actually track you slightly. If you run from your original spot but then stop, you'll dodge the first, but get hit by the other two. You need to remain running (away from other party members) until the third attack lands (hopefully where you aren't).

To prevent two or three characters from being struck simultaneously, keep a fair distance between characters during the fight. Melee classes are stuck to Shirrak, Hunters can stay mobile and take to the southern part of the stairs, while healers and DPS casters stay north, at the base of the steps. Spread out and stick to your jobs unless Shirrak starts looking at you!

Heroic Mode

Shirrak performs in exactly the same manner during Heroic Mode, though his damage is heavily increased. Flawless execution of the normal strategies listen above is the key to success (rather than developing entirely new tricks).

NEARING THE CHAMBER OF THE RESTLESS

THE CRYPT OF REMEMBRANCE

Once Shirrak is dead and looted, rest and proceed along the remainder of the southern hallway. Fight two more Auchenai Monks before the corridor turns east, then prepare for the really fun pulls to start.

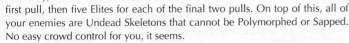

The room ahead of your group is the Chamber of the Restless; although there are only three pulls inside of it, each will test and thrill your party! Normally, there are four Elites in the first pull, then five Elites for each of the final two pulls. On top of this, all of your enemies are Undead Skeletons that cannot be Polymorphed or Sapped. No easy crowd control for you, it seems.

Thus, Shackle Undead and Freezing Traps are your best friends in the world for these pulls; there is a lot of DPS to take otherwise. By Shackling one Skeleton near the door and Freezing another, these fights become rather simple. Note that it's best to get the Angered Skeletons controlled if you have a choice; they love to Enrage and can do major damage in the process.

If you don't have access to Shackle Undead and your group doesn't quite have the armor and survivability to take the larger Skeleton groups all at once, consider using a kite technique. Have a Hunter Multishot the group of Skeletons to pull then run off while the party obliterates two of the foes. Once the Hunter has gotten the Skeletons away from the group and everyone is ready for more fighting, the Hunter can Feign Death and follow the Skeletons back.

Movement debuffs assist in this style of fighting as well. Having the Skeleton group pass through a Frost Trap is useful. Or, a Mage who does not have aggro can land a Frost Nova and Blink back to the group to gain extra time. Because these enemies have no ranged attacks, you have many options to consider by keeping the enemies at a distance.

After you destroy the three groups of Skeletons, walk along the eastern hallway toward the Crypt of Remembrance.

A small patrol of two Auchenai Vindicators tries to stop your party before they reach the final room; it's a pitiful attempt, and you can easily teach them a lesson for their arrogance.

In the last chamber, there are far more frightening encounters to best. Six pulls stand between you and the Exarch. All of these fights contain a large number of Non-Elite Skeletons that are still going to deal heavy damage to their targets. Even worse, half of the pulls are accompanied by a Necromancer. Yikes!

Use crowd control of any sort to get the Necromancers out of the way during the upcoming AoE pulls. You don't want to deal with the Necromancers until after all of the little guys area dead.

As for the AoE part of the pulls, use your tankiest person to collect aggro before starting the big spells and abilities. Having a Warrior use Demoralizing Shout to gather the force then lead them into a trap is quite nice.

Example: Demoralizing Shout from a Warrior, lead Skeletons to an Explosive Trap/Volley or a Frost Nova then Blast Wave/Blizzard.

Whatever the case, your group should prepare their best area-of-effect abilities and use them once the tank has all of the Skeletons in one place. This prevents the nightmare scenario where half of the enemies get nailed by your best AoEs and the other half races into the group's healer while said healer is trying to keep the AoE character alive. That isn't a good scene.

When the Skeletons are down, deal with the Necromancers with a group rush. Have Interrupts ready to break the Drain Soul that these enemies love so much. Unless the casters break their crowd control effect early, it's not too hard to beat them. If control does fail, the tank needs to both get aggro from the Necromancers immediately and to be prepared to Interrupt and beat down the foe.

If you want to use Fear to control Necromancers, pull these fights WAY back. The last thing that a group needs is to have a Necromancer run straight into another party of Skeletons.

And there, at the end of the room, is Exarch Maladaar. He's tough, so you better have your people get some rest before starting any trouble.

EXARCH MALADAAR

HP	83490/131489 (Heroic)	**Damage**	2909-4111/2823-3992 (Heroic)
Abilities	**Stolen Soul**: Decreases target's damage and healing by 50% for 2 minutes. This creates a Dark Side that serves Maladaar. If the Dark Side is killed, the damage and healing debuff is removed.		
	Soul Scream: Disorienting for 2 seconds.		
	Ribbon of Souls: 1.5 second cast. Inflicts 999 to 1351 Shadow damage. **Heroic**: Deals about 1600-1800 Shadow damage.		
	Summon Avatar of the Martyred: At approximately 20% health, Exarch Maladaar will cast Summon Avatar of the Martyred, creating a powerful minion with the Mortal Strike ability.		

ILL-GOTTEN BOOTY

Darkguard Face Mask (Leather Head 208 Armor, +29 Agi, +30 Stam, +20 Hit Rating, +60 Attack Power)

Fetish of the Fallen (Trinket +58 Attack Power, Use: The next opponent killed within 10 seconds that yields experience/honor will restore 900 health)

Ironstaff of Regeneration (Staff 59.3 DPS +33 Stam, +29 Int, +35 Spi, +143 Healing)

Mok'Nathal Beast-Mask (Mail Head 463 Armor +23 Agi, +22 Stam, +15 Int, 2 [red socket], 1 [yellow socket], Socket Bonus: 2 Mana/5 Seconds, +44 Attack Power)

Ring of the Exarchs (Finger +17 Agi, +24 Stam, +34 Attack Power)

Slippers of Serenity (Cloth Feet 94 Armor, +10 Stam, +22 Int, +15 Spi, 1 [red socket], 1 [blue socket], Socket Bonus: +3 Resilience Rating, +35 Healing)

Exarch Maladaar has incredible powers, and your DPS characters need to be ready for the worst. Their role will be the most difficult and important in this encounter, although the tank has some tricky moments to contend with as well.

As the tank engages and starts consolidating aggro, the DPS characters need to help out with damage against Maladaar while watching for a shadowy trail to go between him and one of the characters in the group.

Maladaar creates Dark Side versions of characters, and these start to attack your party as soon as they are summoned. DPSers must switch to these Dark Side versions very quickly; they cannot be hit with crowd control abilities, so it is purely a matter of killing them outright. Besides you always wanted to kill you buddies anyway. Use burst DPS and bring them down!

There is a moderate amount of luck here, as it's far worse for a casting character to be copied as opposed to a melee class. Just cross your fingers and hope for the best as this is a random ability that the Exarch uses.

While all of this is going on, Maladaar does melee damage to the tank and additionally casts Soul Scream to strike random party members with Shadow damage. None of this adds up too quickly, but it will end up being too much for the healer if the Dark Side shadows get to complement Maladaar's output.

The tricky tank moments come when the Exarch uses his area-of-effect Fear. Though very short in duration, the Fear causes Maladaar to choose a new target unless the tank Resists the effect. Fear Ward is always nice to have on the tank to avoid this.

Barring that, the tank must be prepared to Intercept and restore aggro as soon as possible. Some parties prevent Maladaar from going after their healers or casters by having everyone cluster around the Exarch (thus everyone is hit with the Fear). Honestly, this tactic is a bit of a gamble. The less time it takes Maladaar to reach his next victim the less time the tank has to make things right once Fear breaks.

It's often safer to buy the tank a few moments by making a modest retreat if the healer has aggro. Most tanking classes have substantial means to cover distance and restore aggro at this point in their careers, and it's only a moment or two that needs to be earned.

Decide which tactic seems more comfortable for your group and either cluster or use range to buy time for your tanks. Hopefully, the tanks are going to be able to time any Fear-Immunity abilities that they have and have the duration on those running when Maladaar uses his AoE anyway. As the fear doesn't last long, your party doesn't lose any time by stopping all attacks/actions until the tank regains aggro. This avoids the possibility of a large heal or damage spell landing right after the tank has taunted Maladaar.

AVATAR IF THE MARTYRED

HP	30048/47324 (Heroic)	**Damage**	3199-4524/1388-1961 (Heroic)
Abilities	**Mortal Strike**: Inflicts 200% weapon damage and leaves the target wounded, reducing the effectiveness of any healing by 50% for 5 sec.		
	Sunder Armor: Reduces armor by 1608 per Sunder Armor. Can be applied up to 5 times. Lasts 30 sec. **Heroic**: Decreases armor by 1728 per application.		

Once the Exarch reaches 20% health, he'll call the Avatar of the Martyred. This new foe is also Elite, and the Avatar lands Mortal Strikes and heavy normal attacks on his target. If you have an offtank, here is where they will pay for themselves very quickly. Hunter Pets, Voidwalkers, and the Earth Elemental Totem are great for this as this allows the party to keep most of their attention on Maladaar, while the Avatar murders the pet or elemental. Otherwise, have the tank grab both targets and let the rest of the party go DPS-wild on the Exarch.

Though killing the Exarch and wiping is not a good thing, it still means that your group has won. Thus, a painful victory can be established by making it a DPS race at the end. The Exarch will stay dead (and can be looted when the group comes back). The Avatar will remain, but as a solo boss the Martyr is forgetful.

Heroic Mode

The Heroic version of this encounter has few changes, but the DPS increases make it very hard to pull off the encounter without a very well-geared tank or a skilled offtank to help out. A Fury Warrior as an offtank helps to avoid the Fear problems and can switch to a more defensive style later in the fight to grab the Avatar.

SETHEKK HALLS

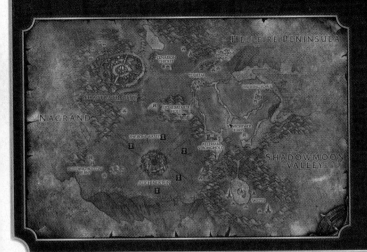

DUNGEON INFORMATION

Name	Sethekk Halls
Location	Terokkar Forest, Auchindoun
Suggested Levels	Group of 5, Levels 67-70
Primary Enemies	Humanoids, Beasts
Damage Types	Physical, Arcane, Nature
Time to Complete	60 to 80 Minutes

WHO TO BRING

JOBS

CLASS	ABILITIES
Druid	Healing, Crowd Control vs. Beasts
Hunter	Very Powerful vs. Ikiss, Trap Use, Emergency Crowd Control vs. Beasts
Mage	Polymorph, Counterspell vs. Prophets and Shadowmages, Spellsteal vs. Time-Lost and Prophet Mobs
Paladin	Secondary Healer, Resistance Auras
Priest	Psychic Scream and Fade, Dispel Polymorph
Rogue	Burst DPS
Shaman	Tremor Totem vs. Prophets, Nature Resistance vs. Cobalt Serpents, Purge vs. Second Boss
Warlock	Anti-Caster and Humanoid Crowd Control
Warrior	Intimidating Shout, Especially Good Tank vs. Prophets, Tank

As with all Instances, every class has a strong place in a 5-man group. Druid Bear tanks and Warriors are both in the higher bracket for holding aggro and surviving against trash and boss encounters here. The Druids can assist with their own healing (useful against both bosses), and they can deal with the second Boss' Polymorph (doubly nice if you don't have a Priest around).

All forms of DPS are useful here. Rogues have some much needed burst DPS. Hunters add extra in-combat crowd control while keeping the damage raining down. Mages are amazing, being potent in all trash pulls and good for freezing or AoEing the Elemental spawns against the first boss. Warlocks don't get as much Elemental or Demon fun in Sethekk, but their Fel Hunter or Succubus pets will bring a great deal to a group.

It's useful to have a primary and a secondary healer here. Though many groups have successfully run Sethekk with just one healer, there are several moments when it becomes risky. Precision is required against the first boss to keep your healer alive, and having a second person there provides leeway! Against the second boss, you want to have a secondary healer because you might have your primary healer Polymorphed if the group isn't careful.

GETTING TO SETHEKK HALLS

Sethekk Halls is on the eastern side of Auchindoun. There are two quests gained just outside of the Instance, and both can be completed in a single run! Your group can fly into the area via normal means, or two members can come in ahead of time and use the Meeting Stone to summon the rest of the group.

REPUTATION GAINS

ACTION	FACTION	REPUTATION GAIN	END POINT
Kill Trash Mobs	Lower City	9	Honored
Kill Bosses	Lower City	90	Honored
Quest: Brother Against Brother	Lower City	350 Points	N/A
Quest: Terokk's Legacy	Lower City	350	N/A

A MURDER OF CROWS

BOSSES

DARKWEAVER SYTH

TALON KING IKISS

ANZU

HP	236120 (Heroic)	Damage	4849-6851 (Heroic)
Abilities	**Heroic ONLY:** He is summoned as a part of the druid epic flight form quest, but otherwise functions as a normal boss (and drops loot, etc).		
	Spell Bomb: Curses the target, causing them to lose mana and take damage when they cast spells. Casting a spell with this debuff active causes 1000 damage and burns 2000 mana.		
	Flesh Rip: This attack inflicts 650 physical damage every 3 seconds for 15 seconds.		
	Paralyzing Screech: Stuns all nearby enemies for 6 seconds.		
	Dive: Charges a distant enemy, inflicting 1850 to 2150 damage, then fears all nearby targets.		
	Cyclone of Feathers: 45 yard range. Temporarily banishes target player.		
	NOTE: Anzu also summons adds periodically throughout the fight. There are also statues in the room that will give the players a buff if a druid casts a healing over time spell on the statue.		

MINIONS

AVIAN DARKHAWK
Notes: Charge, Carnivorous Bite (Physical DOT Every 3 Seconds for 30 Seconds) Can Be Patroller or Grouped

AVIAN RIPPER
Notes: Non-Elite, AoE Fights, Flesh Rip (Physical DOT)

AVIAN WARHAWK
Notes: Sonic Charge, Cleave, Carnivorous Bite (Physical DOT Every 3 Seconds for 30 Seconds), Forward-Facing Knockdown

COBALT SERPENT
Notes: Wing Buffet, Frost Bolt, Lightning Breath

SETHEKK GUARD
Notes: Thunderclap (Over 1.5K Nature Damage, 33% Attack Speed Debuff, 66% Movement Speed Debuff)

SETHEKK INITIATE
Notes: Short-Duration Magic Reflect, Sunder Armor

SETHEKK ORACLE
Notes: Faerie Fire (Armor Debuff), Arcane Lightning (Chain Lightning w/ Silence Debuff)

SETHEKK PROPHET
Notes: Castable/Ranged AoE Fear, Turn Into Ghost On Death

SETHEKK RAVENGUARD
Notes: Howling Shriek (-25% Attack Power/- 50% Movement Speed for 5 Seconds), Enrage on Death of Partner, High DPS, Dual Wielder, Bloodthirst

SETHEKK SHAMAN
Notes: Earth Shock

SETHEKK TALON LORD
Notes: Talon of Justice (Stun), Avenger's Shield (Daze)

TIME-LOST CONTROLLER
Notes: Undead, Shrink (Curse Reduces Str -35%/Stam -44% for 2 minutes), Charm Totem (Mind Control)

TIME-LOST SCRYER
Notes: Undead, Flash Heal, Arcane Missiles, Rejuvenatio, Arcane Destruction

TIME-LOST SHADOWMAGE
Notes: Undead, Curse of the Dark Talon (-50 Stam, +50 Damage Taken), Summon Voidwalker

QUEST LISTING

BROTHER AGAINST BROTHER

Level Requirement	65
Quest Giver	Isfar (Just Outside Sethekk Entrance)
Quest Goal	Kill Darkweaver Syth and Free Lakka
Experience Reward	15,400
Additional Rewards	Torc of the Sethekk Prophet (Neck +18 Int, +19 Damage/Healing, +21 Spell Critical Rating), Sethekk Oracle's Focus (Neck +19 Int, +35 Healing, +8 Mana/5 Seconds), Talon Lord's Collar (Neck +19 Stam, +38 Attack Power, +21 Hit Rating), Mark of the Ravenguard (Neck +40 Stam, +17 Defense Rating)

You can complete this quest and Terokk's Legacy in the same run. This quest is completed after you defeat the first boss of the Instance (Darkweaver Syth). After killing Syth, search his room for a cage. Lakka is trapped inside that cage and can be released without any further trouble. After you leave the Instance, talk to Isfar again for your reward! It's quite simple.

TEROKK'S LEGACY

Level Requirement	65
Quest Giver	Isfar (Just Outside Sethekk Entrance)
Quest Goal	Retrieve Terokk's Mask, Terokk's Quill, and the Saga of Terokk
Experience Reward	15,400
Additional Rewards	The Saga of Terokk (Held-in-Hand +23 Int, +28 Damage/Healing), Terokk's Mask (Leather Head 237 Armor, +66 Attack Power, +30 Critical Strike Rating, +36 Dodge Rating), Terokk's Quill (Polearm 93.3 DPS, +54 Agi, +33 Stam)

Terokk's Legacy is more involved than Brother Against Brother. This quest requires that your group complete the entire Instance of Sethekk. Two of the items you need are taken from the bosses of the Instance, and another is found in the Temple of Shadows (the next-to-final room) as a ground spawn.

After collecting all three items, leave the Instance and give the relics to Isfar for your reward.

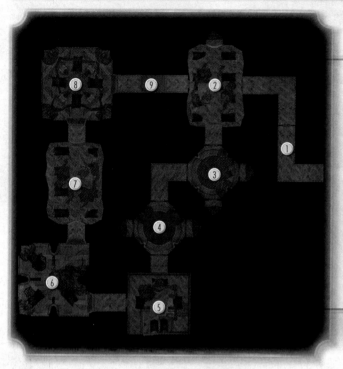

MAP LEGEND	
1	Dungeon Entrance
2	Veil Sethekk
3	Chamber of the Oracles
4	Darkweaver Syth and Prisoner Lakka
5	Stairs
6	Halls of Silence
7	Temple of Shadows
8	Halls of Mourning
9	Quick Exit After Boss

ENTRANCE

Your group will zone into Sethekk Halls on the eastern side of the map (marked as point one on the legend). There are seven major rooms in the Instance, and the whole affair is linear until you are on the way back out after beating the second boss.

Get food and water handed around, finish the buffing, and watch the nearby area. Ahead of your group is a pair of Sethekk Guards; they seem like unassuming melee monsters, and they almost are. However, these two have an area-of-effect Thunderclap that deals extremely high Nature damage, so you don't want to pull them when the patrolling Avian Darkhawk and Sethekk Initiate are close by.

Instead, wait for the patrol to head off, then use crowd control on one of the Sethekk Guards as your group trashes the other. You won't have a ton of room, but if the healers and ranged DPS classes can keep near the Instance portal, it should be enough distance to avoid the Thunderclap (it's 1,500 to 1,800 Nature damage, depending on a few factors). Note that the Thunderclap also debuffs movement and attack speed! Pull the crowd controlled Guard to your group and finish it off next. These living Arakkoa in this Instance are all susceptible to Fear, Polymorph, Sap, Seduce, and Hunter Traps, so you have many choices for crowd control.

SPELLSTEAL IS SO MUCH FUN

If you have a Mage in the group, use Spellsteal on the casters in this Instance. Many of them have Arcane Destruction; it's a 30-minute buff that adds up to 150 Spell Damage.

When that group is gone, pull the patrol. The Initiate is the more troublesome foe here; though it has lower health than the Darkhawk, its Sunder Armor and Spell Reflection can prove irritating. Be certain that your ranged casters know about the Reflect before the fight starts. There is a white hue that surrounds the Initiates when they have their buff going.

For additional practice, a second set of Sethekk Guards is blocking the other end of the hallway. This time there is more room and you won't have to worry about patrols, so the tank can fight the Guard that isn't crowd controlled away from other members of the group.

VEIL SETHEKK

Through the archway is an open chamber with a fair number of pulls. These enemies don't move around much, so the pulls can be made without a high degree of skill or experience in the dungeon; just use range to get the monsters' attention and pull back around the corner into your hallway to break line-of-sight.

The enemies that you see in the room include Sethekk Initiates, Avian Darkhawks, and Time-Lost Controllers. That last monster is the most difficult to handle in these fights because Controllers are Undead! Try to maneuver these foes into Freezing Traps or have a Priest Shackle them if you want the Controllers to be put out of action. Otherwise, use the Controllers as your first kill target while the Beast and Humanoid monsters are controlled!

THEY ARE CALLED CONTROLLERS FOR A REASON

Time-Lost Controllers are quickly dispatched because of their low armor and health. However, they are able to drop Charming Totems; these take control of a character in the group for as long as the Totem lasts. A bright, green light connects the Totem to the character, so it is often clear when the Totem is being used.

Either destroy the Totem immediately or Dispel the effect on the character (Charming Totems have low health, so it's usually more efficient just to blast the Totem with an Earthshock, some fast physical damage, or whatever is at hand). Control immediately returns to the player once the Totem is gone.

There are eight total pulls in the room, though you don't have to clear all of them. Always get the groups near the door; the two nearest groups have three mobs each, and you are certain to have a Time-Lost Controller in each (with a mix of two Initiates or an Initiate and a Darkhawk as buddies). Use your group's mix of crowd control to disable as many enemies as possible; your character composition means a lot here. If you have a Mage and a Priest, Polymorph the Initiate, Shackle the Controller, and bring down the easy Darkhawk first. If you have a Hunter and a Druid, Hibernate the Darkhawk, Freezing Trap the first enemy to approach, and DPS down the remaining target.

The group needs to stay flexible because different crowd control methods are often used, but a solid use of /assist on a character that is declared from the beginning will make a huge difference. In general, the kill order when crowd control isn't a concern is to fell the Controllers, then Initiates, then finally the Darkhawks.

Pull the group of three in the center of the room after the first two groups are cleared. You can keep using the initial hallway for the fights if you need structure (especially useful if anyone is relying on Fear or if enemies are being drawn into Hunter Traps).

Then, unless you spot chests or want additional Reputation gains, ignore the enemies on the right side and start pulling from the left (the southern side of the room).

Pull another group of three from that side, then dispatch the two Sethekk Guards by the next arch. The two pairs of Sethekk Guards on the western side of the room and the trio of general enemies are all guarding the exit. That western passage takes your group out of this Instance after beating the boss, so you don't have to clear it until later.

CHAMBER OF THE ORACLES

The southern hall leads into the Chamber of the Oracles, where there are groups in a somewhat tighter space. Just on the right is a trio of enemies with an Initiate, a Controller, and a Sethekk Oracle. After you've read below about the Oracles and their tricks, pull this group from range and fight them in the hallway to avoid the patrol add.

These Oracles are new targets; their nasty trick is an Arcane Lightning that hits 3-4 people and Silences. This spell takes a brief period to cast and is clearly a Nature Spell (it has a bright Lightning effect during casting). Always Interrupt this! When Oracles cast a green spell, ignore it; that is just Faerie Fire, and it isn't terribly important compared to what the Arcane Lightning can do.

As long as you can either Shackle or Trap the Controller OR Polymorph the Oracle, these are very easy fights. If you can't do that, take out the Controller, then the Oracle, then the Darkhawk. Have one character ready to Interrupt the Oracle when they start casting Arcane Lightning (a Shield Bash from a Warrior does nicely, but a Kick from a Rogue won't get much aggro).

Look for the patrolling Darkhawk next. It's alone and won't be a real bother. Pull that and dispatch it.

Some groups avoid the trio on the left side (often a Controller with two Oracles). If all of your characters are high enough in level to do this without risking future aggro, then go ahead and skip them. That said, it doesn't take long to dispatch the group and it can avoid trouble.

The group in the back of the room is a quartet! Expect a full spread, with an Initiate, a Controller, an Oracle, and a Darkhawk. Use all crowd control that you can, then follow the standard kill order for those that aren't controlled (Controller, Oracle, Initiate, Darkhawk).

If your group is low-level and has trouble taking on four of these monsters at once, clear thoroughly ahead of time so that there is plenty of room. Then, pull at range, go back to the hallway, and use Intimidating Shout/Psychic Scream/other Fear methods to supplement your existing crowd control during this fight.

The western archway has only two Sethekk Guards, and they are old hat by now! Waste them with glee.

The next hallway isn't clear. Wait at the front of it for the patrolling Darkhawk to come say hello. Once that birdie is out of the way, pull the trio of Arakkoa back to your position. Finally, advance to the end of the hall and kill the two Sethekk Guards that protect Darkweaver Syth's chamber.

APPROACHING DARKWEAVER SYTH

Get some rest before heading into Syth's room. This is one of only two boss fights in Sethekk Halls, and it's not an easy one for groups that haven't faced it before. You are going to need high burst DPS, careful control of damage rates, and a healer with brass...eh, baubles.

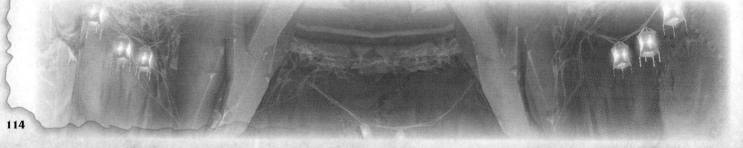

DARKWEAVER SYTH

HP	85194/11352 (Heroic)	Damage	1092-1583/1219-1769 (Heroic)
Abilities	**Chain Lightning**: Spell effects up to 3 targets, dealing roughly 1300 to 1500 Nature damage to each. **Heroic**: This deals about 2000-2800 Nature damage.		
	Shadow Shock: Deals 414 Shadow damage, plus 112 Shadow damage every 3 seconds for 12 seconds. **Heroic**: This deals 878 initial damage and 238 damage every 3 seconds for 12 seconds.		
	Flame Shock: Deals 414 Fire damage, plus 112 Shadow damage every 3 seconds for 12 seconds. **Heroic**: This deals 878 initial damage and 238 damage every 3 seconds for 12 seconds.		
	Frost Shock: Deals 414 Frost damage, plus slowing the target for 8 seconds. **Heroic**: This deals 878 initial damage.		
	Arcane Shock: Deals 414 Arcane damage, plus 112 Shadow damage every 3 seconds for 12 seconds. **Heroic**: This deals 878 initial damage and 238 damage every 3 seconds for 12 seconds.		
	Summon Elementals: Summons a Syth Fire Elemental, a Syth Frost Elemental, a Syth Shadow Elemental, and a Syth Arcane Elemental.		

SYTH'S NESTEGG

Sky-Hunter Swift Boots (Mail Feet 437 Armor, +25 Agi, +19 Stam, +24 Int, +26 Attack Power, 5 Mana/5 Seconds)

Bands of Syth (Plate Wrist 497 Armor, +21 Str, +19 Agi, +18 Stam)

Light-Woven Slippers (Cloth Feet 105 Armor, +24 Int, +13 Spi, +19 Stam, +29 Healing, 10 Mana/5 Seconds)

Libram of the Eternal Rest (Libram +47 to Consecration Damage)

Moonstrider Boots (Leather Feet 196 Armor, +21 Stam, +22 Int, +20 Spell Critical Rating, +25 Damage/ Healing, 6 Mana/5 Seconds)

Sethekk Feather-Darts (Thrown 64.4 DPS, +15 Agi, +22 Attack Power)

Darkweaver Syth deals light melee damage, casts Frost and Fire Shock, and has Chain Lightning. None of these are overly brutal, though the Frost Shock slows and the Fire Shock leaves characters with a DOT. If people bunch together, the Chain Lightning amplifies per target and ends up dealing more harm to the group, so it's good to keep your non-melee folks at a desent range.

None of this is what would wipe a party though. Syth's true glory comes at 75% health. Without pause, he'll summon four Elementals of different types to assist him. These enemies have somewhat low health, but they aren't an instant Aoe death-target either. What is more, they are each immune to damage from their Elemental type, so very few single spells will do the trick to clear them out.

It gets worse. Syth is going to do this again at 50% health at 25% health, so stop the DPS on him right now! When his first group appears, have a Warrior tank use Challenging Shout or have a Mage Frost Nova the pack to try and keep them in place for a short time. This is long enough for the group to start blowing down its new Elemental targets. Use /assist as always, and when the enemy group starts to weaken, blast them with spells like Arcane Explosion to finish them off.

Note that Warlock Banish and Fear works on these guys (though Fear won't work against the Shadow Elementals).

Syth doesn't have any de-aggro abilities, so even your tank can and should help with clearing out the Elementals from this first pack.

Once all is done, have the healer top everyone off (especially themselves), and return full DPS to Syth. Get ready for the rush!

As soon as 50% hits, start a DPS race with Syth. Area-of-effect Fear is amazingly powerful in assisting with this, as it gives your group the time to blast Syth without most of the Elementals going after your healer. Intimidating Shout and Psychic Scream are ideal. Have characters with these abilities declare before the battle who is going to be the 2nd wave Fear and who is going to be the 3rd wave Fear.

If you lack area-of-effect Fear for the third wave, have a Mage Frost Nova to keep the Elementals at bay (it's a very short time between the 3rd wave's arrival and the death of Darkweaver Syth). Failing that, even a Piercing Howl might be enough.

Using this technique, the fight against Syth is almost certain to succeed every time. Executed poorly, you'll probably win but lose your healer. Executed correctly, there won't be a wipe or a single death, even when you only have a single healer for the entire group.

Heroic Mode

The strategy stays the same when fighting against Syth in Heroic Mode. Though he packs only a tad more wallop, his Elementals get the biggest beef-up. In Heroic, the Elementals stack debuffs on their target to make them even more susceptible to damage of their type. This means that healers who don't have the Elemental groups kept off of them will last for only a few moments.

For victory here, it is absolutely essential to have a plan for each of the three Elemental waves and for the execution to go smoothly.

Brother Against Brother can be completed at this point. Darkweaver Syth is dead, and Lakka is trapped in a cage on the left side of the room. Unlock Lakka and your quest will be complete!

Also, remind each person who is doing **Terokk's Legacy** to loot Syth's body. One of the three items that you need was carried by Darkweaver Syth, and all people need to grab it as well as any Spirit Shards if your faction presently controls all the Spirit Towers outside in Terokkar Forest.

THE STAIRS

South from Darkweaver Syth's chamber are the stairs. This chamber has two levels, but most of the enemies are on the bottom floor where you enter.

The first fight is against a small AoE group (several flying birds just to the right of the entrance); Avian Rippers deal a fair amount of Physical damage, but they are so soft that basic area-of-effect methods work wonderfully. Kill this initial group of five. As usual, give the main tank time to pull, gather the enemies around, then start the AoE fun.

Rest and wait for a massive, patrolling snake to come near. These Cobalt Serpents are not meant to be fought while other groups are already in battle with you. Take this thing on solo.

Have your main tank get aggro and give them time to put their backs up against a wall. This prevents the arcing Chain Lightning and Frostbolt attacks of the Cobalt Serpents from damaging other characters in your party. Doing so reduces the damage output of these patrollers by a massive margin and makes the fights very simple.

There aren't any more patrollers on the lower floor now. Pull the two groups of four in the room and fight them anywhere except near the steps themselves. If you need room for Fearing enemies, just pull all the way back to the main hallway.

These groups of four include a Controller, an Initiate, an Oracle, and the new Time-Lost Scryers. As the name might suggest to you, these Scryers are Undead too. If you have Shackle, go ahead and Shackle the familiar Time-Lost Controllers. Scryers are an odd mix, having some light Healing potential and the ability to cast Arcane Missiles. Bring the Scryers down quickly, as they are a soft target, then go after other non-controlled targets. The new kill order is as follows: Controller, Oracle, Scryer, Initiate.

The second group of four has the same composition and necessary tactics.

Climb the steps until you meet the next patrolling Cobalt Serpent. Have your tank stand against the wall of the area to keep from getting knocked off if you are on the steps or up top when you meet the snake.

When the Cobalt is dead, pull the two Sethekk Ravenguards from the western doorway on the upper level. Ravenguards look like the earlier Sethekk Guards except for a slight color difference, but the fights are quite different. For one, the Ravenguards don't have any AoE damage abilities. For another, they are wonderful melee opponents; they hit hard and fast, debuff melee damage and movement, and the second Ravenguard will Enrage when the first one falls.

Use crowd control on the farther Ravenguard, bring down the first one through brute strength, then repeat the process for the second one. Remember to use abilities that debuff Physical damage to assist in the encounter (Thunderclap, Demoralizing Shout, Hex of Weakness, Curse of Weakness, Scorpid Sting, etc.).

HALLS OF SILENCE

Now you get to have the best AoE fight of the dungeon. There are ten Avian Rippers in the front of the Halls of Silence. You have more than enough room in your current hallway to fight them in style, so a ranged pull is going to be easy.

As long as the group waits until all of the Rippers are close together before starting its attacks, this is still rather easy (and fun too).

When the Rippers are gone, your puller can poke a head into the Halls of Silence without getting aggro. Watch and wait for a Cobalt Serpent to patrol to you, kill that, then prepare for the first serous pull.

From the left side, there is a group of four to dispatch. You are facing two Sethekk Prophets, a Sethekk Talon Lord, and a Scryer. Most of these are new foes, so stop a moment and explain to your group what they are to expect. Talon Lords are the easy ones; they are lower DPS, act like half-hearted Paladins, and won't trouble you. Save them for late in a battle.

The Prophets, on the other hand, are a massive pain. These enemies have a castable AoE Fear! You will likely face that Fear a couple of times a pull against groups with two Prophets. Throw up a Fear Ward on the main tank, put down a Tremor Totem, have offtank Warriors in Berserk Stance to go Fear immune, etc.

Luckily, the Prophets don't do a ton of damage on their own. If you can use crowd control on the Time-Lost Scryer via Freezing Trap or Shackle, not much is going to be around to beat on you during the fight against the Prophets. Or, if you have the ability to stop both Prophets with crowd control, do that and kill the Scryer first, then the Talon Lord.

THE PROPHETS AREN'T DONE WITH YOU YET

Prophets continue to be a pain after they die. These enemies turn into ghost that are not killable or even targetable! Run away from the ghost to keep from taking 600+ a shot from their attacks and before too long the enemies will dissipate. A small heal can pull aggro of the ghost toward a healer. This is actually a good idea if the healer is standing at range as the ghost can't reach them before finding their final rest.

A smaller Avian Ripper pull is next, on the right side. Shoot at these from over the rocks and bring them back to the hallway for a quick AoE fight.

As you move north and west through the room, there is another fight against four Elites. This time the Prophet and Scryer are escorted by a Sethekk Shaman and an Avian Warhawk.

Avian Warhawks are meaner than the earlier Darkhawks; these foes Intercept characters randomly and do more Physical damage as well. Warhawks also Cleave, so your rear party should spread out a little to prevent the Warhawks from charging one and getting to critically-hit two!

Because the Warhawks are tougher to control in this way, they are good candidates for Polymorph, Hibernate, Freezing Trap, or even Fear spells (though give your pull from distance if Fear will be used).

The good news is that Shamans are not very powerful compared to some of the other new monsters. Sethekk Shamans use Earth Shock, melee, and die. Like the Talon Lords, they are a good target for later in the fight after more frightening enemies are dispatched.

Pull a final Avian Ripper group, this one also small, then set up another tricky fight against four.

Compared with the big fights you've just done, the two Ravenguards by the doorway will be a walk in the park. Mock them a little as you tear them down, then look carefully into the Temple of Shadows.

TEMPLE OF SHADOWS

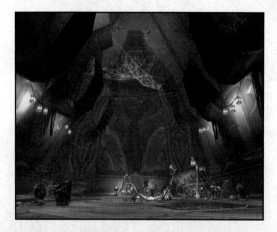

Best the smaller group on the left side, then get the Cobalt Serpent patroller when it comes close to the center of the room (away from your other targets).

The next three pulls are all very similar. You are facing the same types of enemies, and there is a great amount of space to do these fights. If you pull back, adds are not an issue at all, and Prophet ghosts are easy to avoid.

Those doing **Terokk's Legacy** should get their ground spawn from this room; look in the center of the chamber. The Saga of Terokk is there, surrounded by symbols and debris.

The last battle before the final boss is in the hallway to the Halls of Mourning. There are five Elite enemies here, so this is the largest Elite battle in the Instance. Assign all possible crowd control·before the fight begins, and consider the use of Intimidating Shout/Psychic Scream during the fight if any of the monsters break their control early. Mind Control, though always a risk, is also a worthy idea if your group is skittish about fighting five Elites.

The enemy group itself is as follows: Prophet, Shaman, Shadowmage, Talon Lord, Warhawk. Even with only two forms of crowd control, this fight can be made much easier. Get either the Shadowmage and Prophet out of the way and kill the Warhawk, or get the Warhawk and Prophet out of the way and kill the Shadowmage. The Shaman and Talon Lord are both unimportant targets until the end of the fight.

The group on the right, barely inside the room, is able to aggro by proximity unless your puller is very high level. Get a glance at this group from as far back as possible while preparing.

This is another four Elite fight, with a Time-Lost Shadowmage, two Prophets, and a Warhawk. Shadowmages are great to Shackle if you can; otherwise they are the first people to fight while the Prophets are under crowd control.

Time-Lost Shadowmages summon Voidwalkers, deal high damage, and Curse characters to take more damage and lower their Stamina by 50!

HALLS OF MOURNING

With all of his servants slain, the mad Talon King Ikiss must now fight you himself. There can be no question, this Arakkoa still retains all of his Arcane power, and he'll bring it to bear against you shortly. Rest now, and discuss strategics with your group while others look at the chamber from afar.

TALON KING IKISS

HP	80461/113329 (Heroic)	**Damage**	1593-2309/3252-4718 (Heroic)
Abilities	**Polymorph:** Transforms a target into a sheep for up to 6 sec.		
	Arcane Volley: Deals approximately 1800-1900 Arcane damage. **Heroic:** Deals roughly 2800-3260 Arcane damage.		
	Blink: Teleports Talon King Ikiss into the center of his chamber.		
	Slow: (Heroic Mode Only). Increases the time between attacks by 60%, and slows movement by 60% for 8 sec.		
	Arcane Explosion: Deals approximately 5700 Arcane damage. **Heroic:** Deals roughly 7600-8600 Arcane damage.		

THE WEALTH OF SKETTIS

Incanter's Trousers (Cloth Legs 136 Armor, +25 Stam, +30 Int, +17 Spi, +18 Spell Critical Rating, +42 Damage/Healing)

Trousers of Oblivion (Cloth Legs 136 Armor, +42 Stam, +33 Int, +12 Spell Hit Rating, +39 Damage/Healing)

Hallowed Trousers (Cloth Legs 136 Armor, +25 Stam, +33 Int, +16 Spi, +73 Healing, 7 Mana/5 Seconds)

Shoulderpads of Assassinations (Leather Shoulder 219 Armor, +25 Agi, +25 Stam, 2 [yellow socket], Socket Bonus: +4 Stam, +42 Attack Power)

Greaves of Desolation (Mail Legs 570 Armor, +24 Stam, +33 Int, +12 Hit Rating, +22 Critical Strike Rating, +66 Attack Power)

Ravenclaw Band (Finger +20 Agi, +15 Stam, +13 Hit Rating, +30 Attack Power)

Avian Cloak of Feathers (Back 78 Armor, +18 Int, +12 Spi, 5 Mana/5 Seconds, +42 Healing)

Crow Wing Reaper (2h Axe 93.2 DPS, +28 Str, +17 Agi, +33 Stam, 3 [red socket], Socket Bonus: 6 Stam)

Deathforge Girdle (Plate Waist 655 Armor, +22 Str, +25 Stam, 1 [red socket], 1 [blue socket], Socket Bonus: +3 Agi, +20 Critical Strike Rating)

Sky Breaker (Mh Mace 41.4 DPS +13 Stam, +20 Int, +132 Damage/Healing)

Sethekk Oracle Cloak (Back 78 Armor, +18 Stam, +18 Int, +12 Spell Hit Rating, +22 Damage/Healing)

Maneuvering will be essential during the fight against Talon King Ikiss. If you fight him in the wrong spot, your group stands the potential to wipe. If you fight him in the best spot, there is every chance for even a group with lower levels to defeat this Mage.

Ikiss' normal attacks do modest damage in melee. Have your main tank pull Ikiss around to one side of the large pillars that are near the corners of the room. Make it very obvious which side Ikiss is on so that line-of-sight can be blocked quickly, as needed. When tanked by a well-geared character there is very little to heal from Ikiss' melee attacks.

Instead, Ikiss' Arcane Volley is where the normal damage comes from. These AoE spells ignore line-of-sight and do about 1,500 Arcane Damage to everyone. This keeps the healers quite busy, and peripheral DPS character may need to bandage at certain points in the fight; we'll tell you the ideal time to do that in a moment.

Less often, Ikiss will Blink to a different position and start to channel Arcane energies. This is your cue to get behind the pillars and start to bandage. Ikiss will take six seconds then launch an Arcane Explosion that deals massive damage to a character without Arcane Resistance! If everyone is behind the pillars, no damage will be taken at all.

The person who is second on the aggro list will get Polymorphed during this battle. Having a Priest there to Dispel this is very useful. Unless an Arcane Blast is about to go off, be certain to wait until that character is healed before using the Dispel; this Polymorph functions like the normal spell, so characters rest fully while sheeped.

If there is a Rogue or offtank involved in this fight, ranged DPS characters should fully attempt to stay high on the aggro list. Don't try to outdo your main tank, but work hard to outdo the secondary melee unit. That person DOES NOT want to be Polymorphed because Ikiss can start an Arcane Blast afterward and blow the person up before sheep breaks. If you don't have someone to Dispel Polymorph, the best defense is to have a person at range get sheeped (they have a better chance of getting to cover with less time). Also, ranged characters may have PvP Trinkets that remove Polymorph. Melee folks don't.

When Talon King Ikiss gets to low health, he'll raise a Mana Shield with 20,000 points of its own. Dispel/Purge this and keep thumping on the big guy until he falls. He'll leave behind the last quest item for **Terokkar's Legacy** and two pieces of loot as well.

Beyond that, Talon King Ikiss holds the key to the fourth Instance of Auchindoun: The Shadow Labyrinth. You can't go into that Instance until someone in your group or guild has beaten the fight here and looted this key. Everyone who wins the fight gets a copy, so there is no rolling done over it.

Heroic Mode

Besides more hit points and more damage, the Talon King has an AoE Slow Spell.

Use the stairs on the eastern side of the room to leave the dungeon quickly. If you didn't clear the first room way back when, a couple of fights stand in your way, but they are trivial. With a careful run and a Fear or Frost Nova, you can even slip on by without worrying about it if your group likes to play it fast and risky.

Start setting a date for your Shadow Labyrinth run now. That dungeon not only has four bosses, but it is easily one of the coolest locations in Auchindoun. Want more loot? Would you like to gain Reputation point with Lower City all the way up to Exalted? Well, then keep reading and learn more!

SHADOW LABYRINTH

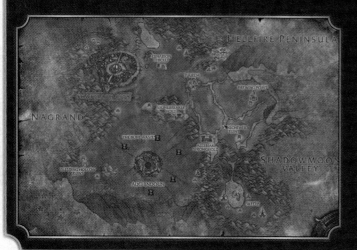

DUNGEON INFORMATION

Name	Shadow Labyrinth
Location	Auchindoun, Terokkar Forest
Suggested Levels	Group of 5, Level 70
Primary Enemies	Humanoids, Demons
Damage Types	Physical, Shadow, Nature
Time to Complete	80 to 110 Minutes

WHO TO BRING

Shadow Labyrinth is an Instance with a surprising amount of variety (several major damage types combine with enemies that are mostly Humanoid but have Demons and Undead in several areas). Then, you end the place with a boss that is a gigantic Elemental. This is certainly not a run-of-the-mill place.

There are four boss and quite a few pulls of varying weaker troops as well, with some considerably large encounters at times. You can (and will) face five Elites with both a non-Elite and the possibility of an add from stealthers. You know that crowd control is going to be essential.

Thus, bring a variety of single-target and AoE abilities into the mix. Fear is very useful, so Warlocks, Warriors, and Priests have considerable use (AoE Fear can be used safely in the areas where it is needed). Polymorph, Freezing Traps, and Seduce are good too. Most of the Instance is quite Sap friendly, so Rogues are just fine.

A single healer can handle Shadow Labyrinth, but they should be specced for healing and geared for it as well. The first two bosses are endurance based, so a lone healer will end up with problems unless they have great +Int gear or the specialization to handle the heals efficiently.

Paladins can handle AoE tanking rather well, so this is a solid Instance for a skilled Protection Pally. This isn't to say that Warriors and Bear Druids can't deal with the problems, but Pallies have an easier run in some of the big trash fights. Of course, Warriors are the best tanks for the final boss, making the whole deal a bit of a wash.

Choose the DPS slots based off of crowd control rather than raw damage. A group with an abundance of crowd control is certainly going to be in better shape than a group that tries to simply burn things down. In addition, the second boss can REALLY punish severe DPS groups (full party Mind Control; it's not pretty).

JOBS	
CLASS	**ABILITIES**
Druid	Can Deal DPS in the Lighter Pulls of the Early and Late Dungeon and Add Backup Healing to Middle Areas, Good Tank for Final Boss
Hunter	Freezing Traps, Huge Benefits Against Most Bosses
Mage	Polymorph is Almost Essential, AoE Against Non-Elite Skeletons, Snare/Root Spells in Large Pulls
Paladin	Good Tanking Option in Trash Fights, Healer
Priest	Mind Control, Sustained Healing in Endurance Fights, Psychic Scream
Rogue	Strong Sap Opportunities, Stunlock of High DPS Trash, DPS Bursting vs. Third Boss, Can Offtank Final Boss At Least for One Round
Shaman	Tremor Totem vs. Fel Overseers, Fire and Nature Resistance, Healing or Backup Healing
Warlock	Seduce, DPS, Howl of Terror, Fear
Warrior	Intimidating Shout, Tank, Good Instance for DPS Warriors/Offtanks

GETTING TO THE SHADOW LABYRINTH

Shadow Labyrinth is on the southern side of Auchindoun. To get past the locked doorway, one person in your group needs to have run Sethekk Halls and gotten the key from the final boss there. Or, you need to have a Rogue at level 70 with 350 Lockpicking.

Quests for this Instance are spread through several areas. One of them involves the search for the Demon-Bane weapons, stared when you kill and loot a Mo'arg Weaponsmith from Shadowmoon Valley (it's a VERY long chain). The Book of Fel Names comes from Altruis the Sufferer in Nagrand, though it too has earlier steps that must be completed ahead of time. The local quests that you get for Shadow Labyrinth before going in are obtained at the Terrace of Light in Shattrath (for the Hearts of the Labyrinth chain) and from the Spy just outside of the Instance itself.

REPUTATION GAINS

ACTION	FACTION	REPUTATION GAIN	END POINT
Kill Trash Mobs	Lower City	12 Points	Exalted
Kill Bosses	Lower City	120 Points	Exalted
Quest: Into the Heart of the Labyrinth (3 Parts)	Lower City	1,000 Points	N/A
Quest: The Soul Devices (2 Parts)	Lower City	600 Points	N/A

MEMBERS OF THE SHADOW COUNCIL

BOSSES

AMBASSADOR HELLMAW

BLACKHEART THE INCITER

GRANDMASTER VORPIL

MURMUR

MINIONS

CABAL ACOLYTE
Notes: Heal, Renew, Shadow Defense

CABAL ASSASSIN
Notes: Stealth, High DPS, Often Found Solo, Backstab

CABAL CULTISTS
Notes: Kick, Thrash

CABAL DEATHSWORN
Notes: Somewhat Low DPS, Black Cleave (Shadow Damage), Knockdown

CABAL EXECUTIONER
Notes: Whirlwind, Enrage, Execute

CABAL FANATIC
Notes: Moderate DPS, Can Shift Aggro, Enrage, Fixate

CABAL RITUALIST
Notes: Can Be Rogues (Gouge, High Melee DPS) or Mages (Three Types: Arcane + Addle Humanoid CC, Frostbolt + Frost Nova, or First Blast and Fire DOTs)

CABAL SHADOW PRIEST
Notes: Very Mean Mind Flay, Shadow Word: Pain, Shadowform

CABAL SPELLBINDER
Notes: Mind Control (Interruptible), Moderate DPS, Spell Shock

CABAL SUMMONER
Notes: Summons Free Elites (Very Scary), Fire Damage, Fireball

CABAL WARLOCK
Notes: Shadowbolt, Seed of Corruption, Non-Elite Pet (Imp, Succubus, or Fel Hunter), Demon Armor

CABAL ZEALOT
Notes: Shadowbolt, Shapeshift Below Half Health, Low Health

FEL OVERSEER
Notes: Very High Health, AoE Fear, Random Intercept, Uppercut (Knockback), Mean Target, Intimidating Shout

MALICIOUS INSTRUCTOR
Notes: High Health, AoE Shadow Nova, Mark of Malice (Increases Melee Damage Taken, Stacks Up to Five Times)

TORTURED SKELETON
Notes: Non-Elite, Solo or in Large Groups, Easy AoE Targets

THE SOUL DEVICES
(STARTS W/ FIND SPY TO'GUN)

Level Requirement	69
Quest Giver	Spy Grik'tha (Just Outside the Instance)
Quest Goal	Find Spy To'gun Then Collect 5 Soul Devices
Experience Reward	30,000
Additional Rewards	Shattrath Wraps (Cloth Wrist 68 Armor, +15 Stam, +15 Int, 1 [red socket], Socket Bonus: +3 Stam, +21 Damage/Healing), Spymistress' Wristguards (Leather Wrist 128 Armor, +18 Agi, +15 Stam, 1 [red socket], Socket Bonus: +2 Dodge Rating, +15 Hit Rating), Auchenai Bracers (Mail Wrist 285 Armor, +15 Int, 1 [red socket], Socket Bonus: 1 Mana/5 Seconds, +36 Attack Power, 4 Mana/5 Seconds), Sha'tari Wrought Armguards (509 Armor, +20 Str, +18 Stam, 1 [yellow socket], Socket Bonus: +3 Stam, +12 Defense Rating)

This is a two-part quest that starts when you speak with Spy Grik'tha outside of Shadow Labyrinth. This NPC asks that your group heads inside and looks for Spy To'gun, who is already well within the Instance (past the first boss).

After your party defeats Ambassador Hellmaw, take the small tunnel that is behind the Demon and speak with To'gun, who is inside a cage. This switches the quest to the second stage, where each person must collect 5 Soul Devices before returning to Shattrath City (to deliver them to Spymistress Mehlisah Highcrown at the Terrace of Light).

Soul Devices are found at the small Shadow Council tents that are set up throughout the Instance. There are a few of these small, purple items in each room, but a group can finish this quest in one full clearing of Shadow Labyrinth because the final room has MANY of these items (and you don't even need to fight Murmur to get them, though there is no reason not to fight him).

INTO THE HEART OF THE LABYRINTH
(STARTS W/ TROUBLE AT AUCHINDOUN)

Level Requirement	69
Quest Giver	Spymistress Mehlisah Highcrown (Shattrath City, Terrace of Light) then to Field Commander Mahfuun (Outside Entrance of Shadow Labyrinth)
Quest Goal	Read From the Codex of Blood
Experience Reward	46,650
Additional Rewards	Shattrath Jumpers (Cloth Feet 107 Armor, +25 Stam, +17 Int, 1 [blue socket], 1 [yellow socket], Socket Bonus: +3 Int, +29 Damage/Healing), Spymistress' Boots (Leather Feet 201 Armor, +15 Stam, 1 [red socket], 1 [blue socket], Socket Bonus: +4 Stam, +36 Attack Power, +27 Dodge Rating), Auchenai Boots (Mail Feet 448 Armor, +25 Stam, +25 Int, 2 [red socket], Socket Bonus: +3 Spell Critical Rating, 10 Mana/5 Seconds), Sha'tari Wrought Greaves (Plate Feet 800 Armor, +24 Str, +21 Agi, +22 Stam, 1 [red socket], 1 [blue socket], Socket Bonus: +3 Resilience Rating)

This is a three-step chain that starts in Shattrath City. Talk to Spymistress Mehlisah when you are there, before going out to Auchindoun. She'll have you report to Field Commander Mahfuun, just outside of the dungeon. This switches the chain to The Codex of Blood.

Complete the next step by clearing the first three bosses of the Shadow Labyrinth. After the third dies (Vorpil), look beneath this Warlock's dias is the Codex of Blood, a book that is waiting to be read. Have each person in the group use the book.

Finally, you are given the third step (Into the Heart of the Labyrinth). Destroy Murmur, the last boss of the dungeon, then return to the Spymistress for your reward!

THE BOOK OF FEL NAMES

Level Requirement	69
Quest Giver	Altruis the Sufferer (Western Nagrand)
Quest Goal	Take the Book of Fel Names from Blackheart the Inciter
Experience Reward	15,800
Additional Rewards	Continues an Awesome Quest Chain

This quest is part of a very fun chain that you start while hunting around in Shadowmoon Valley. Your Scryer or Aldor buddies out there will let you know about Altruis the Sufferer (who you might already have worked with); he and his Nether Drake are found along the small waterway near some of the Demon camps of Nagrand. Talk to Altruis and complete his three early quests, against easier Demons out in the world. Then, he'll give you the mission to retrieve The Book of Fel Names.

Slay the second boss of Shadow Labyrinth (Blackheart the Inciter) and have everyone with the quest loot him to complete this step. Afterward, there is still a step to fight additional Elite foes in Shadowmoon Valley. The story for the quest line is top notch!

THE LEXICON DEMONICA

Level Requirement	69
Quest Giver	David Wayne (Eastern Terokkar Forest)
Quest Goal	Loot the Lexicon Demonica From Grandmaster Vorpil
Experience Reward	12,300
Additional Rewards	Continues Quest Chain

David Wayne's lengthy quest chain to create a Demon-Bane weapon takes your group into Shadow Labyrinth to slay Grandmaster Vorpil (the third boss) and loot the Lexicon Demonica from him. Return to David Wayne afterward for the next step.

ENTRY INTO KARAZHAN

Level Requirement	70
Quest Giver	Khadgar (Shattrath City, Terrace of Light)
Quest Goal	Obtain the First Key Fragment
Experience Reward	N/A
Additional Rewards	Continues Chain to Unlock Karazhan Raid Dungeon

This extends the quest chain that begins in Deadwind Pass (the actual location of Karazhan). There is a Mage there (Archmage Alturus) who begins the quest chain. This soon leads to Shadow Labyrinth, where you need to find this first Key Fragment. Clear all the way to Murmur's area, but you don't need to fight Murmur. Look on the left side of the room for a recessed chest. Open this and pull back the Elite Elemental that spawns, and kill it (with a full group this is extremely easy). Then, loot the body for the Key Fragment.

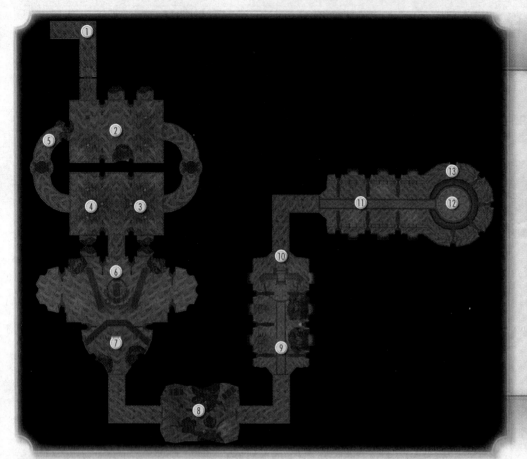

MAP LEGEND	
1	Dungeon Entrance
2	The Front Room
3	The Arcanium
4	Ambassador Hellmaw
5	Spy To'gun
6	The Refectory
7	Blackheart the Inciter
8	The Tomb
9	Sanctum of Shadows
10	Grandmsater Vorpil
11	The Screaming Hall
12	Murmur
13	First Key Fragment

THE FRONT ROOM

Shadow Labyrinth is not the hardest of the level 70 Instances (not by any means), but it isn't as easy to clear as The Steamvault or The Black Morass either. Your group should enter this dungeon with a very solid mix of crowd control and a good block of time. With four bosses to beat, it takes a couple of hours to beat this place before you are well geared and know the pulls extremely well. Add any wipes and it'll take even longer.

None of this will be clear in the first room; things are VERY easy before you advance well into Shadow Labyrinth. After your group buffs and trades consumables, watch the room for the patrolling Cabal Deathsworn; he walks alone and as such should die alone before you advance. Deathsworn are melee enemies and don't have many tricks, but their Cleave deals Shadow damage instead of Physical, they have a short Knockdown, and they also Enrage at low health.

All of that said, Deathsworn are still fairly low on the kill list for this area. Dispatch the solo patroller then pull the group of two Acolytes and a Deathsworn from the left side. Acolytes are good to hit with crowd control, as they have healing abilities. Luckily, Acolytes aren't strong DPSers, so healing is almost all that they have.

A second patrol is seen on the left side, this time with two Deathsworn. Again, it's an easy fight. You can use crowd control on the second Deathsworn if you like, but it's not needed.

Along the southern edge of the room after additional pulls. Your group can avoid these without any danger, as there is plenty of room here. If you are raising Lower City Reputation, clear everything. Otherwise, just ignore the Deathsworn and Acolytes there.

After clearing or sliding along the north wall, watch the groups at the eastern side of the chamber. In front of the corners are two Cabal Warlocks, each with a grouping of pets. The left Warlock has a huge pile of Imps, while the right Warlock keeps a Fel Guardhound and a single Imp Familiar. Warlocks are truly a pain, as they have Firebolts and their Guardhounds have Silence. In these small pulls it's no big deal, but you might learn to hate the Warlocks a couple of rooms from now.

Assign a DPS class for dealing with pets (the Guardhound first, when it is involved with a pull, then the Familiars). Other characters can trash the Warlock. Or, to keep things amazingly simple, use crowd control on the Warlock, kill the pets off, then take the Warlock when he is alone. This works better with the Familiar pull than with the Guardhound.

Remember to use Interrupts and Silence to pull enemies like Warlocks at range. You don't want to engage such foes when they are near possible adds, and having an enemy caster stay at range has many problems.

Once the Warlocks are gone, wait for a patrolling Elite to show himself. This enemy spends most of their time in the corner camps, so it might not even look like there is a patroller (it'll be either a Deathsworn or an Acolyte). Of course, these groups are small enough that you can pull and simply deal with the potential for a single add.

Each corner has three set Elites. One side often has two Acolytes and a Deathsworn; the other has a Warlock, an Acolyte, and a Deathsworn. Hit Warlocks with crowd control, nail Acolytes with additional control or kill them first, and leave Deathsworn for the end while they are tanked.

After the enemies fall, use the eastern hallway that wraps around to the Arcanium.

THE ARCANIUM

Don't enter the Arcanium until you've seen quite clearly what the patrols are doing. There are three wandering Fel Overseers in the area, and any single Overseer can wipe a group if they add during a pull (unless your party is so well geared that you don't need to worry about tactics and safety).

One of the Fel Overseers has a route that takes him to the very front of the room. Pull this Demon first to give your group room for additional clearing. Fel Overseers should be lured way back into the hallway for now, as their AoE Fear could easily rush someone into the groups of Cabal Ritualists nearby. Fear Ward, Tremor Totems, Deathwish, and other such abilities are quite effective for keeping the group's damage going against the Overseer.

If you are the main tank, keep your back fairly close to a wall while fighting Overseers; their Uppercut has a Knockback that tosses you back and can lose you time.

Now, clear the groups of Cabal Ritualists at the front of the room. There are three groups with three members in each. You won't need to worry about adds if you pull back into the hallway, though step back a fair way if your group is using Fear for crowd control.

Ritualists are a bit of a strange foe in that they come in any of four varieties. They can be Rogues, Mages, or a sort-of Warlock variety (with Addle Humanoid as a form of crowd control). None of these have much health, so crowd control and burst DPS makes for easy fights. Have someone with Silence or a ranged Interrupt ready to help with the pull, in case the target you want is taking too long to approach. Also, have the puller use the corners of the hallway to block line-of-sight and force the bulk of the Ritualists forward.

Once all of the early Ritualists are gone, pull the other two Fel Overseers in the room. As before, keep them toward the eastern side of the chamber to prevent add issues.

There are three more groups of Ritualists to clear afterward. For the first two groups, simply blast through them. Then, pull the final group back toward the eastern side of the room. As soon as the last Ritualist of the area dies, Ambassador Hellmaw starts to patrol. Your group can still rest and has not been aggroed, but you won't want to be standing close by for obvious reasons.

Have everyone get ready then engage Hellmaw.

AMBASSADOR HELLMAW

HP	134685/184500 (Heroic)	**Damage**	2330-3295/4705-6653 (Heroic)
Abilities	**Fear**: Strikes all targets within 45 yards, causing them to run in fear for 6 sec.		
	Corrosive Acid: Dealing 1094 to 1406 damage every 3 seconds and reducing armor by 3938 to 5062 for 15 sec.		

DIPLOMATIC PERKS

Dream-Wing Helm (Mail Head 516 Armor, +16 Stam, +25 Int, 6 Mana/5 Seconds, +66 Attack Power, +13 Hit Rating, +20 Critical Rating)

Idol of the Emerald Dream (Idol +88 Lifebloom Healing)

Jaedenfire Gloves of Annihilation (Cloth Hands 95 Armor, +25 Stam, +25 Int, +39 Shadow Damage)

Ornate Boots of the Sanctified (Plate Feet 780 Armor, +24 Str, +18 Stam, +20 Int, +29 Damage/Healing)

Platinum Shield of the Valorous (Shield 3711 Armor, 83 Block, +33 Stam, +24 Defense Rating)

Soul-Wand of the Aldor (Wand 125.3 DPS, +9 Stam, +8 Int, +10 Spi, +22 Healing)

Ambassador Hellmaw is an easy target in Normal Mode; this battle is an endurance fight, but it only gets ugly if your group has bad luck with Fear Resists.

The big ability that Hellmaw relies on is an AoE Fear on roughly a 30-second cooldown. This ability has a huge radius, and pretty much anyone in combat is going to get hit by it. Certainly, your main tank is going to be.

Have Fear Ward on the main tank, if possible, otherwise use Tremor Totem or simply accept that your entire groups NEEDS to be Feared. Don't have anyone except the main tank have Shadow buffs unless your main tank also has the ability to go Fear Immune (e.g. Deathwish).

The reason is that you don't want the main tank to be Feared AND have your healer or a soft DPS class Resist the Fear. That drops aggro off of the main tank and gets Hellmaw onto someone who can't take the heat.

Keep HoTs on your main tank so that healing stays on them even when any and all healers are Feared.

Apart from this issue, Hellmaw only has a few naughty tricks. His Acid Spray debuffs armor and does a fair bit of Nature damage. Have your main tank position Hellmaw so that he is facing away from the group; this mitigates almost all of the danger from Acid Spray.

Basically, this is a standard tanking fight with only slight twists. If the Fear is handled, you are fine. If you keep Shadow Resistance on the main and not on soft targets, you are fine anyway.

Heroic Mode

Hellmaw is slower to kill in Heroic Mode and gets one new ability; a timer. It's always scary to pair an endurance fight with an absolute wipe mark, but that is exactly what happens. If your group takes more than three minutes, Hellmaw wins (he can one-shot almost anything after he Enrages).

To greatly help, raise your main tank's Shadow Resistance. Time lost during Fears is painful, and keeping some damage on the boss during these periods is what it takes to overcome the timer issue.

Before turning south into the Refectory, look down the western passage behind Hellmaw's area; this is where Spy To'gun is located, and those with the quest to find him can quickly exchange that quest for the next stage in the chain.

THE REFECTORY

Cabal Assassin

The Refectory has some of the meanest trash pulls outside of The Shattered Halls. There are a few stealthing Elite Rogues in the room (Cabal Assassins), there are three patrolling Malicious Instructors, and you have to clear eight pulls of Elites that are truly rough.

Have your group set up at the back of the northern hallway that leads into the room, with most of your people still standing in the Arcanium. Except for a couple pulls, it's worth coming all the way back to the Arcanium so that AoE Fears and other wide-area abilities can be used with impunity by your group. Crowd control of any sort is a must!

Wait for the first Malicious Instructor to pass by the hallway, then clear the first two pulls at the front of the room. These are fairly easy compared to what you'll soon face, but there are still four Elites in each group. You must destroy a somewhat random distribution of foes, but the groups are composed of Deathsworn, Cultists, Acolytes, and Shadow Priests. There are Warlocks as well, but they are only in the larger pulls, so you don't have to worry about them yet. Here is a table to give you an idea about the enemies in the Refectory.

AoE Fear is the best tool for staying safe against the pulls of four or five Elites that you fight in the Refectory. Crowd control often removes two enemies from the fight, unless your group is very light on such abilities. Make sure that Shadow Priests and always kept under control or killed directly; their Shadow Word: Pain is bad, and their Mind Flay is many times worse.

For tanks, keep the best possible eye on the Cultists. You don't want anything to peel onto your healers, but these foes are the worst. They Interrupt casting frequently, and their high DPS eats healers alive.

If your group lacks crowd control (ouch), use long pulls to fight the group in two stages. Have a character who can hurry shoot at the larger enemy groups and rush toward the front of the Instance. The party can cherry pick the most dangerous targets out of the bunch then deal with the other foes later. For example, have a Hunter leave a Freezing Trap behind to stop one enemy, Multishot the desired group to start a fight, then run back to the entrance. The party can kill any Warlocks, Cultists, or Shadow Priests that they feel comfortable grabbing, then the slower kills can be grabbed when they snap back (after the Hunter Feigns Death).

Malicious Instructors can be fought at the southern end of the hall; they lack Fear and won't throw you around. These high-health foes take a while to kill but are actually quite easy. Keep as many characters as possible at range to avoid the Shadow damage from Shadow Nova, and beat the big Demons into pulp.

The pull order for the room is such: two fronts groups (5), central Instructor, two rear groups (4), group on right (5 + Non-Elite Pet), right Instructor, small group in right corner (3), Instructor on left, THEN the group on left (5 + Non-Elite Pet), and finally the left corner group (3).

ENEMY LIST

NAME	DANGER LEVEL	WHAT TO DO WITH THEM
Shadow Priest	Immense	Crowd Control (Mind Control, Sap, or Mind Control) or First Kill Target
Warlock	High	Crowd Control
Cultist	High	Good Kill Targets, Tank Until Shadow Priests/Warlocks Dealt With
Warlock Pets	Moderate	Put a Single DPS Character on Them
Acolyte	Low	Keep Them Feared if Possible
Deathsworn	Low	Tank Until Other Targets Are Down

ASSASSINS!

The Assassins in the Refectory can attack while you group is in battle or outside of battle, and sometimes they even aggro from the Arcanium (they spawn in odd places as you approach Blackheart the Inciter).

If you have a Hunter in the group, use Freezing Traps when an Assassin appears at the back of the party. This gives the tank more time to realize what is going on and get back there. Warlocks can Fear, offtanks can aggro the Assassins and pull them back to the main tank (if the main tank is busy), and so forth.

Keep Flares behind the healer(s) so that there is some warning. You don't have to worry about the Assassins coming in from the front, as they will likely aggro on something before they get to the healers.

Only when every visible Elite in the room is dead should your group approach Blackheart the Inciter; otherwise, the Elites will come to aid Blackheart in the boss encounter. It's hard enough to beat this guy when he is by himself!

BLACKHEART THE INCITER

HP	138375/184500 (Heroic)	**Damage**	1889-2672/3528-4990 (Heroic)
Abilities	**War Stomp:** Knocks nearby enemies back, dealing about 1500 damage.		
	Charge: Inflicts normal damage and stunning the target for 2 sec.		
	Incite Chaos: Takes control of all nearby players, forcing them to fight each other.		

TOYS OF A TWO-HEADED OGRE

- Adamantite Figuring (Trinket +32 Defense Rating, Use to Increase Armor by 1280 for 20 Seconds)
- Brooch of Heightened Potential (Neck +15 Stam, +14 Int, +9 Spell Hit Rating, +14 Spell Critical Rating, +22 Damage/Healing)
- Cloak of the Inciter (76 Armor +15 Stam, +16 Hit Rating, +18 Critical Strike Rating, +30 Attack Power)
- Moonglade Handwraps (Leather Hands 183 Armor, +19 Str, +13 Agi, +18 Stam, +20 Int, +17 Spi, +40 Healing)
- Ornate Leggings of the Venerated (Plate Legs 993 Armor, +24 Str, +21 Stam, +25 Int, 1 [red socket], 1 [yellow socket], 1 [blue socket], Socket Bonus: 2 Mana/5 Seconds, +26 Damage/Healing)
- Wand of the Netherwing (Wand 125.3 DPS, +19 Stam, +16 Damage/Healing)

Blackheart is a very specific boss. He's almost worthless by himself, and it first it'll seem like the fight is going to be a total cakewalk. Almost no melee damage, an annoying AoE Knockback that doesn't do damage, and a random Intercept that still isn't very brutal. Is that it?

No. Those are just the minor abilities that Blackheart picked up while working on his masterpiece of mental control. This boss is able to take control of your entire party (frequently). There are many ways to try and deal with this, but it's never going to make Blackheart orderly. This is a chaotic endurance fight like few others!

For the first 20 seconds, you have control. Let your tank get aggro and pull Blackheart to the southern wall of the room. Have all characters keep their backs to the wall as often as possible and thus avoid the troublesome Warstomp Knockback issue.

Next, lay on the DPS while you can. As the 20-second mark approaches, dump Rage into your foe or even throw it away outright by switching Stances. Rogues, do the same to get rid of your free energy. Hunters, place a Freezing Trap under your group's primary healer. This saves a great deal of mana and is the single biggest boost that you can give your group during the Mind Control phase.

Warlocks will want their Succubus pets out for the fight, on Defensive. This gives you the chance for Seduction to take place; another way to save mana.

Dreamless Sleep Potions, Ice Block, and other out-of-battle abilities should be used at this time. If you REALLY have the timing mastered, consider taking off your weapon, changing into less aggressive Stances, Shapeshifting into Bear, etc.

Then the fury hits. Everyone goes after everyone else. It's quite random how bad this can be. If everyone has done what they can to gimp their own damage for the duration of the control, things won't be too rough.

Blackheart runs around madly for a few moments after control breaks. Use this time to have almost everyone Bandage; the main tank shouldn't bother chasing after Blackheart, as he isn't even going after anyone yet. Instead, shoot him at range to give yourself some aggro and try to get him running toward the group again.

The tank is going to get Blackheart near the wall again, and soon the healer can resume healing. Some people will tell you that the first phase is the best period to use your timers, but most timers don't get used randomly by Blackheart. Your group gets more DPS time on the boss during this second phase, so it's worth a bit of a gamble to save Bloodlust, Deathwish, and other timed abilities for those point in the battle (play it safe or go for the gold; it's up to you).

If anyone dies during the fight, have them rush back into the Instance. This is such an endurance match that an unlucky character can make it back into the engagement.

Heroic Mode

In Heroic Mode, Blackheart the Inciter, is much the same except he has a great deal more hit points and deals massive amounts of damage. His charge is frighteningly vicious.

When Blackheart falls, have everyone who needs the Book of Fel Names loot it from his body. Then, take the corridor south, deeper into Shadow Labyrinth.

THE TOMB

There are bone piles here and there along the way, and these can spawn Tortured Skeletons; the non-Elites aren't very tough or high on health, but it's nice to be aware of them. They have a shorter respawn time, so don't assume that these corridors are fully clear if you are wandering back through later. Track Undead reveals the pockets of these Skeletons; Hunters and Paladins should keep that up so that you don't walk into the AoE pulls accidentally.

The first big group of Skeletons is often at the entrance to the Tomb. Make sure not to pull these until the patrolling Demon is off on their own. There are several Demon patrollers in the Tomb area and in the hallway beyond, note that these can be Fel Overseers or Malicious Instructors (chosen at random when you enter the Instance).

Use AoE abilities to knock out the initial group of Skeletons, then take down the patroller. Clear the other bone piles of the room, which doesn't take long, then look at the two groups of Humanoids along the eastern wall. Don't pull these until the next Demon patroller is away, and be just as cautious with the pull itself.

If you shoot at the rear members of the first group, you end up with five Elites at once. Otherwise, you can do these two groups on their own, with three foes and two foes respectively. The enemies are only Acolytes and Cultists. Use crowd control to avoid the Acolytes early in the fights, and burn down the Cultists first.

Leave the Tomb and clear the two Demon patrollers in the next hallway. Leave extra room while fighting any Fel Overseers, as Fear is still very much an issue. The patrolling enemies of the next major room come fairly close to the northern section of hallway, so be aware.

SANCTUM OF SHADOWS

There are five groups of Elites in the Sanctum of Shadows, and four bone piles have Skeleton groups to break down with AoE abilities. This isn't a hard room, but the shifting of the Elite groups make it worthwhile to pull back to the hallway for the initial two fights.

Each Elite group consists of Cultists, Fanatics, and Zealots. Crowd control is very useful on the Zealots, as they are casters throughout most of an encounter. Hit the Cultists first, then slice through the melee-DPS Fanatics. Finally, break crowd control and use ranged Interrupts or Silence to help with mitigating the Zealots.

Zealots sometimes transform at low health, forming melee Demons that take a bit more beating to fell (pun intended). That said, they are very easy foes to slaughter when you don't have Cultists and Fanatics beating on you. A combined group's DPS can obliterate a Zealot is just a few seconds.

Take down the first two groups of patrolling Elites, then clear both of the bone piles ahead (there is one on each side). Follow this with one more Elite group and two more bone piles of Skeletons.

Your group should now be able to see where the Codex of Blood and the next boss are located. You still have two groups of enemies to clear, and they can wander right through each other. Wait for the wanderers to go all the way into the back before taking the forward group. Then, hit the last patrol when it comes back around.

That is the end of the easy part for this room. The pulls were quite easy, but Grandmaster Vorpil is certainly not. Don't aggro and start this fight until you have read the strategies and fully explained the encounter to your group.

GRANDMASTER VORPIL

HP	110681/138720 (Heroic)	**Damage**	1413-1996/1413-1996 (Heroic)
Abilities	**Shadow Bolt Volley**: Deals approximately 1000 to 1400 Shadow damage.		
	Draw Shadows: Teleports Grandmaster Vorpil and all nearby players to the center of his platform.		
	Rain of Fire: Burns all enemies in a selected area for 903 to 997 every 1 sec. for 6 sec. **Heroic**: In Heroic difficulty, this deals 1805 to 1995 Fire damage every 1 sec. for 6 sec.		
	Empowering Shadows: Increases Shadow damage done by 60 for up to 45 seconds. Stacks up to 25 times. **Heroic**: In Heroic difficulty, this increases Shadow damage by 120 per application.		
	Summon Voidwalker: Summons a voidwalker that will travel toward Grandmaster Vorpil. If the voidwalker reaches Vorpil, it will explode, healing Grandmaster Vorpil for approximately 4000-6000 health and giving him the Empowering Shadows buff.		
	Banish (Heroic difficulty only). Banishes a target for 8 sec. Only one target can be banished at a time.		

RICHES OF THE SHADOW COUNCIL

Blackout Truncheon (1h Mace 69.7 DPS, 1 [red socket], 1 [yellow socket], Socket Bonus: +6 Attack Power, Chance on Hit to Add 132 Haste Rating for 10 Seconds)

Breastplate of Many Graces (Plate Chest 1135 Armor, +24 Stam, +33 Int, +75 Healing, 10 Mana/5 Seconds)

Hallowed Pauldrons (Cloth Shoulder 117 Armor, +10 Stam, +17 Int, +20 Spi, 1 [red socket], 1 [blue socket], Socket Bonus: +3 Int, +12 Healing)

Jewel of Charismatic Mystique (Trinket Use to Reduce Your Threat to All Enemies Within 30 Yards)

Wrathfire Hand-Cannon (Gun 64.5 DPS, +15 Critical Rating, +40 Attack Power)

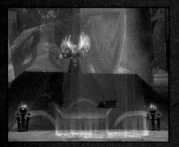

Sustained DPS is very important to have here, though not for Vorpil himself. This Warlock does modest melee damage and can only do Rain of Fire after teleporting the group to his location; this happens periodically, but everyone knows to start running as soon as the screen pauses for the teleportation sequence. Thus, people take one or two ticks of the AoE at most. It's not bad.

What is rough is that Vorpil calls Voidwalkers through a series of Void Rifts during the fight. The number of these Voidwalkers increases as Vorpil gets lower in health.

Each Voidwalker slouches toward their master, and a single one reaching him can be quite painful. Not only do this Demons burst, doing damage to everyone in a large radius; they also heal Vorpil. Not good!

Have two characters assigned to kill the Voidwalkers. Ranged DPS classes are best for this, though Rogues and DPS Warriors can handle the situation if need be. Hunters with Track Demon up are just amazing!

When there aren't Voidwalkers in a DPS character's range, they are free to put damage on the boss until they see a foe. The spawning areas for the Voidwalkers is seen clearly, as they glow brightly.

As a main tank, one trick if a person is letting a Voidwalker through is to lure Vorpil away from the Demon as it approaches. As you have aggro, just back away from it. You won't want to do this very often, as it gets hard to keep DPS on him and avoid other Voidwalkers, but the technique works in a pinch.

Note that all characters should save their best DPS opportunities for the second half of the fight. Once the Voidwalkers start to come in higher numbers, it's time to use all of your trinkets and timed abilities.

Heroic Mode

It gets even harder to keep full DPS on Vorpil when he is able to Banish one of your characters. There isn't much to be done about this, save for peeling a DPS class off of Vorpil to take on the Voidwalkers when someone is Banished.

If the poor person who gets CCed is your only healer, have all non-tanks remember to Bandage, use Health Potions, and pray for the best.

Loot Vorpil when he falls, and remind anyone with the Lexicon Demonica quest to specifically check the body, as it has what they need. Then, read the Codex of Blood for those folks who are doing this dungeon for the first time. That quest chain converts to its final step. There is only a single boss left, and you are almost to it.

THE SCREAMING HALL

Tanks the Executioners while everyone kills the Summoner, then take out the melee troops. Try to keep the Executioners away from the back lines so that Whirlwind hits either the main tank or nobody (if the main tank moves forward quickly enough, the Whirlwind will miss and the Executioners will stick with the main tank).

SUMMONERS HAVE FRIENDS IN LOW PLACES

Surprisingly, Summoners call Elite Humanoids into the fray rather than calling on Demons. This isn't a good thing, as the Elite Humanoids that appear are just as powerful as the ones that you are already fighting. This is why Summoners are always the first ones to be killed off. If you see these casters try to cast a Shadow spell, Interrupt it no matter what. Silence and Interrupts of all sorts are fully effective.

With the runner gone, the other group can be taken a block of four as well. Eventually, however, the runner comes back (meaning that you have to either wait for it to die again or accept a pull of five Elites). Use AoE Fear to help out if you are making a large pull.

Yet one more group of four faces you, though are never any complications with getting that party of foes, then you can take down the trio of Spellbinders at the end of the room. Using two forms of crowd control, this fight is a joke. If you only have one, consider a longer pull that is supplemented with AoE Fear or other methods of secondary crowd control.

Take a few steps north and turn east when the corridor bends. There might be a single Skeleton there to make your characters chuckle a little, but the doors that open reveal a much more impressive scene. There are Cabal leaders in a great battle with the primordial Elemental named Murmur. This creature of sound and energy is wounded, but it is by no means crippled. The Cabal Executioners, Summoners, and Spellbinders in the room are also holding their ground. It's your job to disrupt the balance.

The first fight is against only two Executioners; they are melee targets with Whirlwind and high health (and clearly they've been running Naxxramas a great deal in their free time). Use crowd control on one Executioner, kill the other, and slice the second when you are ready. The next fight is much uglier.

Watch the two groups ahead. There is an extra Elite that runs between them, firing at Murmur from time-to-time. Wait until Murmur kills this extra enemy before doing the next pull. Otherwise, you end up with the four you are pulling, that runner as an add, and the four people behind the runner who add WITH the add. Wipe time!

If you pull when the runner is down, only four enemies come, and the fight is much safer. You have two Executioners, a Spellbinder, and a Summoner. Use ranged Interrupts or Silence to get the Summoner close to the group and lay DPS on that target first. Use crowd control on the Spellbinder to avoids Mind Control (if a Spellbinder does start to use Mind Control, and Interrupt against the Spellbinder will break your buddy out of it).

Look around the room for the many Soul Devices that are here. It's easily a big enough stash to let your group finish off the quest for the Soul Devices, even if all five characters initially needed the items.

Also, look against the northern wall while staying as far away from Murmur as possible. As marked on the map, the chest for the First Key Fragment of Karazhan is there. You need to fight a single Elemental to get it, but it's not a boss challenge or anything like that. A group of five should win without any complications unless someone starts feeling crazy and decides that it's wise to aggro Murmur in the process.

When all buffs are done and rest is complete, position your group and start the daunting and amazing battle against Murmur.

MURMUR

HP	169740/229148 (Heroic)	Damage	3256-4605/3256-4605 (Heroic)
Abilities	**Resonance:** Deals 2000 Nature damage and increases Nature damage taken by 2000 for 45 sec.		
	Sonic Boom: Deals approximately 5000-6000 Nature damage.		
	Magnetic Pull: Pulls targets toward the caster.		
	Murmur's Touch: Explodes for about 3500-3800 Nature damage and silences the player after approximately 10 seconds.		
	Sonic Shock: (Heroic Mode Only). Deals approximately 2000-3000 Nature damage.		

WHISPERS OF GREAT TREASURE

Greatsword of Horrid Dreams (Mh Sword 41.4 DPS, 60 Armor, +15 Stam, +14 Int, +14 Spell Hit Rating, +130 Damage/Healing)

Hallowed Garments (Cloth Chest 156 Armor, +12 Stam, +26 Int, +26 Spi, 1 [red socket], 1 [yellow socket], 1 [blue socket], Socket Bonus: +6 Stam, +57 Healing)

Harness of the Deep Currents (Mail Chest 652 Armor, +28 Stam, +30 Int, +68 Healing, 10 Mana/5 Seconds)

Leggings of Assassination (Leather Legs 256 Armor, +40 Agi, +33 Stam, +22 Hit Rating, +44 Attack Power)

Robe of Oblivion (Cloth Chest 156 Armor, +30 Stam, +20 Int, 1 [red socket], 1 [yellow socket], 1 [blue socket], Socket Bonus: +6 Stamina, +40 Damage/Healing)

Shoulderguards of the Bold (Plate Shoulders 873 Armor, +25 Str, +25 Stam, 1 [yellow socket], 1 [blue socket], Socket Bonus: +3 Dodge Rating, +17 Defense Rating)

Silent Slippers of Meditation (Cloth Feet 107 Armor, +21 Stam, +22 Int, +14 Spi, +20 Spell Critical Rating, +26 Damage/Healing)

Silvermoon Crest Shield (Shield 3806 Armor, +86 Block, +20 Int, +23 Damage/Healing, 5 Mana/5 Seconds)

Sonic Spear (Polearm 93.3 DPS, +35 Agi, +30 Stam, +24 Hit Rating, +62 Attack Power)

Spaulders of Oblivion (Cloth Shoulder 117 Armor, +25 Stam, +17 Int, 1 [yellow socket], 1 [blue socket], Socket Bonus: +3 Spell Hit Rating, +29 Damage/Healing)

Tidefury Kilt (Mail Legs 570 Armor, +39 Stam, +31 Int, +19 Spell Critical Rating, +35 Damage/Healing)

Whispering Blade of Slaying (1h Dagger 71.8 DPS, +21 Stam, +26 Attack Power, +15 Dagger Rating)

Positioning and fast movement are essential for victory in the fight against Murmur. At almost all times, you need to have a person or pet in melee range with this immense boss. If unengaged in melee, Murmur reacts by placing a debuff called Resonance on all of the party (Resonance adds 2000 to Nature Damage per stack of the ability). At long as your party learns how to avoid damage from the other attacks while keeping people in range as often as necessary, you won't ever see this debuff.

During his normal phase, Murmur hits local melee targets for moderate damage (enough to warrant keeping your main tank in their tanking gear, but no more than that). Then, Murmur will toss the Murmur's Touch onto occasional targets.

Murmur's Touch takes ten seconds to develop, at which time the target explodes into the air, taking moderate Nature damage, being struck with Silence for a few seconds, and dealing additional Nature damage to anyone nearby. This is another part of the careful positioning that everyone must maintain. Leave melee targets in the center of the ring, where Murmur always floats. Have a healer at the western side of the circle, then align ranged DPS characters and other healers on the north and south sides of the circle. This keeps everyone in range of the healer but leaves plenty of space so that someone with Murmur's Touch can back off and blow up without hurting the party.

Sometimes Murmur gets lonely and pulls someone out of range and close to himself. This does no direct damage, and there is no change of aggro. That person should simply return to their original spot as soon as they can.

After a short period Murmur begins the chargeup to his Sonic Boom. There is a text message that displays, letting EVERYONE know that this is about to happen. Get out past the 35 yard mark when this happens, then return immediately afterward. Though Murmur can't use Resonance while building up his Sonic Boom, he'll be able to slam the party with this almost as soon as he finishes the Boom.

For Warriors, the trick is to Intervene with a party member who is outside the circle. Chance to Berserk Stance while waiting for the Sonic Boom to enact, then Intercept Murmur as soon as you can.

Paladins can Divine Shield themselves once in the fight to avoid Sonic Boom damage. Rogues can hit Cloak of Shadows and Evasion to stay in melee range for one blast as well, then they can tank Murmur until the proper tank returns.

Once everyone gets the positioning down for Murmur, the fight is stunningly easier to pull off. While still not a simple fight, Murmur is quite fair and does not have any cheap moves. He just requires precision.

Heroic Mode

And then comes Heroic Mode, where Murmur does get a bit more evil. Not only does Murmur throw characters together when using his Touch (so that there is potential for everyone to blow up); he also forces all characters to enter the circle.

Anyone who stays outside of Murmur's circle gets hit with a Sonic Shock that does very high damage. Staying closer to Murmur is not an option; it's the way you are supposed to do the fight in Heroic mode.

Everyone must memorize their placement within Murmur's circle. There is plenty of room there to still avoid the blast from Murmur's Touch, but people NEED to know their spots. Otherwise, there is too much chaos during repositioning and multiple people are going to get hit when a person pops.

During Sonic Boom, everyone is allowed to leave the circle (and has to, to avoid the damage). However, all must return immediately afterward to avoid Sonic Shock deaths. Expect some deaths during the learning curve period; it's not easy to master the fight on Heroic Mode, but you can do it!

You are done with Shadow Labyrinth. With this place on farm status, your group can get to Exalted in Lower City, as desired. It doesn't even take that long to accomplish, if you are serious about getting that level of faction.

If you didn't have any major problems completing the Instance, you are probably ready for The Shattered Halls. Good luck!

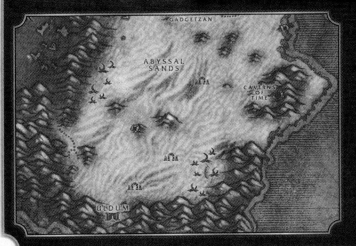

OLD HILLSBRAD FOOTHILLS
(THE ESCAPE FROM DURNHOLDE)

DUNGEON INFORMATION

Name	Old Hillsbrad Foothills (The Escape From Durnholde)
Location	Tanaris, Caverns of Time
Suggested Levels	Group of 5, Levels 66-70
Primary Enemies	Humanoids
Damage Types	Physical, Shadow
Time to Complete	45 to 60 Minutes

WHO TO BRING

The Escape From Durnholde event is very challenging with a level 66 group, as the second half of the Instance is handled as almost one sequence. You often don't have a long time to rest, and things can go wrong very quickly. Yet, with a couple of higher-level characters, this Instance becomes quite easy, and practice always helps too.

If you want to bring everyone into the Instance at its suggested level (around 66), the key is to have everyone ready to go with the proper strategies and a full collection of food/water/bandages/potions. These are going to be needed even more than usual during the escort phase. It's especially good to have a Mage; for the best result, characters will be eating and drinking in bursts, meaning that the bill is quite high for a run without the consumables being "free."

You always want to have a solid tank and healer. Any of the standard tank selections will do nicely (Bear Druids, Warriors, and Paladins). As long as your group is well experienced, a single tank and solo healer should suffice without any problems.

Three DPS classes with a fair supply of in-combat crowd control is desirable. Hunters and Mages bring a great deal to the group, and Warlocks fill this role wonderfully as well. Rogues have fewer opportunities for Sap than in some Instances, so their presence fills burst DPS but not a crowd control slot.

Druids, regardless of whether they are attending for DPS or healing, can make this Instance much easier. Because Old Hillsbrad is primarily outdoors, Druids can Root constantly. There are quite a few melee monsters out there; thus, this is a powerful ability for crowd control. Then, just before the final boss fight, there are three mean waves of Dragonkin. Druids can Hibernate these foes, giving your group more leeway in the frantic encounters. You just can't go wrong with a Druid here (though they aren't required by any means).

Because there aren't many Resistance battles in Old Hillsbrad and the damage is more mundane, Priests bring slightly more than Shamans as a primary healer. Their buffs to health, Shields, Mind Control, and Psychic Scream are all quite effective against the primarily Humanoid host of enemies.

JOBS

CLASS	ABILITIES
Druid	Backup Healer, Hibernate
Hunter	Sustained DPS is Important During Escort Mode, Freezing Traps
Mage	Polymorph, Evocation + Mana Gem During Extended Escort, Free Food/Water
Paladin	Backup Healer, AoE Tanking, Resistance Buffs
Priest	Psychic Scream, Healing
Rogue	DPS
Shaman	Primary or Backup Healing, Ranged Interrupts vs. Casters, Tremor Totem
Warlock	Succubus, DPS
Warrior	Anti-Fear Abilities, Intimidating Shout, Tanking

GETTING TO OLD HILLSBRAD AND THE CAVERNS OF TIME

The Caverns of Time are found in southeastern Tanaris. There are currently three Instances there, with Escape From Durnholde being the first event that you can experience. The Opening of the Dark Portal comes afterward and is unlocked by running this Instance successfully. Finally, there is a 25-man raid (The Battle for Mount Hyjal) that is far beyond the difficulty of these earlier Instances.

The meeting stone for all Caverns of Time dungeons is just outside the cave itself. Form your groups here, then move down the lengthy tunnel into the pre-Instance area. There is a Quartermaster along the way for the Keepers of Time. You can purchase reagents for your classes, repair, and sell here (all useful functions).

To get into Old Hillsbrad Foothills, for the Escape From Durnholde event, you must first run a short quest, as described below, in the quest listing. Once that is done, walk to the western part of the Caverns of Time and look for the large guard tower with Human guards and Peasants nearby. Follow that tunnel to the Instance portal.

REPUTATION GAINS

ACTION	FACTION	REPUTATION GAIN	END POINT
Kill Trash Mobs	Keepers of Time	8 Points	Exalted
Kill Bosses	Keepers of Time	80 Points	Exalted
Old Hillsbrad Quest Chain	Keepers of Time	5,010 Points	N/A

ECHOES OF THE PAST

BOSSES

LIEUTENANT DRAKE

CAPTAIN SKARLOC

EPOCH HUNTER

MINIONS

DURNHOLDE MAGE
Notes: Fire Caster

DURNHOLDE RIFLEMAN
Notes: Ranged Attacker, Scatter Shot, Multi-Shot

DURNHOLDE SENTRY
Notes: Overpower, Hamstring, Moderate Health and Armor

DURNHOLDE TRACKING HOUND
Notes: Detect Stealth, DPS Class, Low Health

DURNHOLDE VETERAN
Notes: Higher DPS Warrior

DURNHOLDE WARDEN
Notes: Psychic Scream, Shadow Word: Pain, Heals, Cleanse

INFINITE DEFILER
Notes: Dragonkin, Caster, Low Health

INFINITE SABOTEUR
Notes: Dragonkin, Melee/DPS

INFINITE SLAYER
Notes: Dragonkin, Melee, High Health

LORDAERON SENTRY
Notes: Low Level, Soft Target, Patrols Roads

LORDAERON WATCHMAN
Notes: Low Level, Soft Target, Patrols Roads

TARREN MILL GUARDSMAN
Notes: Simple Tank

TARREN MILL LOOKOUT
Notes: Ranged Enemy, Serpent Sting

TARREN MILL PROTECTOR
Notes: Paladin Tank

VARIOUS BEASTS OF HILLSBRAD
Notes: Low-level Beasts from Hillsbrad Are Here (and Can Be Killed/Looted)

QUEST LISTING

TO THE MASTER'S LAIR (CHAIN)

Level Requirement	66
Quest Giver	Steward of Time (at the Entrance to the Caverns of Time)
Quest Goal	Meet Andormu and Follow a Short Escort Afterward
Experience Reward	2,400
Additional Rewards	Access to Old Hillsbrad Foothills (The Escape From Durnholde)

The Steward of Time is found at the entrance to the Caverns of Time; just look for the large Drake who wants to have a word with you. Accept **To the Master's Lair** and complete it by speaking with the young child Andormu at the bottom of the cavern. Andormu is obviously not what he appears, and the second stage of this chain is to have the creature spawn a guardian to escort you around the region. Listen to what the escort has to say, and in a few minutes the whole process should be done.

Speak with Andormu again, complete the quest, and then accept **Old Hillsbrad** (the chain described below). If you do not complete this escort quest first, you will not be allowed to enter old Hillsbrad and run the Instance; all members of a group must complete this.

OLD HILLSBRAD (CHAIN)

Level Requirement	66
Quest Giver	Andormu (in the Caverns of Time)
Quest Goal	Complete the Escape From Durnholde Event
Experience Reward	38,300
Additional Rewards	Tempest's Touch (Cloth Hands 88 Armor, +10 Stam, +20 Int, +6 Spi, 2 [blue socket], Socket Bonus: +3 Spell Critical Rating, +27 Damage/Healing, +10 Spell Penetration), Southshire Sneakers (Leather Feet 181 Armor, +16 Stam, 1 [red socket], 1 [blue socket], Socket Bonus: +6 Attack Power, +23 Dodge Rating, +42 Attack Power), Tarren Mill Defender's Cinch (Mail Waist 330 Armor, +19 Stam, +18 Int, 2 [red socket], Socket Bonus: +3 Int, 12 Mana/5 Seconds), Warchief's Mantle (Plate Shoulder 786 Armor, +23 Str, +27 Stam, 1 [red socket], 1 [yellow socket], Socket Bonus: +3 Critical Rating, +18 Parry Rating)

Once your group is allowed into Old Hillsbrad, by completing the chain described above, you can start this event. A successful run through the entire Instance will complete this chain for you in a single pass, so there isn't much complexity here. Just be sure to have each character turn in the steps as you go. See the table below for clarification.

OLD HILLSBRAD CHAIN

QUEST NAME	STARTS AT	ENDS BY	TASK
Old Hillsbrad	Andormu	Erozion	Enter Old Hillsbrad and Talk to Erozion (Just Outside of Starting Cave)
Taretha's Diversion	Erozion	Thrall	Fly to Durnholde, Torch the Internment Lodges, and Speak With Thrall (in the basement of Durnholde Keep)
Escape From Durnholde	Thrall	Erozion	Slay Epoch Hunter and finish the instance
Return to Andormu	Erozion	Andormu	Leave Old Hillsbrad and Talk to Andormu Again

MAP LEGEND	
1	Starting Point (The Yeti Cave in Normal Hillsbrad)
2	Southshore (Lots of Flavor and Two Merchants)
3	Durnholde Keep
4	Tarren Mill

ENTERING HILLSBRAD...AGAIN!

The Instance portal into Old Hillsbrad is lined with the remarkable pine trees of the region. Once you pass through that portal, time itself shifts, as does the appearance of your party. Everyone besides Dwarves and Gnomes (because they were allies with humans in the era of Warcraft II) will appear as a Human in Old Hillsbrad.

Beyond that, all of you have been teleported to the Yeti Cave (marked a map point one in northern Hillsbrad). There are no monsters nearby, and indeed few things pose a threat even when you walk outside. Old Hillsbrad is covered with non-Elite monsters, of the same types that you would expect from any earlier journeys you have made into the present-day region. These can be attacked, slain, and looted, though there is little reason to do so.

Outside of the Yeti Cave is Erozion, an agent of the Keepers of Time. He is there to ensure that Thrall is able to escape from the keep at Durnholde. Though the story as it occurred originally was tragic for Taretha and Thrall, things must proceed for the future to be safeguarded.

Erozion hands everyone who talks to him a Pack of Incendiary Bombs. The five of these need to be planted in each of the buildings beneath Durnholde. Make sure that each person who is doing the quests of Old Hillsbrad talks to Erozion and starts the next step in the chain!

Then you have a choice! Characters can use the nearby Drake, Brazen, to fly over to Durnholde Keep in style. Or, your people can explore Old Hillsbrad. There is much to see and do!

Inside the gates are set groups and patrols, though the bulk of the fighting is down below. Though you can hurry forward and drop down, it's far easier to take the route that we'll outline here (for safety purposes).

The first pair of enemies is by the bridge. A Durnholde Rifleman stands with a Sentry nearby. Watch for the patrol of a Sentry with a Tracking Hound, and avoid pulling the bridge guards when the patrol is near.

Riflemen are better targets to use crowd control against; they have Scatter Shot and Multi-Shot, so their damage is high and their ability to disrupt a group is also considerable. Sap, Polymorph, lay traps, or otherwise disrupt the enemies as best you can.

When those two are dead, eliminate the Sentry and his Tracking Hound to keep your back clear. Tracking Hounds are fairly fast to cut apart, so they are intelligent targets to leave high on the kill list.

THE BEAUTY OF OLD HILLSBRAD

With time reversed, there is more to see here than simply the escape of Thrall. In Southshore, there are many NPCs to hear and observe. The founding members of the Scarlet Crusade are in Southshore, as are some of the members who will later split and form the honorable Argent Dawn.

This flavor is meant to be enjoyed and can be observed even by a single person. There are no enemies to aggro on you in Southshore, so anyone can come into this Instance and watch the speeches and actions of the NPCs at leisure.

For those who are interested in crafting, there are two merchants to seek as well. Thomas Yance wanders the Southshore road; he sells the Riding Crop recipe for only 5 gold. This is a Trinket that improved Mount Speed by 10% (though this is not cumulative with any other items that improve Mount Speed). This works even on Flying Mounts, so you can see why a number of people will be excited to grab this recipe for their Leatherworkers.

Also, there is an Aged Dalaren Wizard who sells the Enchanting Recipe for Enchant Shield-Intellect! This merchant is seen on the east-west road that intersects the map. This Enchant adds 12 Intellect to a Shield, and it only costs 6 gold to purchase!

Cross the bridge and attack the two Riflemen there. Use crowd control, as always, and have your tank engage the first Rifleman directly. These are hard mobs to shoot and pull back from. Thus, it's better to Charge or at least run up to them to start the fight.

Take the path right when you finish crossing the bridge and look for the small set of stairs that is built into the wall of the area. Climb down the steps and take a look at the holding pens before making any pulls. Keep your party against the wall to avoid proximity aggro.

HERE THEY COME

If you have a Hunter, keep them running Track Humanoids so that the patrols are easier to spot. All of your enemies in this Instance are Humanoid up until the very end, so Track Humanoids is never going to let you down.

DURNHOLDE KEEP

When all of the fun and chores are out of the way, have your group meet at Durnholde Keep. Those who are traveling by ground can quickly spot the mounts that are allowed to be used in Old Hillsbrad. This is an outdoor area, which means that mounts and Druid abilities are perfectly legal!

At the entrance to Durnholde is a single Sentry. This light enemy is only able to soak a bit of damage, and doesn't lay much DPS on his target. Pull this Sentry at any time and snuff him out.

There are two patrols that come through the area where you are hiding, and pulling the group of four enemies by the first building is not advisable until both patrols are gone.

Each patrol has a Tracking Hound and a Rifleman escort. Unless you are playing on Heroic Mode, these are very quick, simple fights. Note that in Heroic Mode the Tracking Hound patrols spawn extra Riflemen, so there are four Elites to handle. None of these are controllable via Polymorph in Heroic Mode, so each patrol must be dispatched without additional mobs or extra chaos.

Clear the three southern buildings, then turn to the north and cross under the bridge. There is a fight there with two Sentries and two Wardens. All of the enemies are linked, and this is a mean fight. If you can get crowd control against both Wardens, absolutely do so. In Heroic Mode, Wardens can Cleanse crowd control off of each other (and other members of their groups), so it is essential to wait on crowd control until both Wardens can be hit at the same time. If that isn't an option Wardens must be killed first and quickly!

The two buildings in the north have a patrol group that walks around. It's the usual Tracking Hound and Rifleman duo. Wait until this patrol reaches the northern side of the area and pull from the first building (it's easier to get those enemies first rather than hit the patrol).

Once the area is clear of wandering aggro, look at the first building on the left side. There are five such structures in the lower area beneath the keep, and all of them need to be firebombed. To do that, your group must clear the four enemies in each building, then have someone go inside to plant the explosives.

All of the southern three buildings have the following makeup: two Sentries, one Rifleman, and one Warden. The Riflemen often come out the back of the buildings, so they join the fight later than you might want. Expect them to do this, and your tank can be better prepared to get their attention.

Crowd control must go on the Wardens. These Priest-like enemies deal plenty of damage, Heal on occasion, and use Psychic Scream to Fear your entire party. Have Tremor Totem or other anti-Fear abilities ready ahead of time when engaging groups with Wardens.

Use crowd control on the Warden. Use spare control against the Rifleman in each group, and deal with the weaker Sentries first. You can't pull the two enemies from the front of each buildings; all four Durnholde NPCs are linked in each structure, so don't try to be fancy. Just pull and have your tank engage while the crowd control members wait to do their business.

The fourth building has two Riflemen and two Sentries, so it's usually an easier fight. Pull way back if you are using any Fear abilities against the enemies or if you have trouble getting the Riflemen to approach. Just keep heading backward through your cleared area until the threat of patrol adds is negligible.

Hit the patrol next, when it's entirely safe, and then go after the fifth building (it's the same as the fourth one in terms of enemy composition).

After planting the explosives in the barrel of the fifth building, all of the slave barracks go up in flames. The Orcs realize that things are turning a bit more in their direction, and they'll be rather happy about the affair. Cheer them on, then move back to the southern side. A strong Warrior called Lieutenant Drake is rushing down the stairs to see what is going on. Give him a guided tour of the rebellion.

THE WARDENS ARE ON OUR SIDE

Mind Control is a beautiful thing in this Instance. The Wardens are such dangerous members that it's worth trying to Mind Control them if you have a Priest. This cuts the total number of enemies down to three once you let the other guards kill the Warden, and it means that you won't have to worry about AoE Fear, Heals, or their Shadow Word: Pain. Much better.

138

LIEUTENANT DRAKE

HP	78504/119556 (Heroic)	Damage	1911-2695/7331-10368 (Heroic)
Abilities	**Exploding Shot:** Inflicts 2125-2875 Physical damage and stuns for 6 sec.		
	Intimidating Shout: Paralyzes the target with terror for 6 sec. and causes all other nearby enemies to flee in fear.		
	Whirlwind: Lasts 4 sec. and inflicts normal damage plus 300.		
	Mortal Strike: Inflicts 150% weapon damage and leaves the target wounded, reducing the effectiveness of any healing by 50% for 5 sec.		
	Hamstring: Inflicts 20% of weapon damage, reducing movement speed by 60% for 10 sec.		

AN OFFICER'S MERIT

Cloak of Impulsiveness (Back 70 Armor, +18 Agi, +19 Stam, +40 Attack Power)

Ravenwing Pauldrons (Leather Shoulder 197 Armor, +19 Str, +19 Stam, +13 Int, +14 Spi, 1 [red socket], 1 [yellow socket], Socket Bonus: +3 Int, +26 Healing)

Iron Band of the Unbreakable (Finger 170 Armor, +27 Stam, +17 Defense)

Stormreaver Shadow-Kilt (Cloth Legs 123 Armor, +19 Stam, +26 Int, +14 Spi, +25 Spell Critical Rating, +30 Damage/Healing)

Uther's Ceremonial Warboots (Plate Feet 720 Armor, +19 Str, +21 Stam, +20 Int, +15 Damage/Healing, 8 Mana/5 Seconds)

Ranged DPS and healers should avoid being near Lieutenant Drake at all times. This keeps them out of range for Intimidating Shout and the Whirlwind swings. Your ranged members can either climb the stairs nearby to force Drake to rush up after them if the tanks are Feared, or you can try to stay back on the western side of the area.

If your ranged characters are on the upper tier, make sure to hop down if Lieutenant Drake comes up after you. This wastes enough of his time that even an unlucky tank should have their Fear break and be ready to Intercept or reengage.

Tremor Totem, Fear Ward, Deathwish, and other Anti-Fear abilities make it extremely easy for a tank to hold aggro during this fight. The Intimidating Shout is the only form of aggro dumping that Drake has.

Rest before engaging this boss, and be ready for a fight against a very tradition Warrior opponent. In Normal Mode, Drake has Whirlwind, Mortal Strike, and Intimidating Shout. It's great to have an offtank so that aggro can be traded if your main tank is hit with Mortal Strike and the healer is falling behind. Lacking that, have secondary healers be ready to take up the slack.

Secondary melee types, and even the main tank, should consider quick flight when Drake begins his Whirlwind spin. Getting hit by that attack is extremely mean (and even more so in Heroic Mode, so it's good to practice ducking out of range now).

Heroic Mode

In Heroic Mode, Drake learns how to play the ranged game. All of his normal attacks deal more damage, Whirlwind is horrifying in terms of the damage delivered, and the new Exploding Shot can hit a target for 2,000-3,000 damage and keep the person Stunned for several seconds. Ouch!

Master dodging the Whirlwind, time anti-Fear abilities as well as possible, and Drake shouldn't be too bad for a Heroic party!

TO THE WARCHIEF'S SIDE

With the confusion caused by this fast assault, your group should be clear to enter Durnholde Keep with little difficulty. Climb back up the stairs and walk up the hill toward the main building.

Take a very good look at the front entrance before approaching. There are four guards along the path, and a patrol comes all the way out to them. Wait until you are certain that the patrol is heading away before pulling; this patrol takes a very long time to come back, so you won't have to rush or worry.

The front group has a full mix (Warden, Sentry, Rifleman, and Veteran). As before, Wardens are the biggest threat and defeat proper crowd control. The kill or control list after that is Rifleman, Veteran, Sentry. The Veterans are new; they do more damage than Sentries.

Creep into Durnholde Keep and ambush the patrol on its way back to the front. Dispatch them quickly, then rest for another big fight. Just past the main stairs down is a group with the same configuration as the front door guards. There is no danger of adds, as you've already killed the only patrol. This means that Fear abilities and other crowd control techniques can be used with impunity.

Climb down the stairs on the right side and make sure that all group members who are doing the quest chain in Old Hillsbrad talk to Thrall. He'll complete the second stage of the chain and begin the third. When you've confirmed that everyone is ready, rested, and has turned in the second step, start the escort!

THINGS GET A BIT CRAZY

Thrall is a monster once he is let out of his cage. He'll hurry upstairs and get some gear. After outfitted properly, the young Orc is ready to face the world. He'll run outside and aggro the group of enemies that are waiting by the entrance. Here you will face a Warden, Veteran, Sentry, and Mage. Get that Warden under crowd control as soon as possible, put all DPS onto the Mage, and have your healer keep an eye on Thrall's health.

WARCHIEF THRALL IS VERY NEAT, WARCHIEF THRALL IS MADE OF MEAT

Even young Thrall is as tough as Mithril. He can tank just as well as your best people (better really), and there is no reason to have your tank try and rip aggro off of him unless you lose your healer. That shouldn't happen anyway, and the group is going to focus fire on the casters of these groups while Thrall happily tanks the Veteran/Sentry types.

Have your own group's tanks go into DPS mode to hurry through the softer enemies, then peel aggro from Thrall each time you need a new target to kill. Even a solo healer can often keep Thrall going and prevent your group's tank from getting knocked off.

A word of warning, though. Don't use crowd control on the targets that Thrall is hitting. He'll break Freezing Traps, Polymorph, or just about anything else. He's young and headstrong, and the big guy just doesn't understand that your group is squishier than he is.

There are some vocal cues as to Thrall's health state. As Thrall's health decreases, he'll state "Things are getting grim." That's a big sign for your healers to look to Thrall's health—before he declares that "Today is a good day to die."

If Thrall does die, for whatever reason, you have two spare chances to complete the Instance. Return to the last places where you spoke with Thrall and he'll be there waiting for you (Erozion's magic allows this to happen).

However, if Thrall dies three times, you must restart the Instance from the beginning and try again. Erozion can only do so much, and Thrall's third death spells a final alteration of the timeline. Oops!

There are three more such groups to face in rapid succession. Your characters must sit and eat/drink as quickly as possible when the fight ends to ensure that they get some of their health and mana back. One trick to help with this is to stay slow on DPS with the final enemy and make sure that everyone is ready to rest (rather than have them looking for more targets and such).

You can even let Thrall run ahead and start each engagement. This gives everyone more time to pick out their crowd control and tanking targets anyway, and Thrall has the health to survive it all.

Expect a similar fight at the base of the hill, and then another by the front of the bridge. You might be getting tired by this point, so Innervate/Evocation/Mana Gems and other forms of recuperation are wise. Even the tanks can bandage while Thrall is working on a final enemy in a group, which helps to extend the healer(s) mana supply too.

On the far side of the bridge is the last group fight before the second boss. This time it's all about DPS; there are two Veterans and two Mages. Use crowd control on both Mages, and even consider AoE abilities like Intimidating Shout or Psychic Scream if your group gets into trouble and might lose Thrall or one of your party members.

HE STOPS FOR NOBODY

You can't afford to lose a single person during this phase of the escort. There just isn't time for Resurrection unless you have a Druid who can use their in-combat Rez (yet one more reason why Druids rule with this Instance).

Thrall runs off each time a group is downed, so healers must be at their best. Even DPS classes need to be kept alive.

Those DPS classes must remember not to try and blow through everything and risk themselves during this phase, for the same reasons. Use bandages, avoid getting aggro as best you can, use Healthstones/Potions.

As soon as the Veteran/Mage group falls, rest and do a full med. Thrall will head out of Durnholde, but he'll be stopped by Captain Skarloc. Keep resting! Skarloc likes to monologue, and that will buy your group a few more precious seconds. Tanks and DPS classes should rise first, as the battle starts. Healers can afford to wait just a bit longer to get full mana.

CAPTAIN SKARLOC

HP	62796/95629 (Heroic)	Damage	1636-2304/4452-6290 (Heroic)
Abilities	**Devotion Aura**: Gives all nearby allies 1360 Armor.		
	Cleanse: Cleanses a friendly target, removing 1 poison effect, 1 disease effect, and 1 magic effect.		
	Holy Shield: Increases chance to block by 75% for 8 sec and deals 463 to 537 Holy damage for each attack blocked while active.		
	Hammer of Justice: Stuns an enemy for 6 sec.		
	Consecration: (Heroic Difficulty Only). Deals 15000 Holy damage over 20 sec to enemies who enter the area.		

THRALL ONLY CALLED DIBS ON THE HORSE

Scaled Greaves of Patience (Mail Legs 513 Armor, +28 Agi, +24 Stam, +13 Int, 1 [yellow socket], 1 [red socket], 1 [blue socket], Socket Bonus: +4 Dodge Rating, +46 Attack Power, 4 Mana/5 Seconds)

Stormfront Gauntlets (Mail Hands 367 Armor, +22 Stam, +16 Int, 1 [red socket], 1 [yellow socket], Socket Bonus: +3 Str, +19 Damage/Healing, 6 Mana/5 Seconds)

Northshire Battlemace (Mh Mace 41.3 DPS, +16 Stam, +15 Int, 5 Mana/5 Seconds, +161 Healing)

Amani Venom-Axe (1h Axe 62.8 DPS, +15 Stam, +15 Critical Rating, +26 Attack Power)

Durotan's Battle Harness (Plate Chest 1048 Armor, +31 Str, +34 Stam, 1 [blue socket], 2 [yellow socket], Socket Bonus: +4 Resilience Rating, +16 Critical Rating)

Captain Skarloc has a Warden and a Veteran flanking him. The Veteran isn't important at first, but the Warden sure is. Your first priority is to attack the Warden with all of your group's might, bringing the hapless foe down before they can be healed or heal themselves. Even the tank should be on the Warden, as Thrall will be engaging the Veteran and Skarloc.

Have your healer or at least a backup healer keep a moderate eye on Thrall's health. Heal Thrall as needed, and the group can turn its attention to the Veteran next. Again, this target will go down quite easily compared to the Captain, and it takes the Sentries DPS out of the fight and leaves only a single target to worry about.

Captain Skarloc can Cleanse, which means that you won't be able to use some crowd control methods while doing all this. Because the group is hitting the Warden first, that isn't a huge deal, as the Veteran is not a make-or-break target.

Note that you can Interrupt Captain Skarloc when he tries to heal, but the Captain cannot be Silenced; someone has to use a specific Interrupt while the boss is casting.

Once both of the lesser foes are out of the way, turn all DPS onto Skarloc and start whittling away at him. Though this boss has high health and some major survivability, his damage output is not very impressive. Without a backup healer or additional targets for DPS, he doesn't have much of a chance.

If your healer is very low on mana (because of getting poor rest leading into the boss fight), wait to pull aggro off of Thrall until Thrall's health starts to get quite low. This way, your main tank will have very high health when the Captain starts to beat on them; the delay is enough for the healer to get some mana back and for your group to get Captain Skarloc even lower in health.

Heroic Mode

The good captain has veen in training, because he has gained the Consecrate ability. This changes how long Thrall can be allowed to keep agro.

RIDING TO TARREN MILL

Rest and loot after Captain Skarloc falls, then talk to Thrall again when everyone is ready to go. Thrall will steal the Captain's horse and start riding toward Tarren Mill. Your group should mount and follow Thrall.

There is often a patrolling group along the way that Thrall will dismount and fight: two Lordaeron Watchmen and a Lordaeron Sentry. These foes are lower in level than what you've been fighting, and they pose no real risk to your people or to Thrall.

Follow Thrall to the outside of Tarren Mill and wait until all members of your party are assembled before speaking with Thrall again. The brave Orc storms into Tarren Mill once he is spoken to, and without fear he races into the stables.

Four of the town's defenders spawn outside the stables and converse with each other regarding the noise inside. They take absolutely no note of you, so your group can stay outside the stables and engage them as soon as they become aggressive. Hunters can ready freezing traps as they speak with each other, and any crowd control targets can be easily chosen at this time. Once the fight starts, Thrall rushes outside to help with the battle.

The Tarren Mill Protector and Guardsman are the less dangerous foes, so they can be tanked and ignored at first. Use crowd control on one or both of the Tarren Mill Lookouts. These archers pose more threat to the party.

Thrall won't give you much time once this fight ends, so sit to eat/drink as soon as you can. When ready, follow Thrall's route to the Tarren Mill church and look for another group of foes; this quartet has the same composition and can be defeated using the same crowd control and kill order.

A third such group waits on the upper floor of the inn, though this time your group will be moving into them. Hunters should stay just behind the tanks on the inn's stairs so that any Traps can be dispensed early in the fight without getting proximity aggro.

When the last foe is killed, Thrall will go into the room with Taretha. Have your party rest at this time, and rebuff as needed. Talking to Thrall and Taretha will trigger the final boss of the Instance, and the fighting will be rigorous. Put on as much pre-battle buffing as you can, then rest to restore any mana or health used in the process (e.g., put on Earthshield, use Rage for Battle Shout/Commanding Shout, create Mana Gems that have been used, hand out Healthstones).

The fight itself takes place just outside of the inn, so take that into consideration if placing Lightwells and such. If you have Priests or Paladins around, use buffs to raise the group's Resistance to Shadow damage. There is going to be a lot of it in the fighting ahead.

THE EPOCH HUNTER

HP	98130/149554 (Heroic)	Damage	1536-2165/5227-7393 (Heroic)
Abilities	**Sand Breath**: Inflicts 1700-2300 Arcane damage in a cone in front of the caster, reducing movement and increasing the time between attacks for 10 sec.		
	Frenzy: Increases attack speed by 50% for 8 sec.		
	Impending Death: Inflicts 750 Shadow damage every 3 sec. for 24 sec.		
	Magic Disruption Aura: Periodically removes magic effects from nearby enemies.		
	Wing Buffet: Deals 750 to 1250 Physical damage and knocks the target back.		

TREASURES OF TIME

Mantle of Perenolde (Leather Shoulder 197 Armor, +24 Stam, 2 [red socket], Socket Bonus: +3 Dodge Rating, +23 Hit Rating, +23 Critical Rating, +20 Attack Power)

Broxxigar's Ring of Valor (Finger +21 Str, +19 Stam, +17 Resilience Rating)

Pauldrons of Sufferance (Cloth Shoulder 105 Armor, +18 Stam, +13 Int, +19 Spi, 1 [blue socket], 1 [yellow socket], Socket Bonus: +3 Resilience Rating, +35 Healing)

Diamond Prism of Recurrence (Neck +12 Stam, +18 Int, +20 Spi, +26 Healing)

Time-Shifted Dagger (Mh Dagger 41.3 DPS, +15 Stam, +15 Int, +13 Spell Critical Rating, +85 Damage/Healing)

Thrall heads outside as soon as the final event is triggered. He'll prepare himself to face the Epoch Hunter who is flying above Tarren Mill. Yet, this Epoch Hunter is not a fool; it won't come down and let your group and Thrall have a clean run at it. Instead, it's getting ready to call friends of its own.

Before you get to take a crack at the Epoch Hunter, there are three waves of Dragonkin to defeat. These foes are Immune to Polymorph, but Hunter Traps and Druid Hibernate work perfectly well against them.

DRAGONKIN SPAWNS

- Group One: Three Dragonkin, west side of town
- Group Two: Three Dragonkin, south of the inn
- Group Three: Four Dragonkin, west side of town

Each engagement consists of melee and caster troops. The three types of Dragonkin are Infinite Slayers (high-survivability melee), Infinite Saboteurs (high-DPS melee), and Infinite Defilers (ranged casters, super DPS).

If you have a Druid, use Hibernate on the Defiler, kill the Saboteurs, then go after the Slayer. Otherwise, have all DPS go on the Defiler as soon as it spawns and tank the melee Dragonkin until the group is ready to go after them.

The Dragonkin are not Immune to Fear, so Warlocks can keep some of the Saboteurs off of the group while Defilers are either controlled or dispatched. Also, Intimidating Shout and Psychic Scream are very effective at buying the group time during the early and frantic stages of these fights. If you have access to multiple AoE Fears, decide ahead of time who has group three, then group two, then group one. You count backward because group three is the largest, so that is the engagement where you REALLY want to have an AoE Fear.

When the last Dragonkin is slain, your people have a few moments to eat and drink. Use this time to its fullest! Soon enough, the Epoch Hunter descends and engages the group. Have the group's main tank engage the Epoch Hunter first, then back toward the nearby building. Because of this boss's Knockback, it's very nice to have your tank sheltered by a wall.

Have all melee DPS stay behind the Epoch Hunter during this fight. There are no aggro dumps, so your tank should have aggro very smoothly as long as everyone knows how to control their DPS during the early part of the encounter.

Sand Breath is a castable cone attack that the boss uses with moderate frequency. Anyone in front of the creature takes damage, and a quick tank can run through the Epoch Hunter to avoid taking damage. Yet, if you are at all worried about this, just have the main tank stay in place (even a single healer can keep up if only the main tank is being hit by this).

The Epoch Hunter also uses Pending Doom, a moderate DOT. It uses Knockback as well. Your tank should be able to keep aggro, as they aren't losing time from the Knockbacks, and your healer won't be overhealing by keeping the whole group going.

After you've perfected the fights against the Dragonkin, it's actually fairly easy to beat the Epoch Hunter. Your group gets to start with full resources if you didn't lose anyone to the earlier enemies, and the Epoch Hunter doesn't have enough health to outlast a skilled healer. Thus, you win!

Loot the Epoch Hunter and talk to Erozion again when he appears. This completes the next step of the quest; the only stage remaining is to let Erozion teleport your group back to the present. Speak with Andormu there.

Everyone who completes this quest chain will gain access to The Black Morass (Opening of the Dark Portal). That Instance is also found in the Caverns of Time.

THE BLACK MORASS
(OPENING OF THE DARK PORTAL)

DUNGEON INFORMATION

Name	The Black Morass (Opening of The Dark Portal)
Location	Tanaris, Caverns of Time
Suggested Levels	Group of 5, Levels 68-70
Primary Enemies	Dragonkin and MORE Dragonkin
Damage Types	Physical, Arcane
Time to Complete	30 to 45 Minutes

WHO TO BRING

Any good healer can handle The Black Morass if you have a group that can Dispel/Spellsteal and use Tranquilizing Shot. If your group lacks these things, one of your DPS choices should be someone with backup healing (a Druid would be very nice).

JOBS	
CLASS	**ABILITIES**
Druid	Innervate, Hibernate, Backup Healing
Hunter	Freezing Traps, Tranquilizing Shot
Mage	Spellsteal
Paladin	Backup Healing, Tanking or Offtanking
Priest	Dispel, Prayer of Healing, Health Buff
Rogue	Destroying Adds
Shaman	Purge, Healing or Backup Healing
Warlock	Burning Adds and Keeping DOT DPS
Warrior	Tanking

The Black Morass has very specific boss fights, and certain classes can contribute immensely. For example, having a class to Dispel or Spellsteal during the second boss fight changes the battle from challenging to a cakewalk. Having a Hunter for the final boss fight does the same thing.

Thus, it's very useful to have a Hunter and one of the following for a Black Morass run (Priest, Shaman, or Mage). These aren't mandatory inclusions, but the difference is noticeable.

Beyond that, the Instance has a very intense DPS feel to it. Your group needs to be able to push through the content very quickly to succeed, so a good selection of damage dealers is necessary. Ignore crowd control, for once, and let people know that their damage output is what you are looking for! Try to get characters that sustain their DPS well instead of just having short bursts; Arms and Fury Warriors, Rogues, Warlocks, and Hunters are all good here.

GETTING TO THE CAVERNS OF TIME AND THE BLACK MORASS

The Caverns of Time are found in southeastern Tanaris. There are currently three Instances in there, with Opening of the Dark Portal being the second event that you can experience. To unlock access to this Instance, complete the events in Escape From Durnholde, as outlined in our earlier writeup.

The meeting stone for all Caverns of Time dungeons is just outside the cave itself. Form your groups here, then move down the lengthy tunnel into the pre-Instance area. There is a Quartermaster there for the Keepers of Time. You can purchase reagents for your classes, repair, and sell down there (all useful functions).

The Instance in the southwestern part of the Caverns of Time is the one to use for The Black Morass.

REPUTATION GAINS

ACTION	FACTION	REPUTATION GAIN	END POINT
Kill Trash Mobs	Keepers of Time	1 Point	Exalted
Kill Portal Leaders	Keepers of Time	50 Points	Exalted
Kill Bosses	Keepers of Time	120 Points	Exalted
Quest: The Black Morass (Chain)	Keepers of Time	8,500 Points	N/A

THE NIGHT EVERYTHING CHANGED

BOSSES

CHRONO LORD DEJA

TEMPORUS

AEONUS

MINIONS

BLACKFANG TARANTULA
Notes: Non-Elite, Poison

DARKWATER CROCOLISK
Notes: Non-Elite, High Health

INFINITE ASSASSIN
Notes: Melee Dragonkin, Kidney Shot

INFINITE CHRONOMANCER
Notes: Caster Dragonkin

INFINITE EXECUTIONER
Notes: Melee Dragonkin

INFINITE VANQUISHER
Notes: Melee Dragonkin

INFINITE WHELP
Notes: Comes in Groups of Three, Low Health

RIFT KEEPER
Notes: Controls a Portal, Abilities Vary

RIFT LORD
Notes: Controls a Portal, Abilities Vary

SABLE JAGUAR
Notes: Stealth, Low Health, Non-Elite

THE BLACK MORASS (CHAIN)

Level Requirement	67
Quest Giver	Sa'at
Quest Goal	Defend Medivh
Experience Reward	21,500
Additional Rewards	Band of the Guardian (Finger +11 Int, +17 Spell Critical Rating, +23 Damage/Healing, +15 Spell Penetration), Keeper's Ring of Piety (Finger +18 Spi, +42 Healing, 7 Mana/5 Seconds), Time-Bending Gem (Finger +19 Stam, +21 Dodge Rating, +36 Attack Power), Andormu's Tear (Finger +10 Defense Rating, +26 Dodge Rating, +15 Shield Block Rating)

Once you have completed all of the Escape From Durnholde events, Andormu urges you to enter The Black Morass and speak with Sa'at (who is just inside the Instance). Sa'at hands you a Chrono Beacon to aid in completing the Instance and gives you the next step in the chain (The Opening of the Dark Portal).

Read the strategies in this guide to learn how to beat this Instance comfortably, then do so. Return to Sa'at afterward and accept the final stage of the chain (Hero of the Brood). This takes you back outside the Instance to speak with Andormu. You receive a select of Ring rewards and will be able to start the quest chain for the Battle of Mount Hyjal!

MASTER OF ELIXIRS

Level Requirement	68, Alchemy
Quest Giver	Lorokeem (Northern Side of Lower City/Shattrath)
Quest Goal	Obtain 10 Essence of Infinity (See Below)
Experience Reward	13,900
Additional Rewards	Ability to Choose an Alchemy Mastery

This quest is for Alchemists only, but it is certainly worth doing. Once your Alchemist reaches high level, talk to your Alchemist Trainer in either Thrallmar or Honor Hold (depending on your faction, of course). Your Trainer will give you a choice for masteries, with Elixirs, Potions, and Transmutation being available. The quest that takes you into The Black Morass is the Master of Elixirs. If that is the Mastery you want, continue reading.

The first stage is to seek the Arrakoa Lorokeem in the northern side of Shattrath's Lower City.

Lorokeem wants you to bring 5 Elixirs of Major Defense, 5 Elixirs of Mastery, 5 Elixirs of Major Agility, and 10 Essences of Infinity. Harvest the herbs that you need for the Elixirs whenever you wish, but the Essences of Infinity must be gained from the enemies of the Infinity Dragonflight in the Black Morass. Head to the Caverns of Time and make one or two full runs of that Instance to gather these ingredients. Then, return to Lorokeem for your mastery.

This allows Alchemists to gain extra Elixirs during their crafting. It doesn't always proc, but it's still something that will add up over time and be a great benefit to you and your guild.

Just so that you know, the other two masteries involve Potions and Transmutation (these require you to go on different quests after speaking with your Trainer in Thrallmar/Honor Hold).

THE MASTER'S TOUCH

Level Requirement	68
Quest Giver	Khadgar (Shattrath City, Terrace of Light)
Quest Goal	Talk to Medivh in The Black Morass
Experience Reward	15,800
Additional Rewards	Continue Chain to Open Karazhan

To restore the Apprentice's Key for Karazhan, Medivh must be convinced to help out. The fact that he is no longer around is a slight poser, but it's nothing that can't be circumvented in the long run.

Travel to The Black Morass, complete the Instance normally (as per the walkthrough in this guide), then talk to Medivh when you are done. He'll restore the Apprentice's Key; return to Khadgar afterward to advance the quest chain.

TO BREAK THE WORLD AND TO SAVE IT

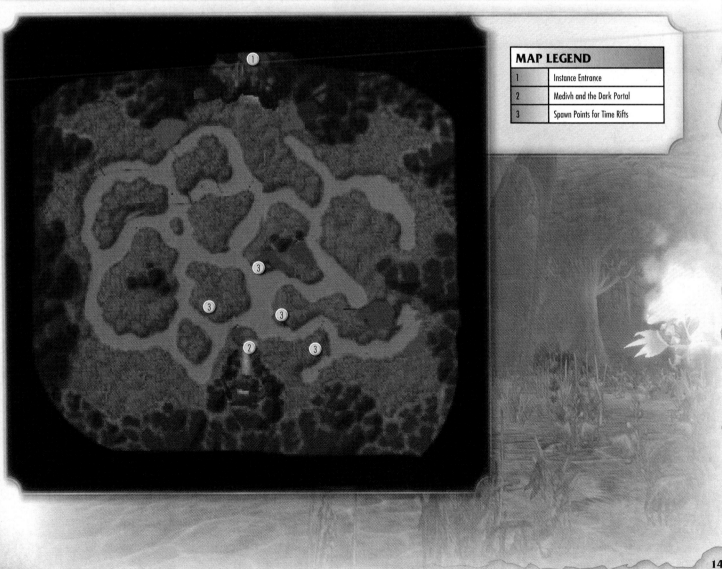

MAP LEGEND	
1	Instance Entrance
2	Medivh and the Dark Portal
3	Spawn Points for Time Rifts

MOVING TOWARD MEDIVH

Your first step into The Black Morass should be followed by looking for Sa'at, a member of the Keepers of Time who is standing close to the Instance portal. This NPC gives characters Chrono Beacons to help out with the Instance events; this is also the person you talk to for The Black Morass chain quest.

Chrono Beacons can't be used against bosses, but these useful items are quite effective for blasting through the non-boss monsters that you face during the events of this Instance. You have five Chrono Beacons to use (one for each character in your group), and each allows the group to gain a Drake ally for about ten seconds. The Drakes slap around the Portal leaders and their adds quite easily.

It's good to plan out when you group is going to use this; this prevents your buddies from using all of their Chrono Beacons at the same time. To give you more to think about, it's time to examine the way this Instance works (The Black Morass is very different from most Instances).

ONCE THINGS GET STARTED

Your group has time to relax and explore The Black Morass right now, before you approach Medivh. However, all of the challenges of this Instance come as an extended event, and once things get started you won't be able to stop in the middle.

Expect to face 18 waves of enemies, each with a powerful, Elite leader. Though only waves 6, 12, and 18 have formal bosses, the Portal leaders of the other waves are still solid opponents who demand most of your group's attention.

After approaching Medivh, at the southern tip of The Black Morass, the Portals start to open. Your group can only close a Portal by killing its leader, and future Portals open whether or not you are ready. In other words, these Portals are timed, and falling behind in the count leads to failure.

Not only must you keep your group alive and in decent health; Medivh must be protected. Though this legendary caster has created a shield around himself, the Dragonkin of the Infinite Dragonflight are able to beat through this over time. Thus, you have to close each Portal AND keep adds from getting to Medivh for very long. It's a lot of fun, but it's challenging until you learn the rhythm.

Make sure that your group stays together by Sa'at until everyone is ready to go. Explain the general idea of the Instance to other characters, and have people buff, have out consumables, and get into a voice communication program if one is available.

Then, travel south as a packet. There are many monsters in the area. Though these Tarantulas, Jaguars, and Crocolisks are non-Elite, they have moderate health and can do enough damage to threaten a softer character. You can mount if you like, but it's easiest to just plow through the monsters, fighting them as they come and having a good time.

You can see Medivh's came from a fair distance; there is a shining light that flickers from the area near the Dark Portal, and that guides you toward Medivh. Don't get too close until everyone is ready to begin the event; you won't even need to speak with Medivh to start things.

Look on the map that we've provided to get an idea where the Rift Portals spawn; there are four places where these appear, and it is random with each run. The only given is that a Portal won't appear in the same place as one that you've just closed (so there are only three places to look each time you shut a Portal).

Each Portal has a bright, golden shine that marks itself clearly in the darkness of The Black Morass. As soon as a character spots a Portal, they should tap the mini-map and alert the rest of the party to its location. This gets everyone moving in the right direction without delay.

PORTALS ONE-TO-SIX

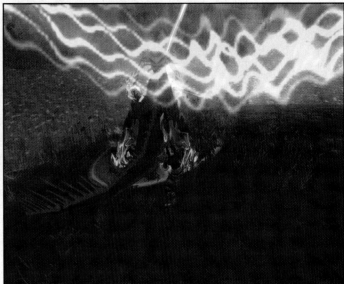

There first six Portals are well-spaced, so groups won't often fall behind in the count unless they are considerably heal-heavy or light on DPS. Use this time to get the flow of battle mastered. Portals without bosses should not get to land a single add against Medivh's shield; once your group is used to fighting off the adds, it should be entirely doable to kill the first boss with the shield at 100% without even using a Chrono Beacon.

Rest between Portals, even if the next Portal is already opening. You can't afford to run out of mana and face a party wipe just because you were worried about Medivh. It takes time for the adds to leave a Portal and reach the shield. Use that time, get your mana back, and move on.

Tanks and melee DPSers should be the first to move in on a Portal, as these characters are the fastest to get their rest completed. If the new Portal has been open for a few moments, intercept the adds and bring them back toward the Portal as you go. Ranged DPS needs its mana but can head in next, then healers should be the final ones to rise.

The Elites that guard each Portal also have a random table that determines which powers they have. Some are casters (Warlock versions have AoE Shadowbolts, Curses for Increased Spell Damage Taken, and Fear while Mage versions have Blast Waves, Frostbolt, Polymorph, and Pyroblast), and some are tankier (Sunder Armor + Thunderclap or Mortal Strike). Of these, only the Warlocks are able to unleash high damage against a party. When these appear it's worth placing even more DPS on them if your group is at all shaky.

When the sixth Portal opens, make sure that every character is full on health and mana, then gather for a bigger fight. The first boss leaves this Portal, but adds continue to spill out during this engagement. Let these beat on the shield, then use a Chrono Beacon when the boss fight ends to help clean up the mess quickly. This often costs only 20% or so of the shield's energy, and the upshot is that the first boss is much easier when all five characters are focused on defeating it.

THE INFINITE!

For the standard Rift Portals (1-5, 7-11, 13-17), there is a fairly standard assortment of enemies. Near the Portal itself will be an Elite Dragonkin with high health and powerful abilities. Though you can sometimes drag these enemies away from their Portals, they won't wander on their own. These Rift Lords and Rift Keepers are the ones to kill when you want to close a Portal.

Over time, non-Elite Dragonkin and Whelps pour through the Portal and immediately rush to attack Medivh. These enemies won't automatically aggro on your party, but you usually want to intercept them and defeat these foes before they have a chance to beat on the shield.

Melee DPS classes are best for intercepting these enemies, but classes that can do damage and get back to the Elite are quite useful too.

The main tank for the group should engage the Rift leader as soon as possible when each Portal opens. The group's healer(s) need to stay in range over there as well, while the DPS characters kill off non-Elites and try to lay damage on the leader when possible.

The Infinite non-Elites include melee Dragonkin, caster Dragonkin, and Whelps. None of these are terribly powerful, though the Whelps come in groups of three. If a character is fighting these adds with area-of-effect attacks, be certain to stay close to the Elite so that your damage nails it as well. (Example: Have an Arms Warrior use Cleaves and Sweeping Strikes to get aggro from the enemies as they leave the Portal. The foes can then be offtanked while damage continues against the Elite)

Instead of trying to have one character take the adds, it's good to let all three DPS characters in a group spend part of their time getting adds. Not only does this even out the damage these characters take; it allows for burst damage against the Elite in-between the kills. Because the main tank is on the Elite the entire time, DPS characters who free themselves from adds for a moment can use ANY and ALL damage attacks on the Elite without fear of getting any aggro at all.

CHRONO LORD DEJA

HP	88545/118060 (Heroic)	Damage	1454-2055/3637-5138 (Heroic)
Abilities	**Time Lapse**: Increases the time between attacks by 60% and slows movement by 60% for 10 sec.		
	Arcane Discharge: Inflicts 2313 to 2687 Arcane damage in an area around the caster. **Heroic**: Inflicts 3700 to 4300 Arcane damage in an area around the caster.		
	Arcane Blast: Blasts with Arcane magic, inflicting normal damage plus 3063 to 3937 and knocks back. **Heroic**: Inflicts normal damage plus 4500 to 5500 and knocks back.		

DEJA LOOT, ALL OVER AGAIN

Ring of Spiritual Precision (Finger +13 Stam, +18 Int, +15 Spi, 7 Mana/5 Seconds)

Mantle of Three Terrors (Cloth Shoulder 197 Armor, +29 Stam, +25 Int, +12 Spell Hit Rating, +29 Damage/Healing)

Mask of Inner Fire (Mail Head 516 Armor, +30 Stam, +34 Int, +22 Spell Critical Rating, +39 Damage/Healing)

Melmorta's Twilight Longbow (Bow 64.5 DPS, +15 Stam, +30 Attack Power)

Sun-Gilded Shouldercaps (Leather Shoulder 214 Armor, +25 Agi, +26 Stam, +15 Hit Rating, +48 Attack Power)

Burnoose of Shifting Ages (Back 216 Armor, +15 Stam, +26 Defense Rating, +29 Shield Block Value)

Deja is the easiest of the three bosses in The Black Morass; he is easy to keep on your main tank, and his damage is often fairly low. Beyond normal melee damage, Deja only attacks other members with his AoE Arcane Blast. This deals Arcane damage to everyone in the group, as the range for it is rather impressive.

Luckily, Arcane Blast only hits for a couple-thousand points per occasion, and Deja can't use it terribly often. The Time Lapse debuff that the Chrono Lord puts on the group is a pain, but it doesn't change the outcome of things and it can be dispelled.

Leave DPS on Deja throughout the fight, then rush to clean up his adds afterward.

Heroic Mode

While Deja doesn't get any new abilities, it is worth mentioning that Arcane Discharge and Arcane Blast both hit much harder in Heroic mode.

PORTALS SEVEN-TO-TWELVE

There is a long lull between the Deja's death and the opening of Portal Seven. Don't worry, as the fun is going to start again before long. If you lost any characters during the boss fight, there is plenty of time to rez now. Otherwise, rest and let any Skinners go about to take care of the lucrative corpses that are sitting around (the Portal leaders are especially nice to Skin).

The fighting during the next set of Portal openings is not too much tougher than the first set. You face very similar foes, and the rate of Portal openings is only slightly higher than it was earlier.

Your real challenge comes when Portal Twelve opens and Temporus comes out. This second boss is a deadly foe until a group learns how to cripple him.

TEMPORUS

HP	110700/147600 (Heroic)	**Damage**	1829-2587/4265-6032 (Heroic)
Abilities	**Blink**: Teleports the caster 20 yd. forward unless something is in the way. Also, frees the caster from any bonds.		
	Hasten: Increases melee and movement speed by 200%.		
	Mortal Wound: Inflicts a wound that reduces all healing effects by 10% for 15 sec. Stacks up to 10 times.		
	Spell Reflection: (Heroic mode only) Reflect all spells for 6 sec.		

THERE IS ALWAYS TIME TO LOOT

Epoch-Mender (Staff 59.9 DPS, +37 Stam, +35 Int, +227 Healing, 12 Mana/5 Seconds)

Khadgar's Kilt of Abjuration (Cloth Legs 133 Armor, +20 Stam, +22 Int, +15 Spi, 1 [yellow socket], 2 [blue socket], Socket Bonus: +5 Spell Damage, +36 Damage/Healing)

Laughing Skull Battle-Harness (Mail Chest 635 Armor, +28 Agi, +29 Stam, +20 Int, 1 [red socket], 1 [yellow socket], 1 [blue socket], Socket Bonus: 2 Mana/5 Seconds, +40 Attack Power)

Hourglass of the Unraveller (Trinket +32 Critical Rating, Chance on Hit to Add 300 Attack Power for 10 Seconds)

Millennium Blade (1h Sword 69.5 DPS, +19 Stam, +21 Resilience Rating)

Star-Heart Lamp (Off-Hand +17 Stam, +19 Int, +12 Spell Hit Rating, +22 Damage/Healing)

Temporus is the hardest boss of the Instance before you know how to do him; taking this foe on without the proper tricks makes him seem amazingly powerful (even cheap at times). Then, you learn about where he is getting his power and everything changes quite suddenly.

Temporus stacks a Mortal Wound on his primary aggro target; this debuffs healing by 10% per stack and can go all the way up to a 90% debuff. That pretty much spells death no matter what the healing situation is. Couple that with this creature's Taunt Immunity and things sound rough. Wait, it gets worse.

Temporus also has a self-Haste that increases his attack speed into the stratosphere. He'll lay on almost 1,000 damage a hit onto your tanks without even a second in-between swings, and each of those blows carries the Mortal Wound farther along. Yikes!

Luckily, that Haste can be Dispelled or taken with Spellsteal. Yes! You can totally destroy Temporus' damage output by doing this as often as he brings the debuff. Have your Mage keep Detect Magic on this boss to know when to cast Spellsteal, have your Priest or Shaman look for the white glow that occurs when the Haste lands.

Not only does this trash the output of your foe; it removes a big part of the Mortal Wound threat. This is because Mortal Wound only has a light cooldown. A good tank can Dodge/Parry enough to let the debuff collapse on its own as long as Haste doesn't enter the equation!

If your group lacks a Mage, Priest, and Shaman, then aggro trading is a must. Temporus will destroy a tank eventually, and Haste makes it all the faster. Have a second target build aggro on Temporus and use a strong push once the main tank gets a second or third Mortal Wound.

Warrior tanks also have the option to Intervene with a distant friendly character and stay away from Temporus long enough to let the debuff collapse.

Don't try to drag Temporus too far away from his Portal; he will hit his tether and snap back to it, healing in the process. It's not a happy experience for a group, though the boss can still be defeated.

Heroic Mode

Besides hitting much harder and having more hit points, Temporus gains the Spell Reflect ability. Be aware when this is up or the party could easily wipe.

THE FINAL SIX

Loot Temporus once he falls and get the last easy rest you have. The final six Portals are going to spawn without much delay at all, and your group is certain to be tested even if they are quite effective at bringing down adds.

Use a Chrono Beacon to clear away the creatures that got past you during the Temporus fight. The shield should still be at very high health, if your group has been solid about taking down enemies apart from the two boss fight. Beyond that, you've only used two of your Chrono Beacons, leaving three more for the final push!

Because the rate of Portal spawns is so high in the next grouping, you want to blow through the first two sets of enemies as quickly as you can. For the next three Portals afterward, use Chrono Beacons to ensure that the Portals are closed quickly and without your group using much of their own resources. As such, there is no threat of having the final Portal open when your group is behind in the fighting.

The last boss is going to step out while you have only brief resting needs. Go ahead and get that short breather as the boss approaches Medivh, then engage as soon as your people are ready.

AEONUS

HP	147600/199260 (Heroic)	**Damage**	2399-3393/5227-7540 (Heroic)	
Abilities	**Sand Breath:** Inflicts 3063 to 3937 Arcane damage in a cone in front of the caster, reducing movement and increasing the time between attacks for 10 sec. **Heroic:** This spell deals 4375 to 5625 Arcane damage.			
	Time Stop: Stuns all nearby targets for 4 sec.			
	Frenzy: Increases melee attack speed by 50% for 8 sec.			
	Cleave: Deals 110% damage to the target and its nearby allies, affecting up to 3 targets.			

TIME HAS RUN ITS COURSE.

Bloodfire Greatstaff (63.0 DPS, +42 Stam, +42 Int, +28 Spell Critical Rating, +121 Damage/Healing)

Cowl of the Guiltless (Leather Head 237 Armor, +28 Stam, +30 Dodge Rating, +31 Resilience Rating, +52 Attack Power)

Handgrips of Assassination (Leather Hands 183 Armor, +25 Agi, +24 Stam, +17 Hit Rating, +50 Attack Power)

Helm of Desolation (Mail Head 530 Armor, +21 Stam, +25 Int, +14 Critical Rating, +66 Attack Power)

Latro's Shifting Sword (1h Sword 71.8 DPS, +15 Agi, +14 Sword Skill, +26 Attack Power)

Legplates of the Bold (Plate Legs 1019 Armor, +31 Str, +19 Agi, +45 Stam, +26 Defense Rating)

Legplates of the Righteous (Plate Legs 1019 Armor, +27 Stam, +24 Int, +26 Defense Rating, 10 Mana/5 Seconds, +28 Damage/Healing)

Mana-Etched Crown (Cloth Head 127 Armor, +27 Stam, +20 Int, 1 [red socket], 1 [meta socket], Socket Bonus: +4 Resilience Rating, +15 Spell Penetration, +34 Damage/Healing)

Moonglade Pants (Leather Legs 256 Armor, +25 Str, +16 Agi, +24 Stam, +25 Int, +23 Spi, +55 Healing)

Pauldrons of the Crimson Flight (Plate Shoulder 873 Armor, +40 Str, +28 Stam)

Primal Surge Bracers (Mail Wrist 285 Armor, +15 Stam, +18 Int, +37 Healing, 6 Mana/5 Seconds)

Scarab of the Infinite Cycle (Trinket +70 Healing, Chance When Casting Healing Spells to Add +320 Spell Haste for 6 Seconds)

Aeonus is large and mean, and he'll be pretty rough if you don't have a Hunter. If you do, Tranquilizing Shot should be used each time Aeonus' claws burn red with energy. Otherwise, expect to see major damage throughout the fight, and your healer is going to need to top off the tank frequently.

The main tank's job is to engage Aeonus and get that creep turned away from the party as soon as possible. This helps avoid the Arcane AoE that Aeonus likes to use; though the tank is still hit with it, nobody else should be. More importantly, it allows melee attacks without the repercussions of Sand Breath and Cleave.

Next, as the tank builds aggro, the healer stays on top of the situation and doesn't have to worry about any of the other characters (Aeonus is quite fixed on who he likes to hurt). DPS characters start lightly, as always, and can built up as soon as the tank starts to get major abilities off.

Don't worry about aggro wipes; Aeonus doesn't have any. Though his ability to Stop Time is scary, it affects everyone equally and as such does nothing to change the aggro list.

Have the tank use abilities on timers and trinkets early in the fight to get extra aggro and have DPS characters save their timed abilities until later on (the best time for important buffs like Deathwish or Bloodlust is just after a Time Stop has ended).

Heroic Mode

Aeonus' Sand Breath is disasterous in Heroic mode. The healer will have to keep a close eye on the main tank. It is more vital than ever to turn Aeonus away from the party.

Without a good plan, The Black Morass is a foul and deadly place to tread. However, the strategies laid out in this guide turn the Instance into a great place for fast farming and easy victories. Return here for more loot, to earn Keepers of Time Reputation, or just to have fun running others through the event.

THE MECHANAR

DUNGEON INFORMATION

Name	The Mechanar
Location	Tempest Keep, Netherstorm
Suggested Levels	Group of 5, Level 70
Primary Enemies	Demons, Blood Elves
Damage Types	Physical, Arcane, Some Fire
Time to Complete	50 to 80 Minutes

WHO TO BRING

AoEs are relatively common by the enemies in The Mechanar, so melee DPS classes should make some extra bandages ahead of time, especially if their gear isn't quite up to snuff yet (though if you have two healers, they can probably heal through many of the problems that come up in the regular encounters).

The volume of Demons here makes it wise to have a Hunter or Warlock along to add some crowd control when Mages and Rogues are prevented from working their best methods.

JOBS

CLASS	ABILITIES
Druid	Innervate and backup Healing
Hunter	Traps add needed CC against Demons, Ranged DPS
Mage	Polymorph, DPS
Paladin	Fully capable of healing or tanking in Mechanar
Priest	Mind Control, Healing, Psychic Scream
Rogue	Sapping, DPS
Shaman	Fire Resistance Totem, Emergency Elemental
Warlock	DPS, Fel Hunter
Warrior	Intimidating Shout, Tank

The Mechanar is a relatively short Instance, with two Mini-Bosses and three normal Bosses. Arcane damage is the damage form to beat in many of the fights, so it is quite wise to carry any Arcane Resistance gear that your characters have; it's obviously most important to do this if you are going to be the main tank.

Almost all of the engagements are quite small, with four enemies being as big as all of the forced encounters get. This means that even modest crowd control will get your people through the day, and a single tank of quality is more than enough to do the job. In addition, a single healer of the appropriate specialization is acceptable!

So, a standard configuration of a main tank, three DPS characters, and one good healer would be great. If you trade a DPS person for a healer/DPS hybrid or a second healer that will be fun as well.

GETTING TO THE MECHANAR

The Mechanar is often listed as the first of the Tempest Keep Instances, though The Botanica is equivalent in difficulty. In any event, your group can seek The Mechanar by flying to the right-most tower of Tempest Keep and walking straight into the dungeon from there. No key is required!

REPUTATION GAINS

ACTION	FACTION	REPUTATION GAIN	END POINT
Kill Trash Mobs	The Sha'tar	20	Exalted
Kill Bosses	The Sha'tar	120 Points	Exalted

WHERE DEMONS TREAD

BOSSES

MECHANO-LORD CAPACITUS

NETHERMANCER SEPETHREA

PATHALEON THE CALCULATOR

MINIONS

TEMPEST-FORGE PATROLLER
Notes: Knockback, Calls for Help at low Health, Charged Arcane Missle

TEMPEST-FORGE DESTROYER
Notes: Charged Fist, Very High Health, Knockdown

SUNSEEKER NETHERBINDER
Notes: Low Health, Summon Two AoE Adds, Starfire, Arcane Nova, Dispel Magic

BLOODWARDER SLAYER
Notes: Whirlwind, Mortal Strike

BLOODWARDER CENTURION
Notes: Shield Bash, High Health

BLOODWARDER PHYSICIAN
Notes: Heals, Anesthetic, Bandage, Holy Shock

MECHANAR DRILLER
Notes: Drill Armor, Glob of Machine Fluid, Short-Term CC

MECHANAR WRECKER
Notes: Short Term CC, Low Health, High Damage Output, Pound, Glob of Machine Fluid

MECHANAR TINKERER
Notes: Non-Elite AoE Mob, Hard to Position, Very High DPS, Netherbomb, Maniacal Charge

MECHANAR CRUSHER
Notes: The Claw, Glob of Machine Fluid

SUNSEEKER ASTROMAGE
Notes: Fire Shield (Use Spellsteal), Solarburn, Scorch

SUNSEEKER ENGINEER
Notes: Super Shrink Ray, Death Ray, Grow Ray

QUEST LISTING

HOW TO BREAK INTO THE ARCATRAZ

Level Requirement	70
Quest Giver	A'dal (Shattrath City, Terrace of Light)
Quest Goal	Defeat Pathaleon and Collect The First Part of The Arcatraz Key
Experience Reward	19,000
Additional Rewards	Key to The Arcatraz

A full dungeon run of The Mechanar is required to complete this quest (as is a full run of The Botanica, which is covered in the next section of the guide). Read through the entire walkthrough and lead a group against Pathaleon the Calculator, at the end of the Instance. Defeating him will get you one section of the key. Once you have both pieces, return to A'dal in Shattrath City and turn these in for future access to The Arcatraz, the final 5-characte dungeon in Tempest Keep.

FRESH FROM THE MECHANAR

Level Requirement	67
Quest Giver	David Wayne (Eastern Terokkar Forest)
Quest Goal	Get an Overcharged Manacell from The Mechanar
Experience Reward	12,300
Additional Rewards	Continues Chain

This step in the chain to create a powerful anti-Demon weapon calls for you to take a group into The Mechanar, though duos of stealthing characters have managed to pull this off as well (Mages with Invisibility, Druids and Rogues with Stealth, etc.). Hunters using Feign Death repeatedly and other classes with Invisibility Potions have also pulled this off. Remember to remove your gear before attempting this, as there is no need to take a Durability hit from any deaths that occur while perfecting the technique.

Seek the Manacells from the area just south of the first boss (Mechano-Lord Capacitus). It is very easy to spot these items as you make your approach. The Manacells are bright purple, so you won't miss them. Return to David Wayne once you have what you need!

THE TURNING OF GEARS AND THE GNASHING OF TEETH

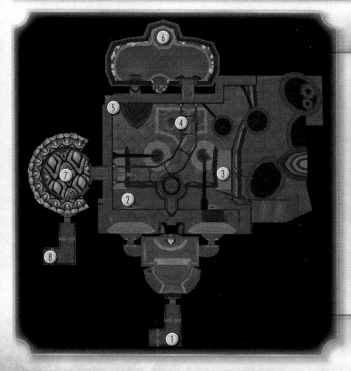

MAP LEGEND	
1	Entrance
2	Gatewatcher Gyro-Kill
3	Gatewatcher Iron-Hand
4	Mechano-Lord Capacitus
5	Cache of the Legion and Elevator to Second Floor
6	Nethermancer Sepethrea
7	Spawning Point for Pathaleon the Calculator
8	Back Exit (Second Floor)

TEMPEST KEEP, AT LAST

There is quite a lot of fighting to do in the first room of The Mechanar, so settle in and make sure that everyone is ready before even trying the first pull. Get all buffs up, and let everyone know who is handling which buffs, totems, blessings, and so forth.

There is a Tempest-Forge Patroller in the center of the far wall. This Patroller has two other Golems of its type that wander all the way out to its position. Pull this Patroller when there is nothing else nearby to keep the first fight simple.

Patrollers are somewhat slow to kill, but they aren't nearly as mean as the Destroyer Golems that you will see later in the dungeon. Their AoE does not do much damage, and its Knockback is more annoying that deadly as long as nobody stands directly behind the Patrollers until the target is all the way over to the group.

REINFORCEMENTS ARE ON THE WAY! BUT NOT FOR YOU!

When low on health, Patrollers do enjoy calling for help, so keep that well in mind. Always pull Patrollers far back and away from anything that could possibly add.

Get the two wandering Patrollers as each reaches the center, where the first foe once stood. Then, when ready, take on the two groups of Blood Elves in the room. Each cluster has a Physician, a Netherbinder, and a Slayer. Kill Physicians first, hit Netherbinders with a long-term crowd control ability like Polymorph, and tank the Slayers away from the group or hit them with secondary crowd control (like Hunter Traps and such).

Never let the evil Netherbinders do what they want. These foul Warlocks can pull out massive damage and summoned non-Elite Elementals that have their own AoEs. It's ugly to see what this can do to a group, so whoever hits the Netherbinder with crowd control should be very clear to let the group know if/when control breaks.

Slayers and Centurions are both seen in this dungeon; they are tanking mobs, with Slayers being the DPS version (Whirlwind and Mortal Strike are their calling cards) and Centurions being more defensive. In each case, these are the lesser foes of any group.

Physicians have Sleep and are a major thorn in your side because of it. Don't let them live for long, and indeed their health is so low that they cannot survive a concerted attack.

When the room is clear except for the side hallways, turn to the right and look ahead. Another Patroller comes all the way out from there, and you must wait for it to get far enough forward to pull safely. If you do not, the group of Blood Elves behind the Golem will aggro as well (exit the dungeon if that happens).

Kill the Physician and Slayer afterward, then advance into the next room.

THE FIRST GATEWATCHER

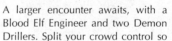

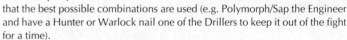

Two more Blood Elves are at the top of the next ramp as the corridor turns north. Kill these by pulling them back to your party, then hug the left wall as everyone advances. This allows the group to get around the pillars, free their line-of-sight, and see the next fight before pulling it!

A larger encounter awaits, with a Blood Elf Engineer and two Demon Drillers. Split your crowd control so that the best possible combinations are used (e.g. Polymorph/Sap the Engineer and have a Hunter or Warlock nail one of the Drillers to keep it out of the fight for a time).

Kill whatever can't be stopped via crowd control, then go after the enemies in order of duration, thus Hunter targets would be first as their traps would be the first to break.

Not far away, the second fight on the top of the ramp has a Crusher and two Tinkerers. This seems like a smaller fight, but it really isn't. Tinkerers are a massive pain in the rear, with their AoE damage and frustrating urge to stand wherever they please. You can't gather them easily for AoE attacks, so single-target DPS is the way to go for taking Tinkerers out.

Thus, use crowd control on the Crusher if available and get all DPS onto the Tinkerers. If crowd control isn't available or if it breaks, have the tank gather the Driller's aggro while the rest of the party continues beating on the little guys until they are both dead. Remember to keep ranged DPS and healers away from the skirmish to prevent deadly incoming damage.

Kill the Physician and the Slayer on the far ramp next while the Gatewatcher is patrolling away. This leaves tons of the room for the Mini-Boss fight coming up.

GATEWATCHER IRON-HAND

HP	121770/164389 (Heroic)	**Damage**	2091-2957/4182-5914 (Heroic)
Abilities	**Stream of Machine Fluid**: 20 yard range, Reduces attack speed by 35% for 10 sec. Reduces armor by 35% for 10 sec.		
	Jackhammer: Inflicts 1568 to 1732 damage every second for 8 secs. **Heroic**: Deals 3135 to 3465 Physical damage every second for 8 secs.		
	Shadow Power: Increases attack speed by 100%. **Heroic**: Increases attack speed by 115%.		
	Hammer Punch: Inflicts weapon damage plus 720 and stuns for 6 seconds.		

Iron-Hand is the nastier of the two Mini-Bosses in The Mechanar, though it's more efficient to take him on first. You have to defeat both of these targets anyway to access the higher level of the dungeon, and the group receives a Rare piece of treasure later on for killing them both anyway.

Iron-Hand should be tanked near the wall of the ramp, though still up top. This leaves tons of room for people to see what is going on and stay at range during the encounter. The tank should keep their back to the wall so that the Stream of Machine Fluid attack Iron-Hand uses won't hit anyone else.

Iron-Hand's Shadow Power doubles his damage output in melee, but it can be healed through and dealt with by a single person, so that isn't the nastier part of the fight.

Instead, this Mini-Boss will give people a five-second warning before using his Jack Hammer. There is a text message and Iron-Hand glows while preparing anyway, so it's very clear that something evil is imminent.

Have all non-tanks and possible the tank as well ditch the area. Iron-Hand won't follow. Extremely tough tanks or groups with extra healing may wish to avoid the hassle and heal through the AoE that follows this charging period.

Don't forget to collect the Crystal that falls when the Gatewatcher dies. This, combined with the second Crystal from the other Gatewatcher, will open a chest soon enough.

Heroic Mode

The primary changes are increased damage from Jackhamer and a vastly more powerful version of Shadow Power.

After resting, move down the ramp and assault the Blood Elves at the base. There is a Centurion guarding a Netherbinder and a Physician. Use the same routine that you've already established to control the Netherbinder and eliminate the others.

Then, pull the two Tinkerers and the two Drillers from the area ahead. Use any crowd control on the Drillers while DPS characters go to town on the Tinkerers (have any non-controlled Drillers get grabbed by the main tank of the party).

For the next and final fight before the first boss, pull the Engineer, Driller, and Wrecker that are slightly on the left. Use one form of control on the Engineer if possible, then Trap/Banish the Driller. Kill the Wrecker, as these foes have low health and will die so quickly that the other enemies will still be under control if you are lucky.

Get another moment to catch your breath afterward, and discuss the color cues with your party. Capacitus is not a good foe to go against without a solid idea of what needs to be done when. And as always, good positioning will save lives and repair bills.

MECHANO-LORD CAPACITUS

HP	121770/258300 (Heroic)	**Damage**	2091-2957/2091-2957 (Heroic)
Abilities	**Head Crack**: Reduces Stamina by 200 for 15 sec.		
	Reflective Damage Shield: Surrounds the caster with a protective shield that inflicts 750 Arcane damage to melee attackers; Lasts 10 sec.		
	Reflective Magic Shield: Surrounds the caster with a protective shield that reflects 100% of harmful spells for 10 sec.		
	Summon Nether Charge: Summons a floating nether charge, deals 2269-3231 Arcane damage in a 15 yard radius every 3 seconds for 18 seconds.		
	Polarity Shift: Heroic Difficulty Only. Places a Positive or Negative on all players which increase the damage when standing near players with the same charge. Deals 2000 damage to nearby players with the opposite charge every 5 sec.		

I HOPE THIS STUFF ISN'T COVERED IN HEAVY METALS

Hammer of the Penitent (Mh Mace 41.4 DPS, +16 Int, +13 Spi, +227 Healing, 6 Mana/5 Seconds)

Lunar-Claw Pauldrons (Leather Shoulder 219 Armor, +23 Stam, +26 Int, +17 Spi)

Plasma Rat's Hyper-Scythe (Polearm 93.3 DPS, +42 Str, +45 Stam, +26 Critical Rating)

Thoriumweave Cloak (Back 318 Armor, +35 Stam)

Warp Engineer's Prismatic Chain (Neck +17 Stam, +18 Int, +16 Spell Critical Rating, +19 Damage/Healing)

Your main tank should be using any Arcane Resistance gear that they have to mitigate as much damage as possible.

When Capacitus glows red, all melee damage must stop. This effect is a damage shield, and all of the incoming melee attacks will just end up biting your people where it hurts. Alternately, Capacitus will glow green. This is the cue for DPS spells to stop, as they will then be reflected. In-between those periods, all damage is acceptable.

Coming in from the angle your group has provides a huge amount of room for the upcoming fight against Capacitus. This is quite useful, as it means that the ranged members of the group can spread out in semi-circle well behind the main tank. This will soon prove invaluable.

Capacitus has a few nice tricks of his own, but honestly, he'd be nothing without his bombs. These flying spawns deal a huge amount of Arcane damage to anything near them when they explode. There is only a brief moment or two from when the fuses light before the detonation occurs.

Though the main tank can only strafe about along the eastern side of Capacitus' area while keeping the boss in range of the DPS, all of the other characters are free to reposition and avoid incoming explosives. This makes the healer(s) job so much easier.

Melee DPS has the worst of things in this fight, and they should endeavor to Bandage, back off and avoid the blasts, and generally consider brief retreats if the healers are fine on mana but are having a tough time keeping up.

Heroic Mode

This fight is really cool in Heroic Mode, as there are actually major changes to the dynamic. Instead of worrying about the melee and magical reflects, your group needs to figure out alternative positioning (before the fight begins). The standard pattern would be to say that positive people should go on the left side of the fight when the shift occurs and that negative characters should run to the right.

What happens is that Capacitus gives each person in the party a charge (positive or negative). You have to get everyone who has the same charge together while keeping opposites from destroying each other. Not only does this save your group from wiping to the damage caused by the charge opposition; it gives your people a bonus to damage from being near those of equal charge!

That is good, because the fight is now on a timer. If you can't kill Capacitus in three minutes, it's time to wipe and start over.

BACK TO THE FRONT

When the group has recovered from its momentous battle, be careful of any bombs that are still in the area; they can blow up if anyone approaches, and they still do full damage. If anyone in the group needs the Manacells, clear the demons on the other side of Capacitus' area and get those now. Otherwise, retreat to the front of the Instance!

Take out the Patroller there (this time from the left side) when it's at the far end of its path. Then, destroy the Slayer and Physician behind that point. Another Physician and Slayer are up the ramp around the corner, and these can be taken out with ease.

Next, hug the right side of the wall and have your tank pull Gatewatcher Gyro-Kill back into the ramp area. There is plenty of room there for the fight.

GATEWATCHER GYRO-KILL

HP	92250/124538 (Heroic)	Damage	2091-2957/4182-5914 (Heroic)
Abilities	**Stream of Machine Fluid**: 20 yard range, Reduces attack speed by 35% for 10 sec. Reduces armor by 35% for 10 sec.		
	Shadow Power: Increases attack speed by 100%. **Heroic**: Increases attack speed by 115%.		
	Saw Blade: 100 yard range. Deals 1758 to 1942 Physical damage and an additional 523 to 577 Physical damage every 2 seconds for 8 seconds to the target and all nearby targets. **Heroic**: Deals 3535-3885 Physical damage and an additional 1045-1155 Physical damage every 2 seconds for 8 seconds.		

The tank should put their back to the wall and ensure that Gyro-Kill faces them at all times; this prevents AoEs from causing major problems.

With that secured, the fight is a very easy one. Gyro-Kill's DPS is rather low, and a single healer can easily keep a decent tank going without any missteps. It's a simple tank-and-trash of the highest order, and the second Crystal will soon be yours.

This kill also opens the elevator to the second floor (the position of this is north from your group's current location).

Heroic Mode

Gyro-Kill functions much the same in Heroic difficulty. The effectiveness of Shadow Power is increased and Saw Blade does significantly more damage

Hug the LEFT side now and move north along that wall. Watch the area ahead and notice the Patroller there. You won't want to pull anything until that Golem is downstairs. When it is, take out the Physician and Slayer at the top of the ramp.

When everything is clear again, kill the Engineer, Tinkerer, and double Wrecker group. Put crowd control on the Engineer and one Wrecker if possible, and have DPS grab the Tinkerer. The main tank can snag any of the Wreckers that aren't under crowd control effects. When the Tinkerer is down, run through the Wreckers, then finish with the Engineer. Do this back along the wall to keep from having the Patroller add.

Toast the Patroller, finally, then clear the Physician, Centurion, and Netherbinder at the bottom (as usual, hit the Netherbinder with crowd control).

Stay on the left to avoid the evil AoE Tinkerer fight nearby (they are safe to skip). Then, pull the Tempest-Forge Destroyer to your location. Don't mistake this for a mere Patroller; these Golems are MUCH meaner.

Destroyers have major Arcane AoE damage, so non-melee characters must stay as far back as they can. Melee DPS should use retreat and Bandage techniques, as needed. And, Arcane Resistance gear is worth putting on, especially in Heroic Mode (where it's just nuts not to).

Collect the Cache of the Legion from the area near the elevator after you kill the two Astromages nearby. These can be stopped with any normal mode of crowd control, so it's pretty much two solo fights. Even better, the vicious Fire Shield that the Astromages use can be stolen w/ Spellsteal! If this is not done, be sure to keep most characters away from the Astromages during the engagement, as the ticks from the Shield are painful!

GOING UP

Take the elevator up to the second floor and stay on the left side until you are certain that all group members are accounted for. Pull the first Destroyer back to your group's location, and tank is near the elevator to avoid AoE problems.

Once this Golem is down, prepare for the fight with two Centurions and two Astromages. Never charge this group, as the second boss is standing just behind them (don't worry, she won't add if you pull at range).

Use the group's crowd control on at least one Astromage, offtank the Centurions, and pull the foes way back if you plan on trying any Fear abilities (this is usually not necessary).

The Destroyer at the back of the area is next. Avoid the boss entirely for now, as you need to have at least this room cleared before fighting her. The final fight is against two more Centurions and two Astromages, in the same vein as the previous encounter.

Beat all of these, then rest. Make sure that nobody approaches the boss or the bridge while others are resting (the bridge triggers a huge fight). Before you get involved with that, question everyone about what they want to do. It's possible to skip this boss for now and go toward the end. This is sometimes wise because it makes the second boss easier when you return to kill her; you will have tons of room to kite her because the bridge will be clear!

In any event, when you do decide to attack the boss, here is how to beat her!

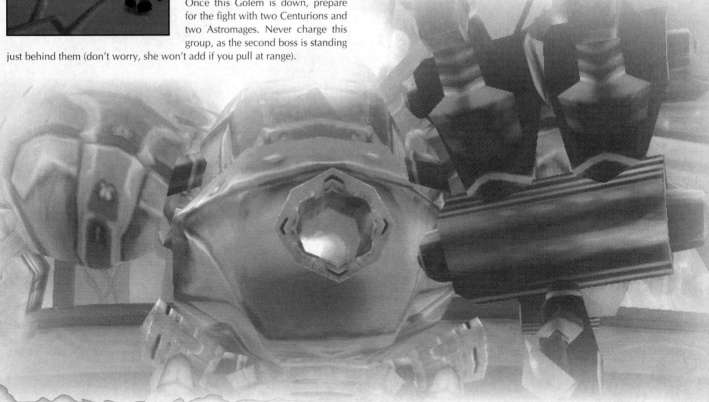

NETHERMANCER SEPETHREA

HP	97400/131489 (Heroic)	**Damage**	1576-2226/2909-4111 (Heroic)
Abilities	**Dragon's Breath**: Deals 684 to 794 Fire damage in front of caster; Disoriented for 3 sec. Any direct damaging attack revives.		
	Arcane Blast: Inflicts normal damage plus 875 to 1125 and knocks back.		
	Summon Raging Flames: Summons two Raging Flame elementals with the Inferno ability. **Heroic**: Summons three Raging Flames.		
	Frost Attack: Slows movement speed by 50% for 8 sec.		

TOYS FOR HER ELEMENTALS

Stellaris (1h Axe 71.6 DPS, +21 Agi, +12 Stam, +22 Attack Power)

Cosmic Lifeband (Finger +57 Healing, 7 Mana/5 Seconds)

Nethershrike (Thrown 66.6 DPS, +15 Stam, +16 Critical Rating)

Jade-Skull Breastplate (Plate Chest 1164 Armor, +30 Str, +50 Stam, +25 Defense Rating, +23 Shield Block)

Manual of the Nethermancer (Off-Hand +12 Stam, +15 Int, +19 Spell Critical Rating, +21 Damage/Healing)

Sepethrea is a very easy boss to defeat if you can get her pinned down, but this girl has a lot of things going in her favor. The biggest is that she has two or three Fire Elementals in her corner (three on Heroic Mode). In Normal Mode, these nasty foes chase random targets around the room after they unleash their AoE Hellfires.

The reason many people read ahead and clear the bridge area is because Sepethrea can be pulled ahead of her Elementals and killed without having to constantly run away from the Elementals, avoiding their fire trails, and so forth.

So, you never bother fighting these Elementals in the least. The trick is to keep kiting them and stay as far away as possible from them while keeping t h e healing and DPS where it needs to me. Having the entire group stay involved in a fight retreat (such as going along the bridge) makes it so much easier to beat this fight!

Remember to don Fire Resistance gear before starting the fight, and use any potions that will give your characters an edge.

When this is accounted for, Sepethrea isn't bad at all. Her Knockback has no value to her if you are doing a fighting retreat (in fact, it helps your tank to keep up with the group). And, her Dragon's Breath does not cause a long enough Disorient effect to throw the plan off.

So, stay in motion, lay on the DPS in bursts as the party retreats, and run in circles once the party gets to Pathaleon's room (this boss won't even make it there if your group has high DPS).

Heroic Mode

A major change occurs in Heroic difficulty. Three Raging Flames are summoned and this changes who can tank these effectively. A Paladin using Righteous Defense is an excellent choice to gain all three Flames' attention.

CROSSING THE BRIDGE

When your party wants to move onto the bridge, be certain that everyone has Bandages ready and full health/mana. Then, have the tank move forward first. Four Blood Elves spawn ahead and start running toward the party. Intercept these and engage the casters of the enemy group while characters with crowd control scramble to eliminate everything they can. Stay on the bridge itself so that Fear is still an option, even if the second boss is alive in her room. Using AoE Fears is very useful for buying the group time to figure out its targets.

Try to keep the last target of the four under crowd control for as long as possible; this allows the group to Bandage, regain a tiny bit of mana, and get themselves mentally ready for what comes next. As soon as the last Blood Elf falls, a Destroyer appears! Keep the main group away from this foe and have the tank do their job. Kill this target as soon as possible, and be ready for

three final Blood Elves to appear. Again, have crowd control ready as soon as possible to save the group from unnecessary damage.

Around the western bend of the bridge is another trio of fights in exactly the same style. These must be completed to spawn the final boss. If your group dies during the event, the enemies that remain will still be there when your party returns to the Instance, so don't worry that your progress has been lost!

As soon as the final wave of Blood Elves is dead, eat and drink. Pathaleon will appear and auto-attack after a short period. Use your time to get everyone up to fighting status as quickly as possible!

PATHALEON THE CALCULATOR

HP	100350/135474 (Heroic)	**Damage**	847-1221/1745-2466 (Heroic)
Abilities	**Disgruntled Anger:** Increases attack speed by 60% and the damage dealt by 213 for 5 min.		
	Mana Tap: Drains 1455 mana from Pathaleon's target and charges him with Arcane energy for 10 min. Stacks three times.		
	Arcane Target: Silences all enemies within 25 yards for 4 sec.		
	Domination: Takes control of a Humanoid of up to level 70 for up to 10 sec.		
	Arcane Explosion: Deals approximately 2700 Arcane damage.		
	Summon Nether Wraith: Summons three Nether Wraiths with the Arcane Bolt ability.		

PATHALEON HAS ALL THE FUN STUFF

Abacus of Violent Odds (Trinket +64 Attack Power, Use to Increase Haste by 260 for 10 Seconds)

Baba's Cloak of Arcanistry (Back 78 Armor, +15 Stam, +15 Int, +14 Spell Critical Rating, +22 Damage/Healing)

Beast Lord Helm (Mail Head 530 Armor, +25 Agi, +21 Stam, +22 Int, 1 [red socket], 1 [meta socket], Socket Bonus: 2 Mana/5 Seconds, +50 Attack Power)

Dath'Remar's Ring of Defense (Finger +15 Stam, +15 Shield Block, +39 Block Value)

Edge of the Cosmos (1h Sword 71.7 DPS, +13 Stam, +16 Critical Strike Rating, +30 Attack Power)

Incanter's Cowl (Cloth Head 127 Armor, +15 Stam, +27 Int, +17 Spi, 1 [yellow socket], 1 [meta socket], Socket Bonus: +4 Spi, +19 Spell Critical Rating, +29 Damage/Healing)

Helm of the Righteous (Plate Head 946 Armor, +30 Stam, +20 Int, 1 [yellow socket], 1 [meta socket], Socket Bonus: +4 Int, +21 Defense Rating, +23 Damage/Healing, 6 Mana/5 Seconds)

Mana Wrath (1h Sword 41.4 DPS, +24 Stam, +18 Int, +126 Damage/Healing)

Molten Earth Kilt (Mail Legs 570 Armor, +24 Stam, +32 Int, +40 Damage/Healing, 10 Mana/5 Seconds)

Moonglade Robe (Leather Chest 292 Armor, +25 Str, +16 Stam, +17 Int, +14 Spi, 1 [red socket], 1 [yellow socket], 1 [blue socket], Socket Bonus: +4 Critical Rating, +55 Healing, +17 Critical Rating)

Tunic of Assassination (Leather Chest 292 Armor, +28 Agi, +21 Stam, 2 [red socket], 1 [blue socket], Socket Bonus: +4 Dodge Rating, +54 Attack Power)

Telescopic Sharprifle (Gun 66.3 DPS, +13 Agi, +28 Attack Power)

Pathaleon is not a very tough final boss as long as you get to enter the fight with all five party members (losing someone late in the spawns on the bridge might hurt you here).

Pathaleon himself is not a heavy hitter, so even a modest tank can do the job without difficulty. Instead, it's his mix of Mind Control (single target and short duration) and adds that give you a hassle.

These adds appear every half-a-minute or so, (they use high-damage Arcane Missiles). If your group has a ton of AoE Fears, it is wise to use them and keep the DPS on Pathaleon; these adds are Fear-able, unlike the Nethermancer summonings.

If you don't have access to major Fear abilities, kill off the first group of adds, then start a major DPS race when the second group spawns. Pathaleon dispels all of his adds when his health reaches 20%, so there is no need to kill off all of the groups.

Another tactic is to use AoEs on the adds when they spawn. Mages are very good for this, but any of the solid AoE classes can down this adds with fair speed.

Once Pathaleon hits 20% of his health, he'll enrage and start to do more melee damage. However, his life is forfeit at that point unless your group is absolutely spent. Pathaleon can't deal enough damage quickly enough to stop a solid burst from killing him off.

And with that, you have all the room you need to kill Sepethrea if she isn't already dead.

Heroic Mode

In Heroic mode Pathaleon doesn't change much. He hits harder, but the real difficulty resides in his Nether Wraiths that are more difficult.

THE BOTANICA

DUNGEON INFORMATION

Name	The Botanica
Location	Tempest Keep, Netherstorm
Suggested Levels	Group of 5, Level 70
Primary Enemies	Humanoid, Plant
Damage Types	Physical, Arcane, Some Nature
Time to Complete	80 to 110 Minutes

WHO TO BRING

JOBS

CLASS	ABILITIES
Druid	DPS while healing, Innervate
Hunter	CC, AoE Assistance, Nature Resistance
Mage	Polymorph, DPS
Paladin	Backup healing, Extra Stun for mobs with CC immunities
Priest	Mind Control, Healer
Rogue	Stunlocking, Sap, DPS
Shaman	Buffs to group DPS are very important (Windfury Totem or Grace of Air depending on group config), Restoration specced, Nature Resistance
Warlock	Fear, DPS, Felhunter
Warrior	Fear, Mortal Strike , Tank

The Botanica requires a party that can deliver damage without breaking their pattern of tanking and healing; this sounds like a generic comment, but those who fight through the dungeon will soon realize what this entails. Much of the trash before the very late stages of the dungeon is quite easy, but there are make-or-break boss fights here, including the second and final bosses. Even with proper aggro consolidation and quality healing, a group that cannot throw a heavy level of damage into a foe will eventually collapse.

As such, shoot for having three DPS slots in The Botanica, and let your tank know that they should bring a set of DPS gear in case it is needed. There may be fights where you prefer to have them in half-tanking or even DPS mode, as the damage coming at them may not be overly high.

That said, a standard group with a dedication healer, a full tank, and three DPS classes will have no problems here. It's only when your group shoots for too much backup healing that things get iffy. Don't worry about falling short on health here, as damage in non-Heroic mode is not bad at all. Even in Heroic Mode, a tank with high-end normal armor and a full set of Arcane Resistance gear can survive the brutal fights.

GETTING TO THE BOTANICA

Your group needs to be level 70, as with all of the dungeons contained by Tempest Keep. This is because only a character with a Flying Mount can reach the Instance portal; fly to the left side (north) of Tempest Keep and enter that tower to reach the dungeon.

There is no lock and key system, so this can be the first or second dungeon of Tempest Keep that you explore. Defeating this one and The Mechanar is needed for taking on the final 5-character Instance of the area, so keep that in mind.

REPUTATION GAINS

ACTION	FACTION	REPUTATION GAIN	END POINT
Kill Trash Mobs	Sha'tar	12 Points	Exalted
Kill Bosses	Sha'tar	120 Points	Exalted
Quest: Breaking Into the Arcatraz	Sha'tar	1,000 Points	N/A

CLIMATE CHANGE GONE HORRIBLY WRONG!

BOSSES

COMMANDER SARANNIS

HIGH BOTANIST FREYWINN

THORNGRIN THE TENDER

LAJ

WARP SPLINTER

MINIONS

BLOODWARDER PROTECTOR
Notes: Crystal Strike (Arcane Version of Mortal Strike), Spell Reflect, Intervene

BLOODWARDER MENDER
Notes: Greater Heal, Mind Blast, Shadow Word: Pain, Has Holy Fury buff if Mind Controlled (30 minutes, +295 Spell Damage)

BLOODWARDER GREENKEEPER
Notes: Light Nature Damage, Greenkeeper's Fury, Nature Shock, Impending Coma

TEMPEST FORGE PEACEKEEPER
Notes: High Physical and Arcane damage, Arcane Missile Volley, MAJOR boost in Heroic Mode (use Arcane Resistance gear on tank), Arcane Explosion, Arcane Blast

BLOODWARDER FALCONER
Notes: Can command attached Falcons to attack a random target, Deterrence, Arcane Shot, Multi-Shot, Wing Clip

SUNSEEKER BOTANIST
Notes: Heals, Rejuvenate Plant, Nature's Rage, Regrowth

SUNSEEKER CHEMIST
Notes: Vial of Poison (ground spawning cloud of Poison), and Fire Breath Potion

SUNSEEKER RESEARCHER
Notes: Poison Shield, Mind Shock (Does Nature Damage and Debuffs Casting Time), Flame Shock, Frost Shock

SUNSEEKER GEOMANCER
Notes: Immune to all CC, Arcane Explosion, Changes Immunities of attached Frayers, Rain of Fire, Blizzard

BLOODWARDER STEWARD
Notes: Arcane Flurry, Immune to Fear and Fear-like effects, Low Health

NETHERVINE REAPER
Notes: Demons, Cleave, Pale Death

NETHERVINE INCITER
Notes: Demons, Poison on Attack, Mind-Numbing Poison, Deadly Poison, Kidney Shot

NETHERVINE TRICKSTER
Notes: Stealthing Elites, Backstab

SUNSEEKER HERBALIST
Notes: Entangling Roots, High Health, Spade Toss

SUNSEEKER HARVESTER
Notes: Polymorph, Summon Adds, Wilting Touch

SUNSEEKER CHANNELER
Notes: Sunseeker Aura, Soul Channel

SUNSEEKER GENE-SPLICER
Notes: AoE Shadow Damage, Summons Adds, Death and Decay

MUTATE FLESHLASHER
Notes: Non-Elite, low health, melee attacks, Vicious Bite

MUTATE FEAR-SHRIEKER
Notes: AoE Fear, Immune to non-Stun CCs

MUTATE HORROR
Notes: Immune to non-Stun CCs, Corrode Armor

FRAYER WILDLING
Notes: Non-Elites, Use AoE attacks to destroy them, their color determines their current Immunities, Lash

HOW TO BREAK INTO THE ARCATRAZ

Level Requirement	67
Quest Giver	A'dal (Shattrath City, Terrace of Light)
Quest Goal	Get the Top and Bottom Shards of the Arcatraz Key
Experience Reward	19,000
Additional Rewards	Key to The Arcatraz, +1,000 Sha'tar Reputation

This quest requires that you take groups through both The Mechanar and The Botanica. Full runs are required in each case, and only when you are done with both sections can you complete the quest and gain access to The Arcatraz.

For this Instance writeup, your only concern is Warp Splinter, the end boss of The Botanica. Take out the dungeon with a good DPS group and you are almost certain of success.

MASTER OF POTIONS

Level Requirement	68
Quest Giver	Lauranna Thar'well (Zangarmarsh)
Quest Goal	Kill and loot the Botanist's Field Guide from High Botanist Freywinn and Craft 5 Super Healing Potions, 5 Super Mana Potions, and 5 Major Dreamless Sleep Potions
Experience Reward	12,650
Additional Rewards	Proc Bonus Potions While Crafting

If you choose Potions as your Alchemy specialization, this is the quest that you will receive to prove yourself. Meet Lauranna Thar'well and let her give you the quest to head into The Botanica. Your target is the second boss of the Instance, but Freywinn offers one of the toughest fights in the entire place. Be sure that your group has a heavy amount of DPS. It is also very useful to have a Mortal Strike Warrior or a Rogue with Wounding Poison. Anything that debuffs Freywinn's ability to regenerate health is a massive boon in the fight.

Once the dungeon run is over, craft the 15 requested Potions and return to Lauranna.

CAPTURING THE KEYSTONE

Level Requirement	67
Quest Giver	Archmage Vargoth (Netherstorm)
Quest Goal	Retrieve the Keystone from Commander Sarannis
Experience Reward	19,000
Additional Rewards	None, Sadly

This quest lies at the end of the Archmage Vargoth chain (the Netherstorm quests that have you restore a staff and run quite a few exciting quests for the Archmage). Though there are no nifty items for doing this final piece, you wouldn't want to leave the mission uncompleted, right? Beyond that, there is an award of gold for the task, and it's fun to run The Botanica anyway.

Your target is Commander Sarannis, and she is the first boss of the Instance. If there are a few people who need this quest, you might even be able to gather a group for just rushing to her. That would make this a VERY fast run indeed, as she is only a couple rooms into the place.

Once Sarannis falls, you can loot the Keystone and return to Vargoth.

WHAT HAVE THEY BEEN GROWING IN HERE?

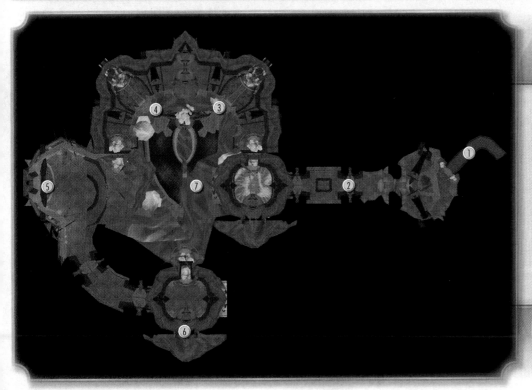

MAP LEGEND	
1	Entrance
2	The Front Hall
3	Commander Sarannis
4	High Botanist Freywinn
5	Thorngrin the Tender
6	Laj
7	Warp Splinter

THE FIRST ROOM

Your group will enter The Botanica on the eastern side of the Instance; the layout of the place is so simple that nobody has a chance to get lose in here. Though the map doesn't make it entirely obvious, the place is essentially just a hallway that leads west then wraps around the central chamber. You fight each boss along the way, and at the end you can take down Warp Splinter.

So, none of the challenges rest on finding your way. Instead, your tests lie in beating the many encounters along the path. This first room starts softly; there are two Bloodwarder Protectors by the western doorway, and a single Tempest-Forge Peacekeepers patrols along the length of the hall.

With for the patroller to leave, then pull the Protectors back to your group's position. Use crowd control on one of the Blood Elves, and tank the other while it is destroyed. These foes have a fairly high-damage Crystal Strike, and this deals Arcane damage. As with many of the fights in here, your tank should consider Arcane Resistance gear if there are any problems.

When this brief fight is over, wait to ambush the patrolling Peacekeeper. In Heroic Mode, these foes are so painful. Without a high level of Arcane Resistance, your group may wipe even on those single foes. If you don't have the right tank/gear for the job, use ranged damage and kiting techniques to bring down the Protector without letting it get a chance to engage anyone in melee. Do so here in the room, where there is enough space!

A LONG HALLWAY

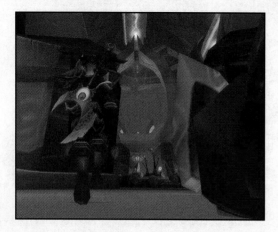

Creep into the hallway past the archway and look for the patroller there. When he heads away, pull the next two Protectors so that they can be cleared out far away from the Peacekeeper. Ambush that Peacekeeper after the Elves are gone, and pull him back to the front room if you need kiting space.

Walk to the west and approach the small room ahead slowly. There are two Protectors near the front, and they are most easily aggroed by having your tank edge up to them. Bring them back to the party so that they can be dispatched, then take a better look at the room.

Directly in front are three Blood Elves. Two of them are Greenkeepers (weak foes really), and one is a Mender. The Mender is a healer and is best placed under crowd control.

If you don't have a Priest, take out the Greenkeepers first then break control of the Mender and finish it off last.

IF YOU DO HAVE A PRIEST

Mind Control is very nice when used on the Menders. These foes can help with healing during a fight, if needed, and they have a buff that you can place on casters for the next 30 minutes; anything that improves Spell Damage is good, right?

The only thing about Greenkeepers that is a major pain is that their Nature Damage debuff has a brief sleep attached to it, and this breaks up the flow of your fight. The debuff then lowers Attack and Movement Speed for a short time, so Impending Coma is annoying. However, the fights are short and it's unlikely that you'll have more than a single target running around for long. There isn't much chance of a wipe here unless you accidentally pull additional enemies or fail to use anticipated crowd control.

Both sides of the passage have additional trios of Blood Elves, in the same configuration. Dispatch as you go, then pull the two Protectors by the far doorway. You might have some problems with line-of-sight in there area because of the railings; as such, ranged characters should be fast to react if they cannot cast/attack and should reposition to a more direct line-of-sight.

TURNING NORTH

Another trio with two Greenkeepers and a single Mender is just past the door. Pull them back to stay safe and have more room for crowd control. Then, peek into the room and look for the Bloodfalcons that are flying about. What looks like patrolling Falcons are actually attached members of the Falconers' groups, so don't try to hit one and think that you will have a small pull.

FALCONERS ARE EVIL

Falconers are able to command their pets to attack targets randomly. This is scary enough on non-Heroic Mode, but you can imagine that this is even more even when the Falcons have a higher damage output. Tanks should be ready to use a variety of AoE abilities to get attention back on themselves.

DPSers with crowd control must assist with this as best they can, especially when a softer member of the group has been targeted. Rogues should hold back on their Energy use to some extent and save the potential for Stunlocking for a Falcon that is being troublesome.

Destroy the darn Falconers early on in the fights to ensure that they cannot sow chaos. Once the Falconers are down, the Bloodfalcons because simple tank-and-trash enemies. It's nice that Falconers have visible text when they declare their targets; this lets the tanks know whether to freak out or stay calm and keep doing whatever they were doing. The Falconers themselves are Hunters, so they have access to Multishot and Wing Clip. Softer characters must stay away from the tanks during the early pull, lest a stray Multishot put your group in dire straights.

A Peacekeeker patrols the bridge area, and it's best to let it come to your. This avoids adds and gives your group the room it might need during the fight.

Pull the two Protectors from the far side of the bridge away from their archway, then kill them in the same fashion that you've been doing. Your next fight against a new opponent is past the archway; two more Protectors are there with a Steward!

Stewards have impressive damage potential, so they are suitable targets for crowd control or for killing first while both Protectors are under crowd control. Either way, your group needs to have all of its damage potential ready to throw at the Stewards. This is because Stewards have an Arcane Whirlwind that can hit many targets for fairly high damage! Though you cannot use Fear and Fear-like effects on Stewards, they can be Stunned! Mind Control also works well, if you have a Priest.

THE COMMANDER'S ROOM

Two more Falconer groups are in the north-east area. Don't have anyone get too close to the archway before you are ready, as both groups of Bloodfalcons leave a member to patrol. Having someone stand too far forward can trigger an encounter with both groups simultaneously, and that is extremely grim news.

Use proximity aggro to lure the first group all the way back through the archway and into your earlier position. There are two Bloodfalcons and a single Falconer to fight. In the event that you do get everything, it is still possible to win without a wipe. Use crowd control to keep the Falconers out of your hair, try to apply AoE Fear on the Bloodfalcons, and remember abilities like Challenging Shout when everything goes foul.

Enter the north-east chamber fully after the Bloodfalcons are gone, and look around. The first boss is on the bridge ahead, and she gets edgy if she stands still. Thus, Sarannis walks back and forth almost constantly. You are going to clear the area in front of the bridge fully before fighting her, but this must be done without aggroing the Commander in the process.

Take out the first trio of Elves (two Protectors and a Steward), then ambush the patrolling Peacekeeper when it comes down the way.

Next, wait for the Commander to clear off and pull another trio of Elves. There is one final pull after that, and they too should be cleared when the Commander is away. This leaves the boss by herself (for the early part of the fight, at least). Rest to full, discuss the strategy of the upcoming encounter, then engage Sarannis.

COMMANDER SARANNIS

HP	110700/149445 (Heroic)	**Damage**	1523-2514/4391-6210 (Heroic)
Abilities	**Arcane Resonance:** Increases Arcane damage taken by 1200 for 30 seconds; stacks.		
	Arcane Devastation: Instant weapon attack that deals 50% of weapon damage plus an additional 1200 damage per application of Arcane Resonance.		
	Summon Reservist: At approximately 50% health, Commander Sarannis will summon three Bloodwarder Reservists and one Bloodwarder Mender.		

IN HER WARCHEST

Towering Mantle of the Hunt (Mail Shoulder 489 Armor, +21 Stam, +23 Int, +21 Critical Rating, +48 Attack Power)

Revenger (1h Sword 71.7 DPS, Chance on Hit: 105-125 Life Steal)

Syrannis' Mystic Sheen (Back 198 Armor, +12 to All Resistances)

Libram of the Lightbringer (Libram +87 to Healing done by Holy Light)

Prismatic Mittens of Mending (Cloth Hands 97 Armor, +23 Stam, +26 Int, +55 Healing, 7 Mana/5 Seconds)

The early part of the battle is a standard tank-and-trash skirmish. Your main tank can hold aggro without much difficulty at all, and the only issue for the healer is in dealing with the debuff that Sarannis uses (it increases Arcane damage taken). It's hard to judge when to Dispel this, as it is stacked often, especially in Heroic Mode.

Even if the group cannot Dispel this debuff, the fight is quite winnable. Your only big test comes at 50% health or somewhat below, when the Commander summons a Mender and three non-Elite support troops. AoE Fear abilities work wonderfully to get rid of this problem for almost as much time as you need. If your group has two of these abilities, it might take care of the issue fully.

In any event, use an in-combat ability for crowd control to remove the Mender from the fight. Without the Mender there to heal and wreak havoc, things aren't too bad at all.

With all of the enemies cleared and your group at full health and mana, it's time to attack. It may be worth putting on your tank's Arcane Resistance suit of armor, as Sarannis deals a fair sum of her damage through Arcane magic and physical attacks, both of which are well mitigated by such a suit.

Heroic Mode

There are two changes to the fight in Heroic Mode, beyond the standard increase in damage output. One of them is an increase in the rate of stacking for the debuff. Having a secondary healer to assist and Dispel is extremely important, and using Arcane Resistance is quite sensible here.

Additionally, a secondary spawn of enemies occurs when the Commander reaches critically low health. Don't fight these; save some for of AoE Fear for them, or at least something to remove their Mender from combat for long enough to rip down their leader.

PLANT ROOM

The room ahead has Elite groups that are mostly spread out; two patrols wander the area, and it's somewhat hard to see what you are pulling the first time you come in here. The color of the room and the muted tones of your enemies confuse things slightly, so look carefully before making any moves.

The group on the left is the best initial pull; grab this Researcher, Botanist, Chemist, and Greater Frayer when the patrols aren't nearby. The Chemist is the AoE member of the group, and it's very useful to hit such target with some form of crowd control. As long as the Chemists don't have free rein, the fights aren't very mean.

Slice through the first forward patrol next (merely a single Botanist with a Frayer), then take out the group on the right. This is one of the few larger groups. There are likely to be two Chemists in the bunch, so they are your crowd control targets. Lacking a second form of crowd control, target one of the Chemists for death while the other is controlled.

Eliminate the other patrol at this time (it is the same as the first one you fought), then position everyone for another somewhat large fight in the center of the room. The ear has a group of four Elites and a Greater Frayer as well.

MAJOR CROWD CONTROL OPPORTUNITIES

These fights are large enough to represent danger to groups that are still gearing up, are disorganized, or who are going through this dungeon in Heroic Mode. As such, it may be worthwhile to add some setup time to the fights in the name of safety.

For doing this, have longer pulls to provide major distance between the groups and the site of battle. Then, consider AoE Fears (Intimidating Shout/Psychic Scream/Howl of Terror) as methods for keeping enemy DPS down in the early part of the engagements.

The last fight in the room is an AoE encounter. There are eight Frayers with a Sunseeker Geomancer controlling them. Watch from a distance as the Geomancer toys with the plants, making them Immune to a given element. While the Blood Elf douses them in flame, they stay Immune to Fire. If the Blood Elf switches to ice, they become Immune to Frost.

Wait until the Frayers are Immune to an element that your group is not going to use heavily, then attack. Don't waste time with crowd control, as the Geomancer is entirely Immune to it.

Instead, have your tank and possible a good Stunlock type of character go after the Geomancer to keep that foe busy, and let your AoE characters go nuts on the Frayers. Challenging Shout is a good way for the tank to grab aggro from the Frayers even while ignoring them with attacks.

DOES SOMEBODY SMELL FERTILIZER?

The approach to the second boss has just three more fights, and none of them are as large as the ones in the previous room. Look for the lone patroller who is on the bridge, and fight the enemies at a time when there is no risk of adds (it's not difficult).

HIGH BOTANIST FREYWINN

HP	92972/125513 (Heroic)	Damage	1413-1996/1413-1996 (Heroic)
Abilities	**Tree Form**: Turns the caster into a tree for 45 sec. While in this form the caster is immune to damage.		
	Tranquility: Regenerates all nearby friendly targets for 925 to 1075 every 2 sec. for 45 sec; channeled.		
	Summon Frayer Protector: Summons three Frayers to protect the caster for 45 sec. **Frayer Protectors**: Shoot Thorns ability.		
	Plant Red Seedling: Summons a seedling to accompany the caster for 3 min.		
	Red Seedlings: Fire Blast.		
	Plant White Seedling: Summons a seedling to accompany the caster for 3 min.		
	White Seedlings: Frozen Touch.		
	Plant Blue Seedling: Summons a seedling to accompany the caster for 3 min.		
	Blue Seedlings: Bind Feet.		
	Plant Green Seedling: Summons a seedling to accompany the caster for 3 min.		
	Green Seedlings: Toxic Pollen.		

WHAT IS IN THE GREENHOUSE?

Aegis of the Sunbird (Shield 3806 Armor, 86 Block, +27 Stam, +19 Defense Rating, +29 Shield Block)

Enchanted Thorium Torque (Neck +27 Stam, +20 Dodge Rating, +16 Hit Rating)

Energis Armwraps (Cloth Hands 97 Armor, +27 Stam, +26 Int, +34 to Damage/Healing)

Obsidian Clodstompers (Plate Feet 800 Armor, +34 Str, +30 Stam, 2 [yellow socket], Socket Bonus: +3 Str)

Stormreaver Warblades (Off Hand Fist 71.6 DPS, +13 Stam, +21 Critical Rating, +22 Attack Power)

This fight is amazingly fun, but it's also one of the most challenging ones in the Instance. Groups that have a Mortal Strike Warrior or a well-prepared Rogue gain a massive boost to their chance of success here, while healing-heavy groups are going to have the worst time of things.

This is a DPS fight, through and through. Freywinn and his summoned plants aren't the best damage dealers in the world, which makes things sound like an endurance fight. It's not what you would expect!

Rather, Freywinn relies on his amazing regenerative properties to win the day. In a sense, the battle is an endurance fight for HIM, but a DPS race for you. If your group cannot deliver a substantial amount of damage at a given rate, you will fail.

Before the fight, assign a single DPS character for add duty. From the very beginning, Freywinn is going to bring occasional non-Elite adds into the fight. These come in different flavors, and all must be destroyed quickly and efficiently. Hunters and Rogues are VERY good at this task. Mainline characters can assist in killing the non-Elites by hitting AoE abilities (such as Sweeping Strikes, which is so wonderful in this dungeon).

The bulk of the group's damage must stay on Freywinn himself. Keep Mortal Strike and Wounding Poison on this boss, as he'll enter his healing phase far too soon.

Roughly twice a minute, Frewinn goes into a trance and Channels Tranquility. As this happens, he goes Immune to all forms of damage and summons three Elite Lashers. These foes deliver moderate damage, and they aren't too much of a threat if your tank is fast in getting their attention.

What makes the situation dire is that Frewinn is healing himself this whole time AND he is also adding health to his Lashers. Some groups try to take the time and pull the Lashers out of Tranquility's range. This does work! Getting the Lashers off the bridge and to the side stops them from healing, and they are more easily dispatched.

But a good DPS group should focus their fire using a main assist for targeting. It takes so little time to down a Lasher when everyone attacks together, that it really isn't worth the effort to pull them away unless the group is known to be healing heavy and DPS light. Heroic Mode has few changes to this encounter.

AFTER BOSS

Give everyone a bit of a breather and a heart handshake. If the last fight went without too many problems, it's likely that your group can have The Botanica on farm status within a run or two. In fact, the final boss of the dungeon is arguable similar in style and can be defeated by any group that can master Freywinn (so things are looking up)!

Start turning south, not that your party has much of a choice. The circle around the outside ring of the dungeon continues, and your next battle is against another Geomancer/Frayer group. Wait for the right element to come up in the rotation and blast these chlorophyll lovers.

Two Protectors guard the next archway, and there are patrols inside the following chamber. Be careful when you pull, and don't approach the arch itself until the fighting is done.

It's good to have a Warlock around in the next area, because Demons abound. Nethervine Inciters tend to wander, and they are Rogues with Deadly Poison, Kidney Shot, and fair DPS.

Get the nearest wanderer when it is very close, then pull the two Channelers from the right side when they are NOT glowing red. That glow isn't just for good looks; it means that the creatures under that influence are buffed for dealing far more damage. Clear the next two Channelers and another Inciter patrol, then rest before descending the steps on the far side.

Reapers and Inciters wander near the ramp itself. The Repeat, not surprisingly, are Warriors with Cleave. They also have a Stamina debuff that is quite heavy (-35%).

Go left from the ramp for a short span to unstealth the nearby Tricksters. These come in pairs and would be awful to aggro at the wrong time.

When those are gone, turn back toward the right side and watch the spread of enemies there before making your first attack. Kill the patrolling Inciter, then attack the group of Reapers and Inciters (two of each) when the group is not glowing red. The Channeler will not add, so that enemy can be killing on its own.

Do everything possible to keep the Reapers facing away from the group. Having two enemies with Cleave is a very bad thing if anyone besides the main tank gets in the way, and in Heroic Mode this can easily cause a wipe if you healer(s) get clipped.

Fight the far group and their Channeler next.

I KNOW WHAT YOU WARLOCKS ARE THINKING

And yes, Enslave is very much fun to use on these Satyrs in the normal dungeon. In Heroic Mode, however, it is not an option. Enslave Demon fails to work on Satyrs in The Botanica when you play on a higher difficulty setting. Sorry, folks!

THORNGRIN THE TENDER

HP	73788/99613 (Heroic)	Damage	2040-2882/3394-4796 (Heroic)
Abilities	**Hellfire:** Causes approximately 1200-1500 Fire damage every 1 sec. for 6 sec. **Heroic:** This ability deals approximately 2000 Fire damage per second.		
	Sacrifice: Stuns the target and deals 642 to 708 damage every second for 8 sec. Damage dealt in this way heals Thorngrin.		
	Enrage: Increases the caster's attack speed by 75% and the Physical damage it deals by 110 for 10 sec.		

THIS GUY WAS TENDING HIS LOOT

Arcane Netherband (Finger +18 Stam, +18 Int, +21 Damage/Healing, +15 Spell Penetration)

Dreamer's Dragonstaff (Staff 63.0 DPS, +46 Str, +27 Agi, +28 Stam, +423 Attack Power in Cat, Bear, Dire Bear, and Moonkin Forms)

Gauntlets of Cruel Intention (Plate Hands 728 Armor, +30 Str, +25 Stam, +21 Critical Rating)

Ring of Umbral Doom (Finger +18 Stam, +20 Critical Rating, +40 Attack Power)

Runed Dagger of Solace (Mh Dagger 41.4 DPS, +24 Stam, +21 Resilience Rating, +227 Healing)

Thorngrin is very easy after a few times defeating him, but he is quite obnoxious if you don't know what to expect. With multiple aggro resets, an effective AoE, and a mix of Fire, Shadow, and Physical damage, this boss seems to have almost too much going for him. Then you find out how crummy his health pool is, and the balance suddenly seems quite fair.

Tanks and melee DPSers should switch to their Fire Resistance gear IF they have up to date equipment. Don't ditch good armor for old suits of gear that were a-okay in the Molten Core days. Thorngrin's Physical DPS is decent normally and can become especially dangerous during his periods of Enrage. Thus, dropping to lower-level armor even for very high Fire Resistance is self-defeating. Other characters should worry more about Shadow damage. We'll explain why shortly.

Have your tank hold Thorngrin in the center of the room. Don't try to build up a ton of excess aggro; instead, stay alert and be ready to Taunt or use other Instant abilities to get aggro. Thorngrin's Sacrifice ability resets aggro immediately, and that is going to necessitate your fast response.

Ranged DPS classes should spread out and start hitting home after giving the tank a short moment to gain momentum. Melee DPSers should start slashing as soon as possible, as they will spend a bit of lost time avoiding AoEs before too long.

Thorngrin's Sacrifice chooses a target that does not have aggro and places them on the dias where this boss was waiting. The attack causes Shadow damage over time, and healers can still help the person while they are taking the damage. Priests are especially useful in this encounter, as they can react faster for the healing and are able to raise the group's Shadow Resistance before the fight.

With some regularity, Thorngrin also uses his Hellfire, which has a fair range and hurts anyone without Fire Resistance. Non-tanks are going to have to flee this attack, and tanks without the appropriate gear will have to back off as well, making for a very aggro-sensitive fight.

THE DARK HARVEST

There are only two more genuine rooms before the end, so things are getting quite intense. After Thorngrin is down, take the route that the Tricksters were guarding and devour the two Protectors by the far archway.

Fights in the following chamber are very dangerous. Not only are the enemies effective, but there is the potential for add summoning (which is always a major pain).

Gene-Splicers are the worst of the bunch; crowd control's first target should always be these guys, as their Shadow AoE obliterates parties, even on normal mode. They can also summon Mutate Fleshlashers.

Harvesters are ugly too, as they have Polymorph, Entangling Roots, and summon potential. Use spare crowd control if you have it, but frankly there won't be enough crowd control to go around. These are going to be your first kill targets.

And, there are Fleshlashers already spawned with these groups, so even without add summoning there are going to be more enemies in each fight. The Mutate Fleshlashers are quick to down, but their damage is fair.

There aren't many Herbalists in here, and when they are found they should be the last target on any kill list.

Each group of enemies has three Blood Elves. Destroy all three groups using the kill order above, and consider pulls back into the following chamber if AoE Fears and other kiting tactics are needed.

Two Protectors guard the far exit, then you can peer into the fourth boss' room.

THEY ARE JUST LAJING AROUND

Three more ugly fights are here before you can attack the boss. Each battle has four Mutate enemies (two Shriekers and two Horrors). The Horror are Immune to crowd control, except for basic Stuns, and they are hard to kill. The Shriekers are exactly the same except for having an AoE Fear! Not good at all.

Ranged DPS is great to have, to avoid the Fear issues. Have your tank use any Fear Immunity that the group can muster, as this greatly diminishes the chaos of the encounter. Beyond that, it's just a mad rush to get the Shriekers down by focused fire on each one. After that, the fight is safe and easy (if you make it that far). Having a Hunter there to kite most of the enemies away for long enough to get the first Shrieker down is a big help if your group has difficulty.

Luckily, the only other trick this boss has is his Enrage, which upgrades his melee damage by a huge margin but only for a short time.

DPS classes must be aware of the difficulty in aggro control for this fight, and be cautious with their aggro for a short time after Sacrifice is used. As long as they degree of control is maintained, Thorngrin won't be too bad. If your group does have problems, so if anyone has some spare Greater Fire Protection Potions for the tank.

Heroic Mode

Besides the normal increase in hit points and basic damage, the primary difference is Hellfire deals almost twice the damage per second.

LAJ

HP	121770/164389 (Heroic)	Damage	1999-2827/4799-6768 (Heroic)
Abilities	**Teleport Self**: Teleports Laj back to his starting platform.		
	Thrash: Gains 2 extra attacks.		
	Allergic Reaction: Diseases an enemy for 18 sec., increases the nature damage by 500. Deals approximately 900-1100 Nature damage every 3 sec for 18 sec. Can be spread.		
	Summon Thorn Flayer: Summons a Thorn Flayer to aid Laj. Thorn Flayers: Mind Flay.		
	Summon Thorn Lasher: Summons a Thorn Lasher to aid Laj. Thorn Lashers: Thorn Missiles.		

DO PLANTS LIKE LOOT?

Boots of the Shifting Sands (Leather Feet 201 Armor, +30 Stam, 1 [red socket], 1 [yellow socket], Socket Bonus: +3 Hit Rating, +19 Critical Rating, +40 Attack Power)

Devil-Stitched Leggings (Cloth Legs 136 Armor, +32 Stam, +28 Int, 1 [red socket], 1 [yellow socket], 1 [blue socket], Socket Bonus: +5 Spell Damage, +29 Damage/Healing)

Spaulders of the Righteous (Plate Shoulder 873 Armor, +22 Stam, +22 Int, 1 [red socket], 1 [blue socket], Socket Bonus: +3 Defense Rating, +20 Defense Rating, +15 Damage/Healing)

Mantle of Autumn (Leather Shoulder 219 Armor, +24 Stam, +31 Int, +27 Spi, +68 Healing)

Mithril-Bark Cloak (Back 78 Armor, +32 Stam, +26 Resilience Rating)

The rest of the group can expect Laj to Disease his primary target and to shift elemental Immunities throughout the fight. None of these become major issues!

Take this creature down and enjoy some easy loot. The real challenge is just ahead.

Laj is arguably the easiest boss of the dungeon. Assign two DPS characters for taking down his adds, and gets your tank, healer, and a backup character to hit Laj directly. This Plant has only moderate DPS and survivability, so most of the fight's challenge rests on having a healer who can split their attention between a few people in a few areas.

The two DPS characters should expect spawns of varying types, but all are focused primarily on damage. Use Stuns if possible to keep them from being very effective, and bursts damage is the key for slaying them. Rogues are the crowned champions here, any skilled DPS character can suffice.

Heroic Mode

Laj has no changes in his abilities; his normal strikes are more than double in Heroic mode. He hits extemely hard. The main healer should keep a closer eye on whoever is tanking.

THE ORIGINAL POWER PLANT

There are a couple of trivial (and wonderful) AoE fights as your group moves into Warp Splinter's lair. These are not intended to wipe your party, and you get plenty of room to pull the little plants without fear of having them bump into each other and grab everything at once.

When those fights are out of the way, Warp Splinter is waiting! This mighty tree could eat an Ancient of War for breakfast, and he's hungry for you.

WARP SPLINTER

HP	132840/179334 (Heroic)	Damage	1999-2827/3136-4435 (Heroic)
Abilities	**Stomp**: Inflicts 2375 to 2625 Physical damage to nearby enemies, stuns them for 5 sec., and increases the Physical damage by 550.		
	Summon Saplings: Attempts to raise a sapling. After 25 sec., if the servant still lives, it will sacrifice itself to heal the caster.		
	Arcane Volley: Deals about 1900 to 2100 Arcane damage. **Heroic**: This ability deals about 3700 to 4200 damage.		
	Sand Breath: Inflicts approximately 2300 Arcane damage in a cone in front of the caster, slows the target's movement and attack speed for 10 sec.		

BAUBLES, BOTANICA, AND BEYOND

Bangle of Endless Blessings (Trinket Equip to have a chance for bonus mana regeneration during casting, Use to increase Spirit by 130 for 20 seconds)

Beast Lord Cuirass (Mail Chest 652 Armor, +20 Agi, +30 Stam, +24 Int, 2 [red socket], 1 [blue socket], Socket Bonus: +4 Agility, +40 Attack Power, 4 Mana/5 Seconds)

Greatsword of Forlorn Visions (2h Sword 93.3 DPS, +26 Str, +28 Stam, Chance to Add +2750 Armor for 10 Seconds)

Incanter's Robe (Cloth Chest 156 Armor, +25 Stam, +22 Int, +22 Spi, 2 [yellow socket], 1 [red socket], Socket Bonus: +4 Int, +10 Spell Critical Rating, +30 Damage/Healing)

Jagged Bark Pendant (Neck +26 Agi, +15 Stam, +30 Attack Power)

Moonglade Cowl (Leather Head 237 Armor, +24 Str, +8 Agi, +18 Stam, +25 Int, +13 Spi, 1 [blue socket], 1 [meta socket], Socket Bonus: +4 Spi, +53 Healing)

Netherfury Cape (Back 78 Armor, +19 Str, +19 Stam, +21 Critical Rating)

Tidefury Helm (Mail Head 530 Armor, +31 Stam, +26 Int, 1 [yellow socket], 1 [meta socket], Socket Bonus: +4 Int, +32 Damage/Healing, 6 Mana/5 Seconds)

Warhelm of the Bold (Plate Head 946 Armor, +24 Str, +22 Agi, 23 Stam, 1 [blue socket], 1 [meta socket], Socket Bonus: +4 Str, +20 Defense Rating)

Warp Infused Drape (Cloth Chest 156 Armor, +27 Stam, +28 Int, 1 [red socket], 1 [blue socket], 1 [yellow socket], Socket Bonus: +4 Spell Critical Rating, +12 Spell Hit Rating, +30 Damage/Healing)

Warp Splinter's Thorn (1h Dagger 71.5 DPS, +16 Agi, +13 Stam, +15 Hit Rating)

Warpscale Leggings (Leather Legs 256 Armor, +32 Agi, +31 Stam, +14 Hit Rating, +21 Critical Rating, +56 Attack Power)

Warpstaff of Arcanum (Staff 63.0 DPS, +37 Stam, +38 Int, +16 Spell Hit Rating, +26 Spell Critical Rating, +121 Damage/Healing)

As the tank is getting early aggro, the group should run deeper into the chamber and get to maximum range. This avoids the damaging War Stomp that Stuns players in a moderate AoE around Warp Splinter.

Lay into the damage onto aggro is clearly on the main tank, and watch for the first spawn of Treants. These six trees don't try to attack much, but instead walk toward the center of the chamber and despawn after about twenty seconds. All of the Treants' health is then transferred to Warp Splinter, healing him considerably.

If your group has major AoE potential, it is best to slam the Treants with major AoE attacks when they are bunched close together in the moments before they despawn. This is very efficient for keeping Warp Splinter from getting much out of them.

If instead your group is better for single-target DPS, it's more effective to just keep the damage on Warp Splinter directly, rather than lose time repositioning to kill each Treant.

Whatever the case, keep Warp Splinter from facing the group; this eliminates the Arcane Valley that the boss unleashes, and only the tank will take damage. With that done, almost all damage in the fight goes onto the tank and nobody else (making for such easy healing that a single healer will be more than aqequate).

Warp Splinter is another boss who will try to run endurance tricks against you while demanding that your group sustain immense DPS. Your tank should draw Warp Splinter to the area near the entrance, by the bridge. If everything goes wrong, this can lead to a fairly fast reset of the fight (allowing your group to escape and rest); Warp Splinter will hit his tether if you take him along the bridge.

Heroic Mode

Lookout for his Arcane Volley. It deals significantly greater damage to all it hits.

Loot Warp Splinter, do a little dance for victory, and realize that you are close to mastering the 5-character dungeons of Tempest Keep. Only The Arcatraz remains virgin territory now.

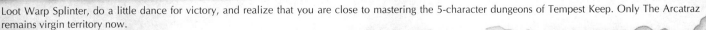

THE ARCATRAZ

DUNGEON INFORMATION

Name	The Arcatraz
Location	Tempest Keep, Netherstorm
Suggested Levels	Group of 5, Level 70
Primary Enemies	Demons, Odd and Ends
Damage Types	Shadow, Fire, Arcane, Physical
Time to Complete	70 to 100 Minutes

WHO TO BRING

The Arcatraz is one of the hardest Instances to deal with if your group relies on strong DPS with tactical crowd control; the problem is that this dungeon is filled with fights that have CC Immunities! Polymorph is less useful, Stuns are sometimes trivialized, and in general the monsters have many special abilities to thwart even a good group.

To counter this, it is very wise to bring two full healers on an Arcatraz run and plan for the long haul. Let your tank know ahead of time that they will likely benefit from Arcane Resistance gear as a backup, and if they have Fire gear as well that is a nice bonus.

Try to make sure that one of your healing classes is a Priest, as their Shadow Resistance is a huge boost to the party at several points in the dungeon. Also, Priests have some of the best healing anyway and can do their work from range (and staying away from these fights is a good thing). Druids, Paladins, and Shamans, on the other hand, may sometimes be healing from closer in toward the action.

Of course, secondary healers are good to have, and Paladins are the best of options in this case, though Druids are wonderful here too. The Paladins add even more Resistance benefits, can offtank if a main tank gets put out of combat temporarily, and can survive it all. This is true for Druids as well.

The Arcatraz is probably one of the more challenging dungeons for melee DPS characters; Fury and MS Warriors and Enhancement Shamans especially end up having to worry about compromising the group with such powerful enemies coming in. Position such characters very carefully to avoid as many AoEs as possible.

JOBS

CLASS	ABILITIES
Druid	Backup Healing and Innervate
Hunter	Traps, Ranged DPS
Mage	DPS
Paladin	Shadow Resistance, Backup Healing, Tanking or Offtanking
Priest	Shadow Resistance, Dispel, Heal
Rogue	Sap, Wounding Poison against Dalliah, Cloak of Shadows
Shaman	Backup healer or DPS dealer with Elemental Combat
Warlock	Felhunter, Succubus, Ranged DPS
Warrior	Tank

GETTING TO THE THE ARCATRAZ

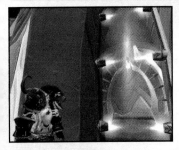

It's on the left side of Tempest Keep (north), and it's higher than the other Instances. Fly up to the highest Tempest Keep dungeon area and use the key that you got from running The Mechanar and The Botanica to unlock the way. Only one person in a group needs to have a key. If nobody has one, ask a Rogue with 350 Lockpicking to open the door or wait for someone in the area to unlock it while taking their group inside. All of this is effective.

REPUTATION GAINS

ACTION	FACTION	REPUTATION GAIN	END POINT
Kill Trash Mobs	The Sha'tar	20-25 Points	Exalted
Kill Bosses	The Sha'tar	120 Points	Exalted
Quest: Seer Udalo	Ashtongue Deathsworn	250 Points	N/A
Quest: The Second and Third Key Fragments	The Violet Eye	350 Points	N/A
Quest: The Harbinger of Doom	The Sha'tar	1000 Points	N/A

THEY ARE NEVER GETTING OFF OF THIS ROCK

BOSSES

ZEREKETH THE UNBOUND

WRATH-SCRYER SOCCOTHRATES

DALLIAH THE DOOMSAYER

HARBINGER SKYRISS

MINIONS

ARCATRAZ DEFENDER
Notes: Light Target

ARCATRAZ SENTINEL
Notes: Energy Discharge

ARCATRAZ WARDER
Notes: Shoot, Arcane Shot, Charged Arcane Shot

DEATH WATCHER
Notes: Immune to All CC, Marked for Death (12 Seconds), Drain Life (1k/second for 5 seconds), Tentacle Cleave

ENTROPIC EYE
Notes: Healing Debuff, Polymorph (to Frog), Shrink, Shadow Resistance Debuff, Disease (Shadow Damage and Mana Loss), Immune to All CC, Tentacle Cleave, Chaos Breath

EREDAR DEATHBRINGER
Notes: Unholy Aura, Knockback, Forceful Cleave

EREDAR SOUL-EATER
Notes: Soul Steal (-45% to Stats and Physical Damage), Soul Chill (AoE Frost Damage and Movement Debuff), Entropic Aura (Casting Times and Movement Times +25%)

ETHEREUM LIFE-BINDER
Notes: Shadow Word: Pain, High DPS, Bind, Shadow Mend

ETHEREUM SLAYER
Notes: Very High Health, Slaying Strike, Impairing Poison

ETHEREUM WAVE-CASTER
Notes: Polymorph, High DPS, Sonic Boom, Arcane Haste

GARGANTUAN ABYSSAL
Notes: Meteor (Damage is divided by number of targets, so let more people get hit oddly enough), Fire Shield, High Health

NEGATON SCREAMER
Notes: Magic Volley, Psychic Scream, Converts to the form of magic that hits them

NEGATON WARP-MASTER
Notes: Summon Negaton Field

PROTEAN HORROR
Notes: Toothy Bite (Physical Damage)

PROTEAN NIGHTMARE
Notes: Cleave, Gaping Maw (Physical DOT), Poison (Incubation), High Health, Immune to All CC, Infectious Poison

PROTEAN SPAWN
Notes: Non-Elite, High Damage Adds for Protean Nightmares (Comes After Incubation Ends), Acidic Bite (Armor Debuff for 30 seconds, Stacks)

SARGERON HELLCALLER
Notes: AoE Hellfire, Immune to CC, Curse of the Elements, Incinerate, Hellrain

SARGERON ARCHER
Notes: AoE Root (Hooked Net), Immune to CC, Shoot, Hooked Net, Scatter Shot, Rapid Fire

SOUL DEVOURER
Notes: Summons Sightless Eyes, Shadow Damage, Sightless Touch Debuff (Reduces Attack Speed by 50%), Frenzy, Fel Breath

SPITEFUL TEMPTRESS
Notes: Spiteful Fury (Adds 500% Threat Generation), Domination, Shadow Bolt

SKULKING WITCH
Notes: Greater Invisibility, Chastise, Lash of Pain (Heroic), Gouge, High DPS

UNBOUND DEVASTATOR
Notes: Deafening Roar (Shadow Damage, Silence, Disarm), Large Aggro Radius, Devastate

UNCHAINED DOOMBRINGER
Notes: War Stomp, Berserker Charge, Agonizing Armor

HARBINGER OF DOOM

Level Requirement	70
Quest Giver	A'dal (Shattrath City, Terrace of Light)
Quest Goal	Slay the final boss of The Arcatraz
Experience Reward	19,000
Additional Rewards	Potent Sha'tari Pendant (Neck +27 Damage/Healing, +24 Resilience), A'dal's Recovery Necklace (Neck +51 Healing, +24 Resilience), Shattrath Choker of Power (Neck +46 Attack Power, +24 Resilience)

This quest requires a complete run of The Arcatraz. Bring a full group with a good tank, two healers, and two DPS characters. Fight all of the bosses, and kill off Skyriss after the full event with the Warden. Return to A'dal when this is complete for your reward.

SEER UDALO

Level Requirement	70
Quest Giver	Akama (Shadowmoon Valley, The Warden's Cage)
Quest Goal	Find Seer Udalo, Near the End of the Instance
Experience Reward	12,650
Additional Rewards	None (But the lore of this quest chain is extremely interesting), Chains to Black Temple

To get this quest, you must complete a small chain that leads into the Ashtongue area at the Warden's Cage. These come from your base camp in eastern Shadowmoon Valley (whether Aldor or Scryer). This begins with Tablets of Baa'ri.

THE SECOND AND THIRD FRAGMENTS

Level Requirement	70
Quest Giver	Khadgar (Shattrath City, Terrace of Light)
Quest Goal	Collect the Second and Third Key Fragments (The Third is here in The Arcatraz)
Experience Reward	15,800
Additional Rewards	Continues Karazhan Chain

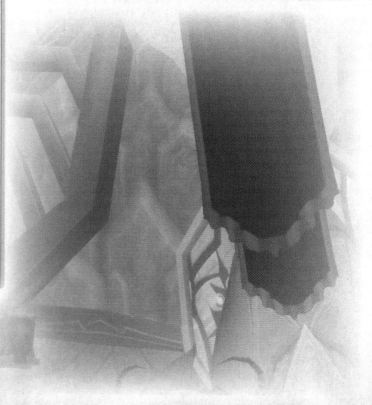

For this part of the quest, your group (or even just a duo of stealthing classes) must get into the dungeon and pass by the first boss' area. There will shortly be a chamber with Voidwalkers, and the right side of that room has a chest.

Opening this chest uncovers the Elemental that carries the Third Fragment. This creature can be duoed safely, but it is imperative to avoid the wandering aggro in the room while doing so.

Once this is done and the portion from The Steamvault is completed as well, you can return to Khadgar and get the next step in the chain (The Master's Touch).

MAP LEGEND	
1	Entrance
2	Butcher's Stand
3	Stasis Block: Trion
4	Zereketh
5	Stasis Block: Maximum (Soccothrates and Dalliah)
6	Containment Core
7	Harbinger Skyriss

BUTCHER'S STAND

The Arcatraz doesn't start off too badly, as the early enemies are more easily controlled with standard CC techniques. In the initial area, your group should find two pairs of Arcatraz Warders. These enemies love to back up and take up space during fights, so they are good to hit with Snares and Roots.

Fight these two pairs of enemies, then set up for the skirmish with three Arcatraz Defenders. They are having their own problems, as you can see. It looks like the containment system of the prison is already failing, and many of the deadly creatures within are breaking out.

Clear the way with a short fight when the enemies are vulnerable, then ahead toward the next encounter. This is where the real trials of the dungeon begin.

Protean Nightmares are just brutal. You must be very careful when pulling these, as even a single Nightmare and its attached Horrors can make for a trying battle. Nightmares cast their Incubate on players to take them out of battle and spawn further Horrors, so it's a very mean debuff.

The best way to deal with the problem is to have DPS characters blow down the Horrors that spawn and return to the central Nightmare; the main tank keeps that Nightmare at bay and uses any AoEs possible to get additional Horrors off of softer party members.

After the initial Nightmare group is down, you have room to look and see what is patrolling. Six wandering Horrors are linked, and they won't provide too ugly a fight. Remind characters without any aggro wipes to hold off on AoE abilities until this group has been thinned a bit (premature blasting is going to rip aggro early and lead to deaths).

STASIS BLOCK: TRION

Continuing into the Stasis Block, there are more enemies. Don't wander quickly, and look at the floors with distrust. The bodies that you see are just waiting to cause problems (Protean Spawns attack when you come too close, so deal with these threats as they come instead of running through).

Pull back when you see the patrol group of a Nightmare and two Horrors nearby. Ensure that the group is prepared before pulling these, then use the previously tested techniques to dispatch the wanderers.

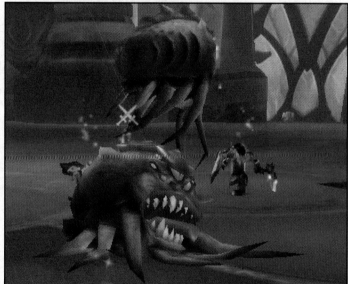

In almost the same area is a fast Horror that loves to add if any groups fight too far forward. A second one can come all of the way forward as well, though with less regularity. Be fully aware of this and use as much distance during the fight with the Nightmare to keep your people see from adds.

With all of those mobile targets done, it's going to be much safer to take care of the fighting. You still won't want to fight inside the main part of the chamber for some time, as almost everything moves around to some extent.

Thus, use ranged pulls and break line-of-sight to keep the foes in the room coming to you. There are Entropic Eyes, Death Watchers, Soul Devourers, and another group of Horrors. Beyond that, there are two bodies in the chamber itself that gives further spawns. Yes, it's quite a place!

KNOW THY ENEMY

The Entropic Eyes in the area have a good mix of crowd control and debuffs. They reduce Shadow Resistance and Healing potential, Polymorph single targets, and use a forward cone breath to deliver their damage. Keep them facing a wall with some smart tanking and it won't be nearly as evil a fight.

Death Watchers cast Marked for Death on the party and use an uninterruptible Drain Life. While they don't have that many tricks, they still give you a mean DPS race.

Soul Devourers come with Horrors and also call Sightless Eyes during the battle. These foes also deal Shadow Damage (and a fair sum of it). Their debuff reduces Attack Speed. The real strategy for survival if for the tank to stay aware of the Horrors and Sightless Eyes and use AoE abilities to generate aggro and keep the attention on themselves. Soul Devourers aren't NEARLY as bad if the tank knows what to expect and avoids chaos.

When every single monster is down, rest and let everyone know about the strategies for defeating Zereketh the Unbound. This Voidwalker holds the left corner and waits for the party's approach before lashing out.

ZEREKETH THE UNBOUND

HP	118060/159381 (Heroic)	Damage	1454-2055/2909-4111 (Heroic)
Abilities	**Shadow Nova:** Deals 1850 to 2150 Shadow damage to all targets within 40 yards; knock back effect. **Heroic:** Deals 3238 to 3762 Shadow damage.		
	Seed of Corruption: Dealing 2400 Shadow damage over 18 sec. When the target takes 2500 total damage, the Seed detonates, dealing 2040 Shadow damage to all within 10 yards. **Heroic:** This deals 3600 damage over 18 sec.		
	Void Zone: Deals 1350 to 1650 Shadow damage every second. **Heroic:** Deals 2250 to 2750 Shadow damage per second.		

THIS VOIDWALKER SWALLOWED A GUILDHALL... WITH ITS MEMBERS STILL INSIDE!

Cloak of Scintillating Auras (Back 76 Armor +12 Stam, +15 Int, +18 Spi, +42 Healing)

Idol of Feral Shadows (Idol +4 Damage per Combo Point for Rip)

Mana-Sphere Shoulderpads (Cloth Shoulder 114 Armor, +23 Stam, +25 Int, +17 Spi, +29 Damage/Healing)

Outland Striders (Mail Feet 448 Armor, +18 Stam, +24 Int, +21 Critical Rating, +50 Attack Power)

Rubium War-Girdle (Plate Waist 655 Armor, +31 Str, +29 Stam, +18 Critical Rating)

Your tank will want to hold Zereketh in the corner while keeping a close eye on the floor. All characters must be ready to move at any time, as this Voidwalker is able to spawn Void Zones on the floor that are very painful if any characters remain within their area of effect.

Shadow Resistance, from potions, Paladin/Priest abilities, and from any possible gear, is very useful in this encounter. Melee attacks from Zereketh, Void Zones, and everything else at his disposal can be reduced in this manner.

In normal mode your ranged DPS can almost directly stay out of Shadow Nova range and keep healers in a very comfortable position; this is not the case in Heroic Mode (where the range of the blast seems to be past just about anyone's healing or DPS potential). This spell does have a casting time, so a very quick reaction can still get people out of range or behind a section of the wall to break line-of-sight. Avoiding this damage also negates the substantial Knockback and delays associated with the Shadow Nova.

Spread out the party; Zereketh finally has Seed of Corruption, and anyone debuffed in this way needs to stay away from allies to keep damage to a minimum. Already being spread out helps this greatly. If the main tank is over by the corner, ranged characters can form a fan that boxes Zereketh into said corner. It works rather well.

Heroic Mode

In Heroic mode Zereketh is extremely tough. Nothing really changes, but every single ability has increased potency.

HEADING UPSTAIRS

Take the ramp up to the top of Zereketh's room and start looking for bodies again; as before, these produce Protean Spawns. Eat them before they eat you, but be more wary of the "destroyed" Golem in the next small chamber. This is an Arcatraz Sentinel, and it's not nearly as trashed as you might expect; rather, it's waiting to give its last hurrah to someone with a side order of pain.

When approached (by the main tank please), the Golem will wake and immediately attack. Almost all of its damage is Arcane, so the main tank should switch to an Arcane suit ahead of time. This is HUGELY beneficial.

Keep the nasty thing away from the party at all times, and DPS should be careful to avoid over-aggroing during the first few moments of the fight. This is not a creature that you want your tank to have to run after. Everything near the Golem takes Arcane damage, and your healers might not be able to keep up. With proper aggro maintained, everything should be fine, and your group can down this lone sentry. Even after death, Sentinels spark and rage for a moment; back off and let the machines finish this phase before having people walk by.

After that your group is back into Void territory. There are Negaton Screamers and Negaton Warp-Masters in the next room. Single, random Horror patrols (though there aren't a huge worry, unlike most patrols in these dungeons). Do what you can to remove them safely, but don't stress yourself out over it.

All Negaton enemies should be pulled back out of the room for battle; this not only ducks the chance for a Horror to add, but it makes it easier to move around during the fight (good for both types of enemies, and we'll explain why).

Screamers have… a Psychic Scream effect! Shocking. Thus, being outside of the room prevent the nightmare of running into adds. Warp-Masters create zones on the floor that heal and buff themselves, so your main tank needs room to pull them around and off of their happy places.

As long as these effects are mitigated, the room is just fine. There are only five of the Negaton enemies, the minor patrollers, and a couple of bodies here and there. If your group is looking for the Fragments (as part of the Karazhan chain), be certain to explore this chamber for the chest you need!

For another treat, your group gets to advance and fight a few Eredar now! These rare enemies are only found in a few interesting places, so it's always good to know that you've met them, discussed the merits of Tauren philosophy, then eradicated the foul, treacherous fiends!

Eredar Deathbringers have a Shadow Damage aura, use Cleave, and also have a Knockback. They deal damage at a high rate, so fighting them feels a bit like a DPS race, though if you have two solid healers it won't be as bad (just ensure that they are ready from the beginning so that they aren't playing catchup with multiple wounded members).

Soul-Eaters have a debuff that is beyond cruel (-45% to stats and Physical Damage for 20 seconds). They also deliver AoE Frost damage and debuff Movement Speed/Casting Time. They aren't quite as scary as the Deathbringers, but they are a wrench in the cogs, as the Gnomes say.

After clearing the first Eredar, grab the bodies from the right side of the room to get the Spawns out of the way. Those Eredar are foul enough without having anything else to worry about while engaging one of them.

Turning south, there are two more enemies before everyone enters Stasis Block: Maximum. They are both Sentinels, so get one-at-a-time and be very careful. Rest between each fight so that your group has full resources to deal with the incoming damage.

STASIS BLOCK: MAXIMUM

Creep toward this Stasis Block when the Sentinels are gone, and let people know that there are Stealthing enemies ahead! The room has a few different demons guarding it, and there are also two bosses inside the chamber; it's not a place for a casual stroll.

There are about half-a-dozen Demons in the room, not counting the actual bosses, who back off from their starting positions and retreat to their respective corners after a moment.

Either use Flare, Detect Invisibility, or actually have a Mage go Invisible to try and find the Skulking Witches, or be extremely hesitant when pulling and retreating from the room. Getting two these Demons at once is a major test for a group, and it can certainly cause a wipe.

Unbound Devastators are quite visible. When safely pulled, your group can focus fire just on them and deal with their AoE Deafening Roar (Shadow damage, Silence, Disarm). Use HOTs when healing during this fights, so that Silence won't leave your healers as far behind. Obviously, you also want to keep people topped off as best as possible.

The Spiteful Temptress, on the right side of the room, has a brief Mind Control and uses Spiteful Fury to add massive Threat generation (+500%) to a target. Tanks should be ready for aggro loss in the event that things go wrong, and Taunt/Mocking Blow/other last-ditch abilities should be prepared. If need be, the Temptress can kited away for a short time while the party goes into full DPS mode on her and works to simply down the target.

When you do find one of the few Witches, pull them in and accept their standard Rogue fair (high DPS, Gouge, etc.). They are very easy on their own. They are the end of the world when they add onto your back while a Devastator is already kicking you around.

When all is done, rest and ponder. Most people choose to fight Dalliah the Doomsayer first, but you are free to take the next two bosses in either order.

DALLIAH THE DOOMSAYER

HP	132840/177120 (Heroic)	Damage	1777-2513/4182-5914 (Heroic)
Abilities	**Whirlwind:** Lasts 6 sec., inflicts normal weapon damage plus 726.		
	Gift of the Doomsayer: Curses an enemy for 10 sec., 100% chance to heal its target by 2313 to 2687 on heal. **Heroic:** This spell heals Dalliah for 4625 to 5375.		
	Heal: 2.5 sec cast. Heals the target for 18500 to 21500 health. **Heroic:** This spell has a 1.5 sec cast.		
	Shadow Wave: Heroic Mode Only. Inflicts 2250 to 2750 Shadow damage. Increases Shadow damage taken by 50% for 15 sec.		

DALLIAH'S JEWELRY BOX

Lamp of Peaceful Repose (Off-Hand +16 Stam, +18 Int, +35 Healing, 6 Mana/5 Seconds)

Nether Core's Control Rod (Wand 129.4 DPS, +9 Stam, +10 Int, +8 Spell Hit Rating, +13 Damage/Healing)

Reflex Blades (Mh Fist 71.7 DPS, +13 Stam, +16 Hit Rating, +32 Attack Power)

Thatia's Self-Correcting Gauntlets (Plate Hands 728 Armor, +16 Str, +35 Stam, +18 Defense Rating, +39 Shield Block)

Worldfire Chestguard (Mail Chest 652 Armor, +33 Stam, +32 Int, +22 Spell Critical Rating, +40 Damage/Healing)

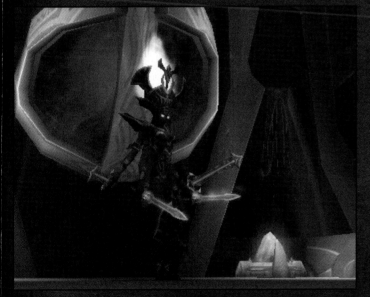

Dalliah is usually the easier of the two bosses in this room. With a basic understand of her ability set, your group is likely to defeat her even on their first attempt!

Dalliah's primary damage output is through standard melee attacks and her frequent Whirlwinds. Each spin of her Whirlwind does heavy damage, so even the main tank needs to back off during this phase. All healers and ranged DPS need to be farther back from the beginning, but that is standard for the majority of boss fights.

Be prepared to use a ranged Interrupt on Dalliah just as soon as her Whirlwind finishes and her casting begins; she has a Heal spell that she uses on herself. Tanks/melee characters can hurry back in to take care of the Interrupt as well. Try to keep Wounding Poison or Mortal Strike on the boss as well, as that will decrease the health she receives when her abilities do succeed.

The other way for Dalliah to restore her health is to place a debuff on her current target. This debuff causes her to receive health whenever that target is healed. This debuff can be Reflected if the main tank is very lucky and on the ball. Shaman Grounding Totems also work to absorb the effect.

Heroic Mode

The only major change in Heroic Mode for Dalliah is that she gains a Shadow Wave that does moderate Shadow damage and increases damage taken by Shadow damage by 50%.

WRATH-SCRYER SOCCOTHRATES

HP	132840/177120 (Heroic)	Damage	2091-2957/4705-6653 (Heroic)
Abilities	**Knock Away:** Normal damage plus knock back.		
	Felfire Shock: Burns 1520 to 1680 Fire damage, an additional 983 Fire damage every 3 sec. for 12 sec. **Heroic:** Deals 2850 to 3150 initial Fire damage and 950 to 1050 additional Fire damage every 3 sec. for 12 sec.		
	Immolation: Deals 414 to 456 Fire damage every 3 sec.		
	Charge: Charges a nearby enemy.		
	Felfire: When Soccothrates charges, he leaves a line of Felfire dealing 1045 to 1155 Fire damage every second.		

AFTER HE DRINKS HIS HEMLOCK, YOU FIND...

Emberhawk Crossbow (Crossbow 66.3 DPS, +18 Critical Rating, +14 Attack Power)

Gloves of the Unbound (Leather Hands 183 Armor, +27 Agi, +20 Stam, 1 [red socket], 1 [blue socket], Socket Bonus: +3 Resilience Rating, +38 Attack Power)

Ryngo's Band of Ingenuity (Finger +12 Stam, +14 Int, +14 Spell Critical Rating, +25 Damage/Healing)

The Sleeper's Cord (Leather Waist 164 Armor, +18 Stam, +24 Int, +21 Spi, +53 Healing)

Warmaul of Infused Light (2h Mace 93.3 DPS, +20 Str, +30 Stam, +28 Int, 1 [red socket], 1 [yellow socket], 1 [blue socket], Socket Bonus: +5 Spell Damage, +21 Critical Rating)

Positioning is the next important step. Let everyone in the group know that the ranged DPS and healers will be forming a line. Soccothrates has a random Charge toward the rear line of the party that he likes to do periodically; if the rear people are close together, this does a huge amount of damage. When people are spread out, this attack is somewhat trivial. The big pain is from the Fire trail that Soccothrates leaves during his charge, and a single pain can withstand a tick of this and get out without crippling the healers' capabilities.

Everyone in melee with Soccothrates has to deal with Fire damage from his aura (this ticks every few seconds and does modest damage). As such, melee DPS character might consider some Fire Resistance gear as well, to reduce healer load. Otherwise, it's likely that such characters will need to retreat and bandage during the fight. Doing so after a charge is the best time, as it won't take as long to get out of the aura's range.

In normal mode, Soccothrates has a Flame Shock that does moderate damage and leaves a substantial DOT on the target; this effect can be Cleansed (and usually should be).

Have your main tank put on any Fire Resistance gear that is available before going after the next boss. Soccothrates has a fair sum of Physical damage, but his Fire output is also very high. If your main tank has a suit that it up-to-date for the occasion, this fight will be much easier.

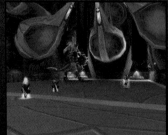

Heroic Mode

Felfire Shock hits for way more damage in Heroic difficulty. Don't waste time trying to Cleanse this effect, as it sticks!

The Fire trail that Soccothrates has gets very ugly. It's frightening how much damage a person can take; the Fire does about 20% more damage per tick. Basically, characters should prepare their escape even before Soccothrates starts his charge. That way you can have your person in motion immediately.

Once both bosses are dead, walk through the door that opens toward the front of the chamber. Climb up to the higher tier from there and deal with Arcane Sentinel and bodies in the next hallway.

Protean Horrors patrol past the northern arch, but they are a trifle. Instead, it is the fallen hulks of two Sentinels that you should fear the most. Both of them are still active, and they are grouped (yes, the feeling of "oh crud" that you just had is shared by all groups).

Fights like this are why you really need to have two healers in The Arcatraz (and Arcane Resistance gear). If your group lacks those things, it's possible to try and kite one of the Sentinels away while the other is killed, but even that takes the Sentinel past your group and is rather ugly in the process.

In fact, you just might have to accept that a poorly-geared group is going to kill one Sentinel, wipe here, and come back for the other. One healer and no Arcane Resistance tends to equal squished tank unless your group is REALLY on their best game.

A lone Sentinel guards the end of the hallway, but that one is a joke after what you just survived.

CONTAINMENT CORE

Finally you get to a room where there is some crowd control (thank all the fates)! Ethereals are here, in three varieties. Wave-Casters are Mages with Polymorph for crowd control, Slayers are trivial but takes a long time to down, and Life-Binders are Priests with AoE Immobilize, Shadow Word: Pain, and Blind.

Hit the Wave-Casters with crowd control, destroy the Life-Binders first, then take out the Slayers. The fights really aren't that bad. Pull the group of four on the right first, when the patrol is farther off. Then kill the patrol, and finish with the four Ethereals around the right corner.

Search the room for the body of Seer Udalo, if your group is trying to complete that quest.

When ready, look into the last area and marvel at the beautiful enemies. They look impressive, and their combat potential is there to match. The Satyrs aren't too vicious (the Archers have an AoE Hooked Net that frustrates melee characters and the Hellcallers use Curse of Elements and Hellfire). You can't use crowd control in these fights, but slapping heavy DPS on the Hellcallers will remove the real threat shortly. Remember to Snare or Root the Archers when cleaning them up at the end.

Pull both groups of Satyrs well into the previous chamber to avoid getting any other Demons involved in the two skirmishes. Do this when the patrolling Abyssal is far off on his route.

Once the Satyrs are cleared, wait for the Abyssal and let the group know that they should bunch together for the fight ahead. It sounds very stupid, but it's actually a good move. The Meteor used by the Abyssals does a set amount of Fire damage. If it hits just one person, that character is either dead or wishing that they were. If it hits an entire group, the spread ensures that nobody will be in particularly bad shape. Once you understand that, the big threat of the Abyssals is done; add Fire Resistance when possible and run a standard tank-and-trash fight.

Doombringers are also in the room, though they are not as scary. These Demons have an AoE Stun, Intercept, Debuff Armor, and melee well. But, they don't have very high health for what they are, and their output isn't enough to suddenly burst a tank down.

Use ranged pulls to grab each solo Demon, win the fights, and get ready for the final boss event once all is done!

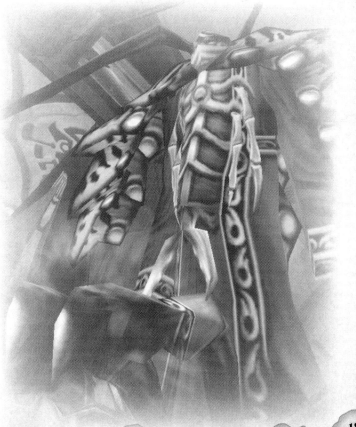

HARBINGER SKYRISS EVENT

HARBINGER SKYRISS

HP	147575/194799 (Heroic)	**Damage**	2182-3083/4364-6166 (Heroic)
Abilities	**Mind Rend**: Deals 1250 Shadow damage every 1 sec and stuns the target for 3 sec. **Heroic**: Deals 1800 damage per second.		
	Fear: Flee in terror for 4 sec.		
	Domination: Takes control of a humanoid enemy up to level 87 for 6 sec.		
	Mana Burn: Heroic Mode Only. For each point of mana consumed by the bolt, the target takes 0.5 damage. Burns 1425 to 1575 mana.		
	Summon Illusion: Creates an illusionary duplicate of Harbinger Skyriss.		
	Teleport: Teleports Harbinger Skyriss, allowing him to switch places with one of his illusionary duplicates.		

YOU'VE EARNED THIS

Breastplate of the Bold (Plate Chest 1164 Armor, +23 Str, +21 Agi, +33 Stam, 1 [red socket], 2 [blue socket], Socket Bonus: +4 Defense Rating, +19 Defense Rating)

Tidefury Chestpiece (Mail Chest 652 Armor, +28 Stam, +22 Int, 1 [blue socket], 2 [yellow socket], Socket Bonus: +5 Spell Damage, +10 Spell Hit Rating, +36 Damage/Healing, 4 Mana/5 Seconds)

Helm of Assassination (Leather Head 237 Armor, +25 Stam, 1 [yellow socket], 1 [meta socket], Socket Bonus: +4 Dodge Rating, +25 Critical Rating, +66 Attack Power)

Hood of Oblivion (Cloth Head 127 Armor, +27 Stam, +32 Int, 1 [blue socket], 1 [meta socket], Socket Bonus: +5 Spell Damage, +40 Damage/Healing)

Hallowed Crown (Cloth Head 127 Armor, +12 Stam, +24 Int, +26 Spi, 1 [blue socket], 1 [meta socket], Socket Bonus: +4 Spi, +57 Healing)

Doomplate Chestguard (Plate Chest 1164 Armor, +30 Str, +27 Stam, 2 [red socket], 1 [blue socket], Socket Bonus: +4 Critical Rating, +19 Critical Rating)

Elementium Band of the Sentry (Finger +24 Stam, +20 Defense Rating, +19 Dodge Rating)

Hungering Spineripper (1h Dagger 71.7 DPS, +13 Stam, +16 Critical Rating, +30 Attack Power)

Choker of Fluid Thought (Neck +15 Stam, +17 Int, +17 Spi, +35 Healing)

Lamp of Peaceful Radiance (Off-Hand +13 Stam, +14 Int, +12 Spell Hit Rating, +13 Spell Critical Rating, +21 Damage/Healing)

Shiffar's Nexus-Horn (Trinket Equip for +32 Spell Critical Rating, Chance on Critical Hit for +225 to Spell Damage for 10 Seconds)

Sigil-Laced Boots (Cloth Feet 107 Armor, +24 Stam, +18 Int, 1 [red socket], 1 [yellow socket], Socket Bonus: +3 Int, +17 Spell Critical Rating, +20 Damage/Healing)

Full rest, rebuff, and use any potions that are needed before approaching Warden Mellichar. You won't be able to fully attack the Warden, as this jailor has the ability to go Immune to all damage for quite some time.

Once you trigger this event, there is a brief period before the pods around the group start to open. Look to the left to see the first pod start to move, then expect two pods from the right to open, then the last one on the left. There will be three fights in this way that lead up to the encounter with the final boss.

Phase One

PHASE-HUNTER

HP	81180/110700 (Heroic)	**Damage**	2352-3326/4182-5914 (Heroic)
Abilities	**Warp**: Teleports the caster behind target.		
	Back Attack: Inflicts normal damage plus 1850 to 2150, but only if attacking from behind.		
	Phase Burst: Increases movement speed and attack speed by 75% for 8 sec.		

BLAZING TRICKSTER

HP	67068/89424 (Heroic)	**Damage**	1434-2026/2868-4052 (Heroic)
Abilities	**Firebolt**: Deals 1980 to 2420 Fire damage. **Heroic**: Deals 2700 to 3300 Fire damage.		
	Fire Shield: Increases Fire resistance by 100 and makes every strike against the target cause 50 Fire damage to the attacker. Lasts 3 min.		

The Trickster is a Fire-base Imp that can target the group randomly with its ranged Fireballs. Healers should be ready to help non-tanks should they have health problems.

The Phase-Hunter is an easier target, but it also more aggro sensitive. Because this enemy has a Blink, you don't want it to be able to go after you back line of characters. Tanks should switch to whatever forms allows them their in-combat charge as soon as the Blink occurs (Pallies will just have to hoof it, but such is the way of things).

Phase Two

SULFURON MAGMA-THROWER

HP	70836/94448 (Heroic)	**Damage**	1731-2446/4452-6290 (Heroic)
Abilities	**Magma-Thrower's Curse**: Reduces healing effects by 50% for 1 min.		
	Rain of Fire: Burns in a selected area for 925 to 1075 Fire damage every 2 sec. for 6 sec. **Heroic**: Deals 1850 to 2150 damage every 2 sec. for 6 sec.		
	Shadow Bolt: Deals 1620 to 1980 Shadow damage. **Heroic**: Deals 2700 to 3300 Shadow damage.		

AKKIRIS LIGHTNING-WAKER

HP	70836/94448 (Heroic)	**Damage**	1607-2271/3637-5138 (Heroic)
Abilities	**Lightning Jump**: Teleports the caster to a specific target.		
	Lightning-Walker's Curse: Increases the magical damage taken by 100% for 1 min.		
	Lightning Discharge: Inflicts 925 to 1075 Nature damage. **Heroic**: Deals 1850 to 2150 Nature damage.		
	Spell Shock: Prevents the target from casting that spell again for 6 sec.		
	Magic Grounding: Reduces damage taken from magic by 50% for 30 sec.		

Have melee DPS move in toward the first pod on the left and stand almost underneath the device as it opens. Shortly, a Blazing Trickster or a Phase-Hunter will appear.

Get more rest and watch happily as an ally joins your ranks. A Gnome Mage pops out from the other pod on the right side and vows to fight the enemies for not showing him enough respect. This NPC can be healed in the following engagements (and should be, as his damage output is a very useful addition).

The second pod on the right sight opens next. Rest as soon as the first enemy falls so that your group will be ready for the next foe will as much of their health and mana as possible. The new mini-boss is either a Sulfuron Magma-Thrower or an Akkiris Lightning-Waker.

The Maga-Thrower is a huge pain if your group relies on melee DPS. The frequent Rain of Fire that this foe uses will force such characters away and reduce damage output. Mages/Druids should be ready to Decurse the healing Debuff that this enemy lands as well.

The Lightning-Waker has a massive-range AoE (Nature damage). It too has a mean Curse, so Mages and Druids must stay aware; this Curse doubles damage taken from magic, and that can be ruinous. Mages are in great shape, because they can stop the Curse AND Spellsteal the nice buff that the Lightning-Waker uses (it halves damage taken).

Phase Three

TWILIGHT DRAKONAAR

HP	86630/118080 (Heroic)	Damage	2132-3016/4182-5914 (Heroic)
Abilities	**Brood Power (Black):** Deals 2125 to 2875 Fire damage within 15 yards.		
	Brood Power (Red): Deals 2625 damage every 1 sec. for 5sec.		
	Brood Power (Bronze): Deals 788 to 1012 Arcane damage to targets within 15 yards. Also decreases casting speed by 50% and increases time between attacks for all affected targets by 33% for 6 sec.		
	Brood Power (Blue): Deals 1313 to 1687 Frost damage to targets within 15 yards and burns 1750 to 2250 mana. Also increases the time between attacks for all affected targets by 100% for 6 sec.		

BLACKWING DRAKONAAR

HP	88560/118080 (Heroic)	Damage	2132-3016/4182-5914 (Heroic)
Abilities	**Brood Power (Black):** Deals 2125 to 2875 Fire damage to targets within 15 yards.		
	Blast Wave: Inflicts 2625-3375 Fire damage to nearby enemies and reduces movement speed for 8 sec. **Heroic:** Deals 3500 to 4500 Fire damage.		
	Mortal Strike: Inflicts 130% weapon damage and reduces any healing by 50% for 5 sec.		

The last pod on the left begins to open, and soon enough you will face either a Blackwing or Twilight Drakonaar.

The Blackwing Drakonaar is a decent test of your group's power. This foe is a heavy melee target with a cruel AoE + Knockback. Combine this with Mortal Strike and you pose a problem for single healer groups (we warned you!). Don't use Fire damage on the Blackwing Drakonaar, as it is Immune to all Fire sources.

Don't tank this enemy against the wall, as the Knockback can cause some Evade bugging (with some consistency).

Have ranged characters stay as far back as possible to avoid the Blastwave. Melee DPS must time their attacks so that they can fight for 10-15 seconds and retreat, then return to hit the enemy again after the Blastwave is used. The main tank cannot escape this effect, so they should not bother to move at all.

If your group faces the Twilight Drakonaar, there is a mix of abilities that can be used (from all of the various types of Dragonkin). The main tank is hit with crowd control rather frequently, so DPS must be cautious of going full tilt and pulling aggro. Otherwise, this isn't too bad a target and is actually a fair bit easier to down than the Blackwing Drakonaar.

Phase Four

Get any rest that you can before Skyriss appears, and know that it is possible for this boss to start its attack before the Drakonaar even goes down (yikes).

The group leader should always put a raid icon (of any sort) on Skyriss as soon as the fight begins. AT 66% and 33% health, this boss spawns an identical image with less health and weaker powers; your people are going to switch to the lesser ones and trash them quickly, and seeing which target DOESN'T have the raid icon gives immediate feedback.

Skyriss is all about crowd control and its Mind Flay. Using Fear and Mind Control, this boss is able to disrupt the party heavily. As before, a second healer or even a backup must be ready. The Mind Flay and the crowd controls may cause your primary healer to be in sudden and dire straights! Anything can happen here, as much of Skyriss' targeting is done without regard to the Threat list.

Know that fleeing the chamber will cause the event to fail. The good news is that you can prevent a full wipe by doing this. If you lose your free Mage or have your healer(s) go down, get out of the room and wait for the Warden to respawn.

As long as your group has the healing potential, this Skyriss isn't a vicious boss. Trying to solo heal this, however, makes for party wipes galore. There is too much of a chance that your healer will take a Mind Flay and not be able to heal themselves. Combine this with the timing for characters that are Mind Flayed, then Mind Controlled, and it gets even harder to stay current with healing unless you have someone on HOTs, someone on full heals, and so forth.

When each Clone appears, switch all DPS and bring the new foe down. It won't take long, and you aren't likely to have any issues will this part of the slaughter.

Heroic Mode

The major difference in Heroic mode is every mini-boss has more hit points and hits a lot harder so it is more difficult to carry hit points and mana between the phases. Be especially wary of Skyriss' Mind Rend.

And that is that! Your party has now cleared what is certainly one of the more challenging 5-character dungeons in the game. You didn't get to rely on crowd control for almost any of the fights, so survival was all about good positioning, rugged healing, an sensible control of aggro. With those skills mastered, it's clear that you have the ability to move on to whatever challenge is next (replay the dungeons in Heroic Mode if you haven't already, finish Attuning for Karazhan and read the walkthrough for that awesome raid, or take a break and hit the Arena). Whatever you do, enjoy!

DOOM LORD KAZZAK

Doom Lord Kazzak packed up and moved to the Outlands when the Dark Portal was reopened. He hasn't changed very much since his days in Blasted Lands, but don't make the mistake of underestimating him.

Kazzak is located in the northern part of Hellfire Peninsula at the Throne of Kil'Jaeden. He is surrounded by several guards: Deathforge Automatons, Greater Fel-Sparks, Throne Hounds, and Throne-Guard Sentinels. The minions around him don't really do anything worth mentioning; tank them and kill them fairly easily.

HP	1214080	Damage	14896-21062

Be careful not to accidentally agro Kazzak when killing the 2 Deathforge Automatons in front of him! He has a large agro radius and you don't want to prematurely start the fight.

Kazzak spawns about 2 times a week. He despawns if not killed after several hours.

It is believed that Kazzak is designed for a 25 person raid group, but there are no drawbacks to bringing a full 40 person raid group to kill him.

LOOT

Ancient Spellcloak of the Highborne: Back, 101 Armor, +15 INT, Equip: Increases damage and healing done by magical spells and effects by up to 36, Equip: Improves spell critical strike rating by 19

Exodar Life-Staff: Staff Two-Hand, 144-294 Damage, Speed 3.20, 68.4 damage per second, +34 INT, Blue Socket, Blue Socket, Yellow Socket, 2 mana per 5 sec., Equip: Increases healing done by spells and effects by up to 364, Equip: Restores 18 mana per 5 sec

Gold-Leaf Wildboots: Leather Feet, 261 Armor, +19 INT, +18 SPI, Yellow Socket, Blue Socket, Socket Bonus: +7 Healing, Equip: Increases healing done by spells and effects by up to 86

Hope Ender: Sword One-Hand, 163-304 Damage, Speed 2.60, 89.8 damage per second, Equip: Increases attack power by 70

Leggings of the Seventh Circle: Cloth Legs, 177 Armor, +22 INT, Red Socket, Yellow Socket, Yellow Socket, Socket Bonus: +5 Spell Damage, Equip: Increases damage and healing done by magical spells and effects by up to 50, Equip: Improves spell hit rating by 18, Equip: Improves spell critical strike rating by 25

Ring of Flowing Light: Finger, Equip: Increases healing done by spells and effects by up to 75, Equip: Improves spell critical strike rating by 23

Ring of Reciprocity: Finger, Equip: Increases attack power by 62, Equip: Improves hit rating by 15, Equip: Improves critical strike rating by 19

Ripfiend Shoulderplates: Plate Shoulder, 1133 Armor, +39 STR, Yellow Socket, Yellow Socket, Socket Bonus: +3 STR, Equip: Improves critical strike rating by 22, Equip: Improves hit rating by 13

Scaled Greaves of the Marksman: Mail Legs, 740 Armor, +37 AGI, Red Socket, Red Socket, Red Socket, Socket Bonus: +4 AGI, Equip: Increases attack power by 76, Equip: Increases bow skill rating by 16, Equip: Increases gun skill rating by 16

Topaz-Studded Battlegrips: Plate Hands, 944 Armor, +49 STA, Yellow Socket, Blue Socket, Socket Bonus: +5 Block Value, Equip: Increases defense rating by 31

ABILITIES

CAPTURE SOUL

Explanation: If anyone dies to damage done by Kazzak, he heals himself for about 10% of his total life. Opposing faction players, players that are not level 70, pets, and totems do not cause him to heal.

Solution: Don't die! Your healers have to keep everyone alive. You might be able to afford one or two deaths that cause him to heal, but even that is questionable.

CLEAVE

Explanation: Kazzak has a cleave attack that hits everyone in front of him for several thousand damage.

Solution: Only the main tank should be in front of Kazzak. All of the melee DPS needs to stay behind him to avoid the Cleave.

ENRAGE

Explanation: 54 seconds after engaging, Kazzak Enrages. His melee attack damage is increased by 25% and he sends 6 waves of Shadowbolt Volleys out. Enrage fades after the last Shadowbolt Volley.

Solution: The ideal solution is to kill him within 54 seconds, but this is very difficult to achieve. Most likely, you just have to heal the damage from Shadowbolt Volley and make sure the main tank doesn't die during the Enrage. You should be able to kill him before a second Enrage happens.

MARK OF KAZZAK

Explanation: Mana-having players randomly get this debuff. It lasts 10 seconds and drains 5% of your mana per second. If you run out of mana with Mark of Kazzak active, you explode and deal several thousand damage to the entire raid. It is not removable.

Solution: Players with mana must remain above 50% mana throughout the fight so they never run out of mana with Mark of Kazzak up. The damage they do if they allow their mana to be drained away entirely is probably going to wipe the raid. They can also drink potions if necessary.

SHADOWBOLT VOLLEY

Explanation: Every 10 seconds or so Kazzak sends a wave of Shadowbolts that hit everyone around him for about 2,000 damage. They have a very long range and ignore LoS, but they are resistible.

Solution: You can't really avoid them altogether. Make sure Shadow Protection is on everyone and heal the damage.

TWISTED REFLECTION

Explanation: Kazzak applies Twisted Reflection to random players throughout the fight. When you have Twisted Reflection on you, any damage that Kazzak does to you causes him to be healed. It is a dispelable magic debuff and it does not have a chance to hit the main tank.

Solution: Cleanse it quickly! You don't want someone to become afflicted by Twisted Reflection and then take damage from the Shadowbolt Volley. Kazzak heals several thousand damage if this happens. Get rid of it as quickly as you can and it shouldn't be a problem.

PREPARATION

The main tank takes significant melee damage throughout the fight so they need a solid group with a Warlock for Blood Pact and maybe a Paladin for Devotion Aura and a Shaman for Grace of Air and Stoneskin.

Put someone who can dispel magic in every group. One of the most important parts of the fight is dispelling Twisted Reflection as quickly as possible.

For the rest of the groups try to maximize DPS by putting Marksmanship Hunters with melee DPS, Shadow Priests with casters, and so on. Kazzak is sort of a DPS based fight with the timed Enrage so you want to squeeze out every bit you can through the group makeup.

Finally, before engaging, buff everyone with Shadow Protection to help reduce the damage caused by Shadowbolt Volley.

STRATEGY

Clear out the various minions surrounding Kazzak before pulling him. You don't need to kill everything, just the ones that are in the area where you fight him.

The main tank starts the fight by engaging Kazzak and turning him away from everyone else. Keep him faced opposite of the raid to avoid damage from the Cleave.

Fairly soon the first Shadowbolt Volley is cast. Most of the raid takes the damage and needs to be healed up. You don't want anyone to die to the damage because their death causes Kazzak to heal himself.

Twisted Reflection is applied to players at random as the fight goes on. The people who can dispel magic need to stay on top of getting it removed as quickly as possible. It really shouldn't be on a player for longer than a second at a time.

And the incurable debuff Mark of Kazzak is applied to players that have mana at random as well. If you have mana, you can't let yourself go below about 50% of your mana pool. You really don't want anyone to run out of mana with Mark of Kazzak on them because, if they do, they explode and deal very significant damage to the entire raid. Make sure you have a mana potion handy in case!

For the first 54 seconds of the fight you DPS him down while keeping the main tank alive, removing Twisted Reflection as quickly as possible, and not dying to Mark of Kazzak. You might be able to kill him within 54 seconds and avoid an Enrage altogether, but this is very hard to accomplish.

Assuming you don't kill him within 54 seconds, he is going to Enrage. When this happens, he shoots 6 waves of Shadowbolt Volley in a row and deals 25% more damage to the main tank. Ideally, your whole raid is at full life—ready to take the Shadowbolts. Healers need to make sure that nobody dies during the Enrage; you don't want anyone to die and heal him.

When the Enrage is over, get everyone healed up and go back to taking Kazzak down. You really should kill him before a second Enrage; healer mana isn't going to last forever, especially with the Mark of Kazzak ability forcing mana users to keep their mana high.

Kazzak is a quick fight with a lot of potential for things to go wrong and a fair amount of damage being dealt to the entire raid. If you wipe to him, the graveyard is next door so you can quickly get ready to go again. Hopefully after a little bit of practice, Kazzak dies and you collect some great loot.

DOOMWALKER

Doomwalker guards the area outside of the Black Temple in the eastern part of Shadowmoon Valley. He is a large mechanical boss similar to a Fel Reaver but not quite the same.

Doomwalker spawns about 2 times a week. He despawns if not killed after several hours.

It is believed that Doomwalker is designed for a 25 person raid group, but there are no drawbacks to bringing a full 40 person raid group to kill him.

HP	2276400	Damage	13940-19710

LOOT

Anger-Spark Gloves: Cloth Hands, 126 Armor, Red Socket, Red Socket, Socket Bonus: +3 Spell Crit Rating, Equip: Increases damage and healing done by magical spells and effects by up to 30, Equip: Improves spell hit rating by 20, Equip: Improves spell critical strike rating by 25

Archaic Charm of Presence: Neck, +23 INT, Equip: Increases healing done by spells and effects by up to 75

Barrel-Blade Longrifle: Gun Range, 147-275 Damage, Speed 2.60, 81.2 damage per second, +16 AGI, Red Socket, Red Socket, Socket Bonus: +3 Crit Rating

Black-Iron Battlecloak: Back, 101 Armor, Equip: Increases attack power by 60, Equip: Improves critical strike rating by 30

Ethereum Nexus-Reaver: Two-Hand Axe Two-Hand, 346-519 Damage, Speed 3.70, 116.9 damage per second, +50 STR, Red Socket, Yellow Socket, Yellow Socket, Equip: Improves critical strike rating by 30

Faceguard of the Endless Watch: Plate Head, 1227 Armor, +49 STA, Blue Socket, Yellow Socket, Yellow Socket, Socket Bonus: +6 STA, Equip: Increases defense rating by 30, Equip: Increases your dodge rating by 37

Fathom-Helm of the Deeps: Mail Head, 687 Armor, +29 INT, Yellow Socket, Blue Socket, Blue Socket, Socket Bonus: +9 Healing, Equip: Increases healing done by spells and effects by up to 106, Equip: Restores 9 mana per 5 sec

Gilded Trousers of Benediction: Cloth Legs, 177 Armor, +15 STA, +16 INT, Yellow Socket, Blue Socket, Blue Socket, Socket Bonus: +9 Healing, Equip: Increases healing done by spells and effects by up to 118, Equip: Restores 12 mana per 5 sec

Talon of the Tempest: Dagger Main Hand, 26-123 Damage, Speed 1.80, 41.4 damage per second, +10 INT, Yellow Socket, Yellow Socket, Socket Bonus: +3 INT, Equip: Increases damage and healing done by magical spells and effects by up to 194, Equip: Improves spell hit rating by 9, Equip: Improves spell critical strike rating by 19

Terrorweave Tunic: Leather Chest, 379 Armor, Red Socket, Yellow Socket, Yellow Socket, Socket Bonus: +4 Crit Rating, Equip: Increases attack power by 96, Equip: Improves hit rating by 21, Equip: Improves critical strike rating by 25

ABILITIES

LIGHTNING WRATH

Explanation: Randomly cast on any player nearby. The initial hit is for about 2,000 damage and the damage doubles every time it chains onto another person within about 8 yards.

Solution: Spread out the entire raid in at least a half circle, preferably a full circle around Doomwalker. Chain Lightning shouldn't hit more than one or two people at a time. Melee DPS is the most susceptible to Chain Lightning and needs to be extra careful about staying spread out.

EARTHQUAKE

Explanation: Every 60 seconds or so Doomwalker pounds the ground stunning everyone while dealing 8,000 damage over 8 seconds.

Solution: Everyone in the raid needs at least 8,000 life or they are probably going to die to Earthquake. Other than that, you can't really avoid it so heal up the damage to prepare for the next one.

ENRAGE

Explanation: At 20% life, Doomwalker Enrages causing his melee damage to double.

Solution: A combination of switching tanks and using Shield Wall should get you through the Enrage. He can easily instantly kill a Warrior while Enraged but a feral Druid with very high armor has a chance of surviving the hits.

OVERRUN

Explanation: Every 45 seconds or so Doomwalker drops his agro and begins to charge players at random.

Solution: Thankfully he is Tauntable. When Overrun starts, the goal is to get him back on a tank and back into his original position. The easiest way to accomplish this is by having tanks get to him, Taunt him, and bring him back into position.

CRUSH ARMOR

Explanation: Decreases armor by 10% for 1 minute. This ability stacks.

Solution: Switch tanks when the damage becomes unmanageable.

PREPARATION

There are several tanks involved in the fight so try to give them the usual groups of Warlocks, Paladins, and Shamans where ever possible.

The only other thing to take into consideration is the positioning. You have to stay spread out to avoid Chain Lightning. Try to use a full circle around Doomwalker but using half a circle can work as well. Setup each group's general position before engaging him.

STRATEGY

The pull is a little weird. For some reason, he doesn't respond well to Misdirect, so I suggest simply having one of the tanks pull him. Make sure the tank that does the pull gets some heals on the way to the position he is going to be tanked in.

Move him into the middle of your circle of groups. Make sure everyone is nicely spread out around Doomwalker and start to DPS him.

Within about 45 seconds, the first Overrun occurs. He goes charging off in a random direction and starts attacking someone new. Sometimes he simply kills whoever his new target is and there isn't much you can do about it. Most of the time someone who can Taunt should pick him up during the Overrun and get him back into position. He hits fairly hard so if you have DPS Warriors helping with the Taunts, have a tanking Warrior take it off of them as quickly as you can.

Shortly after the Overrun is over, or about 60 seconds after Engaging, the first Earthquake hits. While he is using Earthquake he stops doing melee damage to the current tank. Everyone gets stunned and takes 2,000 damage every 2 seconds for 8 seconds, resulting in 8,000 damage to everyone. Since your raid is all above 8,000 life, nobody should die to the Earthquake. Heal up your groups while keeping an eye on the tank.

That is really all there is to the fight until 20%. Overruns are a little chaotic but quick reactions by the tanks will keep him under control. Stay spread out so that Chain Lightning doesn't take out a whole mass of people. And keep everyone's life topped off in preparation for the Earthquakes.

At 20% he Enrages. This is where it gets interesting. His melee damage doubles and this is a huge problem. He can easily instantly kill a tanking Warrior while Enraged, but a well geared feral Druid can usually take the hits. Warriors should probably use Shield Wall for good measure. Be ready to pickup agro with Taunt if the current tank dies.

While Enraged he continues to use Overrun, Chain Lightning, and Earthquake, but the damage done by these abilities is not increased; only his melee damage is.

Get through that last 20% and you'll be picking through the scrap iron that was once Doomwalker for some nice loot.

If anyone dies to Doomwalker, they are afflicted by a 15 minute debuff called Mark of Death. Anyone who has the Mark of Death debuff is instantly killed if they get close to him. Anyone who dies during the fight is out of the fight and you have to wait 15 minutes between attempts after a wipe.

KARAZHAN

Medivh's old home Karazhan has lied abandoned since his death many years ago. Monsters led by a demon Prince have invaded the tower and it's your job to clean it out.

Karazhan is the first 10 person raid instance in The Burning Crusade. It is a fairly big instance with 11 challenging boss encounters and lots of good loot.

DUNGEON INFORMATION

Name	Karazhan
Location	Deadwind Pass
Suggested Levels	Group of 10, Level 70
Time to Complete	5 hours to several days

WHO TO BRING

Karazhan is a very balanced instance. You can build a raid that consists of 1 person from every class and an additional tank. Two tanks (either Warriors or Feral Druids) are essential for many of the normal pulls and a couple of the boss fights. Bringing a well rounded raid of all classes works out just fine, but there are some fights that are made easier by changing one or two people around.

Moroes has four Undead adds that can be Shackled so bringing a couple Priests to help with CC can be very helpful.

Shade of Aran summons some Water Elementals so a Warlock for Fear and Banish is almost essential for this fight.

Prince Malchezaar requires a lot of DPS to kill him as quickly as possible so replacing a second Protection Warrior with a DPS class is advisable.

Nightbane is another DPS intensive fight and bringing a Paladin to handle one of his abilities is required.

The ideal class makeup changes from boss to boss but you really don't need to stack a certain class or bring the perfect group in order to be successful. Everything is fairly flexible and a raid group of people who play well and know the fights are going to succeed.

GETTING TO KARAZHAN

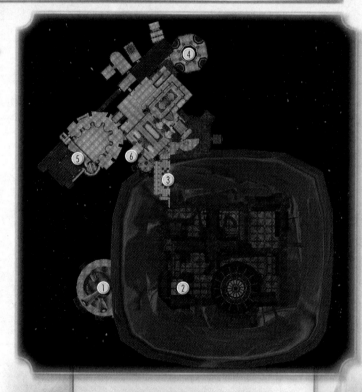

MAP LEGEND	
1	Netherspite
2	Terestian Illhoof
3	Chess Event
4	Maiden of Virtue
5	Opera Event
6	Moroes

Due to the three-dimensional nature of the map all areas cannot be shown.

QUEST CHAIN

ARCANE DISTURBANCES

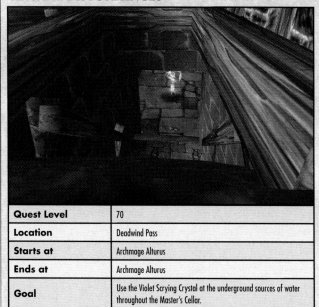

Quest Level	70
Location	Deadwind Pass
Starts at	Archmage Alturus
Ends at	Archmage Alturus
Goal	Use the Violet Scrying Crystal at the underground sources of water throughout the Master's Cellar.

In the burnt down village outside of Karazhan there are two staircases that lead down to the Master's Cellar. The first water source is a large pond down the western staircase. The second water source is a well in a room along the right hand side of the eastern staircase. Use the Violet Scrying Crystal at both water sources and return to Archmage Alturus.

RESTLESS ACTIVITY

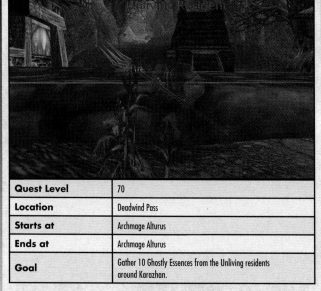

Quest Level	70
Location	Deadwind Pass
Starts at	Archmage Alturus
Ends at	Archmage Alturus
Goal	Gather 10 Ghostly Essences from the Unliving residents around Karazhan.

Kill the Undead creatures around Karazhan until you have collected 10 Ghostly Essences and return to Archmage Alturus.

CONTACT FROM DALARAN

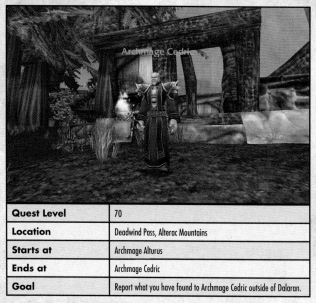

Quest Level	70
Location	Deadwind Pass, Alterac Mountains
Starts at	Archmage Alturus
Ends at	Archmage Cedric
Goal	Report what you have found to Archmage Cedric outside of Dalaran.

Take the report from Archmage Alturus to Archmage Cedric on the northern part of Dalaran in Alterac Mountains.

KHADGAR

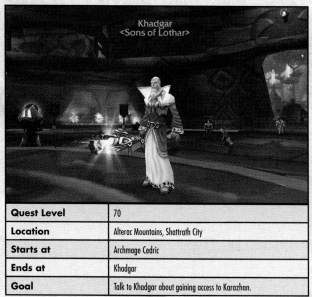

Quest Level	70
Location	Alterac Mountains, Shattrath City
Starts at	Archmage Cedric
Ends at	Khadgar
Goal	Talk to Khadgar about gaining access to Karazhan.

Archmage Cedric sends you to speak with Medivh's apprentice Khadgar who now lives in Shattrath City about gaining access to Karazhan. He is in the middle of the Terrace of Light.

QUEST CHAINI

ENTRY INTO KARAZHAN

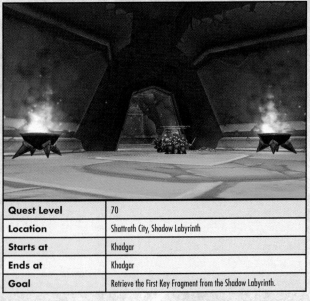

Quest Level	70
Location	Shattrath City, Shadow Labyrinth
Starts at	Khadgar
Ends at	Khadgar
Goal	Retrieve the First Key Fragment from the Shadow Labyrinth.

The First Key Fragment is found at the end of the Shadow Labyrinth. After killing Murmur, click the container on the ledge to the left of him. An elite elemental spawns and drops the First Key Fragment when killed. Return to Khadgar after obtaining it.

THE SECOND AND THIRD FRAGMENTS

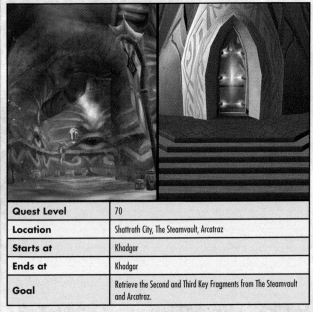

Quest Level	70
Location	Shattrath City, The Steamvault, Arcatraz
Starts at	Khadgar
Ends at	Khadgar
Goal	Retrieve the Second and Third Key Fragments from The Steamvault and Arcatraz.

The Second Key Fragment is in a pool of water near Hydromancer Thespia in The Steamvault. The Third Key Fragment is at the top of the stairs right before Zereketh the Unbound's room in Arcatraz.

Just like the First Key Fragment, an elite elemental spawns when the container is clicked and drops the quest piece for you when killed. As soon as you have collected both Key Fragments, return to Khadgar.

THE MASTER'S TOUCH

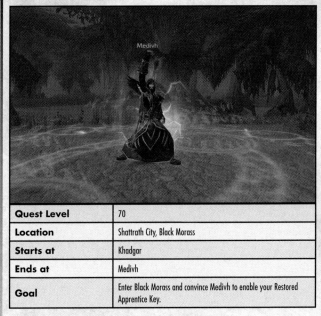

Quest Level	70
Location	Shattrath City, Black Morass
Starts at	Khadgar
Ends at	Medivh
Goal	Enter Black Morass and convince Medivh to enable your Restored Apprentice Key.

The only person who can grant access to Karazhan is Medivh himself. Unfortunately, Medivh is dead, but that is a minor inconvenience because you can still visit him in the Black Morass at the Caverns of Time. Before you can enter Black Morass, you must complete Old Hillsbrad.

Take a strong group to Black Morass and complete the portal opening event there. As soon as you have successfully opened the Dark Portal Medivh is willing to enable your Restored Apprentice Key.

RETURN TO KHADGAR

Quest Level	70
Location	Black Morass, Shattrath City
Starts at	Medivh
Ends at	Khadgar
Goal	Return to Khadgar with your Master's Key.

Medivh has given you his own key to Karazhan. You can now enter Karazhan, but the quest line continues after speaking with Khadgar.

QUESTS IN KARAZHAN

There is only one quest line inside of Karazhan. To begin it you must have at least Honored reputation with The Violet Eye. The line begins at Archmage Alturus outside of Karazhan.

THE VIOLET EYE

Quest Level	70
Location	Shattrath City, Deadwind Pass
Starts at	Khadgar
Ends at	Archmage Alturus
Goal	Report to Archmage Alturus and offer assistance.

Now that you have The Master's Key, report back to Archmage Alturus to see if there is anything you can do to help.

ASSESSING THE SITUATION

Quest Level	70
Location	Deadwind Pass, Karazhan
Starts at	Archmage Alturus
Ends at	Koren
Goal	Koren the Blacksmith can help you recover Keanna's Log of what has been happening in Karazhan.

Koren is located after the first boss in Karazhan—Attumen the Huntsman. Clear the last pack of Undead minions and speak with him.

KEANNA'S LOG

Quest Level	70
Location	Karazhan, Deadwind Pass
Starts at	Koren
Ends at	Archmage Alturus
Goal	Retrieve Keanna's log and return to Archmage Alturus.

Outside of the Maiden of Virtue's room there is a row of bedrooms. The log is located in one of the middle ones on a table. An easy way to complete this quest is by returning to the instance after killing Maiden of Virtue. All of the minions throughout The Guests' Chambers despawn and you can walk right into the bedroom to retrieve the book.

As soon as you have it, return to Archmage Alturus outside of Karazhan.

A DEMONIC PRESENCE

Quest Level	70
Location	Deadwind Pass, Karazhan
Starts at	Archmage Alturus
Ends at	Archmage Alturus
Goal	Destroy the demonic presence at the top of Karazhan.

The log reports that demons have invaded Karazhan and your goal is to kill Prince Malchezaar at the top of Karazhan. He is the final boss of the instance and can be quite the challenge! Details on getting to him and killing him are discussed thoroughly in later sections.

Once you have defeated Malchezaar, return to Archmage Alturus.

THE NEW DIRECTIVE

Quest Level	70
Location	Deadwind Pass, Alterac Mountains
Starts at	Archmage Alturus
Ends at	Archmage Cedric
Goal	Speak with Archmage Cedric to receive your award for helping The Violet Eye.

Report back to Archmage Cedric along the northern border of Dalaran in Alterac Mountains for a nice chunk of gold, 3,000 Violet Eye reputation, and an Arcane Resist trinket.

MEDIVH'S JOURNAL

Quest Level	70
Location	Deadwind Pass, Karazhan
Starts at	Archmage Alturus
Ends at	Wravien
Goal	Speak to Wravien about located Medivh's Journal.

Archmage Alturus is very interested in reading Medivh's Journal but so far nobody has been able to recover it. Talk to Wravien in the library after The Curator about finding the journal.

IN GOOD HANDS

Quest Level	70
Location	Karazhan
Starts at	Wravien
Ends at	Gradav
Goal	Speak to Gradav about Medivh's Journal.

Wravien thinks that Gradav was in charge of locating the journal. Speak to him about it. He is in the same room as Wravien.

KAMSIS

Quest Level	70
Location	Karazhan
Starts at	Gradav
Ends at	Kamsis
Goal	Gradav sends you to talk to Kamsis about Medivh's Journal.

Gradav claims that Kamsis knows where the journal is. Talk to her in the same room as Gradav about finding it.

THE SHADE OF ARAN

Quest Level	70
Location	Karazhan
Starts at	Kamsis
Ends at	Kamsis
Goal	Kill the Shade of Aran and retrieve the journal for Kamsis.

Aran asked for the journal and Kamsis gave it to him. Now he holds it and you must kill him to get it back. Aran is a tough fight that is discussed thoroughly later in the guide.

As soon as you have killed him, return to Kamsis with Medivh's Journal.

DIGGING UP THE PAST

Quest Level	70
Location	Deadwind Pass
Starts at	Archmage Alturus
Ends at	Archmage Alturus
Goal	Retrieve the Charred Bone Fragment from the grounds around Karazhan.

The Charred Bone Fragment is located just south of the front entrance, behind the summoning stone. Note that this isn't a Raid quest so you can't click the fragment while in a raid group. After you have retrieved it, return to Archmage Alturus.

THE MASTER'S TERRACE

Quest Level	70
Location	Karazhan, Deadwind Pass
Starts at	Kamsis
Ends at	Archmage Alturus
Goal	Read the page from Medivh's Journal while on The Master's Terrace and return to Archmage Alturus.

To get to The Master's Terrace, zone in the side entrance, go left after the door, and open the door under the stairs. Outside on that balcony area is The Master's Terrace. Once you are there, click the journal and watch the event to complete the quest. After you have done this, return to Archmage Alturus outside of Karazhan.

A COLLEAGUE'S AID

Quest Level	70
Location	Deadwind Pass, Netherstorm
Starts at	Archmage Alturus
Ends at	Kalynna Lathred
Goal	Bring the Charred Bone Fragment to Kalynna Lathred at Area 52 in Netherstorm.

The Charred Bone Fragment has no life left in it but Kalynna Lathred can help you restore it. She is located at Area 52 in Netherstorm.

KALYNNA'S REQUEST

Quest Level	70
Location	Netherstorm, Shattered Halls, Sethekk Halls
Starts at	Kalynna Lathred
Ends at	Kalynna Lathred
Goal	Gather the Book of Forgotten Names and the Tome of Dusk and return to Kalynna.

The Book of Forgotten Names drops off of Darkweaver Syth in Sethekk Halls and the Tome of Dusk drops off of Grand Warlock Nethekurse in Shattered Halls. This is a Heroic quest so the items only drop if you kill the bosses on Heroic difficulty.

As soon as you've gathered both items, return to Kalynna.

NIGHTBANE

Quest Level	70
Location	Netherstorm, Karazhan, Deadwind Pass
Starts at	Kalynna Lathred
Ends at	Archmage Alturus
Goal	Bring the Faint Arcane Essence from Nightbane to Archmage Alturus.

Nightbane

For the final part of the quest line you have to kill Nightbane. Nightbane is a challenging fight that is covered later in the guide. As soon as you've successfully killed Nightbane, loot the Faint Arcane Essence and return to Archmage Alturus.

Keep the Blackened Urn! It is the only way to summon Nightbane for future kills.

DOWN THE VIOLET PATH

Archmage Leryda

Starting at Friendly you can receive a new ring for each level of reputation gained. To get your first ring, talk to Archmage Leryda outside of Karazhan. She asks which path you want to follow and you can return to her as your reputation increases to get your ring upgraded.

PATH OF THE VIOLET ASSASSIN

Friendly	
Violet Signet	Finger, +19 STA, Equip: Improves hit rating by 18, Equip: Increases attack power by 42
Honored	
Violet Signet	Finger, +27 STA, Equip: Improves hit rating by 22, Equip: Increases attack power by 50
Revered	
Violet Signet	Finger, +27 STA, Equip: Improves hit rating by 24, Equip: Increases attack power by 52
Exalted	
Violet Signet of the Master Assassin	Finger, +28 STA, Equip: Improves hit rating by 25, Equip: Increases attack power by 58

PATH OF THE VIOLET MAGE

Friendly	
Violet Signet	Finger, +18 STA, +18 INT, Equip: Improves spell critical strike rating by 12, Equip: Increases damage and healing done by magical spells and effects by up to 22
Honored	
Violet Signet	Finger, +19 STA, +21 INT, Equip: Improves spell critical strike rating by 15, Equip: Increases damage and healing done by magical spells and effects by up to 26
Revered	
Violet Signet	Finger, +22 STA, +22 INT, Equip: Improves spell critical strike rating by 17, Equip: Increases damage and healing done by magical spells and effects by up to 28
Exalted	
Violet Signet of the Archmage	Finger, +24 STA, +23 INT, Equip: Improves spell critical strike rating by 17, Equip: Increases damage and healing done by magical spells and effects by up to 29

PATH OF THE VIOLET PROTECTOR

Friendly	
Violet Signet	Finger, 294 Armor, +27 STA, Equip: Improves defense rating by 13
Honored	
Violet Signet	Finger, 350 Armor, +33 STA, Equip: Improves defense rating by 14
Revered	
Violet Signet	Finger, 371 Armor, +36 STA, Equip: Improves defense rating by 18
Exalted	
Violet Signet of the Great Protector	Finger, 393 Armor, +37 STA, Equip: Improves defense rating by 19

PATH OF THE VIOLET RESTORER

Friendly	
Violet Signet	Finger, +18 STA, +18 INT, +12 SPI, Equip: Increases healing done by magical spells and effects by up to 42
Honored	
Violet Signet	Finger, +24 STA, +21 INT, +15 SPI, Equip: Increases healing done by magical spells and effects by up to 46
Revered	
Violet Signet	Finger, +24 STA, +22 INT, +17 SPI, Equip: Increases healing done by magical spells and effects by up to 51
Exalted	
Violet Signet of the Grand Restorer	Finger, +24 STA, +23 INT, +17 SPI, Equip: Increases healing done by magical spells and effects by up to 55

THE TWO ENTRANCES TO KARAZHAN

There are two ways to get into Karazhan. The obvious way is through the front gate.

The second entrance is north of the front entrance, across the river. Enter the building and go up the stairs and over the bridge that leads to the side gate.

The side entrance door does not open until the Opera Event has been completed. To start your journey into Karazhan, go in the front entrance.

MAKING YOUR WAY THROUGH KARAZHAN

Not every group clears Karazhan in the same order. You can make your way through the dungeon in a variety of ways. The order presented here is the quickest way to get every boss down. Alternate routes and optional areas to clear are noted between each section.

After zoning in the front entrance you want to take the path to the left and begin clearing the packs of Spectral Chargers and Spectral Stable Hands to get to the first boss. Make sure you wait for the patrols before clearing too far. All of the minions are Undead and can be CC'ed.

After clearing the packs you arrive at a neutral horse named Midnight. He does not agro right away but when you attack him the first boss fight begins.

ATTUMEN THE HUNTSMAN

The first boss in Karazhan! At first only Attumen's horse Midnight is there, and he isn't hostile. Attack Midnight to begin the fight and be ready for Attumen to show up eventually.

Vambraces of Courage: Plate Wrist, 634 Armor, +33 STA, Yellow Socket, Socket Bonus: +2 Dodge Rating, Equip: Increases the block value of your shield by 33, Equip: Increases defense rating by 15

Whirlwind Bracers: Mail Wrist, 355 Armor, +19 STA, +20 INT, Equip: Increases healing done by spells and effects by up to 46, Equip: Restores 7 mana per 5 sec

Worgen Claw Necklace: Neck, +20 AGI, +21 STA, Equip: Increases attack power by 42, Equip: Improves hit rating by 17

ABILITIES

ATTUMEN THE HUNTSMAN

HP	39400	Damage	5310-7508
Abilities	**Intangible Presence:** Reduces an enemy target's chance to hit with spells and attacks by 50%.		
	Shadow Cleave: Inflicts weapon damage plus 1500 to an enemy and nearest allies, affecting up to 3 targets.		
	Charge: Attumen only uses this ability while mounted (phase 2). 8-25 yard range. Charges an enemy, inflicting normal damage and stunning the target.		

MIDNIGHT

HP	379400	Damage	4248-6007
Abilities	**Knockdown:** Deals 1500 damage to the current enemy target, knocking them down for 3 sec.		

CHARGE

Explanation: When Attumen is mounted, he charges people outside of melee range at random. The Charge hits for up to 6,000 and knocks the player down for a few seconds.

Solution: Keep everyone's life topped off so that they don't get killed instantly when charged. A quick Priest can Power Word: Shield them before they take damage. Heal the people who get damaged as quickly as you can.

CLEAVE

Explanation: Attumen has a standard Cleave attack that hits everyone in front of him for up to 4,000 damage.

Solution: Only the main tank should be in front of Attumen. Additionally, Attumen can be disarmed rendering him unable to Cleave.

INTANGIBLE PRESENCE

Explanation: Attumen randomly puts Intangible Presence on players. It reduces their chance to hit with melee attacks, ranged attacks, and spells by 50%. It can be removed by a Druid or Mage.

Solution: Remove it as quickly as possible. Healers are a low priority target.

LOOT

Bracers of the White Stag: Leather Wrist, 159 Armor, +16 STA, +18 INT, +22 SPI, Equip: Increases damage and healing done by magical spells and effects by up to 26

Gauntlets of Renewed Hope: Plate Hands, 906 Armor, +19 STA, +29 INT, Blue Socket, Blue Socket, Socket Bonus: +3 INT, Equip: Restores 5 mana per 5 sec, Equip: Increases healing done by spells and effects by up to 62

Gloves of Dexterous Manipulation: Leather Hands, 228 Armor, +35 AGI, +22 STA, Red Socket, Blue Socket, Equip: Increases attack power by 42

Gloves of Saintly Blessings: Cloth Hands, 121 Armor, +27 STA, +25 INT, +25 SPI, Red Socket, Blue Socket, Socket Bonus: +7 Healing, Equip: Increases healing done by spells and effects by up to 40

Handwraps of Flowing Thought: Cloth Hands, 121 Armor, +24 STA, +22 INT, Yellow Socket, Blue Socket, Socket Bonus: +3 Spell Hit Rating, Equip: Increases damage and healing done by magical spells and effects by up to 35, Equip: Improves spell hit rating by 14

Harbinger Bands: Cloth Wrist, 85 Armor, +21 STA, +21 INT, +14 SPI, Equip: Increases damage and healing done by magical spells and effects by up to 26

Spectral Band of Innervation: Finger, +22 STA, +24 INT, Equip: Increases damage and healing done by magical spells and effects by up to 29

Stalker's War Bands: Mail Wrist, 355 Armor, +21 AGI, +18 STA, +17 INT, Equip: Increases attack power by 44

Steelhawk Crossbow: Crossbow Range, 155-288 Damage, Speed 2.80, 79.1 damage per second, Equip: Increases attack power by 30, Equip: Improves hit rating by 16

PREPARATION

Assign one tank to Attumen and one tank to Midnight and split the healing up evenly on them.

Make sure the DPS understands that they are taking Midnight down first.

STRATEGY

Begin the fight by having Midnight's tank attack him. Give the tank a few moments to build threat, then start to DPS it down.

When Midnight gets to 95% life, Attumen joins the fight. Attumen's tank should have some Rage from beating on Midnight and should be able to pick up Attumen quickly. Get him on a tank and pointed away from everyone to avoid damage from the Cleave. Tank both bosses a little distance away from each other and never face Attumen towards the raid.

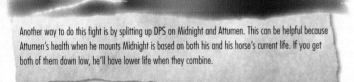

Another way to do this fight is by splitting up DPS on Midnight and Attumen. This can be helpful because Attumen's health when he mounts Midnight is based on both his and his horse's current life. If you get both of them down low, he'll have lower life when they combine.

Keep both tanks alive and continue to DPS Midnight. It doesn't hurt to throw a few DoTs on Attumen but all DPS should be focused on Midnight.

When Midnight is at 25% life, Attumen mounts him. Attumen's HP is based on his previous HP while unmounted and he resets his threat list. One of the tanks needs to pick him up and point him away from the raid as quickly as they can. Give the tank a few seconds to build threat before starting DPS.

As soon as he is mounted he gains the Charge attack. Make sure everyone is at full life incase they get charged and top them off after it happens.

Keep Attumen's tank alive; don't let anyone die to Charge, and DPS him down the remaining percent.

FROM THE GATEHOUSE TO THE GRAND BALLROOM

Koren the Blacksmith is located just after Attumen. You have to pull one more pack of minions to get to him. You can repair at him once you've reached Honored reputation with The Violet Eye and he is part of the quest *Assessing the Situation*.

After killing Attumen, go back to the front entrance and go up the stairs into The Grand Ballroom. There are a handful of single pull patrols, a couple packs of non-elite Phantom Guests and some packs of Phantom Attendants. For now you only need to kill all of the patrols and enough packs to safely get the raid into the next room to the left.

Pull them one pack or one patrol at a time and make your way to the left into the Banquet Hall. Pull the tables (don't worry, the big table is split into 2 pulls), the Skeletal Waiters, and Ghostly Stewards. You have to clear out the entire Banquet Hall for the next fight with Moroes.

MOROES

Moroes is a Rogue boss who has four Undead adds with him. He can be a challenging fight because his main ability—Garrote—deals significant damage over a long period of time.

LOOT

Belt of Gale Force: Mail Waist, 457 Armor, +27 STA, +28 INT, Equip: Restores 10 mana per 5 sec, Equip: Increases healing done by spells and effects by up to 59

Boots of Valiance: Plate Feet, 997 Armor, +28 STA, +28 INT, Equip: Increases healing done by spells and effects by up to 55, Equip: Improves spell critical strike rating by 25

Brooch of Unquenchable Fury: Neck, +24 STA, +21 INT, Equip: Increases damage and healing done by magical spells and effects by up to 26, Equip: Improves spell hit rating by 15

Crimson Girdle of the Indomitable: Plate Waist, 816 Armor, +16 STR, +36 STA, Red Socket, Yellow Socket, Socket Bonus: +3 Parry Rating, Equip: Increases defense rating by 24, Equip: Increases your shield block rating by 20

Edgewalker Longboots: Leather Feet, 250 Armor, +29 AGI, +28 STA, Red Socket, Yellow Socket, Socket Bonus: +3 Hit Rating, Equip: Increases attack power by 44, Equip: Improves hit rating by 13

Emerald Ripper: Dagger One-Hand, 126-189 Damage, Speed 1.80, 87.5 damage per second, +19 AGI, +18 STA, Equip: Increases attack power by 36

Idol of the Avian Heart: Idol Relic, Equip: Increases the amount healed by Healing Touch by 136

Moroes' Lucky Pocket Watch: Trinket, Use: Increases dodge rating by 300 for 10 seconds, Equip: Increases your dodge rating by 38

Nethershard Girdle: Cloth Waist, 109 Armor, +22 STA, +30 INT, +22 SPI, Equip: Increases damage and healing done by magical spells and effects by up to 35

Royal Cloak of Arathi Kings: Back, 97 Armor, +26 STR, +31 STA, Equip: Improves hit rating by 16

Shadow-Cloak of Dalaran: Back, 97 Armor, +18 INT, +19 STA, Equip: Increases damage and healing done by magical spells and effects by up to 36

Signet of Unshakable Faith: Held In Hand, +19 STA, +21 INT, +22 SPI, Equip: Increases healing done by spells and effects by up to 37

PREPARATION

Take a look at what adds have spawned for you. There are six possible adds of different classes and talent specs. It is pretty easy to figure out which add is which by looking at their equipment.

ABILITIES

HP	386988	Damage	6193-8172
Abilities	**Gouge:** Inflicts 950 to 1050 damage and stuns for up to 6 sec.		
	Garotte: Garrote the enemy, causing damage over 18 sec.		
	Vanish: Puts the caster in stealth mode for 12 sec.		
	Blind: Blinds the target, causing it to wander confused for up to 10 sec.		
	Deadly Throw: Deals 250% weapon damage.		
	Enrage: Physical damage dealt is increased by 20%.		

BLIND

Explanation: Moroes Blinds the second person on his threat list randomly. It is a curable Poison.

Solution: Cure it quickly. You don't want the current tank to get Gouged with the offtank Blinded.

ENRAGE

Explanation: At 30% life Moroes becomes Enraged causing him to deal additional melee damage.

Solution: Extra heals on the tanks!

GARROTE

Explanation: Every 30 seconds or so Moroes Vanishes and Garrotes a random player upon reappearing. The Garrote lasts for 5 minutes and does 1,000 damage every 3 seconds. His threat does not reset.

Solution: Remove the Garrote if you can. A Dwarf's Stoneform ability gets rid of it. Mages with Iceblock can use that you remove it. And Paladins can use Divine Shield and Blessing of Protection. If you can't get rid of it, heal the damage with a couple HoTs. It's important to not let anyone die from Garrote damage.

GOUGE

Explanation: Every 15 seconds or so Moroes Gouges his current target and begins attacking the second highest person on the threat list.

Solution: An offtank is needed. The second highest person on the threat list should be a tank who can take the hits. DPS classes need to mind their threat and not take the second place position.

BARON RAFE DREUGER
Retribution Paladin. Dispels debuffs (like Shackle Undead) and blesses.
BARONESS DOROTHEA MILSTIPE
Shadow Priest. Deals mainly shadow damage and casts Mana Burn.
LADY CATRIONA VON'INDI
Holy Priest. Dispels debuffs and heals.
LADY KEIRA BERRYBUCK
Holy Paladin. Dispels debuffs, blesses, and heals.
LORD CRISPIN FERENCE
Protection Warrior. High AC, lots of life.
LORD ROBIN DARIS
Mortal Strike Warrior. Has lots of life, Mortal Strikes, and deals significant melee damage.

Bringing two Priests to this fight makes it easier because you can keep two adds Shackled the entire time. Other CC options are Turn Undead and Freezing Trap. Definitely Shackle the Warriors if you get either of them; they take too long to kill. Beyond that it doesn't really matter what you decide to Shackle but keep in mind the Paladins and the Holy Priest are going to try to dispel any CC spells unless they are also CC'ed. If you choose to kill an add that can dispel, fight it far away from any CC'ed adds.

Setup as much CC as you can and assign a tank to anything not being CC'ed. The Priests don't hit very hard so a Paladin can tank them. Remember that Moroes needs two tanks throughout the entire fight; some tanks might have to pull double duty by handling Moroes and an add.

It really depends on exactly what classes you bring but in general you are going to have two adds CC'ed and two adds killed. One of the adds being killed is tanked by a Paladin. The other add is tanked by Moroes' offtank.

Make sure the CC is setup, the tanking is ready, and the DPS knows the order you are going to kill the adds in before the fight starts.

STRATEGY

Start the fight by having the main tank pull or by using Misdirection. As soon as the adds come into LoS, get them CC and tanked. Give the tank on the first add you plan to kill a few moments to build agro, then tear into it.

The offtank on Moroes should start to build threat with him very early in the fight. You never want someone else to be second on the agro list when he Gouges the current tank.

Kill off the adds that aren't CC quickly and start DPS on Moroes. The adds that are CC stay like that until Moroes is dead. Never let them get loose!

Gouge hits the main tank fairly early in the fight. The offtank should have built some threat and now be tanking Moroes. As soon as the Gouge wears off, the main tank should go back to building threat in preparation for the next Gouge. This switching of the tanks after Gouge continues throughout the entire fight and everyone needs to mind their threat, taking care not to overtake the second position on the threat list.

Eventually Moroes uses Vanish and is gone for a few seconds. When he reappears, someone at random is Garroted. Think about removing it with Stoneform, Iceblock, Divine Shield, or Blessing of Protection, or just heal it away. Eventually you won't be able to remove it and really need to keep some HoTs on anyone afflicted by Garrote.

Crispin Ference

His agro does not reset after a Vanish so nothing really changes about the tanking. Keep those adds CC, help offtanks maintain the second agro position by watching your threat, and heal up anyone who is taking damage from Garrote. The hardest part of the fight is getting the adds down without any problems; as soon as you're working on the boss with the remaining adds under control with CC, getting him down shouldn't be much of a problem.

FROM THE GRAND BALLROOM TO THE GUESTS' QUARTERS

Turn around the way you came into the Banquet Hall and pull the remaining packs of Phantom Guests from The Grand Ballroom. Stay along the left hand wall and go up the stairs at the end of the room.

At the top of the stairs there are more pulls just like the ones you have been clearing so far. Start pulling the room one pack or one patrol at a time. Your goal is the hallway along the right hand side of the room.

Killing Maiden of Virtue is completely optional. She is a challenging fight and many raids choose to skip her and continue onward to the Opera Event. If your raid decides to do this, skip ahead for information on getting to and defeating the Opera Event.

Don't enter the hallway too early. There are several patrols of Concubines, Wanton Hostesses, and Night Mistresses. Clear out the patrols before entering the hallway. As soon as you're in, hug the right hand side of the wall. There are several packs of minions in the rooms along the left that can be skipped.

Continue clearing out the hallway and at the end of it the Maiden of Virtue awaits you.

MAIDEN OF VIRTUE

Maiden of Virtue is a tough boss with Paladin and Priest abilities. She can deal a lot of damage to everyone around her so your raid's healing and dispelling has to be on the ball.

ABILITIES

HP	424900	Damage	6156-896
Abilities	**Repentance**: Puts all nearby enemy targets in a state of meditation, incapacitating them for 12 sec.		
	Holy Ground: Periodically silences all targets within 12 yards; deals 240 to 360 Holy damage per second.		
	Holy Fire: Burns for 3238 to 3762 Fire damage and inflicting 1750 additional Fire damage every 2 sec. over 12 sec.		
	Holy Wrath: Deals 1950 to 2050 Holy damage, then arcs to other nearby targets dealing greater damage each time the spell jumps.		

HOLY FIRE

Explanation: Every 10 seconds or so Maiden hits a random player not in melee range with Holy Fire. The initial hit does about 3,000 damage and the DoT debuff ticks for about 1,700 damage every 2 seconds. The DoT part is a dispelable magic debuff.

Solution: Dispel the DoT as quickly as possible. Make sure everyone is within range for dispel. Heal up the damage done; don't let anyone be under 3,000 life or they might get killed if hit.

HOLY GROUND

Explanation: Throughout the fight the ground around Maiden is consecrated with Holy Ground. It does about 300 damage per tick and interrupts non-instant spell casts. It also breaks her Repentance ability.

Solution: Anyone who can stay out of the Holy Ground should avoid it. It has a small area of effect; avoiding it is not very hard. Melee classes are going to have to take the damage so keep them healed up.

HOLY WRATH

Explanation: Every 20 seconds or so one player is hit by Holy Wrath. The initial hit does around 2,000 damage chains to other players within 10 yards of the target, increasing the damage dealt by about 1,000 per chain.

Solution: You can't avoid the initial hits but you should stay spread out enough that it very rarely chains to anyone else. Ranged classes can spread out in a circle around her but melee classes have limited space and should do their best to spread out.

REPENTANCE

Explanation: Every 15-25 seconds everyone but Maiden's current target is afflicted by Repentance. It does about 1,700 damage when it hits and incapacitates the player for 10 seconds. If you take any damage while afflicted, Repentance is broken.

Solution: The biggest problem Repentance causes is when all of the healers are incapacitated and the main tank dies. One of the best ways to prevent this is by having a Paladin use Blessing of Sacrifice on the main tank. The Paladin's Repentance is removed when they take damage from the blessing. Another possible way to break it is by having one healer stay in the Holy Ground. The damage from Holy Ground breaks the Repentance. The main tank should save their health potion, Health Stone, Last Stand, and any other HP restoring abilities for the Repentances incase they get low.

LOOT

Bands of Indwelling: Cloth Wrist, 85 Armor, +22 STA, +18 INT, +20 SPI, Equip: Increases healing done by spells and effects by up to 46

Bands of Nefarious Deeds: Cloth Wrist, 85 Armor, +27 STA, +22 INT, Equip: Increases damage and healing done by magical spells and effects by up to 32

Barbed Choker of Discipline: Neck, +39 STA, Equip: Increases your dodge rating by 21, Equip: Increases defense rating by 16

Boots of Foretelling: Cloth Feet, 134 Armor, +27 STA, +23 INT, Red Socket, Yellow Socket, Socket Bonus: +3 INT, Equip: Increases damage and healing done by magical spells and effects by up to 26, Equip: Improves spell critical strike rating by 19

Bracers of Justice: Plate Wrist, 634 Armor, +22 STA, +22 INT, Equip: Increases healing done by spells and effects by up to 46, Equip: Improves spell critical strike rating by 16

Bracers of Maliciousness: Leather Wrist, 159 Armor, +25 STA, Equip: Increases attack power by 50, Equip: Improves critical strike rating by 22

Gloves of Centering: Mail Hands, 507 Armor, +25 STA, +20 INT, Blue Socket, Red Socket, Socket Bonus: +3 INT, Equip: Increases healing done by spells and effects by up to 62, Equip: Restores 6 mana per 5 sec

Gloves of Quickening: Mail Hands, 507 Armor, +22 STA, +24 INT, Blue Socket, Red Socket, Socket Bonus: +3 AGI, Equip: Increases attack power by 52, Equip: Restores 4 mana per 5 sec, Equip: Improves critical strike rating by 17

Iron Gauntlets of the Maiden: Plate Hands, 906 Armor, +39 STA, Red Socket, Yellow Socket, Socket Bonus: +4 Block Rating, Equip: Increases the block value of your shield by 38, Equip: Increases defense rating by 16, Equip: Increases your shield block rating by 17

Mitts of the Treemender: Leather Hands, 228 Armor, +25 STA, +22 INT, +14 SPI, Blue Socket, Yellow Socket, Socket Bonus: +3 SPI, Equip: Increases healing done by spells and effects by up to 64

Shard of the Virtuous: Mace Main Hand, 28-129 Damage, Speed 1.90, 41.3 damage per second, +22 STA, +20 INT, Equip: Increases healing done by spells and effects by up to 348, Equip: Restores 6 mana per 5 sec

Totem of Healing Rains: Totem Relic, Equip: Increases the base amount healed by Chain Heal by 87

PREPARATION

Positioning is the only real thing to worry about before engaging Maiden. Staying spread out to avoid Holy Wrath chaining is one of the key parts of the fight.

Notice she stands in the middle of a circle and that there are pillars along the edge. One ranged class player can stand between each pillar. Unless you have an unusual amount of ranged classes in your raid, between the pillars should be plenty of room for everyone to spread out. Melee classes obviously can't stand that far from the boss so they should just do their best to spread out around the main tank.

Make sure everybody knows where they are going to be positioned before the fight starts.

STRATEGY

Start the fight by having the tank run in. She is tanked in the middle of the room and does not move. All of the ranged classes should head to their proper position between the pillars around Maiden. Melee DPS heads in and stays spread out around her as best they can.

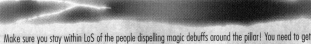

Make sure you stay within LoS of the people dispelling magic debuffs around the pillar! You need to get the Holy Wrath DoT removed as quickly as possible so make it easy on the dispellers by staying nearby and within LoS.

Give your tank a few moments to generate threat and start DPS. Stay in your position, stay spread out from other players, and keep the tank alive.

Holy Ground is active throughout most of the fight. Ranged classes can easily stay out of it but make sure the melee classes are getting the occasional heal. Spell casting classes should always avoid the Holy Ground because of its interrupting component.

Holy Fire is probably the most damaging of all her abilities. The initial damage hits fairly hard but the DoT debuff is brutal. Dispel it as quickly as you can and heal up the damage done. Make sure nobody stays too low on life; you don't want them to get instantly killed by Holy Fire. Since everyone is spread out around the pillars, everyone has to help cleanse the DoT and heal. It's impossible for just one person to take care of it completely.

Holy Wrath shouldn't be too big of a deal because you're staying spread out and it's only hitting one person at a time. Heal up the various players getting hit by Holy Wrath and avoid chaining it as best you can.

About 20 seconds into the fight the first Repentance hits everyone but Maiden's current target. The worst thing that can happen is all of the healers stay incapacitated for the full 10 second duration and the tank dies because of it. At least one healer should have a way to break the Repentance. The best way is having a Paladin use Blessing of Sacrifice on the tank before Repentance hits. When they take damage from the blessing, the incapacitation is removed. The other option is having one healer stand in the Holy Ground. The damage taken from Holy Ground breaks the Repentance. Point is, one healer needs to be able to heal the tank while everyone else is incapacitated.

Heal up the damage from all of Maiden's abilities while keeping the tank alive. Stay spread out, make sure a healer is breaking Repentance, and cleanse those Holy Wraths. With a little bit of practice and some good healing, you should be able to get her down.

FROM THE GUESTS' QUARTERS TO THE OPERA HOUSE

Turn around down the hallway you cleared out and head back to the big room. Your next destination is through the archway to your right as you come out of the hallway.

These Skeletal Ushers are probably the hardest minions in Karazhan. They have a freezing ability that causes them to drop agro off whoever is tanking them and charge the next highest person on the threat list. And they hit very hard. Thankfully you can use Shackle Undead to keep one of them controlled while you kill the others. Have both tanks fight for agro in preparation for their freeze attack.

It doesn't always work this way so be ready to use those life saving abilities like Iceblock, Blessing of Protection, Feign Death, and so on.

After you clear the Skeletal Ushers, start clearing out the Opera House and hug the right wall. As you get closer to the stage along the right wall you come to a stairway. Enter the stairway to get backstage.

Once you're backstage there's only one path you can take. Continue down it pulling the Phantom Stagehands and Spectral Performers. Eventually you get to a locked door with Barnes standing in front of it. Talk to him when you're ready to begin the Opera Event.

OPERA HOUSE

The Opera House is a really fun event that comes in three different flavors depending on the show being put on that week. After a short speech by Barnes, the curtain opens and the fight begins.

The Big Bad Wolf is probably the easiest of the encounters with The Wizard of Oz close behind. Romulo and Julianne is definitely the most challenging.

The event you get remains the same for the whole week. You can't change it by resetting the instance.

BIG BAD WOLF

At first all you see is a Grandma. She can't be very hard, right? Let's go talk to her. Oh no, lookout! It's a Big Bad Wolf! Who saw that coming?!

LOOT

Beastmaw Pauldrons: Mail Shoulder, 609 Armor, +24 AGI, +22 STA, +23 INT, Equip: Increases attack power by 46, Equip: Restores 8 mana per 5 sec

Big Bad Wolf's Head: Mail Head, 659 Armor, +42 STA, +40 INT, Equip: Increases damage and healing done by magical spells and effects by up to 47, Equip: Improves spell critical strike rating by 28

Big Bad Wolf's Paw: Fist Weapon Main Hand, 153-285 Damage, Speed 2.50, 87.6 damage per second, +17 AGI, +18 STA, Equip: Improves critical strike rating by 20

Earthsoul Leggings: Leather Legs, 319 Armor, +25 STA, +30 INT, +24 SPI, Yellow Socket, Blue Socket, Blue Socket, Socket Bonus: +4 SPI, Equip: Increases healing done by spells and effects by up to 81

Eternium Greathelm: Plate Head, 1178 Armor, +31 STR, +48 STA, Red Socket, Yellow Socket, Blue Socket, Socket Bonus: +4 Dodge Rating, Equip: Increases defense rating by 34

Libram of Souls Redeemed: Libram Relic, Equip: Increases the benefit your Flash of Light and Holy Light spells receive from Blessing of Light by 105

Red Riding Hood's Cloak: Back, 97 Armor, +16 STA, +22 INT, Equip: Increases healing done by spells and effects by up to 48, Equip: Restores 7 mana per 5 sec

Ribbon of Sacrifice: Trinket, Use: For the next 20 seconds, your direct heals grant Fecundity to your target, increasing the healing received by the target by up to 20. Fecundity lasts 10 seconds and stacks up to 5 times, Equip: Increases healing done by spells and effects by up to 73

Trial-Fire Trousers: Cloth Legs, 170 Armor, +42 STA, +40 INT, Yellow Socket, Yellow Socket, Yellow Socket, Socket Bonus: +5 Spell Damage, Equip: Increases damage and healing done by magical spells and effects by up to 49

Wolfslayer Sniper Rifle: Gun Range, 149-278 Damage, Speed 2.70, 79.1 damage per second, +15 AGI, Equip: Increases attack power by 32

ABILITIES

HP	379400	Damage	4142-5856
Abilities	**Terrifying Howl:** Causes nearby enemies to flee in terror for 3 sec.		
	Wild Swipe: Stuns the target for 4 sec.		

LITTLE RED RIDING HOOD

Explanation: Every 30 seconds or so a random player is turned into Little Red Riding Hood. This causes the Big Bad Wolf to chase that player. You can not attack while turned into Little Red Riding Hood but your movement speed is increased by 50%.

Solution: The player who is turned into Little Red Riding Hood has to kite the Big Bad Wolf around the stage for the duration of the debuff. As soon as it wears off, the Big Bad Wolf goes back to his previous target. Since this is the big part of the fight, details on positioning and where to kite is covered in depth in the strategy section.

TERRIFYING HOWL

Explanation: Every 30 seconds or so the Big Bad Wolf Fears everyone within melee range.

Solution: Fear Ward, Tremor Totem, an offtank with Berserker Rage available, use all of the usual anti-Fear tactics.

PREPARATION

Positioning is a key part of the fight. Assign a tank to the Big Bad Wolf and keep him tanked in the north east corner of the stage. All ranged classes should stay in the north west corner.

When someone gets turned into Little Red Riding Hood they are going to kite the Big Bad Wolf counter clockwise from the north east corner around the edge of the stage.

STRATEGY

Begin the fight by talking to the Grandma and spawning the Big Bad Wolf. Get him tanked and bring him into the north east corner. The ranged DPS should already be positioned in the north west corner.

The Fear goes off every 30 seconds or so. Make sure you keep Fear Ward up on the main tank, or Tremor Totem down in the main tank's group, or that your offtank is using Berserker Rage and tanking the Big Bad Wolf until the main tank's Fear wears off.

Start DPS and be ready for someone to get turned into Little Red Riding Hood. The moment this happens they need to start running, especially if they are melee DPS and right next to the wolf. Kite him counter clockwise around the edge of the stage until the debuff wears off and he returns to attacking the tank.

When you're kiting the Big Bad Wolf you can't run as quickly as possible. If you do this, he is going to cut across the stage and catch up. You have to wait a second in each corner so that he stays out of melee range. It can take a little practice to master the kiting without getting killed.

Get good at kiting the Big Bad Wolf around; don't let him catch you! As soon as you are good at this you should be able to slay the wolf and have a happy ending.

ROMULO AND JULIANNE

Romulo and Julianne is undoubtedly the hardest of the Opera Events.

When the fight begins you only fight Julianne. After she has been killed, Romulo appears and you fight him. Once he has been slain, both Romulo and Julianne come back to life and you take them on at the same time.

They must be killed within about 10 seconds of each other or the one you killed is resurrected by the other.

LOOT

Beastmaw Pauldrons: Mail Shoulder, 609 Armor, +24 AGI, +22 STA, +23 INT, Equip: Increases attack power by 46, Equip: Restores 8 mana per 5 sec

Blade of the Unrequited: Dagger One-Hand, 112-168 Damage, Speed 1.60, 87.5 damage per second, +13 STA, Red Socket, Yellow Socket, Blue Socket, Socket Bonus: +8 Attack Power, Equip: Increases attack power by 18, Equip: Improves critical strike rating by 9

Despair: Two-Hand Sword Two-Hand, 319-479 Damage, Speed 3.50, 114.0 damage per second, +52 STR

Earthsoul Leggings: Leather Legs, 319 Armor, +25 STA, +30 INT, +24 SPI, Yellow Socket, Blue Socket, Blue Socket, Socket Bonus: +4 SPI, Equip: Increases healing done by spells and effects by up to 81

Eternium Greathelm: Plate Head, 1178 Armor, +31 STR, +48 STA, Red Socket, Yellow Socket, Blue Socket, Socket Bonus: +4 Dodge Rating, Equip: Increases defense rating by 34

Libram of Souls Redeemed: Libram Relic, Equip: Increases the benefit your Flash of Light and Holy Light spells receive from Blessing of Light by 105

Masquerade Gown: Cloth Chest(Robe), 194 Armor, +34 STA, +32 INT, Equip: Increases healing done by spells and effects by up to 88, Equip: Chance on spell cast to increase your SPI by 145 for 15 secs

Ribbon of Sacrifice: Trinket, Use: For the next 20 seconds, your direct heals grant Fecundity to your target, increasing the healing received by the target by up to 20. Fecundity lasts 10 seconds and stacks up to 5 times, Equip: Increases healing done by spells and effects by up to 73

Romulo's Poison Vial: Trinket, Equip: Your melee and ranged attacks have a chance to inject poison into your target dealing 200 to 300 Nature damage, Equip: Improves hit rating by 35

Trial-Fire Trousers: Cloth Legs, 170 Armor, +42 STA, +40 INT, Yellow Socket, Yellow Socket, Yellow Socket, Socket Bonus: +5 Spell Damage, Equip: Increases damage and healing done by magical spells and effects by up to 49

ABILITIES

JULIANNE

HP	151750	Damage	2955-4147
Abilities	**Powerful Attraction:** Stuns the target for 6 sec.		
	Devotion: Increases the Holy damage dealt by the caster by 50% and the caster's attack speed by 50% for 10 sec.		
	Blinding Passion: Inflicts 1500 initial Holy damage and an additional 750 Holy damage per second for 4 seconds.		
	Eternal Affection: Heals an ally for 46250 to 53750 hit points.		

BLINDING PASSION

Explanation: Hits a random player for around 1,500 damage followed by a DoT debuff that ticks for 750 damage. Has a 2 second casting time.

Solution: Don't interrupt it. Save the interrupts for Eternal Affection. Heal up the random players hit by Blinding Passion.

DEVOTION

Explanation: A self buff that increases Holy damage by 50% and reduces spell casting time by 50%. It can be removed by a Priest or Shaman with Dispel Magic and Purge respectively, or a Mage using Spell Steal. Lasts 10 seconds.

Solution: Get it off of her as quickly as possible. You don't want her to hit someone with Blinding Passion while Devotion is up. She doesn't buff herself with it that often so removing it quickly every time isn't very difficult.

ETERNAL AFFECTION

Explanation: Heals Romulo for about 50,000 life. Has a 2 second casting time.

Solution: Interrupt it. Part of the preparation for this fight is putting the best spell interrupters on Julianne. You have to interrupt Eternal Affection every time it is cast.

POWERFUL ATTRACTION

Explanation: Stuns random targets for 6 seconds.

Solution: You can't remove it or prevent it.

ROMULO

HP	189700	Damage	3282-5631
Abilities	**Backward Lunge:** Strikes at an enemy behind the caster, inflicting 1900 to 2100 Physical damage and knocking the enemy away.		
	Deadly Lunge: Strikes at nearby enemies in front of the caster, inflicting weapon damage plus 110.		
	Poisoned Thrust: Deals weapon damage plus 100 and decreases all stats by 10% for 30 sec.		
	Daring: Increases the Physical damage dealt by the caster by 35% and the caster's attack speed by 35% for 8 sec.		

BACKWARD LUNGE

Explanation: Knocks back players behind Romulo and does a little bit of damage.

Solution: Heal up anyone who needs it after being knocked back. His abilities are hard to predict so avoiding it altogether isn't really an option.

DARING

Explanation: Increases melee damage and attack speed by 35%. Can be removed.

Solution: A Priest or a Shaman or a Mage needs to remove it as quickly as possible. He already hits fairly hard and leaving Daring up can easily get your tank killed.

DEADLY SWATHE

Explanation: Knocks back players in front of Romulo and does a little bit of damage.

Solution: Only the tank should be in front of Romulo to minimize the amount of people Deadly Swathe hits. Tank him against a wall so the tank isn't knocked back.

POISONED THRUST

Explanation: Poison debuff that reduces all stats by 10%. Stackable up to 8 times. Can be removed with Cure Poison.

Solution: Druids, Paladins, and Shamans should cleanse anyone who is afflicted by Poisoned Thrust and not allow it to stack.

PREPARATION

Your best geared tank should tank Julianne, then Romulo, then Romulo again. Your second best tank handles Julianne when both are present.

You have to split up the DPS when both Julianne and Romulo are up. Julianne has her Eternal Affection heal that must be interrupted every time she casts it. Put your best spell interrupters on Julianne. Romulo has a nasty self buff that needs to be removed as quickly as possible so if you have a Shaman or Mage doing DPS, consider putting them on Romulo.

Split the DPS evenly keeping their abilities in mind for when they are both onstage.

STRATEGY

At the start of the fight it is only Julianne. Get her tanked and start to DPS her. Since the entire raid is on her you can probably interrupt both Blinding Passion and Eternal Affection, but Eternal Affection has priority. Keep the tank up and kill her without pulling agro.

After Julianne dies Romulo appears in hopes of avenging her death. Have the tank pick him up and move so that their back is against a wall in order to avoid the knock back from his Deadly Swathe ability. Start to DPS after he is in position. Romulo's self buff Daring must be removed as quickly as possible. He can easily kill a tank if you let Daring stay on him. Heal the melee getting hit by the knock back and cleanse the poison quickly without letting it stack on anyone. Slowly take him down.

After Romulo is dead you have to fight both of them at the same time. None of their abilities have changed; they behave exactly like they did when they were by themselves. Romulo's tank should pick him up and move against a wall. Julianne's tank should grab her and build some threat.

DPS is split up so that the best spell interrupters are on Julianne and not letting her cast Eternal Affection. Don't try to interrupt the Blinding Passion at this point. Healers, keep in mind Blinding Passion does a fair amount of damage and you need to heal up anyone who gets hit by it; don't let anyone die to it.

Kill them as quickly as you can but remember they have to die within about 10 seconds of each other. Stop DPS when your target gets to about 10% life. Go help take the other boss down to about 10% if necessary and then finish both of them off quickly.

It is a hard fight because they are both powerful bosses that must be killed at the same time. Stay on top of those Eternal Affection interrupts, get rid of Romulo's Daring as quickly as possible, don't let anyone die to Blinding Passion, and you should have them both dead after a little practice.

WIZARD OF OZ

This is a multi-opponent, multi-stage fight. Everything you know to be true is: Roar is a coward, the Strawman hates fire, and Tito...Tito needs to be punted off a bridge.

LOOT

Beastmaw Pauldrons: Mail Shoulder, 609 Armor, +24 AGI, +22 STA, +23 INT, Equip: Increases attack power by 46, Equip: Restores 8 mana per 5 sec

Blue Diamond Witchwand: Wand Range, 169-314 Shadow Damage, Speed 1.50, 161.0 damage per second, +13 INT, +11 SPI, Equip: Increases healing done by spells and effects by up to 29

Earthsoul Leggings: Leather Legs, 319 Armor, +25 STA, +30 INT, +24 SPI, Yellow Socket, Blue Socket, Blue Socket, Socket Bonus: +4 SPI, Equip: Increases healing done by spells and effects by up to 81

Eternium Greathelm: Plate Head, 1178 Armor, +31 STR, +48 STA, Red Socket, Yellow Socket, Blue Socket, Socket Bonus: +4 Dodge Rating, Equip: Increases defense rating by 34

Legacy: Two-Hand Axe Two-Hand, 319-479 Damage, Speed 3.50, 114.0 damage per second, +46 STA, +40 AGI, Equip: Increases attack power by 80, Equip: Restores 8 mana per 5 sec

Libram of Souls Redeemed: Libram Relic, Equip: Increases the benefit your Flash of Light and Holy Light spells receive from Blessing of Light by 105

Ribbon of Sacrifice: Trinket, Use: For the next 20 seconds, your direct heals grant Fecundity to your target, increasing the healing received by the target by up to 20. Fecundity lasts 10 seconds and stacks up to 5 times, Equip: Increases healing done by spells and effects by up to 73

Ruby Slippers: Cloth Feet, 134 Armor, +33 STA, +29 INT, Equip: Increases damage and healing done by magical spells and effects by up to 35, Use: Returns you to $z. Speak to an Innkeeper in a different place to change your home location, Equip: Improves spell hit rating by 16

Trial-Fire Trousers: Cloth Legs, 170 Armor, +42 STA, +40 INT, Yellow Socket, Yellow Socket, Yellow Socket, Socket Bonus: +5 Spell Damage, Equip: Increases damage and healing done by magical spells and effects by up to 49

Wicked Witch's Hat: Cloth Head, 158 Armor, +37 STA, +38 INT, Equip: Increases damage and healing done by magical spells and effects by up to 43, Equip: Improves spell critical strike rating by 32

PREPARATION

Assign one person to chain Fear Roar. He is a Beast so a Hunter using Scare Beast works.

Assign a Mage to kite Tinhead around using Frostbolt.

Assign a tank to Strawman and make sure they also pickup Tito when he is summoned.

ABILITIES

DOROTHEE

HP	151750	Damage	2462-3478
Abilities	**Water Bolt:** Deals 2025 to 2475 Frost damage.		
	Frightened Scream: Causes up to 3 nearby enemies to flee for 2 sec.		
	Cleanse: Cleanses a friendly target, removing 1 poison effect, 1 disease effect, and 1 magic effect. Also removes special impairments on Oz creatures.		
	Summon Tito: Summons Tito- Annoying Yipping ability, which prevents the target from attacking or casting spells for 2 sec.		

ENRAGE

Explanation: If Tito is killed while Dorothee is alive, she Enrages causing her damage to be increases and her casting time to be reduced. Lasts until another Tito is summoned.

Solution: Ideally, kill Dorothee before Tito. It isn't absolutely necessary but it does minimize the damage done by her.

FEAR

Explanation: Fears everyone within melee range.

Solution: Since she can't be tanked the best solution is to stay away from her. Melee DPS is going to get feared while attacking her so you can use the usual anti-Fear abilities like Fear Ward, Tremor Totem, and Berserker Rage to counter it.

TITO

Explanation: Dorothee summons her faithful dog Tito throughout the fight. He has a single target ability called Annoying Yip that makes the player unable to attack for 2 seconds.

Solution: Eventually you have to kill him. Since Dorothee resummons him and Enrages when he is killed, it's smart to kill her and then kill him. He can be tanked normally and doesn't hit very hard at all.

WATER BOLT

Explanation: Hits random players for around 2,000 damage. Has an uninterruptible 1.5 second casting time.

Solution: Water Bolt replaces Dorothee's normal melee attack and you can't really do anything about it. Heal the random players that are hit and don't let anyone die to it.

ROAR

HP	110700	Damage	2509-3548
Abilities	**Mangle:** Rake the target for 1600 to 2400 damage and an additional 2500 damage over 15 sec.		
	Shred Armor: Reduces armor by 5000 for 8 sec.		

STRAWMAN

HP	110700	Damage	4182-5194
Abilities	**Brain Bash:** Stuns the target for 3 sec.		
	Brain Wipe: Silences the target for 4 sec. and drains 713 to 787 mana.		

BRAIN BASH

Explanation: Stuns the player for 6 seconds.

Solution: You can't remove it or prevent it.

BURNING STRAW

Explanation: Fire based attacks against Strawman have a high chance of disorientating him for 6 seconds.

Solution: This ability is to your advantage! Use those Fire spells on him and keep him disorientated as much as possible.

THE CRONE

HP	151750	Damage	4925-6956
Abilities	**Chain Lightning:** Affects up to 5 targets, inflicting greater Nature damage to each successive target. The first target takes 2775 to 3225 Nature damage.		
	Fiery Broom: Each attack by the Crone has a chance to deal an additional 2375 to 2625 Fire damage.		
	Cyclone: A cyclone moves around the stage, tossing targets into the air.		

CYCLONE

Explanation: Summons a cyclone that knocks players into the air, interrupting spells.

Solution: This isn't a targeted ability. You can avoid the cyclone by moving away from it.

CHAIN LIGHTNING

Explanation: Hits a random target for around 3,000 damage and chains to additional players within 5 yards, increasing the damage dealt with each leap.

Solution: Stay spread out so it doesn't chain to any other players. Only one person at a time should take damage from the Chain Lightning; heal them up.

TINHEAD

HP	110700	Damage	4182-5194
Abilities	**Cleave:** Inflicts Physical damage to an enemy and its nearby allies, affecting up to 3 targets.		

CLEAVE

Explanation: A standard Cleave that hits everyone in front of Tinhead for melee damage.

Solution: Stay out of the area in front of Tinhead.

STRATEGY

As soon as the fight starts get Roar Feared and Tinhead kited by a Mage. They are going to be ignored for the time being.

Strawman should get picked up by a tank and kept under control.

DPS focuses on Dorothee first. She can't be tanked and does the most damage out of the group. When she summons Tito have the person tanking Strawman pick him up for the time being. DPS Dorothee down with no regard for agro as quickly as you can.

As soon as Dorothee is dead switch to Tito and finish him off. Once Tito has been slain take down Strawman. Remember to use any fire based spell you have against Strawman to keep him disorientated.

Once Strawman is dead you can kill either Roar or Tinhead first. Get them tanked and focus them down one at a time. Don't let the DPS be split on both targets; make sure everyone is assisting one person.

As soon as all four bosses are dead, The Crone appears in the middle of the stage. She has a Chain Lightning ability so try to spread out around the stage, staying at least 5 yards away from everyone. Her other ability summons a Cyclone that roams around the stage and tosses people into the air. It doesn't do any damage but you can't move and can't use anything but instant cast spells.

Keep The Crone tanked, spread out, and avoid the Cyclone. Take her down and you win!

FROM THE OPERA HOUSE TO THE GALLERY

After the Opera Event you have two possible routes to take. You can go through the exit on the opposite side of the stage, up into the balcony seats. Or you can zone out, reenter Karazhan through the side entrance, and clear The Broken Stair. Going to the side entrance is definitely quicker, but the Ghostly Philanthropists in the balcony seats drop a lot of gold. Both routes lead to The Menagerie where the next boss is located.

If you choose to exit the stage and head to the balcony, go through the door. From here there is only one possible route to take. There are many pulls of Spectral Patrons and Ghostly Philanthropists along the way. The Ghostly Philanthropists drop a lot of gold; make sure they get looted! As soon as you go down a stairway and see the pulls turn into Undead ghosts called Trapped Souls, you've reached The Broken Stair.

If you choose to zone out and reenter Karazhan through the side entrance, take a left as soon as you zone in and start pulling the Trapped Souls. Follow the stairs up until you get to the top and see a pair of Arcane Watchman guarding The Menagerie.

Pull the Arcane Watchmen; make sure the person who gets the Overload debuff quickly moves away from the raid until it's gone. Clear out the Arcane Anomaly and Syphoner packs. Once the last pack of these has been pulled, you are safe to engage The Curator.

THE CURATOR

The Curator is a very unique fight that lets you unload a lot of damage periodically. Having a well equipped tank is one of the key parts because Curator hits harder than any boss in Karazhan thus far.

LOOT

Dragon-Quake Shoulderguards: Mail Shoulder, 609 Armor, +28 STA, +28 INT, Equip: Restores 8 mana per 5 sec, Equip: Increases healing done by spells and effects by up to 64

Forest Wind Shoulderpads: Leather Shoulder, 273 Armor, +22 STA, +28 INT, +24 SPI, Equip: Increases healing done by spells and effects by up to 66

Garona's Signet Ring: Finger, +20 AGI, +25 STA, Equip: Increases attack power by 40, Equip: Improves hit rating by 18

Gloves of the Fallen Champion: Classes: Shaman Rogue Paladin

Gloves of the Fallen Defender: Classes: Druid Priest Warrior

Gloves of the Fallen Hero: Classes: Warlock Mage Hunter

Pauldrons of the Solace-Giver: Cloth Shoulder, 146 Armor, +28 INT, +22 SPI, Equip: Increases healing done by spells and effects by up to 57, Equip: Restores 10 mana per 5 sec

Staff of Infinite Mysteries: Staff Two-Hand, 143-290 Damage, Speed 3.20, 67.7 damage per second, +61 STA, +51 INT, Equip: Increases damage and healing done by magical spells and effects by up to 185, Equip: Improves spell hit rating by 23

Wrynn Dynasty Greaves: Plate Legs, 1269 Armor, +24 STR, +48 STA, Red Socket, Yellow Socket, Yellow Socket, Socket Bonus: +6 STA, Equip: Increases defense rating by 27, Equip: Increases your dodge rating by 29

ABILITIES

HP	698050	Damage	5467-7722
Abilities	**Hateful Bolt**: Deals 4435 to 5999 Arcane damage.		
	Evocation: Regenerate 5% mana per second for 20 sec. Damage taken while Evocating is increased by 200%.		
	Arcane Infusion: Adds 1500 to 2500 Arcane damage.		
	Summon Astral Flare: Summons Astral Flares- Arcing Sear ability, deals 675 to 825 Arcane damage to all targets within 10 yards periodically.		

ASTRAL FLARE

Explanation: Every 10 seconds an Astral Flare is summoned. This causes Curator to use 10% of his mana. The Astral Flare has a lightning attack that hits up to 3 people in melee range. Curator stops summoning Astral Flares when he Enrages at 15% life.

Solution: Summoning Astral Flares is how Curator runs out of mana for the eventual Evocation. If there is an Astral Flare up, the entire raid should be focused on killing it. You never want to have more than one Astral Flare up at a time. Target and kill them as quickly as possible. Their lightning attack does do noticeable damage so assign a healer to keeping the melee DPS alive as they kill Astral Flares.

BERSERK

Explanation: After 12 minutes Curator goes Berserk and kills everyone.

Solution: You have to kill him within 12 minutes. Doing tons of damage while he is Evocating is essential to the fight.

ENRAGE

Explanation: When Curator reaches 15% life he Enrages causing him to deal more melee damage. He no longer summons Astral Flares while Enraged.

Solution: Since he does a ton of damage while Enraged the tank should save all their cool downs for the last 15%. All DPS needs to focus on taking that last 15% off as quickly as possible. All healers should switch to the tank during the Enrage.

EVOCATION

Explanation: When Curator runs out of mana by summoning Astral Flares he Evocates to restore it back to full. Evocate lasts 20 seconds. While he is Evocating he stops doing melee damage to the tank and takes greatly increased damage from attacks against him.

Solution: Quickly kill the last Astral Flare that was summoned and open up as much damage as you can on him while Evocate is up. He takes a ton of damage while Evocating. You should really get take off at least a fourth of his life every Evocate.

HATEFUL BOLT

Explanation: The second highest person on the threat list is hit by Hateful Bolt every 10 seconds or so. It hits for about 5,000 damage.

Solution: Since all of the DPS is focused on the Astral Flares, controlling who is second on the threat list is pretty easy. You want Hateful Bolt to always hit the same person who has a decent amount of life and can take the hits such as a Warlock or a Hunter. It's probably not a good idea to have a melee DPS class take the Hateful Bolts since they are already taking damage from the Astral Flare's lightning attack. One healer should be assigned to healing the person taking the Hateful Bolts.

PREPARATION

There really isn't much preparation but everyone needs to understand that killing the Astral Flares as quickly as possible is top priority.

Figure out who is going to maintain second on the threat list and be focused by the Hateful Bolt.

Assign one healer to take care of the melee DPS and maybe another healer for the person getting hit by Hateful Bolt (one can probably do both jobs). All remaining healing, at least two healers, should be on the tank.

STRATEGY

Start the fight by getting Curator Misdirected onto the tank or by simply having the tank run up and attack him. Bring him all the way back against the north west wall.

The person designated to taking Hateful Bolts should do some damage to the boss. It doesn't need to be much, just enough to stay above all the healers in threat. Even this person is mainly focused on Astral Flares.

The first Astral Flare is summoned after 10 seconds. They can't be Taunted but they do have a threat list and attack the highest person on it. Don't let it run all over the place and kill it as quickly as possible.

KARAZHAN

Kill the Astral Flares, keep the tank alive, keep the person taking Hateful Bolts alive, and make sure nobody dies to the lightning damage. For 10 Astral Flares there is nothing else to the fight.

After the 10th Astral Flare is summoned Curator begins to Evocate. Kill the last Astral Flare before focusing all damage onto the boss. Use all of your cool downs such as trinkets, Arcane Power, Heroism—everything you've got. Do as much damage as you can while he is Evocating.

> Priests! Use your Shadowfiends during the Evocate. Since the amount of mana you get back is based on how much damage the Shadowfiend deals, you can restore a lot of mana by using it then.

After the Evocate ends, go right back to what you were doing. A new Astral Flare is summoned and nothing about the fight has changed. Keep repeating this pattern until you get him down to 15%.

At 15% life Curator Enrages. While Enraged he no longer summons Astral Flares but does increased melee damage to the tank. Focus all heals on the tank and keep them alive. After cleaning up any Astral Flares that may be spawned, DPS switches to Curator and finishes him off.

FROM THE GALLERY TO THE LIBRARY

Continue down the hallway until you see the next pair of Arcane Watchmen guarding a large library.

There are a lot of different types of pulls throughout The Library. In the first room wanders several Arcane Protectors and packs of Chaotic Sentiences and Mana Feeders. The Mana Feeders are immune to all magic attacks. Pull them one pack or one patrol at a time making your way along the left wall and up the ramp. You can skip several of the packs but all of the patrols must be killed.

At the top of the ramp there are new pulls of Mana Warps and Magical Horrors. When the Magical Horrors get under 10% life they begin to explode dealing around 5,000 damage to everyone. Fear them at low life to prevent the explosion. Kill the Mana Warps first. Clear out the room as move into the next.

In the next room are Sorcerous Shades and Spell Shades. The Spell Shades can be CC'ed with Shackle and Turn Undead so use CC as much as possible. The Sorcerous Shades have some nasty AoE abilities; they need to be killed first. Continue along the ramps and through the rooms of these pulls until you get to the packs of imps and Shadow Pillagers.

Pull the Shadow Pillagers and their imps killing the caster first. In this room there is a Suspicious Bookcase that opens when clicked. Down the hallway behind the bookcase is an optional boss, Terestian Illhoof.

217

TERESTIAN ILLHOOF

Illhoof is a one of the harder fights in Karazhan; thankfully you can skip him if you want. Having a Warlock with high fire resistance makes this fight fairly easy.

ABILITIES

HP	698600	Damage	5049-7140
Abilities	**Fiendish Portal:** Periodically summons demonic minions to aid the caster in battle.		
	Shadow Bolt: Inflicts 3188 to 4312 Shadow damage.		
	Summon Fiendish Imp: Summons an imp minion to aid the caster.		
	Amplify Flames: Increases the Fire damage taken by an enemy by 500 for 25 sec.		
	Sacrifice: Stuns the target and leeches 1500 health per second for 30 sec. This can be cancelled early by breaking the Demon Chains that are summoned by this spell.		

LOOT

Breastplate of the Lightbinder: Plate Chest, 1450 Armor, +28 STA, +40 INT, Equip: Increases healing done by spells and effects by up to 88, Equip: Restores 13 mana per 5 sec

Cincture of Will: Cloth Waist, 109 Armor, +24 STA, +28 INT, +25 SPI, Equip: Increases healing done by spells and effects by up to 59

Cord of Nature's Sustenance: Leather Waist, 205 Armor, +24 STA, +30 INT, +16 SPI, Equip: Increases healing done by spells and effects by up to 64, Equip: Restores 6 mana per 5 sec

Fool's Bane: Mace Main Hand, 159-296 Damage, Speed 2.60, 87.5 damage per second, Yellow Socket, Socket Bonus: +3 STA, Equip: Increases attack power by 30, Equip: Improves critical strike rating by 24

Gilded Thorium Cloak: Back, 385 Armor, +30 STA, Equip: Increases defense rating by 24

Girdle of the Prowler: Mail Waist, 457 Armor, +25 AGI, +21 STA, +22 INT, Equip: Increases attack power by 48, Equip: Restores 6 mana per 5 sec, Equip: Improves hit rating by 17

Malefic Girdle: Cloth Waist, 109 Armor, +27 STA, +26 INT, Equip: Increases damage and healing done by magical spells and effects by up to 37, Equip: Improves spell critical strike rating by 21

Mender's Heart-Ring: Finger, +18 STA, +21 INT, +19 SPI, Equip: Increases healing done by spells and effects by up to 44

Shadowvine Cloak of Infusion: Back, 97 Armor, +21 INT, +22 SPI, Equip: Restores 9 mana per 5 sec

Terestian's Stranglestaff: Staff Two-Hand, 133-271 Damage, Speed 3.00, 67.3 damage per second, +38 STR, +37 AGI, +48 STA, Equip: Increases attack power by 647 in Cat, Bear, Dire Bear, and Moonkin forms only, Equip: Improves hit rating by 25

The Lightning Capacitor: Trinket, Equip: You gain an Electrical Charge each time you cause a damaging spell critical strike. When you reach 3 Electrical Charges, they will release, firing a Lightning Bolt at your current target for 925 to 1075 damage

Xavian Stiletto: Thrown Throwing, 88-133 Damage, Speed 1.40, 78.9 damage per second, Equip: Improves critical strike rating by 20, Equip: Improves hit rating by 12

BERSERK

Explanation: After 10 minutes Illhoof goes Berserk and kills everyone Shadowbolts.

Solution: He must be killed within 10 minutes.

BROKEN PACT

Explanation: When Illhoof's pet Kil'Rek dies it causes Illhoof to take 25% increased damage.

Solution: Kill the pet every time it's up and take full advantage of the Broken Pact debuff after it has been killed.

SACRIFICE

Explanation: Every 30 seconds or so Illhoof Sacrifices a random player. This stuns the target and causes them to take 1,500 damage per second which then heals Illhoof. The Demon Chains that bind the player can be killed, freeing the player. The player who is Sacrificed can be healed.

Solution: You have to kill the Demon Chains as quickly as possible every time someone is being Sacrificed. The moment Sacrifice happens everyone needs to target the Demon Chains and free the trapped player. Toss them some heals while they are being Sacrificed; don't let them die!

SUMMON FIENDISH IMPS

Explanation: There are two portals in the room that summon a steady stream of little, non-elite Fiendish Imps. The Fiendish Imps have a fire based attack that does a few hundred damage.

Solution: The best strategy for the Fiendish Imps is having a caster with fire resistance gear continually AoE them down throughout the fight. A Warlock using Seed of Corruption or Hellfire is ideal. You can't let the Fiendish Imps get out of control because healers can get into trouble when a handful of imps are attacking them.

SUMMON KIL'REK

Explanation: Kil'Rek is Illhoof's pet. When he is killed Illhoof summons him again. Kil'Rek's attacks cause the Amplify Flames debuff that increases damage taken by fire.

Solution: Tank and kill him as quickly as you can. The Demon Chains for Sacrifice are a higher priority, but he definitely needs to get killed. If the person handling the Fiendish Imps gets the Amplify Flames debuff, make sure they get extra healing until it wears off.

PREPARATION

Figure out who is going to deal with all of the Fiendish Imps. A Warlock wearing fire resistance gear is the best choice. A Mage with fire resist works too, but they are going to need at least one Innervate. It has to be someone with some fire resistance and AoE abilities. Put them in a Paladin or Shaman group for the fire resistance aura or totem.

Assign your best tank to Illhoof. He doesn't hit very hard but healers are going to be very busy. The same tank, or another offtank depending on your raid makeup, needs to grab Kil'Rek when he spawns as well.

Make sure everybody knows what to target first. Demon Chains around a Sacrificed player are always top priority. Help with the Fiendish Imps if they ever get out of control. Kill Kil'Rek anytime he is spawned. And finally DPS Illhoof if that's the only choice.

STRATEGY

Start the fight by charging in and getting Illhoof and Kil'Rek tanked. Right away the portals that summon Fiendish Imps open up and start sending them in. The person assigned to handling them should get agro on all of them and kill them with AoE throughout the entire fight.

Make sure Kil'Rek stays tanked and never targets the person killing Fiendish Imps. His attack afflicts you with a debuff that increases damage taken from fire. Since all of the imps are shooting fireballs, you don't want it to hit the person killing them.

Kil'Rek should die fairly quickly and cause Illhoof to take 25% more damage until he summons another Kil'Rek. Start to DPS Illhoof as soon as Kil'Rek dies.

Very soon someone is going to be Sacrificed. All DPS needs to switch targets to the Demon Chains holding the player in place and free them as quickly as possible. The person being Sacrificed probably needs a couple heals as well; don't let them die! Always target and kill the Demon Chains quickly. Since the Demon Chains heal, keeping Mortal Strike or Wound Poison on Illhoof could be helpful.

Illhoof summons another Kil'Rek. Get him tanked and switch to him. Kill Kil'Rek again and then switch to Illhoof, always keeping in mind any player being Sacrificed.

As DPS switches between the Demon Chains, Kil'Rek, and Illhoof, the person tanking the Fiendish Imps AoEs them down throughout the fight.

That is all there is too the fight. It can be chaotic because DPS has to switch targets around constantly as the Fiendish Imps are kept under control. Switch targets quickly and kill those imps and you should get Illhoof down. Having someone who can AoE with a lot of fire resistance makes the fight fairly easy.

FROM ILLHOOF TO ARAN

Go back up the secret passageway and through the bookshelf. Continue along the path through The Library and pull a few more packs of Undead Shades.

Eventually you get to a room that has a second path off to the left leading to a Private Library Door. Behind that door is another optional boss—Shade of Aran.

SHADE OF ARAN

Shade of Aran is one of the most enjoyable and difficult fights in Karazhan. There are a lot of abilities to counter and it requires a great deal of execution by the raid to get him down.

LOOT

Aran's Soothing Sapphire: Held In Hand, +22 INT, Equip: Increases healing done by spells and effects by up to 51, Equip: Restores 8 mana per 5 sec

Boots of the Incorrupt: Cloth Feet, 134 Armor, +24 STA, +24 INT, +23 SPI, Equip: Restores 8 mana per 5 sec, Equip: Increases healing done by spells and effects by up to 57

Boots of the Infernal Coven: Cloth Feet, 134 Armor, +27 STA, +27 INT, +23 SPI, Equip: Increases damage and healing done by magical spells and effects by up to 34

Drape of the Dark Reavers: Back, 97 Armor, +24 AGI, +21 STA, Equip: Increases attack power by 34, Equip: Improves hit rating by 17

Mantle of the Mind Flayer: Cloth Shoulder, 146 Armor, +33 STA, +29 INT, Equip: Increases damage and healing done by magical spells and effects by up to 35, Equip: Increases your spell penetration by 23

Pauldrons of the Justice-Seeker: Plate Shoulder, 1087 Armor, +23 STA, +26 INT, Equip: Increases healing done by spells and effects by up to 57, Equip: Restores 7 mana per 5 sec, Equip: Improves spell critical strike rating by 22

Pendant of the Violet Eye: Trinket, +40 INT, Use: Each spell cast within 20 seconds will grant a stacking bonus of 21 mana regen per 5 sec. Expires after 20 seconds. Abilities with no mana cost will not trigger this trinket

Rapscallion Boots: Leather Feet, 250 Armor, +26 STA, Equip: Increases attack power by 82, Equip: Improves critical strike rating by 24

Saberclaw Talisman: Neck, +21 AGI, +33 STA, Equip: Increases attack power by 46

Shermanar Great-Ring: Finger, 223 Armor, +36 STA, Equip: Increases defense rating by 23

Steelspine Faceguard: Mail Head, 659 Armor, +36 AGI, +34 STA, +34 INT, Equip: Increases attack power by 62, Equip: Restores 9 mana per 5 sec

Tirisfal Wand of Ascendancy: Wand Range, 169-314 Shadow Damage, Speed 1.50, 161.0 damage per second, +10 STA, +9 INT, Equip: Increases damage and healing done by magical spells and effects by up to 15, Equip: Improves spell hit rating by 11

ABILITIES

HP	849760	Damage	2062-2992
Abilities	**Mass Polymorph:** Transforms all nearby enemies into sheep, forcing them to wander around for up to 10 sec.		
	Summon Water Elemental: Summons 4 Water Elementals to protect the caster. Shade of Aran uses this ability at approximately 40% health.		
	Blizzard: Deals 1313 to 1687 damage every 2 sec. and slows movement speed by 65%.		
	Blink: Teleports the caster into the center of the Karazhan library.		
	Mass Slow: Reduces all nearby enemy's attack speed by 35% and slows their movement by 60% for 10 sec.		
	Flame Wreath: Creates a circle of flame that will detonate if a player passes through it. This detonation causes 3238 to 3762 Fire damage and knocks the effected targets into the air.		
	Fireball: Inflicts 3910 to 5290 Fire damage to an enemy.		
	Pyroblast: Inflicts 6800 Fire damage to nearby enemies.		
	Counterspell: Prevents any spell from that school of magic from being cast for 10 sec.		
	Frost Bolt: Inflicts 3500 to 4500 Frost damage to an enemy and reduces its movement speed for 4 sec.		
	Arcane Explosion: Explodes with arcane power, dealing 9000 to 11000 arcane damage.		
	Arcane Missiles: Launches magical missiles at an enemy, inflicting 1260-1540 Arcane damage each second for 5 sec.		
	Conjure Water: Conjures water, which restores the Shade of Aran's mana.		

ARCANE EXPLOSION

Explanation: Pulls everyone to Aran, casts Slow on the raid, and detonates a 10,000 damage Arcane Explosion after 10 seconds. You can dispel the Slow.

Solution: Immediately start running out of range. The Slow is a dispelable magic debuff but if you start moving instantly you can get out of the Arcane Explosion's range even while slowed. Nobody should ever get hit by the Arcane Explosion.

ARCANE MISSILES

Explanation: Lasts 5 seconds, deals 1,500 damage per missile.

Solution: Arcane Missiles is the weakest of his three spell attacks. Since you want to save your interrupts for the Fireball and the Frostbolt, let Arcane Missiles cast and heal the player being targeted.

BLIZZARD

Explanation: Large Blizzard that deals just under 2,000 damage per tick. Starts in one part of the room and moves clockwise around the room's edge. Additionally, Aran casts Chains of Ice on random players. This is a dispelable magic attack that prevents the player from moving.

Solution: Dispel any Chains of Ice that he casts and stay away from the Blizzard. Since it moves almost a full circle around the edge of the room, you have to keep moving ahead of it. Always be aware of where the Blizzard is and where it's going to be. Stay ahead of it and nobody should take any damage from the Blizzard.

CONJURE WATER

Explanation: If Aran gets under 20% mana, he Polymorphs everyone, conjures a drink, and restores his mana. After the Polymorph breaks, everyone takes around 7,500 damage from a Pyroblast.

Solution: Avoiding this is a balance of interrupting the Fireballs and Frostbolts—preventing him from using mana, and having enough DPS to kill him quickly. If he does this it isn't a guaranteed wipe, but that Pyroblast after the Polymorph breaks really hurts. Save your Health Stones for this and get everyone healed up as quickly as possible. If you are low on hit points, using a fire resistance potion can be helpful.

COUNTERSPELL

Explanation: Aran regularly interrupts the spells of everyone within 10 yards of him.

Solution: All casters should stay at least 10 yards away from him or you are probably going to get interrupted. Occasionally, like when you're dodging a Blizzard, you don't have a choice. At least try not to cast any spells while you're forced to be near him.

FLAME WREATH

Explanation: 5 second cast, puts a ring of fire around 3 random players. If anyone touches the fire, from the inside or the outside, everyone in the raid takes around 3,500 damage and is tossed in the air.

Solution: Keep it simple, do not move. Absolutely everyone should stop moving from the moment Flame Wreath begins casting until the flames disappear. Logically you just need to avoid stepping in the fire, but they are really big and it's easiest to just forbid moving altogether during Flame Wreath. Pets do not trigger the damage from Flame Wreath.

FROSTBOLT

Explanation: 3 second cast, hits the targeted player for around 4,000 damage.

Solution: Interrupt it. Two people are assigned to interrupting the Frostbolt. You want to interrupt it to prevent him from using any mana. The occasional Frostbolt might get off but the vast majority of them should be caught.

FIREBALL

Explanation: 3 second cast, hits the targeted player for around 4,000 damage.

Solution: Just like the Frostbolt, assign two people to interrupt it (two people on each ability). Keep up those interrupts because it does a fair amount of damage and you want to prevent him from using as much mana as possible.

WATER ELEMENTALS

Explanation: At 40% life Aran summons 4 Water Elementals. They have a ranged frost attack that hits for around 1,500 damage. They despawn after 90 seconds.

Solution: Bringing a Warlock to Aran is very important. They can keep one Water Elemental Banished and another Feared. The remaining 2 should be CC'ed by any means available. Psychic Scream, Hammer of Justice, anything you can do. Don't bother killing them, CC and wait for the despawn.

PREPARATION

Split up everyone who can interrupt spells into two teams. Assign one of them to Fireballs and the other to Frostbolts. Try to make then equally capable of interrupting spells. Shamans have the best interrupt but if they are healing it is very hard to consistently Earth Shock. Rogues and Warriors have the second best. And Mages are the worst because of the long cool down. Silencing Shot and a Priest's Silence do not work.

Make sure everyone has a health potion, Health Stone, and maybe a fire resistance potion just incase Aran runs low on mana and uses Conjure Water.

Other than that, it's a matter of knowing how his abilities work and how you are supposed to counter them.

STRATEGY

Start the fight by having anyone attack him. Aran can not be tanked in the traditional sense. He targets random players and uses Arcane Missiles, Fireball, and Frostbolt.

Your two teams of interrupters should stay on top of interrupting the Fireball and the Frostbolt to prevent him from using as much mana as possible. Let the Arcane Missiles cast and heal up the player they hit.

All of his special abilities are completely random. It's up to the raiders to know what they do and how to counter them.

When he pulls you to him and Slows everyone, an Arcane Explosion is coming. Get away from him as quickly as you can. Even if nobody removes the Slow you can still get away from him. After the Arcane Explosion goes off it is safe to get near him again.

When Blizzard is cast, take note of where it starts, remember that it's going to move clockwise around the edge of the room, and stay ahead of it. Dispel anyone who gets hit by Chains of Ice so they can avoid the Blizzard. If you get in trouble, head towards the middle of the room. But keep in mind that he Counterspells everyone within 10 yards; try to avoid casting spells while near him.

When Flame Wreath is cast, stop moving! Don't move at all. Technically you only have to avoid stepping in the flames around the players, but it is safer and easier to simply not move at all during Flame Wreath.

If at any time Aran goes under 20% mana, he Polymorphs everyone and takes a drink to restore his mana. After he is done drinking, everyone gets Pyroblasted for about 7,500 damage. Save your health potions and Health Stones for this if it happens. Use a fire resistance potion when he gets low on mana if you have low hit points. It's fairly common for him to do this once during the fight but a second time is trouble. The Pyroblast does too much damage. Your interrupters should be on top of stopping Fireball and Frostbolt, reducing the amount of mana Aran uses and the risk that he uses this ability.

At 40% life Aran summons 4 Water Elementals. They have a ranged attack and do about 1,500 damage. A Warlock should be able to keep 2 of them under control with Banish and Fear. The remaining Water Elementals should be CC'ed any way you can. Don't try to kill them; they have too much life. Keep them from killing anyone for 90 seconds and they despawn.

If you can make it passed the Water Elementals, you're well on your way to killing Aran. He is a really tough fight and a lot of things can go wrong, but if the raid knows the abilities and is prepared to counter them correctly, you can kill him.

FROM ARAN TO NETHERSPITE

After you have killed Shade of Aran it is always quickest to zone in the front entrance and ask Berthold the Doorman to teleport you to Aran's room.

After Aran's room are some new pulls of Ethereal Thieves. They have an AoE debuff that reduces everyone's Agility and Strength by 3% per stack. And they have the tendency to drop agro.

Pull them one at a time and continue onward until you get to a room where there are two options. You can go up the stairs to Netherspite, or you can go down the stairs to the Chess Event.

Either way you want to go is fine, but if you go up the stairs be prepared to battle Netherspite.

NETHERSPITE

Netherspite is unlike any boss you've ever fought. It's going to sound really complicated because there is a lot going on, but once you engage him and everyone gets a feel for the fight he becomes very manageable.

LOOT

Cowl of Defiance: Leather Head, 296 Armor, +34 AGI, +33 STA, Equip: Increases attack power by 100, Equip: Improves hit rating by 24

Earthblood Chestguard: Mail Chest, 812 Armor, +40 STA, +41 INT, Equip: Increases healing done by spells and effects by up to 86, Equip: Restores 11 mana per 5 sec

Girdle of Truth: Plate Waist, 816 Armor, +28 STA, +29 INT, Equip: Increases healing done by spells and effects by up to 66, Equip: Restores 8 mana per 5 sec

Jewel of Infinite Possibilities: Held In Hand, +19 STA, +18 INT, Equip: Increases damage and healing done by magical spells and effects by up to 23, Equip: Improves spell hit rating by 21

Mantle of Abrahmis: Plate Shoulder, 1087 Armor, +21 STR, +43 STA, Red Socket, Yellow Socket, Socket Bonus: +3 Dodge Rating, Equip: Increases defense rating by 23

Mithril Band of the Unscarred: Finger, +26 STR, +24 STA, Equip: Improves critical strike rating by 22

Pantaloons of Repentence: Cloth Legs, 170 Armor, +27 STA, +34 INT, +26 SPI, Red Socket, Blue Socket, Blue Socket, Socket Bonus: +4 SPI, Equip: Increases healing done by spells and effects by up to 68

Rip-Flayer Leggings: Mail Legs, 710 Armor, +18 STA, +30 INT, Red Socket, Yellow Socket, Blue Socket, Socket Bonus: +6 STA, Equip: Increases attack power by 56, Equip: Restores 8 mana per 5 sec, Equip: Improves critical strike rating by 28

Shining Chain of the Afterworld: Neck, +18 STA, +21 INT, +19 SPI, Equip: Increases healing done by spells and effects by up to 46

Skulker's Greaves: Leather Legs, 319 Armor, +32 AGI, +28 STA, Red Socket, Red Socket, Blue Socket, Socket Bonus: +4 Dodge Rating, Equip: Increases attack power by 64, Equip: Improves hit rating by 28

Spiteblade: Sword One-Hand, 165-308 Damage, Speed 2.70, 87.6 damage per second, +14 AGI, +16 STA, Equip: Increases attack power by 46

Uni-Mind Headdress: Cloth Head, 158 Armor, +31 STA, +40 INT, Equip: Increases damage and healing done by magical spells and effects by up to 46, Equip: Improves spell critical strike rating by 25, Equip: Improves spell hit rating by 19

ABILITIES

HP	1117800	Damage	7514-8186
Abilities	**Nether Portal - Dominance**: Damage dealt is increased by 5%. Healing recieved reduced by 1%. Damage taken by spells is increased by 8%. Stacks.		
	Nether Portal – Serenity: Healing done is increased by 5%. Spell cost reduced by 1%. Maximum mana reduced by 200. Stacks.		
	Nether Portal - Perseverance: Damage taken is reduced by 1%. Defense increased by 5. Health increased by 29000. The defense and damage taken portions of this buff stack, however, the health bonus decreases until it goes negative.		
	Void Zone: Creates a void zone that damages targets within it for approximately 1000-1200 Shadow damage.		
	Netherbreath: Inflicts 4163 to 4837 Arcane damage to enemies in a cone in front of the caster. Knocks back.		

BERSERK

Explanation: After 9 minutes Netherspite goes berserk and kills everyone with massive damage from Nether Burn.

Solution: You must kill him within 9 minutes. This is around the 6th Nether Rage.

NETHERBREATH

Explanation: When Netherspite is in a Nether Rage he can use the Netherbreath ability that hits everyone in front of him for around 4,000 damage and knocks them away. Netherbreath is a targeted ability so expect him to change where he is facing often.

Solution: There are a few different ways to counter Netherbreath. The easiest way is to out range it; his room is really big and getting out of range is fairly easy no matter where he is positioned. The only problem with that is you lose DPS on Netherspite. If you are having trouble killing him before the Berserk, you need to stay within range of Netherbreath and continue to deal damage. It's fairly easy to dodge the attack entirely by quickly moving away from the area he casts it in. Even though it targets a specific player, even they can get out of the way if they move fast. Occasionally someone is hit by Netherbreath; get them healed as quickly as you can.

NETHER BURN

Explanation: Throughout the fight everyone within LoS of Netherspite is hit for up to 1,200 damage every 5 seconds. It is shadow damage and can be partially and fully resisted.

Solution: Make sure Priests buff Shadow Protection and Paladins use their Shadow Resistance Aura. Beyond that there isn't much you can do about it; heal up the damage done to the raid.

NETHER RAGE

Explanation: Every 60 seconds Netherspite goes into a Nether Rage. While in this state the portals disappear, he doesn't move, and he doesn't use Void Zones or Nether Burn, but he begins using Netherbreath. Nether Rage lasts 30 seconds.

Solution: This is the second part of the fight so it is gone over in detail in the strategy section. To sum it up, you can dodge the Netherbreath or out range it.

VOID ZONE

Explanation: Netherspite randomly places Void Zones under players. They appear as black circles and do 1,000 damage per second while standing in them.

Solution: Move out of the Void Zones as quickly as possible. Nobody should take more than one or two ticks of damage from them.

THE PORTALS

Explanation: When Netherspite isn't in a Nether Rage there are 3 portals in his room. The location of the portals never changes but the colors are randomly assigned after a Nether Rage has ended. The Portals emit a beam pointed directly toward Netherspite. When the beam hits Netherspite, he gains a powerful buff. When the beam hits a player, they gain a powerful buff (with some consequences). A major part of the fight is having players intersect this beam and pass off the beam to other players when they can't stay in it any longer. After a player leaves the beam they gain the debuff Nether Exhaustion preventing them from using the same colored beam again for 90 seconds. Using the portals correctly is discussed thoroughly in the strategy section.

BLUE:

Netherspite: Increases damage dealt by 1% per stack.

Player: Increases damage dealt by 5%, decreases healing received by 1%, and increases damage taken from spells by 8% per stack.

GREEN:

Netherspite: Heals 4,000 health per stack. The first stack heals 4,000, the second 8,000, the third 12,000, and so on.

Player: Increases healing done by 5%, reduces cost of spells by 1%, reduces maximum mana by 200 per stack.

RED:

Netherspite: Reduces damage taken by 1% per stack.

Player: Reduces damage taken by 1%, increases Defense by 5, and gives the player 31,000 health which is reduced by 1,000 per stack.

This fight is fairly complicated. You might not understand the Preparation section fully until you've read the Strategy section. If it's still unclear, try engaging the boss a couple times to get a feel for exactly how the fight is and then reread both sections.

Assign four people split up into two groups to each of the three portals. The players assigned to each portal should match what the beam benefits; healers should be in Green portal groups, DPS classes in Blue portal groups, and tanks in Red portal groups.

You need to assign two groups because of the Nether Exhaustion debuff. Each group alternates after every Nether Rage. For example, the first Blue group handles the Blue portal until the first Nether Rage. After the Nether Rage is over, the second Blue group handles the Blue portal until the next Nether Rage.

The best way to explain the portal group setup is by making up a fake raid. The raid consists of 10 players, one player from each class, two Warriors. A sample of how you could setup the portal groups is:

Blue: 1: Rogue, Mage, 2: Hunter, Warlock
Green: 1: Priest, Paladin, 2: Druid, Shaman
Red: 1: WarriorA, Druid, 2: WarriorB, Paladin

The Blue group is straightforward. There are four people who primarily do DPS, put all of them on Blue portal duty.

The Red group needs four people with high AC in it. There is going to be some overlap as you poach Druids, Paladins, and maybe Shaman from other groups to handle the Red portal. Make sure any player who is in two different groups never has overlap where they are somehow supposed to deal with two portals at the same time.

Put all of the healers into the Red group and keep in mind any overlap you have doesn't cause someone to do two things at once.

Before the fight starts the two portal groups for each color must be assigned.

STRATEGY

Wait until Netherspite wanders to the middle of his room before engaging him. Start the fight by having the first person in the Red group charge in and get agro.

Immediately the portals are spawned. After about 10 seconds they begin to emit their beam. The first players in each group need to be positioned between the portal and Netherspite so that the beam hits them instead of the boss.

Netherspite automatically attacks whoever is in the Red beam. The player currently tanking doesn't have to worry about building agro and as long as the Red beam is being switched off correctly, the DPS doesn't ever have to worry about pulling agro.

Now you should have the first person of the first group for each portal intersecting the beam coming out of the portal. The next person in line—the second person of the first group—for each portal needs to position themselves in front of the player currently taking the beam. This allows the player currently taking the beam to move slightly to the left or right to get out of the beam and pass it to the next person who is standing right in front of them when the time comes.

Players in the Green beam want to get out of it after about 30 stacks. Players in the Blue and Red beams want to get out earlier, around 25 stacks at the most. When it's time to get out of the beam hopefully the next player to take it is standing right in front of you so you can just move to the side.

That's how you handle the beams. The first player gets between the portal and Netherspite before the beam is there, catching it as it starts being emitted. The next player gets in front of the first player ready to take it over as soon as the first player has to get out of the way and pass it onto them. Everything is assigned and everyone needs to know where they are in the beam rotation.

While the portals are being dealt with there is the Nether Burn to heal and the Void Zones to avoid. Healers have a tough time because Nether Burn does a fair amount of damage and the current tank—the person in the red beam—is going to need heals as it gets stacked higher. Keep everyone alive and make it easier on the healers by getting out of the Void Zones that appear under random people as quickly as possible.

After 60 seconds Netherspite goes into a Nether Rage. The portals disappear, the Netherburn stops and the Void Zones stop happening.

As soon as he is in a Nether Rage you have a couple options to handle it. The easiest way is by running out of range of his new attack Netherbreath. Netherbreath targets a random player and hits everyone in that direction for around 4,000 damage, knocking them back in the process. If your DPS is high you can just run out of range and avoid the attack entirely. But if your DPS is low you are going to need to stay in and do damage during the Nether Rage. Spread out around Netherspite and move out of the way if he faces you to avoid getting hit by the Netherbreath. It's not an instant cast spell; there is time to move out of the way if you are quick.

After 30 seconds of being in a Nether Rage the portals respawn and everything starts over. The location of the portals never changes but their colors are randomly assigned. Call out which portal is where so that the second group of people who handle the portals know where to go. The first player of the second group should intersect the beam and the next play should move in front of them ready for the switch.

Continue the fight and keep switching people off.

The top priority is preventing the beams from hitting Netherspite. Sometimes the player who is supposed to pick up the beam isn't able to do so because they are too far away. If this happens, a random person can temporarily hold the beam until the correct person shows up to take it over.

Dealing with the beams is going to take some practice. You might hit the Enrage timer a couple times because DPS is being lost as everyone gets familiar with the beam rotations. Get through a couple full rotations without any trouble and you're well on your way to slaying Netherspite.

FROM NETHERSPITE TO THE GAME ROOM.

After you go down the stairs there are a few pulls of Ethereal Spellfilchers. These have an aura just like their Thief counterparts, but it reduces Intellect and Spirit instead. Pull them one at a time and continue on the path.

In the room before the Game Room is a friendly NPC named Ythyar who sells reagents and can repair your gear.

As soon as you see a big chess board with all the pieces laid out, you've reached the Chess Event.

CHESS EVENT

Develop your pieces! Castle early! Put pressure on the middle squares! Just kidding, the Chess Event has little to do with a real game of chess. It is an easy and fun event where the goal is to kill the opposite team's King.

LOOT

Battlescar Boots: Plate Feet, 997 Armor, +18 STR, +28 STA, Red Socket, Blue Socket, Socket Bonus: +3 Parry Rating, Equip: Increases defense rating by 23

Bladed Shoulderpads of the Merciless: Leather Shoulder, 273 Armor, +30 STA, Yellow Socket, Yellow Socket, Socket Bonus: +3 Hit Rating, Equip: Increases attack power by 58, Equip: Improves hit rating by 13, Equip: Improves critical strike rating by 21

Fiend Slayer Boots: Mail Feet, 558 Armor, +26 AGI, +24 STA, +16 INT, Red Socket, Blue Socket, Socket Bonus: +3 AGI, Equip: Increases attack power by 34, Equip: Improves hit rating by 17

Forestlord Striders: Leather Feet, 250 Armor, +24 STA, +27 INT, +16 SPI, Blue Socket, Blue Socket, Socket Bonus: +7 Healing, Equip: Increases healing done by spells and effects by up to 55

Girdle of Treachery: Leather Waist, 205 Armor, +18 AGI, +37 STA, Red Socket, Red Socket, Socket Bonus: +3 AGI, Equip: Increases attack power by 58

Headdress of the High Potentate: Cloth Head, 158 Armor, +37 STA, +38 INT, +32 SPI, Equip: Increases healing done by spells and effects by up to 81

Heart-Flame Leggings: Mail Legs, 710 Armor, +36 STA, +33 INT, Blue Socket, Blue Socket, Yellow Socket, Socket Bonus: +4 INT, Equip: Increases healing done by spells and effects by up to 90

King's Defender: Sword One-Hand, 182 Armor, 98-182 Damage, Speed 1.60, 87.5 damage per second, +28 STA, Equip: Increases defense rating by 13, Equip: Improves hit rating by 17

Legplates of the Innocent: Plate Legs, 1269 Armor, +24 STA, +32 INT, Yellow Socket, Blue Socket, Blue Socket, Socket Bonus: +4 INT, Equip: Increases healing done by spells and effects by up to 66, Equip: Restores 8 mana per 5 sec, Equip: Improves spell critical strike rating by 21

Mithril Chain of Heroism: Neck, +28 STR, +22 AGI, +22 STA

Ring of Recurrence: Finger, +15 INT, +15 STA, Equip: Increases damage and healing done by magical spells and effects by up to 32, Equip: Improves spell critical strike rating by 19

Triptych Shield of the Ancients: Shield Off Hand (Shield), 4872 Armor, 122 Block, +24 STA, +21 INT, Equip: Increases healing done by spells and effects by up to 42, Equip: Restores 8 mana per 5 sec

PIECES

Each piece has two abilities in addition to changing the way they face and moving around the board.

BISHOP
Heals friendly pieces and hits all enemies in front of it for 3,000 damage.
KING
Cleaves everyone in front of it for 4,000 damage and increases damage dealt by all nearby friendly pieces by 50%.
KNIGHT
Deals 3,000 damage to current target and reduces damage of all nearby enemy units by 50%.
PAWN
Deals 1,000 damage to current target and absorbs 500 damage.
ROOK
Hits every enemy piece next to it for 3,000 damage and reduces the damage done to itself by 50%.
QUEEN
Deals 4,000 damage to current target and deals 6,000 damage to current target plus all targets next to it.

PREPARATION

Make sure everyone is ready to control a piece and start the event by taking control of the King.

It's helpful to have someone ready to control the Pawns in front of the King and Queen in order to move them out of the way.

STRATEGY

The quick and dirty way to do this is by taking control of the King and Queen and charging them into battle with the opponent's King right away. Your King might need a heal or two so have someone controlling a Bishop ready to take care of it.

These two can really just go up and kill the opponent's King, but it takes a while.

Go attack other pieces and use all your abilities to kill everything you feel like killing. Don't let your King die; keep him healed if he takes damage. There really isn't much else to it!

After the opponent's King is dead a chest appears with your reward.

You can play another game and control both sides of the board now if you choose.

FROM THE GAME ROOM TO THE TOP

Pull the first two Fleshbeasts and the Greater Fleshbeast patrol before leaving the Game Room. They hit fairly hard so watch those tanks.

Both the left and the right paths lead to the same place. The right path is much quicker but less scenic. Continue up the stairs killing the Fleshbeasts one pack at a time until you get to the top. At the very top awaits Prince Malchezaar.

PRINCE MALCHEZAAR

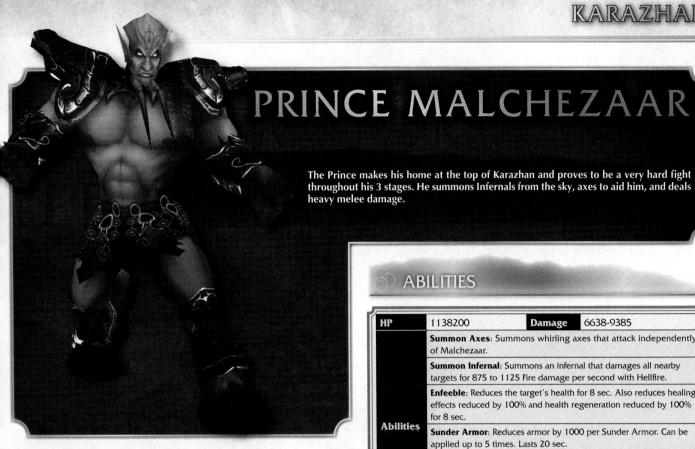

The Prince makes his home at the top of Karazhan and proves to be a very hard fight throughout his 3 stages. He summons Infernals from the sky, axes to aid him, and deals heavy melee damage.

ABILITIES

HP	1138200	Damage	6638-9385

Abilities

Summon Axes: Summons whirling axes that attack independently of Malchezaar.

Summon Infernal: Summons an infernal that damages all nearby targets for 875 to 1125 Fire damage per second with Hellfire.

Enfeeble: Reduces the target's health for 8 sec. Also reduces healing effects reduced by 100% and health regeneration reduced by 100% for 8 sec.

Sunder Armor: Reduces armor by 1000 per Sunder Armor. Can be applied up to 5 times. Lasts 20 sec.

Shadow Word: Pain: Inflicts 1500 Shadow damage to an enemy every 3 sec. for 18 sec.

Shadow Nova: Deals 3000 Shadow damage and knocks back.

Amplify Damage: Increases all forms of damage taken by an enemy by 100% for 10 sec.

LOOT

Adornment of Stolen Souls: Neck, +20 INT, +18 STA, Equip: Increases damage and healing done by magical spells and effects by up to 28, Equip: Improves spell critical strike rating by 23

Farstrider Wildercloak: Back, 105 Armor, +36 STA, Equip: Increases attack power by 70

Gorehowl: Two-Hand Axe Two-Hand, 345-518 Damage, Speed 3.60, 119.9 damage per second, +49 STR, +43 AGI, +51 STA

Helm of the Fallen Champion: Classes: Shaman Rogue Paladin

Helm of the Fallen Defender: Classes: Druid Priest Warrior

Helm of the Fallen Hero: Classes: Warlock Mage Hunter

Jade Ring of the Everliving: Finger, Equip: Increases healing done by spells and effects by up to 68, Equip: Restores 12 mana per 5 sec

Light's Justice: Mace Main Hand, 25-125 Damage, Speed 1.80, 41.7 damage per second, +16 STA, +21 INT, +20 SPI, Equip: Increases healing done by spells and effects by up to 382

Malchazeen: Dagger One-Hand, 132-199 Damage, Speed 1.80, 91.9 damage per second, +16 STA, Equip: Increases attack power by 50, Equip: Improves hit rating by 15

Nathrezim Mindblade: Dagger Main Hand, 25-125 Damage, Speed 1.80, 41.7 damage per second, +18 STA, +18 INT, Equip: Increases damage and healing done by magical spells and effects by up to 203, Equip: Improves spell critical strike rating by 23

Ring of a Thousand Marks: Finger, +21 STA, Equip: Increases attack power by 44, Equip: Improves critical strike rating by 23, Equip: Improves hit rating by 19

Ruby Drape of the Mysticant: Back, 105 Armor, +22 STA, +21 INT, Equip: Increases damage and healing done by magical spells and effects by up to 30, Equip: Improves spell hit rating by 18

Stainless Cloak of the Pure Hearted: Back, 105 Armor, +22 STA, +23 INT, Equip: Increases healing done by spells and effects by up to 53, Equip: Restores 7 mana per 5 sec

Sunfury Bow of the Phoenix: Bow Bow, 169-314 Damage, Speed 2.90, 83.3 damage per second, +19 AGI, Equip: Increases attack power by 34

The Decapitator: Axe Main Hand, 167-312 Damage, Speed 2.60, 92.1 damage per second, Use: Hurls your axe in an attempt to decapitate your target causing 513 to 567 damage, Equip: Improves critical strike rating by 27

ENFEEBLE

Explanation: About every 30 seconds Prince Enfeebles 5 random players. This reduces their life to 1 and reduces healing effects on them by 100%. When it wears off everyone's life is put back where it was. It does not hit his current target and he stops using Enfeeble under 30% life.

Solution: By itself Enfeeble doesn't really do any damage. The problem occurs when you get hit by Shadow Nova or an Infernal's fire nova with only 1 life, getting yourself killed. Enfeeble usually comes shortly before a Shadow Nova so any melee DPS should immediately back out and wait for the Shadow Nova to happen or for Enfeeble to wear off before going back in.

SHADOW NOVA

Explanation: Shortly after an Enfeeble, or about every 30 seconds, Shadow Nova hits everyone within 30 yards for around 3,000 damage and knocks you back quite a ways.

Solution: Since it only hits people within 30 yards all ranged classes should be able to avoid it. When it hits melee the worst thing that can happen is that they are knocked back into an Infernal's fire nova. Try to position yourself so that you are thrown against a nearby wall. And never get hit by Shadow Nova while you are Enfeebled or you are going to die.

SHADOW WORD: PAIN

Explanation: Prince randomly casts Shadow Word: Pain on nearby targets. It does about 1,250 damage per tick and is a dispelable magic debuff.

Solution: Dispel it as quickly as possible. Keep in mind the Shadow Nova if you are moving in closer to dispel it off of melee classes. Try to time it so that you don't take damage from the Shadow Nova.

SUMMON INFERNAL

Explanation: Prince summons Infernals from the sky throughout the fight. When they land they begin to pulse a fire nova around them that does about 1,750 damage per tick. Their location is completely random and not necessarily on top of where a player is currently positioned. They despawn after 180 seconds.

Solution: The main idea is to stay out of the fire nova. Since their position is so random a lot of things can go wrong related to the Infernals. Sometimes you just get unlucky and they land in all the wrong places, sometimes you barely notice they are there. The tank might need to adjust their position depending on where Infernals land to allow ranged classes to stay at max range and avoid the Shadow Novas. Communication, watching where they land, and avoiding them while they are up are the keys.

Make sure the tank has a stacked tanking group with Blood Pact and maybe a Shaman for Grace of Air. Devotion Aura isn't really an option since the Paladins are staying at max range throughout the fight.

Assign one healer to heal the damage from the axes in the last phase of the fight.

STRATEGY

Have the main tank charge in, get agro, and position Prince in the middle of the east wall. The tank should always have their back against a wall to avoid being knocked back by Shadow Nova. All ranged classes should stay at max range throughout the fight.

The tank takes a ton of melee damage so keep those heals on them. Move into range to dispel the Shadow Word: Pain when it is applied.

The first thing that happens is an Enfeeble. Five random players are now at 1 life. If any melee classes get Enfeebled, they need to run away from Prince before the Shadow Nova hits. Taking a Shadow Nova while Enfeebled is a guaranteed death.

Shortly after the Enfeeble Prince uses Shadow Nova dealing about 3,000 damage to everyone within 30 yards and knocking them back in the process. Ranged classes should never get hit by Shadow Nova; they should be able to stay out of range.

The first Infernal is summoned and lands in a random spot. Sometimes it lands far away and you can ignore it, but other times it lands in a bad spot. If it lands on the melee, move Prince to the north or south as necessary. Ranged classes should get out of the Infernal's Fire Nova if it lands near them.

Dodging the Infernals can become a huge hassle as the fight goes on. Sometimes they land in all the wrong places and there's little you can do to prevent wiping to them. Usually they land in places where you can adjust your positioning and move around them. As long as the positioning is setup so that ranged classes can stay at least 30 yards away to avoid the Shadow Nova, it works. Adjust positions around the Infernals as they spawn keeping the goal in mind.

DPS him down to 60% life. At 60% he summons his axes to his hands and starts dealing increased melee damage to the tank. Nothing else about the fight changes but he starts doing a ton of damage so keep that tank alive. This is the best time to start using cool downs like Heroism and the like. You want to get him down to 30% as quickly as possible.

At 30% he drops his axes. The axes start targeting random players and hitting them for about 200-500 damage. They can't be targeted, so they can't be killed or tanked. One healer needs to heal anyone who is getting hit by the axes. Use Evasion, Deterrence, and maybe even Limited Invulnerability potions to help reduce the damage from the axes.

Under 30% he no longer uses Enfeeble but Shadow Nova continues to happen. Stay at max range to avoid it.

Don't let anyone die to axes, keep dodging those Infernals, and take him down the last 30%.

Even the most experienced raid can wipe to bad luck. Dodging the Infernals is probably the hardest part of the fight since it is so random where they land. There is a lot of damage being dealt to the tank but healing only really suffers when all of the healers have to move to dodge an Infernal. Keep your positioning intact and don't let anyone die to Shadow Nova.

Prince deals tons of damage and it takes some practice to master adjusting positions around the Infernals, but as soon as everyone knows the fight the only thing that can kill you is bad luck.

THE MASTER'S TERRACE

After zoning in the side entrance and going left there is a door under the first ramp up The Broken Stair.

Behind that door is The Master's Terrace where Nightbane is fought.

NIGHTBANE

Nightbane is summoned using the Blackened Urn on The Master's Terrace. He is an Undead Dragon and a fairly challenging fight. He is also part of the attunement quest to Serpentshire Cavern: Coilfang Reservoir.

ABILITIES

HP	1327900	Damage	9028-12764
Abilities	**Cleave:** Inflicts normal damage plus 365 to an enemy and its nearest allies, affecting up to 2 targets.		
	Tail Sweep: Inflicts 450 damage on enemies behind the caster, knocks back. Also deals an additional 450 Fire damage every 3 sec. for 15 sec.		
	Smoldering Breath: Inflicts 3700 to 4300 Fire damage to enemies in a cone in front of the caster. Also deals 1688 to 1912 damage every 3 sec. for 15 sec.		
	Summon Bone Skeletons: Summons a large group of Bone Skeletons.		
	Searing Blast: Deals 1850 to 2150 physical damage to the target. (See Searing Cinders for the additional fire damage.)		
	Searing Cinders: Deals 3000 fire damage over 18 sec.		
	Distracting Ash: Reduces the chance to hit with spells and abilities by 30% for 40 sec.		
	Charred Earth: Deals 2188 to 2812 Fire damage every 3 seconds for 30 sec.		
	Fireball Volley: Deals 2550 to 3450 Fire damage to targets over 40 yards away. Nightbane does not use this ability when being fought normally.		
	Immolation: Burns nearby enemies for 950 to 1050 Fire damage every 3 seconds.		
	Rain of Bones: Deals 352 to 408 Physical damage per second for up to 30 sec. Summons 3 skeletons in the process.		

LOOT

Chestguard of the Conniver: Leather Chest, 364 Armor, +37 AGI, +36 STA, Equip: Increases attack power by 90, Equip: Improves hit rating by 22

Dragonheart Flameshield: Shield Off Hand (Shield), 4872 Armor, 122 Block, +19 STA, +21 INT, Equip: Increases damage and healing done by magical spells and effects by up to 23, Equip: Restores 7 mana per 5 sec

Emberspur Talisman: Neck, Equip: Increases healing done by spells and effects by up to 66, Equip: Restores 11 mana per 5 sec

Ferocious Swift-Kickers: Mail Feet, 558 Armor, +22 STA, +21 INT, Yellow Socket, Blue Socket, Socket Bonus: +6 Attack Power, Equip: Increases attack power by 58, Equip: Improves critical strike rating by 16

Ironstriders of Urgency: Plate Feet, 997 Armor, +33 STR, +20 AGI, +28 STA, Red Socket, Yellow Socket, Socket Bonus: +3 STR

Nightstaff of the Everliving: Staff Two-Hand, 143-290 Damage, Speed 3.20, 67.7 damage per second, +33 STA, +34 INT, +55 SPI, Equip: Increases healing done by spells and effects by up to 348

Panzar'Thar Breastplate: Plate Chest, 1450 Armor, +51 STA, Yellow Socket, Blue Socket, Blue Socket, Socket Bonus: +4 Block Rating, Equip: Increases the block value of your shield by 39, Equip: Increases defense rating by 26, Equip: Increases your shield block rating by 24

Robe of the Elder Scribes: Cloth Chest(Robe), 194 Armor, +27 STA, +29 INT, +24 SPI, Equip: Increases damage and healing done by magical spells and effects by up to 32, Equip: Gives a chance when your harmful spells land to increase the damage of your spells and effects by up to 130 for 10 seconds, Equip: Improves spell critical strike rating by 24

Scaled Breastplate of Carnage: Mail Chest, 812 Armor, +33 STA, +38 INT, Equip: Increases attack power by 80, Equip: Restores 8 mana per 5 sec, Equip: Improves critical strike rating by 24

Shield of Impenetrable Darkness: Shield Off Hand (Shield), 4872 Armor, 122 Block, +33 STA, Equip: Increases the block value of your shield by 33, Equip: Increases defense rating by 22

Stonebough Jerkin: Leather Chest, 364 Armor, +34 STA, +35 INT, +31 SPI, Equip: Increases healing done by spells and effects by up to 77, Equip: Restores 9 mana per 5 sec

Talisman of Nightbane: Held In Hand, +19 STA, +19 INT, Equip: Increases damage and healing done by magical spells and effects by up to 28, Equip: Improves spell critical strike rating by 17

BELLOWING ROAR

Explanation: Every 30-45 seconds Nightbane fears everyone within 30 yards.

Solution: Bellowing Roar is the standard dragon fear spell. Counter it with Fear Ward, Tremor Totems, or an offtank in Berserker Stance.

CHARRED EARTH

Explanation: Throughout the fight random areas become Charred Earth. When a player is in the Charred Earth they take a few thousand damage per tick.

Solution: It's really obvious where the Charred Earths are. You have to avoid them and stay out of them until they disappear.

CLEAVE

Explanation: A standard Cleave attack that hits everyone in front of Nightbane for several thousand damage.

Solution: Only the tank should ever be in front of Nightbane. Keep him pointed away from the raid.

DISTRACTING ASH

Explanation: Nightbane periodically hits everyone within about 20 yards with Distracting Ash. This reduces the range of spells and abilities by 50%. It is a dispelable magic debuff.

Solution: Ranged classes need to stay away from him. It has a pretty small range so only melee should ever get hit by Distracting Ash and since they have no mentionable ranged abilities, it isn't a big deal and doesn't need to be dispelled. If a ranged class ever gets hit by Distracting Ash, dispel it as soon as you can, but it really shouldn't happen.

FIREBALL BARRAGE

Explanation: If someone goes very far away from Nightbane while he is in the air, he begins shooting Fireballs at the entire raid that deal about 3,500 damage each.

Solution: Stay relatively close to him while he is in the air. This ability only exists so that you can't get everyone out of range of the Smoking Blast attack. You really shouldn't ever see it unless someone is moving very far away from him while he is in the air.

RAIN OF BONES

Explanation: After Nightbane takes flight a random player is afflicted by Rain of Bones. This causes a Rain of Fire type of attack to damage the area around them for about 300 damage per tick and it is where the skeletons spawn.

Solution: Heal the person who gets Rain of Bones. Move away from them; only one person should take damage from Rain of Bones.

SMOKING BLAST

Explanation: While Nightbane is in the air he casts Smoking Blast mainly on the healer with the highest threat, but it can also hit other players at random. Smoking Blast hits for 2,000-5,000 damage depending on AC and afflicts the person he hits with a DoT debuff. The DoT can stack up to 4 times and is a dispelable magic debuff.

Solution: Since the damage from Smoking Blast is based on your AC, you want a Paladin to take them. Who Smoking Blast is going to hit is fairly controllable through healing threat, and Paladins also have Righteous Fury to generate a lot of threat quickly. Smoking Blast is discussed more thoroughly in the strategy section, but the general idea is to get it hitting a Paladin and heal through it.

SMOLDERING BREATH

Explanation: A breath attack that hits everyone in front of Nightbane for about 4,000 damage and deals an additional 2,000 damage per tick for 15 seconds afterwards.

Solution: Just like the Cleave, nobody but the tank should ever be in front of Nightbane.

TAIL SWEEP

Explanation: Hits everyone behind Nightbane for a few hundred damage and knocks them back. Has a DoT debuff that lasts 25 seconds.

Solution: Don't stand directly behind him and you'll never get hit by Tail Sweep. Melee DPS should attack the side of him. Think back to those Onyxia and Vaelastrasz days!

PREPARATION

The best place to fight Nightbane is in the middle of the balcony; right about where he lands when he is summoned with the Blackened Urn.

At the start of the fight have the raid split up onto each side of him by group. As the fight goes on this positioning is going to get a little messy and staying split up evenly on each side is not completely necessary; it just helps spread out the damage from Charred Earth.

The tank needs to be in the best possible tanking group with a Warlock for Blood Pact, Paladin for Devotion Aura, and Shaman for Grace of Air. Nightbane does a ton of melee damage; mitigate as much of it as possible.

STRATEGY

Begin the fight by using the Blackened Urn and summoning Nightbane. After flying around for a few seconds he lands in the middle of the balcony and becomes attackable. The tank should be waiting where he lands ready to pick him up right away. Give the tank a few moments of building agro before opening up the DPS.

The Fear happens throughout the fight. Deal with it like any other dragon Fear with Fear Ward, Tremor Totem, or an offtank using Berserker Rage. Since the Fear only has a 30 yard range all ranged classes should be able to avoid it entirely.

Charred Earths appear under random players and lasts for about 30 seconds. Get out of them quickly and wait until they despawn.

Distracting Ash is going to hit everyone close to Nightbane but since it only really effects ranged classes—all of which are staying far away to avoid the fear; you can pretty much just ignore it. Dispel it off any ranged class that manages to get it for whatever reason.

The tank is taking a ton of damage but the ground phases are fairly easy. Don't let the tank die, dodge those Charred Earths, and DPS him down to 75%.

At 75% Nightbane takes flight. When he does this his threat list is reset. The first thing that happens is a random player gets the Rain of Bones debuff and begins taking about 300 damage per second from a Blizzard-like spell raining down on them. Additionally, 5 Restless Skeletons are summoned around the player who has Rain of Bones.

Heal the player who has Rain of Bones and start killing the Restless Skeletons as quickly as possible. They can be CC'ed through any available means but your best bet is to simply tear them apart one at a time. Don't use AoE; single target DPS them down as quickly as you can.

As the Restless Skeletons are being dealt with the healer with the highest threat is targeted by the Smoking Blast attack. It hits for a few thousand and stacks a DoT debuff that can do significant damage, but its damage is reduced by AC. A Paladin is the perfect person to take the Smoking Blasts because they have high AC and can use Righteous Fury to guarantee themselves a high spot on the healer threat list.

Smoking Blast is a little unpredictable—on occasion it may hit players at random—but the healer with the highest threat takes most of them. Keep everyone who gets hit by Smoking Blast alive and dispel the debuff as quickly as you can. Don't let anybody die to it!

Get the Restless Skeletons dead and don't let anyone die to Smoking Blast. When Nightbane lands he comes down further to the north of where he originally spawned. The tank should be waiting under him ready to pickup agro the moment he lands. Agro is a little touchy when he's landing so it's a good idea to not do anything what so ever until he is tanked. A Hunter using Misdirect on the tank can really help when he lands as well.

Go back into your ground positions and the fight continues just like before. At 50% he takes flight again, the Rain of Bones hits, the Restless Skeletons spawn, and the Smoking Blasts begin; deal with it the same way. The third and final time he takes to the air is at 25%.

If you can get through one ground phase and one air phase without much trouble, it's just a matter of repeating it three times. Nightbane is healing intensive and certainly not an easy fight by any means, but a well geared raid of players who understand the phases should be able to kill him.

SERVANT QUARTERS

The Servant Quarters is a seldom traveled area immediately to the right after zoning in the front entrance of Karazhan. There are various Undead beasts guarding the area.

A random boss spawns in the Servant Quarters once a certain number of creatures have been killed.

HYAKISS THE LURKER

Hyakiss is a spider boss with a web attack that immobilizes the target for 10 seconds and a poison attack that deals 500 damage per second and stacks on the current melee target.

Since there is a stacking poison debuff, it is wise to use two tanks. If the poison gets stacked really high on one tank, the other can pull agro and tank Hyakiss until it is reset.

The web attack isn't a very big deal because it is a dispelable magic debuff. Cleanse it as necessary.

LOOT

Lurker's Belt: Mail Waist, 457 Armor, Random Enchant

Lurker's Cord: Cloth Waist, 109 Armor, Random Enchant

Lurker's Girdle: Plate Waist, 816 Armor, Random Enchant

Lurker's Grasp: Leather Waist, 205 Armor, Random Enchant

ROKAD THE RAVAGER

Rokad is a wolf boss without any notable abilities. Get him tanked and kill him.

LOOT

Ravager's Bands: Mail Wrist, 355 Armor, Random Enchant

Ravager's Bracers: Plate Wrist, 634 Armor, Random Enchant

Ravager's Cuffs: Cloth Wrist, 85 Armor, Random Enchant

Ravager's Wrist-Wraps: Leather Wrist, 159 Armor, Random Enchant

SHADIKITH THE GLIDER

Shadikith is a bat boss, probably the hardest of the bunch. He has a close range AoE silence ability, knocks the tank backwards with a Wing Buffet, and charges the player furthest away from him.

Spell casters should stay away from him to avoid the silence. The tank is being knocked back so watch your agro; don't overdo it on this guy and get yourself killed. And the furthest away player should be someone like a Hunter who can take the potentially serious damage from the charge.

LOOT

Glider's Boots: Leather Feet, 250 Armor, Random Enchant

Glider's Foot-Wraps: Cloth Feet, 134 Armor, Random Enchant

Glider's Greaves: Plate Feet, 997 Armor, Random Enchant

Glider's Sabatons: Mail Feet, 558 Armor, Random Enchant

GRUUL'S LAIR

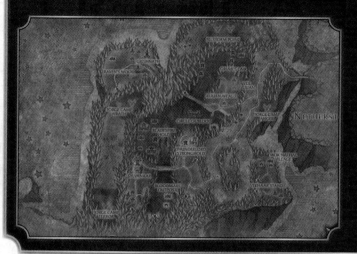

DUNGEON INFORMATION

Name	Gruul's Lair
Location	Blade's Edge Mountains
Suggested Levels	Group of 25, Level 70
Time to Complete	30-45 minutes per boss

GRUUL'S MINIONS

The trash in Gruul's Lair is all Ogres that are either Lair Brutes or Gronn-Priests. There are a total of two pulls prior to the High King Maulgar encounter, and a total of five pulls after High King to reach Gruul the Dragonkiller. Any of the multi-mob packs can come in any variation of the two types of Ogres, i.e. 1 Brute and 1 Priest, 2 Brutes, 2 Priests, etc. The Lair Brutes have three main attacks which are Mortal Strike, Cleave and a Charge attack, while the Gronn-Priests use an interruptible Heal, Psychic Scream, and Renew. Both types will call for aid around 25% health to any nearby Ogres.

The trash pulls prior to High King Maulgar will be a single Lair Brute followed by a two-pack of random makeup. Lair Brutes can seem overwhelming at first, but if you keep your raid inside of 8 yards or outside of 25 yards, you will keep the Brute from charging random party members and killing them. For the two-pack, if you have two Lair Brutes, face them both towards opposite walls with each tank having its back against the wall. This will let your raid stand in  between both Ogres to stay inside of 8 yards to avoid the Charge from both of them. Make sure your melee don't go stand in front of the Lair Brutes, as their Cleave attack can and will kill them. If the two-pack is two Gronn-Priests, just split them up and have your tanks ready to break Psychic Scream when it happens. Be sure to Dispell or Purge Renew if its on the kill target and keep an eye out for each one trying to heal the other; ranged interrupts, such as Earth Shock and Counterspell, should be ready to interrupt in case the melee get feared. If you have one Lair Brute and one Gronn-Priest, keep an extra tank back towards the raid to catch the Lair Brute if it uses Charge against a raid member and drag it back out of the raid while everyone else focuses on the Gronn-Priest.

The trash pulls after High King will come as a two-pack, a single roamer, another two-pack, another single roamer, and a three-pack. Use the same strategy as before on any of the single or two-pack pulls; you will have much room for the two-pack pulls, so it is possible to keep one Lair Brute far away from anyone else to keep him from using his Charge and use 2-3 healers to standing right behind the Lair Brute as they heal the tank on it away from the raid.

For the three-pack pull, the best thing to do is to split up into three sections being one tank and a couple healers near the hallway, one tank and a couple healers over in the Northern area, and everyone else to the East. Have a Hunter use misdirect on the eastern tank to begin the pull, but the makeup of the three-pack will determine the kill order. If you have one Gronn-Priest and two Lair Brutes,  use extra Hunters to misdirect the two Brutes to the two tanks that are away from the rest of the raid or have those tanks tag their mobs for themselves as the raid kills the Gronn-Priest. If you have two Gronn-Priests and 1 Lair Brute, send one Gronn-Priest to the raid while the other Gronn-Priest is tagged or Misdirected to one of the tanks away from the raid, and the Lair Brute should be tagged or Misdirected to the better geared extra tank away from the raid. If you have three Lair Brutes, simple send one to each tank and make sure they are all spread out so that each group has more than 40 yards between it and any of the other two groups.

232

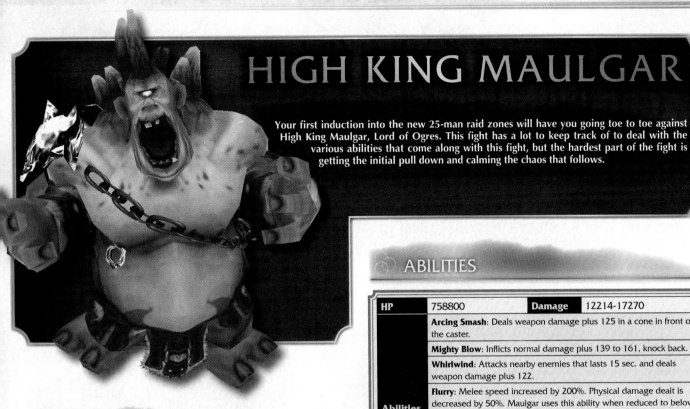

HIGH KING MAULGAR

Your first induction into the new 25-man raid zones will have you going toe to toe against High King Maulgar, Lord of Ogres. This fight has a lot to keep track of to deal with the various abilities that come along with this fight, but the hardest part of the fight is getting the initial pull down and calming the chaos that follows.

ABILITIES

HP	758800	Damage	12214-17270
Abilities	**Arcing Smash**: Deals weapon damage plus 125 in a cone in front of the caster.		
	Mighty Blow: Inflicts normal damage plus 139 to 161, knock back.		
	Whirlwind: Attacks nearby enemies that lasts 15 sec. and deals weapon damage plus 122.		
	Flurry: Melee speed increased by 200%. Physical damage dealt is decreased by 50%. Maulgar uses this ability when reduced to below 50% health.		
	Intimidating Roar: Paralyzes the target for 8 sec., and causes all nearby enemies to run in fear. Maulgar uses this ability when reduced to below 50% health.		
	Berserker Charge: Charges, knocking the target back and inflicting normal damage plus 300. Maulgar uses this ability when reduced to below 50% health.		

LOOT

Belt of Divine Inspiration: 118 Armor, +27 Stamina, +26 Intellect, 1 Yellow Socket, 1 Blue Socket, Socket Bonus: +4 Spell Damage, +43 Spell Damage and Healing

Bladespire Warbands: 687 Armor, +20 Strength, +16 Stamina, 1 Blue Socket, 1 Red Socket, Socket Bonus: +3 Strength, +24 Critical Strike Rating

Brute Cloak of the Ogre-Magi: 105 Armor, +18 Stamina, +20 Intellect, +23 Spell Critical Strike Rating, +28 Spell Damage and Healing

Hammer of the Naaru: 345-518 Damage, 3.60 Speed, 119.9 Damage Per Second, +30 Strength, +41 Stamina, +37 Intellect, 2 Red Sockets, 1 Blue Socket, Socket Bonus: +4 Intellect, +33 Spell Damage and Healing

Malefic Mask of the Shadows: 321 Armor, +45 Stamina, +31 Hit Rating, +42 Critical Strike Rating, +84 Attack Power

Maulgar's Warhelm: 715 Armor, +43 Stamina, +31 Intellect, +42 Critical Strike Rating, +86 Attack Power

Pauldrons of the Fallen Champion: Classes: Paladin, Rogue, Shaman.

Pauldrons of the Fallen Defender: Classes: Warrior, Priest, Druid.

Pauldrons of the Fallen Hero: Classes: Hunter, Mage, Warlock.

HIGH KING MAULGAR 100%-51%

Inflicts extremely heavy physical damage with normal attacks that hit for around 5,000-6,500 damage on a well geared Warrior.

Arcing Smash: A frontal cleave attack that hits for between 8,000-12,000 damage on plate, and has a 10-12 second refresh.

Mighty Blow: A single target attack that hits for between 6,000-11,000 damage on plate with a small knockback effect, and is on about a 15 second refresh.

Whirlwind: Every 40-45 seconds, Maulgar will begin to Whirlwind for about 10 seconds, hitting for 4,000-5,000 damage on plate every 2-3 seconds. His Whirlwind is targeted, so if you are his primary agro target and you try to run, he will follow you.

HIGH KING MAULGAR 50%-0%

Damage reduced by 50% but his attack speed triples and he puts his weapon away, resulting in no further Arcing Smash or Mighty Blow attacks.

Fear: Every 30 seconds or so, Maulgar will do an AE fear attack that has a range of about 10 yards.

Charge: A charge attack that goes to a random raid member outside of his AE fear range causing them to become the new primary agro target.

Whirlwind: Similar to his earlier version, Whirlwind is AE physical damage to anyone around Maulgar, and he will chase whoever is his primary agro target, which can be very bad if it happens when your MT is feared.

Dealing with High King Maulgar: You will need to use a well geared Protection spec Warrior to tank High King or a very well geared Feral Druid. The MT should make sure he/she has over 18,000 HPs at all times, and should be using Ironshield Potions to help give a boost in mitigation during the encounter until High King reaches 50%. You will want to tank High King away from your raid in the western area with your back on a wall or the fallen pillar so that the knockback doesn't send you out of range of your healers. Keep Thunderclap and Demoralizing Shout on High King at all times, make sure Shield Block is refreshed immediately, and be ready to use Last Stand or Shield Wall at a moment's notice (this abilities tip the MT favor in the Warrior's favor). High King should be killed last.

KING MAULGAR'S MINIONS

KIGGLER THE CRAZED

HP	303500	Damage	6834-9652

Abilities

Greater Polymorph: Sheep for up to 10 sec.

Arcane Shock: Inflicts 647-843 Nature damage and interrupts the spell being cast for 5 sec; also disarms for 5 sec.

Arcane Explosion: Deals 1750 to 2250 Arcane damage; knocks back.

Lightning Bolt: Inflicts 1488 to 2012 Nature damage.

Inflicts moderate to heavy Nature damage mixed in with a Hex spell and an AE knockback. He will occasionally melee his primary target for around 3,000, but it is mostly unknown when he chooses to melee.

Lightning Bolt: Inflicts 1,000-2,500 Nature Damage, before resists, to his primary agro target. Kiggler chain casts this spell.

Wild Polymorph: Every so often Kiggler will cast this spell, turning his primary agro target into a random critter causing Kiggler to turn his attacks towards his second highest agro target. You cannot dispel this debuff.

Arcane Shock: 2,500 Arcane damage AE knockback that has a range of about 10-15 yards outside of Kiggler. It has an agro reduction component as is standard with knockback effects.

Dealing with Kiggler the Crazed: Kiggler is best dealt with by two ranged classes, preferably Hunters because they can use Aspect of the Wild to help mitigate the incoming damage from Lightning Bolts. Kiggler's use of Hex forces you to use two ranged classes, but it is possible to use a Moonkin Druid or feral Druid to solo tank it if necessary. Arcane Shock forces you to keep him away from your raid, and you have a few options for that depending on where you tank the other Ogres. The best location is having two Hunters pull him towards the zone in area, as one Hunter stays to one side of the hallway and the other stays on the other side, both with their backs angling towards the walls so as not to get launched out of the zone on a knockback. One healer between these two Hunters is more than sufficient. Kiggler should be killed fourth.

BLINDEYE THE SEER

HP	303500	Damage	1723-2434

Abilities

Greater Power Word: Shield: Shields against physical and magical damage; immune to spell interruption and stun. Lasts 30 sec.

Heal: Heals a nearby ally for 46250 to 53750.

Prayer of Healing: Heals nearby party members for 92500 to 107500.

This Ogre Priest doesn't deal much damage, but he does provide a single target heal and a group heal for his fellow Ogres.

Shield: Similar to the Priest ability Power Word: Shield, this puts up a protective shield around Blindeye and makes his spells become uninterruptible.

Heal: A single target heal that heals for about 5-10% of Blindeye's HPs. This heal is interruptible

Prayer of Healing: A group heal that heals all of the Ogres for around 33%, but has a much longer casting time. This heal is interruptible.

Dealing With Blindeye the Seer: Since Blindeye heals, and at certain points his heals can't be interrupted, he should be killed first. He should be tanked by either a Warrior or a Feral Druid. He should be tanked normally, and because he has no AE attacks, you can freely stack the raid on him to leave more room for the other Ogres who do have AE attacks. Save your 5-point combos and insta-casts to blow up his shield as fast as you can when he puts it up so that you can interrupt Prayer of Healing. Use Mortal Strike or Wound Poison to help reduce the amount healed if you do miss interrupting any heals.

OLM THE SUMMONER

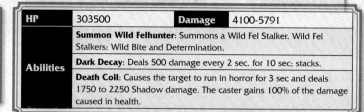

HP	303500	Damage	4100-5791

Abilities

Summon Wild Felhunter: Summons a Wild Fel Stalker. Wild Fel Stalkers: Wild Bite and Determination.

Dark Decay: Deals 500 damage every 2 sec. for 10 sec; stacks.

Death Coil: Causes the target to run in horror for 3 sec and deals 1750 to 2250 Shadow damage. The caster gains 100% of the damage caused in health.

This Warlock can be one of the most difficult of the Ogres to get under control, and you will need at least two Warlocks or two tanks to deal with him.

Death Coil: A single target attack towards his current agro target that deals 2,000 damage, sends the target fleeing, and also heals Olm for 4,000 HP.

Dark Decay: A stackable debuff that deals 500 damage every 2 seconds for 10 seconds, and it can only be removed by using his own Wild Fel Stalker's Devour Magic ability . He will use this on random raid members.

Summon Wild Fel Stalker: At the start of the fight and every 60 seconds thereafter, Olm will summon a Wild Fel Stalker to his side (he can have more than one). They should be enslaved as they are immune to Death Coil and can remove Dark Decay, making them ideal for tanking Olm.

Dealing with Olm the Summoner: Once you begin this encounter, Olm will immediately start to summon a Wild Fel Stalker. You should have someone who has a relatively high agro insta-cast grab him and bring him back towards the raid while one of your Warlocks enslaves the newly summoned Fel Stalker. Olm's melee attacks hit for around 3,000-4,000, but he is fully tauntable by Tanks or the Fel Stalker. Olm has no AE attacks, so you should be afraid to have him tanked on the raid, but you should have a back up tank ready to help keep him under control and pick up the next Wild Fel Stalker when it is summoned. Your second Warlock should enslave this new Fel Stalker as your healers let the first one die, then the new one should taunt and begin tanking. You can also use two tanks to tank Olm, but Healers will have to rotate between two targets rather than just the healing the Wild Fel Stalker. If you use two tanks, the tanks will also have to let the Wild Fel Stalker taunt at some point to get itself killed before Olm goes to summon another pet. Olm should be killed second.

KROSH FIREHAND

HP	303500	Damage	4100-5791

Abilities

Spell Shield: Reduces magic damage received by 75% for 30 sec.

Greater Fireball: Inflicts 8550 to 9450 Fire damage to an enemy.

Blast Wave: Inflicts 6013 to 6987 Fire damage and reducing their movement speed by 70% for 6 sec.

This Mage packs incredible fire power, and if you don't keep the initial tank alive who is tanking Krosh, your raid will most likely wipe.

Blastwave: An AE fire attack that deals ~7,000 damage to all characters within about 20 yards of Krosh and has a 10-15 second recast time. Similar to the Mage spell Blastwave, it will also slow your movement speed.

Spell Shield: A self-buff that reduces the amount of Fire damage taken drastically. Krosh will cast this on himself whenever it fades.

Greater Fireball: An extremely powerful fireball that deals ~9,000 fire damage, and cannot be reduced by way of Fire Resist gear. This spell has a 4 second cast time and is chain cast by Krosh.

Dealing with Krosh Firehand: Krosh is tricky to position at the start of the fight because he will take about three or four steps in the direction of his primary agro target before he will stop and begin to chain cast his Greater Fireball mixed with some Blastwaves. The only class that can deal with Krosh as far as tanking goes is the Mage class. The Mage tank should have over 10,000 HPs buffed (use PvP gear or some extra high STA gear to help) and simply makes sure to use Spellsteal every time Krosh casts Spell Shield. This will prevent most of the Greater Fireball damage, but the Mage will need to be topped off and it is possible for Krosh to resist Spellsteal as well as finish casting a fireball after Spell Shield fades off of the Mage; this is why the Mage should have over 10,000 HPs. Krosh must be kept away from the raid at all times, and should only be killed by ranged classes because of the Blastwave attack. Krosh should be killed third.

PREPARATION

As far as your Raid make-up goes, to be on the safe side and to provide the largest comfort zone, it is best that you come with at least the following class balance:

- 2 Defensive Tanks (1 Prot Warrior + 1 Other)
- 2 Warlocks
- 2 Hunters
- 1 Mage (High HPs/STA gear)
- 8 Assorted Healers (2 of each healing class is a great mix)
- 10 Assorted DPS (a mix of ranged and melee DPS is the best choice, but melee classes will not be attacking two of the five Ogres)

As far as tanking goes, your MT on High King Maulgar will need to have over 18,000 HPs full buffed with a Flask of Fortification and a healthy supply of Ironshield Potions to chug during Phase 1. Use any other elixirs that will raise your MTs avoidance and mitigation. Your Mage tank will need to have over 10,000 HPs buffed, but shouldn't need any supplemental flasks or potions to chug. The other members of the raid should be in normal gear, using potions and flasks to increase their damage, mana, and mana regeneration is always a good thing.

All of the Ogres are tauntable, so as the fight goes on and you get to Phase 2 of High King, if your MT dies, do not call a wipe as one of your OTs can easily pick him up and begin tanking.

THE PULL

The hardest part of this encounter is the pull because of the chaos that exists as each Ogre has to be taken to a specific area depending on your raid, and each one must be under control. The number of Hunters you have to Misdirect can drastically affect the ease of the pull, but you should have at least two. The pull for each Ogre should go as follows:

High King Maulgar: MT runs in first towards High King Maulgar to begin the encounter and uses Sunder Armor and/or Shield Slam to get initial agro on High King. The MT then begins to drag High King over towards the western side of the room and has to make sure that High King is well out of range of Whirlwinding any raid members while keeping his back against a wall or pillar.

Kiggler the Crazed: One of the Hunters should tag Kiggler with Distracting Shot and begin to drag him up towards the hallway that leads to the zone line, but be sure to avoid getting Wild Polymorph on you before you are up in the hallway.

Blindeye the Seer: If you have three Hunters, have one misdirect Blindeye to the tank assigned to this Ogre. He should be pulled to the South/Southwest area near the wall and the raid should move on top of him so that they can maintain range on multiple healing targets while still giving plenty of room for the Ogres who have AE attacks to be placed. If you do not have an extra Hunter, have a Shaman tag Blindeye with a lower rank Earthshock and your tank should then taunt Blindeye off of the Shaman.

Olm the Summoner: If you happen to have four Hunters, you can use another Hunter to misdirect Olm towards the OT who will be picking up the extra Wild Fel Stalker spawns. If you do not, have that OT and/or the second Warlock attempt to agro Olm and just keep him off the healers until the first Warlock can get the first Wild Fel Stalker spawn enslaved and tanking on Olm. This part can be tricky, as there will be multiple targets to heal just from Olm Death Coiling and meleeing various people. Olm should be tanked near Blindeye since he has no AE attacks.

Krosh Firehand: This is where your second Hunter will use misdirect to send Krosh towards the Mage tank who should be on the right side of the hallway as it opens up into the cave where the five Ogres are standing. If your Hunter is quick, Krosh should be a good distance away from your raid, but your healers will have to make sure they keep your Mage tank in range in case the Mage has to backup or move slightly to guarantee avoiding Blastwave. Have your Mage tank make a hotkey or say over voice communication when he/she needs to be topped off because the Spell Shield may fade before the Greater Fireball hits.

STRATEGY

Once you have the pull down, you should begin to kill each Ogre one at a time. Start off with Blindeye the Seer, making sure to save up 5-point combos and insta-nukes for when his Shield is up, and be sure to interrupt every heal he tries to cast.

After Krosh dies, ranged classes should head up the hallway a bit and they should finish off Kiggler the Crazed. By this time, Kiggler should be at around 60% HPs or less, so he should be taken down pretty quickly. Melee need to make sure they do not take High King Maulgar to 50% before all of the other Ogres are dead, but once they are all dead, ranged and healing classes should spread out inside the cave and get ready for Phase 2. Once Phase 2 starts, having a tank back out and wait for Fear or Charge attacks is always a good thing. Avoid Whirlwinds as best you can and keep whoever it tanking him alive. If you get to Phase 2 with 20+ people alive, you should be able to down him with ease.

Once he is dead, move on to Olm the Summoner, but make sure your Warlocks are paying attention so that if someone pulls agro off of the Wild Fel Stalker, they can immediately taunt and get it back on the pet. Depending on your raid make-up, you may want to have some ranged classes begin damaging Krosh Firehand as Olm gets low.

With Olm dead, melee should head in and start on High King Maulgar, but making sure they stay behind him to avoid Arcing Smash and running out immediately to avoid Whirlwind. Ranged classes should begin taking down Krosh Firehand as well as the left over enslaved Wild Fel Stalker.

GRUUL

The most well-known of the brutish Ogre, Gruul the Dragonkiller is the most feared and the most powerful of all the Gronn. He resides to the North of Blade's Edge Mountains and is protected by the Lord of Ogres, High King Maulgar and his advisors.

High King Maulgar and Gruul the Dragonkiller are 25 person raids located in Blade's Edge Mountains. There is no attunement required for either encounter and looting a quest item from Gruul is half of what is needed to complete the quest The Cudgel of Kar'desh. The completion of this quest will attune players to the Serpentshrine Cavern dungeon.

LOOT

Aldori Legacy Defender: 5279 Armor, 137 Block, +39 Stamina, 1 Blue Socket, Socket Bonus: +2 Defense Rating, +19 Defense Rating, +15 Hit Rating

Axe of the Gronn Lords: 345-518 Damage, 3.60 Speed, 119.9 Damage Per Second, +66 Stamina, +124 Attack Power

Bloodmaw Magus Blade: 35-136 Damage, 1.80 Speed, 47.7 Damage Per Second, +16 Stamina, +15 Intellect, +25 Spell Critical Rating, +203 Spell Damage and Healing

Collar of Cho'gall: 171 Armor, +42 Stamina, +36 Intellect, +68 Spell Damage and Healing

Cowl of Nature's Breath: 321 Armor, +34 Stamina, +42 Intellect, +34 Spirit, +92 Healing

Dragonspine Trophy: +40 Attack Power, Equip: Your melee attacks have a chance to increase your haste rating by 325 for 10 sec.

Eye of Gruul: +44 Healing, Equip: Each healing spell you cast has a 2% chance to make the next healing spell cast within 15 sec. cost 450 less mana.

Gauntlets of Martial Perfection: 982 Armor, +36 Strength, +34 Stamina, 1 Blue Socket, 1 Yellow Socket, Socket Bonus: +3 Strength, +23 Critical Strike Rating

Gauntlets of the Dragonslayer: 550 Armor, +24 Agility, +27 Stamina, +27 Intellect, 2 Red Sockets, Socket Bonus: +3 Intellect, +48 Attack Power

Gronn-Stitched Girdle: 222 Armor, +27 Stamina, 1 Blue Socket, 1 Yellow Socket, Socket Bonus: +3 Critical Strike Rating, +25 Critical Strike Rating, +72 Attack Power

Shuriken of Negation: 70-105 Damage, 1.20 Speed, 72.9 Damage Per Second, +16 Stamina, +36 Attack Power

eeth of Gruul: +21 Intellect, +19 Spirit, +46 Healing, +8 Mana/5 Sec.

Windshear Boots: 605 Armor, +37 Stamina, +32 Intellect, +18 Spell Hit Rating, +39 Spell Damage and Healing

ABILITIES

HP	3414600	Damage	6903-9761
Abilities	**Cave In**: Deals 2700 every 3 seconds for 15 seconds.		
	Reverberation: Silences nearby enemies for 4 sec.		
	Grow: Increases damage by 15%. Stacks up to 30 times.		
	Ground Slam: Smashes the ground, knocking all nearby players back and begins to turn them to stone.		
	Gronn Lord's Grasp: Immediately after a Ground Slam, the movement speed of affected players is reduced by 20% every 1 sec. for 5 sec. After 5 sec., the player is turned to stone.		
	Stoned: Prevents the player from moving, attacking, casting spells, or taking any other action.		
	Shatter: Shatters the stone surrounding petrified players, dealing damage to the player based on the number of other players nearby and their distance apart.		
	Hurtful Strike: An instant attack that deals 12350 to 13650 Physical damage to Gruul's secondary target.		

GRUUL THE DRAGONKILLER

GROWTH

Explanation: Every 30 seconds after the encounter is started, Gruul will gain this self-buff that increases his damage by 15% and increases his size by 10%. This buff can stack up to 30 times and will effect all of his other abilities that deal damage except for Shatter.

Solution: This buff puts a soft-cap timer on this fight, as anything above 20 stacks will be unhealable for any tank who is appropriately geared from previous zones. You should arrange healing on your MT and OT accordingly, as the start of the fight requires less tank healing than latter parts of the fight. When Gruul gets to about 10 growths, you will want to make sure your healers never cancel a heal on your MT from that point on as it is entirely possible to get 2-shotted.

CAVE IN

Explanation: This is a targeted AoE ability that will deal about 2,800 damage in an 8 yard radius around the targeted player every 3 seconds for 15 seconds. This damage is considered to be physical damage and can therefore be mitigated by armor. Cave In damage increases as Gruul gains more Growth buffs.

Solution: Players should be very aware of their surroundings and be sure to move out of Cave In the moment they see it appear on or near them. A good way to avoid it ever hitting more than one player, is by spreading out and keeping at least 8 yards between you and any other players. It is entirely possible to completely avoid Cave In damage or at most take one round of damage from it, anything more can be lethal.

REVERBERATION

Explanation: Every 60-75 seconds after the encounter begins, Gruul will use this ability that causes his whole room to be silenced for 4 seconds.

Solution: There is no way to avoid this ability, but it can be resisted if you are lucky. The best thing to do is make sure that the MT is topped off and has multiple regens and a shield when Reverberation is eminent. The MT can also use a Healthstone or Healing Potions to help during this time, but save Shield Wall and Last Stand until later in the fight when Gruul is at around 11+ Growths.

HURTFUL STRIKE

Explanation: Every so often Gruul will use this ability against the person with the second highest threat who is in Gruul's melee range. This ability cannot land as a Crushing Blow or a Critical Strike, and it is a physical attack. It starts off hitting for around 5,000 (12,350 – 13,650 base damage) on a tank when the encounter starts; at 10 Growths it will hit for 10,000 – 11,000.

Solution: Assign a Hurtful Strike OT who must stay second highest on threat of all the melee. A Feral Druid is often times superior in this role as they have higher base Armor values than a Warrior in equal gear, and Feral Druids do not suffer from Rage generation issues or from lack of threat due to lack of Rage like Warriors do. If you use a Warrior to OT, it is very helpful to have your Hunters use Misdirect on the OT every time they can to keep the OT's threat high.

GROUND SLAM

Explanation: This ability occurs about 50 seconds after the encounter starts, and about every 70 seconds thereafter. Ground Slam is a zone-wide effect that will cause all affected players to be knocked up to 20 yards in a random direction. Once a player lands after Ground Slam, they will be affected by Gronn Lord's Grasp.

Solution: There are a few locations around Gruul's cave in which you can prevent yourself from being knocked around by Ground Slam, but the most important thing is to make sure everyone stays spread out when Ground Slam is about to happen. It is important to note that Ground Slam is on about a 70 second timer, but Gruul can choose not to use the effect and he has been known to sometimes do it before 70 seconds or sometimes he won't use it for close to 2 minutes after the previous one. Maximizing the free space in his cave is paramount to successfully dealing with Ground Slam, and if you have ranged classes who can find the "safe" spots (typically objects that you can wedge yourself between or behind), they can also help bring some control to the chaos that occurs afterwards.

GRONN LORD'S GRASP

Explanation: Once a player lands after being affected by Ground Slam, this ability triggers and slows movement speed by 20% every second. Once the movement speed has been slowed by 100%, this debuff will be replaced with the Stoned debuff.

Solution: After players land from Ground Slam, they must do whatever it takes to spread out away from other characters while this debuff ticks away before they get the Stoned debuff. . There is no way to remove this effect.

STONED

Explanation: This debuff causes affected players to be frozen in place and players will be unable to move, attack or use any abilities, spells or items.

Solution: You cannot remove this debuff, and all players should be spread out from other players as much as they can before they are Stoned and they must be topped off as well.

SHATTER

Explanation: Once all players have been Stoned, Gruul will use this ability that causes all Stoned players to Shatter from their locked state. Damage is dealt to players based upon their proximity to other players. If one player is 0 yards from another player, they will take around 5,000 damage; if one player is 15+ yards from another player, neither player will take any damage from the other. This damage does not increase as Gruul gains more Growth buffs.

Solution: The goal of dealing with Shatter is to reduce the amount of damage that all players take, which is why you must spread out as much as possible before Ground Slam and move as fast as you can to open areas after Ground Slam. Players do not need to try and get 15 yards away from all other players, obviously this is ideal, but is highly unlikely. Players should try to minimize the damage they take from Shatter, but if any player thinks they may die to Shatter, they should use a Healthstone, Healing Potion or any ability in their arsenal to stay alive.

PREPARATION

Preparation for Gruul is fairly simple as the fight is basically a DPS race; the faster you kill Gruul, the less Shatters and Growths you will have to deal with. That being said, you will want your DPS classes to have a full array of potions and flasks, as well as using a Flask of Fortification on your MT and OT. The use of potions and flasks for Healers really depends on your raid makeup; if you are light on mana regen for your healers, have them use potions and a Flask of Mighty Restoration. You will also want a Flask of Fortification for your MT and OT as well as an ample supply of Ironshield Potions that they should be using whenever possible beyond 10+ Growths.

Other than preparing to burn him down as fast as you can, the only other preparation that you can take is by knowing the layout of his room so that you can spread out appropriately and so that some Ranged DPS or Healers can use a few of the objects in the room to help avoid the effects of Ground Slam. Make sure you set up your groups to maximize DPS and keep people in the same general area as the rest of their group, but be sure to have Healers spread out throughout the whole cave to help keep people alive.

STRATEGY

As your raid prepares to engage Gruul, make sure that everyone is inside of the gate because once he is engaged, the gate will shut and no one will be allowed to enter or exit. Have the groups that will be on the eastern and western sides of the cave cheat to their sides a bit to save them an extra second or two while running to the positions. Once everyone is set up, have your MT countdown and rush Gruul with your OT following closely and the rest of the raid moving to their positions in the lair once the MT takes off. DPS, especially melee, should use this run time to allow the MT and OT to generate threat on Gruul while he is pulled back to the middle of his room and the Healers and Ranged DPS spread out and get to their positions. It is vital that the OT stays within melee range of Gruul to eat Hurtful Strikes.

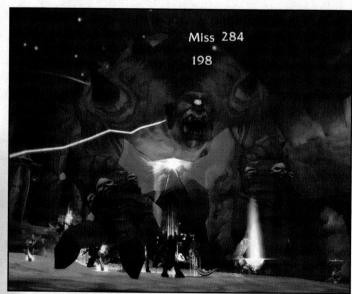

Positions Everyone

Gruul is a very large boss, and like most large bosses, he does not move smoothly when he walks, but rather, he moves more in clips when the MT tries to walk him backwards into position. To avoid any range issues with Hurtful Strike, the OT should do his/her best to walk backwards with the MT. Ranged DPS should be free to begin once they reach their spots, but Melee should wait until Gruul is moved into the middle of the room so that the OT has enough time to build threat as well.

After everyone is in position, they should begin to pay attention to the most important factors of the fight which are maximizing DPS while not pulling agro, keeping the MT and OT alive, moving out of Cave In immediately, keeping your HPS topped off, and staying spread out for Ground Slam. Ranged DPS should try to be at max range to provide for more free space, Mages particularly should be able to find a location that is generally free of people that they can turn and Blink to once Ground Slam happens, and be sure to keep threat levels below that of the MT. Melee DPS should try to be at max range and stay spread out while moving around Gruul to avoid Cave In, but being sure to stay below the OT on threat.

After about 30 seconds, the raid should be prepared for the first Ground Slam. Any Healers or Ranged DPS who have found safe spots using terrain/objects in the lair should try to get to their spot but maintain healing and damage as best as possible. Keep the raid topped off as best as possible until Ground Slam hits.

Stand and Scan

Once Ground Slam occurs, all Warriors and Feral Druids should use Intercept/Feral Charge to get right back to Gruul and then move away from each other, all other classes should use their judgment based upon where they landed in relation to others to determine which way to move. It is best to move away from any other player in the direction that you are in relation to other players; if you land to the left of someone else, keep moving left and pan your camera around to see if anyone else is approaching you.

Once everyone is Stoned and Gruul uses Shatter, anyone who can should use a bandage to regain as many HPs as possible, and any non-MT/OT healers for the early parts of the fight should help top everyone off. About 5-10 seconds after Shatter, once everyone is in position again, everyone should use their cooldown abilities (except Warriors), trinkets, and all Shamans should use Bloodlust to maximize DPS at this time while everyone is most likely alive.

As the fight continues, Healers need to make sure that they watch for their timers on Reverberation to make sure the MT and OT are topped off when its about to go off, as well as shielded and have every HoT possible. About 60-70 seconds after the first Ground Slam, the raid should be prepared for the next one, making sure to constantly watch positioning and avoiding Cave In.

After 5 minutes, when Gruul gets to 10 Growths, about 5 Healers should be on the MT and 3 on the OT, and no Healer should ever cancel a heal on the MT at this point. The MT should make sure that Shield Block is up at all times at this point, and should not be wasting Rage on other abilities unless he/she has an abundance of Rage to spare. Both the MT and OT should drink an Ironshield Potion from this point on whenever the timer is up. Healers should be especially mindful of Reverberation at this time, making sure the MT and the OT are topped off before the silence occurs, but the MT and OT should be ready to hit Last Stand, a Nightmare Seed or even Shield Wall at a moment's notice.

At 20%, any DPS Warriors should use Recklessness while they spam Execute and all DPS should use whatever they have left to finish him off. If either the MT or the OT dies before 10%, you will probably wipe, but if either dies after 10%, you can bounce Gruul around for the last 5+% to finish him off. If this does happen, Rogues should be prepared to use Evasion to buy a few extra seconds, and if a Hunter has agro, he/she can Feign Death as Gruul gets close to send him to the next highest agro player to buy a few seconds without having someone get killed. Many Gruul fights often end in such a way, so don't feel discouraged if your raid happens to kill him like this. Stay focused and pay attention to your surroundings for a smooth kill.

MAGTHERIDON'S LAIR

Once the mighty ruler of the Outlands, Magtheridon has been overthrown by Illidan and enslaved by the Fel Orcs deep below Hellfire Citadel.

Magtheridon is a 25 person raid located in Hellfire Peninsula. There is no attunement required to fight him and he completes the quest Trial of the Naaru.

DUNGEON INFORMATION

Name	Magtheridon's Lair
Location	Hellfire Citadel
Suggested Levels	Group of 25, Level 70
Time to Complete	At least 1 hour

CLEARING TO MAGTHERIDON

There are 4 groups of Hellfire Warders with 3 mobs in each pack. The Warders cast Shadow Word: Pain, Unstable Affliction, Rain of Fire, Shadow Bolt Volley, Shadow Burst (an AoE knock back), Fear, and Death Coil. They respawn after 45 minutes. The final two packs are within agro range of Magtheridon's room.

Assign a tank to each Warder and pull one pack at a time. Offtank two of the Warders away from the raid, out of LoS as the remaining Warder is killed. Use the ramps in the lair to break LoS and minimize the damage from the Shadow Bolt Volley. Try to keep Fear Ward up on as many offtanks and healers as possible to absorb the Fears and use Tremor Totems where available.

Assist and kill them one at a time while interrupting the Shadow Bolt Volley, staying out of the Rain of Fire, and cleansing the Shadow Word: Pain. As the first Warder dies, bring the next one up to the top of the ramp and kill it.

These Warders are very nasty but with a little practice you should blow through the pulls in no time at all.

FELL THE FALLEN

HELLFIRE CHANNELER

HP	242800	Damage	4925-6956

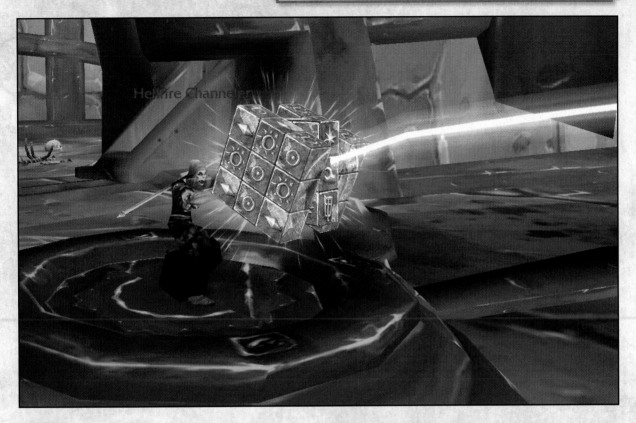

For the first 2 minutes of the fight the only thing to worry about is the Hellfire Channelers. There are 5 of them spread throughout the room, one on each Manticron Cube. You want to kill at least 3 of them in the first 2 minutes of the fight.

DARK MENDING

Explanation: The Channelers regularly try to heal themselves and others nearby. Dark Mending heals for about 75,000 HPs and has a 2 second cast time. It can be interrupted.

Solution: A rotation of interrupts must be setup to consistently interrupt the Dark Mending. It isn't cast all that often; you should be able to interrupt it all the time without exception. Additionally, tank the Channelers far apart so that they don't try to heal each other. Tanking them on top of their Cube platform works perfectly.

SHADOW VOLLEY

Explanation: Every 10 seconds or so the Channelers cast Shadow Volley. It hits everyone within 30 yards for about 2,000 shadow damage. It has a 2 second cast time and is interruptible. It can also be both partially and fully resisted.

Solution: Shadow Volley should be interrupted just like Dark Mending when you're killing a Channeler. However, the Channelers that are being off-tanked only have 1 person on them to interrupt (the offtank themselves), so you are only able to consistently interrupt one Channeler at a time. For this reason, healers need to try to stay at least 30 yards away from any off-tanked Channeler to avoid taking unnecessary damage from Shadow Volley.

SOUL TRANSFER

Explanation: As each Channeler dies, they transfer their souls to the remaining live ones. Soul Transfer increases each Channeler's damage by 30% and decreases their casting time by 20%. It stacks up to 4 times.

Solution: The offtanks on the final two Channelers need to be pretty beefy tanks to survive the damage. They can hit a well geared tank for well over 5,000 damage with 4 stacks of Soul Transfer. Additionally, since their casting time is reduced with each application, Warlocks must keep Curse of Tongues up on the Channelers and everyone needs to be very careful with their spell interrupts.

BURNING ABYSSAL

Explanation: Every Channeler has the ability to summon up to two Infernals. It is an instant cast and can not be prevented. When an Infernal is summoned, they land on top of a random player and do about 2,500 fire damage to everyone within 10 yards on impact. Their melee damage hits fairly hard and they have a Fire Blast ability that does about 3,000 fire damage. They can be CC'ed and despawn after 60 seconds.

Solution: Warlocks are in charge of keeping the Infernals under control. Warlocks are more focused on banishes and fearing Infernals than they are on doing damage to the Channelers (but a DoT here and there certainly doesn't hurt!). Any Warlock can easily keep 2 Internals under control with Banish and Fear. Anyone else with a CC ability like Freezing Trap, Hammer of Justice, and Psychic Scream should help out as well. Don't try to tank them, don't try to kill them, CC them in every way possible and wait for them to despawn.

MAGTHERIDON

2 minutes after engaging, Magtheridon becomes free. At least 3 Channelers should be dead at this point and a tank needs to pick him up as quickly as possible.

LOOT

Aegis of the Vindicator: Shield Off Hand (Shield), 5279 Armor, 137 Block, +21 INT, Equip: Increases healing done by spells and effects by up to 53, Equip: Restores 11 mana per 5 sec

Chestguard of the Fallen Champion: Classes: Shaman Rogue Paladin

Chestguard of the Fallen Defender: Classes: Druid Priest Warrior

Chestguard of the Fallen Hero: Classes: Warlock Mage Hunter

Cloak of the Pit Stalker: Back, 105 Armor, +28 STA, Equip: Increases attack power by 56, Equip: Improves critical strike rating by 24

Crystalheart Pulse-Staff: Staff Two-Hand, 143-297 Damage, Speed 3.20, 68.8 damage per second, +51 STA, +50 INT, Equip: Increases healing done by spells and effects by up to 382, Equip: Restores 16 mana per 5 sec

Eredar Wand of Obliteration: Wand Range, 177-330 Shadow Damage, Speed 1.50, 169.0 damage per second, +10 STA, +11 INT, Equip: Increases damage and healing done by magical spells and effects by up to 16, Equip: Improves spell critical strike rating by 14

Eye of Magtheridon: Trinket, Equip: Increases damage and healing done by magical spells and effects by up to 54, Equip: Grants +170 increased spell damage for 10 seconds when one of your spells is resisted

Girdle of the Endless Pit: Plate Waist, 884 Armor, +34 STR, +30 STA, Red Socket, Blue Socket, Socket Bonus: +3 Crit Rating, Equip: Improves critical strike rating by 28

Glaive of the Pit: Polearm Two-Hand, 354-532 Damage, Speed 3.70, 119.7 damage per second, Red Socket, Red Socket, Red Socket, Socket Bonus: +4 Crit Rating

Karaborian Talisman: Held In Hand, +23 STA, +23 INT, Equip: Increases damage and healing done by magical spells and effects by up to 35

Liar's Tongue Gloves: Leather Hands, 247 Armor, +31 STA, Blue Socket, Blue Socket, Socket Bonus: +3 Crit Rating, Equip: Increases attack power by 72, Equip: Improves critical strike rating by 26

Magtheridon's Head: Use: Begin Quest *The Fall of Magtheridon*

Soul-Eater's Handwraps: Cloth Hands, 132 Armor, +31 STA, +24 INT, Yellow Socket, Blue Socket, Socket Bonus: +4 Spell Damage, Equip: Increases damage and healing done by magical spells and effects by up to 36, Equip: Improves spell critical strike rating by 21

Terror Pit Girdle: Mail Waist, 495 Armor, +18 STA, +22 INT, Blue Socket, Red Socket, Socket Bonus: +4 STA, Equip: Increases attack power by 44, Equip: Restores 8 mana per 5 sec, Equip: Improves critical strike rating by 21

Thundering Greathelm: Plate Head, 1276 Armor, +50 STR, +43 AGI, +49 STA

ABILITIES

HP	4818380	Damage	14604-20649

BLAST NOVA

Explanation: Blast Nova is on a 60 second cooldown. When Magtheridon emotes that he begins to cast it, he pulses fire damage on everyone in the lair for 10 seconds, dealing 2188-2812 damage every 2 seconds.

Solution: This is where the Cubes spread throughout the room come into play. If each Cube is activated at the same time, Blast Nova is stopped. Since this is a key aspect of the fight, it is explained in detail in the Strategy section. But if you activate the Cubes correctly, no one takes any damage at all from Blast Nova.

DEBRIS

Explanation: At 30% life Magtheridon slams the walls of his lair and causes everyone to take about 6,000 damage, knocks them to the ground, and stuns them for one second. After this has happened, the room begins to Debris on top of random players. If they do not move out of the Debris as soon as they see it happening, they are killed instantly.

Solution: The first part of the Debris is unavoidable. Everyone is going to take around 6,000 damage when Magtheridon gets to 30% life. Don't let anybody die to it and top everyone's life off afterwards. After that, the smaller and much deadlier Debris are completely avoidable. As soon as someone sees the animation happening on top of them, they need to get away as quickly as possible. The animation is the same one as the Debris at Gruul and once you have seen one they are fairly easy to avoid.

CLEAVE

Explanation: Magtheridon has a standard Cleave attack that hits everyone in front of him for several thousand damage.

Solution: Only the main tank should ever be in front of Magtheridon.

CONFLAGRATION

Explanation: Magtheridon randomly sets parts of the lair on fire just like our old friend Magmadar. If a player steps into this fire, they gain the Conflagration debuff and take 750 Fire damage per second over 8 seconds.

Solution: Stay out of the fires. Heal anyone who accidentally steps into one. Most importantly, don't stand on the Cube platforms until it's your turn to click a Cube because the fires are targeted at players when they are spawned; you don't want to set an entire Cube platform on fire!

MANTICRON CUBES

Explanation: There are 5 Cubes spread throughout the lair. The Cubes are used to stop Blast Nova. If all 5 Cubes are activated when Blast Nova is casting, it is stopped. When a player clicks a Cube to activate it, they take 800 damage per second while channeling the Cube. After they stop channeling, they gain the Mind Exhaustion debuff that prevents them from using a Cube again for 1 minute 30 seconds.

Solution: Using the Cubes correctly is a core part of the fight and is discussed thoroughly in the Preparation and Strategy sections. Explained very quickly, a group of 3 people (2 clickers that rotate and 1 healer) is assigned to each Cube and the Cubes should all be clicked at the same time the moment Magtheridon begins to cast Blast Nova.

QUAKE

Explanation: Quake is on a 45 second cool down. During a Quake, everyone in the room is knocked around at random. They can't really move and each knock back interrupts spells.

Solution: There really isn't anything you can do about it. Since it doesn't do any damage, it isn't that big of a deal. One of the bad things that can happen is someone gets tossed in front of Magtheridon and gets killed by Cleave; try to stay well out of Cleave range to avoid this. Another possible problem is the healers can't use non-instant heals on the tank; make sure they have plenty of HoTs during the Quake. And the final thing that can go wrong is when he uses Blast Nova right after Quake, preventing people from getting to their Cube in time; always move to your Cubes a little early just incase!

After the tanking, assign the initial healing. As Channelers die, the healing changes. Upon engaging, every tank only really needs 1 healer; the Channelers aren't doing much damage yet. Once there are only 2 Channelers left, the final offtanks need at least 2 healers on them. This leaves 5 healers free to take care of the main tank once Magtheridon becomes free.

At this point you have a tank assigned to every Channeler, one healer for each tank on the first 3 Channelers to die, and two healers for the tanks on the last 2 Channelers.

Now it's time to think about the Cubes. Each Cube needs a group of 3 people assigned to it: 2 clickers and 1 healer. The clickers must rotate because of the Mind Exhaustion debuff and the healer keeps them topped off as they take damage while channeling the Cube.

The best clickers are ranged DPS because they can get to the Cubes faster than anyone else. The second best are tanks who aren't who aren't going to do that much damage to Magtheridon. After you run out of those, fill up the rest of the clicker spots with various DPS.

The healers for each cube can be anyone who isn't going to be busy while the last Channeler is dying. The off-tank on the last Channeler needs 2 dedicated healers on them until it dies and the main tank needs at least 2 healers on them. The remaining 5 healers are assigned to a Cube group.

Finally, anyone who isn't assigned to a Cube group should know they are a backup. Make a backup order for both clickers and healers. If anyone in a Cube group dies, have them announce what they were doing and what position their Cube is in so that the backups know they need to get on Cube duty.

In summary, before the fight begins you should have assigned: 5 Channeler tanks (one of which is also tanking Magtheridon), 1 healer on the first 3 Channeler tanks, 2 healers on the last 2 Channeler tanks, 2 healers assigned to Magtheridon's tank, and 5 Cube groups that consist of 2 clickers and 1 healer each.

PREPARATION

Preparing for Magtheridon is fairly complicated. You need the following in your raid group: 3 Warlocks for CC'ing the Infernals, 3 high quality tanks for the final 2 Channelers and Magtheridon himself (Protection Warriors or Feral Druids with good gear), 1 decent tank for the second Channeler (like a DPS spec Warrior with a little bit of tanking gear on), and 1 fake tank for the first Channeler (like a Paladin with some talents in Protection and some tanking gear), and, at least 9 Healers. The remaining 8 slots are filled by DPS classes. It doesn't hurt to be a little Rogue-heavy since they have the best interrupt ability for the Channelers.

To sum that up, bring 3 Warlocks, 3 real tanks, 2 sort-of tanks, 9 healers, and 8 DPS with at least 3 Rogues.

Mark the Channelers

Use the Raid Icons to mark each Channeler while setting up the fight! This makes it very easy to assign the tanking and Cube clicking.

Setup the tanking first. Put the least capable tank on the first Channeler to die. Put the second least capable tank on the second Channeler to die. Magtheridon's tank should be on the third Channeler to die; this ensures their Channeler is dead before Magtheridon becomes free. The fourth and fifth Channelers need high quality tanks because Soul Transfer gets stacked up and they begin to hit hard.

STRATEGY

Have the tanks move into position next to their Channeler and make sure the healers get their targets. Begin the fight by attacking a Channeler and immediately get all of them tanked.

After a few moments of establishing agro, begin DPS on the first Channeler to die. Announce when you use your interrupts on the Shadow Volley and Dark Mending and avoid having more than one or two people interrupt at a time. Keep the Channeler you are killing locked down casting-wise and open up the DPS.

As soon as the first Channeler is dead, move onto the next one. As each Channel dies, the Soul Transfer buff is applied to the remaining Channelers causing them to cast spells more rapidly and deal extra melee damage.

The first 3 Channelers should die without much trouble. Keep the interrupts consistent, don't let them heal, minimize the amount of Shadow Volleys, and kill them quickly.

Use the Entire Room

When the fight starts, the only place healers can outrange all of the Shadow Volleys is in the middle of the room—under Magtheridon. Since the Inferals fall on random targets, having all of the healers in the same place isn't a good idea. As the Channelers die, more room opens up for the healers to spread out and outrange Shadow Volleys. Use the entire room to your advantage!

While the Channelers are killed, the Warlocks and, to a lesser extent, the Hunters, Paladins, and Priests, are CC'ing Infernals that spawn. Don't let them get out of control; they can easily kill a cloth wearer. Keep them Feared, Trapped, Banished, Stunned, anything you can do to prevent them from running off and killing someone. Warlocks are responsible for the vast majority of Infernal CC so if you are having problems with the Infernals, bring an additional Warlock along to help. Also, take a look at your damage meters; if one Warlock is dealing significantly more damage than all of the others in the first 2 minutes of the fight, chances are they could pay more attention to Infernal CC and less attention to doing damage to the Channelers.

2 minutes into the fight Magtheridon becomes free. At this point you should have at least 3 Channelers dead and are working on the fourth. The main tank's Channeler should be dead leaving them free to pickup Magtheridon when he becomes attackable. The remaining off-tanks are taking significant melee damage and need at least 2 healers each. All of the remaining healers should focus their attention on the main tank.

As soon as Magtheridon becomes free, the main tank needs to establish agro and position him against the closest wall, facing away from the raid. The main tank takes very heavy damage from Magtheridon but everyone else can ignore him for the time being. There are still Channelers alive so continue killing them as quickly as you can.

45 seconds after Magtheridon has become free the first Quake occurs. By then all of the Channelers should be dead or, at worst, the last one very close to dying. The Quake hits and everyone is tossed around for a few seconds. Keep HoTs up on the main tank to ensure they don't die during a Quake. Immediately after the Quake ends, the first group of Cube clickers and their designated healers should move to their Cube and be ready to click.

The Early Clicker Saves the Raid

Always move to your Cube early! As the fight goes on, there is eventually a point where Blast Nova is used almost immediately after the Quake ends. If you aren't waiting by your Cube when this happens, Magtheridon is likely to pulse Blast Nova at least once while you get to it and click it.

About 10 seconds after the first Quake ends, or about 60 seconds after Magtheridon has become free, the first Blast Nova happens. The first group of Cube clickers and their healers better be at their Cubes ready to click the instant Magtheridon emotes that he is casting Blast Nova. Don't click too early; wait until he is actually casting it. As soon as all 5 Cubes are activated at the same time, Magtheridon is momentarily banished and Blast Nova ceases. Stop channeling the Cube as soon as he is banished; there is no reason to stay on it and take additional damage from the Cube. If you time the clicks correctly, not a single pulse of Blast Nova will hit the raid.

Up until Magtheridon is at 35% health, the strategy remains consistent as described above. Keep the main tank alive, especially during the Quakes, and alternate groups of clickers on the Cubes keeping those Blast Novas under control. Keep the people clicking the Cubes healed, and watch out for any Conflagrate fires that are started. It is pretty straight forward.

As long as the main tank gets heals and everyone is clicking their Cube at the right time, not much can go wrong. If someone who is in a Cube group dies, they need to announce what they were doing and what position they were in. Someone has to come replace them because continuing to click the Cubes correctly is the key part of the fight.

At 35% it's time to start thinking about the Debris. Stop casting DoTs and prepare to stop DPS completely at about 31%. You want him to go down to 30% right after a Blast Nova so you have the maximum amount of time to heal everybody up before the next one. As soon as he is at about 31% and Blast Nova ends, open up the DPS and continue to take him down.

At 30% he slams the walls and causes about 6,000 damage to everyone in the lair. Use Healthstones and get everyone healed up as quickly as possible. After the walls have been slammed they randomly begin to crumble on top of players. Anyone who sees the Debris animation happening on top of them needs to move out of the way as quickly as they can or they die instantly. You can't avoid the 6,000 damage everyone takes initially, but avoiding the Debris happening in the room is fairly easy as soon as you know what to look for (they have the same animation as Gruul's Debris).

Other than avoiding the new Debris, nothing else has changed. Continue to keep the tank alive and click those Cubes. If you have gotten this far and everything is still under control, you have a very good chance of taking off that last 30% as long as everyone stays focused!

MAGTHERIDON'S HEAD

Like our old friends Onyxia and Nefarian, Magtheridon drops his head every time he is killed. The head is used to start a quest called *The Fall of Magtheridon*. Turn the quest in at Honor Hold for Alliance players or Thrallmar for Horde players. You can choose one of four rewards:

A'dal's Signet of Defense: Finger, 367 Armor, +34 STA, Equip: Increases defense rating by 20

Band of Crimson Fury: Finger, +22 STA, +22 INT, Equip: Increases damage and healing done by magical spells and effects by up to 28, Equip: Improves spell hit rating by 16

Naaru Lightwarden's Band: Finger, +21 STA, +25 INT, Equip: Increases healing done by spells and effects by up to 55, Equip: Restores 8 mana per 5 sec

Ring of the Recalcitrant: Finger, +24 AGI, +27 STA, Equip: Increases attack power by 54

SERPENTSHRINE CAVERN

Played & Written by: Andrei "Bloodshot" Ionescu of <Death and Taxes> on Korgath

Water levels are falling in Zangarmarsh and an unnatural corruption has taken hold over its native flora. All the signs seem to point to a recently discovered series of caverns deep beneath Serpent Lake, occupied by the sinister Naga and their minions. Led by Lady Vashj herself, the Naga appear to be working towards the construction of a new Well of Eternity, under direct orders from Illidan Stormrage, the Betrayer. One can only start to imagine the implications this would have, should they be successful.

The dungeon is non-linear, and early encounters can be attempted in any order based on the strengths and weaknesses of the group. The path lined out on the following pages is therefore just a suggestion. However, in the end all paths lead to Lady Vashj who awaits you on her seemingly unreachable platform.

DUNGEON INFORMATION

Location	Serpent Lake, Zangarmarsh
Region	Contested
Quests	Alliance and Horde
Suggested Level	70 (25-person raid)
Enemy Types	Naga, Broken, Murlocs
Time to Complete	4-8 hours (1-2 days)

MAP OF SERPENTSHRINE CAVERN

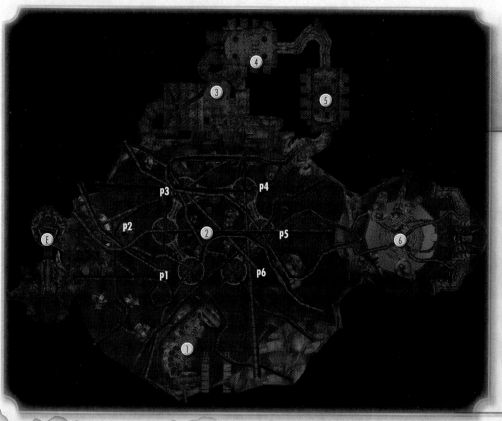

MAP LEGEND	
1	Hydross The Unstable
2	The Lurker Below
Strange Pool	
3	Leotheras the Blind
4	Fathom Lord Karathress
Seer Olum	
5	Morogrim Tidewalker
6	Lady Vashj
E	Entrance
p#	Pumping Station

QUEST

THE CUDGEL OF KAR'DESH

Quest Level	70
Location	The Slave Pens (Heroic)
Starts at	Skar'this the Heretic
Ends at	Skar'this the Heretic
Goal	Obtain the Earthen and Blazing Signets by defeating Gruul the Dragonkiller and Nightbane.

Skar'this the Heretic can only be accessed on the "Heroic" difficulty setting. This requires the "Reservoir Key" which can be purchased from the Cenarion Expedition quartermaster in Zangarmarsh by players that have reached Revered reputation with the Cenarion Expedition. After defeating the first boss in The Slave Pens, go up the ramp then jump in the water, Skar'this will be on your left as you emerge from the pool.

CREATURES OF THE CAVERN

The elevator at the entrance of the cavern has claimed many victims on long raiding nights, but if your guild has managed to survive it, they will be faced with the first creatures in the cavern on the path to Hydross the Unstable. The Underbog Colossi are a common appearance throughout the zone, so a raid should be aware of their abilities. Although they all look the same the colossi can be one of three types, depending on the combination of abilities that they use. The first type uses Spore Quake, which deals 1291-1499 nature damage every 3 seconds to targets in a 30 yard range, and Rampant Infection, which inflicts nature damage to a random target in the raid, then jumps to the nearest player, dealing increased damage every time it jumps. This is classed as a disease and should be cleansed off a player before it jumps to another target. The second type uses Acid Geyser, a channeled ability that picks a random target and inflicts nature damage to the target and every player in the target's proximity. This type of colossus also spawns parasites which usually attack healers but are easily killed off. The third and least dangerous type of colossus uses Frenzy which increases damage to the tank, but can be removed by Hunters with Tranquilizing Shot. These also use Atrophic Blow on the tank, which deals a small amount of damage and reduces strength and stamina by 30 per application.

In order to avoid Spore Quake the raid must run out of its 30 yard range. Avoiding Acid Geyser is best done by having everyone in the raid close to the colossus run away behind it if they are the target selected for geyser. If the selected target moves rapidly behind the colossus, they will be the only one taking damage from the geyser, while the rest of the raid will be safe. Because these two types of colossus require opposite strategies (everyone standing close vs. everyone at range) it is extremely important to identify the type of colossus as early as possible. This can be done by looking for their secondary ability. Rampant Infection is a sign that a colossus will use Spore Quake while parasites are an indication an Acid Geyser type. Using detect magic on a colossus will quickly identify it as the third type if that is the case while making it easier for Hunters to remove the effect. Detect magic can also reveal vulnerabilities to elemental magic.

Many times the death of a colossus does not mean the end of the fight. Some of them spawn two Colossus Ragers upon death, while others will spawn a large group of small creatures that must be grouped up and killed with area of effect spells. A colossus death can also spawn a Toxic Pool that persists on the ground for a few seconds, dealing massive damage. On the other hand, there is a chance that a patch of mushrooms will spawn that helps regenerate the raid's hit points and mana. Remember that colossus corpses can be searched for plants and motes of life by skilled herbalists.

Apart from colossi, the path to Hydross is blocked by 3 identical packs of creatures, consisting of two Coilfang Hate-Screamers, two Serpentshrine Sporebats and one Coilfang Beast Tamer. Two tanks can easily handle a hate-screamer and sporebat each, ideally with a Hunter helping them out by misdirecting the sporebat. Kill the sporebats first since they have relatively low hit points, but their random charge ability can be near fatal for cloth classes. With the sporebats dead kill the hate-screamers next, which the tanks must face away from the raid to avoid silencing the casters, and finally, the beast tamer.

Boots of Courage Unending: Feet / Plate: 1105 Armor, +19 Stamina, +20 Intellect, Equip: Improves spell critical strike rating by 31, Equip: Increases healing done by spells and effects by up to 90.

Spyglass of the Hidden Fleet: Trinket: +40 Stamina, Use: Heals 1300 damage over 12 sec.

Pendant of the Perilous: Neck: +32 Strength, +24 Stamina, Equip: Improves critical strike rating by 23.

Totem of the Maelstrom: Relic: Equip: Reduces the mana cost of Healing Wave by 24.

Wildfury Greatstaff: Two-Hand Staff: 135 - 282 Damage, Speed 3.00, (69.4 DPS), 500 Armor, +70 Stamina, Equip: Increases your dodge rating by 50, Increases attack power by 731 in Cat, Bear, Dire Bear, and Moonkin forms only.

Serpentshrine Shuriken: Thrown: 94 - 142 Damage, Speed 1.40, (84.3 DPS), +12 Stamina, Equip: Improves hit rating by 11, Improves critical strike rating by 20.

TIME IS PRECIOUS

Remember that throughout the entire zone creatures will respawn two hours after they are killed, unless the nearest boss has been defeated.

HYDROSS THE UNSTABLE

Despite his positioning at the beginning of the zone, Hydross is not the easiest of encounters. He requires specific gear, perfect execution, and challenges all departments in the raid: tanking, healing, and DPS.

ABILITIES

HP	3146000	Damage	5974-8447
Abilities	**Purify Elemental**: Turns a Tainted Water Elemental into a Purified Water Elemental.		
	Water Tomb: Inflicts 3600 Frost damage over 4 sec. and stuns all targets in a 5 yard radius.		
	Water Nova: Inflicts 1080-1320 Frost damage within 20 yards.		
	Summon Corrupted Spawn: Summons 4 Corrupted Spawn of Hydross.		
	Summon Purified Spawn: Summons 4 Pure Spawn of Hydross.		
	Mark of Corruption: Increases Nature damage taken by 10%. This effect stacks and increases in power significantly each time; the first additional stack increases Nature damage by 25%, then 50%, 100%, 250%, and finally 500%.		
	Mark of Hydross: Increases Frost damage taken by 10%. This effect stacks and increases in power significantly each time; the first additional stack increases Frost damage by 25%, then 50%, 100%, 250%, and finally 500%.		
	Vile Sludge: Decreases damage by 50% and deals 500 Nature damage every 3 sec. for 24 sec.		

LOOT

Ranger-General's Chestguard: Chest/Mail: 900 Armor, +36 Agility, +19 Stamina, +30 Intellect, Blue Socket, Red Socket, Yellow Socket, Socket Bonus: +4 Agility

Equip: Improves critical strike rating by 14, Increases attack power by 88.

Scarab of Displacement: Trinket, Equip: Increases defense rating by 42, Use: Increases your defense rating by 165, but decreases your melee and ranged attack power by 330. Effect lasts for 15 sec.

Living Root of the Wildheart: Trinket, Classes: Druid, Equip: Your spells and attacks in each form have a chance to grant you a blessing for 15 sec.

Pauldrons of the Wardancer: Shoulder / Plate: 1206 Armor, +38 Strength, +21 Stamina, Red Socket, Blue Socket, Socket Bonus: +3 Crit Rating, Equip: Improves critical strike rating by 29.

Boots of the Shifting Nightmare: Feet/Cloth: 148 Armor, +41 Stamina, +22 Intellect, Equip: Improves spell hit rating by 18, Increases damage done by Shadow spells and effects by up to 59.

Shoulderpads of the Stranger: Shoulder / Leather: 303 Armor, +33 Agility, +28 Stamina, Red Socket, Socket Bonus: +2 Agility, Equip: Improves critical strike rating by 16, Increases attack power by 60, Increases dagger skill rating by 10.

Blackfathom Warbands: Wrist / Mail: 394 Armor, +21 Stamina, +23 Intellect, Blue Socket, Socket Bonus: 1 Mana per 5 sec., Equip: Increases healing done by spells and effects by up to 62.

Fathomstone: Off-hand: +16 Stamina, +12 Intellect, Equip: Improves spell critical strike rating by 23, Increases damage and healing done by magical spells and effects by up to 36.

Idol of the Crescent Goddess: Relic: Equip: Reduces the mana cost of Regrowth by 33.

Ring of Lethality: Ring: +24 Agility, +19 Stamina, Equip: Improves hit rating by 19, Increases attack power by 50.

Brighthelm of Justice: 1306 Armor, +36 Stamina, +44 Intellect, Equip: Increases healing done by spells and effects by up to 101, Restores 14 mana per 5 sec.

Robe of Hateful Echoes: Cloth / Chest: 215 Armor, +34 Stamina, +36 Intellect, Red Socket, Yellow Socket, Yellow Socket, Socket Bonus: +6 Stamina, Equip: Improves spell critical strike rating by 25, Increases damage and healing done by magical spells and effects by up to 50.

OVERVIEW

While under the influence of the Naga-built machines, Hydross stays in water elemental form dealing frost damage, but when drawn away from the beams above the initial position it turns into nature elemental form, dealing poison damage. The longer it stays in one form, the more damage inflicted to the tank, due to the aura that affects every player engaged. Named Mark of Hydross in water elemental form and Mark of Corruption in nature elemental form, this aura will increase damage taken by frost, and nature abilities respectively. Starting with a small 10% increase in damage, the auras ramp up quickly to 25%, 50%, then 100%. At 250% the increase in damage is so high it makes healing the tank a game of luck, while at 500% any tank is obliterated almost instantly. To avoid the aura damage from ramping up, the tanks must switch Hydross back and forth between frost and nature incarnations by dragging Hydross into and out of the area of effect of the light beams at the spawn point. However, every time Hydross is transitioned from one phase to the other, four elemental spawn: Corrupted Spawns of Hydross when transitioned to nature, and Purified Spawn of Hydross when transitioned to water form. This prevents the raid from switching too often and forces the raid to deal with Hydross with the aura up to the 100% increased damage mark.

RESISTANCE GEAR

Since all damage done by Hydross is elemental damage, conventional high armor item sets for tanks are useless for this encounter. Gearing the tanks with items high in nature and frost resistance is a basic requirement for this encounter. The source for these items are reputation based vendors in Karazhan for The Violet Eye, and Zangarmarsh for the Cenarion Expedition items.

ITEM	DESC	STATS	SOURCE
Iceguard Breastplate	Chest / Plate	1268 Armor, +21 Stamina, +60 Frost Resistance	The Violet Eye – honored
Equip: Increases defense rating by 10.			
Iceguard Helm	Head / Plate	1030 Armor, +42 Stamina, +50 Frost Resistance	The Violet Eye – Honored
Equip: Increases defense rating by 20.			
Iceguard Leggings	Legs / Plate	1110 Armor, +55 Stamina, +60 Frost Resistance	The Violet Eye – Revered
The Frozen Eye	Finger	+12 Stamina, +35 Frost Resistance	The Violet Eye – Honored
Wildguard Breastplate	Chest / Plate	1450 Armor, +45 Stamina, +60 Nature Resistance	Cenarion Expedition – Exalted
Equip: Increases defense rating by 14.			
Wildguard Helm	Head / Plate	1178 Armor, +58 Stamina, +50 Nature Resistance	Cenarion Expedition - Revered
Equip: Increases defense rating by 28.			
Wildguard Leggings	Legs / Plate	1269 Armor, +55 Stamina, +60 Nature Resistance	Cenarion Expedition - Revered
The Natural Ward	Finger	+12 Stamina, +35 Nature Resistance	Cenarion Expedition - Exalted
Further Nature resistance gear can be obtained from killing the Dragons of Nightmare Ysondre, Taerar, Emeriss, Lethon, or from Cenarion Circle reputation patterns.			
Further Frost resistance gear can be obtained from Naxxramas, either as boss drops or crafted by using frozen runes.			

RAID COMPOSITION

Four tanks are required for this encounter. One to tank Hydross in frost phase, one for the nature phase, and two to tank the adds that spawn between transitions. While protection Warriors are more suited for tanking Hydross, the adds are best tanked by feral Druids since they usually find it easier to generate threat on two targets at the same time. Seven healers can easily be enough, but for early learning attempts eight is probably better. This leaves room for 13-14 DPS classes. Hydross in frost form is not very melee-friendly. Compounded with the need to deal with multiple adds at the same time, the encounter skews in the favor of ranged classes, particularly those who can use area of effect abilities. If possible, a raid should consist of at least six AoE damage capable classes, and no more than three melee DPS classes. Two shadow Priests are also highly recommended, due to the mana regeneration they provide to classes that expend their mana rapidly with area of effect spells. Finally, two Hunters add a high degree of control to a raid group attempting this difficult to execute encounter.

CONSUMABLES

Consumables is generally low, but when learning the encounter using Flasks of Fortification for the tanks is very helpful. Flasks for the DPS classes should only really be used if the raid can control the encounter, but cannot defeat it without consumables before the 10 minute enrage timer.

THE PULL

The pull is a key element of the encounter. Having a tank run up towards Hydross is not recommended, since as soon as the tank has entered her aggro range, Hydross will start moving towards the tank, away from the cleansing beams, and therefore switch to nature form immediately, spawning 4 adds in the process. With a bit of practice it is possible to have the tank approach from the side around a pillar, use Bloodrage, then Intercept as soon as Hydross enters line of sight. An even easier strategy is to have the tank use an invisibility potion to approach Hydross and to cancel the effect once standing in front of the boss, starting the event.

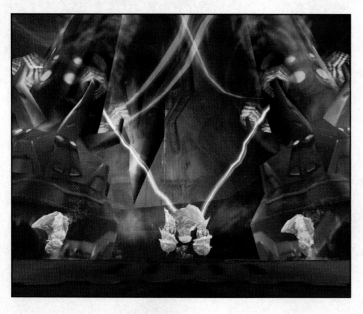

STRATEGY

Starting the encounter in frost form without adds gives the raid about a minute of uninterrupted damage time on the boss. This is particularly handy, considering her 3.4 million HPs and the 10 minute enrage timer. While in frost form, apart from hitting the main tank and affecting every player in the raid with the Mark of Hydross, Hydross has a random secondary target ability, named Water Tomb. The target and all other players within an 8-yard range from the target will be stunned and take 4500 damage over 5 seconds. This number is amplified by the Mark of Hydross, and can therefore be extremely dangerous, especially when more than one player is affected. This can be avoided by spreading everyone out, avoiding as much as possible situations where players are within eight yards of each other. This can be achieved by having ranged classes at maximum range, and positioning a part of the raid behind Hydross.

Mark of Hydross stacks every 15 seconds, from 10%, to 25%, 50% and then 100%. With 10 seconds to go before the 250% aura stack, the tank must start moving Hydross away from the beams of light. At this point all DPS must stop. Once Hydross transitions to nature phase, all aggro is wiped and the nature-geared tank must pick Hydross up. Hunters can make this transition easy by using their Misdirect skill on the new tank. Four nature elementals spawn. These must be picked up by the two offtanks. To help them, Mages can use Frost Nova to freeze them in place, or they can be stunned by Paladins using Hammer of Justice. After giving the offtanks time to build aggro on the adds, these can be positioned by the offtanks on top of the boss. Once in position, area of effect damage classes can take them down while at the same time doing damage to Hydross. Mages can use any AoE spell available to them, depending on their talent choice, while Warlocks should use Seed of Corruption. Once the four adds have been dealt with, the raid can resume single target damage to Hydross. While in nature phase, Hydross uses a secondary target ability named Vile Sludge. It inflicts a small amount of periodic damage, but reduces damage and healing done by 50% for 24 seconds.

Just like Mark of Hydross, Mark of Nature stacks every 15 seconds. As before, Hydross must be transitioned back to frost phase a few seconds before the aura reaches 250% increased damage. And once again, adds will spawn. This time four frost-immune purified spawns of Hydross. Compared to the nature stage, the frost stage is slightly more difficult, since dealing with the four adds and Water Tomb at the same time can create quite challenging situations. Healers that are "tombed" must be healed and so do their assigned targets. The raid must particularly avoid getting the offtanks tombed by standing too close to them. While tombed, a tank cannot dodge incoming attacks, cannot build aggro, and also takes the additional periodic frost damage, therefore requiring additional healing.

The rest of the encounter consists of alternating between the nature and frost stage until Hydross dies, or hits the 10 minute enrage timer, whichever comes first.

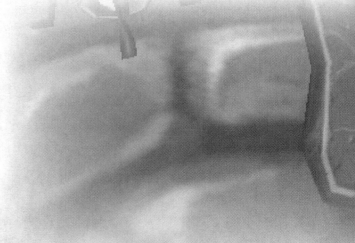

TANKS

For tanks, this is a difficult encounter that requires perfect execution. After acquiring the resistance gear outlined above, try maximizing stamina and avoidance in the other available gear slots. Enchant your new pieces of gear, every little helps. While it is fairly easy to transition Hydross from one phase to another at the 100% mark, it is recommended that you do it with as little time as possible before the 250% mark, in order to maximize DPS.

Make sure you communicate with the rest of your raid while doing that, since they will need to stop damage. Immediately after a transition is probably the most sensitive moment of the encounter. Hydross has reset the aggro table, and will move towards the next DPS class that attacks it, or the next healer that heals, unless you can pick him up in time. Ask a Hunter to Misdirect you after every transition. Do not be afraid to use your cooldowns (Shield Wall/Last Stand) since the death of one of the two main tanks practically always results in a wipe.

As far as the offtanks are concerned, you must use a combination of frost and nature resistance gear, as you will be tanking both types of adds. Once they spawn, build some aggro on both, and remember that they can be taunted, should you lose aggro temporarily. Once you feel confident about your threat level, let the DPS classes know that you are ready for them to AoE. While during the nature phase it is more efficient to tank the adds directly on top of Hydross, during the frost phase grouping up very tightly can cause both offtanks, and sometimes the main tank too, to be encased in water tombs. Avoid this at all costs. If positioned carefully, all the adds and Hydross can still be close enough to be affected by AOE spells, while the offtanks and main tank are far enough from each other as not to get water tombed.

HEALING

Tanks with good resistance gear are not terribly difficult to heal on this encounter, unless they are affected by Water Tomb. Remember that not only will they take the added DoT damage, but they will also be unable to dodge or parry or use abilities that will help them stay alive. Ask for help if your tank is tombed during the frost stage, or if you are affected by vile sludge during the nature stage. Due to the increased damage from the aura, damage taken by both main tank and offtanks will ramp up between transitions, so be prepared to compensate. The same is true about players affected by Water Tomb. With the aura at 100%, these are likely to die unless healed within 5 seconds of the effect.

Be careful with the timing of your heals, particularly during a transition. Landing a big heal immediately after Hydross has switched stages will pull aggro from the boss, potentially wiping the raid.

DPS

This is a difficult encounter for DPS classes, because it combines the requirement of high DPS to beat the enrage timer, with frequent threat resets. It is extremely important to stop DPS when your main tank announces that he is about to move and transition Hydross. If you use damage over time (DoT) spells, stop applying them well ahead of time. Once Hydross has transitioned, do not start DPS immediately. Give your new tank a few seconds to start building aggro again. For Warlocks, shadow Priests, or fire Mages that have landed a big crit before the transition make sure you are always standing ahead of the tank, in the direction he is pulling Hydross towards. Even if after the transition, you will pull aggro because of your DoTs. Hydross will continue moving towards you, staying in the same form. Standing behind the tank, or in the direction Hydross is coming from, is dangerous because pulling aggro after a transition will make Hydross turn back towards you, transitioning again and spawning an additional 4 adds, which guarantees a wipe.

Shadow Priests should keep damage on Hydross at all times, in order to provide mana regeneration to Warlocks and Mages which are using area of effect spells on the adds. Seed of Corruption on Hydross is the best way to do damage to the adds, which must be tanked within a 15 yard range of the boss. Mages can use Blast Wave, Dragon's Breath and Arcane Explosion for the nature adds, while more conservative spells such as Flamestrike are better for the frost stage, since you can use them from a distance, without putting the offtanks at risk of being water tombed.

Serpentshrine Consoles

With the first boss in the cavern defeated, the console behind him becomes unlocked. There are 5 consoles in Serpentshrine Cavern, one for every early boss. Once a boss is defeated, their respective console becomes unlocked and can be activated by players. Activating all 5 consoles unlocks the larger, Lady Vashj Bridge console at pumping station #5, which unfolds the large bridge leading to her otherwise inaccessible island.

Going for a swim in Serpentshrine Cavern can be quite hazardous, due to the water's inhabitants, Coilfang Frenzies. These vicious fish only appear when unsuspecting players jump in the water, and larger numbers of fish are attracted if several players are in the water. They deal about 1000 damage per hit to cloth wearing classes, and attack very fast. While it may be tempting to take a shortcut, it's probably best to just stay out of the water.

THE PUMPING STATIONS

Immediately to the left of Hydross is the first of six water pumping stations. They are all manned by large groups of enemies that must be defeated in order to attempt the next boss, the Lurker Below. These packs each consist of four rather harmless Greyheart Technicians, two Coilfang Priestesses, two Coilfang Shatterers and one Vashj'ir Honor Guard that controls the operation of the steam pump.

Priestesses and Technicians can be polymorphed, while the Shatterers and the Honor Guard need to be tanked. Since raids will probably not have six Mages, prioritize polymorphing the two Priestesses preventing them from healing other mobs in the pack. DPS can eliminate the remaining technicians without the need of a real tank, feral Druids can tank them easily in cat form, alternatively Hunter pets can be used. The other 3 remaining mobs however need a well geared tank each. The Honor Guard will periodically fear all nearby targets and also has a Cleave attack that can deal huge damage to the raid. It must be positioned away from the raid. Fear Ward the tank if a Dwarf/Draenai Priest is available, or drop a tremor totem in case the tank fails to avoid an intimidating shout. Tanks on the aptly named Shatterers must also be very careful when tanking, since these mobs have an ability called Shatter Armor. This ability reduces an enemy's armor by 50% as well as their damage by 35% for 15 sec. Fortunately this ability can be reflected back to the Shatterer, causing him to deal less damage and becoming more vulnerable to physical attacks from players in the raid.

Once the Honor Guard is defeated, the pumping station is disabled until the Honor Guard respawns, two hours later. Disabling all six pumping stations causes the water in the cavern to heat up close to boiling point. The scalding water will kill off all the Coilfang frenzies swimming in the waters, thus allowing players to swim through while only taking 500 damage every 3 seconds. From the 6th pumping station players can jump down to the Strange Pool, the spawning place of the Lurker Below.

THE LURKER BELOW

The Lurker Below is one of the best designed encounters in early Burning Crusade raids. It is not easy and takes good execution from everyone in the raid, although individual mistakes usually only lead to the loss of the person at fault, as opposed to the whole raid. In order to coerce the boss to emerge from the depths, players must fish in the strange pool. Fishing here, just like in other areas of the game is fairly unpredictable, and players are more likely to come up with smaller fish or random crates before they land the lurker himself. However, the more characters in the raid start fishing in the pool, the faster the Lurker can be spawned. A base fishing skill of about 250 is recommended, and this can be enhanced by using special fishing poles such as the quest reward from the Stranglethorn Fishing Extravaganza weekly event, or Seth's Graphite Fishing Pole from the quest in Shattrath City. Fishing skill can be further increased by using fishing lures from fishing supplies vendors around major lakes, or engineering-created fish attractors.

ABILITIES

HP	3794000	Damage	11948-16894
Abilities	**Sprout**: Deals 3238 to 3762 Frost damage per second and knocks the target back 100 yards.		
	Summon Coilfang Guardians: Summons 3 Coilfang Guardians and 6 Coilfang Ambushers.		
	Whirl: Deals 4375 to 5625 Physical damage and knocks them back 25 yards.		
	Water Bolt: Blasts a single target with a bolt of frost for 8750 to 11250 Frost damage. This ability is used when no targets are currently in melee range.		

OVERVIEW

Like Hydross, the Lurker Below is essentially a two-stage encounter with alternating stages. The first stage starts with the Lurker emerging after being "fished" by a player. Periodically the Lurker will submerge, summoning adds on the large inner ring platform around the strange pool, as well as on the adjacent smaller three platforms. One minute later, the lurker re-emerges from the depths, and stays above the water for 90 seconds. This pattern continues until either the raid wipes or the lurker is defeated. There is no enrage timer.

RAID COMPOSITION

Three tanks are recommended for this encounter, as well as three Mages for crowd controlling adds. Additional Mages or Hunters (for freezing trap) will increase the raid's ability to deal with the adds in stage two. The encounter can be healing intensive at times, therefore eight healers are recommended.

LOOT

Grove-Bands of Remulos: Wrist/Leather: 177 Armor, +21 Stamina, +14 Intellect, +21 Spirit, Equip: Increases healing done by spells and effects by up to 68.

Velvet Boots of the Guardian: Feet/Cloth: 148 Armor, +21 Stamina, +21 Intellect, +15 Spirit, Equip: Improves spell critical strike rating by 24, Increases damage and healing done by magical spells and effects by up to 49.

Glowing Breastplate of Truth: Chest/Plate: 1607 Armor, +39 Stamina, +40 Intellect, Equip: Improves spell critical strike rating by 42, Restores 10 mana per 5 sec, Increases healing done by spells and effects by up to 53.

Libram of Absolute Truth: Relic: , Equip: Reduces the mana cost of Holy Light by 27.

Mallet of the Tides: Main Hand Mace: 111 - 207 Damage, Speed 1.70, (93.5 DPS), +33 Stamina, Equip: Increases defense rating by 15, Increases mace skill rating by 14.

Cord of Screaming Terrors: Waist/Cloth: 121 Armor, +34 Stamina, +15 Intellect, Yellow Socket, Yellow Socket, Socket Bonus: +4 Stamina, Equip: Improves spell hit rating by 24, Increases damage and healing done by magical spells and effects by up to 50.

Boots of Effortless Striking: Feet/Leather: 278 Armor, +42 Agility, +41 Stamina, Equip: Increases attack power by 58.

Tempest-Strider Boots: Feet/Mail: 619 Armor, +25 Stamina, +26 Intellect., Equip: Increases healing done by spells and effects by up to 51, Restores 16 mana per 5 sec.

Ancestral Ring of Conquest: Finger: +32 Strength, +21 Agility, +30 Stamina

Bracers of Eradication: Wrist/Plate: 703 Armor, +25 Strength, +12 Stamina, Blue Socket, Socket Bonus: Strength +2, Equip: Improves hit rating by 17, Improves critical strike rating by 24.

Earring of Soulful Meditation: Trinket: Equip: Increases healing done by spells and effects by up to 66, Use: Increases your Spirit by +300 for 20 sec.

Choker of Animalistic Fury: Neck: +24 Stamina, Equip: Improves critical strike rating by 23, Increases attack power by 64.

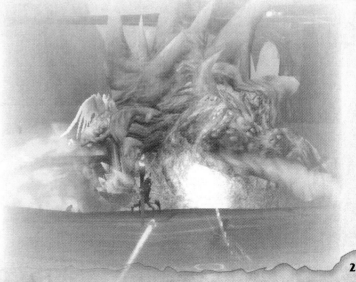

CONSUMABLES

Consumables is generally low although using a flask on the main tank can help keep him alive against the lurker's very powerful melee attacks.

 ## POSITIONING

This is an encounter that requires good positioning of the raid, using both the large inner island around the strange pool and the three smaller islands (a diagram is provided to help with positioning). Particularly important is the positioning of the main tank and that of his healers on island A. Other than that, all ranged DPS must be spread among the three small islands, with one Mage per island, and two other ranged classes. Also adding a Paladin to every island can help tremendously when it comes to the second stage. All melee DPS are spread along the inner island, on the opposite side from the main tank. One of the healers on island B is assigned to healing them.

Ranged

Ranged 1 MTH

2 H MT

Lurker

Melee OT

OTH

3

H

Ranged

MAP LEGEND	
MT	Main Tank
MTH	Main Tank Healers
OT	Off tank
OTH	Off tank healer
Ranged	Mages, Warlocks, Hunters, Shadow Priests
H	Healers
1,2,3	Island Locations
Lurker	The Lurker Below

STRATEGY

In stage one, the lurker below uses three main abilities, apart from attacking the main tank. These are Spout, Whirl, and Geyser, and will be explained in detail below. It is important to note that he will always attack a target in melee range if one is available, even if ranged targets on the islands have more threat. If no targets are available in melee range he will use a powerful ranged ability named Water Bolt, which deals 8750-11250 frost damage to one target. This must be avoided at all costs by making sure that at least one tank is always in melee range. Unlike most other bosses in the zone, the lurker below is not immune to Taunt.

Spout is the lurker's most important ability. The raid will experience it for the first time about 35 seconds after he is fished. The ability has a 50 second cooldown, and can only be used while the lurker is above the water, in stage one. The cooldown on the ability will always expire during stage two. Every time the lurker re-emerges to start a new stage one, he will use the Spout ability. The Lurker will drop his primary target when he is about to Spout. Spout is a powerful, rotating beam of water that starts off in the direction the lurker is facing, then rotates either clockwise, or counterclockwise 400 degrees. A Spout takes about 20 seconds to complete.

The easiest way to avoid it is to dive under the water. Players that are fully submerged will not be hit by the Spout, but those that are hit, will take bursts of around 3500 frost damage and be knocked back a long distance, which for most players is equivalent with death. Remember that the Spout does not only cover a full 360 degree circle, but it overlaps beyond its starting point. If a player is standing in the area where the Spout starts off, he will need to dive at the beginning, re-emerge, then dive again after the Spout has gone around the room or risk being hit by the last few seconds of Spout.

Whirl is a knockback that Lurker will perform on all targets in melee range every 17 seconds. Players standing on the inner edge of the inner platform will be knocked back to the outside edge, but will not fall into the water. Geyser also knocks targets back, but it only affects the targeted player and those immediately around him. When knocked away from the main platform, swim back as fast as possible to avoid taking too much damage from scalding water.

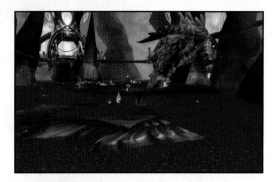

Stage two will begin 90 seconds into the encounter the lurker. In this stage nine additional mobs will spawn. Two Coilfang Ambushers, an archer type mob with about 28,000 hit points, on each of the three small islands. Three Coilfang Guardians, a powerful Warrior type mob with around 68,000 hit points, on the large inner island. Ideally the raid should finish off all these mobs in one minute, the time available before the lurker re-emerges.

On the small islands Mages should sheep one Ambusher each, with the Paladin, or a Shaman, tanking the second one. This one must be killed first, by the ranged damage classes on the islands. Once the first one dies, the Paladin/Shaman tank can break Polymorph and the ranged classes can kill off the second Ambusher. They do moderate damage with their bows, and also have a Multishot ability that will hit several targets.

On the inner island, the main tank and the two other tanks must pick up one Guardian each. These have a powerful melee attack and a frontal Cleave. They are significantly more dangerous than Ambushers. A healer must be assigned to every tank for this stage, and the tanks must pay close attention to the positioning of the Guardians or risk cleaving the melee classes to death. While the ranged classes are dealing with the Ambushers on the islands, melee damage classes can start killing the three tanked Guardians. Because of their hit points, Ambushers will always die first. Then the ranged classes must help the melee classes finish off the Guardians. In a raid where deaths have occurred, or with fewer DPS classes available, it might be impossible to finish off all the adds in time for the lurker's re-emergence. In these cases a Mage can Polymorph a target, and keep it polymorphed for the entire duration of the encounter. This is made possible because during the next stage two one of the adds will not spawn to replace the polymorphed one. (i.e., if a Guardian is polymorphed, only two new ones will spawn).

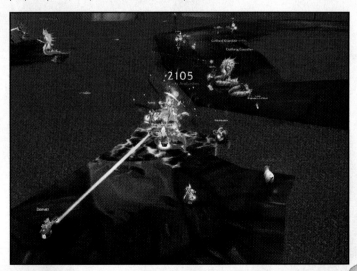

TANKING

Use Intercept to get back to the Lurker if you get knocked away. As the offtank, you can Taunt the Lurker if the main tank gets knocked away. As the main tank you need to be very quick to dive when a Spout is coming up, especially since most of the time the Spout will start on top of you. In stage 2 pick up the 3 Guardians and be careful not to point them in the direction of the other melee classes.

HEALING

Paladins must be spread out among the platforms to tank the Ambushers in stage 2. One additional healer on each platform will help with the healing during that stage. The remaining 2 healers must watch the main tank and therefore stand on the platform closest to him. It is also very important to assign a healer to every tank for the second stage, since the Guardians do serious damage.

DPS

Ranged classes, enjoy the ability to do damage without ever worrying about threat! In stage 2, kill the Ambushers as fast as possible, even if you do pull aggro. The Ambusher will die before you do, and the Paladin tank can always regain agro. As soon as you have cleared your island, start shooting the Guardians on the inner island.

With the lurker defeated, the raid can now climb out of the water to the platform with the lurker's console, in between the 3rd and 4th pumping station.

CHOICES

The path to the left leads to Leotheras the Blind, while the path to the right leads to Morogrim Tidewalker. The two paths meet again in the furthest room in the instance, where Fathom Lord Karathress and his prisoner can be found. Before the raid reaches either of them a new set of enemies must be taken out. Apart from the Colossi, there are multiple packs of Naga on the bridge area consisting of Coilfang Serpent Guards and Fathom-witches. Take out the Fathom-witches first, and beware of their Shadow Nova attack which knocks targets away. To avoid accidents with players being knocked into the scalding water, the tanks must place their backs against a wall and have only ranged targets attack fathom witches. Melee targets on Serpent Guards will help deal with their Mind Control ability. If there are no melee targets around them, they will Mind Control the tank and attack someone else in the raid.

Beyond them, the path to Leotheras is littered with packs of Broken, consisting of combinations of Greyheart Skulkers, Tidecallers, Shield Bearers and Nether-Mages.

Skulkers pose the smallest threat and can be tanked normally, but the other three types of mobs require a bit of effort. Tidecallers will occasionally place down a Water Elemental totem, which summons a water elemental. Kill the totem immediately to despawn the elemental. Shield Bearers throw their shield at random targets, but will also periodically drop their current target and charge the furthest available target in their range. This can result in instant death for cloth classes, so make sure that a plate wearer is the furthest target at all times, in order to take the charge attack.

Finally, Nether-Mages come in three varieties, frost, fire and arcane mages. These are the most dangerous types of mobs and must always be polymorphed while the raid deals with the others. While they are polymorphed, Mages can try to use Spellsteal on them to determine the damage type. Nether-Mages buff themselves with one of either frost, fire or arcane destruction spells. By spellstealing their buff, a Mage can gain a damage boost, reduce the damage done by the Nether-Mage, and also determine the type of damage it will do once Polymorph is broken.

Fire Nether-Mages will use Rain of Fire, frost mages have a Cone of Cold, while arcane mages have a powerful Arcane Burst ability as well as the ability to Teleport around the raid. Always leave arcane mages last, and heal the whole raid before breaking a polymorphed arcane Nether-Mage.

Finally, the last type of mob that the raid will encounter, first on its own and later as a part of the Greyheart packs, is the Serpentshrine Lurker. These elementals can be banished, and when they are group should be the last mob attacked. Once you get around to fighting them, they spawn mushrooms on top of players in the raid. Once the mushrooms have grown, players standing near them will be enveloped in a spore cloud that does progressive amounts of damage to them. Move away from grown mushrooms.

LEOTHERAS THE BLIND

This powerful Demon Hunter is probably the most difficult encounter in the zone, besides Lady Vashj. Like Hydross he requires specific gear, as well as careful execution from every player in the raid. Mistakes always result in deaths, and a death usually means that the raid will be unable to defeat the encounter before the 10 minute enrage timer. However, if successful the raid will be rewarded with very high quality loot, among them two glove tokens that can be turned into Tier 5 set pieces.

ABILITIES

HP	3794000	Damage	7169-10136
Abilities	**Whirlwind**: Lasts 12 sec. and inflicts normal damage plus 50. Inflicts 2500 additional Physical damage every 3 sec. for 15 sec.		
	Metamorphosis: Transforms Leotheras into a demon with additional abilities for 1 minute. While under the effects of Metamorphosis, Leotheras does not use his Whirlwind ability.		
	Summon Shadow of Leotheras: Summons the Shadow of Leotheras, a demon that uses the Insidious Whisper and Chaos Blast abilities. Once this creature is summoned, Leotheras will not use the Metamorphosis ability.		
	Insidious Whisper: Creates an Inner Demon from the target. If this Inner Demon is not slain quickly, it will take control of the target for 10 min.		
	Chaos Blast: Inflicts 1675 Fire damage and increases Fire damage taken by 1675 for 45 sec.		

LOOT

Gloves of the Vanquished Champion: Classes: Paladin, Rogue, Shaman: Tier 5 Glove Token

Gloves of the Vanquished Hero: Classes: Hunter, Mage, Warlock: Tier 5 Glove Token

Gloves of the Vanquished Defender: Classes: Warrior, Priest, Druid: Tier 5 Glove Token

Girdle of the Invulnerable: Waist/Plate: 904 Armor, +37 Stamina, Red Socket, Blue Socket, Socket Bonus: +4 Stamina, Equip: Increases defense rating by 22, Increases your dodge rating by 19, Increases your parry rating by 29.

Tsunami Talisman: Trinket: Equip: Improves hit rating by 10, Improves critical strike rating by 38, Chance on critical hit to increase your attack power by 340 for 10 secs.

Coral-Barbed Shoulderpads: Shoulder Mail: 675 Armor, +22 Stamina, +33 Intellect, Blue Socket, Blue Socket, Socket Bonus: +7 Healing, Equip: Restores 6 mana per 5 sec, Increases healing done by spells and effects by up to 73.

Fang of the Leviathan: Main Hand/Sword: 23 - 125 Damage, Speed 1.80, (41.3 DPS), +28 Stamina, +19 Intellect, Equip: Improves spell critical strike rating by 20, Increases damage and healing done by magical spells and effects by up to 209.

Orca-Hide Boots: Feet Leather: 278 Armor, +19 Stamina, +27 Intellect, +19 Spirit, Blue Socket, Blue Socket, Socket Bonus: +3 Spirit, Equip: Increases healing done by spells and effects by up to 73.

True-Aim Stalker Bands: Wrist/Mail: 394 Armor, +18 Stamina, +12 Intellect, Yellow Socket, Socket Bonus: +3 Stamina, Equip: Improves critical strike rating by 24, Increases attack power by 50.

OVERVIEW

The three Greyheart Spellbinders that keep Leotheras banished must be killed before he can be engaged. Once released Leotheras will attack the raid in his Elf form. While for most of the time he can be tanked normally. Periodically he performs Whirlwind randomly, rapidly changing targets, hitting all players in his path. Once the Whirlwind stops, his threat table resets and he must be picked up once again.

Leotheras will switch into demon form, once again clearing his threat table. In this form he will attack his primary target with Chaos Blast, a fireball that does relatively little damage initially, but increases the fire damage taken by subsequent spells making it hit for more and more damage on the tank and all other targets in an eight yard radius. Also during his demon stage, five players will be affected by Inner Demons. The demons will spawn from the affected targets and attack those players with their melee attack and Shadow Bolts.

They are unusual creatures that follow very specific rules. They can only attack and be attacked by the target they spawned from; therefore, every player must fight his own inner demon. Players that fail to defeat their inner demon will be Mind Controlled by Leotheras for the duration of the encounter. Leotheras will switch between his Elf and demon form until he reaches 15% health, at which point he will split in two, with the raid having to face both his Elven and his demon form at the same time during this third stage. The raid must kill the Elf before the 10 minute enrage timer to complete the encounter.

RESISTANCE GEAR

In order to deal with the increased damage caused by Chaos Blast, a tank needs to be geared up in fire resistance armor. Including party buffs such as a Paladin's fire resistance aura or a Shaman's fire resistance totem, the aim is to reach 375 fire resistance. The best fire resistance gear available is purchased with tokens dropped by bosses in 5-man heroic instances. A full set costs a whopping 100 tokens and can be purchased from G'eras in the middle of Shattrah City. The stats on all the pieces are the same, whether they are cloth, plate, mail or leather. Good choices for completing the fire resistance set are the Phoenix-Fire Band, the reward for the Trial of the Naaru: Magtheridon quest, the Wyrmcultist's Cloak sold by the Wyrmcult Provisioner in Blade's Edge Mountains and the Pendant of Frozen Flame that can be obtained from skilled jewelcrafters.

The raid has a choice, to go with a protection Warrior tank or with a more unusual Warlock tank. While the Warrior tank will have more hit points as well as the option to use Last Stand and Shield Wall, the Warlock tank has a number of important perks that make him particularly suitable for the task. Most importantly, a melee tank must tank the demon form from melee range, which makes it practically impossible for melee classes to do damage to the demon form without taking damage from the Chaos Blast. Choosing the Soul Link talent, the Warlock can also split damage taken with his pet, reducing burst damage and making healing more manageable.

EPIC FIRE RESISTANCE GEAR

ITEM	STATS
Inferno Tempered Boots/Infernoweave Boots	+45 Fire Resistance, +36 Stamina
Inferno Tempered Chestguard/Infernoweave Robe	+54 Stamina, +60 Fire Resistance
Inferno Tempered Gauntlets/Infernoweave Gloves	+52 Stamina, +40 Fire Resistance
Inferno Tempered Leggings/Infernoweave Leggings	+69 Stamina, +55 Fire Resistance

RAID COMPOSITION

Apart from one melee tank and the one fire resistance tank, raid composition can be very flexible, an eight healer group should perform well. A minimum of two Hunters will make transitions between demon and Elf easier by misdirecting the main tank. Due to the Whirlwind mechanic, ranged DPS classes tend to outperform melee DPS classes, as they can spend less time adjusting and more time dealing damage.

CONSUMABLES

Consumable use is generally high for this encounter, particularly during the learning stages. Consumables can help the DPS stay above the required limit even with a few casualties in the raid, so Flasks of Relentless Assault and Supreme Power should be used until the raid becomes comfortable with the encounter. The damage on well-geared tanks is usually not high enough to warrant the use of a Flask of Fortification, and healers end up not expending all their mana, but tanks and healers can consider consumables as a means to help them defeat their inner demons.

STRATEGY

The Greyheart Spellbinders at the beginning of the encounter are very easy to defeat and should be used by the raid to their advantage. Keep them spread out to avoid having them target the same player with their mind blast. Apart from that, the most important thing to remember is that the time spent fighting them does not count towards the 10 minute enrage timer. Therefore, casters should use their mana conservatively, while the main tank should use them as an opportunity to gain full rage which can be used on Leotheras as soon as he is released.

With Leotheras positioned in the center of his large room, the raid must surround him in a circle, at the maximum range of their abilities. DPS can start off in force if the tank started off with a full rage bar. His Whirlwind attack during this stage is lethal, and must be avoided as much as possible. Apart from the initial damage, players hit during the Whirlwind stage will be affected by Rend damage over time effect that deals 2250 damage every 3 seconds for 15 seconds. This is very difficult to heal when several people in the same area are hit, and must be healed by the same healer. Melee classes should run away as soon as they see the Whirlwind animation, while ranged classes can continue doing damage and run only when Leotheras is whirlwinding towards them. It is very important to stop attacking as the Whirlwind ends, because Leotheras will wipe his threat list and attack the first person that performs a hostile action. Hunters using Misdirect on the main tank when Whirlwind ends are instrumental in getting Leotheras under control, especially when the tank is not near Leotheras when the Whirlwind ends.

Another threat list reset occurs at the transition between Elf and demon stage. DPS must stop and allow the fire resistance geared tank to pick him up and build aggro before attacking again. Once the fire resistance tank begins taking Chaos Blasts, everyone must move away from him to avoid being collateral damage. Even with optimal resistance gear the tank will be hit often and the damage taken per Chaos Blast will increase over time until the end of the demon phase.

INNER DEMONS

As far as inner demons are concerned, the random factor in the selection of targets will significantly affect the difficulty of the encounter. Obviously, damage dealing classes usually have little trouble dealing with their demons within the 30 second window, while healers and tanks are usually at risk of failing and being Mind Controlled. Several little steps can be taken to help the less fortunate classes defeat their demons.

One important thing to realize is that being hit by a demon pushes back spell channeling, reducing the DPS of a target fighting a demon. This is why having a Priest shield them can help a lot. Healers that normally put out little DPS must be healed exclusively by another healer, and never heal themselves as this reduces the amount of damage they can do to the demon. Finally, the best solution for a tank is to switch from a 1-handed weapon and shield to two weapons and use skills such as devastate to quickly bring the demon down. The use of cooldowns while fighting demons is usually a good idea, as is the use of consumables such as Haste Potions for melee classes and Destruction Potions for healers. Wearing a few good pieces of damage gear over healing or tanking gear can also make a big difference. Should someone fail and be Mind Controlled, it is best to kill them as soon as possible, as they can be brought back into combat by Druids casting rebirth on them.

Threat resets yet again at the transition back to Elf. This is usually not very dangerous, as the stage one tank can stand close to the demon and pick Leotheras up again, as he turns into an Elf. Also, after this transition Leotheras can sometimes go directly into a Whirlwind, where aggro is not an issue until the end of the Whirlwind.

At the 15% health mark, the raid will get a short breather as Leotheras transitions into stage 3, which is essentially a combination of the first two stages. The fire resistance tank must pick up the demon, and as in the second stage, players need to move away from him. The main tank must pick up Leotheras in his Elf form and the raid must deal with both of them at the same time. The demon cannot be killed, but he does not use his Insidious Whisper that causes inner demons to spawn. All the raid needs to do is kill the Elf form of Leotheras before the 10 minute mark.

TANKING

This is a difficult encounter for tanks, as they must deal with a moving target that often clears its threat table. Follow Leotheras around during the Whirlwind, and save up rage which must be used when the Whirlwind has stopped. Use Intervene to save another player if they were the first to attract Leotheras' attention. During the demon phase, stand on top of the demon and save rage that you can release once he reverts back into Elf form. As a Warlock tank, use Searing Pain to generate enough threat on the demon form, and try to position yourself away from other players. Soulstone yourself, as your death will otherwise result in a wipe.

HEALING

The main challenge in this encounter is saving the players that have been hit by Whirlwind, and are now taking damage from rend. As a Shaman, Chain Heal is a good means of keeping your group alive if several players are hit, while an affected Paladin can use his Shield to be able to concentrate on other members of the group. For the Warlock tank, healers must be assigned both to him and his pet. Also, in stage 2, remember that you must heal those fighting their inner demons, even if they are a healer class.

DPS

The challenge of this encounter is doing enough damage so that the raid can defeat Leotheras before the enrage timer, but also knowing when to stop doing damage to prevent you from getting killed. Try and avoid the Whirlwind as much as possible, as it places a big strain on healing. Remember not to damage Leotheras as a Whirlwind ends, or at a transition between stages. Always give the tanks a few seconds to build aggro before opening up with damage abilities. If you can stay alive until the end of the encounter, those extra seconds will be insignificant, and the raid will have ample time to defeat Leotheras.

FATHOM LORD KARATHRESS

Fathom Lord Karathress is considered by many to be the easiest encounter in Serpentshrine Cavern. Due to his positioning it is time consuming to reach him before defeating any of the previous bosses, but this does remain an option for raids that are having difficulties with Hydross, Leotheras or the Lurker Below. The items obtained from this encounter, particularly the two Tier 5 leg piece tokens can be put to good use in the other encounters in the zone.

ABILITIES

FATHOM-LORD KARATHRESS

HP	1821000	Damage	8866-12522
Abilities	**Cataclysmic Bolt:** 80 yard range. Blasts with shadow, dealing damage equal to half their total health.		
	Sear Nova: Inflicts 2850 to 3150 Fire damage.		
	Spitfire Totem: Summons a Searing Totem with 25000 health for 60 sec that repeatedly attacks a nearby enemy for 2550 to 3450 Fire damage. Karathress gains this ability when Tidalvess is killed.		
	Tidal Surge: Knocks the target up in the air and encases them in ice for 3 sec. Deals 1663 to 1837 Frost damage. Karathress gains this ability when Caribdis is killed.		
	The Beast Within: Increases your damage by 30%. Karathress gains this ability when Sharkkis is killed.		

FATHOM-GUARD SHARKKIS, FATHOM-GUARD CARIBDIS, AND FATHOM-GUARD TIDALVESS

HP	861600	Damage	8866-12522

LOOT

Leggings of the Vanquished Champion: Classes: Paladin, Rogue, Shaman: Tier 5 Leg Token

Leggings of the Vanquished Defender: Classes: Warrior, Priest, Druid: Tier 5 Leg Token

Leggings of the Vanquished Hero: Classes: Hunter, Mage, Warlock: Tier 5 Leg Token

Soul-Strider Boots: Feet / Cloth: 148 Armor, +20 Stamina, +19 Intellect, +33 Spirit, Red Socket, Blue Socket, Socket Bonus: +7 Healing, Equip: Increases healing done by spells and effects by up to 64.

World Breaker: Two-Hand / Mace: 360 - 541 Damage, Speed 3.70, (121.8 DPS), +46 Strength, +46 Stamina, Chance on hit: Increases the critical strike rating of your next attack made within 4 seconds by 900.

Frayed Tether of the Drowned: Neck: +45 Stamina, Equip: Increases defense rating by 24, Improves hit rating by 18.

Fathom-Brooch of the Tidewalker: Trinket: Equip: Your Nature spells have a chance to restore 335 mana.

Bloodsea Brigand's Vest: Chest / Leather: 404 Armor, +24 Stamina, Yellow Socket, Yellow Socket, Blue Socket, Socket Bonus: +8 Attack Power, Equip: Improves hit rating by 27, Improves critical strike rating by 36, Increases attack power by 92.

Sextant of Unstable Currents: Trinket: Equip: Improves spell critical strike rating by 40, Your spell critical strikes have a chance to increase your spell damage and healing by 190 for 15 sec.

OVERVIEW

Fathom Lord Karathress is surrounded by three of his minions: Fathom-Guard Sharkkis the Hunter, Fathom-Guard Tidalvess the Shaman, and Fathom-Guard Caribdis, the Priest. The encounter is very dynamic, and the strategies that can be used to defeat him vary widely. This is caused by the fact that killing off one of his minions makes one of that respective fathom guard's abilities available to Karathress himself. It is up to the raid to choose the order in which to kill the guards, and therefore the order in which he learns new abilities.

QUESTION???

So why kill off the adds and make Karathress stronger, when we could just offtank the adds and focus all the damage on the boss? Good idea, but unfortunately Karathress doesn't seem to appreciate it. Attempting to offtank the guards while killing Karathress will cause him to enrage at the 75% HP mark, increasing his damage to an unhealable level with current itemization. Maybe a challenge for the future?

RAID COMPOSITION

A standard raid with four tanks, eight healers and a good mix of DPS classes including two Hunters for Misdirect and two to three shadow Priests for mana regeneration and additional group healing.

CONSUMABLES

Practically not required, an Elixir of Major Fortitude or Flask of Fortification on the Tidalvess tank is all that is necessary.

THE PULL

As with most encounters that involve multiple mobs and multiple tanks, the pull is a key factor in determining success or failure. Four tanks are required to deal with Karathress. Two of the tanks can pick up their own target fairly easily, while the other two should be helped by a Hunter using Misdirect. Karathress and Sharkkis can be tanked close to their spawn point, while Hunters can Misdirect Tidalvess to a tank at the side of the room leading to Leotheras, and Caribdis to a tank waiting at the opposite end of the room, leading towards Morogrim.

STRATEGY

For exact positioning, a diagram is provided. Throughout the encounter Karathress has a secondary target ability named Cataclysmic Bolt. It deals damage equal to half its target's maximum hit points and stuns that target for 2 seconds. Therefore every player in the raid must be above 50% health at all times or risk dying to Cataclysmic Bolt. The order in which adds are killed is obviously very important and many strategies are possible, but for most guilds the kill order outlined below should be the easiest to manage.

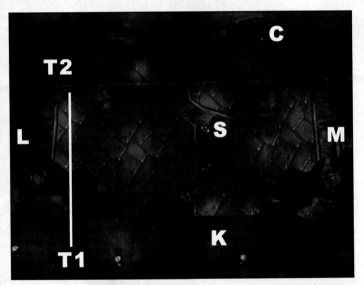

FATHOM-GUARD CARIBDIS

Fathom-Guard Caribdis can easily be killed first. Otherwise, she will attempt to heal the other fathom guards. Apart from her Healing Wave, which can be kicked or counterspelled, she casts a Water Bolt Volley which does around 3000 damage to targets in a 45 yard range. She will also periodically throw in the air and then freeze the targets around her, including her tank. Gusting Winds disorient nearby targets and increase their casting time by 50%.

While fighting her, healing can get very intensive, due to combinations of Water Bolt Volley and Cataclysmic Bolt. Three healers are usually assigned to this corner of the room in order to heal the tank and the damage classes on Caribdis. It is important to keep Curse of Tongues on her to slow down the cast of her Healing Wave. Also, the task of interrupting her casting should fall to Mages, because of the Tidal Surge. Melee classes may be frozen and therefore unable to interrupt her. Upon her death, Karathress will learn the Tidal Surge ability.

FATHOM-GUARD SHARKKIS

With Caribdis dead, the tank on Sharkiss can pull him towards the raid, so that he can be killed quicker. During the encounter, usually before Caribdis dies, Sharkkis will spawn a Hunter pet. The tank on Sharkkis must also pick up the pet. Periodically he will use the Beast Within which increases his and his pet's damage by 30% for 18 seconds. He also has a secondary Leeching Throw ability which will drain 3150 health and mana from its target over 12 seconds. The raid must first kill Sharkkis, then kill his pet. Upon his death, Karathress with learn the Beast Within ability.

FATHOM-GUARD TIDALVESS

Tidalvess is the final add to be killed, and also the most challenging one to deal with. He will periodically drop Grounding and Spitfire totems. These latter ones have 25,000 hit points and periodically attack 5 targets within a 45 yard range with fireballs dealing 2550 to 3450 damage. Assign your best tank to him, as his damage output is significantly higher than that of Karathress himself, due to his Windfury attacks, Spitfire totems and Shock abilities.

It takes at least two healers to keep this tank alive, and for early attempts three are recommended. Start by tanking him in the right corner of the room, as you enter the room coming from Leotheras. Healers must be positioned close to this entrance, but in range to heal the tank. Once he drops a Spitfire totem, the tank must move away towards the healers, and position Tidalvess in the left corner of the room. Healers must follow him until they are all out of the totem's 45 yard range. The first totem will despawn, and be replaced by another totem, close to Tidalvess. Once again, the tank and healers must move to the opposite corner to outrange it. Repeat this until the raid has killed both Caribdis and Sharkkis. Once the raid is in position to kill Tidalvess, there is no need to keep moving him around. Instead, the raid must immediately destroy any Spitfire totems, while ignoring other totem types. After the Spitfire totem has been destroyed, attack Tidalvess until a new totem spawns. Repeat until his death, upon which Karathress will learn the Spitfire totem ability.

With all three guards dead, the raid returns to the center of the room to fight Karathress, who will now use his new abilities in addition to his original Cataclysmic Bolt. If the raid has managed to get so far without heavy losses, the rest of the encounter should be easy to complete before the end of the 10 minute enrage timer. Just like with Tidalvess, always kill Spitfire totems as soon as they spawn, then attack Karathress. After you defeat him, do not forget to talk to Seer Olum.

TANKING

The tanking experience varies widely depending on the assignment, while the tank on Tidalvess will take huge burst damage and must constantly re-adjust, the tank on Karathress basically has to wait four to five minutes for the raid to finish off the adds. As the tank on Caribdis, the main challenge is building aggro. A little trick that prevents you from being thrown too high up in the air is to position yourself under the roof of the little tent in the corner you are assigned. The tank on Sharkiss must build threat on the pet as well, or the healing will pull aggro off you. Do not hesitate to use cooldowns if your hit points drop too low, especially while the Beast Within is active.

HEALING

Initially healers are split, with one each on the Karathress and Sharkkis tanks, two or three on the Tidalvess tank and the remaining healing of the raid on the tank assigned to Caribdis. Heal people up after every Water Bolt Volley, and let nobody in the raid stand at less than 50% hit points. With Caribdis and Sharkkis dead, healers need to be re-assigned. The tank on Karathress will need an additional one or two healers to cope with the increase in damage caused by the Beast Within, while all other available healers must move and heal the raid that is now taking damage from the Spitfire totem.

DPS

Ranged DPS should be careful not to pull aggro on Caribdis. If you are a Mage, be ready to interrupt her Healing Wave. She will only attempt to cast it when her hit points drop below 50%. Do not hesitate to bandage if your hit points are low for too long. You next target is Sharkkis. Do not attack his pet until Sharkkis has died and the tank has had the chance to build some aggro. After that, Tidalvess and Karathress both follow the same rules. Almost always it will be your responsibility to destroy the Spitfire totem as soon as it spawns.

If you completed the Ashtongue Deathsworn series of quests in Shadowmoon Valley, you will now be able to pick up a new quest from Seer Olum, the broken that was imprisoned behind Karathress. The quest series starts either at the Sanctum of the Stars or at the Altar of Sha'tar, depending on whether you have chosen to be an ally of the Aldor or the Scryer.

The Secret Compromised is a very important quest line, after returning to Akama, players will have to defeat Al'ar in Tempest Keep and then Rage Winterchill in Mount Hyjal in order to gain Black Temple attunement.

THE SECRET COMPROMISED

Quest Level:	70
Location:	Serpentshrine Cavern
Starts at:	Olum the Seer
Ends at:	Akama, Warden's Cage, Shadowmoon Valley
Goal:	Speak to Akama and deliver Seer Olum's Warning

No matter what direction you choose to approach Morogrim from, you will have to deal with the packs of Murlocs on the way to him and in his room. Tidewalker Warriors should be killed first, as they are the most unpredictable type of Murloc. They will occasionally go into a frenzy which can be removed by Hunters with Tranquilizing Shot. However, it is their de-aggro that makes them dangerous. Take them out first. Tidewalker Depth-Seer should be killed next as they heal the rest of the pack with Tranquility. Tidewalker Shamans use Chain Lightning and Lightning Shield against the raid and should be killed to reduce the damage output of the pack. Tidewalker Hydromancers and Tidewalker Harpooners can be killed towards the end; their main abilities are used to immobilize players with Frost Novas and nets.

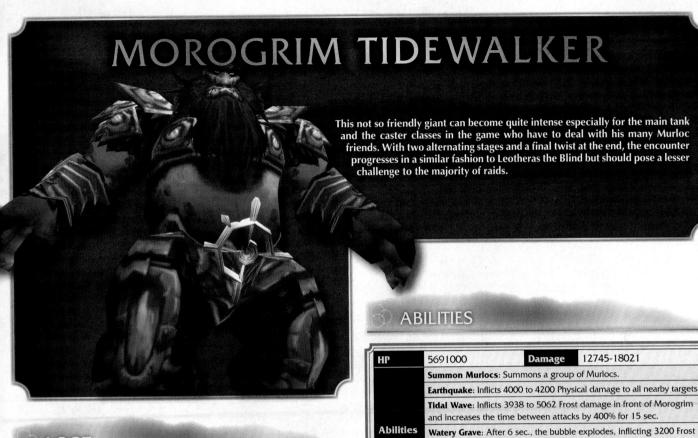

MOROGRIM TIDEWALKER

This not so friendly giant can become quite intense especially for the main tank and the caster classes in the game who have to deal with his many Murloc friends. With two alternating stages and a final twist at the end, the encounter progresses in a similar fashion to Leotheras the Blind but should pose a lesser challenge to the majority of raids.

ABILITIES

HP	5691000	Damage	12745-18021
Abilities	**Summon Murlocs:** Summons a group of Murlocs.		
	Earthquake: Inflicts 4000 to 4200 Physical damage to all nearby targets.		
	Tidal Wave: Inflicts 3938 to 5062 Frost damage in front of Morogrim and increases the time between attacks by 400% for 15 sec.		
	Watery Grave: After 6 sec., the bubble explodes, inflicting 3200 Frost damage and 4625 to 5375 Frost damage to nearby allies.		
	Summon Water Globule: Summons a Water Globule for 35 sec. **Freeze:** Water Globules have the Freeze ability, which inflicts 6563 to 7437 Frost damage and stuns the target for 8 sec.		

LOOT

Razor-Scale Battlecloak: Back: 108 Armor, +33 Strength, +23 Agility, +22 Stamina

Serpent-Coil Braid: Trinket: Equip: Improves spell hit rating by 12, Improves spell critical strike rating by 30, You gain 25% more mana when you use a mana gem. In addition, using a mana gem grants you 225 spell damage for 15 sec.

Pauldrons of the Argent Sentinel: Shoulder late: 1206 Armor, +34 Intellect., Equip: Improves spell critical strike rating by 32, Increases healing done by spells and effects by up to 75.

Pendant of the Lost Ages: Neck: +27 Stamina, +17 Intellect, Equip: Increases damage and healing done by magical spells and effects by up to 36, Reduces the duration of any Silence or Interrupt effects used against the wearer by 20%. This effect does not stack with other similar effects.

Girdle of the Tidal Call: Waist/Mail: 506 Armor, +35 Strength, +30 Stamina, +20 Intellect, Equip: Improves critical strike rating by 33.

Gnarled Chestpiece of the Ancients: Chest/Leather: 404 Armor, +48 Stamina, +32 Intellect, +34 Spirit, Equip: Increases healing done by spells and effects by up to 110.

Ring of Sundered Souls: Finger: +45 Stamina, Equip: Increases defense rating by 18, Increases your dodge rating by 25.

Talon of Azshara: One-Hand/Sword: 177 - 329 Damage, Speed 2.70, (93.7 DPS), 168 Armor, +14 Agility, Equip: Improves hit rating by 19, Increases attack power by 40.

Mantle of the Tireless Tracker: Shoulder/Mail: 675 Armor, +22 Agility, +23 Intellect, Equip: Improves critical strike rating by 33, Increases attack power by 64.

Luminescent Rod of the Naaru: Wand: 180 - 336 Shadow Damage, Speed 1.50, (172.0 DPS), +13 Intellect, Equip: Increases healing done by spells and effects by up to 33, Restores 5 mana per 5 sec.

Warboots of Obliteration: Feet/Plate: 1105 Armor, +44 Strength, +29 Stamina, Equip: Improves critical strike rating by 31.

Illidari Shoulderpads: Shoulder/Cloth: 161 Armor, +34 Stamina +23 Intellect, Yellow Socket, Yellow Socket, Socket Bonus: +4 Stamina, Equip: Improves spell critical strike rating by 16, Increases damage and healing done by magical spells and effects by up to 39.

OVERVIEW

When compared to the other encounters in the zone, Morogrim Tidewalker is a fairly simple encounter, which is why many guilds decide to attempt him before Leotheras the Blind especially if they can bring an adequate raid composition to it. He has a frontal ability called Tidal Wave which deals frost damage and slows down the attack speed of affected targets, and periodically sends four players to the waterfalls in the middle of his room. There they will be frozen in place and take a large amount of damage before they are allowed to reenter combat. Periodically Morogrim uses his Earthquake ability which deals around 4000 damage to nearby players and alerts two packs of Murlocs. After killing the Murlocs, the raid can continue to damage Morogrim until the next Earthquake and Murloc spawn. Below 25%, Morogrim will stop sending people to the waterfalls, because the waterfall begins to spawn a number of watery globules which float toward the raid. He continues using his Earthquake ability and the Murloc reinforcements never cease until his death. This encounter does not have an enrage timer.

RAID COMPOSITION

A main tank and two secondary tanks, seven to eight healers and heavy area of effect damage classes. A total of seven Mages and Warlocks are sufficient, but the more that are available the easier the encounter becomes. Two shadow Priests are generally considered a requirement in order to replenish the mana of casters using area of effect spells.

CONSUMABLES

Low, with the exception of the main tank who should use a Flask of Fortification. Since this encounter tests the endurance and the depth of the mana pools of your caster classes come well stocked up with Super Mana Potions.

STRATEGY

The most important thing to remember about positioning Morogrim is that at all times, only the main tank should be in front of him, and therefore the only one hit by Tidal Wave. Apart from the 4000-5000 damage dealt by the ability, it also reduces melee attack speed, and therefore the tank's threat generation will be affected throughout the encounter. Raids can compensate by giving the tank Windfury totem. The first players will be sent to the watery graves 20 seconds into the encounter, with more following every 30 seconds. Healers must be assigned to the waterfalls, but they must stand a few feet away or be hit by the burst. Normally the watery grave explosion only deals between 4625 and 5375 damage, however, the selected player's spell damage is taken into account. Mages, Warlocks and shadow Priests are therefore always hit for more than that, often for more than 6000 damage. Additionally, after the burst, they may also take falling damage. Healers must therefore make sure they have full hit points before the burst, and enough hit points to survive the landing. Healing them back to full afterwards is recommended, since they cannot run back to the raid with less than 5000 hit points or risk being killed in one hit by Earthquake.

The first Earthquake occurs 40 seconds into the encounter. This brings the first two packs of Murlocs. Additional packs are summoned by the Earthquake every 45 seconds throughout the encounter. These packs, consisting of 6 Murlocs each, must be picked up by the two offtanks. It is very hard to build good aggro on so many targets, but Warriors must do their best using Demoralizing Shout and Thunderclap, while feral Druids and Paladins have a slightly easier

task with Swipe and Consecration. These two packs will converge on the raid, where Mages and Warlocks can kill them with AoE spells. It is recommended to wait a few seconds to give the offtanks a better chance of holding aggro. Once area of effect spells are started, they must be very coordinated. Everyone has to use them at the same time, and continue using them until all Murlocs are dead. Losing AoE classes to Murlocs will make further waves of Murlocs more and more difficult to deal with, so avoid that at all costs. Use rebirth to bring the casualties back to battle. Using soulstones on Mages before the encounter begins is also a good option. Positioning the bulk of the raid behind but in close proximity to Morogrim is very efficient, as AoE spells will damage him along with the Murlocs.

At 25% Morogrim stops sending targets to their watery graves and the healers assigned to those spots can now re-join the raid. Watery globules will spawn and float towards the raid. These cannot be targeted nor killed. They are mostly harmless, dealing minimal amounts of damage to players that they hit. The raid can shift further towards the entrance of the room to give the globules a longer travel time. Murlocs must be dealt with as before, until Morogrim dies. For a raid that has sustained heavy casualties, it is possible to offtank the last packs of Murlocs until Morogrim has died, or use challenging shout while casters use AoE spells to minimize further deaths.

TANKING

Due to the Tidal Wave ability it can be quite challenging to generate good aggro on Morogrim, but most of the time, his damage output results in enough rage for special abilities that can compensate for some of the drop in threat caused by the slowdown of melee attacks. Offtanks have a pretty challenging job with the large number of targets involved, but apart from Demoralizing Shout and Thunderclap, try to land a few normal attacks on every Murloc before the Mages and Warlocks start killing them.

HEALING

Two healers, ideally Druids, should be assigned to heal the players that are sent to their watery graves. Placing heals over time on them after the explosion ensures their health will be replenished before they re-join the raid. Prioritize Mages and Warlocks as their survival is essential to success in this encounter, and also because they take more damage than other classes.

Shamans using Chain Heal are excellent at healing the Earthquake damage, and their nature's swiftness can save the life of a caster who has attracted the attention of too many Murlocs. Paladins and holy Priests can be assigned to heal the main tank.

DPS

Be aware of your main tank's threat generation issues. shadow Priests particularly generate massive amounts of aggro. Apart from doing uninterrupted damage to Morogrim, they also generate a lot of healing aggro. Wait until the offtanks have built sufficient aggro before you start attacking the Murlocs. If you do not get healed immediately after a watery grave, stop and bandage yourself before rejoining the raid.

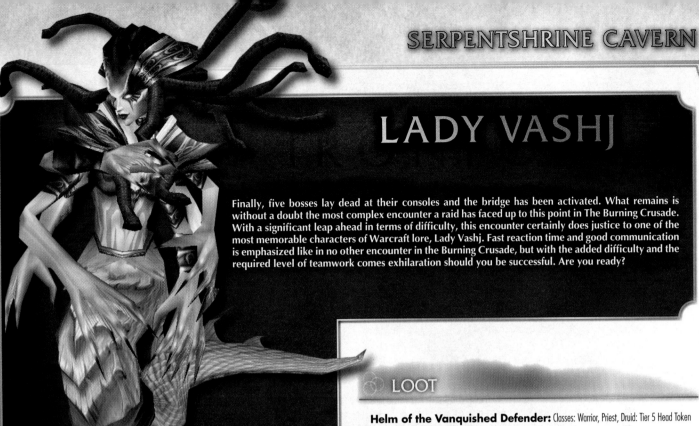

LADY VASHJ

Finally, five bosses lay dead at their consoles and the bridge has been activated. What remains is without a doubt the most complex encounter a raid has faced up to this point in The Burning Crusade. With a significant leap ahead in terms of difficulty, this encounter certainly does justice to one of the most memorable characters of Warcraft lore, Lady Vashj. Fast reaction time and good communication is emphasized like in no other encounter in the Burning Crusade, but with the added difficulty and the required level of teamwork comes exhilaration should you be successful. Are you ready?

ABILITIES

HP	4856000	Damage	11082-15653
Abilities	**Multi-Shot:** Strikes up to 5 targets for normal damage plus 6475 to 7525.		
	Forked Lightning: Inflicts 2313 to 2687 Nature damage in front of the caster.		
	Magic Barrier: Renders the target immune to all attacks and spells. Lady Vashj uses this ability during Phase 2.		
	Shock Blast: Inflicts 8325 to 9675 Nature damage and stuns for 5 sec.		
	Entangle: Inflicts 500 Nature damage every 2 sec. and immobilizes for up to 10 sec.		
	Static Charge: Deals 1619 to 1881 damage to surrounding allies every 2 sec.		
	Shoot: Between 8 and 40 yards, inflicting 13875 to 16125 Physical damage.		

LOOT

Helm of the Vanquished Defender: Classes: Warrior, Priest, Druid: Tier 5 Head Token

Helm of the Vanquished Champion: Classes: Paladin, Rogue, Shaman: Tier 5 Head Token

Helm of the Vanquished Hero: Classes: Hunter, Mage, Warlock: Tier 5 Head Token

Fang of Vashj: One-Hand/Dagger: 142 - 213 Damage, Speed 1.80, (98.6 DPS), +19 Stamina, Equip: Increases attack power by 54, Increases dagger skill rating by 21.

Lightfathom Scepter: Main Hand/Mace: 22 - 136 Damage, Speed 1.90, (41.4 DPS), +27 Stamina, +19 Intellect, Equip: Increases healing done by spells and effects by up to 431, Restores 10 mana per 5 sec.

Krakken-Heart Breastplate: Chest / Plate: 1728 Armor, +61 Strength, +43 Agility, +42 Stamina, Equip: Improves hit rating by 30.

Vestments of the Sea-Witch: Chest/Cloth: 231 Armor, +28 Stamina, +28 Intellect, Yellow Socket, Yellow Socket, Blue Socket, Socket Bonus: +5 Spell Damage, Equip: Improves spell hit rating by 27, Improves spell critical strike rating by 31, Increases damage and healing done by magical spells and effects by up to 57.

Coral Band of the Revived: Finger: +21 Stamina, +14 Intellect, +27 Spirit, Equip: Increases healing done by spells and effects by up to 75.

Runetotem's Mantle: Shoulder/ eather: 326 Armor, +31 Stamina, +22 Intellect, +32 Spirit, Equip: Increases healing done by spells and effects by up to 101.

Prism of Inner Calm: Trinket: Equip: Reduces the threat from your harmful critical strikes.

Ring of Endless Coils: Finger: +31 Stamina, Equip: Improves spell critical strike rating by 22, Increases damage and healing done by magical spells and effects by up to 37.

Serpent Spine Longbow: Bow: 214 - 321 Damage, Speed 3.00, (89.2 DPS), +15 Stamina, Equip: Improves critical strike rating by 15, Increases attack power by 38.

Belt of One-Hundred Deaths: Waist Leather: 244 Armor, +29 Agility, +25 Stamina, Red Socket, Blue Socket, Socket Bonus: +3 Agility, Equip: Increases attack power by 74, Increases dagger skill rating by 25, Increases sword skill rating by 25, Increases mace skill rating by 25, Increases fist skill rating by 25.

Cobra-Lash Boots: Feet:/Mail, 665 Armor, +33 Agility, +25 Stamina, +25 Intellect, Blue Socket, Red Socket, Socket Bonus: +3 Agility, Equip: Increases attack power by 66.

Glorious Gauntlets of Crestfall: Hands/Plate: 1080 Armor, +25 Stamina, +26 Intellect, Yellow Socket, Blue Socket, Socket Bonus: +7 Healing, Equip: Improves spell critical strike rating by 28, Increases healing done by spells and effects by up to 81.

Nether Vortex: Crafting Component:

Vashj's Vial Remnant: Quest Item: "Contains a small amount of water from the Well of Eternity."

OVERVIEW

The Lady Vashj encounter consists of three distinct stages. While she faces the raid alone during the first stage, the other two stages introduce a number of her minions, all with their own distinct abilities. Spawning at a rapid rate, the speed at which the raid deals with them is the key to this encounter. It will take several attempts for raids to learn how to deal with the adds, and several more to attain the level of execution that is required by the encountered, but do not be disheartened. Let's start at the beginning:

RAID COMPOSITION

Raid composition is fairly flexible for this encounter, apart from two tanks and seven to eight healers there are no specific class requirements.

CONSUMABLES

The consumable requirement for this encounter is high. Apart from the usual flasks for the tanks, the damage classes need to use flasks and oils to increase their damage to their maximum potential. Not because of damage that needs to be done to Vashj, but because otherwise a raid's kill speed will probably fall below the spawn rate of the adds in stage 2.

STAGE 1

The first phase of the Lady Vashj encounter is straightforward and should only take a few attempts for any raid to perfect. It starts upon engaging her and ends when she hits the 70% HP mark. Apart from her hitting the main tank rather vigorously, or shooting him with her bow and her Shock Blast ability, she has a number of secondary abilities that the raid must get accustomed to. Static Charge is an ability that can be placed on anyone in the raid. It deals 1619 to 1881 damage every 2 seconds to that target and all other targets in an 8 yard range for 20 seconds. With good positioning in a circle around Lady Vashj at the maximum range of abilities, Static Charge requires only minimum readjustment to make sure the player affected does not damage those around him.

Things get a little more complicated with the addition of her Entangle ability that roots all players in her melee range in place. If a rooted target is affected by Static Charge, a Paladin can cast Blessing of Freedom, to allow that target to move away and stop dealing damage to the other melee classes. If the main tank is affected by Static Charge, the only option is having all the other melee classes run away until the effect expires.

Lady Vashj will also occasionally use Multi-Shot, hitting three targets for up to 6000 damage. These must be healed rapidly to avoid deaths to multi-shot and Static Charge combinations. In order to minimize the effect of Shock Blast which deals 8325 to 9675 damage and stuns the tank, a Grounding totem can be placed in the main tank group.

STAGE 2

As she reaches 70% HP Lady Vashj runs to the middle of her platform and activates four shield barriers from the shield generator pillars around her. These make her immune to attacks and must be brought down in order to end stage 2. Just because Lady Vashj is immune to your attacks doesn't mean she cannot do damage. While she stops attacking the main tank, she begins using her Forked Lightning ability. She selects a target anywhere in the lair and hits every target in a cone around that target for 2313-2687 damage. This can sometimes be challenging to heal, especially if she selects targets that are near each other in succession. However, the main challenge of the second stage is defeating her minions that start spawning all around the edge of her platform.

The most common type of mob that spawns in this stage are Enchanted Elementals. With around 7000 health, these are very easy to kill. Also, they do not have an aggro table, and do not attempt to attack players. Instead, after spawning they start slowly moving towards Lady Vashj. If they reach her, they despawn and cast a spell on her called Surge. Surge increases her size and damage by 10%, and stacks. The buff persists into stage three. There several stacks will be lethal. It is imperative that she not be allowed to surge.

Coilfang Striders are a dangerous type of creature that spawns every 63 seconds during stage two. They hit extremely hard and can usually kill a player not wearing plate armor in one hit. It is impossible to tank them effectively because they pulse an AoE Fear in a short range around them. However, they move very slowly and should be further slowed down by Warlocks casting Curse of Exhaustion. With 170,000 HP they need to be killed as soon as possible and should be the focus of all the ranged DPS in the raid. While they can be tanked by a ranged class, such as a Warlock or Hunter, that isn't necessary. Apply Curse of Exhaustion, and DPS as hard as possible. If a player has aggro he can run away. While he is running he isn't generating any threat and therefore another ranged class will pull aggro off him. Repeat until the Strider is dead.

Coilfang Elites are Naga Warrior type of creatures similar to the Guardians in the Lurker Below event. With a powerful Cleave attack, players should always avoid standing in front of them. They can be tanked normally, and should be killed immediately after Striders are dead. Throughout stage two the raid has to kill Striders and Elites at a constant rate without falling behind.

A Tainted Elemental will spawn 60 seconds into stage three, and every 60 seconds after that. With a little more HP than enchanted elementals, these also have a Poison Bolt attack that can hit a random target anywhere in the area. The Poison Bolt's damage is insignificant, but it does serve the purpose of alerting the raid that a Tainted Elemental has spawned. These must be killed as soon as possible because they each drop a Tainted Core, which can be used to take down a shield generator.

Tainted Elementals will despawn less than 30 seconds after spawning, so they must be killed or the raid will have to wait for another one to spawn, extending the duration of stage two. Looting a Tainted Core makes a player unable to move but they can right click the Core in their inventory while targeting a friendly player, which will throw the Tainted Core to that player. Throwing a Tainted Core requires the target to be in line of sight and in range. It takes at least three people to get the Core to the generator: one to pick up the Core, one at the top of the stairs, and another one standing next to the generator pillar. Right clicking the pillar with a Tainted Core in your inventory will destroy the Core and power down that shield. Destroying a generator also reduces Lady Vashj's health by 5%. With all four shields brought down and Lady Vashj at 50% the spawn of creatures will stop and stage three begins.

STAGE 3

It is important to note that none of the mobs that have spawned during stage two despawn. They all need to be killed, and that is what the raid should be focusing on while the main tank picks up Vashj and starts building aggro. In this stage Spore Bats begin spawning and flying around the room above the raid. Their attacks do not cause direct damage, but a toxic pool will spawn at the feet of players that are targeted, dealing around 3000 damage every second to players that fail to move out of it. Around four minutes into the third stage, bats will start shooting players much more often, a mechanic that takes the place of an enrage timer. By the time the four minutes are up, Lady Vashj should be dead, or very close to dying.

Apart from the bats, stage three is identical to stage one in terms of abilities used, with the difference that these abilities will be doing more damage if any Enchanted Elementals reached her during stage two.

An important survival tip for the end of this encounter is that the toxic pools and their effects can be dealt with. Once the bats have started throwing massive amounts of Toxic Spores, the raid must keep moving at all times. Standing in one spot is no longer an option, as areas where players are standing will immediately be covered by toxic pools. However, if the tank keeps moving Vashj out of the pools, melee DPS classes can follow, while ranged classes and healers can also readjust. A raid on the move takes fairly little damage from the toxic pools and old pools will eventually despawn creating new safe areas. Healing on the move is of course a lot more challenging, but by using this strategy the raid can extend the encounter at least another minute during which they can finish off the last of her health.

TANKING

The encounter is not difficult for the tanks. Stage 1 is very straight forward, especially with grounding totems absorbing her most powerful attack, Shock Blast. Tanks need to pay attention and pick up the Coilfang Elites as soon as they spawn, as these will usually target healers. After they are picked up they need to be moved to the center of the room where all ranged classes can hit them. In stage three, the main tank needs to move Vashj quickly if he or any other melee class is the target of the spore bats and a toxic pool forms at their feet.

HEALING

The best healing assignments are location based, with two healers watching half of the raid each for Static Charge in stage one, and the rest of the healers on the main tank. For stage two, main tank healers can switch to the tank covering the Elites, with the other healers covering assigned areas and healing the ranged DPS. In stage three, just like in stage one, at least four healers need to focus on the main tank at all times.

DPS

Different assignments are possible based on raid composition. Hunters are particularly good at dealing with elementals in stage one, where the pet can contribute significant damage, especially for beast mastery Hunters. In a raid with four Hunters, they can easily control the elemental spawns for the whole room. In raids with fewer Hunters, melee classes are usually assigned to deal with the elementals, since they cannot do any damage to the Striders and can get cleaved by the Elites. A raid with a good number of ranged classes can alternate between killing Striders and Elites without having more than two up at the same time. For the last stage it is usually best to ignore bats and focus all damage on her, and even with a few losses a raid will do enough damage to kill her before the bats become a problem.

QUEST

THE VIALS OF ETERNITY

Quest Level	70
Location	Serpentshrine Cavern / Tempest Keep
Starts at	Soridormi, Caverns of Time
Ends at	Soridormi, Caverns of Time
Goal	Obtain Vashj's Vial Remnant and Kael's Vial Remnant to gain access to the Caverns of Time.

Soridormi
<The Scale of Sands>

Chances are that this quest has been in your log for a few months. Some progress on it has been long overdue. By picking up Vashj's Vial Remnant, which is available to every player in the raid, you are now half-way to being attuned to Mount Hyjal. Only Kael'Thas Sunstrider remains in your way. Onwards, to Tempest Keep!

TEMPEST KEEP: THE EYE

Home to the Lord of the Blood Elves, Kael'thas Sunstrider, The Eye is the largest of the ensemble of Naaru fortresses that are floating through the twisting nether, on the eastern end of Netherstorm.

In terms of raid progression, the dungeon is on the same tier with Serpentshrine Cavern, and should be the focus of guilds that have completed Karazhan, Magtheridon and Gruul's Lair. While compared to these instances it is a step upwards in terms of difficulty and rewards, it is just another stepping stone towards the last tier of raiding in The Burning Crusade, which consists of Mount Hyjal and The Black Temple.

Progression through the instance is non-linear, with the raid being given the choice of what order to attempt the first three encounters. However, defeating all three is required before the raid can meet Prince Kael'Thas Sunstrider.

DUNGEON INFORMATION

Location	Twisting Nether, Netherstorm
Region	Contested
Quests	Alliance and Horde
Suggested Level	70 (25-person raid)
Enemy Types	Humanoid, Mechanical, Dragonhawk
Time to Complete	4 hours

MAP OF TEMPEST KEEP: THE EYE

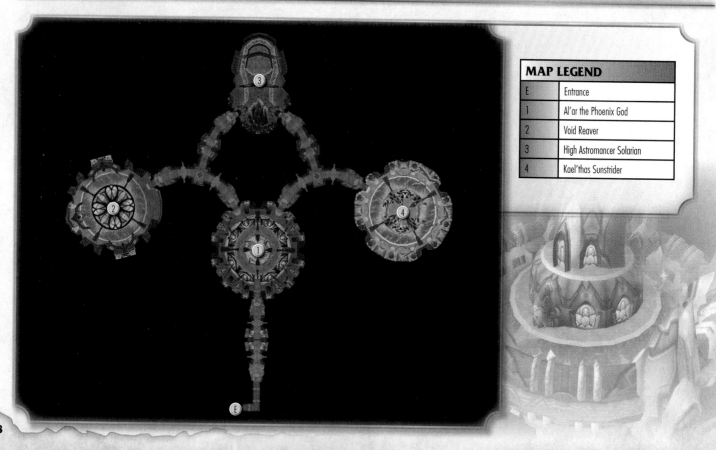

MAP LEGEND

E	Entrance
1	Al'ar the Phoenix God
2	Void Reaver
3	High Astromancer Solarian
4	Kael'thas Sunstrider

QUEST CHAIN

While completing the attunement quest that has been in place since the release of the Burning Crusade is no longer required to enter Tempest Keep, this long series of quests is still available to players seeking a challenge and an insight in the storyline behind Tempest Keep.

Upon completing the Cipher of Damnation quest line in Shadowmoon Valley, players receive a letter from Khadgar, summoning them to Shattrah City. Here, A'dal will offer three quests in three heroic mode 5-man instances, also known as the Trials of the Naaru.

For "Trial of the Naaru: Mercy" players must complete The Shattered Halls in Hellfire Citadel, on heroic mode, against a 55 minute timer that starts after defeating the first boss in the zone, Grand Warlock Nethekurse.

"Trial of the Naaru: Strength" is a two-part quest. It first takes players to heroic mode Shadow Labyrinth in Auchindoun where they must defeat Murmur, then sends them to destroy the leader of the Coilfang Steamvaults in Zangarmarsh, Warlord Kalithresh.

Finally, in order to complete "Trial of the Naaru: Tenacity" players must venture to the Arcatraz in Tempest Keep and rescue the gnome, Millhouse Manastorm, once again using the heroic setting for the dungeon's difficulty.

After completing all three trials, A'dal will give players a final task, defeating the pit lord Magtheridon in the 25-man wing of Hellfire Citadel. A follow-up quest with substantial rewards is soon to be implemented to reward players that have completed the now obsolete attunement quest line.

THE INNOCUOUS INHABITANTS

Upon zoning in the raid is faced with a number of Blood Elf groups, guarding the tunnel that leads to Al'ar's room. While these are not very difficult to defeat, the lack of available room in the narrow tunnel together with their many area of effect spells, can sometimes cause problems.

The stationary packs consist of Star Scryers, Astromancers, Bloodwarder Vindicators and Legionnaires. Star Scryers and Astromancers use powerful area of effect spells such as Starfall and Fireball Volley, and should be crowd controlled on the pull by mages using polymorph. Legionnaires can also be polymorphed, but for raids lacking mages they can be offtanked away from the raid to prevent them from cleaving or whirlwinding several players at once. Finally, Bloodwarder Vindicators must be picked up by tanks and killed first, since they cannot be controlled by players.

Once the first pack has been defeated the raid must wait for the Marshall to patrol to them and engage them before proceeding down the corridor. Place the Marshall away from the raid to avoid his whirlwind, while taking down the Squires.

With all the humanoid packs out of the way, the raid will reach a large open room that acts as a hub for the rest of the instance. Al'ar the Phoenix God circles the room, far above the ground. Do not worry about engaging him by accident, as the only way to start the encounter is to attack him directly.

Two patrols consisting of two Tempest Falconers and several Phoenix-Hawk Hatchlings guard the ground level of the room, while 4 fully grown Phoenix-Hawks circle the top level of the room. For the Falconer packs crowd control as many of the Hatchlings as possible using polymorph, and offtank the remaining ones while killing the two Falconers. The larger Phoenix-Hawks above them must be killed one by one. They have a powerful "dive" ability which attacks the furthest target in their range. Because it also mana burns nearby targets, it is best to have a tank stand away from the raid in order to take the damage from dive while the rest of the raid kills the Phoenix-Hawk rapidly.

With the room cleared, the raid now has the option to attempt Al'ar the Phoenix God, or continue on, either through the western corridor towards Void Reaver or through the eastern corridor, towards the High Astromancer Solarian.

TIME IS PRECIOUS

Remember that throughout the entire zone creatures will respawn two hours after they are killed, unless the nearest boss has been defeated.

LOOT

Bark-Gloves of Ancient Wisdom: Hands/Leather: 252 Armor, +28 Stamina, +25 Intellect, +33 Spirit, Equip: Increases healing done by spells and effects by up to 73.

Seventh Ring of the Tirisfalen: Finger: +37 Stamina, Equip: Increases defense rating by 17, Increases your shield block rating by 24, Increases the block value of your shield by 24.

Mantle of the Elven Kings: Shoulder/Cloth: 161 Armor, +27 Stamina, +18 Intellect, +17 Spirit, Equip: Improves spell hit rating by 18, Improves spell critical strike rating by 25, Increases damage and healing done by magical spells and effects by up to 39.

Fire-Cord of the Magus: Waist/Cloth: 121 Armor, +21 Stamina, +23 Intellect, Equip: Improves spell critical strike rating by 30, Increases damage done by Fire spells and effects by up to 60.

Bands of the Celestial Archer: Wrist / Mail: 394 Armor, +17 Agility, +24 Intellect, Equip: Improves critical strike rating by 17, Increases attack power by 48.

Girdle of the Fallen Stars: Waist / Mail: 506 Armor, +26 Stamina, +18 Intellect, Yellow Socket, Yellow Socket, Socket Bonus: +7 Healing, Equip: Increases healing done by spells and effects by up to 73, Restores 10 mana per 5 sec.

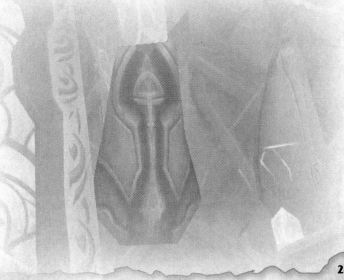

AL'AR THE PHOENIX GOD

Al'ar, one of Prince Kael'thas Sunstrider's most prized possessions is the first encounter players will be able to access after setting foot in Tempest Keep. However, most raids choose to avoid him at first due to his difficult learning curve and effort required.

Contrary to popular belief, while it is a difficult encounter requiring careful execution, defeating Al'ar does not require any specific gear, such as fire resistant armor, as was believed initially.

ABILITIES

HP	3035200	Damage	11789-16669
Abilities	**Flame Quills:** Incinerates the upper platform in Al'ar's chambers, dealing 6563 to 8437 Fire damage per tick.		
	Flame Buffet: Deals 1750 to 2250 Fire damage to all enemy targets in Al'ar's chamber and increases Fire damage taken by 10% for 10 sec. This ability is only used when no one is in melee range of Al'ar.		
	Rebirth: Deals 4375 to 5625 Fire damage and heals Al'ar to full health. This signals the start of Phase 2 of the encounter. Note that Al'ar uses Rebirth again later in the fight, but later uses do not heal him.		
	Flame Patch: Deals 2188 to 2812 Fire damage and increases Fire damage taken by 20% for 20 sec.		
	Meteor: Deals 5700 to 6300 Fire damage to all targets in a 10 yard area of effect.		
	Charge: Inflicts 4500 to 5500 Fire damage and stuns for 3 sec.		
	Melt Armor: Reduces armor by 80% for 1 minute.		

LOOT

Talon of Al'ar: Trinket: Equip: Your Arcane Shot ability increases the damage dealt by all other damaging shots by 40 for 6 sec.

Talisman of the Sun King: Off-hand: +27 Stamina, +24 Intellect, Equip: Increases healing done by spells and effects by up to 59, Restores 6 mana per 5 sec.

Band of Al'ar: Ring: +24 Stamina, +23 Intellect, Equip: Increases damage and healing done by magical spells and effects by up to 37.

Gloves of the Searing Grip: Leather: 252 Armor, +33 Agility, +37 Stamina, Equip: Increases attack power by 66. Increases sword, fist, mace and dagger skill rating by 18.

Phoenix-Wing Cloak: Cloth: 108 Armor, +37 Stamina, Equip: Increases defense rating by 22, Increases your dodge rating by 27.

Mindstorm Wristbands: Cloth: 94 Armor, +13 Stamina, +13 Intellect, Equip: Improves spell critical strike rating by 23, Increases damage and healing done by magical spells and effects by up to 36.

Arcanite Steam-Pistol: Gun: 171 - 319 Damage, Speed 2.90, (84.5 dps), +19 Agility, Equip: Improves hit rating by 17.

Phoenix-Ring of Rebirth: Ring: +24 Intellect, Equip: Increases healing done by spells and effects by up to 55. Restores 10 mana per 5 sec.

Fire Crest Breastplate: Mail: 900 Armor, +36 Stamina, +34 Intellect, Equip: Improves spell critical strike rating by 34. Increases healing done by spells and effects by up to 81. Restores 10 mana per 5 sec.

Tome of Fiery Redemption: Trinket: Classes: Paladin, Equip: Each time you cast a spell, there is chance you will gain up to 290 spell damage and healing.

Netherbane: One-Handed Axe: 170 - 317 Damage, Speed 2.60, (93.7 dps), +24 Agility, +19 Stamina, Equip: Increases attack power by 38.

Claw of the Phoenix: Off hand, Fist Weapon: 98 – 183 Damage, Speed 1.50, (93.7 dps), +20 Agility, +28 Stamina, Equip: Increases attack power by 38.

Talon of the Phoenix: Main Hand, Fist Weapon: 177 – 329 Damage, Speed 2.70, (93.7 dps), Equip: Improves hit rating by 14, Improves critical strike rating by 19, Increases attack power by 48.

OVERVIEW

Al'ar is a fairly difficult and time consuming encounter when compared to other early bosses in Serpentshrine Cavern or Tempest Keep, which is why he is routinely skipped in favor of Void Reaver. The encounter consists of two different stages, both in which the tanks play the key role and bear most of the responsibility for success or failure. During the first stage Al'ar flies around the room summoning Embers of Al'ar until he is defeated. The phoenix will then rise from its own ashes, starting the second stage, during which it uses a completely different set of abilities while being tanked on the ground floor of his large room.

Ruse of the Ashtongue is part of the Black Temple attunement quest line. To prove his allegiance to Illidan, Akama is tasked to send his Ashtongue followers into Tempest Keep to slay Al'ar. By using magical Ashtongue Cowls that disguise players as followers of Akama, you must now perform Illidan's bidding.

QUEST

RUSE OF THE ASHTONGUE

Quest Level:	70
Location:	Tempest Keep
Starts at:	Akama, Warden's Cage, Shadowmoon Valley
Ends at:	Akama
Goal:	Kill Al'ar while disguised as an Ashtongue

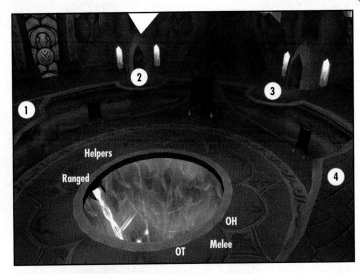

RAID COMPOSITION

Three tanks are the bare minimum for this encounter, but a fourth backup tank is highly recommended. Seven healers are usually sufficient, with the rest of the raid consisting of DPS classes. Fire specialized mages are not recommended since Al'ar is fire immune. A number of melee-unfriendly abilities discourage heavy melee DPS based raids, leaving hunters, warlocks and shadow priests as the best choices for this encounter.

CONSUMABLES

A 10 minute enrage timer starts with Al'ar's rebirth at the beginning of the second stage, so DPS classes should consider using consumables. Tanks are also encouraged to use them due to the high amount of damage taken, and the fact that the loss of a tank usually results in a raid wipe.

THE PULL

Before pulling Al'ar, tanks must be in position on the platforms on the top level of the room. Al'ar can be engaged either by a tank using his ranged weapon or a hunter shooting him from the ground level. No matter who engages Al'ar, he will always fly to the platform on the western side of the room first. For more details see the positioning diagram.

STRATEGY

Starting at the western platform after the pull, Al'ar will periodically switch to the next platform in a clockwise direction. Unless she has a target in melee range to attack, Al'ar will perform her Flame Buffet ability. This inflicts 1750-2250 fire damage to every player in the raid, and places a debuff on them that increases fire damage taken by 10% per stack. This is why a tank must always wait for her on the platform she is about to fly to, at all times. For ranged classes, threat is not an issue during this stage, as Al'ar ignores all targets standing on the lower level of her room. This is where healers also have to be positioned, as their healing spells can reach the tanks on the top level if they are positioned at the edge of the platform.

After reaching the fourth tanking position on the eastern side of the room, the next transition will be across the room, restarting at position one. During platform transitions Al'ar can summon Embers of Al'ar. These must be picked up by the offtank on the ground level. Killing an Ember of Al'ar reduces her hit points by 3%, but these also explode upon dying causing massive damage and knocking back every player in their vicinity.

Periodically in stage one, Al'ar will fly high in the air, in the middle of her room and perform her Flame Quills ability. This engulfs the top level of the room in flames, killing all the tanks that do not jump down fast enough. After a Flame Quill, tanks must hurry back to the top level to tank Al'ar again, preventing Flame Buffet damage.

Overall, when compared to the second stage, the first stage is quite easy. First of all, ensure that casters are close to full mana at the end of stage one. Since the first stage has no time limit and there is very little raid-wide damage, a good option is not killing any Embers of Al'ar, and bringing her down only by direct damage. Multiple Embers can be offtanked by a single offtank, perhaps as many as 15, but Al'ar will usually be dead by the time 10 adds are being offtanked. Melee DPS classes should attack the Embers and reduce all their hit points to around the 15% mark, while being careful not to kill one by accident. The offtank should always mark the active target for the rogues, to minimize aggro issues. With 8-10 adds at low health, Al'ar usually dies, ending stage one.

The raid must now clear the center of the room, where Al'ar will be reborn, and let the tanks pick her up. AoE damage capable classes should now head towards the offtank, and use their ranged AoE abilities (Blizzard, Seed of Corruption) to quickly kill off the adds. The offtank needs to use Shield Wall as soon as the adds are about to die, or he will be killed by the series of explosions. If executed well, even with only eight adds, Al'ar will be immediately reduced to 76% of his health, giving the raid a good head start on the enrage timer.

At least two tanks must keep Al'ar under control during this stage. Once again, if there is no target in melee range, Al'ar performs her Flame Buffet, which does very significant amounts of damage to the raid. Periodically she casts Melt Armor on her primary target which will drastically increase the damage taken by that tank. Another tank must then taunt her, until Melt Armor has worn off the main tank one minute later.

Periodically Al'ar will charge a random target in the raid and inflict around 5,000 damage, which requires every player to be as close to full hit points as possible, at all times. This also helps save the lives of players affected by Flame Patch, a circle of flames that is placed on the ground about every 30 seconds, which inflicts 2188-2812 fire damage every second to players standing in it. It also increases the fire damage taken by players from subsequent attacks.

However, Al'ar's trademark ability during the second stage is Meteor. Periodically, he will turn into a huge fireball which targets a random player and inflict 5,000 fire damage to everyone in its area of effect. Spreading out during meteor ensures only one player is affected by its damage. Al'ar re-emerges from the Meteor's ashes and with him two Embers of Al'ar. After they are picked up by the offtank, these can be killed by the ranged DPS classes, while melee classes do direct damage to Al'ar. Like their counterparts in stage one, these Embers also explode, but careful positioning will ensure the offtank is the only one taking the damage. With all ranged DPS on Embers it is possible to kill both off until the next meteor when two more will spawn. Maintain this pace, and killing Al'ar within the enrage timer should be no problem.

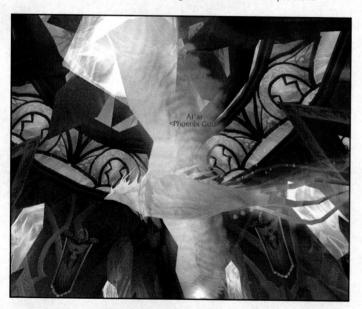

Al'ar
<Phoenix God>

TANKS

Success in both stages rests upon your shoulders more than upon any other class. During the first stage it is imperative to pay attention to Al'ar's movement and jump down as soon as you see her reach the top of her room. Flame Quill consists of five bursts of flame, so as soon as you have seen the last one, rush up to minimize the time she is not tanked and inflicting Flame Buffet damage to the raid.

During the second stage, apart from taunting off the target affected by Melt Armor, you must always be ready to reposition Al'ar in case a Flame Patch is cast on the ground under her. This allows the melee DPS classes to continue doing damage.

As the offtank you need to communicate, both with your healer announcing your movement when you need to pick up an Ember that spawned across the room, and with the DPS classes attacking the Embers. Remember that Embers always follow you as you move through the raid, but an Ember's death in the middle of the raid can potentially kill off several people. Let DPS classes know when they need to stop doing damage.

HEALING

Stage one healing is extremely easy. Have one healer assigned to the Ember offtank and one additional healer under the platform Al'ar is about to transition to in order to heal the next tank.

During the second stage it is important to spread out around the room, to avoid having several people take damage at the same time from Flame Patches or Meteors. Healing is also much more intensive, and the pressure to keep everyone at maximum health is much higher. Main tank healers must also pay attention to the frequent tank changes, as the offtank will taunt off the tank affected by Melt Armor.

DPS

Again, stage one is extremely straightforward as threat on Al'ar is not an issue. Do not kill off any Embers at this stage, as killing them in the second stage is much more beneficial to the raid.

During the second stage spread out and bandage if you are not at full health, to relieve the pressure on your healers. Do mind your aggro during this stage, as it is possible to draw Al'ar's attention from the main tank to yourself.

IT IS ALWAYS DARKEST...

The tunnel towards Void Reaver is guarded mostly by mechanical opponents. Crystalcore Sentinels should be approached from range, as they trample targets in melee range as well as cast a powerful Arcane Explosion. Their Overcharge ability is extremely damaging but can be spell reflected by the tank.

All humanoid Tempest Smiths need to be polymorphed until all other enemies are defeated, as they will boost the damage done by the mechanical units and also have a powerful fragmentation bomb attack that also stuns targets.

Crystalcore Mechanics are demon-type creatures and can therefore be banished. They will otherwise throw Saw Blades at players in a cone around a randomly selected target. These inflict over 3500 damage upon hitting their target and another 1200 over 2 seconds after that.

Since humanoids and demons can be crowd-controlled by the raid, for all the packs of enemies in the tunnel, as well as in Void Reaver's room that must be fully cleared, the kill order should be mechanical units first, then demons, and finally humanoids.

VOID REAVER

Void Reaver is a very popular choice of encounter for guilds working their way through Serpentshrine Cavern and Tempest Keep. He is easier to defeat than any other early encounter in either zone, and his loot is easily among the best, certainly when compared to Al'ar or High Astromancer Solarian.

Most guilds should be able to defeat him after only one day of learning how to deal with him, at the end of which they will be rewarded with two Tier 5 shoulder piece tokens, and a third random epic item.

ABILITIES

HP	4552500	Damage	8866-12522
Abilities	**Pounding**: Damages all in an 18 yard radius for 1350 to 2250 Arcane damage.		
	Arcane Orb: Deals 4675 to 6325 Arcane damage to all targets in a 20 yard radius and silences them for 6 sec.		
	Berserk: Increases attack speed by 150% and damage by 500%.		

LOOT

Pauldrons of the Vanquished Champion: Tier 5 shoulder token (Paladin, Rogue, Shaman)

Pauldrons of the Vanquished Defender: Tier 5 shoulder token (Warrior, Priest, Druid)

Pauldrons of the Vanquished Hero: Tier 5 shoulder token (Hunter, Mage, Warlock)

Cowl of the Grand Engineer: Head/Cloth: 175 Armor, +22 Stamina, +27 Intellect, Yellow Socket, Yellow Socket, Blue Socket, Socket Bonus: +5 Spell Damage, Equip: Improves spell hit rating by 16, Improves spell critical strike rating by 35, Increases damage and healing done by magical spells and effects by up to 53.

Fel Reaver's Piston: Trinket: Equip: Your direct healing spells have a chance to place a heal over time on your target, healing 500 over 12 sec, Restores 16 mana per 5 sec.

Girdle of Zaetar: Waist/Leather: 227 Armor, +22 Stamina, +23 Intellect, +24 Spirit, Blue Socket, Blue Socket, Socket Bonus: +7 Healing, Equip: Increases healing done by spells and effects by up to 73.

Void Reaver Greaves: Legs/Mail: 787 Armor, +37 Agility, +33 Stamina, +24 Intellect, Red Socket, Yellow Socket, Blue Socket, Socket Bonus: +4 Agility, Equip: Increases attack power by 88.

Fel-Steel Warhelm: Head Plate: 1306 Armor, +46 Strength, +46 Stamina, Equip: Improves hit rating by 30, Improves critical strike rating by 44.

Warp-Spring Coil: Trinket: Class: Rogue, Equip: Improves hit rating by 21, Your special attacks have a chance to give you 1000 armor penetration for 15 sec.

Wristguards of Determination: Wrist/Plate: 703 Armor, +37 Stamina, Equip: Increases defense rating by 24, Increases your dodge rating by 19, Increases your shield block rating by 13.

OVERVIEW

Void Reaver is a one-stage encounter, a boss that uses the same abilities from 100% to 0%. He is not particularly friendly to melee classes as he periodically stops attacking and pounds every target in his close proximity. Targets at range are not safe either, due to his Arcane Orb ability which can inflict up to 6,000 damage to players in a 20 yard radius of the explosion, and temporarily prevent them from casting spells. Tanks and their healers are also kept on their toes by his single target knock back ability which permanently reduces the threat of his current target, often resulting in aggro changing to a secondary tank. A 10 minute enrage timer requires the majority of the raid to survive until the end, to ensure the raid group has enough DPS to cause the Void Reaver's timely demise.

RAID COMPOSITION

Due to his knock back ability, three tanks are required for this encounter. A melee-heavy group is extremely healing intensive, so bringing more than four melee classes is not recommended. Like with most encounters on this tier of raiding, seven healers seem to be optimal. Complete the raid with ranged DPS classes.

CONSUMABLES

Consumables are generally not needed but DPS classes can use them in the eventuality that the raid cannot defeat Void Reaver before he reaches his 10 minute enrage timer.

POSITIONING

Good positioning on this encounter is easy to achieve, mainly due to the large amount of space available to the raid. Tank Void Reaver as close to the center of the room as possible, with the raid spread out in a circle around him, at the maximum range of their abilities. While players in the 5-man groups should be standing relatively close to facilitate healing and benefit from totems and auras, they should not be grouped up too closely to minimize the risk of being hit by Arcane Orb.

STRATEGY

With the raid already in position around the room, start by misdirecting the main tank. Everyone should start attacking as soon as possible.

His two main damage abilities are both on very short cooldowns, so the raid experiences both early in the encounter.

Pounding is used every 12 seconds, and inflicts 1350 to 2250 arcane damage every second to targets in an 18 yard range of Void Reaver, who will pound the ground for 3 seconds at a time. Melee classes have the option to run out to avoid the damage, then run back in and do about 10 seconds of damage before running out again, or, in the case of a healer-heavy raid, stay in and attack even while taking the damage. A shaman's chain heal ability is an excellent choice for healing a melee group that takes damage from pounding.

Arcane Orb cannot target players in melee range, so avoiding it is only an issue for ranged DPS classes and healers. Orbs do significant damage, anywhere between 4675 and 6325, and affect every target in a 20 yard range. Because the affected targets are unable to cast spells for 6 seconds, this can easily result in deaths, especially when considering that Orbs can be fired every 3 seconds.

Therefore, avoid taking damage at all costs. The easiest way to avoid it is to watch Void Reaver's target. He will always de-select the tank, and select a secondary ranged target. About 5 seconds later he launches the slow-moving Arcane Orb towards that target's initial position. Therefore, once you are selected as an Arcane Orb target start moving immediately, and have all players around you move as well. Please bear in mind that because of latency, the visual effect of the Orb moving towards you is not always consistent with the timing of its explosion and the area of effect. The only way to make absolutely sure you are not hit by an Arcane Orb is to move at least 15-20 yards, as soon as you are targeted. As a general not, avoid grouping up, because the more people are grouped up, the more likely Void Reaver is to target a player in that area, causing everyone to move, thus being unable to heal or do damage while running. Always being spread out ensures that generally only one target needs to move to avoid an Arcane Orb.

Void Reaver's knockback adds another dimension to this encounter. With the tank's threat being periodically reduced, pulling aggro as a DPS class becomes a very real possibility. Because of his enrage timer, slowing down damage is not a real option, and the raid must consider other means of keeping aggro on the tanks at all times.

First of all, as far as tanks and offtanks are concerned, build maximum threat at all times, whether you are main tanking or offtanking. The damage taken while Void Reaver is pounding should generate a good amount of rage that can be converted into more threat. After the main tank has been misdirected on the pull, Hunters should use Misdirect on one of the offtanks every time their cooldown has expired. The challenge here is not to ensure that the main tank keeps aggro at all times, that is impossible since all his accumulated threat will be periodically reduced, but that when he does lose aggro, an offtank is second on Void Reaver's threat list.

Obviously, all DPS classes should use their threat reducing abilities, Rogues should Vanish, Hunters should Feign Death often, Warlocks can Soulshatter while Mages can use Invisibility. Generally, with tanks building good threat, using a threat wiping ability once during the encounter, with Void Reaver around the 50% mark, should be enough.

This leaves shadow Priests as the unfortunate class that does not have an ability to reduce accumulated threat. Due to the damage done and group healing done to targets that have taken Arcane Orb damage, shadow Priests are always in danger of pulling aggro. Especially towards the end of the encounter when the tanks have been knocked back multiple times. There is no real solution to the problem, but in order to reduce healing threat Vampiric Embrace healing can be turned off. Using a soulstone on shadow Priests before the encounter is started ensures that they can rejoin the battle even after being killed by an angry Void Reaver.

TANKING

While the damage taken by off-spec tanks does not prevent them from being viable tanks for this encounter, their reduced threat generation certainly does. Apart from a heavy protection or feral specialization, gear selection should emphasize threat generation over mitigation. Also, adding additional tanks does not necessarily make the encounter easier. With 4 tanks (or more) the threat reducing knockback occurs less often on a particular tank, but tanks will also take their turn to main tank less often. Adding tanks also increases the requirement for healing, while reducing the available spots for DPS classes which makes the encounter last longer.

HEALING

One healer per 5 man group should be more than enough, therefore group healers can also keep an eye on the tanks, together with the dedicated tank healers. Shamans make very good healers for the melee and tank groups, where they can also provide windfury totem to help with threat generation. As a healer, avoid being hit by Arcane Orb, as this will make you unable to heal for 6 seconds, putting your assigned group or tank at risk.

DPS

As a melee DPS class in a raid where you have to run out to avoid pounding damage the challenge is to learn to estimate the range and timing of pounding. Running out too soon reduces you DPS output, running out too late makes you take too much damage. Moving too far away makes you a potential target for Arcane Orb, which can endanger you and all the melee classes around you, so try not to run further than 20 yards from the boss.

As a ranged DPS class your task is to maximize your damage output while avoiding all Arcane Orbs. If you do get hit, as a caster you have nothing to do for 6 seconds since you are silenced, so take the time to bandage yourself so you can survive if you are hit a second time. Do not forget to use your threat reducing abilities and soon you and your raid group will be facing the pleasant dilemma of distributing some high quality pieces of loot.

...BEFORE THE DAWN.

The raid must now make their way back to Al'ar's room where they must take the eastern tunnel, towards High Astromancer Solarian. The packs guarding the way are easier to defeat than those protecting Void Reaver.

The large caster groups can easily be tanked by a protection Paladin and then brought down by area of effect spells. Once in Solarian's room all the caster groups on the room's perimeter must be cleared, as well as the two patrols. Do not underestimate them, even if they only consist of 3 mobs, these can mind control several players at a time. Always do the patrols without pulling additional mobs.

HIGH ASTROMANCER SOLARIAN

Despite her short list of abilities and simple mechanics, Solarian is not an easy encounter. Most importantly she is almost impossible to defeat without encounter-specific gear crafted for at least 2 players in the raid. Because of this, her positioning in the instance, and her less than spectacular loot she is usually attempted last, once Void Reaver and Al'ar have been defeated.

LOOT

Heartrazor: One-Hand/Dagger: 118 - 219 Damage, Speed 1.80, (93.6 dps), +18 Agility, +25 Stamina.

Chance on hit: Increases attack power by 270 for 10 sec.

Trousers of the Astromancer: Legs/Cloth: 188 Armor, +33 Stamina, +36 Intellect, +22 Spirit, Blue Socket, Yellow Socket, Blue Socket, Socket Bonus: +5 Spell Damage, Equip: Increases damage and healing done by magical spells and effects by up to 54.

Star-Strider Boots: Feet/Mail: 619 Armor, +33 Agility, +13 Stamina, +18 Intellect, Blue Socket, Blue Socket, Socket Bonus: +6 Attack Power, Equip: Increases attack power by 66, Restores 4 mana per 5 sec.

Star-Soul Breeches: Legs/Cloth: 188 Armor, +27 Stamina, +27 Intellect, +52 Spirit, Equip: Increases healing done by spells and effects by up to 101.

Vambraces of Ending: Wrist Leather: 177 Armor, +24 Agility, +24 Stamina, Blue Socket, Socket Bonus: +4 Attack Power, Equip: Increases attack power by 52.

Wand of the Forgotten Star: Wand: 180 - 336 Shadow Damage, Speed 1.50, (172.0 dps), Equip: Improves spell hit rating by 9, Improves spell critical strike rating by 13, Increases damage and healing done by magical spells and effects by up to 21.

Boots of the Resilient: Feet/Plate: 1105 Armor, +51 Stamina, Red Socket, Yellow Socket, Socket Bonus: +4 Stamina, Equip: Increases defense rating by 25, Increases your shield block rating by 25.

Worldstorm Gauntlets: Hands/Mail: 562 Armor, +21 Stamina, +22 Intellect, Blue Socket, Yellow Socket, Socket Bonus: +4 Stamina, Equip: Improves spell critical strike rating by 15, Increases healing done by spells and effects by up to 73, Restores 9 mana per 5 sec.

Ethereum Life-Staff: Two-Hand/Staff: 143 - 301 Damage, Speed 3.20, (69.4 dps), +41 Stamina, +40 Intellect, +60 Spirit, Equip: Increases healing done by spells and effects by up to 386.

Girdle of the Righteous Path: Waist/Plate: 904 Armor, +27 Stamina, +33 Intellect, Equip: Improves spell critical strike rating by 27. Increases healing done by spells and effects by up to 77.

Solarian's Sapphire: Trinket: Classes: Warrior +30 Stamina, Equip: Your Battle Shout ability grants an additional 70 attack power.

Void Star Talisman: Trinket: Classes: Warlock, Equip: Increases your pet's resistances by 130 and increases your spell damage by up to 48.

Greaves of the Bloodwarder: Legs/Plate: 1406 Armor, +49 Strength, +46 Stamina, Red Socket, Yellow Socket, Blue Socket, Socket Bonus: +4 Strength, Equip: Improves critical strike rating by 31.

ABILITIES

HP	3035000	Damage	6156-8696
Abilities	**Blinding Light:** Inflicts 2280-2520 Arcane damage.		
	Mark of Solarian: Reduces Arcane Resistance by 15 for 2 minutes.		
	Wrath of the Astromancer: Causes target to harm nearby allies for 5400 to 6600 Arcane damage after 6 sec.		
	Arcane Missiles: Inflicts 3000 Arcane damage.		
	Summon Astromancer Adds: Summons several minions.		
	Solarian Transform: Transforms Solarian into a Void Lord.		
	Void Bolt: Inflicts 4394 to 5106 Shadow damage. Used after transforming.		
	Psychic Scream: Causes up to 5 creatures to run in fear for 4 sec. Used after transforming.		

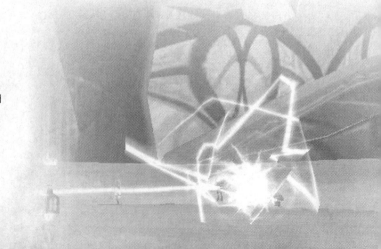

OVERVIEW

Despite the fact that the encounter has 3 stages, Solarian is one of the shortest, fastest-paced encounters in the Burning Crusade. Whether the raid defeats her, or she turns out triumphant, the encounter will be over in well under 10 minutes. During stage one the raid takes vast amounts of arcane damage. In the alternating stage two, the raid will have to deal with two Solarium Priests and 12 Solarium Agents before the Astromancer returns. At 20% Solarian transforms into her void walker form, and uses shadow-based spells until her death.

RESISTANCE GEAR

A variety of strategies exist for Solarian, and they all revolve around different strategies for dealing with the arcane damage done in stage one. It is certainly possible to defeat Solarian using absolutely no resist gear and a raid group heavily skewed towards damage classes that can bring her down before the raid loses too many players. Conversely, it is possible to gear out every player in the raid with around 200 arcane resistance, which makes her damage healable for a long time, gives the raid better control of the encounter, but also makes it last significantly longer.

Arcane resistance gear also does not grow on trees, and gearing up a full raid can be an expensive, time-consuming process. This guide suggests a middle of the road strategy that gives the raid significant control of the encounter, at the cost of gearing up only two players with arcane resistance. However, for these two players the "shopping list" is extensive, as they will benefit from arcane resistance past the traditional cap of 365. Around 450 arcane resistance should be the target for these two players. Due to talents such as improved defensive stance, and their ability to use last stand and shield wall, protection warriors are an ideal choice for arcane resistance tanks.

ARCANE RESISTANCE GEAR

SLOT	ITEM	TRADE SKILL	ARCANE RESISTANCE
Neck	Pendant of the Null Rune	(Jewelcrafting)	+30
Shoulders	Soulcloth Shoulders	(Tailoring)	+30
Cloak	Cloak of Arcane Evasion	(Tailoring)	+32
Cloak Enchant	Greater Arcane Resistance	(Enchanting)	+15
Chest	Soulcloth Vest	(Tailoring)	+45
Bracers	Arcanoweave Bracers	(Tailoring)	+25
Gloves	Enchanted Felscale Gloves	(Leatherworking)	+30
Waist	Enchanted Adamantite Belt	(Blacksmithing)	+30
Legs	Enchanted Felscale Leggings	(Leatherworking)	+40
Feet:	Arcanoweave Boots	(Tailoring)	+35
Finger:	Ring of Arcane Shielding	(Jewelcrafting)	+30
Trinket:	Violet Badge	(Quest Item)	+45
Arcane Armor Kit	Chest/Leg/Hands/Feet	(Leatherworking)	+8

RAID COMPOSITION

Apart from the two arcane tanks, Solarian does not require an additional specialized tank. A DPS warrior or feral Druid can tank Solarian adequately. Solarian has very little armor, and melee DPS classes perform extremely well.

However, for the second stage adds, AoE caster classes are needed, so the raid needs to be balanced with this in mind. In a raid with several shadow Priests and chain healing Shamans, six to seven healers are enough. Although it can be healing intensive, bringing more DPS classes usually helps end the encounter faster. A protection Paladin is ideal for tanking stage two, but any Paladin equipped for tanking can perform well.

CONSUMABLES

Solarian is a DPS race, therefore consider using consumables for your DPS classes.

STRATEGY

After Solarian is engaged, the raid has a 50 second window for pure DPS. Aggro is not a concern here, so use cooldowns to bring her as low as possible. Before she disappears, Solarian casts Light of Solarian on the raid. This inflicts 2280-2520 Arcane damage to every player in the raid.

Periodically she casts Wrath of the Astromancer on a random player, infusing the target with arcane power, causing them to harm nearby allies for 5400 to 6600 arcane damage, 6 seconds after the spell is cast. The affected player must run away from the raid as soon as possible since the explosion deals massive damage to everyone in a 10 yard radius. The explosion also causes the target to be knocked very far away.

During her first stage, she will also randomly choose targets for her Arcane Missiles, a burst of 3 missiles dealing 3,000 damage per. Without using arcane resistance, the damage dealt will be challenging to heal. Healers should always watch Solarian's target so that they can quickly adapt and save the targeted player.

Fifty seconds after engaging Solarian, she vanishes and opens three portals. A dozen Solarium Agents come out of the portals and attack the raid. A Paladin with Consecration can build enough aggro on all of them so that a raid consisting of several area of effect damage classes can kill them off quickly.

About 30 seconds after she disappears, Solarian re-emerges from one of the three portals. Two Solarium Priests spawn from the other two portals. These do not need to be tanked, as they hit for very little damage. They do cast Smite on their target which causes Holy damage but can easily be healed through. Additionally, they attempt to heal themselves, each other, or Solarian herself. The spell can and should be interrupted.

The Agents should always be dead before the Priests spawn, and these should be killed before re-starting DPS on Solarian, who fights the raid for 90 seconds at a time, before vanishing again.

Three or four transitions later the raid should have Solarian at the 20% mark. It is at this point that stage 3 begins. Solarian transforms into a Voidwalker and attacks her primary target with a Void Bolt, dealing 4394-5106 damage. She also uses Psychic Scream to fear up to 5 nearby targets. Fear Ward on the main tank negates Psychic Scream, as will all other fear breaking mechanics.

A raid that has brought Solarian to 20% will almost always end up killing her.

TANKING

As mentioned above, Solarian can be tanked by a variety of classes and specializations as her melee attacks are very weak against armored classes. The arcane resistance tanks also have very little responsibilities, other than being ready to use Shield Wall or Last Stand in case their hit points drop too fast.

HEALING

Healing during this encounter is considerably more difficult than tanking. One well-geared restoration Druid can single-handedly heal both arcane resistance tanks, although they may request additional help towards the end of the encounter. The real challenge lies in quickly healing the target of her Arcane Missiles. Ideally keep Solarian targeted and watch her target, then assist her to heal it.

DPS

The pressure to finish the encounter quickly, before the arcane damage overwhelms the raid rests with the DPS classes. Remember that aggro is not an issue during this encounter and always maximize your damage by using your longer cooldowns during the stages where you can do damage to Solarian. During the Agent phase, allow your Paladin tank to build sufficient aggro before you use area of effect spells, and upon the priests spawning watch them closely in order to be able to interrupt their heals.

SUNSTRIDER'S MINIONS

With the fall of the third boss in the zone, the barriers blocking the way to Kael'thas fall. However, a number of Blood Elf packs need to be cleared before the raid can engage their master. Four of these packs are in Kael's room, and two of them patrol the two corridors. However, the only challenging packs are the three groups of six casters that guard the way. Crimson Hand Centurions are by far the most dangerous caster type. Fortunately these can be Polymorphed by mages, and dealt with when every other mob type has died. Their Arcane Flurry ability spells death for all melee classes, but mages can continuously cast Polymorph on them to interrupt Arcane Flurry. While the target is being constantly attacked by the raid, Polymorph does not replenish its hit points but will interrupt the spell being cast. Crimson Hand Battle Mages can also be Polymorphed, but if the raid doesn't have enough Mages, Warlocks and Priests can control them through Fear. Do not attempt to tank these from melee range, as they can kill tanks in one hit. Instead kill them from a distance while using Fear and Death Coil to keep them away from players.

KAEL'THAS SUNSTRIDER

With Al'ar, Void Reaver and Solarian defeated, the defenses protecting the Lord of the Blood Elves have now fallen, yet he is far from being defenseless. Guarded by his closest four advisors and an arsenal of powerful weapons, Kael'Thas is still a threat.

Many consider this the best raid encounter in the Burning Crusade. With five stages, it is certainly epic in length but also in terms of complexity and rewards.

ABILITIES

HP	3642000	Damage	11082-156533
Abilities	**Resurrection:** Kael'thas resurrects all four of his guardians. This signals the beginning of Phase 3.		
	Phoenix: Summons a Phoenix.		
	Mind Control: Takes control of the target, increasing the target's damage by 100%, movement speed by 50%, and healing done by 1000%.		
	Shock Barrier: Absorbs 80000 damage and makes the caster immune to spell interruption.		
	Pyroblast: Inflicts 45000 to 55000 Fire damage. Interruptible. Used while Kael'thas is under the effects of Shock Barrier.		
	Fireball: Inflicts 18000 to 22000 Fire damage.		
	Arcane Disruption: Disorients all enemies in Kael'thas' chamber and deals them 1750 to 2250 Arcane damage.		
	Gravity Lapse: Knocks a target into the air and prevents the target from landing.		
	Nether Vapor: Decreases total health by 10% and deals 875 to 1125 Shadow damage within 8 yards of Kael'thas during a Gravity Lapse.		
	Nether Beam: Deals 1850 to 2150 Arcane damage to the first target and jumps to nearby targets for increasingly greater damage.		
	Flamestrike: Burns all enemies in a selected area for 115625 to 134375 Fire damage and inflicts 3000 additional Fire damage every 1 sec. for 8 sec.		

LOOT

Chestguard of the Vanquished Hero: Tier 5 Chest token: (Hunter, Mage, Warlock)

Chestguard of the Vanquished Champion: Tier 5 Chest token: (Paladin, Rogue, Shaman)

Chestguard of the Vanquished Defender: Tier 5 Chest token: (Warrior, Priest, Druid)

Verdant Sphere: Quest Item: Various neck piece rewards

Rod of the Sun King: One-Hand / Mace: 186 - 347 Damage, Speed 2.70, (98.7 dps)

Chance on hit: Chance on melee attack to gain 10 Energy or 5 Rage, Equip: Increases attack power by 50.

Crown of the Sun: Head / Cloth: 188 Armor, +39 Stamina, +38 Intellect, +49 Spirit, Equip: Increases healing done by spells and effects up to 108.

Leggings of Murderous Intent: Legs / Leather: 380 Armor, +45 Agility, +31 Stamina, Equip: Improves critical strike rating by 37, Increases attack power by 92.

Gauntlets of the Sun-King: Hands / Cloth: 145 Armor, +28 Stamina, +29 Intellect, +20 Spirit, Equip: Improves spell critical strike rating by 28, Increases damage and healing done by magical spells and effects by up to 42.

Sunhawk Leggings: Legs / Mail: 847 Armor, +39 Stamina, +31 Intellect, Blue Socket, Blue Socket, Yellow Socket, Socket Bonus: +9 Healing, Equip: Increases healing done by spells and effects by up to 108, Restores 13 mana per 5 sec.

The Nexus Key: Two-Hand Staff: 144 - 310 Damage, Speed 3.20, (71.0 dps), +73 Stamina, +52 Intellect, Equip: Improves spell critical strike rating by 50, Increases damage and healing done by magical spells and effects by up to 229.

Thalassian Wildercloak: Back: 116 Armor, +28 Agility, +28 Stamina, Equip: Increases attack power by 68.

Twinblade of the Phoenix: Two-Hand / Sword: 369 - 555 Damage, Speed 3.60, (128.3 dps), +51 Stamina, Red Socket, Yellow Socket, Blue Socket, Socket Bonus: +8 Attack Power, Equip: Improves critical strike rating by 36, Increases attack power by 108.

Band of the Ranger-General: Finger: +27 Stamina, Equip: Improves hit rating by 18, Improves critical strike rating by 28, Increases attack power by 56.

Sunshower Light Cloak: Back: 116 Armor, +18 Stamina, +24 Intellect, +20 Spirit, Equip: Increases healing done by spells and effects by up to 77.

Royal Gauntlets of Silvermoon: Hands / Plate: 1080 Armor, +57 Stamina, Yellow Socket, Blue Socket, Socket Bonus: +3 Dodge Rating, Equip: Increases defense rating by 24, Increases your dodge rating by 32.

Royal Cloak of the Sunstriders: Back: 116 Armor, +27 Stamina, +22 Intellect, Equip: Increases damage and healing done by magical spells and effects by up to 44.

OVERVIEW

Kael'thas Sunstrider is a five stage encounter that usually takes in excess of 20 minutes to complete. The stages are intertwined, and how well the raid performs during one stage usually influences the next one.

During the first phase the raid faces Kael's four advisors, one by one. After the death of the fourth advisor, Kael'thas summons his legendary weapons. As they are killed, players can loot them and use them for the remainder of the encounter. The start of phase three is timed, and Kael'thas will resurrect his advisors. The raid now faces all of them at the same time with the weapons that are left from the previous stage. During stage four Kael'thas finally enters the battle, joining any advisors that are still alive. He uses Fireball and Pyroblast on the main tank and summons a phoenix add to help him in battle. The fifth and final stage starts when Kael'thas reaches the 50% mark. He flies up into the air, periodically removes the gravity in the room sending players floating through the air, while continuing to attack the main tank and summoning phoenixes.

RAID COMPOSITION

Three or four tanks are required, of which two protection warriors are mandatory for this encounter. A standard seven healers are sufficient, together with a good mix of DPS classes. While every class has its strengths and should be represented, bringing several area of effect damage classes makes the encounter significantly easier. The raid cannot be completely stacked with casters, as at least one hunter and three melee DPS classes are recommended.

CONSUMABLES

DPS is key to this very complex encounter. The faster you can kill advisors and weapons, the faster you can reduce the complexity of the encounter. Therefore all DPS classes should use full consumables. The main tank will also be hit extremely hard, therefore any consumables that increase his or her hit points should be used.

THALADRED THE DARKENER

While he does have an aggro table, this is not how Thaladred normally selects his targets. Instead, Thaladred sets his gaze upon a random target and relentlessly follows it for 12 seconds, then picks another target and repeats the process. While a melee hit from Thaladred will kill most non-plate wearers, he can be avoided. Thaladred moves slower than a player's run speed. The fact that he sometimes attacks his target with a Psychic Blow that deals around 5,000 damage and knocks it away from him, makes it even less likely that he will land a melee hit on his target. On plate wearers, Thaladred's attacks inflict about 4,000 damage and leave behind a Rend effect that causes an additional 2,500 damage every 2 seconds for 12 seconds. Additionally, Thaladred will silence caster classes in his vicinity.

LORD SANGUINAR

Lord Sanguinar can be picked up and tanked normally. He hits tanks for around 4,000 damage every hit. His only noteworthy ability is Bellowing Roar, an area of effect fear that will send all targets in a 35 yard range fleeing in panic. This occurs around every 30 seconds.

THE CAST OF CHARACTERS

GRAND ASTROMANCER CAPERNIAN

Capernian is one of the more dangerous advisors of Kael'Thas. She attacks her primary target with a powerful Fireball, while periodically using Conflagration on a random target. Conflagration sets an enemy aflame, inflicting 9000 Fire damage over 10 sec. and sends it into a state of panic. While the target is affected, the flames periodically scorch nearby players as well. More importantly, the initial effect of the Conflagration will be applied to all players within an 8 yard range of the main target which can result in several casualties if Conflagration hits a group of players. Capernian cannot be controlled by a classic tank or attacked from melee range, as she will use her Arcane Burst ability, which will hit targets in a 10 yard range for over 4,000 arcane damage and knock them away.

MASTER ENGINEER TELONICUS

The final advisor, Telonicus can also be tanked normally. In addition to his melee attack he throws bombs at his primary target, which also do splash damage to targets around it. Melee classes should stay away from the Telonicus' tank. Every 15 seconds he will place a debuff called Remote Toy on a random target in the raid. This will last for a minute, during which that target is periodically stunned.

STAGE ONE

Stage one consists of the raid fighting the advisors one by one. While not difficult, this is an excellent opportunity for the whole raid to get acquainted with all their abilities. Because of the duration of the encounter, it is recommended to re-apply Paladin buffs at the end of stage one.

For Thaladred it is important to stay well away from him, especially when he is about to switch targets. If he switches to a cloth class in his melee range then that class is guaranteed to die. Do not use immunities except as a last resort, because this will cause Thaladred to attack his primary aggro target, which will always be a lightly armored ranged class. If possible, try to kill Thaladred in the south side of the room, as the spot where he dies will be the spot where he gets resurrected in stage three.

Pull Lord Sanguinar to a corner, while giving the tank Fear Ward or Tremor Totem in case he fails to avoid the Fear himself. Ranged DPS can kill Sanguinar easily while outranging the Fear. Killing him in a corner ensures that once resurrected his Fear will only hit a minimal number of targets.

Capernian is potentially very dangerous to the raid due to her Conflagration ability. Since she cannot be tanked from melee range, it is best to have her misdirected to a Warlock tank. To minimize the damage taken, the Warlock should be using fire resistance gear, or have the soul link talent. It is possible for the tanking Warlock to be affected by Conflagration and disoriented, which will cause Capernian to switch target. Healers must quickly adjust to the change in target until the Warlock can regain aggro. Kill Capernian as close to the south edge of the room as possible.

Finally, while the raid is attacking Telonicus the raid should take the time to refresh short duration buffs, and regain most of their mana back. The beginning of stage two is not timed, but instead triggered by the engineer's death. No matter what time the raid chooses to kill Telonicus, a number of targets in the raid will be affected by Remote Toy, and can therefore get stunned at any time. Do not kill Telonicus if an essential member of the raid, such as a tank, is affected by Remote Toy. Once Telonicus is defeated, after a short break, stage two will start.

A good example of where to position each advisor can be found in the diagram below:

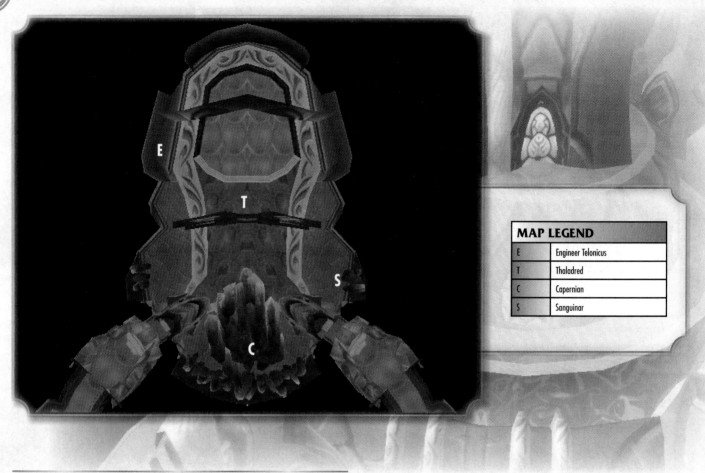

MAP LEGEND

E	Engineer Telonicus
T	Thaladred
C	Capernian
S	Sanguinar

MAP LEGEND

E	Engineer Telonicus
T	Thaladred
C	Capernian
S	Sanguinar

STAGE TWO

THE LEGENDARY ARSENAL

DEVASTATION

This is a two-handed axe that hits plated classes for around 4,000 damage and has a Whirlwind area of effect attack that does around 5,000 damage to tanks. Hits on cloth classes are devastating. Upon defeating it, players in the raid can loot:

Devastation	Two hand / Axe	496 - 744 Damage, Speed 3.90, (159.0 dps), +75 Stamina
Equip: Improves critical strike rating by 50, Increases attack power by 150.		
Chance on hit: Increases your movement speed by 50%, and your melee attack speed by 20% for 30 sec.		

COSMIC INFUSER

This one handed mace has a weak melee attack but will instantly cast its Holy Nova ability every 15 seconds, which will heal the nearby weapons and damage the nearby players. It will also attempt to heal itself and other weapons with a powerful channeled healing spell, but this can be interrupted. Upon defeating it, players in the raid can loot:

Cosmic Infuser	Main Hand / Mace	14 - 221 Damage, Speed 2.80, (41.8 dps), +40 Stamina, +40 Intellect, +40 Spirit
Equip: Restores 30 mana per 5 sec, Increases healing done by spells and effects by up to 600, Friendly targets of the caster's heals gain an effect that reduces the damage taken by Fire and Shadow spells by 50% for 30 sec.		

THE LEGENDARY ARSENAL

STAFF OF DISINTEGRATION

The Staff will launch Frostbolt volleys at the raid unless interrupted, and also casts a Frost Nova that immobilizes players. It can be tanked normally and does very little damage to a plated class. Unless interrupted it will continuously cast Frostbolts at the raid, dealing large amounts of damage. The staff also has considerably fewer hit points than the rest of the weapons. Upon defeating it, players in the raid can loot:

Staff of Disintegration	Two-Hand Staff	131 - 310 Damage, Speed 2.80, (78.6 dps), +75 Stamina, +50 Intellect
Equip: Improves spell critical strike rating by 75, Increases damage and healing done by magical spells and effects by up to 325, Increases attack power by 1125 in Cat, Bear, Dire Bear, and Moonkin forms only.		
Use: Places a mental protection field on friendly targets within 30 yards, granting immunity to Stun, Silence, and Disorient effects.		

PHASESHIFT BULWARK

Due to the shield's spikes, hitting it with melee attacks will cause damage to the attacker. The shield's other ability is Shield Bash which can hit players in its melee range. With more hit points than the other weapon the shield usually takes longer to kill. Upon defeating it, players in the raid can loot:

Phaseshift Bulwark	Shield	7313 Armor, 208 Block, +40 Stamina
Equip: Increases defense rating by 40.		
Use: Shields the caster, absorbing 100000 damage and making the caster immune to Fear and Snare effects for 4 sec.		

THE LEGENDARY ARSENAL

WARP SLICER

This is a one handed sword that does a good amount of damage and therefore needs to be picked up by a well geared tank. In addition to the direct damage, the target will be affected by a stacking Rend debuff that inflicts 500 damage every 3 seconds per stack. Upon defeating it, players in the raid can loot:

Warp Slicer	One-Hand Sword	248 - 461 Damage, Speed 2.90, (122.2 dps), +35 Stamina
Equip: Improves critical strike rating by 25, Increases attack power by 70.		
Chance on hit: Increases your movement speed by 50%, and your melee attack speed by 20% for 30 sec.		

INFINITY BLADES

This pair of daggers is similar to the sword in the way they deal a good amount of physical damage to their tank. While the damage per hit is slower, they attack considerably faster than the sword and therefore put out more damage. Upon defeating it, players in the raid can loot:

Infinity Blade	One-Hand Dagger	171 - 318 Damage, Speed 2.00, (122.3 dps), +35 Stamina.
Equip: Improves critical strike rating by 25, Increases attack power by 70.		
Chance on hit: Increases magical damage taken by the target by 5%, and dispels a special magical effect. Can be applied up to 5 times. Lasts 30 sec.		

NETHERSTRAND LONGBOW

Finally, the bow will shoot at its main target with both physical damage arrows and Arcane Shot. It will also occasionally use Multishot, hitting several players at the same time. In addition to that it has the ability to teleport a short distance, making it difficult to control. Upon defeating it, players in the raid can loot:

Netherstrand Longbow	Bow	256 - 385 Damage, Speed 2.90, (110.5 dps), +20 Stamina, Classes: Hunter
Equip: Improves ranged critical strike rating by 50, Increases ranged attack power by 70, Increases your ranged weapon critical strike damage bonus by 50%.		
Use: Summons a bundle of Nether Spikes for use as ammo.		
Chance on hit: Increases Physical damage taken by the target by 5%. Can be applied up to 5 times. Lasts 30 sec.		

LEGENDARY LIMITATIONS

Once one of the weapons has been defeated, every player in the raid can loot the corpse and pick one up. Since corpses only last about one minute, players should do so at the earliest opportunity. Sadly, not only are the looted weapons only usable inside Tempest Keep, but they also despawn 15 minutes after they are picked up. Since without them the encounter is virtually impossible to beat, consider their duration as an enrage timer to the encounter.

A wide variety of strategic options are available for this stage, both in terms of tanking and killing the weapons. Speed is of the essence, since regardless of the raid's performance stage three will start with the advisors being resurrected only a little over two minutes after the weapons have spawned. A good protection Warrior or feral Druid should easily be able to tank two weapons at a time.

A tank will usually be solely dedicated to the axe, because repositioning it in search for a second weapon to tank can easily result in deaths due the axe's Whirlwind.

The bow should be tanked by a ranged class, usually a Hunter, who can easily build aggro on it even after random teleports.

The mace's damage output is so low it does not warrant a protection tank, and is therefore usually picked up by a damage dealing Warrior.

Immediately after the weapons have spawned, the staff will start channeling Frostbolts which must be interrupted by Mages casting counterspell.

All weapons can be stunned, a prime candidate being the mace, which will otherwise heal the other weapons with its Holy Nova. While a few Holy Novas do not make a big difference, its single target heal is very powerful, and must always be interrupted.

After picking their targets up, the tanks can position all weapons in a tight cluster. Exceptions are the bow, which teleports around, and the axe, which should be positioned about 10 yards away from the other weapons.

Mages and Warlocks can now start using area of effect spells to bring down the weapons, while single target classes focus down weapons one by one. A good choice for a first target is the mace, because the faster it is killed, the less it will heal the other weapons.

Once this has been killed, single target damage classes can bring down the other weapons which already have low hit points from the area of effect damage spells. Shadow Priests can target the shield, which has the highest amount of hit points left, while Rogues can go on any other weapon. Once most of the weapons are dead, area of effect spells become less efficient. Usually the shield, axe and bow will be left, at which point Mages and Warlocks can also switch to single target abilities. The shield is a good choice, since Rogues attacking it take damage because of the shield's spike.

283

If the axe was positioned well during the area of effect stage (far enough as not to whirlwind anyone but the tank but close enough to be hit by at least some area of effect spells), it will quickly be killed next by the ranged classes. Rogues can concentrate on the bow.

A well executed stage two will see most if not all weapons killed before stage three begins. Every weapon that is left alive at this point complicates the encounter further and gives the raid fewer strategic options.

At the beginning of the third stage, Kael'thas resurrects all his four advisors. These must be dealt with at the same time and will use the same abilities they used in stage one. Fortunately, the raid now has the legendary weapons to help them defeat the advisors for a second time.

It is essential to remember that advisors get resurrected in the position where they were killed. It is therefore very important not to stand close to Thaladred's corpse, as his gaze can be fatal for lightly armored classes.

STAGE THREE

Stage three is again about speed and efficiency, as 3 minutes later, whether the raid is prepared for it or not, Prince Kael'thas attacks the raid. The most efficient way of dealing with the advisors is to have the Rogues attack Telonicus, while a Hunter using the legendary bow applies the debuff that increases melee damage taken.

At the same time, one of the tanks, using the legendary dagger can apply the debuff that increases magical damage taken to Thaladred, which is attacked by all the caster classes in the raid.

During this time, a tank using the legendary shield and Berserker Rage to avoid Sanguinar's Bellowing Roar can easily keep him controlled in the same position where he was tanked during the first stage, with the aid of a healer.

Only one healer is required for the Warlock tank, due to the mace's buff that reduces the fire damage taken by the Warlock. The legendary staff in the hands of the Warlock will completely cancel out the confusing effect of the Conflagration, which effectively ensures Capernian will never switch targets. With Thaladred and Telonicus dead, the raid must switch their attention to Sanguinar. Once Sanguinar has been defeated, the melee classes must head towards Kael'thas, as he is about to enter the battle, while the ranged classes can finish off Capernian.

STAGE FOUR

With Kael'thas engaged, the encounter now enters stage four. He attacks his main target with Fireballs which would normally deal in excess of 20,000 damage. This will be reduced by half if the tank has been given the damage reduction buff by a healer with the legendary mace, and is further reduced by talents such as improved defensive stance. These Fireballs can also be interrupted, which should be the main priority for Rogues and damage dealing Warriors.

Kael'thas also uses his Arcane Disruption ability, which deals 1750-2250 damage to everyone in the raid and disorients them. If the main tank becomes disoriented the raid almost inevitably wipe, so it is highly imperative that the aura from the legendary staff is active on the main tank at all times.

Another easy to avoid ability is Kael's Flamestrike. A large visual effect will mark the spot where the Flamestrike will be cast, and players should move out of it. Beware of the lingering effects of the Flamestrike, which persists a few seconds after the initial spell has been cast.

To make matters more interesting, Kael'thas periodically Mind Controls several players in the raid. Fortunately, this effect can be removed by players using the legendary dagger to attack the mind controlled targets. One of the protection Warriors that has been relieved of his tanking duties is ideal for this task, as they can Intercept to the Mind Controlled target and hit it for relatively low damage to remove the Mind Control effect.

One minute after he is engaged, and every minute after that, Kael'thas shields himself with a Shock Barrier spell which absorbs 80,000 damage. While shielded, Kael's spells cannot be interrupted, and he will take advantage of that by attempting to cast a chain of three powerful Pyroblasts on the main tank. With a 4 second cast time, the base damage on his Pyroblasts is an enormous 45,000 – 55,000 damage. Even with this halved by the effects of the legendary staff, Pyroblasts can still obliterate a tank. Surviving them is the key to the fourth stage. With all the raid focused on taking down his shield, the main tank can use the legendary shield to absorb the first of the 3 Pyroblasts. With all the raid concentrating damage on Kael'thas it should be possible to take the shield down and interrupt his Pyroblast before the second one has completed its 4 second cast time.

If the raid is unable to break the shield, the tank has a number of emergency options, which must often be used in conjunction to survive a second Pyroblast. Using long cooldown abilities such as Last Stand and Shield Wall only work once, so use them sparingly. Instead the tank can use a Major Fire Protection Potion to absorb up to 4,000 of the Pyroblast's damage, while at the same time using a secondary item, such as a Frozen Rune or Nightmare Seed. While Nightmare Seeds are fairly easily obtained by herbalists, Frozen

Runes can only be found in Naxxramas and usually require the effort of several players to obtain.

After his Pyroblast sequence has been interrupted, Kael'thas will spawn a Phoenix to help him in battle. He will do so every minute, whether the previous Phoenix has been defeated or not. It is important to give a tank the opportunity to build some threat on the Phoenix, since it can otherwise not be taunted. The Phoenix continuously casts a damage dealing fire spell in a point blank range around it, which players must avoid. This ability seems to damage the Phoenix too, as it continuously loses health whether it is attacked or not. Once dead, the Phoenix spawns a Phoenix Egg. If the egg is not destroyed within 15 seconds, the Phoenix re-emerges at full health. This must be avoided at all costs, therefore all the ranged damage classes must attack the egg and destroy it as soon as possible.

Since summoning the Phoenix and Kael's Shock Barrier and Pyroblast sequence are both on a one minute timer, ideally the raid should always switch from full damage on Kael to break his shield to full damage on the egg to prevent the Phoenix from respawning. Keeping this rhythm up without losing players rapidly brings Kael's health down to the 50% mark, where stage 5 begins.

STAGE FIVE

While the encounter's final stage introduces several new abilities, a raid that was capable of defeating the previous four stages should have no problems at this point. Kael'thas starts by teleporting all players close to him and casting Gravity Lapse. This spell effectively removes the effects of gravity in his chambers, causing players to fly in the air. He then starts attacking players with his Nether Beam, which only deals between 1850 and 2150 damage but jumps from player to player if they stand close to each other. Therefore, immediately after a Gravity Lapse, players must fly away from Kael'thas, spreading out to avoid chaining the Nether Beam between them. At the same time it is recommended that they fly close to the ground, to avoid taking falling damage once the gravity is reinstated.

During this stage Kael will continue to use most of his stage four abilities, such as Fireball, Arcane Disruption and Shock Barrier. He also continues to summon Phoenixes. All these must be dealt with just like in the previous stage.

Additionally, Kael'thas will summon a number of Nether Vapor clouds, usually in close proximity to him. Standing in these clouds inflicts only a small amount of damage, but reduces the maximum hit points of the affected players by 10% per stack, which can be very dangerous, particularly for the main tank. Simply float away from them to avoid the debuff.

Keep a cool head and deal with all his abilities you have learned from the previous stages, and you will soon have defeated one of the most difficult and exhilarating encounters in the Burning Crusade.

QUEST

THE VIALS OF ETERNITY

Quest Level	70
Location	Tempest Keep / Serpentshrine Cavern
Starts at	Soridormi, Caverns of Time
Ends at	Soridormi, Caverns of Time
Goal	Obtain Vashj's Vial Remnant and Kael's Vial Remnant to gain access to the Caverns of Time.

If you have already defeated Lady Vashj, it is finally time to complete one of the most challenging quests in The Burning Crusade. Pick up Kael's Vial Remnant and head to the Caverns of Time, the next step in your challenges. Apart from granting you access to the Battle of Mount Hyjal, Soridormi will also offer players a Band of Eternity, a choice between four powerful rings that will gain even more power as your standing with the Scales of the Sands improves. Congratulations on your well-deserved reward!

THE VIALS OF ETERNITY REWARDS

ITEM	TYPE	STATS
Band of Eternity (Tanking)	Finger	+37 Stamina
Equip: Increases defense rating by +25, Increases the block value of your shield by 38.		
Band of Eternity (Healing)	Finger	+24 Stamina, +22 Intellect
Equip: Increases healing done by spells and effects by up to 55, Restores 8 mana per 5 sec.		
Band of Eternity (Caster DPS)	Finger	+24 Stamina, +22 Intellect
Equip: Improves spell critical strike rating by 21, Increases damage and healing done by magical spells and effects by up to 29.		
Band of Eternity (Physical DPS)	Finger	+25 Agility, +37 Stamina
Equip: Increases attack power by 50.		

THE BATTLE FOR MOUNT HYJAL

In Caverns of Time, the gateway that provides access to key moments in Warcraft history, a new portal has opened under the watchful eyes of the Infinite Dragonflight. It gives adventurers the chance to be a part of the pivotal moment in the battle that united horde and alliance races against the Burning Legion.

Starting at the side of Jaina Proudmoore raids will then continue the battle alongside the Warchief Thrall, to set up a final battle with Archimonde under the shadow of the world tree, Nordrassil.

The Battle of Mount Hyjal is a tier 6 raid instance, the highest in The Burning Crusade. Although comparable to the Black Temple in terms of difficulty and reward, the instance is completely unique in format, with the raid having to defend the horde and alliance bases instead of the classic progression through a dungeon. If successful, the raid has the opportunity to fight Archimonde himself, at the summit of Mount Hyjal.

DUNGEON INFORMATION

Location	Caverns of Time, Tanaris
Region	Contested
Quests	Alliance and Horde
Suggested Level	70 (25-person raid)
Enemy Types	Undead, Demons
Time to Complete	4 hours

MAP OF MOUNT HYJAL

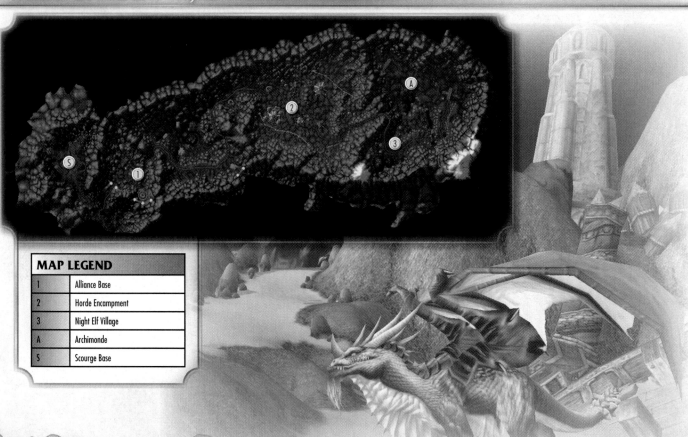

MAP LEGEND

1	Alliance Base
2	Horde Encampment
3	Night Elf Village
A	Archimonde
S	Scourge Base

QUEST

THE VIALS OF ETERNITY

Quest Level	70
Location	Tempest Keep / Serpentshrine Cavern
Starts at	Soridormi, Caverns of Time
Ends at	Soridormi, Caverns of Time
Goal	Obtain Vashj's Vial Remnant and Kael's Vial Remnant to gain access to the Caverns of Time.

Upon zoning in, players find themselves in a preparation area where three portals lead to the alliance, horde and night elf base. Two vendors are also to be found here, offering repairs, tier 6 armor pieces and a number of new gem designs that teach jewelcrafters how to cut the epic gems that can be found both in Mount Hyjal and in Black Temple.

For a raid zoning in for the first time, the horde and night elf base portals will be locked. The human missions must be completed first. Take the portal on the left to find yourself alongside Jaina Proudmoore and her troops, inside the human encampment.

AN INSTANCE WITH A DIFFERENCE

As mentioned earlier, the usual set of rules do not apply inside Hyjal. Instead of normal progression through a dungeon, Hyjal offers a set of four missions that are more similar in format to those in Warcraft III. As opposed to players being on the offensive, they must take on the role of defenders, fighting alongside horde and alliance leaders against waves of Burning Legion invaders.

Missions are started by talking to the base leaders, Jaina Proudmoore in the case of the alliance base. Every mission consists of eight waves of invaders, followed by a boss. The waves are timed and follow one another whether the previous wave has been cleared or not. A mission is won when the boss is defeated, or lost when the base leader dies. If the base leader has died, the raid has to start again at the first wave. If a boss is killed, progress is saved up to that point and the raid can continue on to the next mission.

AN UNUSUAL HERO

An instance with a difference lends itself to a unique approach, and in the case of Mount Hyjal it's time for an unusual hero to step up—the protection Paladin. While protection Paladins are normally not to be found inside of raid instances where protection Warriors and feral Druids are used as the tanks of choice, inside Hyjal things are different. Their unusually high chance to block attacks gives them good survivability, while their aggro generation on groups of mobs is unparalleled while using Holy Shield, Consecration and Retribution Aura. In Hyjal, while under attack by waves of undead enemies a protection Paladin can easily replace two protection Warriors while dealing a considerable amount of damage at the same time and allowing AoE damage classes to do their job without the fear of dying.

RAID COMPOSITION

While not absolutely required, one protection Paladin tank is a great addition for the raid. For a raid lacking a Paladin tank, feral Druids are recommended, due to their ability to hold better aggro on several targets when compared to protection Warriors. One protection Warrior at least is also recommended since they are the best choice for tanking the bosses in the zone. Including a protection Paladin, bring no more than 3 or 4 tanks, while raids without one should consider bringing up to 5 tanks. 7-8 healers are a good number for most encounters in the zone, while the 14 DPS spots should be distributed favoring area of effect damage classes such as Warlocks and Mages in order to deal with the invading mobs as effectively as possible. Bring at least 7-8 AoE caster classes, and the 2 shadow Priests that are needed to help the other casters sustain the mana consumption of AoE abilities. Shadow Priests should always be assisting the remaining DPS classes in the raid, Rogues and Hunters, to bring down single targets rapidly.

MISSION 1: RAGE WINTERCHILL

HP	4249000	Damage	11304-15966
Abilities	**Death and Decay**: Reduces the health of all targets in the area of effect by 15% per second.		
	Frost Armor: Lasts 10 sec. Increases armor by 3000, slows melee attackers' movement to 50%, and increases the time between attacks by 25%.		
	Icebolt: Causes 4250 to 5750 Frost damage immediately and 10000 Frost damage over 4 sec.		
	Frost Nova: Inflicts 2775 to 3225 Frost damage to nearby enemies, immobilizing them for up to 10 sec.		

Upon zoning in, get acquainted to the base layout first. Most importantly, on the southwestern side of the base is the gate which will soon to be under assault by the burning legion's forces. Behind the line of footmen guarding the gate stands a line of riflemen, sorcerers and Priests. Behind the second line, Jaina stands near her tower, with the rest of the alliance army consisting mostly of knights, further to the southeast.

With everyone buffed and ready, it's time to talk to Jaina and start the mission. The invading forces consist of Ghouls, Crypt Fiends, Abominations and Necromancers. Ghouls are the most common type of invading mob. They have a good amount of hit points but do not hit very hard on plate armored targets. However, when low on hit points they will attempt to cannibalize a nearby corpse and regain considerable strength. No matter how many Ghouls spawn as part of a wave, they can all be tanked easily by the Paladin tank. After a few seconds of aggro generation, Warlocks can start using Seed of Corruption, which will be triggered by Mage attacks such as Blast Wave or Arcane Explosion. Mages should save Dragon's Breath to disorient Ghouls attempting to cannibalize, while other classes should also attempt to stun them to interrupt them from gaining health. All single target DPS should focus on the same target and bring Ghouls down one by one.

Crypt Fiends have slightly more hit points and do slightly more damage. They also summon small Crypt Scarabs that run towards a target and attack it for a small amount of damage. Overall they pose very little threat and can be tanked by the protection Paladin together with the Ghouls. On packs consisting of Ghouls and Fiends, the other tanks can pick up 2-3 of the fiends. Have all the DPS classes kill one while the Paladin builds threat on all the Ghouls, then have the other tanks move their targets

Early casualties

Players that die during the 8 waves of invaders can rejoin the battle, either by being Resurrected when the raid gets out of combat at the end of a wave, or by simply running back from the graveyard. However, once Rage Winterchill is engaged, those options will no longer be available and the raid will have to rely on Druids casting Rebirth to Resurrect the fallen.

Abominations are a more dangerous type of invader, the main enemy for your Paladin tank as well as the allied forces in the base. They have more hit points than a Crypt Fiend and hit for more damage, easily twice as hard as Ghouls. Wherever they go, they are followed by their nature damage aura which in time becomes fatal to the defenders of the base. Fortunately they can be shackled by Priests, while the remaining ones should be picked up by the protection Warriors and feral Druids. The danger these pose to the Paladin tank is not due to their direct damage, but due to the fact that they can knock targets down, which makes them unable to dodge or block attacks. Since the Paladin is constantly attacked by 6-10 mobs, tanking more than one Abomination together with them almost always is fatal. On melee-only waves, consisting of combinations of Ghouls, Crypt Fiends, and Abominations, use single target DPS to kill one of the Abominations as soon as possible. The Paladin and the off-tanks need to generate enough threat to make AoE spells viable. While Abominations are being off-tanked, keep them spread out, so several defenders are not affected by poison clouds at the same time.

Necromancers are the final type of invaders before the Rage Winterchill event. They have few hit points, less than any other invading creature type, but do relatively high damage with their Shadow Bolts. These mobs can and should be Polymorphed by Mages as soon as possible. However, while they are approaching the raid without having aggro on a player they can be extremely dangerous as they tend to focus fire either on the closest target or the healer that generates threat first. The most effective way of dealing with waves consisting of multiple casters is to have a protection Warrior meet them in front of the line of defenders, with Spell Reflect active to counter the Shadow Bolts. After the Necromancers have selected the Warrior as their target, Mages can move up from behind him and Polymorph their targets. On waves consisting of a mix of casters and melee invaders, always kill all the caster first, with all the ranged DPS classes in the group assisting one player that is calling out the targets. No tank is necessary for bringing down Necromancers. Their Shadow Bolt can be interrupted, using Counterspell or Kick, but these abilities should mostly be used to counter their Raise Dead spell, which summons 2 helpers, either Skeleton Mages or Skeleton Warriors. While not terribly dangerous, these take additional time to kill, which gives the raid less time to prepare for the next wave.

Getting help

The alliance base is defended by a large number of Footmen, Riflemen, Sorcerers, Priests and Knights. While the first line of defense consisting of Footmen is always involved in the thick of the battle, most of the troops towards the back of the base are normally too far away to get involved. They only enter the battle if an enemy comes close to them. Involve them early by having a tank followed by a healer pull one of the invading mobs close to the groups of defenders, then back to the raid fighting the rest of the mobs. After killing the initial target they stay and help until the entire wave has been cleared.

The strategies employed when dealing with invading mobs are the same for every mission in Hyjal. The key elements are keeping the Paladin tank alive at all costs, as he brings a huge amount of control to the raid. Have a healer watch the protection Warrior moving ahead to Intercept Necromancers, and whether you are a Priest attempting to shackle or a Mage attempting to Polymorph, do not move ahead of either the tank, or the first line of defenders. The main objective of every wave is to have it cleared completely with 20 seconds before the next one, as this gives the raid the ability to leave combat, Resurrect the dead, rebuff, eat and drink. Falling behind the spawn rate is usually fatal, as casters reach the end of their mana pool within two waves of invaders, unless they are able to leave combat to drink. Involve the base defenders as early as possible, as they can help you out particularly when you are falling behind in terms of kill speed. To help raids prepare for the 8 invading waves, here is a breakdown of their composition:

INVADING WAVES – RAGE WINTERCHILL

WAVE #	INVADING MOBS	TOTAL NUMBER
1	10 Ghouls	10
2	10 Ghouls, 2 Crypt Fiends	12
3	6 Ghouls, 6 Crypt Fiends	12
4	6 Ghouls, 4 Crypt Fiends, 2 Necromancers	12
5	2 Ghouls, 6 Crypt Fiends, 4 Necromancers	12
6	6 Ghouls, 6 Abominations	12
7	4 Ghouls, 4 Necromancers, 4 Abominations	12
8	6 Ghouls, 4 Crypt Fiends, 2 Abominations, 2 Necromancers	14

Rage Winterchill follows the eighth wave of invaders. Have a Hunter use Misdirection on the main tank as soon as possible and engage him early, away from Jaina's tower. Apart from his melee swing which hits the main tank for around 5,000 damage, Rage Winterchill has 3 main abilities.

The first one, named Death & Decay is a ranged area of effect ability. It deals damage equal to 15% of a target's health every second to every player in the 20 yard radius of the spell's area of effect. Players should minimize the damage taken as much as possible by moving out of the affected area.

His second ability is a powerful ranged Frost Nova that targets a random player; inflicting 2775-3225 damage to him and all other targets in a 20 yard range. Affected targets will be immobilized for 10 seconds but the effect can be removed using abilities such as Escape Artist, Blink or Blessing of Freedom.

His third ability is his most dangerous one, a random target Icebolt that hits for 4250-5750 damage, stuns players and deals a further 2500 damage every second. Players need to always be healed up to max to survive the initial damage. The damage over time component can be removed by abilities such as Blink, Divine Shield or items such as the PvP reward trinkets, the Insignia/Medallion of the Horde/Alliance. Players that do not have access to any of the above must be healed immediately. The only method of guaranteeing their survival is to watch Rage Winterchill's target and immediately start channeling a Heal if the target switches from the main tank to another player.

NPC's that have survived the 8 waves of invaders contribute some damage but usually die fairly quickly to Death & Decay, therefore players in the raid must deal most of the damage themselves. With this in mind, deaths must be avoided at all costs, which is usually achieved by keeping everyone at full hit points at all times, moving out of Death & Decay and rapidly healing Rage Winterchill's target. Spreading the 5 groups out in a circle with Rage Winterchill in the middle is the most efficient positioning, as it minimized damage taken from his two area of effect spells.

Threat generation can be an issue for the main tank since Winterchill swings rather slowly and stops attacking altogether while casting Death & Decay. One option for the rage-starved tank is to stay in Death & Decay in order to continue generating rage and threat. This enables your DPS dealing classes to go all out, ensuring Winterchill's rapid demise.

An Artifact from the Past is part of the Black Temple attunement quest line. With Illidan's attention now focused on Kael'thas after the completion of the Ruse of the Ashtongue quest, it is now time to retrieve a final magical item, the Phylactery of Rage Winterchill. While this is not the end of the quest line which continues through Black Temple, it is the last step in attunement line and with Rage Winterchill defeated, the players can enter Illidan's domain, the Black Temple.

QUEST

AN ARTIFACT FROM THE PAST

Quest Level:	70
Location:	Mount Hyjal, Caverns of Time
Starts at:	Akama, Warden's Cage, Shadowmoon Valley
Ends at:	Akama
Goal:	Obtain the Time-Warped Phylactery of Rage Winterchill

Apart from the Time-Warped Phylactery and two random epic items, Rage Winterchill and all other bosses in the instance can drop epic jewelcrafting designs that will complement those sold by Indormi in the preparation area of the instance.

LOOT

Bracers of the Pathfinder: Wrist / Mail, 432 Armor, +25 Agility, +24 Stamina, +24 Intellect, Blue Socket, Socket Bonus: +2 Crit Rating, Equip: Increases attack power by 48.

Cuffs of Devastation: Wrist / Cloth, 103 Armor, +22 Stamina, +20 Intellect, +19 Spirit, Yellow Socket, Socket Bonus: +3 Stamina, Equip: Improves spell critical strike rating by 14, Increases damage and healing done by magical spells and effects by up to 34.

Deadly Cuffs: Wrist / Leather, 194 Armor, +28 Stamina, Yellow Socket, Socket Bonus: +3 Stamina, Equip: Improves hit rating by 12, Improves critical strike rating by 28, Increases attack power by 58.

Blessed Adamantite Bracers: Wrist / Plate, 772 Armor, +22 Stamina, +22 Intellect, Yellow Socket, Socket Bonus: +3 Stamina, Equip: Improves spell critical strike rating by 21, Increases healing done by spells and effects by up to 62.

Rejuvenating Bracers: Wrist / Leather, 194 Armor, +16 Stamina, +20 Intellect, +28 Spirit, Blue Socket, Socket Bonus: +4 Healing, Equip: Increases healing done by spells and effects by up to 64.

Howling Wind Bracers: Wrist / Mail, 432 Armor, +29 Stamina, +21 Intellect, Blue Socket, Socket Bonus: 1 Mana per 5 sec., Equip: Increases healing done by spells and effects by up to 62, Restores 8 mana per 5 sec.

Blood-stained Pauldrons: Shoulder / Plate, 1324 Armor, +47 Strength, +34 Stamina, Equip: Improves hit rating by 23, Improves critical strike rating by 32.

Stillwater Boots: Feet / Mail, 679 Armor, +39 Stamina, +36 Intellect, Equip: Increases healing done by spells and effects by up to 84, Restores 10 mana per 5 sec.

Bracers of Martyrdom: Wrist / Cloth, 103 Armor, +15 Stamina, +20 Intellect, +28 Spirit, Blue Socket, Socket Bonus: Healing +4, Equip: Increases healing done by spells and effects by up to 64.

Furious Shackles: Wrist / Plate, 772 Armor, +35 Strength, +28 Stamina, Yellow Socket, Socket Bonus: +3 Stamina, Equip: Improves critical strike rating by 19

Tracker's Blade: One-Hand / Dagger, 105 - 196 Damage, Speed 1.50, (100.3 dps), Equip: Improves hit rating by 20, Improves critical strike rating by 23, Increases attack power by 44.

Chronicle of Dark Secrets: Off-hand, +16 Stamina, +12 Intellect, Equip: Improves spell hit rating by 17, Improves spell critical strike rating by 23, Increases damage and healing done by magical spells and effects by up to 42.

MISSION 2 - ANETHERON

Lady Jaina Proudmoc

Alliance Sorceress

Guardian Water Elemental
<Lady Jaina Proudmoore's Guardian>

HP	4249000	Damage	12313-17392
Abilities	**Sleep**: Puts enemies in a small area to sleep for up to 10 sec. Any damage caused will awaken sleeping targets.			
	Vampiric Aura: Melee attacks heal the caster for 300% of the damage dealt.			
	Carrion Swarm: Deals 4250 to 5750 Shadow damage and reduces all healing by 75% for 20 seconds in a cone. 65 yard range.			
	Inferno: Summons an Infernal.			

Anetheron is the second boss attacking the human encampment, but just like Rage Winterchill he is preceded by 8 waves on invaders. After Winterchill's defeat, players can talk to Jaina once again to start the second mission.

The invading packs consist of the same type of mobs as in the first mission, with the addition of Banshees, a second caster-type mob, in many ways similar to Necromancers. Banshees cannot be Polymorphed but can be shackled, and should always be killed first when they appear as part of a wave. Just like with Necromancers, a tank should be the first to welcome them and Spell Reflect their Banshee Wail, a fast cast shadow bolt that deals up to 3,000 damage. Like most invaders, these are stunnable. Stuns should be use to interrupt their cast of Anti-magic Shell, a shield that absorbs up to 200,000 magic damage before it is removed. As they only have around 80,000 hit points, having casters attack them through the shield is inefficient. They should be finished off by Rogues and Hunters while casters pick a Necromancer to attack. Banshees also have a curse which does not affect casters but will reduce a player's chance to hit by 66% for 5 minutes. Remove this off your Rogues, Warriors, and feral Druids as soon as possible. To help prepare for the 8 invading waves, here is a breakdown of their composition:

INVADING WAVES – ANETHERON

WAVE #	INVADING MOBS	TOTAL NUMBER
1	10 Ghouls	10
2	8 Ghouls, 4 Abominations	12
3	4 Ghouls, 4 Crypt Fiends, 4 Necromancers	12
4	6 Crypt Fiends, 4 Necromancers, 2 Banshees	12
5	6 Ghouls, 2 Necromancers, 4 Banshees	12
6	6 Ghouls, 4 Necromancers, 2 Abominations	12
7	2 Ghouls, 4 Crypt Fiends, 4 Abominations, 2 Banshees	12
8	4 Ghouls, 2 Crypt Fiends, 2 Necromancers, 4 Abominations, 2 Banshees	14

Once again, Anetheron will follow the 8th wave, but this time it is absolutely imperative that every single mob is defeated before Anetheron is engaged. His first ability is a Vampiric Aura. This benefits all his allies within a 25 yard range. Melee attacks dealt by him and allies that are in range of his aura will heal the attacker for 3 times the damage dealt, which makes any mobs that are left over particularly hard to kill.

His second ability is equally powerful. Carrion Swarm deals 4250-5750 shadow damage to enemies in a wide cone area of effect. Additionally, affected players will have the effects of their healing spells and abilities reduced by 75% for 20 seconds. Spreading out is therefore as important as in the Rage Winterchill encounter. Not only will the raid take less damage from Carrion Swarm, but more importantly it will prevent fatal situations where several healers are affected by it at the same time, possibly resulting in the main tank's death. To prevent that, not only must the groups be spread around, but the healers assigned to the main tank must not stand in the same area. If one of them is affected by Carrion Swarm, another must be able to heal without the debuff, at all times.

Anetheron's third ability is a Sleep spell that puts random targets to sleep for 10 seconds or until they take damage. Healers affected by it should be backed up until the effect has worn off.

Additionally, every 50 seconds Anetheron summons a Towering Infernal to aid him in battle. Infernals are summoned on top of a random player, who then takes 2,500 damage and becomes temporarily stunned. They have a very damaging Immolation aura that burns nearby players for 3325 to 3675 fire damage every 2 seconds. Infernals also swing at a plate armored tank for about 2,000 damage. While they are close enough to Anetheron they benefit from his aura and heal on every attack they land. Infernals must be picked up by an off-tank and killed as soon as possible by all the ranged DPS classes in the raid, since melee classes are kept at bay by their Immolation aura. Fire resistance gear is not required for the tank but it can help reduce the damage taken. Once an Infernal has been killed players must all return to their original position, spread out around Anetheron and resume dealing damage until the next Infernal spawn. While Infernals can be moved away from Anetheron's Vampiric Aura, this is usually not recommended as the amount they heal for does not warrant repositioning the ranged DPS classes in the raid which both lowers their damage output and risks more people being hit by Carrion Swarm at the same time.

SAVING JAINA

Unfortunately, no matter how good the raid performs, Jaina's death results in the mission being failed. Therefore watch her hit points at all times. Generally she is safe, unless in melee range of the Infernals, which will cause her to take Immolation damage. Always standing away from her will ensure Infernals will not spawn close enough to her to get her attention.

The key to this encounter is keeping up high damage on Anetheron and even more importantly, the Towering Infernals. A 25-man raid should have absolutely no problem keeping up with the spawn rate of the Infernals, but losses especially among ranged DPS classes can make this more difficult and must be avoided at all costs. Make sure they are kept close to full health at all times to survive Carrion Swarm, and always move away from Infernals as soon as possible to avoid the Immolation aura, as these are the only deadly sources of damage in the encounter.

Continue the cycle of killing Infernals and DPS on Anetheron until his hit points drop below 10% at which point all DPS can focus on him until he is dead, while the last Infernal can just be offtanked.

LOOT

Enchanted Leather Sandals: Feet / Leather, 305 Armor, +34 Stamina, +29 Intellect, +37 Spirit, Equip: Increases healing done by spells and effects by up to 84.

Don Alejandro's Money Belt: Waist / Leather, 249 Armor, +29 Agility, +37 Stamina, Red Socket, Yellow Socket, Socket Bonus: +4 Stamina, Equip: Improves critical strike rating by 19, Increases attack power by 76.

Bastion of Light: Off Hand / Shield, 5930 Armor, 160 Block, +28 Stamina, +28 Intellect, Red Socket, Socket Bonus: 1 Mana per 5 sec., Equip: Increases healing done by spells and effects by up to 62.

Archbishop's Slippers: Feet / Cloth, 162 Armor, +29 Stamina, +30 Intellect, +37 Spirit, Equip: Increases healing done by spells and effects by up to 84.

Golden Links of Restoration: Chest / Mail, 988 Armor, +51 Stamina, +35 Intellect, Equip: Increases healing done by spells and effects by up to 118, Restores 19 mana per 5 sec.

The Unbreakable Will: One-Hand / Sword, 112 – 209 Damage, Speed 1.60, (100.3 dps), 308 Armor, +33 Stamina, Equip: Increases defense rating by +21

Blade of Infamy: One-Hand / Sword, 182 - 339 Damage, Speed 2.60, (100.2 dps), +28 Agility, Equip: Increases attack power by 56.

Quickstrider Moccasins: Feet / Mail, 679 Armor, +28 Agility, +30 Stamina, +31 Intellect, Red Socket, Yellow Socket, Socket Bonus: +3 Agility, Equip: Improves hit rating by 15, Increases attack power by 58.

Pillar of Ferocity: Two-Hand / Staff, 136 - 293 Damage, Speed 3.00, (71.5 dps), 550 Armor, +47 Strength, +96 Stamina, Equip: Increases attack power by 826 in Cat, Bear, Dire Bear, and Moonkin forms only.

Glimmering Steel Mantle: Shoulder / Plate, 1324 Armor, +26 Stamina, +27 Intellect, Blue Socket, Yellow Socket, Socket Bonus: +3 Spell Crit Rating, Equip: Improves spell critical strike rating by 29, Increases healing done by spells and effects by up to 84.

Hatefury Mantle: Shoulder / Cloth, 177 Armor, +15 Stamina, +18 Intellect, Blue Socket, Yellow Socket, Socket Bonus: +3 Spell Crit Rating, Equip: Improves spell critical strike rating by 24, Increases damage and healing done by magical spells and effects by up to 55, Increases your spell penetration by 23.

Anetheron's Noose: Waist / Cloth, 133 Armor, +22 Stamina, +23 Intellect, Yellow Socket, Blue Socket, Socket Bonus: +4 Spell Damage, Equip: Improves spell critical strike rating by 24, Increases damage and healing done by magical spells and effects by up to 55.

With the second mission complete it is time to talk to Jaina again, but not before distributing all the loot. A large force of Burning Legion forces is inbound, and Jaina will gather all her remaining troops and use Mass Teleport to bring them to safety. Follow her example by leaving the human base behind, taking the path east out of the base. This will lead you to the horde base, but on your way miners should activate their Find Minerals ability, as epic gem deposits can be found in these hills.

Shadowy Necromancer

MISSION 3: KAZ'ROGAL

HP	4249000	Damage	12313-17392
Abilities	**Mark of Kaz'rogal**: Drains 600 mana. Lasts 5 sec. Targets without sufficient mana to drain detonate, dealing 10213 to 11287 damage in an area.		
	Cripple: Increases the time between attacks by 75% and movement by 75%, in addition reduces Strength by 75%. Lasts 12 sec.		
	War Stomp: Inflicts normal damage plus 2250, stunning them for 5 sec.		
	Malevolent Cleave: Deals 22800 to 25200 Physical damage divided up evenly among all affected targets.		

After arriving in the horde encampment, take the time to meet the locals and learn your way around the base. Once again, there is a heavily guarded gate which is where most of the invaders will be attempting to strike. It is guarded mostly by Grunts and Headhunters. Thrall stands in front of the Great Hall with a small force of Shamans and Grunts. There are two more notable groups of horde troops, a mix of Headhunters, Witchdoctors and Shamans on the hill on the northeastern side of the base, and the amazing Tauren Warriors, most of which can be found north of the Great Hall.

The invaders are the same type of mobs that have already been encountered during the first two missions, with the addition of two airborne creatures, Frost Wyrms and Gargoyles. The first is a large flying creature that must be tanked and killed by ranged classes. Have a Hunter or Warlock pick up aggro on it and move away from the raid, as the Frost Wyrm's breath inflicts between 2,550 and 3,450 damage to all the targets in an 8 yard radius. It also slows down movement speed by 50% for a short time. Frost Wyrms are a good target particularly for shadow Priests, because with their vast amount of hit points they provide a target that will live long enough for them to do a good amount of damage and thus return health and mana to players in their group.

Gargoyles have a ranged ability named Gargoyle Strike, which inflicts around 1,000 nature damage. It has a short cast time, and several gargoyles can pose danger to a healer that has attracted their attention before others can perform a hostile action. As opposed to Frost Wyrms which must be dealt with exclusively by ranged classes, Gargoyles can be brought to the ground, by using Counterspell while they are casting Gargoyle Strike. While this will enable melee classes to quickly kill them, tanks should try and pick them up, as once on the ground they can hit cloth and leather wearing classes for over 3,000 damage. They can and should be shackled, even when in mid-air, which will take them out of battle until it is their turn to be killed.

An important note about airborne creatures is that they do not follow the same rules as the other invaders, most importantly they do not attempt to force the entrance through the gate. Most of the time they will attack coming from the east and should be Intercepted by ranged classes together with 2 healers above the horde camp on the northeastern hill, where players will be helped by Witchdoctors and Headhunters. To help prepare for the 8 invading waves, here is a breakdown of their composition:

INVADING WAVES – KAZ'ROGAL		
WAVE #	**INVADING MOBS**	**TOTAL NUMBER**
1	6 Ghouls, 4 Abominations, 2 Necromancers, 2 Banshees	14
2	10 Gargoyles, 4 Ghouls	14
3	6 Ghouls, 6 Crypt Fiends, 2 Necromancers	14
4	6 Crypt Fiends, 2 Necromancers, 6 Gargoyles	14
5	4 Ghouls, 6 Abominations, 4 Necromancers	14
6	9 Gargoyles, 1 Frost Wyrm	10
7	6 Ghouls, 4 Abominations, 1 Frost Wyrm	11
8	4 Ghouls, 4 Crypt Fiends, 2 Necromancers, 4 Abominations, 2 Banshees	16

With the final wave defeated, Kaz'rogal now approaches the gate of the encampment. More so than the previous two bosses, once engaged Kaz'rogal is a DPS race which influences the way he should be approached. Even with very good execution, by the time the 8th wave has been cleared, most if not all of the horde troops guarding the gate have fallen. It is therefore better to retreat to the middle of the base, close to the Great Hall and Thrall's camp. If any horde troops are left at the gate, let them fall prey to Kaz'rogal. After killing them, the encounter will reset, with the raid given another short breather to eat and drink while Kaz'rogal approaches the Great Hall. Because of his limited abilities, Kaz'rogal does not pose any threat to Thrall, therefore getting Thrall involved in the battle is always a good idea. Have your main tank engage Kaz'rogal close to the Great Hall which always attracts Thrall's attention and that of his nearby troops. After Thrall has been involved in the battle, start dragging Kaz'rogal towards the Tauren Warrior camp. Stop once these have started attacking him and join them in bringing down the demon. If the pull is executed correctly, horde defenders can end up doing at least 1 million damage to the boss, greatly reducing the overall difficulty of the encounter.

Kaz'rogal has 3 melee attacks. His normal swing hits the tank for an average of 4,500 damage. He also has a powerful strike named Malevolent Cleave which he uses frequently to hit targets standing in front of him. This hits the tank for around 8,000 damage but can kill most other targets. This Cleave deals less damage if it hits multiple targets. As such, it is smart to have at least three targets in front of Kaz'rgal. Therefore, be very careful and always stand behind him, particularly while he is being positioned during the pull. Every 10 to 30 seconds he will use his War Stomp ability which will stun every target in a 15 yard range for 5 seconds, while also dealing around 2,500 damage. Every healer and ranged DPS class should always be outside the range of this ability. Melee classes can also avoid it because of the size of his hitbox, but only if they are standing at the absolute maximum of their melee range.

While these 3 abilities are easy to deal with, the main challenge is an ability named Mark of Kaz'rogal. This drains 600 mana every second from affected targets for 5 seconds. However, targets without sufficient mana to drain detonate, dealing 10213 to 11287 damage in a 15 yard range. The application of the debuff can be resisted as can the detonation, where even small amounts of shadow resistance can ensure at least part of the shadow damage is resisted. Wearing shadow resistance gear is not recommended for the DPS classes as it reduces raid DPS, but healers can wear a moderate amount, as the encounter does not place a big strain on their classes. While in the beginning the delay between applications of the Mark can be as long as 1 minute, as time progresses he starts casting it faster and faster. About 3 minutes into the encounter the Mark will be cast as fast as every 10 seconds, and unlucky players that have been affected will run out of mana causing them to explode. To minimize the effects of the Mark, use anything that restores your mana. Mana potions should be used as early as possible in the encounter, to start the 2 minute timer so that another one can be used close to the end when mana is an even bigger issue. Mages should have their mana gems ready and be prepared to use Evocation when their mana is low. Mana Tide and Spring totems help a lot during this encounter, as will the Druid ability to Innervate characters that are running low on mana. However, even with maximum consumable usage it is still likely that some players will run out of mana. Spreading out to avoid the effects of the explosion is therefore extremely important. If your mana pool is under 3,000 and you have no option to replenish it, make sure you move away from the raid, even if this will put you out of Kaz'rogal's range as the next Mark is guaranteed to cause you to detonate. Wait until your mana has reached a safe level before rejoining the raid.

High DPS and good management of the Mark of Kaz'rogal debuff ensures the demon's demise, the only other element of the encounter that needs to be watched for is the main tank. The Cleave and auto-attack can do a lot of damage, and while affected by War Stomp, the tank cannot dodge or parry incoming attacks. Watch his health closely and you will be on your way to victory.

Kaz'rogal's Hardened Heart: Off Hand / Shield, 5930 Armor, 160 Block, +43 Stamina, Yellow Socket, Socket Bonus: +3 Stamina, Equip: Increases defense rating by +28, Improves hit rating by 21.

Blue Suede Shoes: Feet / Cloth, 162 Armor, +37 Stamina, +32 Intellect, Equip: Improves spell hit rating by 18, Increases damage and healing done by magical spells and effects by up to 56.

Sun-touched Chain Leggings: Legs / Mail, 864 Armor, +39 Stamina, +28 Intellect, Yellow Socket, Blue Socket, Blue Socket, Socket Bonus: +9 Healing, Equip: Increases healing done by spells and effects by up to 110, Restores 16 mana per 5 sec.

Hammer of Atonement: Main Hand / Mace, 19 - 129 Damage, Speed 1.80, (41.1 dps), +31 Stamina, +21 Intellect, Equip: Improves critical strike rating by 23, Increases healing done by spells and effects by up to 443.

Black Featherlight Boots: Feet / Leather, 305 Armor, +41 Stamina , Equip: Improves hit rating by 34, Increases attack power by 98.

Beast-tamer's Shoulders: Shoulder / Mail, 741 Armor, +39 Agility, +38 Stamina, Equip: Increases attack power by 78, Increases damage dealt by your pet by 3%, Increases your pet's critical strike chance by 2%.

Angelista's Sash: Waist / Cloth, 133 Armor, +29 Stamina, +30 Intellect, Equip: Improves spell haste rating by 37, Increases healing done by spells and effects by up to 84.

Belt of the Crescent Moon: Waist / Leather, 249 Armor, +25 Stamina, +27 Intellect, +19 Spirit, Equip: Improves spell haste rating by 36, Increases damage and healing done by magical spells and effects by up to 44.

Belt of Seething Fury: Waist / Plate, 993 Armor, +48 Strength, +37 Stamina, Equip: Improves haste rating by 38.

Leggings of Channeled Elements: Legs / Cloth, 207 Armor, +25 Stamina, +28 Intellect, +28 Spirit, Yellow Socket, Yellow Socket, Blue Socket, Socket Bonus: +5 Spell Damage, Equip: Improves spell hit rating by 18, Improves spell critical strike rating by 34, Increases damage and healing done by magical spells and effects by up to 59.

Razorfury Mantle: Shoulder / Leather, 333 Armor, +28 Agility, +55 Stamina, Equip: Improves critical strike rating by 23, Increases attack power by 76.

Valestalker Girdle: Waist / Mail, 556 Armor, +27 Agility, +25 Stamina, +18 Intellect, Equip: Improves haste rating by 36, Increases attack power by 76.

MISSION 4: AZGALOR

INVADING WAVES – AZGALOR

WAVE #	INVADING MOBS	TOTAL NUMBER
1	6 Abominations, 6 Necromancers	12
2	8 Gargoyles, 5 Ghouls, 1 Frost Wyrm	14
3	6 Ghouls, 8 Giant Infernals	14
4	6 Fel Stalkers, 8 Giant Infernals	14
5	4 Necromancers, 4 Abominations, 6 Fel Stalkers	14
6	6 Necromancers, 6 Banshees	12
7	2 Ghouls, 2 Crypt Fiends, 8 Giant Infernals	12
8	4 Crypt Fiends, 4 Abominations, 4 Fel Stalkers, 2 Banshees, 2 Necromancers	16

HP	4249000	Damage	21352-30158
Abilities	**Rain of Fire**: Burning all enemies in a selected area for 1619 to 1881 Fire damage every 2 sec. for 10 sec.		
	Unquenchable Flames: Burns all enemies affected by Rain of Fire with an additional 1250 Fire damage every 1 sec. for 5 sec.		
	Doom: Causes the target to die and spawn a Lesser Doomguard after 20 sec.		
	Cleave: Inflicts weapon damage plus 1750 to an enemy and its nearest allies, affecting up to 5 targets and knocking them back.		
	Howl of Azgalor: Silences nearby enemies for 5 sec.		

With the demon Kaz'rogal defeated, it's time to face the pit lord, Azgalor, but not before defeating 8 more waves of invaders. These are again comprised of mobs that previously made their appearance, with two new additions, Fel Stalkers and Giant Infernals.

Fel Stalkers have relatively few hit points, but they have very high resists to magical damage which allows them to partially resist most spells. They hit tanks for under 1,000 damage per hit, but casters need to stay away from them, as Fel Stalkers have a Mana Burn ability which can render casters useless. Have melee classes and Hunters attack them and if all other mobs are dead, casters can attack them using ranged area of effect spells.

Giant Infernals just like airborne creatures do not attack the gate of the horde base. Instead they will fall from the sky and attack the nearest target. Their melee attacks inflict fire damage and can hit for up to 1,800 per swing. Additionally they have an Immolation Aura that also deals fire damage, hitting nearby targets for 700 damage every 2 seconds. Every wave that Infernals are a part of consists of 8 Infernals, which makes it very hard to get all of them tanked as they land all over the base. However, they can be Feared, Deathcoiled, trapped, or snared by Frost Nova or Entangle.

Like with Kaz'rogal, there is no timed enrage, but the encounter does become gradually harder to the point where the raid will wipe due to attrition. Damage done to Azgalor is therefore extremely important, which influences the pull and positioning. The horde base defenders can contribute substantially to the damage done, however, due to the Azgalor's area of effect abilities, Thrall can potentially die resulting in failure. The raid's positioning must therefore allow him and the other horde defenders to attack the boss, while minimizing his chance to die.

As with Kaz'rogal, there are 2 main camps of horde troops that should be involved in battle, the first is Thrall's camp while the second is the Tauren Warrior camp to the north of it. The few remaining defenders of the gate to the base will serve as a distraction for Azgalor, while the raid can retreat towards Thrall, eat, drink, and rebuff. Let Azgalor approach Thrall's camp, and once he and his followers have entered battle, start moving Azgalor towards the Tauren Warrior camp. Once they have engaged Azgalor as well it is time to stop and position him so that no players or horde defenders are in danger of being hit by his Cleave attack. This is usually done by having Azgalor face the gate with Thrall on the south and the Tauren Warriors on the north.

Apart from his Cleave, the main danger to players and horde defenders alike, comes from his Rain of Fire ability. This has a large 20 yard area of effect and inflicts 1,619 to 1,881 damage every 2 seconds to those hit by it. Those affected by the Rain of Fire take additional damage over time from Unquenchable Flames, which burns all enemies affected by Rain of Fire for 1,250 Fire damage every second for 5 seconds. This ability is always targeted, either on a player or on a horde defender. Spreading out is therefore recommended, as is moving out of it as soon as possible. Thrall however will not move if affected by the Rain of Fire which can cause his death if the area he stands in is chosen repeatedly for Rain of Fire. To minimize the chance of that happening, all players must stand 20 yards away from Thrall. Melee classes in the raid must always attack from the opposite side, while ranged classes should stand at the maximum range of their abilities.

The tank can be hit very hard during this encounter, for up to 9,000 damage by Azgalor's melee attack, and over 8,000 by his Cleave. While he does not attack very fast, Azgalor can pose a very serious threat to the tank, due to an ability named Howl of Azgalor. This is a 5 second silence effect that leaves every caster in a 100 yard range from Azgalor temporarily unable to cast spells. Keep the tank as close to full hit points as possible and keep healing over time spells on him at all times. These include Renew, Rejuvenation and Regrowth. Heal the tank to back full as soon as the silence ends.

His final ability is what causes the raid to fail. Simply named Doom, it kills a player 20 seconds after it is applied. Moreover, a Lesser Doomguard will spawn from the player's corpse and attack the raid. These can be picked up by tanks which take about 1,500 damage per hit from their attacks. Lesser Doomguards also use War Stomp. This ability temporarily stuns players in melee range, which can make it difficult for a tank to move around attempting to pick up additional Doomguards. Ideally have those affected by Doom run towards the offtank dealing with them, to make picking them up an easier task. A diagram of the suggested positioning is provided for clarification. Doom is cast around every 50 seconds, but it is not required to kill the resulting Doomguards, at least not until Azgalor has died. Keep all the DPS classes on Azgalor until he dies, then deal with the Doomguards.

Reactive Soulstoning

A Warlock's Soulstone ability is mostly used to act as wipe recovery, allowing a class that can Resurrect others to return from the dead and start Resurrecting others, saving the raid precious time. However, this is not necessary in Hyjal. Wipes will result in Jaina or Thrall dying, which causes a 5 minute cooldown until the event is reset. Soulstoning for recovery is therefore not necessary. However, Soulstones can be used reactively (or offensively) in several raid encounters. For Azgalor, quickly Soulstone those affected by Doom. Even though they will die and spawn a Doomguard, they can rejoin the battle immediately by accepting the Soulstone Resurrection.

With Azgalor dead and two lucky members of your raid equipped with brand new Tier 6 gloves, it's time to talk to Thrall and evacuate the horde base. Take the path east towards the Night Elf base, while keeping an eye out for the epic gem deposits. Once at the Night Elf base, find Tyrande Whisperwind and prepare to face Archimonde himself.

LOOT

Gloves of the Forgotten Conqueror: Tier 6 Glove token
(Paladin, Priest, Warlock)

Gloves of the Forgotten Vanquisher: Tier 6 Glove token
(Rogue, Mage, Druid)

Gloves of the Forgotten Protector: Tier 6 Glove token
(Warrior, Hunter, Shaman)

Shady Dealer's Pantaloons: Legs / Leather, 388 Armor, +50 Agility, +61 Stamina, Equip: Increases attack power by 102, Your attacks ignore 175 of your opponent's armor.

Bow-stitched Leggings: Legs / Mail, 864 Armor, +42 Agility, +28 Stamina, +28 Intellect, Red Socket, Yellow Socket, Blue Socket, Socket Bonus: +4 Crit Rating, Equip: Improves critical strike rating by 20, Increases attack power by 100.

Glory of the Defender: Chest / Plate, 1765 Armor, +75 Stamina, Equip: Increases defense rating by +35, Increases your dodge rating by 51, Improves hit rating by 34.

Girdle of Hope: Waist / Plate, 993 Armor, +38 Stamina, +27 Intellect, Yellow Socket, Yellow Socket, Socket Bonus: +3 Intellect, Equip: Improves spell critical strike rating by 21, Increases healing done by spells and effects by up to 84.

Don Rodrigo's Poncho: Chest / Leather, 444 Armor, +39 Stamina, +31 Intellect, +52 Spirit, Equip: Increases healing done by spells and effects by up to 118.

Boundless Agony: One-Hand / Dagger, 144 - 217 Damage, Speed 1.80, (100.3 dps), Equip: Improves critical strike rating by 24, Your attacks ignore 210 of your opponent's armor.

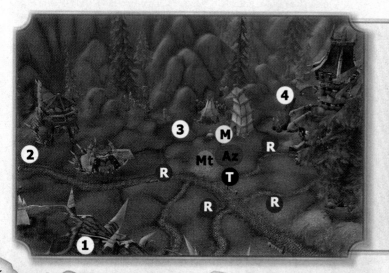

MAP LEGEND	
1	Great Hall
2	Entrance Gate
3	Tauren Warrior Camp
4	Headhunter Camp, Doomguard tanking position
Az	Azgalor
Mt	Main Tank
M	Melee classes, Tauren Warriors
T	Thrall
R	Healers, Ranged DPS Classes

MISSION 5: ARCHIMONDE

HP	4552500		Damage	20724-29271
Abilities	**Doomfire Strike:** Calls down a pillar of flame that moves around randomly, burning everything in its path.			
	Doomfire: Deals diminishing damage (starting at 2400 Fire damage) every 3 sec. for 45 sec.			
	Red Soul Charge: Deals 4500 Fire damage and silences in a 200 yard radius for 4 sec.			
	Yellow Soul Charge: Deals 4500 Physical damage and increases all damage taken by 50% for 8 sec. to all targets in 200 yards.			
	Green Soul Charge: Burns 2250 Mana and deals 4500 Nature damage over 4 sec. to all targets in 200 yards.			
	Grip of the Legion: Inflicts 375000 Shadow damage over 5 min. (2500 Shadow damage every 2 sec.)			
	Finger of Death: Inflicts 20000 Shadow damage. Used when no one is in Archimonde's melee range.			
	Air Burst: Inflicts 3000 Nature damage and knocks targets high in the air.			
	Fear: Strikes fear into all enemies within 99 yards, causing them to flee in terror for up to 8 sec.			
	Hand of Death: Instantly kills all enemies. This occurs if the raid has not defeated Archimonde within 10 minutes.			

The final mission sees raiders take on Archimonde himself at the summit of Mount Hyjal, near the world tree, Nordrassil. Unlike the previous 4 bosses, there are no invading waves to clear, just Archimonde. Before you engage him, every member of your raid must talk to Tyrande Whisperwind and obtain the Tears of the Goddess, an item without which the encounter is impossible. After obtaining it, follow the path around the world tree and prepare for the final battle on Mount Hyjal.

RAID COMPOSITION

While for the previous encounters a raid always needed several tanks to deal with the invading waves, for Archimonde only one tank is needed. The encounter is still possible with a sub-optimal raid group consisting of several tanks, but a raid looking to optimize the composition of the group should drop additional tanks in favor of other classes. Shamans are particularly useful during this encounter, therefore consider bringing as many as 4-5 if they are available. The encounter's difficulty is considerably higher if only 1-2 Shamans are in the raid. Also needed are a good number of decursers, Druids and Mages. Four or more are a good number, while the total number of healers for the raid should be around 8-9.

STRATEGY

Archimonde has an array of damage-dealing abilities, starting with his melee swing on the main tank, which can hit for over 8,000 damage! Apart from that, he has spells that inflict fire, nature, and shadow damage. He Enrages 10 minutes after being engaged, but if he is brought to under 10% of his hit points before that, the raid will be victorious. The encounter is by no means a DPS race, but a survival challenge for every player in the raid.

The first ability a raid should learn to work with is named Air Burst. It targets a random player in the raid, then inflicts 3,000 nature damage to him and all other players in a 13 yard range. It will then throw them high in the air away from Archimonde. Players affected by it always die from falling damage, unless they take measures to avoid it. Mages, Priests and Rogues have a number of options available to them, such as Slow Fall, Blink, Levitate or Safe Fall, but other classes only have one option, activate their Tears of the Goddess to temporarily slow down their speed. These are not easy to use or guaranteed to always save your life, but practice makes perfect and until every player in the raid has mastered using them you will be unable to kill Archimonde.

The limitation of the Tears of the Goddess is that it only slows down the rate of descent for 2 seconds. Activating it too early sees the user lose the effect too early, plummeting to the ground. Activating it too late can also kill the affected target due to their latency. Ideally the Tears should be activated after a player has reached the peak of their trajectory through the air, and has already fallen about half the distance to the ground. Even if the effect wears off before landing, the damage taken will be minimal.

Normally, losing one or more players during a boss encounter does not automatically result in failure, but with Archimonde the chance of that happening is very high. He has a series of abilities that punish the raid, should a player die. The aptly named Soul Charge. Every time a player dies, Archimonde gains a Soul Charge, which can come in one of three different varieties. A green Soul Charge is obtained after the death of a Druid, Hunter or Shaman. A red Soul Charge is obtained after the death of a Paladin, Priest or Warlock. And a yellow Soul Charge follows the death of a Mage, Rogue or Warrior.

Archimonde will gain the charges as a buff and unleash their effect shortly after. The color of the charge determines the effect. A green Soul Charge inflict 4,500 nature damage over 8 seconds to every player in the raid, while also draining 2,250 mana from every caster. A red Soul Charge inflicts 4,500 fire damage to every player in the raid, and silences every caster for 6 seconds. Finally, a yellow Soul Charge inflicts 4,500 physical damage to every player in the raid and increases all damage taken by players by 50% for the next 8 seconds.

As you can see, Soul Charges have very powerful effects and together with Archimonde's other abilities they usually result in other deaths which trigger further Soul Charges. These cascading Soul Charges are hard to interrupt, therefore do your best to prevent the first death.

Archimonde's other abilities include Grip of the Legion, a curse that inflicts 375,000 Shadow damage over 5 minutes, unless removed. We'll do the math; it roughly works out to 2,500 damage every 2 seconds.

Doomfire Strike is another ability which can have devastating effects on the raid. It is spawn as a patch of fire on the ground which inflicts 2,400 fire damage to affected targets and places a damage over time effect named Doomfire on them. This inflicts a further 2,250 damage every 3 seconds for 45 seconds and cannot be removed. The Doomfire moves around randomly, burning players standing in its path. Several trails of Doomfire will be active at any one time during the Archimonde event.

Archimonde will also periodically fear every player in the raid for up to 8 seconds. This can be avoided or interrupted by all the usual fear-breaking abilities or items, such as Berserker Rage, Fear Ward, Tremor Totem, Divine Shield, etc. It is extremely important that the tank does not get feared, or Archimonde will start looking for another target. Alliance raids can use Fear Ward to avoid the fear on the tank, while horde raids must rely on the tank using berserker rage while Archimonde is casting the fear. With the tank avoiding the fear, it is still possible for him to die if the entire raid is feared. Tremor totems in healer groups will ensure that at least some of the healers will break out early from the fear effect and are able heal the main tank. The fear further complicates the existence of every class in the raid, as it is possible to be feared into the Doomfire that is moving on the ground. While feared, healers cannot heal, damage classes cannot do direct damage, and decursers cannot remove Grip of the Legion. Therefore, the more Shamans are present to lay down Tremor Totems, the easier the encounter becomes. Healers will be able to resume healing earlier, DPS classes will have more time to DPS and are less likely to take Doomfire damage, while decursers can remove Grip of the Legion early. With 3 Shamans in the raid, give one to a melee group that will be your primary source of DPS, and put the remaining two in groups consisting of healers and Mages, who act as decursers. Spread these two groups out, to make sure that healers and Mages that benefit from Tremor Totem are in range of every other player in the raid. Heal early and decursers at the earliest opportunity, as that opportunity will be lost if Archimonde fears or Air Bursts the affected target away.

Archimonde's final ability usually signals the raid's demise. Named Finger of Death, it inflicts 20,000 shadow damage to the affected target, but is only performed when no targets are available in melee range, typically during a wipe.

Die in a fire

While this is rarely a sound piece of advice, during the Archimonde encounter dying in a Doomfire does not cause a durability hit. Therefore, once several players are dead and a wipe is imminent, look for the nearest Doomfire and bathe in it.

Positioning plays an important role in the encounter. Players must always be in range of a healer and a decurser, however, standing too close will result in several people being affected by Air Burst every time. The nearby presence of the Well of Eternity does not make matters easier, as any caster hit by Air Burst that lands in the water will be unable to cast any spells for 30 seconds. A diagram with suggested positioning is provided for guidance, but positioning of individual players during the attempt has to be very flexible, in reaction to Doomfire spawns. When positioning himself, every player must follow a long list of guidelines. Everyone should always be in range of a healer and a decurser, and those in a group with a Shaman should always be in range of his Tremor Totem. While observing these range restrictions, spread out as well as possible to minimize the number of players affected by Air Burst. Always move well away from Doomfires, ideally in excess of 15 yards, as Archimonde's next fear can send you running towards it.

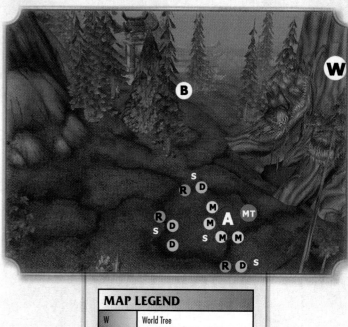

MAP LEGEND	
W	World Tree
A	Archimonde
B	Buff spot
MT	Main Tank
M	Melee classes
S	Shaman
D	Decurser
R	Ranged classes

Other than positioning, the key in this encounter is ensuring everyone's survival. This starts with gear selection, by using pieces with high stamina. Consider a target of 11,000 hit points (when fully buffed) for every player in the raid. Apart from the selection of gear, prioritize healing and decursing at all times. Mages that see a target affected by Grip of the Legion should interrupt their current spell and decurse immediately. Targets affected by Doomfire or Grip of the Legion that are hit by Air Burst and knocked away, should announce this immediately in order to have a healer or decurser move towards them, and be prepared to use Healing Potions, Health Stones or Fire Protection Potions to survive until their arrival.

In the event of someone's death, do your best to salvage the attempt, as wipe recovery is not possible and everyone will die in a wipe. Green Soul Charges can usually be healed through. Red and Yellow Soul Charges are much harder to live through, but attempt it by having the main tank use Shield Wall and focusing the raid's healing towards having every player in the raid at full health.

The objective of the encounter is to bring Archimonde's hit points to 10 percent, at which time an event will take place which will result in Archimonde's death. This is started by Archimonde running away from the raid, in order for him to use his Finger of Death ability. Fortunately, powerful allies are watching over, and players will be granted the Protection of Elune, which will make them immune to all of Archimonde's abilities. Ancient Wisps will spawn from all directions and run towards Archimonde then detonate, which will cause the mighty Eredar's demise. Congratulations, you have completed the Battle of Mount Hyjal.

LOOT

Helm of the Forgotten Conqueror: Tier 6 helm token (Paladin, Priest, Warlock)

Helm of the Forgotten Vanquisher: Tier 6 helm token (Rogue, Mage, Druid)

Helm of the Forgotten Protector: Tier 6 helm token (Warrior, Hunter, Shaman)

Cataclysm's Edge: Two-Hand / Sword, 386 - 580 Damage, Speed 3.50, (138.0 dps), +75 Strength, +49 Stamina, Equip: Your attacks ignore 335 of your opponent's armor.

Legguards of Endless Rage: Legs / Plate, 1650 Armor, +70 Strength, +61 Stamina, Equip: Improves hit rating by 19, Improves critical strike rating by 46.

Savior's Grasp: Chest / Plate, 1886 Armor, +69 Stamina, +48 Intellect, Equip: Improves spell critical strike rating by 46, Increases healing done by spells and effects by up to 106.

Midnight Chestguard: Chest / Leather, 474 Armor, +64 Stamina, Blue Socket, Red Socket, Yellow Socket, Socket Bonus: +8 Attack Power, Equip: Improves hit rating by 29, Improves critical strike rating by 46, Increases attack power by 106.

Bristleblitz Striker: Ranged / Bow, 201 - 374 Damage, Speed 3.00, (95.8 dps), +28 Stamina , Equip: Improves critical strike rating by 25.

Mail of Fevered Pursuit: Chest / Mail, 1055 Armor, +49 Agility, +66 Stamina, Equip: Improves critical strike rating by 29, Increases attack power by 108, Restores 8 mana per 5 sec.

Apostle of Argus: Two-Hand / Staff, 145 - 322 Damage, Speed 3.20, (73.2 dps), +62 Stamina, +59 Intellect, Equip: Increases healing done by spells and effects by up to 486, Restores 23 mana per 5 sec.

Antonidas's Aegis of Rapt Concentration: Off Hand / Shield, 6336 Armor, 174 Block, +28 Stamina, +20 Intellect, Equip: Improves spell critical strike rating by 20, Increases damage and healing done by magical spells and effects by up to 42.

Tempest of Chaos: Main Hand / Sword, 16 - 131 Damage, Speed 1.80, (41.0 dps), +30 Stamina, +22 Intellect, Equip: Improves spell hit rating by 17, Improves spell critical strike rating by 24, Increases damage and healing done by magical spells and effects by up to 259.

Scepter of Purification: Off-hand, +24 Stamina, +17 Intellect, +25 Spirit, Equip: Increases healing done by spells and effects by up to 77.

Leggings of Eternity: Legs / Cloth, 221 Armor, +45 Stamina, +38 Intellect, Blue Socket, Blue Socket, Blue Socket, Socket Bonus: +9 Healing, Equip: Increases healing done by spells and effects by up to 121, Restores 16 mana per 5 sec.

Robes of Rhonin: Chest / Cloth, 253 Armor, +55 Stamina, +38 Intellect, Equip: Improves spell hit rating by 27, Improves spell critical strike rating by 24, Increases damage and healing done by magical spells and effects by up to 81.

BLACK TEMPLE

Once a place of worship for the Draenai, the Temple of Karabor served as the focal point of their faith. Since then it has changed hands many times, first falling under the control of the Warlocks of the Shadow Council and their demonic magic, the temple was later to become the demon general Magtheridon's seat of power. Under the name bestowed to it by the orcish spellcasters, the Black Temple would become the scene of a battle between Magtheridon and Illidan, the Betrayer. Illidan would finally claim the temple as his own. What remains of the proud Draenai temple is now a darkened shell from where Illidan and his minions rule the remains of Draenor, now known as the Outlands.

The Black Temple is a tier 6 raid instance, the highest in the Burning Crusade expansion. Just like Mount Hyjal, entrance to it is granted only to those who have fully completed the previous tier of raiding, and are now looking for the ultimate challenge, a showdown with Illidan Stormrage himself.

DUNGEON INFORMATION

Location	Shadowmoon Valley
Region	Contested
Quests	Alliance and Horde
Suggested Level	70 (25-person raid)
Enemy Types	Demons, Naga, Orcs, Humanoids
Time to Complete	6-8 hours

MAP OF THE BLACK TEMPLE

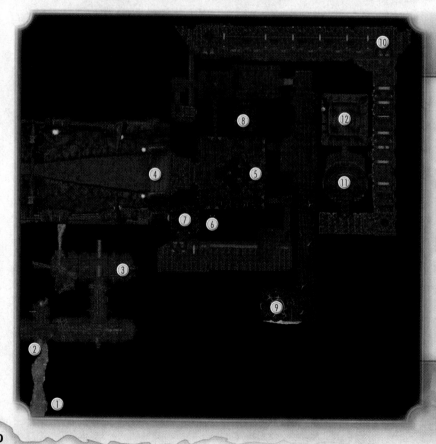

MAP LEGEND	
1	Entrance
2	Spirit of Olum
3	High Warlord Naj'entus
4	Supremus
5	Ashtongue Camp
6	Shade of Akama
7	Teron Gorefiend
8	Gurtogg Bloodboil
9	Reliquary of Souls
10	Mother Shahraz
11	Illidari Council
12	Illidan Stormrage

ATTUNEMENT

The attunement process to the Black Temple is without a doubt the hardest and longest for any dungeon currently in the game. For those allied with the Scryers it begins at the Sanctum of the Stars, while those who have sworn allegiance to the Aldor must go to the Altar of Sha'tar, both of which can be found in Shadowmoon Valley. Players must first recover the Tablets of Baa'ri, then obtain Akama's orders from Oronu the Elder, and finally obtain the four medallion fragments given to the Ashtongue Corruptors before they are sent to the Warden's Cage, where Akama resides. Before they are granted an audience, players must slay the satyr known as Zandras who patrols the prison walls. Akama now reveals the secret of the Medallions of Karabor, which eventually allow players entrance into the Black Temple. However, Seer Udalo, the brave deathsworn that found the final missing piece is now held by Kael'thas inside the Arcatraz in Tempest Keep.

While every step of the quest so far can be completed by individual players, breaking into Arcatraz requires a group. Seer Udalo can be found in the room before Harbinger Skyriss, the final boss in Arcatraz, but regrettably adventurers will reach him too late. An inscription covered by his fallen body guides the group to the Ata'mal terrace where they must defeat Shadowlord Deathwail and obtain the Heart of Fury from him.

The completed Medallion of Karabor must now be brought to A'dal in Shattrath City, where players are rewarded for the completion of this set of quests.

Attunement however is far from complete, and further steps require the full strength of a 25-man raid. Seer Olum has been imprisoned by Fathom Lord Karathress inside Serpentshrine Cavern. Upon his release, he sends players back to Akama to deliver his warning. Akama's plan involves sending the raid of adventurers to Tempest Keep, where they must slay Al'ar while wearing the Ashtongue Cowls as a disguise. The final challenge for the raid group is retrieving the phylactery of Rage Winterchill in Mount Hyjal, which of course requires the completion of both Serpentshrine Cavern and Tempest keep.

With this final artifact in their hands, players return to A'dal in Shattrath City, where a plan is hatched. The Naaru will create a distraction in front of the Black Temple, which allows Akama and Maiev to enter the temple. With their part in the distraction fulfilled, players are rewarded with Medallions of Karabor a sign of trust from both the Ashtongue and the Naaru, but also the key to enter the Black Temple.

Attunement is now complete, but the quest line is not. Adventurers must now make contact with Akama's followers, inside the Black Temple, a task not as easy as it seems. Onward, to the Black Temple!

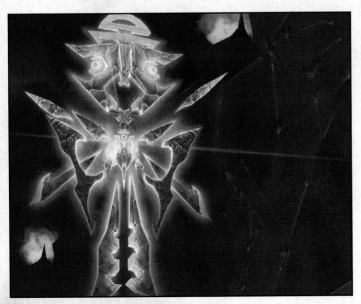

THE TEMPLE'S DEFENDERS

The first inhabitants of the sewers below the Black Temple should not pose a threat to the raid. Clearing the packs of mobs between boss encounters is generally a painless process when compared to Serpentshrine Cavern or Tempest Keep.

For the packs containing Aqueous Lords, start by Polymorphing their Naga companions. Turn the Lords away from the raid and kill them as fast as possible, as they periodically summon Aqueous Spawns, which, when left alone for a long period of time attempt to Heal their master.

The only pack of mobs that can be problematic is located in the room that also houses High Warlord Naj'entus. There are always 6 mobs in the pack, of which two are always Coilskar Generals. These are immune to crowd-controlling effects and do significant damage. The rest of the pull can consist of a mix of Coilskar Soothsayers, Harpooners, and their Dragon Turtle pets, or Aqueous Surgers. All these can be crowd controlled, but Generals have the ability to both remove all types of crowd control, as well as make their allies immune to them for a short duration. To avoid this, place the two tanks that will control the Generals at the bottom of the ramp that leads to this room and use Hunters to misdirect the Generals to them. Crowd control everything else on the spot, by Polymorphing Soothsayers, Sleeping the Turtles, and Banishing the Surgers. Kill the Generals first, then the rest of the pack.

HIGH WARLORD NAJ'ENTUS

Although considered by many to be an easy "reward" boss for players who have just completed the previous tier of raiding, Naj'entus is certainly not a walk in the park. Particularly not for your healers, as the raid-wide damage taken during this encounter is one of the highest in the game.

HP	3794000	Damage	11152-15768
Abilities	**Needle Spine**: Deals 2890 to 3910 damage and an additional 2280 to 2520 damage to nearby enemies.			
	Horseshoe Swipe: Inflicts weapon damage plus 1 to an enemy and its nearest ally.			
	Impaling Spine: Deals 4513 to 4987 initial Physical damage plus an additional 2750 Physical damage every 3 sec. for 30 sec. Stuns the target for 30 sec. or until the spine is removed.			
	Tidal Burst: Deals 8500 Frost damage to all targets in the area.			
	Tidal Shield: Protects the caster from most attacks and spells. In addition, the caster regenerates health.			

LOOT

Ring of Calming Waves: Finger, +19 Stamina, +27 Intellect, Equip: Improves spell critical strike rating by 24, Increases healing done by spells and effects by up to 64.

Halberd of Desolation: Two-Hand / Polearm, 365 - 548 Damage, Speed 3.50, (130.4 dps), +51 Agility, +57 Stamina, Equip: Improves hit rating by 30, Increases attack power by 100.

Eternium Shell Bracers: Wrist / Plate, 772 Armor, +52 Stamina, Equip: Increases defense rating by +24, Increases your dodge rating by 26.

Guise of the Tidal Lurker: Head / Leather, 360 Armor, +39 Stamina, +35 Intellect, Meta Socket, Red Socket, Socket Bonus: 2 mana per 5 sec., Equip: Increases healing done by spells and effects by up to 103, Restores 15 mana per 5 sec.

Ring of Captured Storms: Finger, Equip: Improves spell hit rating by 19, Improves spell critical strike rating by 29, Increases damage and healing done by magical spells and effects by up to 42.

Helm of Soothing Currents: Head / Mail, 803 Armor, +40 Stamina, +42 Intellect, Blue Socket, Meta Socket, Socket Bonus: +9 Healing, Equip: Increases healing done by spells and effects by up to 118, Restores 10 mana per 5 sec.

Fists of Mukoa: Hands / Mail, 617 Armor, +25 Agility, +24 Stamina, +17 Intellect, Equip: Improves haste rating by 37, Increases attack power by 76.

Rising Tide: One-Hand / Axe, 208 - 313 Damage, Speed 2.60, (100.2 dps), +33 Stamina, Equip: Improves hit rating by 21, Increases attack power by 44.

The Maelstrom's Fury: One-Hand / Dagger, 37 - 110 Damage, Speed 1.80, (41.3 dps), +33 Stamina, +21 Intellect, Equip: Improves spell critical strike rating by 22, Increases damage and healing done by magical spells and effects by up to 236.

Slippers of the Seacaller: Feet / Cloth, 162 Armor, +25 Stamina, +18 Intellect, +18 Spirit, Yellow Socket, Blue Socket, Socket Bonus: +4 Spell Damage, Equip: Improves spell critical strike rating by 29, Increases damage and healing done by magical spells and effects by up to 44.

Boots of Oceanic Fury: Feet / Mail, 679 Armor, +28 Stamina, +36 Intellect, Equip: Improves spell critical strike rating by 26, Increases damage and healing done by magical spells and effects by up to 55.

Pearl Inlaid Boots: Feet / Plate, 1213 Armor, +37 Stamina, +27 Intellect, Equip: Improves spell critical strike rating by 28, Increases healing done by spells and effects by up to 84, Restores 8 mana per 5 sec.

Tide-stomper's Greaves: Feet / Plate, 1213 Armor, +56 Stamina, Red Socket, Yellow Socket, Socket Bonus: +4 Stamina, Equip: Increases defense rating by +19, Increases your dodge rating by 29, Increases damage and healing done by magical spells and effects by up to 30.

Mantle of Darkness: Shoulder / Leather, 333 Armor, +34 Stamina, Equip: Improves hit rating by 22, Improves critical strike rating by 33, Increases attack power by 94.

RAID COMPOSITION

Because of the attunement process, on your first visit to the Black Temple you are unlikely to be able to choose a particular raid composition and may even have to attempt Naj'entus without a full 25-man raid. It is indeed possible to defeat him with 21-22 players, but not if the ones who are missing are healers. Only one tank is necessary, but 7 healers should be considered a minimum. Ranged DPS classes are preferable over melee DPS classes due to area of effect abilities.

STRATEGY

Apart from his melee attack on the main tank which usually does around 4,000 damage, the most common ability used by Naj'entus is Needle Spine. It inflicts 2,890 to 3,910 damage to its primary target and an additional 2,280 to 2,520 damage to every player in a 6 yard range from the primary target. This ability has a large impact on the positioning of the raid. The groups should be arranged in a circle around Naj'entus, with players spaced out at least 6 yards from each other. The melee group should be divided in two camps in order to avoid everyone being hit by Needle Spine at the same time. A diagram is provided for further detail.

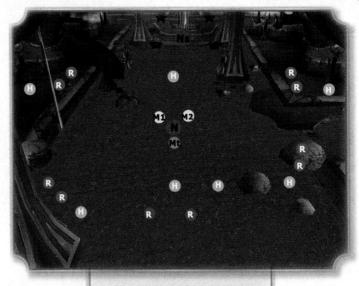

MAP LEGEND	
Ns	Naj'entus Spawn Point
N	Naj'entus (Tanking Position)
MT	Main Tank
M1	Melee Group 1
M2	Melee Group 2
R	Ranged DPS classes
H	Healers

Naj'entus' trademark ability however is named Impaling Spine. This fires off a massive spine at a random secondary target impaling it to the ground. The initial impact inflicts 4,513 to 4,987 damage but the spine also causes the target to bleed for 2,750 damage every 3 seconds while it is impaled. Impaled targets can be saved by nearby players who right click the spine going through their body. This stops the bleed effect and the spine will be transferred to the inventory of the rescuer who clicked it.

The only other ability used during this encounter is named Tidal Shield. This ability is used exactly every 60 seconds. It encases Naj'entus in a shield that makes him immune to all attacks. While shielded, Naj'entus heal 1% of his hit points every 2 seconds. To break the shield, one of the players that has picked up a Naj'entus Spine must throw it back at him. This is done by using the item in their inventory. The shield will break with a massive Tidal Burst, which deals 8,500 Frost damage to every player in the raid. This process is repeated every minute, with Naj'entus always impaling two players in between shielding himself. The raid wide damage taken when the shield is Broken is enormous but the timing of it is in the hands of the players. Wait until everyone has full health before throwing the spine. Allowing Naj'entus to heal a few percent of his health is not a big issue, while losing several members of the raid certainly is. When Naj'entus shields himself, everyone must be healed as soon as possible. If you are not at full health, bandage yourself, use a healthstone, or a Frost Protection potion if they are available. Power Word: Shield, Frost Ward, and Mana Shield should also be used to absorb some of the damage caused by the explosion. After the explosion, heal everyone as soon as possible, starting with the main tank.

The key elements in the defeating this encounter are patience, positioning, itemization choices, and good healing. First of all, always be patient with throwing the spine until you are sure everyone will survive the Tidal Burst. Spreading out adequately minimizes raid wide damage from Needle Spine, and quick healing ensures people will not die from Tidal Burst or combinations of abilities such as a Needle Spine following an Impaling Spine.

Items with higher than average stamina can make a huge difference for this encounter. Over 8,500 hit points is obviously a basic requirement, but through careful gear selection most players in the raid should easily be able to reach 10,000 to 11,000 hit points, which will dramatically increase their chance to survive. While patience is a virtue, you need to break his shield as soon as you are sure nobody will die from Tidal Burst. Allowing him to heal too much every time he shields himself will see the raid reaching the 8 minute enrage timer, although that is unlikely for a raid with the level of itemization required to reach the Black Temple.

DEEPER INTO THE DARK

Keep your high stamina items equipped for the next room and stay spread out because the Aqueous Spawns have an area of effect Sludge Nova that can inflict large amounts of damage to groups of players. Shamans can use Greater Earth Elementals to tank them with great success as they are immune to the nature damage dealt by the Spawns.

Move through the pipe on the western side of the room and you find yourself in a large courtyard known as the Illidari training grounds which are occupied by a large variety of enemies.

Illidari Fearbringers temporarily stun players in a wide area around them which makes it difficult to move out of the area of effect of their Illidari Flames. Pulling two Fearbringers at the same time is a recipe for disaster, so avoid that all costs. The groups of Bonechewer Workers can easily be tanked by a Paladin, but protection Warriors or feral Druids should tank the hard hitting Bonechewer Taskmasters that lead the groups of workers. Finally, be aware that attacking the patrolling Dragonmaw Wyrmcallers causes them to summon the flying Dragonmaw Windreavers. Move out of the range of their abilities to force them to land, enabling melee DPS classes to bring them down.

SUPREMUS

Supremus is without a doubt the easiest encounter you will face, not only in Black Temple, but across this 6th tier of raiding. Every mechanic used during this encounter has already been seen before, and despite his high hit points, in the area of 4.5 million, he has a very generous 15 minute enrage timer.

HP	4552800	Damage	14936-21118
Abilities	**Molten Punch**: A trail of fire travels lasting 8 sec. and deals 3325 to 3675 Fire damage to any players that make contact with it.		
	Hateful Strike: Strikes a target between the 2nd and 4th highest on Supremus hate list for 27750 to 32250 Physical damage.		
	Volcanic Eruption: Deals 4163 to 4837 Fire damage in a 15-yard radius.		
	Charge: Charges at a target and knocks it back.		

🌀 LOOT

Nether Shadow Tunic: Chest / Leather, 444 Armor, +36 Agility, +52 Stamina, Red Socket, Yellow Socket, Blue Socket, Socket Bonus: +8 Attack Power, Equip: Improves hit rating by 35, Increases attack power by 86.

Legionkiller: Crossbow, 184 - 342 Damage, Speed 2.90, (90.7 dps), +21 Agility, +30 Stamina

Idol of the White Stag: Idol, Equip: Your Mangle ability also increases your attack power by 94 for 12 sec.

Naturalist's Preserving Cinch: Waist / Mail, 556 Armor, +22 Stamina, +30 Intellect, Equip: Improves spell haste rating by 37, Increases healing done by spells and effects by up to 66.

The Brutalizer: One-Hand / Axe, 128 - 193 Damage, Speed 1.60, (100.3 dps), +33 Stamina, Equip: Increases defense rating by +22, Increases axe skill rating by 21.

Syphon of the Nathrezim: One-Hand / Mace, 196 – 365 Damage, Speed 2.80, (100.2 dps), Equip: Increases attack power by 50.

Chance on hit: Fills you with fel energy allowing all melee attacks to drain life from opponents.

Pauldrons of Abyssal Fury: Shoulder / Plate, 1324 Armor, +72 Stamina, Equip: Increases defense rating by +28, Increases your dodge rating by 36.

Wraps of Precise Flight: Wrist / Mail, 432 Armor, +18 Agility, +28 Stamina, +20 Intellect, Equip: Improves critical strike rating by 19, Increases attack power by 58.

Felstone Bulwark: Off Hand / Shield, 5930 Armor, 160 Block, +28 Stamina, +21 Intellect, Equip: Improves spell critical strike rating by 27, Increases healing done by spells and effects by up to 64.

Waistwrap of Infinity: Waist / Cloth, 133 Armor, +31 Stamina, +22 Intellect, Equip: Improves spell haste rating by 32, Increases damage and healing done by magical spells and effects by up to 56.

Bands of the Coming Storm: Wrist / Mail, 432 Armor, +28 Stamina, +28 Intellect, Equip: Improves spell critical strike rating by 21, Increases damage and healing done by magical spells and effects by up to 34.

Choker of Endless Nightmares: Neck, Equip: Improves hit rating by 21, Improves critical strike rating by 27, Increases attack power by 72.

Band of the Abyssal Lord: Finger, +53 Stamina, Equip: Increases defense rating by +27, Improves hit rating by 21.

RAID COMPOSITION

Two tanks are required for this encounter, with the rest of the raid composition being largely irrelevant. Six healers are sufficient, with the rest of the raid spots available to DPS classes. Due to the mechanics of the encounter, while certainly avoidable, deaths among classes in melee range are significantly higher than deaths among ranged classes.

STRATEGY

The Supremus encounter consists of two alternating stages, each lasting around one minute each. During the first stage he can be tanked normally, and hits the tank for around 5,000 damage. Periodically he will use his Hateful Strike ability on the target in his melee range with the most hit points apart from the main tank. A well armored off-tank will be hit in the area of 9,000 damage, but the hit can be fatal to non-tanks. To avoid other players from getting hit, the off tank must be healed to full as soon as possible and always be in melee range of Supremus.

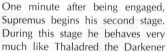

Throughout the encounter, Supremus launches trails of blue Molten Flame on the ground, towards a random player in the raid. All players in its path must move or they suffer 3,325 to 3,675 Fire damage every second they are standing in it.

One minute after being engaged, Supremus begins his second stage. During this stage he behaves very much like Thaladred the Darkener during the Kael'thas encounter, which all players in the raid will be familiar with. He drops aggro from the main tank, set his gaze on a random target and start chasing it. Since he moves slower than player run speed he should be easy to avoid, but players that are caught will usually die in one swing. Just like Thaladred, he occasionally throws the player he is chasing a large distance across the courtyard. Frequently during this stage he will switch targets to another player and the process is repeated.

During this second stage only, Supremus will cause the ground to crack open into volcanoes that erupt in fireballs. Volcanoes always appear on top of a player in the raid who together with all others in a 15 yard range must move away immediately. Failure to leave the area in time results in 4,163 to 4,837 Fire damage every second.

During this stage it is recommended that the tanks follow Supremus around as he chases random players, and conserve rage for when the stage has finished. One minute after entering stage 2, Supremus switches back to his initial stage, wiping all aggro in the process. Using the accumulated rage, tanks can easily stay ahead of the damage dealing classes. This is repeated until either Supremus dies or he reaches his 15 minute enrage timer.

The key to defeating Supremus is rapidly healing the tank and offtank, and avoiding too many deaths to volcanoes. Both are easily achievable goals. With him dead, players will now be able to reach their allies, the Deathsworn, and gain access to the depths of the Black Temple.

QUEST

SEEK OUT THE ASHTONGUE

Quest Level	70
Location	Black Temple, Shadowmoon Valley
Starts at	Xi'ri, Shadowmoon Valley
Ends at	Seer Kanai, Black Temple
Goal	Find Akama's followers and talk to Seer Kanai.

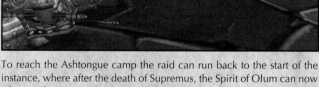

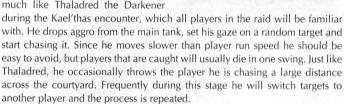

To reach the Ashtongue camp the raid can run back to the start of the instance, where after the death of Supremus, the Spirit of Olum can now teleport players into the depths of the Temple.

The quest line continues, with the raid being asked to help Akama free his soul by defeating the Shade of Akama. This is only one of several options now open to the raid. From the Ashtongue camp, the raid can head southwest to reach the Refectory where the Shade of Akama can be found, or southeast to face Teron Gorefiend. The path west leads back to the Illidari Training grounds and the corpse of Supremus, while the door to the Den of Mortal Delights to the northwest stays locked until the first six bosses in the temple have been slain. Heading northeast through the Halls of Anguish, the raid can choose between heading to the Shrine of Lost Souls which is host to the Reliquary of Souls Encounter. Opposite to it lies the path to Gurtogg Bloodboil, the last of the encounters in the inner temple. They can be attempted in any order, and therefore the path described below is just a suggestion. However, most guilds find it the most rewarding route.

SHADE OF AKAMA

The Shade of Akama is yet another boss that can be defeated even without a full raid. Killing the Shade of Akama is also the next step in the Black Temple quest line.

HP	1001616	Damage	23897-33789

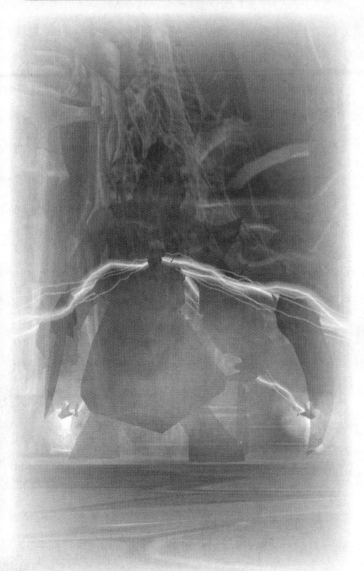

LOOT

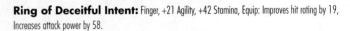

Ring of Deceitful Intent: Finger, +21 Agility, +42 Stamina, Equip: Improves hit rating by 19, Increases attack power by 58.

Spiritwalker Gauntlets: Hands / Mail, 617 Armor, +38 Stamina, +27 Intellect, Equip: Improves spell haste rating by 37, Increases healing done by spells and effects by up to 84.

Kilt of Immortal Nature: Legs / Leather, 388 Armor, +40 Stamina, +42 Intellect, Blue Socket, Yellow Socket, Blue Socket, Socket Bonus: +9 Healing, Equip: Increases healing done by spells and effects by up to 118, Restores 10 mana per 5 sec.

Grips of Silent Justice: Hands / Plate, 1103 Armor, +40 Strength, +37 Stamina, Red Socket, Red Socket, Socket Bonus: +4 Stamina, Equip: Improves hit rating by 15, Your attacks ignore 175 of your opponent's armor.

Wristbands of Divine Influence: Wrist / Cloth, 103 Armor, +24 Stamina, +21 Intellect, +28 Spirit, Equip: Increases healing done by spells and effects by up to 62.

Praetorian's Legguards: Legs / Plate, 1544 Armor, +75 Stamina, Yellow Socket, Yellow Socket, Red Socket, Socket Bonus: +6 Stamina, Equip: Increases your dodge rating by 35, Increases your parry rating by 43, Improves hit rating by 18.

Shoulders of the Hidden Predator: Shoulder / Mail, 741 Armor, +38 Agility, +37 Stamina, Equip: Improves critical strike rating by 26, Increases attack power by 76.

Shadow-walker's Cord: Waist / Leather, 249 Armor, +27 Agility, +38 Stamina, Equip: Improves haste rating by 37, Increases attack power by 76.

Myrmidon's Treads: Feet / Plate, 1213 Armor, +56 Stamina, Yellow Socket, Red Socket, Socket Bonus: +3 Dodge Rating, Equip: Increases defense rating by +30, Increases your dodge rating by 26, Improves hit rating by 17.

Focused Mana Bindings: Wrist / Cloth, 103 Armor, +27 Stamina, +20 Intellect, Equip: Improves spell hit rating by 19, Increases damage and healing done by magical spells and effects by up to 42.

Amice of Brilliant Light: Shoulder / Cloth, 177 Armor, +38 Stamina, +27 Intellect, +37 Spirit, Equip: Increases healing done by spells and effects by up to 84.

Flashfire Girdle: Waist / Mail, 556 Armor, +27 Stamina, +26 Intellect, Equip: Improves spell critical strike rating by 18, Improves spell haste rating by 37, Increases damage and healing done by magical spells and effects by up to 44.

The Seeker's Wristguards: Wrist / Plate, 772 Armor, +43 Stamina, Equip: Increases defense rating by +21, Increases your shield block rating by 28, Increases damage and healing done by magical spells and effects by up to 22.

Blind-Seers Icon: Off-hand, +25 Stamina, +16 Intellect, Equip: Improves spell hit rating by 24, Increases damage and healing done by magical spells and effects by up to 42.

QUEST

REDEMPTION OF THE ASHTONGUE

Quest Level	70
Location	Black Temple, Shadowmoon Valley
Starts at	Seer Kanai, Black Temple
Ends at	Seer Kanai, Black Temple
Goal	Help Akama free his soul and he will grant access to Illidan's sanctum.

RAID COMPOSITION

Three tanks are required for this encounter where once again, good planning and execution ensures only minimal healing is needed. Six healers are sufficient, with the rest of the raid spots available to DPS classes. In terms of dealing damage, all DPS classes are equally useful, but the need to crowd control during this encounter makes Mages the class of choice. Four Mages effectively neutralizes the major threat, but the encounter is easily possible even with fewer Mages. Two Hunters are also recommended.

STRATEGY

The Shade of Akama encounter consists of two distinct stages. The first one is started by talking to Akama who is hiding in the shadows close to the entrance of the Refectory. The objective of the first stage is to kill the Channelers that are keeping the Shade of Akama banished on the platform to the south of the room. These will not attack players and just focus on keeping the Shade of Akama controlled.

During this stage a constant stream of mobs enter the battle through the gateways on the eastern and western sides of the room. Every 30-40 seconds, through each of the gates, a group of three Broken enter the battle. These groups consist of an Ashtongue Rogue, an Ashtongue Elementalist and an Ashtongue Spiritbinder, each with around 25,000 hit points. Rogues attack players with their daggers which can also apply Debilitating Poison, a debuff that deals 1,665 to 1,935 Nature damage every 2 seconds, while also slowing down attacks and spellcasting speed by 50%. Ashtongue Elementalists cast Rain of Fire on nearby players who need to move out of its area of effect. Spiritbinders attempt to heal their allies.

On each side, have a Hunter place down a Frost Trap in front of the doorways. The groups of 3 mobs will be slowed as they enter the room, and a tank can pick up the Spiritbinder, while the Rogue and Elementalist are Polymorphed by Mages. Kill the Spiritbinder, then assist the tank as he attacks the Rogue and finally the Elementalist. One healer should be enough to keep the entire group up. Two Mages and one Hunter should be enough to finish off all 3 mobs before a new wave spawns.

Between the waves, solitary Ashtongue Sorcerers and Defenders also enter the battle. Sorcerers always enter through the eastern gate and head straight to the Shade of Akama, ignoring all players. Once next to the Shade it will help the Channelers in their attempt to keep the Shade of Akama banished. Defenders always enter through the western gateway and must be picked up by the third tank. Apart from their moderately strong melee attack, they also hit the tank with Debilitating Strike, an ability which reduces the melee damage done by that tank by 75%. Each Defender has around 75,000 hit points. It is not necessary to kill them, as one tank, with the help of one healer at the beginning, can easily control all the defenders that will spawn during the encounter. A second healer should be added once more than four Defenders are being tanked.

While the waves of mobs are being dealt with by the Defender tank and the two groups positioned at the gates, the remaining DPS classes in the raid must kill the Channelers keeping Akama banished, as well as the Sorcerers that are trying to help them. Affliction Warlocks are particularly suitable for this task, as they can apply their damage over time spells to every Channeler. Shadow Priests should also be attacking these, as their constant damage helps the mana regeneration of all players in their groups. Rogues are also able to do large amounts of damage to these stationary targets, particularly when grouped with Shamans that drop Windfury Totems. Once the Channelers and Sorcerers have been killed, the Shade of Akama begins walking towards Akama, starting the second stage.

During the second stage, adds no longer enter the battle, but those that are already inside the Refectory will stay for the remainder. Any remaining Rogues or Elementalists can be chain-polymorphed, while the raid attacks the Shade of Akama. The Shade has a very powerful melee attack, averaging around 15,000 damage per swing. Fortunately, the Shade will be tanked by Akama and because of its low hit points will be finished off by the raid in around a minute, before Akama's demise.

CRY HAVOK

Leave the Refectory and head east up the stairs, towards Teron Gorefiend. On your way are a number of Shadowmoon Houndmasters and their Riding Hounds. Kill the Hounds first, as they enrage should their masters fall in battle first. Shadowmoon Deathshapers and Bloodmages should be polymorphed and dealt with on an individual basis, as uncontrolled Deathshapers can Deathcoil players as well as summon undead helpers. Bloodmages have powerful frontal abilities such as Bloodbolt, an area of effect damage spell or Blood Siphon, an ability that will drain player hit points while healing the Bloodmage. Shadowmoon Soldiers can easily be tanked by a Paladin, as long as the Weapon Master is split from the group and offtanked by a dedicated tank.

TERON GOREFIEND

For most raiding guilds, this is where the walk in the park ends and serious progress begins. Teron Gorefiend is not exceptionally difficult, but the encounter has a unique mechanic which must be mastered by everyone in the raid.

HP	5007750	Damage	19702-27827

Abilities	
Summon Doom Blossom: Doom Blossom fires Shadow Bolts at nearby targets.	
Incinerate: Deals 2775 to 3225 Fire damage on impact and an additional 8325 damage over 3 sec.	
Shadow of Death: Applies a 60 second debuff to a random player. When the debuff is removed via the player dying or 60 seconds have passed, the player is removed from the fight and granted control of a Vengeful Spirit. This also spawns several Shadowy Constructs at the player's current position. The Vengeful Spirit lasts 60 seconds, after which it dissipates, killing the player. Players killed this way can be ressed after their Vengeful Spirit has dissipated.	
Crushing Shadows: Increases Shadow damage dealt to them by 60% for 15 sec.	
Destroy Spirit: Destroys a target Vengeful Spirit.	

LOOT

Gauntlets of Enforcement: Hands / Plate, 1103 Armor, +70 Stamina, Equip: Increases defense rating by +32, Increases the block value of your shield by 36, Increases sword, mace and axe skill ratings by 21.

Shadowmoon Destroyer's Drape: Back, 118 Armor, +24 Stamina, Equip: Improves hit rating by 17, Improves critical strike rating by 24, Increases attack power by 72.

Insidious Bands: Wrist / Leather, 194 Armor, +28 Agility, +28 Stamina, Yellow Socket, Socket Bonus: +2 Agility, Equip: Improves hit rating by 12, Increases attack power by 58.

Rifle of the Stoic Guardian: Gun, 120 - 224 Damage, Speed 1.90, (90.5 dps), +31 Stamina, Equip: Increases your dodge rating by 20.

Twisted Blades of Zarak: Thrown, 101 - 152 Damage, Speed 1.40, (90.4 dps), +23 Agility, Equip: Improves critical strike rating by 16.

Robe of the Shadow Council: Chest / Cloth, 236 Armor, +37 Stamina, +36 Intellect, +26 Spirit, Equip: Improves spell critical strike rating by 28, Increases damage and healing done by magical spells and effects by up to 73.

Botanist's Gloves of Growth: Hands / Leather, 277 Armor, +34 Stamina, +29 Intellect, Yellow Socket, Blue Socket, Socket Bonus: +7 Healing, Equip: Improves spell haste rating by 37, Increases healing done by spells and effects by up to 84.

Cowl of Benevolence: Head / Cloth, 192 Armor, +39 Stamina, +27 Intellect, +42 Spirit, Meta Socket, Blue Socket, Socket Bonus: +9 Healing, Equip: Increases healing done by spells and effects by up to 118.

Totem of Ancestral Guidance: Totem, Equip: Increases damage done by Chain Lightning and Lightning Bolt by up to 85.

Soul Cleaver: Two-Hand / Axe, 386 - 579 Damage, Speed 3.70, (130.4 dps), +65 Strength, +63 Stamina, Equip: Your attacks ignore 315 of your opponent's armor.

Softstep Boots of Tracking: Feet / Mail, 679 Armor, +27 Agility, +29 Intellect, Equip: Improves hit rating by 17, Improves critical strike rating by 26, Increases attack power by 76.

Girdle of Lordaeron's Fallen: Waist / Plate, 993 Armor, +32 Stamina, +32 Intellect, Equip: Improves spell haste rating by 38, Increases healing done by spells and effects by up to 70.

RAID COMPOSITION

Only one tank is necessary for this encounter, and considering the high requirements for healing and DPS, bringing more than one is wasteful. Eight healers are recommended for this encounter where dispelling and fast healing are required. There is no specific advantage to any DPS class, however Warlock Soulstones come in very handy.

STRATEGY

Compared to the previous three bosses, damage to the tank is very high. Teron swings at the tank for an average of 7,000 damage, and can land crushing blows in excess of 10,000 damage. In addition, he will incinerate a random target in the raid every 20-30 seconds. That target takes an initial 2,775 to 3,225 fire damage on impact, and an additional 8325 to 9675 damage over 3 sec unless the debuff is dispelled.

Throughout the encounter Teron Gorefiend will summon Doom Blossoms: shadowy clouds that fire hundreds of Shadow Bolts at the raid over the duration of the encounter. Doom Blossoms cannot be killed and while the base damage of their Shadow Bolts averages around 1,600 damage, Teron Gorefiend periodically places a debuff named Crushing Shadows on random players in the raid. This increases the damage dealt by Shadow Bolts by 60%, turning them from a minor nuisance into a real threat.

However, the unique aspect of this encounter lies in an ability named Shadow of Death. Used for the first time 10 seconds into the encounter and every 30-40 seconds after that, Shadow of Death targets a random player that inevitably loses control of their character 55 seconds later and subsequently dies. After the 55 seconds have elapsed or upon the player's death, four Shadowy Constructs spawn in a square around the player. In the middle of the square, a Vengeful Spirit will spawn, that is controlled by the player. The Shadowy Constructs will float towards the raid and attack random players who are completely defenseless against them. Those hit by Constructs will be affected by Atrophy: a stacking ability which deals damage and weakens the target, decreasing melee, ranged, and spell casting speed by 5% per hit. The only way to kill the Shadowy Constructs is to use the Vengeful Spirits against them. These have a range of abilities which can be accessed via a pet bar.

REQUIREMENT: A PET BAR

While Hunters and Warlocks will usually have a fully configured and functional pet bar, this is less common for other classes, particularly those using customized interface modifications. Before engaging Teron Gorefiend, make sure everyone is the raid either has a tried and tested pet bar, or shortcuts to the abilities used by the Vengeful Spirits.

VENGEFUL SPIRITS HAVE THE FOLLOWING ABILITIES:

1) Spirit Strike, a melee range ability that deals 638-862 frost damage and weakens the target, reducing the damage it deals by 10% for 5 sec.

2) Spirit Lance is a ranged, single target ability that can only be used against Shadowy Constructs. It fires a burst of spirit energy dealing 6,175 to 6,825 damage to its target, temporarily slowing its movement speed by 30%.

3) Spirit Volley is a powerful, area of effect version of Spirit Lance. It will not slow its targets down, but will inflict 9,900 to 12,100 damage to all Constructs in a 12 yard radius.

4) Spirit Chains shackles Constructs in a 12 yard range in chains of spirit energy, preventing all action for 5 sec. Any damage caused will break the effect.

5) Spirit Shield protects a friendly target with a barrier of spirit, absorbing 11400 to 12600 Shadow damage. Lasts 30 sec.

Properly managing the Vengeful Spirits is essential to mastering the encounter. This starts with good positioning. Since the Constructs start moving towards the raid once they spawn, positioning should ensure that the distance between their spawn point and the raid is as long as possible. Tank Teron Gorefiend on the spot where he spawns on the balcony, and have players affected by Shadow of Death run towards the door, on the opposite side of the room. Since it takes 55 seconds before Constructs spawn, players affected by Shadow of Death can safely continue attacking Teron or healing the raid, until they have about 15-20 seconds left on their debuff, then run out to the door and wait for control of the Vengeful Spirit. Because of this delay, using Warlock Soulstones reactively on players affected by Shadow of Death will ensure they can rejoin the battle after they control their Vengeful Spirit.

Fight Against the Night

Ideally, a player gaining control of his Vengeful Spirit near the door should have enough time to kill all the Constructs before they reach the raid and do any damage. The most efficient way to do that is to start by using Spirit Volley as early as possible, which inflicts a decent amount of damage to each of the Constructs. Use Spirit Chains next to shackle all four Constructs. Switch to Spirit Lance next, while waiting on the cooldowns of Spirit Volley and Chains. Shoot each Construct two or three times, rapidly switching targets to slow them all down. By the time the last Construct has been slowed down, Spirit Volley and Chains should be available again. Use them in quick succession, then finish off any remaining Constructs.

Do not waste the time remaining on your Vengeful Spirit. Help the next player that was affected by Shadow of Death kill his Constructs. If all Constructs are dead, you can use Spirit Shield on a player affected by Shadow of Death, to minimize the chance of an early death or use Spirit Strike on Teron Gorefiend to reduce the damage done to the main tank.

Even with reactive Soulstones on players affected by Shadow of Death and having Druids use Rebirth, the raid eventually starts to dwindle in numbers. DPS on the boss is therefore very important so a full set of consumables should be used, particularly for raids doing early attempts on this boss. The tank also needs to consider using every consumable available to him.

ONTO THE RELIQUARY

With both encounters on the south side of the temple defeated, it is time to backtrack, visit the Deathsworn camp for repairs and restocking on reagents, and head for the northeast corner towards Gurtogg Bloodboil and the Reliquary of Souls.

On the way to Gurtogg, watch out for the Bonechewer Behemoths. They can stun the tank, which makes the tanks very vulnerable to the Behemoths' rapid attacks, as well as lowers their ability to generate threat. Their Fiery Comets do damage to the entire raid, which needs to group up around the Behemoths or risk getting charged. Leaving a second tank as the furthest target from the Behemoth ensures no other player can be charged and killed.

On the level below them Bonechewer Combatants and Brawlers like to engage in sparring matches which are eagerly watched by the groups of Bonechewer Spectators. Time your attack to catch the Combatants and Brawlers at low health after fighting each other, assign a tank to each of them, and use a Paladin to tank the Spectators who should be killed first.

GURTOGG BLOODBOIL

Gurtogg, like Teron Gorefiend is an average difficulty encounter when compared with the other bosses inside the Black Temple. It is also very healing intensive, but additionally requires extremely accurate raid movement.

HP	5691000	Damage	11948-16894
Abilities	**Arcing Smash:** Inflicts normal damage plus 125 in a cone in front of the caster.		
	Acidic Wound: Inflicts 300 Nature damage every 3 sec. and reduces armor by 500. Stacks up to 60 times, lasts 60 sec.		
	Eject: Inflicts normal damage plus 1000 and knocks back.		
	Bewildering Strike: Confuses the target for 8 sec.		
	Fel Geyser: Deals 3238 to 3762 Nature damage to the target and all targets within an 18-yard radius.		
	Fel-Acid Breath: Inflicts 2850 to 3150 Nature damage and an additional 2750 damage every 5 sec. in a cone in front of the caster.		
	Bloodboil: Deals 600 damage every 1 sec for 24 sec.		
	Fury: While in a Fel Rage, Gurtogg has a chance on every successful melee hit to increase his attack speed by 10%. This effect stacks.		

LOOT

Messenger of Fate: One-Hand / Dagger, 112 - 169 Damage, Speed 1.40, (100.4 dps), +22 Agility, +31 Stamina, Equip: Increases attack power by 44.

Leggings of Divine Retribution: Legs / Plate, 1544 Armor, +51 Strength, +51 Stamina, Equip: Improves critical strike rating by 35, Your attacks ignore 350 of your opponent's armor.

Girdle of Stability: Waist / Plate, 993 Armor, +56 Stamina, Red Socket, Yellow Socket, Socket Bonus: +4 Stamina, Equip: Increases defense rating by +19, Increases your dodge rating by 18, Increases the block value of your shield by 56.

Vest of Mounting Assault: Chest / Mail, 988 Armor, +58 Agility, +27 Stamina, +18 Intellect, Equip: Increases attack power by 116.

Unstoppable Aggressor's Ring: Finger, +36 Strength, +28 Stamina, Equip: Improves critical strike rating by 30 (1.4%).

Shroud of Forgiveness: Back, 118 Armor, +27 Stamina, +19 Intellect, +20 Spirit, Equip: Increases healing done by spells and effects by up to 79.

Blood-cursed Shoulderpads: Shoulder / Cloth, 177 Armor, +25 Stamina, +19 Intellect, Equip: Improves spell hit rating by 18, Improves spell critical strike rating by 25, Increases damage and healing done by magical spells and effects by up to 55.

Belt of Primal Majesty: Waist / Leather, 249 Armor, +34 Stamina, +29 Intellect, Equip: Improves spell haste rating by 37, Increases healing done by spells and effects by up to 84.

Garments of Temperance: Chest / Cloth, 236 Armor, +51 Stamina, +34 Intellect, Equip: Increases healing done by spells and effects by up to 118, Restores 20 mana per 5 sec.

Girdle of Mighty Resolve: Waist / Plate, 993 Armor, +56 Stamina, Yellow Socket, Blue Socket, Socket Bonus: +3 Dodge Rating, Equip: Increases defense rating by +26, Increases your shield block rating by 25, Increases damage and healing done by magical spells and effects by up to 30, Increases the block value of your shield by 38.

Wand of Prismatic Focus Wand, 193 - 360 Shadow Damage, Speed 1.50, (184.3 dps), +21 Stamina, Equip: Improves spell hit rating by 13, Increases damage and healing done by magical spells and effects by up to 26.

Staff of Immaculate Recovery: Two-Hand / Staff, 145 - 312 Damage, Speed 3.20, (71.5 dps), +73 Stamina, +51 Intellect, +35 Spirit, Equip: Increases healing done by spells and effects by up to 443, Restores 14 mana per 5 sec.

Shadowmoon Insignia: Trinket, Equip: Increases defense rating by +36, Increases your dodge rating by 32, Use: Increases your maximum health by 1750 for 20 sec.

RAID COMPOSITION

Two tanks are the bare minimum for this encounter, with a 3-tank strategy also being viable. A minimum of eight healers are required, nine are recommended but raids can compensate by using several Shadow Priests to contribute to raid healing. All DPS classes can perform equally well.

STRATEGY

Similar to the Teron Gorefiend encounter, damage to the main tank is high, not only due to his melee attacks that average around 3,500 damage, but also due to a stacking debuff named Acidic Wound. This reduces armor by 500 and inflicts 300 physical damage every 3 seconds per stack. The speed at which it stacks varies and is largely based on a tank's avoidance.

In addition to his melee attacks and Acidic Wound, periodically Gurtogg will hit targets in front of him with an Arcing Smash. This hits for about 25% more damage than his normal attacks, additionally placing a debuff on affected targets that reduces all healing effects received by 50% for 4 seconds. Gurtogg also has the ability to temporarily disorient his main target, which is why threat generation by the secondary tank is very important. Both the tanks will be thoroughly tested in their ability to generate good threat because of Gurtogg's Eject ability. This knocks his main target back, reducing threat already generated.

Tanking Gurtogg is very demanding as it requires constant observation and adjusting to the randomness of every attempt. Tanks cannot blindly build aggro, because should a tank avoid Disorient and Eject several times in a row he finds himself with an unhealable stack of Acidic Wound. If the active tank already has eight or more stacks of Acidic Wound, he should consider stopping and allowing the offtank to catch up in terms of threat. This encounter also challenges DPS classes to stay below both tanks in terms of threat generation or risk being killed when the main tank gets hit by Eject or Disorient.

The ability that takes the most effort to avoid is named Bloodboil. Fortunately for the tanks who already have their hands full, Bloodboil is an ability that only hits the five targets that are furthest away from Gurtogg. Targets hit take 600 damage every second for 24 seconds. This stacks, so if a target is hit for a second time during the 24 seconds, the timer will reset and the target will start taking 1,200 damage per second. It is therefore imperative that the targets hit by Bloodboil are constantly changing to avoid the debuff from stacking. With Bloodboil cast about every 10 seconds, a rotation of 3 groups of 5 players must be set up to take turns at being hit by Bloodboil. This can be achieved by having two moving groups and a static group, at medium range.

Starting with group one being hit as the furthest away, this group should move into close range, leaving the stationary group 2 as the furthest away. Once these are hit, the third Bloodboil group can move out, becoming the furthest target and taking the third Bloodboil hit. By the time Bloodboil is cast for a fourth time, the debuff will have faded from the first group who can now run out and be hit again.

MAP LEGEND	
Gs	Gurtogg Spawn Point
G	Gurtogg (Tanking Position)
Mt	Main Tank
Ot	Off-Tank
M	Melee Classes
R	Ranged DPS
H	Healer

It should be noted that ranged DPS classes and their healers make the best choices for the first and third Bloodboil groups, as they can do damage to Gurtogg even while far away and taking Bloodboil damage. The second, stationary Bloodboil Group should consist of the players healing the main tank plus an additional healer to compensate for the Bloodboil damage the stationary group will take. This assignment works best because the healers assigned to the tanks can ill afford to move and heal at the same time.

Melee classes are safe from Bloodboil, as they are never among the five furthest targets. However, they are valid targets for Fel-Acid Breath, which inflicts 2,850 to 3,150 direct Nature damage and further periodic Nature damage. Only targets that are within a 15 yard range of Gurtogg can be selected for Fel-Acid Breath, but this includes Hunter or Warlock pets. Since it has a 2 second casting time, it is possible for the selected target to move into one direction, while the other melee targets move in the opposite direction, so that only one player is affected at any one time.

After the fifth Bloodboil is cast and about a minute into the encounter, Gurtogg will cast Fel Rage on a random target in the raid. This target grows in size, gaining 30,000 hit points and 15,000 armor as well as a very significant boost to their damage and healing done. However, they also become Gurtogg's target for the next 30 seconds. Everyone else in the raid will be affected by a debuff named Insignificance and any actions they perform generate no threat. While people still need to be healed from Bloodboil ticks and the offtanks are still taking Acidic Wound damage, most of the healers in the raid must now focus on keeping this target alive. To make matters worse, upon selecting his Fel Rage target Gurtogg immediately hits everyone around the target with Fel Geyser.

This inflicts around 3,500 damage. Throughout this stage Gurtogg deals more damage than usual and gradually increases his attack speed. Should the target die, Gurtogg returns to the main tank, who has little chance of survival unless he uses Shield Wall. Should the target live, the encounter will return to normal with a fresh Bloodboil following 10 seconds later and every 10 seconds for one minute until a new Fel Rage stage. This cycle continues until Gurtogg dies or reaches his 10 minute enrage timer, which makes the encounter difficult to beat if there are early fatalities to Fel Rage.

The main points to focus on during this encounter are healing, threat management and perfecting the movement of the Bloodboil groups. Bloodboil groups are best healed by a holy Priest using Prayer of Healing, but a Chain Healing Shaman can also help, if needed. Paladins can keep up the main tank, while the offtank's Acidic Wound is best compensated for by a restoration Druid. During Fel Rage the Paladins need to switch over to the random target picked by Gurtogg together with the Shamans in the raid. Both tanks must still be healed or they will die from their Acidic Wound. This damage over time effect should fade at some point during this stage. Once the Priests in the Bloodboil groups have completely healed their groups, they can also join in the healing of the Fel Rage tank.

Threat management should be as much a worry for DPS classes as it is for tanks. While tanks are trying to switch aggro between them, DPS classes must always stay behind both of them in terms of aggro generation. A good time to use aggro reduction abilities such as Vanish, Soulshatter or Invisibility is towards the end of the second Fel Rage stage. Rogues, Warlocks and Mages should be able to do all-out damage after using their threat reducing ability. Hunters can feign death more often. Shadow Priests are not as lucky and must keep a very close eye on their aggro generation throughout the encounter. One way of reducing the threat they are generating is not using Vampiric Embrace to heal their groups. A holy Priest should have no trouble keeping these groups up and will never run into the same threat generation issues a shadow Priest would.

With threat and healing under control, it comes down to practice until the Bloodboil groups move flawlessly, avoiding the double stacking of the debuff. Maintain a good level of execution with the focus on minimizing casualties, and Gurtogg will always fall before the critical ten minutes have elapsed.

SOUL SEARCHING

All that remains in the inner temple is the Reliquary of Souls event. In order to access it, the raid needs to complete a short gauntlet of fast respawning mobs. Hungering and Suffering Soul Fragments must be tanked as they can hit cloth classes rather hard. Classes that can interrupt spell casting should watch the Suffering Soul Fragments and break their casting. Area of effect damage spells are the most effective way to clear the path through the gauntlet.

While moving through it, stay as close as possible to the eastern wall, until you reach the southeast corner of the room. If necessary, use this as a resting space allowing your casters to drink, if not, proceed along the southern wall until you reach the top of the ramp that leads to the Reliquary. Here, kill the Suffering and Hungering Soul Fragments as soon as possible, and start eating and drinking. Melee DPS classes can kill the Angered Soul Fragments before they interrupt the mana break the casters need. Have Warlocks cast Detect Invisibility on the melee classes to enable them to see the stealthed Angered Fragments. Once close to full mana run down the ramp, killing any mobs that follow you down.

RELIQUARY OF SOULS

Reliquary of Souls is without a doubt the most technical and difficult to execute encounter in the Burning Crusade. If your raid can defeat this, it can defeat any other encounter in the game, including Illidan Stormrage.

LOOT

Grips of Damnation: Hands / Leather, 277 Armor, +27 Agility, +38 Stamina, Equip: Improves haste rating by 37, Increases attack power by 76.

The Wavemender's Mantle: Shoulder / Mail, 741 Armor, +37 Stamina, +26 Intellect, Equip: Increases healing done by spells and effects by up to 84, Restores 15 mana per 5 sec.

Touch of Inspiration: Off-hand, +24 Stamina, +21 Intellect, Equip: Increases healing done by spells and effects by up to 64, Restores 12 mana per 5 sec.

Torch of the Damned: Two-Hand / Mace, 396 - 595 Damage, Speed 3.80, (130.4 dps), +51 Strength, +45 Stamina, Equip: Improves critical strike rating by 38, Improves haste rating by 50.

Gloves of Unfailing Faith: Hands / Cloth, 148 Armor, +25 Stamina, +33 Intellect, Red Socket, Blue Socket, Socket Bonus: 1 Mana per 5 sec., Equip: Increases healing done by spells and effects by up to 75, Restores 11 mana per 5 sec.

Translucent Spellthread Necklace: Neck, Equip: Improves spell hit rating by 15, Improves spell critical strike rating by 24, Increases damage and healing done by magical spells and effects by up to 46.

Crown of Empowered Fate: Head / Plate, 1434 Armor, +39 Stamina, +27 Intellect, Meta Socket, Blue Socket, Socket Bonus: +4 Spell Crit Rating, Equip: Improves spell critical strike rating by 42, Increases healing done by spells and effects by up to 118.

Pendant of Titans: Neck, +43 Stamina , Equip: Increases defense rating by +21, Increases your dodge rating by 25, Improves hit rating by 20.

Boneweave Girdle: Waist / Mail, 556 Armor, +38 Agility, +26 Intellect, Equip: Improves hit rating by 17, Improves critical strike rating by 24, Increases attack power by 76.

Naaru-Blessed Life Rod: Wand, 193 - 360 Shadow Damage, Speed 1.50, (184.3 dps), +12 Stamina, +12 Intellect, +16 Spirit, Equip: Increases healing done by spells and effects by up to 37.

Elunite Empowered Bracers: Wrist / Leather, 194 Armor, +27 Stamina, +22 Intellect, Equip: Improves spell hit rating by 19, Increases damage and healing done by magical spells and effects by up to 34, Restores 6 mana per 5 sec.

Naturewarden's Treads: Feet / Leather, 305 Armor, +39 Stamina, +18 Intellect, Yellow Socket, Blue Socket, Socket Bonus: +4 Spell Damage, Equip: Improves spell critical strike rating by 26, Increases damage and healing done by magical spells and effects by up to 44, Restores 7 mana per 5 sec.

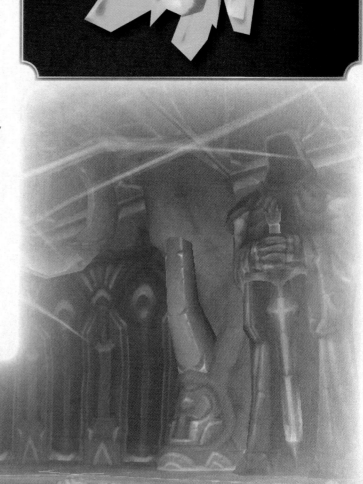

RAID COMPOSITION

The encounter is feasible with only one tank, but raids should consider bringing a second one for backup. The DPS requirement to defeat this encounter is higher than for any other boss in the zone, but since the encounter is also very healing-intensive, replacing healers with DPS classes is usually not possible. Consider bringing seven healers, and a good mix of DPS classes, they all have something to contribute to this encounter.

STRATEGY

The Reliquary of Souls encounter is divided in three distinct stages, with the raid having to face the Essence of Suffering first, followed by the Essence of Desire, and finally the Essence of Anger. Every Essence has unique abilities and requires a different strategy. Therefore each essence can be treated as a unique encounter.

ESSENCE OF SUFFERING

HP	2276400	Damage	1062-1501
Abilities	**Aura of Suffering**: Reduces the effect of healing spells by 100%, regeneration by 100%, armor by 100%, and defense by 500. This effects all targets engaged with the Essence of Suffering.		
	Fixate: The Essence of Suffering focuses on a specific target.		
	Soul Drain: Deals 2625 to 3375 damage every 3 sec. for 30 sec. Burns 2625 to 3375 mana every 3 sec. for 30 sec.		
	Enrage: Increases Physical Attack damage by 97% and Attack Speed by 50%.		

While the Essence of Suffering is engaged, the raid will be permanently affected by the Aura of Suffering. Most importantly, this aura prevents any healing or health regeneration effects on players. There is only one direction your health bar will be moving, and that is down. The Aura of Suffering also reduces every player's defense by 500 and their armor to zero.

The fact that no healing can be done, does not mean that healers should idle during this stage. Their primary responsibility will be removing the Soul Drain debuff that the Essence of Suffering places on five targets simultaneously every 20 seconds. Unless dispelled, this drains 2,625 to 3,375 health and mana from the affected targets every 3 seconds.

However, the most unique aspect of the Essence of Suffering encounter is that it cannot be tanked by any one player. Instead, most players in the raid will have to take their turn and tank for a short time period. The Essence of Suffering selects its target based on proximity, fixates on that target, and ignores threat.

Approximately five seconds later it will once again select the nearest target and repeat the process. Its melee damage is low, only causing around 1,200 damage per swing. Around 45 seconds after being engaged and every 45 seconds after that, the Essence of Suffering will Enrage, which increases its physical damage dealt by 25% and its attack speed by 50%. The Enrage lasts 15 seconds, during which she continues to switch targets by fixating on the nearest one every 5 seconds.

Obviously, the key to defeating the first stage is controlling the target that the Essence of Suffering is attacking, at all times. Generally, classes that have low hit points can only be fixated once, a second fixate is likely to cause their death. Controlling this stage is easier to achieve if the Essence is stationary at all times, do your best not to move it around. To optimize damage done, start with your Hunters as the first targets for Fixate. Once the Essence has selected a Hunter as its first target, have the entire raid stand inside the visual model of the boss, as close to its center as possible. Five seconds later, the Essence selects the closest target and the Hunter is free to go outside his dead zone and attack the Essence. The selected target should inch out towards the edge of the Essence's body, to make sure that five seconds later, another target is closer to its center, so that it can be selected with the next Fixate.

While fixated, do not run away from the Essence of Suffering and the rest of the raid, or it will follow you around the room and you will remain its closest target causing your death. While fixated, stand on the edge of the Essence's model until a new target has been selected, after which you are free to move away. Melee classes that have been fixated can stand and attack from the maximum melee range, while ranged classes and healers should stand a few feet away, safe from Fixate but close enough to the raid in case they need to have Soul Drain dispelled.

Dealing with the periodic Enrage requires additional measures. During the Enrage, the Essence deals out significantly more damage which is usually fatal to classes with low hit points. You should attempt to have the essence tanked by a protection Warrior or feral Druid for the duration of the Enrage. Rogues are also a viable option, since they can activate Evasion to dodge most of the Essence's attacks. To control the target that will tank during the Enrage, have the raid run away from the Essence when an Enrage is close. The only players remaining inside the model should be the current fixated target, which ensures the Essence does not move and, at the center of the Essence's model, the targets with high hit points that are intended to tank the Essence during the Enrage. About 10 seconds after the Enrage has been cast, the raid can move back in and resume the normal rotation.

With good DPS a raid only needs to go through 2 Enrages before the Essence of Suffering dies. While there is no hard timer to the first stage, eventually the raid dies due to the lack of healing. Consider the third Enrage, around the 2 minute 15 seconds mark as your deadline to finish off the Essence of Suffering.

Following its death, there is a short break for the raid which will be surrounded by Enslaved Souls. They are very easy to kill, and on death casts Soul Release on the raid which replenishes health and mana. With the raid at fully rejuvenated, it's time to face the Essence of Desire.

ESSENCE OF DESIRE

HP	3035200	Damage	11948-16894
Abilities	**Aura of Desire**: Causes all nearby targets to take damage when they deal damage. Increases Healing by 100%. Decreases maximum mana over time.		
	Spirit Shock: Deals 9250 to 10750 Arcane damage and confuses for 5 sec.		
	Deaden: Increases damage taken by 100% for 10 sec.		
	Rune Shield: Absorbs 50000 damage. Grants immunity to spell interrupt effects. Increases attack speed by 100%. Increases casting speed by 100%.		

Just like the Essence of Suffering, while the Essence of Desire is engaged the raid will be affected by its aura. The Aura of Desire doubles healing spells and effects, however every time a player deals damage to the Essence of Desire, he takes half the amount of damage himself. The Aura of Desire also decreases maximum mana over time, and about three minutes after being engaged the maximum mana of players in the raid reaches zero.

This is probably the most difficult of the three stages in the Reliquary of Souls encounter. Throughout this stage, the Essence of Desire attempts to cast Spirit Shock on its primary target. This is a powerful arcane bolt that inflicts 9,250 to 10,750 damage and disorients the target for 5 seconds. It can be interrupted by all spell interrupting abilities. Unless it is interrupted during its one second cast time, the Shock hits the main tank and disorient it, causing the Essence to switch to the secondary target on its aggro list. Bringing a second tank can be very effective, in case the raid fails to interrupt a Spirit Shock, provided of course the secondary tank can maintain secondary aggro. Due to the short cooldown on Kick, Rogues make the ideal class for interrupting Spirit Shock. A rotation of three Rogues each taking turns at kicking the Shocks is usually sufficient.

To further complicate matters, 10 seconds after being engaged and every 15 seconds after that, the Essence of Desire casts Rune Shield upon itself. The shield is an extremely powerful ability that absorbs 50,000 damage, doubles the Essence's attack, increases casting speed, and makes it immune to spell interrupt effects. The shield must be dispelled immediately, in order to allow the Rogues to interrupt Spirit Shock. Priests can dispel it. It can also be removed by Mages using Spellsteal. However, the easiest and fastest way to remove it is to have Warlocks assign their Felhunter pets to use Devour Magic on the Essence of Desire. Due to their relatively high chance of being resisted, a minimum of two Felhunters is required with three being the recommended number.

With the Shield rapidly removed every time it is cast, Rogues should have little trouble interrupting every Spirit Shock. Unfortunately, a further ability makes their task significantly more difficult. Twenty seconds after being engaged, and every 33 seconds after that, the Essence of Desire attempts to cast Deaden on its primary target. This debuff doubles the damage taken by the target it is placed on. Since this stage is effectively a DPS race to ensure the Essence dies before the raid runs out of mana, interrupting Deaden is not the ideal solution. Instead, Rogues should allow Deaden to be cast at the main tank, who can reflect it back on to the Essence of Desire, effectively doubling raid DPS for 10 seconds.

BE CAREFUL WHAT YOU WISH FOR.

Reflecting Deaden on the Essence of Desire does indeed double the damage it takes, but due to the Aura of Desire it also doubles the damage taken by DPS classes. While Deaden is active on the target, avoid doing sudden bursts of damage or you risk killing yourself before the raid healers have a chance to save you.

The end of the raid's mana pools usually equates with a wipe. No mana means there is no healing, and most importantly, without mana the Felhunters are unable to dispel the Essence's Rune Shield. This allows it to use Spirit Shock freely, disorienting the tanks and killing other players in one hit. It is pretty much a dominoe effect to oblivion.

However, a number of tricks allow the raid to survive a number of additional seconds even without mana. The Rune Shield must be dispelled by Priests using Inner Focus to cast a "free" Dispel Magic. Taking into account the three minute cooldown on Inner Focus, the raid can only dispel as many Shields as there are Priests in the raid. The tank will continue taking damage, and the only way to heal him without mana is either by having Paladins use their Lay on Hands ability or by having the Draenai members of the raid use their Gift of the Naaru healing effect. Even though this can extend the encounter, the raid is still limited in terms of its ability to do damage to the Essence of Desire, because of the 50% returned damage the aura causes. Caster classes can use their wands to do some damage without mana, with the main limitation being the depth of their ever decreasing health pool. Do not expect to be able to do more than 5% damage after the raid has run out of mana.

If successful in defeating the Essence of Desire, the raid gets another chance to refill health and mana with the help of Enslaved Souls, before being faced with the final stage of the Encounter, the Essence of Anger.

ESSENCE OF ANGER

HP	3035200	Damage	14604-20649
Abilities	**Aura of Anger:** Deals 100 damage every 3 seconds and increases damage dealt by 5%. This effect stacks and gradually increases over the course of the fight.		
	Spite: Makes the target immune to damage for 6 sec. Deals 7444 to 7556 Nature damage to three targets after 6 sec.		
	Soul Scream: Deals 2625 to 3375 Shadow damage and burn 4375 to 5625 mana in a 10-yard radius.		
	Seethe: When effected by Taunt, the Essence of Anger's Attack Speed increases by 100% for 10 sec. and all threat generated against him is increased by 200%.		

Similar to the previous two stages, the Essence of Anger is another DPS race with an unique aura effect. The Aura of Anger deals increasing amounts of shadow damage over time to every player in the raid, but also gradually increases the damage dealt by players. Every three seconds the raid takes shadow damage, which increases by 100 every time it is applied. Therefore, 90 seconds after the start of this stage, the raid takes in excess of 3,000 damage every 3 seconds, making it extremely difficult to survive past the 100 second mark. Damage is also increased, by the rate of 5% per application making survival of the DPS classes until the end of the stage when they can deal in excess of double their normal DPS very important.

Aggro generation by the main tank is extremely important, as he is competing against DPS classes with an increased damage modifier. While tank DPS also increases, causing an increase in threat generation, the Essence of Anger has a unique ability which can be extremely detrimental to threat generation. Soul Scream deals a base damage of 2,625 to 3,375 in a cone around the main tank, but additionally it also consumes the mana or rage of affected targets, dealing additional damage based on the amount of rage or mana consumed.

For example, if the tank has 100 rage when he is hit by Soul Scream in addition to the 3,000 shadow damage, he will take an additional 100 damage for every point of rage. Even when reduced by talents such as Improved Defensive Stance, Soul Scream can hit the tank for well in excess of 10,000 damage. Not only is it a challenge for the healers, but also for the main tank who needs the rage to build aggro. With Soul Scream being cast around every 11 seconds, try to have as little rage as possible when it hits.

Apart from the constant shadow damage taken by the raid, the Essence of Anger has another ability that can inflict massive damage. Spite is cast alternatingly every 7 or 14 seconds on a random target in the raid. For six seconds the target will be immune to all damage, but at the end of the immunity the target takes 7,444 to 7,556 nature damage. Heal the affected target to full before and after the Spite damage hits.

Cauldrons and Consumables

Due to the very high DPS requirement, flasks and oils are highly recommended for your DPS classes. To increase survivability against Spite and the shadow damage dealt by the Essence of Anger, Shadow and Nature Protection potions are recommended. Have an alchemist put down two cauldrons before starting the gauntlet, an inexpensive method of providing your entire raid with both a Shadow and a Nature protection potion. Use the Nature Protection potion during the invulnerability period if you are affected by Spite, or else save the potion cooldown for the end of the encounter, when shadow damage is at its highest.

During this final stage, healing is very intensive. Use Chain Heal on the main tank to help the Paladins that are the main tank's primary healers. Melee classes that are close to the main tank benefit from Chain Heal as well. Group healing abilities such as Prayer of Healing and Tranquility can make a big difference, as can the use of Shadow Priests with Vampiric Embrace. Keep the main tank alive, and do not lose players early to Spite. Watch threat closely, and do not pull off the main tank and you will soon have defeated the last remaining boss in the inner temple.

DEN OF MORTAL DELIGHTS

With the last boss in the inner temple, the door to the Den of Mortal Delights is now open. This is where you will find Mother Shahraz. On your way there, use a protection Paladin, if available, to tank the multiple Concubine pulls. Always have a dedicated tank pick up the hard hitting Servants. For the double Sister of Pleasure/Sister of Pain pulls be very careful when attacking the latter. Their Shell of Pain reflects spells back to their attacker while melee classes are returned 2,500 shadow damage per hit. None of these pulls should be a challenge.

MOTHER SHAHRAZ

After defeating the difficult to execute Reliquary of Souls event, it is hard to imagine an encounter that can be more challenging to a raid. Mother Shahraz certainly comes close, not necessarily because it is more difficult to execute, but because of the numerous random elements that can derail very promising attempts. While a raid can never fully remove all of them, the impact of these random elements can be mitigated by gear selection, positioning, strategy, consumables, and flawless execution.

HP	4552500	Damage	22165-31306

Abilities	**Prismatic Aura:** Decreases damage dealt by one damage type (i.e. Fire) by 25% and increases the damage dealt by another damage type by 25% (i.e. Frost). The aura rotates resistances every 15 sec.
	Fatal Attraction: Links three targets with demonic energy. This causes Shadow damage to be inflicted to nearby allies every 1 sec.
	Saber Lash: Deals 76000 to 84000 Physical damage, divided equally among three targets in front of Shahraz.
	Sinful Beam: Strikes an enemy with shadow energy that arcs to another nearby enemy, dealing 6938 to 8062 Shadow damage. The spell affects up to 10 targets.
	Sinister Beam: Strikes an enemy with shadow energy that arcs to another nearby enemy, dealing 2000 Shadow damage and knocking the targets back. The spell affects up to 10 targets.
	Vile Beam: Strikes an enemy with shadow energy that arcs to another nearby enemy, dealing 2500 Shadow damage every 2 sec. for 8 sec. The spell affects up to 10 targets.
	Wicked Beam: Strikes an enemy with shadow energy that arcs to another nearby enemy, burning 1000 mana. The spell affects up to 10 targets.
	Silencing Shriek: Silences all nearby enemies for 10 sec.

LOOT

Pauldrons of the Forgotten Protector: Tier 6 Shoulder Token, Warrior, Hunter, Shaman

Pauldrons of the Forgotten Vanquisher: Tier 6 Shoulder Token, Rogue, Mage, Druid

Pauldrons of the Forgotten Conqueror: Tier 6 Shoulder Token, Paladin, Priest, Warlock

Heartshatter Breastplate: Chest / Plate, 1765 Armor, +63 Strength, +45 Stamina, Equip: Improves hit rating by 30, Improves critical strike rating by 44.

Shadowmaster's Boots: Feet / Leather, 305 Armor, +30 Agility, +38 Stamina, Red Socket, Yellow Socket, Socket Bonus: +3 Crit Rating, Equip: Improves critical strike rating by 17, Increases attack power by 76.

Leggings of Devastation: Legs / Cloth, 207 Armor, +40 Stamina, +42 Intellect, Yellow Socket, Yellow Socket, Blue Socket, Socket Bonus: +5 Spell Damage, Equip: Improves spell hit rating by 26, Increases damage and healing done by magical spells and effects by up to 60.

Tome of the Lightbringer: Libram, Equip: Your Judgement ability also increases your shield block value by 93 for 4 sec.

Blade of Savagery: One-Hand / Sword, 98 - 183 Damage, Speed 1.40, (100.4 dps), +19 Stamina, Equip: Improves hit rating by 15, Improves critical strike rating by 22, Increases attack power by 44.

Nadina's Pendant of Purity: Neck, +16 Stamina, +14 Intellect, Equip: Improves spell critical strike rating by 19, Increases healing done by spells and effects by up to 79, Restores 8 mana per 5 sec.

RAID COMPOSITION

Three tanks are required for this encounter, together with a minimum of eight healers (nine are recommended and even ten healers brings improvement in reliability). As far as DPS classes are concerned, caster classes are severely outperformed by physical damage classes such as Rogues, arms/fury Warriors, Hunters, or feral Druids.

RESISTANCE GEAR

Throughout the encounter, Mother Shahraz deals massive amounts of Shadow damage to everyone in the raid. Everyone needs to be close or over the cap of 365 Shadow resistance. This can only be achieved by wearing crafted items using the Hearts of Darkness that drops inside the Black Temple from random mobs. There are, of course, cloth, leather, mail and plate versions, but the shadow resistance and stamina boost they provide is identical. The only difference is their armor value. A list can be found below:

EPIC SHADOW RESISTANCE GEAR	
ITEM	**STATS**
Night's End Cloak	+40 Shadow Resistance, +30 Stamina
Wrist Slot	+40 Shadow Resistance, +30 Stamina
Feet Slot	+54 Shadow Resistance, +40 Stamina
Leg Slot	+72 Shadow Resistance, +54 Stamina
Waist Slot	+54 Shadow Resistance, +40 Stamina
Medallion of Karabor	+40 Shadow Resistance, +49 Stamina

Further optimize your gear with additional shadow resistance and stamina either with the help of an enchanter or that of a leatherworker. Finally, to complete preparations, an alchemist will be needed to mix a large number of Greater Shadow Protection Potions.

STRATEGY

The first thing raids notice about the Mother Shahraz encounter is the very high damage output on the main tank. Melee hits average over 6,000 damage and she swings at the tank very frequently. In addition, she uses a powerful melee attack named Saber Lash against melee targets in front of her. The base damage of Saber Lash is 76,000 to 84,000. If several targets or more are in front of Mother Shahraz up to three of them share the damage from the hit. Having all three tanks stand in front of her will bring the damage taken by each tank down to the 7,500–9,500 range.

While the tanks have to deal with Saber Lash, the rest of the raid will be under constant assault by one of Mother Shahraz's many beam abilities.

Vile Beam is a damage over time effect that inflicts 2,500 damage every 2 seconds for 8 seconds. Sinful Beam is a direct damage spell that deals 6,938 to 8,062 damage. Sinister Beam throws the affected target high in the air causing it to take falling damage when landing in addition to a base of 2,000 shadow damage. Finally, Wicked Beam is a mana burn that consumes 1,000 mana from the affected target.

It is important to note that all these abilities can chain from player to player, to a maximum of up to 10 targets. However, the chain will stop if a player fully resists the beam, and in a raid where everyone has maximum Shadow resistance, it is extremely unlikely that any beam will chain past the 3rd or 4th target.

The key mechanic of the encounter however is named Fatal Attraction. Three random players in the raid are teleported to a random position in a large circular area around Mother Shahraz. These targets become linked together by demonic energy and while they are within a 15 yard range of each other, they deal 2,775 to 3,225 shadow damage every second to themselves, each other, and any other nearby player.

While all the damage values appear to be very high, partial resists are practically guaranteed when wearing high shadow resistance. With healers assigned to heal the raid, the beam damage can be outhealed very reliably. However, Fatal Attraction can be more difficult to deal with, since it is very likely that the three players that are chosen will be ported far away, out of the range of any healers.

As a rule of the thumb, those affected by Fatal Attraction must survive on their own, without the help of a healer. To ensure survival, the 3 players must start spreading out immediately after they get teleported. The demonic energy that links them breaks if they spread out more than 15 yards from each other. Some classes can cover that distance faster than others, such as Mages using Blink or Rogues using Sprint. While moving away, players take significant amounts of shadow damage. This is a very good time to use a Shadow Protection Potion or a Healthstone. The location players get ported to is random, and can have a great impact on the damage they deal and take. Being teleported near a wall restricts the available directions to run in, while being ported near the raid or the tank causes several more players to take damage. Through practice both those ported and the rest of the raid will learn to adapt, and to move rapidly away from each other to break the Fatal Attraction link.

A better perspective

Being teleported with Fatal Attraction can be confusing at first, but it is very important to be aware of the position you are ported to and the direction in which the other two players are running. A helpful tip is to zoom out the view of your character to get a better perspective. For the best results use the "Max Camera Distance" slider under interface options.

Occasionally the raid has to adjust and move away from players affected by Fatal Attraction to avoid taking damage. With the raid on the move, nobody would be able to heal the main tank which could cause his death due to the enormous amount of damage he is taking. Therefore, positioning two healers out of the raid who can heal the tank if the raid has to adjust, is highly recommended. A positioning diagram is provided to better illustrate this.

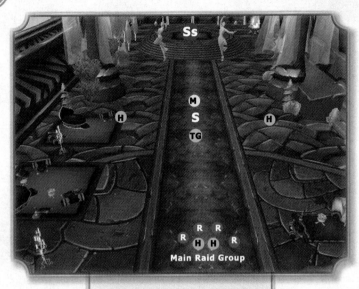

MAP LEGEND	
Ss	Mother Shahraz spawn point
S	Mother Shahraz tanking position
TG	3 Tanks
M	Melee Classes
H	Healer
R	Ranged DPS classes

CHAMBER OF COMMAND

Heading towards the Chamber of Command the raid encounter several packs of high ranked Illidari elves. Archons are the group healers and should be killed first, while the Blood Lords are picked up by tanks. These Paladin-type mobs use Divine Shield when low on health, which is a good time to switch to another target. Rogues can be Polymorphed, but once free of crowd control they periodically Vanish and switch to another target. Always polymorph the Battle-Mages as they have a variety of both area of effect and single target spells in their arsenal. Kill them last, and move away from their Blizzard and Flamestrike.

The key to defeating this encounter, apart from coming prepared with Shadow resistance gear and potions, is dealing with Fatal Attraction and healing the main tank. In time, practice and quick thinking enable players to spread out faster and faster, minimizing the damage taken by Fatal Attraction. As far as healing is concerned, assign one healer per group and one healer per off-tank with the remaining 3 or 4 healers assigned exclusively to the main tank. Consider having some of the main tank healers cast fast heals such as Flash of Light, to compensate for the longer pauses between longer heals such as Greater Heal or Holy Light. Adjust the group composition as best as possible, especially for early kills, favoring physical DPS classes to speed up the process of killing Mother Shahraz. Her final trick, an Enrage after she reaches the 10% hit points mark, should have little impact on a tank that has saved long cooldown abilities such as Shield Wall and Last Stand. Take her down and enjoy the Tier 6 spoils.

ILLIDARI COUNCIL

Defeating four enemies at the same time may seem like a daunting task at first, but a raid that can defeat the Reliquary of Souls Event and Mother Shahraz should have little trouble with the members of the Illidari Council. The encounter-specific gear and consumable requirements are minimal, but what is required is a solid piece of execution.

RAID COMPOSITION

Four tanks are required for this encounter, one for each of the council members. However, there is a good amount of flexibility in terms of classes and talent specializations for those assigned to tank. Since the requirement for DPS during this encounter is relatively low, raids can afford to bring 8-9 healers to increase survivability. As far as DPS classes are concerned, this is an equal opportunity encounter but at least one Mage is required, and a Hunter or two can make the pull smoother.

LOOT

Leggings of the Forgotten Conqueror: Tier 6 Leg Token, Paladin, Priest, Warlock

Leggings of the Forgotten Vanquisher: Tier 6 Leg Token, Rogue, Mage, Druid

Leggings of the Forgotten Protector: Tier 6 Leg Token, Warrior, Hunter, Shaman

Helm of the Illidari Shatterer: Head / Plate, 1434 Armor, +51 Strength, +29 Stamina, Meta Socket, Yellow Socket, Socket Bonus: +6 Stamina, Equip: Improves hit rating by 34, Improves critical strike rating by 42.

Forest Prowler's Helm: Head / Mail, 803 Armor, +42 Agility, +29 Stamina, +28 Intellect, Red Socket, Meta Socket, Socket Bonus: 2 mana per 5 sec., Equip: Increases attack power by 100, Improves critical strike rating by 20.

Veil of Turning Leaves: Shoulder / Leather, 333 Armor, +29 Stamina, +29 Intellect, +38 Spirit, Equip: Increases healing done by spells and effects by up to 84.

Belt of Divine Guidance: Waist / Cloth, 133 Armor, +35 Stamina, +24 Intellect, +32 Spirit, Yellow Socket, Blue Socket, Socket Bonus: +7 Healing, Equip: Increases healing done by spells and effects by up to 73.

Cloak of the Illidari Council: Back / Cloth, 118 Armor, +24 Stamina, +16 Intellect, Equip: Increases damage and healing done by magical spells and effects by up to 42, Improves spell critical strike rating by 25.

Madness of the Betrayer: Trinket, Equip: Improves hit rating by 20, Increases attack power by 84, Your melee and ranged attacks have a chance allow you to ignore 300 of your enemies' armor for 10 secs.

THE PULL

As with all other encounters involving several mobs (e.g. High King Maulgar and Fathom Lord Karathress) the pull is one of the more sensitive moments in the encounter. It is important to get every council member to attack their assigned tank as soon as possible and without casualties. If Hunters are available, Misdirection can be used to split the council members to their assigned tanks. If you are lacking several Hunters, a Warrior can engage the Council by running in with Shield Wall active to prevent him from dying until the other 3 tanks are in control of their mobs.

STRATEGY

Unlike other multiple mob encounters in the Burning Crusade, but in a similar fashion to the Twin Emperors in Anh'Qiraj, the four council members share their health. Doing damage to one council member damages all four of them equally, but it is impossible to kill one of them before the others. All four must therefore be tanked throughout the encounter and die simultaneously at the end.

GATHIOS THE SHATTERER

HP	1746500	Damage	18470-26088
Abilities	**Seal of Command**: Gives the caster a chance to deal additional Holy damage equal to 70% of normal weapon damage. Lasts 30 sec. Judging this Seal deals 6175 to 6825 Holy damage.		
	Seal of Blood: Melee attacks deal additional Holy damage over time. Judging this Seal deals 1200 Holy damage per second for 9 sec.		
	Consecration: Consecrates the land beneath Paladin, doing 15000 Holy damage over 20 sec to enemies who enter the area.		
	Devotion Aura: Gives 20% additional armor to nearby party members for 30 sec.		
	Chromatic Resistance Aura: Increases the resistance of nearby group members to all schools of magic by 250 for 30 sec.		
	Hammer of Justice: Unable to move or attack for 6 sec.		
	Blessing of Protection: Protected from all physical attacks for 15 sec.		
	Blessing of Spell Warding: Protected from all magical attacks for 15 sec.		

This is a retribution Paladin that can deal out severe damage while helping the other council members with his blessings and auras. He must be picked up by your main tank, as his melee swings will, on average, dish out in excess of 6,000 damage. His Seal of Blood cause his melee attacks to deal additional Holy damage. His Judgments cause the tank to take around 1,200 damage every second for 9 seconds.

Additional burst damage comes in the form of Judgement of Command, which hit the tank for 6,175 to 6,825 Holy damage, while constant damage is provided by his consecration, which will deal 2,250 damage every 3 seconds to targets in its area of effect.

Apart from his direct damage abilities, Gathios has two auras that he can switch between and two powerful blessings that he can put on the other council members. His Devotion Aura gives 20% additional armor to council members in a 30 yard radius of him, while his Chromatic Resistance Aura increases their resistance to all schools of magic by 250. Blessing of Spell Warding makes an ally of his choice immune to magical attacks for 15 seconds, while his Blessing of Protection gives another council member physical immunity for 15 seconds.

HIGH NETHERMANCER ZEREVOR

HP	1746500	Damage	3940-5565
Abilities	**Flamestrike**: Burns all enemies in a selected area for 4625 to 5375 Fire damage and inflicts 2806 to 3194 additional Fire damage every 2 sec. for 12 sec.		
	Blizzard: Inflicts 4375 to 5625 Frost damage every 2 sec. in a selected area.		
	Arcane Bolt: Deals 12950 to 15050 Arcane damage.		
	Fireball: Inflicts 6300 to 7700 Fire damage, plus 200 additional damage every 1 seconds for 3 sec.		
	Frostbolt: Inflicts 5250 to 6750 Frost damage and reduces movement speed for 4 sec.		
	Arcane Explosion: Inflicts 8550 to 9450 Arcane damage.		
	Dampen Magic: Decreases damage taken from spells by up to 75% and healing spells by up to 500. Lasts 5 min.		

Zerevor is a powerful caster that must be tanked from a distance by a Mage. His primary attack which is used very frequently is an Arcane Bolt that inflicts between 12,950 and 15,050 damage. Fortunately, the Dampen Magic ability that he casts on himself can be stolen by the Mage tank using Spellsteal. This reduces the damage taken by the Mage by 75%, bringing his Arcane Bolt to a range where healing the Mage becomes feasible.

Additionally, Zerevor has two area of effect abilities he frequently uses against the raid. The first is a Flamestrike that deals 4,625 to 5,375 direct damage and a further 2,806 to 3,194 damage every 2 seconds for 12 seconds to those that stand in its area of effect. The second ability is a Blizzard that also lasts for 12 seconds, dealing 4,375 to 5,625 damage every 2 seconds.

LADY MALANDE

HP	1746500	Damage	6156-8696
Abilities	**Circle of Healing**: Heals nearby party members for 95000 to 105000 hit points.		
	Renew: Heals the target for 20000 hit points every 3 sec. for 15 sec.		
	Empowered Smite: Smites an enemy, inflicting 5463 to 6037 Holy damage.		
	Divine Wrath: Burns for 5000 Holy damage and inflicts 2500 additional Holy damage every 2 sec. over 8 sec.		
	Reflective Shield: Wraps the target in a shield that lasts up to 20 sec., absorbing a maximum of 25000 Physical or magical damage. While the shield holds, spells will not be interrupted by Physical attacks. In addition, half the damage dealt to the target is reflected while the shield is active.		

She is a Priest that casts both offensive damage spells on the raid, as well as attempts to heal herself and other council members. Her healing spell is a powerful Circle of Healing that heals for 95,000 to 105,000. This has a 2.5 second cast time and should be interrupted every time she attempts to cast it. Her offensive spells are Empowered Smite which is cast on her primary target, dealing 5,463 to 6,037 holy damage, while all other targets in the raid can be attacked with Divine Wrath, 5,000 direct damage and a further 2,500 Holy damage inflicted every 2 seconds for 8 seconds. Defensively she occasionally protects herself with a Reflective Shield which lasts for 20 seconds, absorbing a maximum of 25,000 damage. While the shield is active, her attackers take damage back based on the damage they deal themselves.

VERAS DARKSHADOW

HP	1746500	Damage	10621-15017
Abilities	**Vanish**: Puts the caster in stealth mode for 30 sec.		
	Deadly Strike: Strikes an enemy target with Deadly Poison, inflicting 1000 Nature damage every 1 sec. for 4 sec.		
	Envenom: Consumes the Deadly Poison on the target and deals 4250 to 5750 instant Nature damage.		

This Blood Elf Rogue must also be picked up by a tank, although his damage output is significantly lower than that of Gathios the Shatterer. Apart from attacking the tank, about once a minute Darkshadow Vanishes and attacks 4 random targets in succession. The targets all take 1,000 damage per second for 5 seconds from his Deadly Poison, which is immediately followed by Envenom, a finishing move that consumes the Deadly Poison on the target and deals an instant 4,250 to 5,750 nature damage. After attacking four targets he waits a few seconds before re-emerging, giving his tank an opportunity to pick him up again. Use Intercept or Feral Charge to close the distance quickly. After every Vanish, his threat will be reset.

Although this may seem like a complicated encounter at first, most guilds that have made it so far will take little time to master it once they have experienced all the abilities that the Council can throw at them. After mastering the pull it only takes reliable healing, moving away from avoidable damage sources and well timed spell interrupts.

At the pull, misdirect Zerevor to the Mage tank who must immediately use Spellsteal to gain the Dampen Magic effect. Slowly move Zerevor away from the raid toward the ramp on the western side of the entrance. Positioning him far away at the base of the ramp seems to have an effect on the duration of the channeling of his area of effect spells. As the Mage tank on Zerevor, your main priority is to have Zerevor's Dampen Magic on yourself at all time. He casts it on himself around every minute, and it has a 2 minute cooldown. However, Blessing of Spell Warding from Gathios not only makes him temporarily immune to Spellsteal, but it also removes the Dampen Magic effect. Therefore, always steal it as soon as it is cast. Due to Blessing of Spell Warding and unlucky timing you may not have another chance. One healer is usually enough to heal the Mage tank.

Mage Tank – Gear Selection

In terms of gear selection, the objective of the Mage tank is to have a hit point pool that is deep enough to allow him to be effortlessly healed by 1 healer. The one statistic that matters is Stamina, and with a good mix of Arena PvP gear and "of Stamina" items, the Mage can easily reach in excess of 16,000 hit points. Arcane Resistance gear is ineffective against Zerevor's Arcane Bolt.

Once he has been picked up by a tank, Veras Darkshadow makes a good target for your physical DPS classes due to his low armor. His habit to periodically Vanish restricts the opportunities to do damage to him, as will his aggro table reset each time he returns. Allow the tank a few seconds to rebuild aggro once he reappears. Targets hit by his Deadly Poison must be healed immediately, and beware the Envenom damage that follows the five seconds of Deadly Poison damage.

The alternative target for DPS classes is Gathios the Shatterer. Due to his high damage output, threat generation should never be an issue, but melee classes attacking him should be mindful of his Consecration damage. Three healers should be watching the tank on Gathios to compensate for the high amount of damage taken.

The main challenge with Lady Malande lies in interrupting her Circle of Healing ability. Failing to do so extends the encounter's duration significantly. The tank assigned to her takes minimal damage which can be managed with the help of only one healer. Two Rogues should be assigned to her, using Kick to interrupt her spells. You can allow her to cast Empowered Smite on the tank, but Divine Wrath should definitely be interrupted. It is a large unpredictable source of damage that can kill a player in the raid in conjunction with another source of damage, such as Envenom or one of Zerevor's area of effect spells. Always interrupt Circle of Healing. If Malande is affected by Blessing of Protection, request the help of a Mage or Shaman to interrupt her should she attempt to cast during the 15 seconds of melee immunity.

Keep all the tanks healed, react quickly to Deadly Poison, move away from Consecration, Blizzard, and Flamestrike. Finally, make sure you interrupt Circle of Healing. Observe these priorities for 10 minutes and the Council falls, giving you the opportunity to meet their master, Illidan Stormrage.

ILLIDAN STORMRAGE

Congratulations on making it this far. With the Council slain, your Deathsworn allies are now be able to teleport you from the temple entrance directly to their Chamber of Command. The Illidan Stormrage encounter that awaits you at the temple's summit is an epic 5-stage battle, befitting its place in Warcraft lore and its position at the pinnacle of Tier 6 raiding. Enjoy it!

LOOT

Chestguard of the Forgotten Conqueror: Tier 6 Chest Token, Paladin, Priest, Warlock

Chestguard of the Forgotten Vanquisher: Tier 6 Chest Token, Rogue, Mage, Druid

Chestguard of the Forgotten Protector: Tier 6 Chest Token, Warrior, Hunter, Shaman

Shard of Azzinoth: One-Hand / Dagger, 161 - 242 Damage, Speed 1.90, (106.1 dps), Equip: Increases attack power by 64., Chance on hit: Calls forth an Ember of Azzinoth to protect you in battle for a short period of time.

The Skull of Gul'dan: Trinket, Equip: Improves spell hit rating by 25, Increases damage and healing done by magical spells and effects by up to 55., Use: Tap into the power of the skull, increasing spell haste rating by 175 for 20 sec.

Cursed Vision of Sargeras: Head / Leather, 385 Armor, +39 Agility, +46 Stamina, Meta Socket, Yellow Socket, Socket Bonus: +6 Stamina, Equip: Improves hit rating by 21, Increases critical strike rating by 38, Increases attack power by 108., Use: Shows the location of all nearby demons on the minimap until cancelled.

Memento of Tyrande: Trinket, Equip: Increases healing done by spells and effects by up to 118, Each time you cast a spell, there is chance you will gain up to 76 mana per 5 for 15 sec.

Stormrage Signet Ring: Finger, +33 Stamina, Equip: Improves hit rating by 30, Increases attack power by 66, Your attacks ignore 126 of your opponent's armor.

Faceplate of the Impenetrable: Head / Plate, 1532 Armor, +82 Stamina, Meta Socket, Red Socket, Socket Bonus: +6 Stamina, Equip: Increases defense rating by +30, Increases your dodge rating by 38, Increases your shield block rating by 29, Increases the block value of your shield by 45.

Black Bow of the Betrayer: Ranged / Bow, 201 - 374 Damage, Speed 3.00, (95.8 dps), Equip: On successful melee or ranged attack gain 8 mana and if possible drain 8 mana from the target, Increases attack power by 26.

Zhar'doom, Greatstaff of the Devourer: Two-Hand / Staff, 145 - 322 Damage, Speed 3.20, (73.2 dps), +70 Stamina, +47 Intellect, Equip: Improves spell critical strike rating by 36, Improves spell haste rating by 55, Increases damage and healing done by magical spells and effects by up to 259.

Bulwark of Azzinoth: Off Hand / Shield, 6336 Armor, 174 Block, +60 Stamina, Equip: Increases defense rating by +29, When struck in combat has a 2% chance of increasing your Armor by 2000 for 10 secs.

Cowl of the Illidari High Lord: Head / Cloth, 205 Armor, +33 Stamina, +31 Intellect, Meta Socket, Blue Socket, Socket Bonus: +5 Spell Damage, Equip: Improves spell hit rating by 21, Improves spell critical strike rating by 47, Increases damage and healing done by magical spells and effects by up to 64.

Crystal Spire of Karabor: Main Hand / Mace, 16 - 131 Damage, Speed 1.80, (41.0 dps), +22 Stamina, +15 Intellect, Equip: Increases healing done by spells and effects by up to 486, Restores 6 mana per 5 sec, If your target is below 50% health, your direct healing spells will cause your target to be healed for an additional 180 to 220 health.

Shroud of the Highborne: Back, 126 Armor, +24 Stamina, +23 Intellect, Equip: Improves spell haste rating by 32, Increases healing done by spells and effects by up to 68.

Warglaive of Azzinoth: Main Hand / Sword, 214 - 398 Damage, Speed 2.80, (109.3 dps), +22 Agility, +29 Stamina, Classes: Warrior, Rogue, Equip: Improves hit rating by 21, Increases attack power by 44.

Warglaive of Azzinoth: Main Hand / Sword, 214 - 398 Damage, Speed 2.80, (109.3 dps), +22 Agility, +29 Stamina, Classes: Warrior, Rogue, Equip: Improves hit rating by 21, Increases attack power by 44.

Warglaive of Azzinoth: Off Hand / Sword, 107 - 199 Damage, Speed 1.40, (109.3 dps), +21 Agility, +28 Stamina, Classes: Warrior, Rogue, Equip: Improves critical strike rating by 23, Increases attack power by 44.

Set Bonuses: The Twin Blades of Azzinoth

Your melee attacks have a chance to increase your haste rating by 450 for 10 sec.

Increases attack power by 200 when fighting Demons.

RAID COMPOSITION

Four tanks must be used for this encounter: a Warrior in his normal gear, two offtanks in optimized fire protection gear and a Warlock tank with shadow protection gear. Nine healers are recommended, but the encounter can be completed with only eight. Frost specialized Mages are highly recommended both for their damage against fire-immune targets and the utility of their defensive abilities. An over-abundance of melee DPS classes is not recommended, otherwise any DPS class setup is possible.

STAGE 1

HP	6070400	Damage	19914-28157
Abilities	**Shear**: Deals melee damage and reduces the target's maximum health by 60% for 7 sec.		
	Flame Crash: Deals 925 to 1075 Fire damage in an area in front of Illidan, as well as creating an area of fire in the same location. This area deals 5000 Fire damage to anyone who steps into it.		
	Draw Soul: Deals 4500 to 5500 Shadow damage to everyone in front of Illidan, regardless of range. Illidan will gain 100,000 health for every target that is affected by this.		
	Parasitic Shadowfiend: Deals 3000 Shadow damage every 2 sec. for 10 sec. This also summons a Parasitic Shadowfiend at the end of the duration of the damage over time spell.		

The encounter is started by talking to Akama who finally reveals the betrayal of his master and joins the raid in battle. The first stage is fairly simple, but the abilities used here are seen again later in the encounter, so the raid should take the time to get well acquainted to them.

The biggest killer during this stage is an ability named Shear. Illidan attempts to use it on the main tank every 12 seconds. If the tank is hit, his hit points are reduced by 60% for 7 seconds. This lowers his health to a level where Illidan can potentially kill him in two hits. However, the ability can be Shield Blocked. Since it is cast at regular intervals and has a 1.5 second cast time, the tank should never fail to block it.

Draw Soul is a Shadow based spell that is cast in a frontal cone in the direction Illidan is facing. All players hit by it take 4,500 to 5,500 Shadow damage and heal Illidan for up to 100,000 health. Always face Illidan away from the raid. With constant Mortal Strike or Wound Poison debuffs on Illidan, he will only heal for 50,000 every time he casts Draw Soul.

Flame Crash is an ability that places down a circle of blue flame at Illidan's feet. Standing in it deals 5,000 Fire damage every 2 seconds. To avoid it, the tank needs to shift Illidan away from the 7 yard radius of its area of effect.

The final ability used during this stage is Parasitic Shadowfiend. Often, a random target in the raid is affected by it and takes 3,000 damage every 2 seconds for 10 seconds. At the end of the 10 seconds two Parasitic Shadowfiends spawn and attack the raid. They have around 3,500 hit points and hit for very little damage. The catch is those hit become infected, spawning 2 more parasites 10 seconds later. The first target affected by parasites should move away from the raid, in order to have the parasites spawn a good distance away. A freezing trap can immobilize a Shadowfiend, but Frost Nova is the more efficient ability, especially the one that can be cast from a distance by a Mage's Water Elemental. Use Ice Lance to rapidly kill the Parasites trapped in a Frost Nova.

When his health reaches 90%, Illidan calls for the help of his minions which will be dealt with by Akama. The first stage continues until Illidan reaches the 65% mark, at which point he will fly in the air, starting stage 2.

STAGE 2

HP	6070400	Damage	19914-28157
Abilities	**Fireball**: Deals 2550 to 3450 Fire damage in a 10 yard radius.		
	Dark Barrage: Targets a random person in the raid and deals 3000 shadow damage per second for 10 sec.		
	Eye Blast: Deals a stream of damage across Illidan's chamber, incinerating targets with 19750 to 20250 Shadow damage in 6 yard radius around the blast. On top of this instant damage dealt, the eye blast also leaves behind a trail of fire that will damage players if they touch it.		

This is one of the more difficult stages of the encounter. Illidan is flying above the temple and cannot be attacked but he will throw down his two Blades of Azzinoth on opposite sides of the circle that marks the center of the Black Temple's summit. Each blade spawns a Flame of Azzinoth, a powerful fire elemental with over 1 million hit points. These must each be tanked by Warriors using Fire protection gear. The best Fire resistance gear available is purchased with tokens dropped by bosses in 5-man heroic instances. A full set can be obtained at a cost of 100 tokens and can be purchased from G'eras in the middle of Shattrah City. Good choices for completing the fire resistance set are the Phoenix-Fire Band, the reward for the Trial of the Naaru: Magtheridon quest, the Wyrmcultist's Cloak sold by the Wyrmcult Provisioner in Blade's Edge Mountains, and the Pendant of Frozen Flame that can be obtained from skilled Jewelcrafters.

For this healing intensive stage assign 3 healers to each of the offtanks which should have healing over time effects on them at all times. The raid is best healed by Shamans using Chain Heal, helped by shadow Priests and their Vampiric Embrace.

The second stage ends when both Flames of Azzinoth are dead. The raid's healers will not be able to cope with healing both tanks and the entire raid for very long, so the sooner the Flames die, the better. Move away from the inner circle and prepare for stage 3.

STAGE 3

HP	6070400	Damage	19914-28157

Abilities	**Agonizing Flames:** This is an area effect fire spell that deals damage over time to everyone affected. Deals a total of 36000 Fire damage over 60 sec. It hits a random player outside of 15 yards, unless it cannot find anyone, then it just hits anyone it can find. The damage it deals increases over time, similar to Curse of Agony.
	Flame Burst: Throws fireballs to everyone in the raid outside of 15 yards. Deals 3238 to 3762 Fire damage to the target and all targets in a 5 yard radius.
	Summon Shadow Demons: Summons 4 Shadow Demons to aid the caster. These demons cast Paralyze on a random target and move towards them slowly, ignoring everyone else. If they get to their target, they instantly kill them and choose a new target.
	Uncaged Wrath: Increases Illidan's damage by 500% and movement speed by 200%.
	Demonic Transformation: Turns Illidan into a massive demon with different abilties.
	Shadow Blast: Deals area damage around the target and all friends of the target. This one will be fired off constantly during this phase, it has zero cooldown.

This stage starts with Illidan landing at the center of the terrace where he must be met by the main tank who has to start dragging him north, towards the position where he was tanked during stage 1. To begin with, Illidan uses all his stage 1 abilities, Shear, Flame Crash, Draw Soul and Parasitic Shadowfiend. The raid should already know how to deal with all of them. Additionally he will start using a new ability named Agonizing Flames. This causes an initial 4,000 damage and a further 3,000 damage every 5 seconds for 1 minute. The target for it is randomly selected. However, Agonizing Flames also affects all players in a 5 yard range around that target, so it is very important to have the raid spread out at least 5 yards away from each other. The damage over time debuff caused by Agonizing Flames can be removed by Iceblock, Cloak of Shadows, or Divine Shield, but other classes will need to be healed for the one minute duration of the debuff.

Seventy five seconds after the death of the second Shard of Azzinoth, which ended the second stage Illidan turns into his demon form, effectively announcing the fourth stage of the encounter.

EPIC FIRE RESISTANCE GEAR

ITEM	STATS
Inferno Tempered Boots	+45 Fire Resistance, +36 Stamina
Inferno Tempered Chestguard	+54 Stamina, +60 Fire Resistance
Inferno Tempered Gauntlets	+52 Stamina, +40 Fire Resistance
Inferno Tempered Leggings	+69 Stamina, +55 Fire Resistance
Phoenix Fire Band	+34 Stamina, +30 Fire Resistance
Wyrmcultist's Cloak	+14 Stamina, +24 Fire Resistance
Pendant of Frozen Flame	+18 Stamina, +30 Fire Resistance
Use: Absorbs 900 to 2700 fire damage on all nearby party members.	

A tank with over 365 Fire resistance takes fire-based melee hits averaging 3,000 damage, and on average resist about half of the 7,000 to 9,000 damage normally inflicted by Flame Blast. Periodically, the Flames of Azzinoth cast a frontal spell named Blaze. This spell places a circle of flames on the ground that inflicts up to 5,000 damage per second. This requires the tanks to constantly readjust to avoid taking too much Blaze damage. While repositioning always be aware of the position of the Flames of Azzinoth. The elementals cannot be tanked too far away from the center of the room, or they charge at their furthest target. This in turn can cause them to enrage, often with fatal consequences.

During this stage Illidan is not idle. He continuously casts Fireball on the raid. His fireballs deal 2,550 to 3,450 damage to all players within a 10 yard radius of their primary target. To reduce the damage taken, the players should spread out in the inner circle at the top of the temple. Occasionally he stops casting Fireball to use Dark Barrage against a random player. This is a very powerful spell that deals 3,000 damage every second for 10 seconds. It can be avoided using Iceblock, Cloak of Shadows or Divine Shield, but classes lacking those abilities need to be healed as soon as the Barrage has started.

The biggest threat to tanks and melee classes during this stage is Illidan's Eye Blast. This blue beam will always be cast on the outskirts of the inner circle. It is slow and easy to avoid, but those failing to move out of its way will be instantly killed by its 19,750 to 20,250 damage. Eye Blast leaves behind a blue trail of flame named Demon Fire, which only tanks can afford to move through as it deals around 2,000 damage per second. If the path to a Flame of Azzinoth is blocked by Demon Fire, melee classes must shift to the other Flame until the Demon Fire has subsided.

STAGE 4

As he transforms into Demon Illidan will wipe his threat table which gives the Warlock tank the opportunity to generate enough threat to focus Illidan's attention upon him. Illidan's primary attack during this stage is Shadow Blast, 8,750 to 11,250 damage in a 20 yard radius around its target. The Warlock, using the same Shadow resistance set he used for the Mother Shahraz encounter will, on average, resist half the damage. It is very important for the Warlock to position himself in the northwestern side of the temple's summit, a smart distance from the raid and from Illidan, but not out of the range of his healers. Moving too close to the Warlock tank usually spells instant death for anyone not wearing Shadow resistance. It is impossible to tank Illidan with a melee class during this stage, as anyone in a 15 yard radius around Illidan is affected by his Aura of Dread, which deals Shadow damage but also places a stacking debuff that increases Shadow damage by 30% per stack.

During this stage the raid must handle Flame Burst, which deals 3,238 to 3,762 Fire damage. While the direct damage is impossible to avoid, this spell causes splash damage around every player in the raid. Effectively, a group of two players within a 5 yard range of each other take double damage, with the damage increasing with each additional player. It is therefore important to keep some distance between any two players in the raid.

Thirty seconds after turning into a demon, Illidan summons five Shadow Demons. These have around 21,000 hit points and as soon as they spawn they link with a random player, paralyzing them in the process. They quickly begin moving towards their chosen targets. If they reach their target they will kill it, then choose another target. It is therefore very important that they are all killed before they reach their first target. They can be slowed down by any means such as Frostbolts, Hamstring, Crippling Poison, or Frost Traps.

Ideally, during the transformation stage at the beginning of Stage 4, a Hunter can place a Frost Trap near Illidan, in order to slow down the demons that he spawns 30 seconds later. Earthbind Totems are also a good option. One important thing to note is that after summoning demons, Illidan will continue to perform his stage 4 abilities, including Shadow Blast and Flame Burst. Therefore, while killing the demons the raid has to continue avoiding these abilities by staying away from the Warlock tank, and at least 5 yards from each other. Melee classes particularly should avoid attacking the same target and should let ranged classes deal with the Demons that approach the Warlock tank.

The demon stage lasts for 60 seconds at the end of which Illidan will turn back into his normal form, effectively starting a new stage 3. This will last for 75 seconds which is then followed by another 60 second long demon stage. Stages 3 and 4 alternate until Illidan reaches 30% health.

STAGE 5

As Illidan reaches 30% health, Maiev Shadowsong enters the battle. She periodically blinks to a player in the raid and places down a trap that can be used against Illidan. In this stage, Illidan enters an enraged state which significantly increases his damage to the point of being unhealable. The tank needs to drag Illidan towards the trap, click it to activate it, and position Illidan on top of it.

While he is trapped, Illidan takes additional damage from every player attacking him. Even during this stage he will continue his transitions from normal to demon form that define stages 3 and 4. Always stop doing damage while he transitions to give the new tank the chance to build some aggro. Even as his hit points approach zero, be patient and keep control of the encounter, it's only a matter of time before you stand victorious. Focus, and with a bit of luck Illidan's legendary Warglaives of Azzinoth may soon be yours to wield. Congratulations on completing the Black Temple!

QUEST

THE FALL OF THE BETRAYER

Quest Level:	70
Location:	The Black Temple, Shadowmoon Valley
Starts at:	Seer Kanai
Ends at:	Seer Kanai
Goal:	Defeat Illidan Stormrage inside the Black Temple.

Following the death of your mightiest opponent, return to Seer Kanai for your reward, a Blessed Medallion of Karabor that allows the wearer to teleport to the footsteps of what used to be Illidan's impenetrable fortress.

NAXXRAMAS

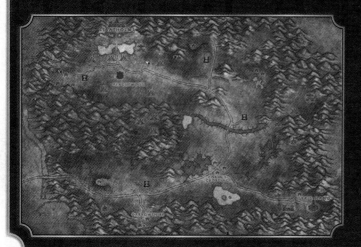

In a floating necropolis high above Eastern Plaguelands, Kel'Thuzad works to spread The Scourge across Lordaeron. Naxxramas is the highest level 40 person raid instance in the game. It is a giant dungeon with 15 challenging bosses, full sets of Tier 3 armor for every class, and many other high level drops.

Name	Naxxramas
Location	Eastern Plaguelands
Suggested Levels	Full raid group, levels 60-70
Reputation	Argent Dawn
Primary Enemies	Undead and Demons
Damage Types	All types, mainly shadow
Time to Complete	2-7 Days

BRIEF OVERVIEW

Naxxramas is divided into 5 wings.

SPIDER WING

Arguably the easiest wing; a good place to start your adventures and get a feel for Naxxramas.

- Anub'Rekhan
- Grand Widow Faerlina
- Maexxna

PLAGUE WING

The first two bosses are fairly manageable, but the final boss takes your raid to the high level of execution required from here on out.

- Noth the Plaguebringer
- Heigan the Unclean
- Loatheb

ABOMINATION WING

Home to the infamous Patchwerk, a challenging wing with many fun encounters.

- Patchwerk
- Grobbulus
- Gluth
- Thaddius

DEATHKNIGHT WING

After the first boss this is arguably the hardest wing.

- Instructor Razuvious
- Gothik the Harvester
- The Four Horsemen

FROSTWYRM LAIR

The final wing with only two bosses; it is only accessible after the previous four wings are clear.

- Sapphiron
- Kel'Thuzad

You are free to clear the wings in any order you choose, except for Frostwyrm Lair.

ATTUNEMENT

Every player who wishes to enter Naxxramas must first become attuned. Depending on your reputation with the Argent Dawn, the materials required for attunement are different. You must be at least Honored to attune.

HONORED

5 Arcane Crystals
2 Nexus Crystals
1 Righteous Orb
60 Gold

REVERED

2 Arcane Crystals
1 Nexus Crystal
30 Gold

EXALTED

Free!

Bring the required items to Archmage Angela Dosantos inside of Light's Hope Chapel and accept the quest **"The Dread Citadel – Naxxramas."**

WHO TO BRING

Every 40 person fight in the game is logically designed around bringing 4-6 players of each class to the raid. This holds true for most of Naxxramas but each boss is slightly different.

In order to know who to bring you should know what bosses you plan on killing. Study the information provided for each boss you plan to kill to get a closer idea on who to bring.

GETTING TO NAXXRAMAS

You teleport up to Naxxramas by entering the transporter in the northwestern part of Eastern Plaguelands. You must be attuned, at least level 60, and in a raid group before the portal sends you anywhere.

You can not zone into Naxxramas while a boss is engaged.

QUESTS IN NAXXRAMAS

ECHOES OF WAR

Quest Level	60 (Raid)
Location	Eastern Plaguelands, Naxxramas
Starts at	Commander Eligor Dawnbringer
Ends at	Commander Eligor Dawnbringer
Goal	Slay 8 Deathknight Captains, 3 Venom Stalkers, 5 Living Monstrosities, and 5 Stoneskin Gargoyles

Echoes of War is a very important quest because it must be completed before you can obtain any of the quests for Tier 3 armor. Commander Dawnbringer wants you to kill a few of the minions from each of the 4 wings. Complete this and return to him at Light's Hope Chapel. After finishing this quest, Father Inigo Montoy at Light's Hope Chapel now offers you the quests for Tier 3 armor.

THE FATE OF RAMALADNI

Quest Level	60 (Raid)
Location	Eastern Plaguelands, Naxxramas
Starts at	Korfax, Champion of the Light
Ends at	Korfax, Champion of the Light
Goal	Search Naxxramas to learn what happened to Ramaladni

Kill enough minions in Naxxramas and eventually a quest starter drops called The Fate of Ramaladni; it looks like a ring. Take this quest item back to Korfax at Light's Hope Chapel.

CRYPTSTALKER ARMOR – HUNTER

TIER 3 SETS

Naxxramas works on a token based loot system. Every boss drops different tokens that can be turned in, along with some other easily obtainable things, for the appropriate piece of Tier 3 armor.

DREAMWALKER RAINMENT – DRUID

SET BONUSES

2 pieces: Your Rejuvenation ticks have a chance to restore 60 mana, 8 energy, or 2 rage to your target.

4 pieces: Reduces the mana cost of your Healing Touch, Regrowth, Rejuvenation, and Tranquility spells by 3%.

6 pieces: Your initial cast and Regrowth ticks will increase the maximum health of your target by up to 50, stacking up to 7 times.

8 pieces: On Healing Touch critical hits, you regain 30% of the mana cost of the spell.

Dreamwalker Boots: Leather Feet, 195 Armor, +20 INT, +14 SPI, +20 STA, Equip: Increases healing done by spells and effects by up to 46, Equip: Restores 5 mana per 5 sec

Dreamwalker Girdle: Leather Waist, 162 Armor, +14 STA, +23 INT, +13 SPI, Equip: Increases healing done by spells and effects by up to 51, Equip: Restores 4 mana per 5 sec

Dreamwalker Handguards: Leather Hands, 180 Armor, +16 SPI, +17 STA, +22 INT, Equip: Increases healing done by spells and effects by up to 53

Dreamwalker Headpiece: Leather Head, 235 Armor, +20 SPI, +31 INT, +25 STA, Equip: Increases healing done by spells and effects by up to 66

Dreamwalker Legguards: Leather Legs, 253 Armor, +20 SPI, +26 INT, +22 STA, Equip: Increases healing done by spells and effects by up to 66, Equip: Restores 8 mana per 5 sec

Dreamwalker Spaulders: Leather Shoulder, 212 Armor, +12 SPI, +22 INT, +18 STA, Equip: Restores 5 mana per 5 sec, Equip: Increases healing done by spells and effects by up to 48

Dreamwalker Tunic: Leather Chest, 299 Armor, +19 SPI, +29 INT, +29 STA, Equip: Increases healing done by spells and effects by up to 66, Equip: Restores 8 mana per 5 sec

Dreamwalker Wristguards: Leather Wrist, 126 Armor, +14 STA, +16 INT, Equip: Increases healing done by spells and effects by up to 40, Equip: Restores 5 mana per 5 sec

SET BONUSES

2 pieces: Increases the duration of your Rapid Fire by 4 secs.

4 pieces: While your pet is active, increases attack power by 50 for both you and your pet.

6 pieces: Your ranged critical hits cause an Adrenaline Rush, granting you 50 mana.

8 pieces: Reduces the mana cost of your Multi-Shot and Aimed Shot by 20.

Cryptstalker Boots: Mail Feet, 425 Armor, +22 AGI, +19 STA, +8 INT, Equip: Increases your hit rating by 10, Equip: Increases attack power by 44

Cryptstalker Girdle: Mail Waist, 355 Armor, +16 AGI, +22 STA, +12 INT, Equip: Increases your hit rating by 10, Equip: Increases your critical strike rating by 14, Equip: Restores 3 mana per 5 sec

Cryptstalker Handguards: Mail Hands, 395 Armor, +16 AGI, +15 INT, +21 STA, Equip: Increases your critical strike rating by 14, Equip: Restores 4 mana per 5 sec, Equip: Increases attack power by 32

Cryptstalker Headpiece: Mail Head, 513 Armor, +21 AGI, +30 STA, +12 INT, Equip: Increases your critical strike rating by 28, Equip: Restores 3 mana per 5 sec, Equip: Increases attack power by 40

Cryptstalker Legguards: Mail Legs, 552 Armor, +28 AGI, +26 STA, +10 INT, Equip: Increases your critical strike rating by 14, Equip: Restores 6 mana per 5 sec, Equip: Increases attack power by 56

Cryptstalker Spaulders: Mail Shoulder, 464 Armor, +20 AGI, +23 STA, +10 INT, Equip: Increases your critical strike rating by 14, Equip: Increases attack power by 38

Cryptstalker Tunic: Mail Chest, 658 Armor, +30 AGI, +27 STA, +15 INT, Equip: Increases your hit rating by 10, Equip: Increases your critical strike rating by 14, Equip: Restores 4 mana per 5 sec

Cryptstalker Wristguards: Mail Wrist, 276 Armor, +18 AGI, +16 STA, Equip: Increases your hit rating by 10, Equip: Increases attack power by 34

FROSTFIRE REGALIA – MAGE

REDEMPTION ARMOR – PALADIN

SET BONUSES

2 pieces: Reduces cooldown on your Evocation by 1 minute.

4 pieces: Gives your Mage Armor a chance when struck by a harmful spell to increase resistance against that school of magic by 35 for 30 seconds.

6 pieces: Your damage spells have a chance to cause your target to take up to 200 increased damage from subsequent spells.

8 pieces: Your damage spells have a chance to displace you, causing the next spell cast to generate no threat.

Frostfire Belt: Cloth Waist, 85 Armor, +10 SPI, +19 STA, +21 INT, Equip: Increases damage and healing done by magical spells and effects by up to 28, Equip: Increases your spell hit rating by 8

Frostfire Bindings: Cloth Wrist, 66 Armor, +14 STA, +15 INT, Equip: Increases your spell penetration by 10, Equip: Increases damage and healing done by magical spells and effects by up to 27

Frostfire Circlet: Cloth Head, 123 Armor, +22 STA, +23 INT, Equip: Increases damage and healing done by magical spells and effects by up to 35, Equip: Increases your spell hit rating by 8, Equip: Increases your spell critical strike rating by 28

Frostfire Gloves: Cloth Hands, 95 Armor, +17 STA, +19 INT, +10 SPI, Equip: Increases damage and healing done by magical spells and effects by up to 36

Frostfire Leggings: Cloth Legs, 133 Armor, +10 SPI, +26 INT, +25 STA, Equip: Increases your spell hit rating by 8, Equip: Increases damage and healing done by magical spells and effects by up to 46

Frostfire Robe: Cloth Chest(Robe), 158 Armor, +21 STA, +27 INT, Equip: Increases damage and healing done by magical spells and effects by up to 47, Equip: Increases your spell hit rating by 8, Equip: Increases your spell critical strike rating by 14

Frostfire Sandals: Cloth Feet, 102 Armor, +10 SPI, +18 INT, +17 STA, Equip: Increases your spell critical strike rating by 14, Equip: Increases damage and healing done by magical spells and effects by up to 28

Frostfire Shoulderpads: Cloth Shoulder, 111 Armor, +17 STA, +18 INT, +9 SPI, Equip: Increases damage and healing done by magical spells and effects by up to 36

SET BONUSES

2 pieces: Increases the amount healed by your Judgement of Light by 20.

4 pieces: Reduces cooldown on your Lay on Hands by 12 min.

6 pieces: Your Flash of Light and Holy Light spells have a chance to imbue your target with Holy Power.

8 pieces: Your Cleanse spell also heals the target for 200.

Redemption Boots: Plate Feet, 756 Armor, +22 STA, +18 INT, Equip: Increases healing done by spells and effects by up to 42, Equip: Increases your spell critical strike rating by 14, Equip: Restores 5 mana per 5 sec

Redemption Girdle: Plate Waist, 632 Armor, +19 STA, +29 INT, Equip: Increases healing done by spells and effects by up to 40, Equip: Restores 5 mana per 5 sec

Redemption Handguards: Plate Hands, 702 Armor, +23 STA, +22 INT, Equip: Restores 8 mana per 5 sec, Equip: Increases healing done by spells and effects by up to 33

Redemption Headpiece: Plate Head, 913 Armor, +28 STA, +26 INT, Equip: Increases healing done by spells and effects by up to 64, Equip: Increases your spell critical strike rating by 14, Equip: Restores 8 mana per 5 sec

Redemption Legguards: Plate Legs, 983 Armor, +30 STA, +31 INT, Equip: Increases your spell critical strike rating by 14, Equip: Increases healing done by spells and effects by up to 42, Equip: Restores 8 mana per 5 sec

Redemption Spaulders: Plate Shoulder, 825 Armor, +22 STA, +20 INT, Equip: Increases your spell critical strike rating by 14, Equip: Increases healing done by spells and effects by up to 40, Equip: Restores 4 mana per 5 sec

Redemption Tunic: Plate Chest, 1172 Armor, +25 STA, +31 INT, Equip: Increases healing done by spells and effects by up to 59, Equip: Increases your spell critical strike rating by 14, Equip: Restores 10 mana per 5 sec

Redemption Wristguards: Plate Wrist, 492 Armor, +22 STA, +15 INT, Equip: Increases healing done by spells and effects by up to 31, Equip: Restores 4 mana per 5 sec

VESTMENTS OF FAITH – PRIEST

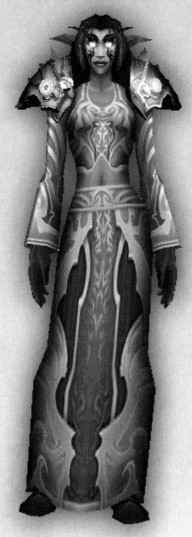

BONESCYTHE ARMOR – ROGUE

SET BONUSES

2 pieces: Reduces the mana cost of your Renew spell by 12%.

4 pieces: On Greater Heal critical hits, your target will gain Armor of Faith, absorbing up to 500 damage.

6 pieces: Reduces the threat from your healing spells.

8 pieces: Each spell you cast can trigger an Epiphany, increasing your mana regeneration by 24 for 30 seconds.

Belt of Faith: Cloth Waist, 85 Armor, +23 INT, +18 STA, +17 SPI, Equip: Increases healing done by spells and effects by up to 48

Bindings of Faith: Cloth Wrist, 66 Armor, +11 STA, +15 INT, +17 SPI, Equip: Increases healing done by spells and effects by up to 40

Circlet of Faith: Cloth Head, 123 Armor, +22 SPI, +22 INT, +22 STA, Equip: Increases healing done by spells and effects by up to 75, Equip: Restores 5 mana per 5 sec

Gloves of Faith: Cloth Hands, 95 Armor, +22 SPI, +21 INT, +16 STA, Equip: Increases healing done by spells and effects by up to 40, Equip: Restores 4 mana per 5 sec

Leggings of Faith: Cloth Legs, 133 Armor, +28 SPI, +26 INT, +25 STA, Equip: Increases healing done by spells and effects by up to 66

Robe of Faith: Cloth Chest(Robe), 158 Armor, +21 SPI, +27 INT, +26 STA, Equip: Increases healing done by spells and effects by up to 64, Equip: Restores 5 mana per 5 sec

Sandals of Faith: Cloth Feet, 102 Armor, +13 SPI, +19 STA, +22 INT, Equip: Restores 6 mana per 5 sec, Equip: Increases healing done by spells and effects by up to 44

Shoulderpads of Faith: Cloth Shoulder, 111 Armor, +17 SPI, +18 INT, +17 STA, Equip: Increases healing done by spells and effects by up to 51, Equip: Restores 3 mana per 5 sec

SET BONUSES

2 pieces: Your normal melee swings have a chance to Invigorate you, healing you for 90 to 110.

4 pieces: Your Backstab, Sinister Strike, and Hemorrhage critical hits cause you to regain 5 energy.

6 pieces: Reduces the threat from your Backstab, Sinister Strike, Hemorrhage, and Eviscerate abilities.

8 pieces: Your Eviscerate has a chance per combo point to reveal a flaw in your opponent's armor, granting a 100% critical hit chance for your next Backstab, Sinister Strike, or Hemorrhage.

Bonescythe Bracers: Leather Wrist, 126 Armor, +26 AGI, +14 STA, Equip: Increases your critical strike rating by 14

Bonescythe Breastplate: Leather Chest, 299 Armor, +29 STA, Equip: Increases your critical strike rating by 28, Equip: Increases attack power by 80, Equip: Increases your hit rating by 10

Bonescythe Gauntlets: Leather Hands, 180 Armor, +20 STA, Equip: Increases your hit rating by 10, Equip: Increases attack power by 66, Equip: Increases your critical strike rating by 14

Bonescythe Helmet: Leather Head, 235 Armor, +30 AGI, +29 STA, +18 STR, Equip: Increases your hit rating by 10, Equip: Increases your critical strike rating by 28

Bonescythe Legplates: Leather Legs, 253 Armor, +32 AGI, +25 STA, +31 STR, Equip: Increases your critical strike rating by 14, Equip: Increases your hit rating by 10

Bonescythe Pauldrons: Leather Shoulder, 212 Armor, +22 AGI, +15 STA, +22 STR, Equip: Increases your critical strike rating by 14, Equip: Increases your hit rating by 10

Bonescythe Sabatons: Leather Feet, 195 Armor, +18 STA, Equip: Increases your hit rating by 10, Equip: Increases your critical strike rating by 14, Equip: Increases attack power by 64

Bonescythe Waistguard: Leather Waist, 162 Armor, +24 AGI, +20 STA, +23 STR, Equip: Increases your critical strike rating by 14

THE EARTHSHATTERER – SHAMAN

DREADNAUGHT'S BATTLEGEAR – WARRIOR

SET BONUSES

2 pieces: Reduces the mana cost of your totem spells by 12%.

4 pieces: Increases the mana gained from your Mana Spring totems by 25%.

6 pieces: Your Healing Wave and Lesser Healing Wave spells have a chance to imbue your target with Totemic Power.

8 pieces: Your Lightning Shield spell also grants you 15 mana per 5 sec. while active.

Earthshatter Boots: Mail Feet, 425 Armor, +20 STA, +25 INT, Equip: Increases healing done by spells and effects by up to 37, Equip: Restores 6 mana per 5 sec

Earthshatter Girdle: Mail Waist, 355 Armor, +25 INT, +18 STA, Equip: Restores 7 mana per 5 sec, Equip: Increases healing done by spells and effects by up to 42

Earthshatter Handguards: Mail Hands, 395 Armor, +21 STA, +28 INT, Equip: Increases healing done by spells and effects by up to 35, Equip: Restores 6 mana per 5 sec

Earthshatter Headpiece: Mail Head, 513 Armor, +26 STA, +30 INT, Equip: Increases healing done by spells and effects by up to 68, Equip: Restores 8 mana per 5 sec

Earthshatter Legguards: Mail Legs, 552 Armor, +28 STA, +30 INT, Equip: Increases healing done by spells and effects by up to 59, Equip: Restores 9 mana per 5 sec

Earthshatter Spaulders: Mail Shoulder, 464 Armor, +24 STA, +19 INT, Equip: Increases healing done by spells and effects by up to 42, Equip: Restores 6 mana per 5 sec

Earthshatter Tunic: Mail Chest, 658 Armor, +26 STA, +32 INT, Equip: Increases healing done by spells and effects by up to 59, Equip: Restores 12 mana per 5 sec

Earthshatter Wristguards: Mail Wrist, 276 Armor, +17 STA, +18 INT, Equip: Increases healing done by spells and effects by up to 33, Equip: Restores 4 mana per 5 sec

SET BONUSES

2 pieces: Increases the damage done by your Revenge ability by 75.

4 pieces: Improves your chance to hit with Taunt and Challenging Shout by 5%.

6 pieces: Improves your chance to hit with Sunder Armor, Heroic Strike, Revenge, and Shield Slam by 5%.

8 pieces: When your health drops below 20%, for the next 5 seconds healing spells cast on you help you to Cheat Death, increasing healing done by up to 160.

Dreadnaught Bracers: Plate Wrist, 492 Armor, +14 STR, +28 STA, Equip: Increases defense rating by 7

Dreadnaught Breastplate: Plate Chest, 1172 Armor, +21 STR, +43 STA, Equip: Increases defense rating by 20, Equip: Increases your dodge rating by 12, Equip: Increases your hit rating by 20

Dreadnaught Gauntlets: Plate Hands, 702 Armor, +27 STA, +17 STR, Equip: Increases defense rating by 13, Equip: Increases your block rating by 13, Equip: Increases the block value of your shield by 21

Dreadnaught Helmet: Plate Head, 913 Armor, +45 STA, +21 STR, Equip: Increases your dodge rating by 12, Equip: Increases defense rating by 21

Dreadnaught Legplates: Plate Legs, 983 Armor, +23 STR, +37 STA, Equip: Increases defense rating by 19, Equip: Increases your dodge rating by 12, Equip: Increases the block value of your shield by 32

Dreadnaught Pauldrons: Plate Shoulder, 825 Armor, +29 STA, +16 STR, Equip: Increases your hit rating by 10, Equip: Increases the block value of your shield by 21, Equip: Increases defense rating by 13

Dreadnaught Sabatons: Plate Feet, 756 Armor, +15 STR, +34 STA, Equip: Increases defense rating by 13, Equip: Increases your dodge rating by 12

Dreadnaught Waistguard: Plate Waist, 632 Armor, +20 STR, +26 STA, Equip: Increases the block value of your shield by 18, Equip: Increases your block rating by 13, Equip: Increases defense rating by 13

PLAGUEHEART RAINMENT – WARLOCK

SET BONUSES

2 pieces: Your Shadow Bolts now have a chance to heal you for 270 to 330.

4 pieces: Increases damage caused by your Corruption by 12%.

6 pieces: Your spell critical hits generate 25% less threat. In addition, Corruption, Immolate, Curse of Agony, and Siphon Life generate 25% less threat.

8 pieces: Reduces health cost of your Life Tap by 12%.

Plagueheart Belt: Cloth Waist, 85 Armor, +23 STA, +12 INT, Equip: Increases damage and healing done by magical spells and effects by up to 34, Equip: Increases your spell critical strike rating by 14

Plagueheart Bindings: Cloth Wrist, 66 Armor, +23 STA, +14 INT, Equip: Increases damage and healing done by magical spells and effects by up to 23

Plagueheart Circlet: Cloth Head, 123 Armor, +28 STA, +25 INT, Equip: Increases damage and healing done by magical spells and effects by up to 33, Equip: Increases your spell critical strike rating by 28, Equip: Increases your spell hit rating by 8

Plagueheart Gloves: Cloth Hands, 95 Armor, +25 STA, +17 INT, Equip: Increases your spell critical strike rating by 14, Equip: Increases damage and healing done by magical spells and effects by up to 26

Plagueheart Leggings: Cloth Legs, 133 Armor, +30 STA, +25 INT, Equip: Increases your spell critical strike rating by 14, Equip: Increases damage and healing done by magical spells and effects by up to 37, Equip: Increases your spell penetration by 10

Plagueheart Robe: Cloth Chest(Robe), 158 Armor, +27 STA, +22 INT, Equip: Increases your spell hit rating by 8, Equip: Increases damage and healing done by magical spells and effects by up to 51, Equip: Increases your spell critical strike rating by 14

Plagueheart Sandals: Cloth Feet, 102 Armor, +20 STA, +16 INT, Equip: Increases damage and healing done by magical spells and effects by up to 32, Equip: Increases your spell critical strike rating by 14

Plagueheart Shoulderpads: Cloth Shoulder, 111 Armor, +22 STA, +12 INT, Equip: Increases your spell hit rating by 8, Equip: Increases damage and healing done by magical spells and effects by up to 36

MISCELLANEOUS NAXXRAMAS LOOT

The following items have a small chance to drop off of any minion in Naxxramas.

Belt of the Grand Crusader: 612 Armor, +18 Strength, +18 Stamina, +18 Intellect, +21 Spell Damage and Healing, +7 Mana/5 sec.

Ghoul Skin Tunic: Leather Chest, 446 Armor, +20 STR, +22 STA, Equip: Increases your critical strike rating by 28

Harbinger of Doom: Dagger One-Hand, 83-126 Damage, Speed: 1.60, 65.3 damage per second, +8 AGI, +8 STA, Equip: Increases your critical strike rating by 14, Equip: Increases your hit rating by 10

Leggings of Elemental Fury: Mail Legs, 535 Armor, +26 STA, +27 INT, Classes: Shaman, Equip: Increases damage and healing done by magical spells and effects by up to 32, Equip: Increases your spell critical strike rating by 28

Leggings of the Grand Crusader: 952 Armor, +21 Strength, +21 Stamina, +21 Intellect, +26 Spell Damage and Healing, +28 Critical Strike Rating

Misplaced Servo Arm: Mace One-Hand, 128-238 Damage, Speed: 2.80, 65.4 damage per second, Equip: Chance to discharge electricity causing 100 to 150 Nature damage to your target

Necro-Knight's Garb: Cloth Chest, 467 Armor, +32 STA, Classes: Priest, Mage, Warlock, Equip: Increases damage and healing done by magical spells and effects by up to 37

Ring of the Eternal Flame: Finger, +10 INT, Equip: Increases damage done by Fire spells and effects by up to 34, Equip: Increases your spell critical strike rating by 14

Spaulders of the Grand Crusader: 816 Armor, +18 Strength, +18 Stamina, +17 Intellect, +4 Mana/5 Sec., +14 Critical Strike Rating, +20 Spell Damage and Healing

Stygian Buckler: Shield, 3570 Armor, 78 Block, Equip: When struck has a 15% chance of reducing the attacker's movement speed by 50% for 5 secs. Chance to fizzle against targets over level 60

SPIDER WING

The Spider Wing is home to three bosses. This is arguably the easiest wing to clear and most raid groups should head to the Spider Wing to get themselves acquainted with Naxxramas. Anub'Rekhan is a fight that relies on the main tank kiting the boss during the Locus Swarm. Grand Widow Faerlina is about dodging her AoE abilities and using Mind Control to sacrifice her adds which weakens her. And Maexxna is a strict timing-based fight with a nasty enrage at the end.

SPIDER WING MINIONS

CARRION SPINNER	BEAST
CRYPT GUARD	UNDEAD
CRYPT REAVER	UNDEAD
DREAD CREEPER	BEAST
INFECTIOUS GHOUL	UNDEAD
INFECTIOUS SKITTERER	BEAST
NAXXRAMAS ACOLYTE	HUMANOID
NAXXRAMAS CULTIST	HUMANOID
PLAGUED GHOUL	UNDEAD
SHADE OF NAXXRAMAS	UNDEAD
SPIRIT OF NAXXRAMAS	UNDEAD
STONESKIN GARGOYLE	UNDEAD
TOMB HORROR	UNDEAD
VENOM STALKER	BEAST

ANUB'REKHAN

Anub'Rekhan is commonly the first boss that a raid group takes down in Naxxramas. This fight boils down to being able to deal with the Locus Swarm correctly. It should only take a few tries to master this fight and start your adventures into Naxxramas!

LOOT

Band of Unanswered Prayers: Finger, +11 INT, +11 STA, +12 SPI, Equip: Increases healing done by spells and effects by up to 51

Cryptfiend Silk Cloak: Back, 212 Armor, +14 STA, Equip: Increases defense rating by 10, Equip: Increases your dodge rating by 12, Equip: Increases your hit rating by 10

Desecrated Bindings: Classes: Warlock, Mage, Priest

Desecrated Bracers: Classes: Rogue, Warrior

Desecrated Wristguards: Classes: Shaman, Druid, Hunter, Paladin

Gem of Nerubis: Held In Hand, +14 STA, +10 INT, Equip: Increases your spell penetration by 10, Equip: Increases damage and healing done by magical spells and effects by up to 25

Touch of Frost: Neck, +20 STA, +24 Frost Resistance

Wristguards of Vengeance: Plate Wrist, 465 Armor, +24 STR, +10 STA, Equip: Increases your critical strike rating by 14

ABILITIES

HP	1665500	Damage	3844-5096
Abilities	**Locust Swarm:** Deals 875 to 1125 nature damage every 2 sec. for 20 sec. and prevents attacking and casting of spells in a 30 yard radius. The damage component of this effect stacks.		
	Impale: Inflicts 3938 to 5062 Physical damage to the target and other nearby targets, knocking them into the air.		
	Summon Crypt Guard: Summons Crypt Guard to aid the caster.		
	Summon Corpse Scarabs: Summons Corpse Scarabs based on the number of corpses in Anub'Rekhan's room.		

IMPALE

Explanation: Sends out an impaling bolt towards any player on the agro list. The impale travels about 35 yards and can do up to 4000 damage to cloth wearers. Additionally, you are tossed into the air and take another 1000 damage from falling.

Solution: Since Impale only has a 35 yard range, all healers and most ranged DPS can outrange it and not worry about it. Make sure anyone within range of Impale is topped off. Be prepared to use Levitate and Safe Fall and drink healing potions midair so that you don't die from fall damage. Impale is going to hit people and you can't really stop it or control it, but you shouldn't see anyone die as long as they are topped off on health and have at least 1 emergency midair consumable to save themselves.

LOCUS SWARM

Explanation: Every 90 seconds or so (it is not entirely predictable), Anub'Rekhan begins to channel Locus Swarm. Once it has cast, the area within 30 yards around him starts dealing a stackable DoT debuff. The debuff silences you and ticks for 1200 damage per stack. Additionally, Anub'Rekhan's movement speed is reduced to 40%.

Solution: This is the most important part of the encounter. When Locus Swarm starts the main tank needs to start running and the Hunter in the group needs to turn Aspect of the Pack on. The main tank should kite Anub'Rekhan along the right side of the room while staying at least 30 yards away from him. Use the very edge of the room—on the far side of the green slime. Don't move too quickly or he cuts across the room and catches up to the tank too quickly; you want to keep him along the sides as much as possible. The main tank usually takes one or two stacks of the DoT debuff so the healers should rotate alongside the kiter. The main tank should go all the way back up against the door, by the time Anub'Rekhan catches up Locus Swarm is over.

CORPSE SCARABS

Explanation: Every time a player dies their corpse explodes with scarabs. Additionally, every time a Crypt Guard body disappears, their corpse spawns about 10 scarabs.

Solution: These are non-elite and should be AoEed down very quickly. Try to use spells like Frost Nova to prevent any of them from running off and attacking a healer or the main tank. You always have to deal with scarabs from decaying Crypt Guard bodies, but you shouldn't have to deal with many scarabs from dead players—they shouldn't die in the first place!

PREPARATION

Group 1 needs to have a Priest, a Paladin, a Warlock, a Hunter, and the Main Tank. All of the other groups don't need anything special. Distribute the classes evenly.

STRATEGY

Assign one tank to the left Crypt Guard—the one you plan on killing first. Assign two tanks to the right Crypt Guard. You want two tanks on the second Crypt Guard because they have a stacking DoT debuff that really hurts; having a second tank available when the debuff gets stacked up too high on the first makes it easier to succeed. Finally, assign one Hunter to peel each Crypt Guard onto the appropriate tanks, but make sure the main tank has their target first.

The main tank should charge in and bring Anub'Rekhan to the far side of the room. The tank needs to position himself or herself so that they are ready to take off along the right side of the room when Locus Swarm is cast.

The Crypt Guards should be dragged to the left side of the room and killed one at a time as quickly as possible. Be aware, they have a net ability that hits everyone within melee range.

After the Crypt Guards are down, the main tank should be in position and have plenty of threat built up. The Hunter in group 1 should be along the right edge of the room within aura range of the main tank, ready to activate Aspect of the Pack as soon as Locus Swarm begins.

Start to DPS Anub'Rekhan; keep everyone topped off so that nobody dies to Impale and make sure the main tank is getting steady heals.

About 90 seconds into the fight the first Locus Swarm happens. The moment Anub'Rekhan starts casting all DPS should retreat to the left side of the room. When the Crypt Guard spawns at the far end of the room, it should be pulled to the waiting DPS and killed quickly.

The main tank needs to start moving quickly. Move along the right side of the room. Stay at least 30 yards away from Anub'Rekhan, but don't move too quickly because you don't want him to cut across the room and catch up to you. Make sure the kiting tank gets a few heals because he or she might get hit with the DoT debuff once or twice. The Hunter just needs to make sure Aspect of the Pack is on the main tank during the kiting.

Reacting to Locus Swarm is the key to this fight. Nobody but the main tank should get hit by the debuff, and even then they should only get hit by two stacks at the very most.

Later in the fight, you need to stay on top of the scarabs that spawn when players die or when Crypt Guards decay, because you can't have the scarabs attacking anyone in group 1 when Aspect of the Pack active.

Once the main tank arrives at the doorway, they should run all the way back against the door and let Anub'Rekhan come to them, Locus Swarm is over. The Crypt Guard should be long dead by this point and the main tank needs to position themselves so they are ready to run along the right wall again; the Hunter also needs to get into position along the right edge. The rest of the raid should spread out, stay at max range, and be ready for Impales.

Approximately 90 seconds after the first Locus Swarm ends, he does it again. Kite him along the right edge the same as before. Deal with the Crypt Guard that spawns and be ready to resume the fight in the position you started in. There is no enrage and nothing else to worry about other than the Swarm. After four or five Locus Swarms you should have a dead bug at your feet.

GRAND WIDOW FAERLINA

Grand Widow seems like an intimidating fight with so many powerful adds to deal with, but you will find if you dodge the Rain of Fire, cleanse the Poison Bolt Volley, and use the Sacrifice ability efficiently, it is a very manageable fight.

LOOT

Desecrated Bindings: Classes: Warlock, Mage Priest

Desecrated Bracers: Classes: Rogue, Warrior

Desecrated Wristguards: Classes: Shaman, Druid, Hunter, Paladin

Icebane Pauldrons: Plate Shoulder, 797 Armor, +18 STA, +9 STR, +33 Frost Resistance, Equip: Increases defense rating by 10

Malice Stone Pendant: Neck, +8 INT, +9 STA, Equip: Increases damage and healing done by magical spells and effects by up to 28, Equip: Increases your spell penetration by 15

Polar Shoulder Pads: Leather Shoulder, 207 Armor, +25 STA, +33 Frost Resistance

The Widow's Embrace: Mace Main Hand, 42-115 Damage, Speed 1.90, 41.3 damage per second, +12 INT, +12 STA, +14 SPI, Equip: Increases healing done by spells and effects by up to 161

Widow's Remorse: Sword One-Hand, 100 Armor, 70-131 Damage, Speed 1.60, 62.8 damage per second, +17 STA, Equip: Increases your hit rating by 10

ABILITIES

HP	1332400	Damage	5491-7780
Abilities	**Enrage:** Increases attack speed by 75% and the Physical damage by 150% for 30 min.		
	Rain of Fire: Burns all in a selected area for 1850 to 2150 Fire damage every 2 sec. for 6 sec.		
	Poison Bolt Volley: Inflicts 1225 to 1575 Nature damage, then 417 to 483 damage every 2 sec. for 8 sec.		

ENRAGE

Explanation: This is on a 60 second cooldown. When she enrages, she does significantly more melee damage and has increased attack speed.

Solution: When you mind control a Naxxramas Worshipper, they have an ability called Sacrifice that destroys the Worshipper and removes enrage from Faerlina. It is very important that you only use Sacrifice when Faerlina is enraged. If you silence her before she enrages, the next enrage happens in 30 seconds. If you silence her while she is enraged, the next enrage happens in 60 seconds. You need that extra 30 seconds to damage her or you are going to run out of Worshippers to Sacrifice before she dies.

POISON VOLLEY

Explanation: Every 5-10 seconds she hits 10 random people for about 1500 poison damage and applies a curable poison DoT debuff that ticks for additional damage.

Solution: Cleanse the debuff and heal anyone who gets hit. Thankfully, when Faerlina has been silenced by a Worshipper's Sacrifice, she doesn't cast Poison Volley for 30 seconds. A little bit of quality Nature Resist gear helps mitigate the damage.

RAIN OF FIRE

Explanation: Just like Gehennas, she casts Rain of Fire in a random area. This hits fairly hard, 2000 damage per tick.

Solution: Move out of it as quickly as possible, especially when it is cast on the melee DPS/main tank. It is resistible so a little bit of Fire Resist can help reduce the damage.

Balance is the Key

Don't sacrifice too much gear for Nature and Fire resistance! You still need a lot of damage to take her down.

PREPARATION

Five things need to be tanked: Faerlina and 4 Worshippers. One tank can usually handle two Worshippers by themselves if necessary, but having 5 tanks is ideal. With this in mind, setup 5 tanking groups. Give them Devotion Aura and quality healing.

Assign a tank to each Worshipper and the main tank to Faerlina. You kill the two Followers first, so they don't even really need tanks; a Paladin or Rogue using Evasion can take care of them.

One Priest is in charge of Mind Controlling the Worshippers and Sacrificing them when Faerlina Enrages. Make sure that Priest is not healing anyone who plans on taking a lot of damage. The Mind Controlling Priest should use at least 30 spell hit rating worth of gear as well to help reduce the chances of a resist or an early break on the Mind Control.

Try to have someone who can cleanse poison in every group. Spread out Fire Resistance Auras.

STRATEGY

Make sure everybody knows their target, knows which Follower is going to die first, and when the tank is going to charge the boss.

Kill the two Followers as quickly as possible. Faerlina should be positioned somewhere in the middle of the room. 60 seconds into the fight, she Enrages. Have your first Worshipper positioned near Faerlina and the Priest assigned to Mind Controlling Worshippers ready to start casting.

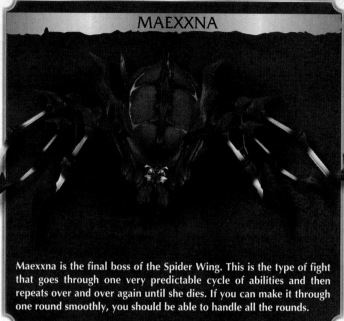

MAEXXNA

Maexxna is the final boss of the Spider Wing. This is the type of fight that goes through one very predictable cycle of abilities and then repeats over and over again until she dies. If you can make it through one round smoothly, you should be able to handle all the rounds.

Worship Me

The Priest who is Mind Controlling needs to have the Worshipper controlled and ready to Sacrifice a good 5 seconds before the Enrage actually happens. You want to immediately Sacrifice the moment she Enrages.

When the first Enrage happens, your Mind Controlling Priest should quickly Sacrifice the first Worshipper and, assuming all goes smoothly, it really won't be very difficult.

Continue to dodge the Rain of Fire and cleanse the Poison Bolt Volley. Top off people's life so that they don't die to any of the various AoE abilities, and get ready for the second Enrage by bringing a Worshipper close to Faerlina. Have your Mind Controlling Priest ready to Sacrifice another Worshipper.

This is how the fight continues until she is dead. Don't let anyone die to the AoE damage spells Faerlina casts, stay on top of those Sacrifices, and she bows to your raid in time.

LOOT

Crystal Webbed Robe: Cloth Chest(Robe), 147 Armor, +25 STA, +19 INT, Equip: Increases damage and healing done by magical spells and effects by up to 53

Desecrated Gauntlets: Classes: Rogue, Warrior

Desecrated Gloves: Classes: Warlock, Mage, Priest

Desecrated Handguards: Classes: Shaman, Druid, Hunter, Paladin

Kiss of the Spider: Trinket, Equip: Increases your critical strike rating by 14, Equip: Increases your hit rating by 10, Use: Increases your haste rating by 200 for 15 seconds

Maexxna's Fang: Dagger One-Hand, 94-141 Damage, Speed 1.80, 65.3 damage per second, +8 STA, Equip: Increases attack power by 36, Equip: Increases your hit rating by 10

Pendant of Forgotten Names: Neck, +18 SPI, +18 INT, Equip: Restores 7 mana per 5 sec

Wraith Blade: Sword Main Hand, 38-109 Damage, Speed 1.80, 40.8 damage per second, +10 STA, +8 INT, Equip: Increases damage and healing done by magical spells and effects by up to 95, Equip: Increases your spell hit rating by 8, Equip: Increases your spell critical strike rating by 14

ABILITIES

HP	1498950	Damage	5491-7280
Abilities	**Web Wrap:** Stuns and deals 657 to 843 damage every 2 sec. for 1 minute. Other players can destroy the Web Wrap by attacking it.		
	Necrotic Poison: Reduces healing effects by 90% for 30 sec.		
	Poison Shock: Instantly shocks for 1750 to 2250 Nature damage.		
	Summon Maexxna Spiderling: Summons a group of spiders.		
	Web Spray: Stuns all nearby targets for 10 sec.		
	Enrage: Increases physical damage by 100% and attack speed by 50%.		

ENRAGE

Explanation: At 30% life Maexxna gains significantly increased damage and attack speed.

Solution: Get ready to heal that tank! Use Shield Wall if you are going to get a Web Spray during the Enrage or the main tank might die while everyone is stunned.

NECROTIC POISON

Explanation: Only cast on current target. This spell reduces all healing effects by 90% for 30 seconds. This is a cleansable Poison spell.

Solution: Always have Abolish Poison up on the main tank. This needs to be cleansed immediately at all times.

POISON SHOCK

Explanation: Deals about 2,000 damage to everyone in front of her.

Solution: Never point Maexxna towards the raid. If this rule is followed to the letter then only the main tank should ever take damage from Poison Shock.

WEB SPRAY

Explanation: Everyone is hit for about 2,000 damage and stunned for 8 seconds.

Solution: Make sure nobody is under 2,000 health and stack a lot of Heal-Over-Times on the main tank so they don't die during the stun. Web Spray is unavoidable.

WEB WRAP

Explanation: Three random players are tossed onto the wall and put inside of a cocoon. The cocoon does around 700 damage per tick and has about 6,000 life.

Solution: You have to kill the cocoons to free the players. Otherwise, they are going to die. Depending on where they are cocooned along the wall, you can heal them. Some places do not have LoS to heal.

PREPARATION

The main tank group needs a Paladin for Devotion Aura, a Warlock for Blood Pact, a Hunter for Aspect of the Wild, and maybe a Druid for Abolish Poison (that can be done outside of group without much trouble).

All ranged DPS is split up into three groups to kill the cocoons after a Web Wrap. Assign three assists and spread the ranged DPS out to each assist. Then, assign each assist a general area of the wall. For example, the first assist is on the left side, the second assist is on the middle, and the third assist is on the right side. You won't always have someone in your specific area; be ready to pickup a target and kill a cocoon regardless of where your designated area of the wall is.

Additionally, assign one healer per ranged DPS group. They are going to try to heal the person inside of the cocoon if they can.

STRATEGY

The pull is fairly straightforward. The main tank engages Maexxna and pulls her back towards the spider-webbed wall that players are flung onto by Web Spray. Once she is close to that wall, turn her around so that she is facing away from the wall and only the main tank is getting hit by Poison Spray. The rest of the raid should position themselves in-between the spider-webbed wall and Maexxna—behind her.

Once she is positioned correctly, the fight is all about timing. You know what is coming and you should be ready to react to it.

20 seconds: Web Wrap. Three players are cocooned. The ranged DPS groups you assigned prior to the fight need to assist and kill all of the cocoons as quickly as possible. The healers assigned to each group should try to heal the person inside of the cocoon their group is killing. As soon as the cocoon is destroyed, the player is released and falls to the ground. Heal them up!

30 seconds: Spider Spawn. About 10 non-elite spiders spawn under Maexxna. Get a well timed Frost Nova off and AoE them down very quickly. You don't want any of them to be alive when she Web Sprays in 10 seconds.

40 seconds: Web Spray. Everybody takes about 2,000 damage and be stunned for 8 seconds. Stack up those HoTs and get a fresh Abolish Poison on the main tank so they don't die while everyone is stunned. Hopefully no spiders are running around hitting people.

And then it starts over. 20 seconds after the Web Spray ends, three players are thrown to the wall and cocooned again. This is how the fight goes start to finish.

At 30% she Enrages and do a lot more damage to the main tank. You want to time it so that she is at 31% when Web Spray wears off, giving you a full 40 seconds to kill her while Enraged before the next Web Spray. When she Enrages, start ignoring people on the wall. You want all of your DPS on Maexxna to take her down as quickly as possible. However, you still need to kill the non-elite spiders that spawn at the 30 second mark.

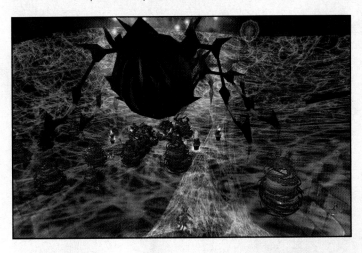

More likely than not, you are not be able to kill her within 40 seconds and she is going to Web Spray while Enraged. The main tank needs to pop Shield Wall for this or they are probably going to die while everyone is stunned. Make it thought that last Web Spray and take her down before the next one.

PLAGUE WING

The Plague Wing starts out fairly easy but the end boss—Loatheb—is a major challenge for any raid group. Noth the Plaguebringer is a fight with a nasty curse and many adds to deal with. Heigan the Unclean requires everyone to learn how to dance in order to avoid the exploding floor. And Loatheb requires everyone to come prepared with consumables and be ready to execute their job near flawlessly.

PLAGUE WING MINIONS

DISEASED MAGGOT	BEAST
FRENZIED BAT	BEAST
MUTATED GRUB	NOT SPECIFIED
PLAGUED BAT	BEAST
PLAGUE BEAST	ELEMENTAL
PLAGUE SLIME	NOT SPECIFIED
PLAGUED GARGOYLE	UNDEAD
ROTTING MAGGOT	BEAST

NOTH THE PLAGUEBRINGER

Noth is a fight that is all about the timing. Lots of things are going on but they are all fairly predictable. The pitfalls are not decursing Curse of the Plaguebringer quickly enough, having too many DPS die after a Blink, or letting the adds get out of control.

LOOT

Band of the Inevitable: Finger, Equip: Increases damage and healing done by magical spells and effects by up to 36, Equip: Increases your spell hit rating by 8

Cloak of the Scourge: Back, 72 Armor, +23 STA, Equip: Increases attack power by 30, Equip: Increases your hit rating by 10

Desecrated Belt: Classes: Warlock Mage Priest

Desecrated Girdle: Classes: Shaman Druid Hunter Paladin

Desecrated Waistguard: Classes: Rogue Warrior

Hailstone Band: Finger, +18 STA, +20 Frost Resistance, Equip: Increases your dodge rating by 12

Hatchet of Sundered Bone: Axe One-Hand, 119-221 Damage, Speed 2.60, 65.4 damage per second, Equip: Increases attack power by 36, Equip: Increases your critical strike rating by 14

Libram of Light: Libram, Equip: Increases healing done by Flash of Light by up to 83

Noth's Frigid Heart: Held In Hand, +12 INT, +13 SPI, Equip: Increases healing done by spells and effects by up to 53

Totem of Flowing Water: Totem, Equip: Regain up to 10 mana each time you cast Lesser Healing Wave

ABILITIES

HP	1665500	Damage	5491-7280
Abilities	**Cripple**: Increases the time between attacks by 100%, movement by 50%, and reduces Strength by 50%. Lasts 15 sec.		
	Curse of the Plaguebringer: If not dispelled, the target will become infected along with all nearby allies with the Wrath of the Plaguebringer.		
	Wrath of the Plaguebringer: Infects nearby allies, inflicting 1758 to 2042 Nature damage, then 875 to 1125 additional damage every 2 seconds for 10 sec.		
	Blink: Teleports Noth to another part of his chamber.		
	Summon Skeletons: Summons several skeletons to aid the caster.		

BLINK

Explanation: Noth Blinks every 25-35 seconds. His threat list is entirely wiped after every Blink.

Solution: You can not prevent the Blink from happening but you should be prepared for dealing with it. The fact that the threat list is cleared is the biggest problem. To deal with that, have your DPS stop attacking 25 seconds after the last Blink and wait until he does it. Immediately after the Blink happens, one or two main tanks should be trying to get agro back. Ideally no one should die because a tank gets agro very quickly after a Blink. Sometimes one or two people get instantly killed before the tank reestablishes agro. This is sometimes not all that preventable but your DPS needs to be really careful around the time a Blink is expected to happen. You don't want that last big-damage attack to hit Noth right after he Blinks or you are going to die before a tank can get agro back. Be careful around the Blinks, have an attentive main tank or two, and these shouldn't be too big of a deal.

CRIPPLE

Explanation: After every Blink, Noth casts Cripple on everyone within melee range. This is a dispelable Magic debuff that slows movement, attack speed, and reduces Strength.

Solution: Since Cripple is a dispelable Magic debuff, you just want to cleanse it as quickly as possible. The top priorities for dispel are the tanks who are trying to get agro after the Blink. It is almost impossible for them to get agro back if they are Crippled.

CURSE OF THE PLAGUEBRINGER

Explanation: Every 45 seconds or so Noth applies this curse to everyone within 40 yards of him. This is a cleansable curse but doesn't actually do anything unless you let it stay on a player for longer than 10 seconds. If this happens, you are affected by Wrath of the Plaguebringer which does about 1000 damage every 2 seconds for 10 seconds to everyone within 40 yards.

Solution: Cleanse the curse as quickly as possible and do not miss anyone. You never want it to run the full 10 seconds and afflict someone with Wrath of the Plaguebringer. More likely than not, if a single person does not get cleansed, you are going to wipe. Wrath of the Plaguebringer simply does too much damage to be dealt with.

SUMMONING OF ADDS (WHILE ON BALCONY)

Explanation: 90 seconds after Noth is engaged he teleports to the balcony in the room and summons waves of adds. The next wave comes 110 seconds after he has returned from the balcony. And the final wave comes 180 seconds after he returns the second time.

Solution: This is a key aspect of the fight and is discussed in detail in the strategy section. Long story short, you have to kill the adds as quickly as possible!

SUMMONING OF ADDS (WHILE NOT ON BALCONY)

Explanation: When Noth is being fought on the ground he summons an elite skeleton in 3 different corners every 30 seconds. They spawn in the south west, north west, and north east corners.

Solution: You want to have a tank in each of these corners ready to pick the add up. Additionally, you want to have 4 or 5 DPS classes assigned to killing these skeletons while Noth is on the ground. There should not be any alive when Noth teleports to the balcony.

PREPARATION

Make sure there is someone who can decurse in every group. Curse of the Plaguebringer is very dangerous and needs to be removed as quickly as possible.

You have at least 4 tanks during this fight. At least one for Noth (it can sometimes help to have more than one on Noth because of the Blinks), and 3 more for the skeleton spawns while he is not on the balcony. Setup some solid tanking groups and assign healers to each tank. Assign which corners the 3 skeleton spawn tanks are in. Finally, assign the 4 or 5 DPS classes that are killing skeleton spawns while he isn't on the balcony.

STRATEGY

Noth is wandering around in the middle of the room. You want to tank him in the south east corner—the corner that does not have any skeleton spawns. Start your 25 second Blink timer and your 90 second balcony teleport timer as soon as he is engaged. Drag him to the south east corner, let the tank build some agro, and start the DPS.

The 3 tanks and DPS assigned to killing the skeletons should move into position and be ready to pickup the skeletons as they spawn every 30 seconds.

The first Curse of the Plaguebringer happens shortly after he is engaged. Cleanse it as quickly as possible!

The first Blink occurs within about 35 seconds at the most. Hopefully your DPS is being careful and does not immediately pull agro after a Blink. Cleanse the Cripple from the tanks and let them reestablish agro. After the Blink, make sure you start your 25 second Blink timer again. After Noth is back on a tank, open up DPS again and be ready for the next Blink.

He's Not Quite Dead

Sometimes it is helpful to have a Hunter use Distracting Shot after a Blink. They can pop Deterrence, bring Noth to a tank, let the tank build threat for a couple seconds, and then Feign Death. Ideally the Hunter won't die and Noth starts attacking the tank after the Feign Death.

You want to get him down to at least 75% before he teleports to the balcony the first time. If your DPS seems low, maybe the DPS is being a little too careful about the Blinks. Or maybe they aren't being careful enough and are dying after a Blink.

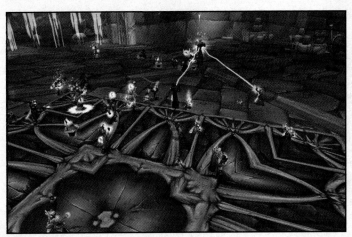

90 seconds after he is engaged, the first teleport happens. At this point Noth becomes invulnerable and adds begin to spawn. The skeleton adds that spawn while he is on the ground should be dead or almost dead. The entire raid needs to focus on the 3 add spawn points now-the same 3 corners as before. 6 Plagued Champions are the first to spawn. They are Undead, can be Shackled, and have an AoE shadow damage attack. Every tank needs to try and pick them up. They hit fairly hard and should not be allowed to run around uncontrolled. Frost Nova can help keep them under control as well. Get them tanked or CC'ed and kill them one or two at a time. 35 seconds after the first spawn of 6 Plagued Champions, a second wave comes. Deal with them the same way.

70 seconds after he teleports to the balcony, he returns to the room. He spawns in the center of the room. Have your tanks waiting to get agro. Additionally, he Blinks almost immediately after returning to the room. And finally, he uses Curse of the Plaguebringer within about 10 seconds. DPS should not touch him until he has Blinked and is being tanked. Decursers should be ready to get rid of the curse as quickly as possible (make sure everyone stays within range). Obviously, a lot is going on after he returns to the room, but there is nothing new to deal with.

Noth should get tanked and moved back into the south east corner. The 3 tanks assigned to skeleton adds move back into their designated corner. The DPS assigned to killing the skeletons gets ready to keep them under control. Go back to what you were doing for the first 90 seconds of the fight.

110 seconds after he has returned to the room, he ports back up to the balcony. The raid should focus on the add spawn points and kill what comes out. Since this is the second balcony teleport, there is a new type of spawn in addition to the 6 Plagued Champions you had before. This time 2 Plagued Guardians come out. They are pretty dangerous and have a nasty arcane based AoE spell. Thankfully, they have low hit points and can be killed very quickly. Focus them first then move onto the Plagued Champions. Deal with both of the waves and wait for Noth to port back into the middle of the room.

Handle Noth as you did last time he returned to the room. At this point, if your DPS has been good, you should kill him long before he ports to the balcony a third time (in 180 seconds). There is a long gap before the third teleport and you really should be able to kill him before it happens.

But if you don't get him down within 180 seconds after he returns to the room, be prepared for a third wave of adds. In addition to the 6 Plagued Champions and the 2 Plagued Guardians, there are 3 Plagued Constructs. These new adds have Mortal Strike, hit like a truck, and move very fast. You don't want to have to deal with this third wave of spawns; it is very difficult to defeat. If you can get through both waves, Noth returns to the room and you should continue the fight until he dies.

BREAKDOWN OF FIGHT

This fight may seem complicated because a lot is going on, but as you can tell from the strategy section the vast majority of the fight is very predictable. This table should help you learn what to expect as the fight progresses.

0:00 – Noth is engaged
0:10 – First Curse of the Plaguebringer, expect the next within 45 seconds
0:25 – First Blink, expect the next within 35 seconds
1:30 – First teleport, 6 adds are spawned
2:40 – Noth returns to the room, Blink and Curse follow soon after
4:30 – Second teleport, second round of 8 adds are spawned
6:00 – Noth returns to the room, Blink and Curse follow soon after
9:00 – Third teleport, third round of 11 adds are spawned (he should be dead already!)
10:50 – Noth returns to the room, Blink and Curse follow soon after

HEIGAN THE UNCLEAN

I hope you're ready to dance. Heigan may sound complicated but the whole fight really comes down to one thing: the ability to avoid Eruption. It is going to take some practice to learn the Heigan dance but overall you shouldn't find this to be too hard of a fight.

LOOT

Desecrated Belt: Classes: Warlock Mage Priest

Desecrated Girdle: Classes: Shaman Druid Hunter Paladin

Desecrated Waistguard: Classes: Rogue Warrior

Icebane Helmet: Plate Head, 864 Armor, +24 STA, +12 STR, +44 Frost Resistance, Equip: Increases defense rating by 12

Icy Scale Coif: Mail Head, 486 Armor, +24 STA, +18 AGI, +44 Frost Resistance

Legplates of Carnage: Plate Legs, 930 Armor, +42 STR, +18 STA, Equip: Increases your critical strike rating by 28

Necklace of Necropsy: Neck, +10 SPI, +11 INT, +10 STA, Equip: Increases healing done by spells and effects by up to 53

Preceptor's Hat: Cloth Head, 117 Armor, +18 STA, +24 INT, Equip: Increases damage and healing done by magical spells and effects by up to 51

ABILITIES

HP	1832050	Damage	5491-7280
Abilities	**Teleport:** Teleports the target to another part of Heigan's chamber.		
	Teleport Self: Teleports Heigan to the center of his starting platform.		
	Fear: Flee in terror for up to 6 sec.		
	Plague Cloud: Deals 4000 Nature damage every 5 sec.		
	Decrepit Fever: Deals 500 nature damage every 3 seconds and decreases maximum health by 50% for 21 sec.		
	Mana Burn: For each point of mana consumed, the target takes 1 damage. This spell burns 2313 to 2687 Mana.		
	Eruption: The cracks around Heigan's rooms periodically erupt with jets of poison, dealing 3500 to 4500 Nature damage.		

DECREPIT FEVER

Explanation: If you get hit by the eruptions from the floor, you are afflicted by Decrepit Fever. This reduces your maximum health by 50% and causes you to take 500 nature damage every 3 seconds. It is a cleansable Disease.

Solution: As much as you can avoid it, don't get hit by Eruption in the first place. Mind your position and you can avoid Decrepit Fever altogether. However, sometimes the main tank seems to get Decrepit Fever even when they don't get hit by Eruption. For this reason, always be prepared to cleanse it as quickly as possible.

ERUPTION

Explanation: Every 10 seconds or so Noth makes the ground burst with green slime; similar to the lava that comes out of the ground during Onyxia's third phase. If you are hit by one of these, you take around 4,000 damage and are afflicted by Decrepit Fever.

Solution: Thankfully, the Eruption follows a predictable pattern. It is the job of the raid to study and remember the proper safe area for each of the 4 possible Eruption positions. You have to be in the right spot and ready to avoid Eruption at all times.

MANA BURN

Explanation: Heigan steals your mana if you get too close to him. It can cause a caster to run out of mana very quickly.

Solution: Never bring Heigan too close to the mana users. Keep him tanked about 25 yards away.

TELEPORT

Explanation: Heigan teleports 3 random people to a room that is filled with maggots and Eye Stalks. The maggots hurt a lot when they hit you. The Eye Stalks cast a powerful Mind Flay.

Solution: You can't prevent the teleport but you can make it out of the room without dying. All 3 players need to help each other a little bit. The Eye Stalks have very low hit points and can be killed almost instantly. Start moving to the end of the room—back to Heigan—and kill the Eye Stalks along the way. The maggots move very slowly so they can be kited without any trouble. Once you reach the end of the room, make sure an Eruption isn't about to happen and get back into your original position.

PREPARATION

There really isn't anything special as far as groups go for this fight. Most of the raid is simply on their own in learning how to avoid the Eruption.

STRATEGY

Heigan begins at the trash. Much like Broodlord Lashlayer, the trash is an important part of the encounter and has to be killed again before every attempt. Some general tips are: Don't have Druids heal, they build too much agro with no way to dump it; don't use AoE spells, it is better to kill them individually; don't die! It is very hard to get out of combat to resurrect you.

You start out in Noth's room and you see a bunch of Grubs, Bats, and a few wandering Plague Beasts. Once everyone is ready to go, pull the first group of Grubs and Bats. Quickly move forward until you get to the wall and clean the adds up; usually you want to kill the Grubs first because they have an AoE damage spell and a slow.

Start hugging the wall and get ready for your first Plague Beast. These have a very nasty AoE spell and must be tanked away from the raid. Melee DPS should focus on the Grubs and Bats while ranged DPS focuses on the Plague Beast. Kill it as quickly as possible and continue moving along the wall to the corner. At the corner, clean up all the adds that have probably followed you and kill the next two Plague Beasts one at a time.

Continue hugging the wall, killing adds, and keeping Plague Beasts out of the raid until you get to Heigan's door. Sometimes he agros but you can easily reset him by retreating back to the wall. Make sure you have no adds left (or maybe a couple) and charge into Heigan's room to begin the fight.

The main tank needs to pick up Heigan right away and move into the first safe position. Ranged DPS and healers head over to the platform where Heigan was standing; this is where they stay for the time being. Melee DPS should start attacking Heigan and be ready to move with the tank.

The first Eruption occurs fairly soon. Immediately after the first Eruption, the main tank and all of the melee DPS should move to the next safe position. Cleanse anyone who accidentally got hit by the Eruption of Decrepit Fever. Continue to do DPS and be ready to move to the next safe spot after the next Eruption.

Keep in mind while this is happening 3 random players are teleported to the Eye Stalk room. These players should move together, kite the maggots, and kill the Eye Stalks. Pause for a moment before leaving the Eye Stalk room to make sure you aren't hit by Eruption on the way back to your appropriate position.

After 8 Eruptions, the second phase of the fight begins. Heigan teleports to the platform. Now the speed of the Eruptions has been greatly increased and the entire raid must avoid them. You can not get within about 15 yards of Heigan while he is on the platform or you take significant damage from a shadow based aura.

Don't Be Hasty

Occasionally after teleporting to the platform Heigan pauses for a moment and causes the entire floor to Erupt with no safe spots available. You can tell when this is going to happen because there is a 2-3 second pause before the first Eruption. If this happens, simply wait on the platform until it is safe to move to the first position.

The moment he teleports to the platform, the entire raid moves into the first position. After the Eruption happens, the raid moves to the next position. This continues for another 8 Eruptions. Heigan does not become immune to anything so it is very possible to damage him during this phase (mostly via instant cast spells since you don't really have time to cast anything), but the majority of your attention should be on successfully avoiding the Eruptions. That extra DPS during the second phase can help but is not completely necessary.

After 8 quick Eruptions that the entire raid has been avoiding, Heigan starts attacking the main tank again; agro is not cleared. The main tank should move back to the first safe position, the melee DPS should follow them, the ranged DPS and healers head back to the platform, and everything starts over again.

The major challenge during this fight is learning how to avoid the Eruptions. It can take a little bit of practice to master where the safe spots are and learn the patterns, but that is really the only hard part of the fight. Study the Eruptions, practice avoiding them correctly, and you will be dancing over the corpse of Heigan in no time.

LOATHEB

Loatheb is an intimidating boss that requires everyone to come prepared with Greater Shadow Resistance potions and know exactly what their job is throughout the fight. A lot of people think Loatheb is a very fun fight because you get to do a ton of damage, but others find it to be a frustrating fight since the smallest mistakes by an individual person can make the difference between a kill and a 2% wipe.

LOOT

Band of Unnatural Forces: Finger, Equip: Increases your critical strike rating by 14, Equip: Increases your hit rating by 10, Equip: Increases attack power by 52

Brimstone Staff: Staff Two-Hand, 140-250 Damage, Speed 3.20, 60.9 damage per second, +31 STA, +30 INT, Equip: Increases your spell hit rating by 16, Equip: Increases damage and healing done by magical spells and effects by up to 113, Equip: Increases your spell critical strike rating by 14

Desecrated Leggings: Classes: Warlock Mage Priest

Desecrated Legguards: Classes: Shaman Druid Hunter Paladin

Desecrated Legplates: Classes: Rogue Warrior

Loatheb's Reflection: Trinket, +13 Fire Resistance, Use: Increases resistances to all schools of magic by 40 for 20 seconds

Ring of Spiritual Fervor: Finger, +14 INT, +11 STA, Equip: Restores 10 mana per 5 sec

The Eye of Nerub: Polearm Two-Hand, 251-378 Damage, Speed 3.70, 85.0 damage per second, +30 AGI, +22 STA, Equip: Increases Bow skill rating by 9, Equip: Increases Crossbow skill rating by 9, Equip: Increases gun skill rating by 9

ABILITIES

HP	5329600	Damage	5491-7280
Abilities	**Corrupted Mind:** Forces target to only cast one healing spell every 60 seconds.		
	Remove Curse: Removes up to 32 curses from an allied target.		
	Poison Aura: Inflicts 196 Nature damage every 6 seconds for 12 sec.		

CORRUPTED MIND

Explanation: A few seconds after Loatheb is engaged he places this debuff on everyone in the room. Corrupted Mind only allows you to cast 1 healing spell every 60 seconds; this includes cleansing type spells.

Solution: There is no way to avoid Corrupted Mind so you simply have to base your healing around the fact that healers can only heal once every 60 seconds. This is a key part of the fight and is discussed in detail in the strategy section. Simply put, a healing rotation that loops around every 60 seconds is needed; this allows the main tank to get a big heal every 3-4 seconds.

INEVITABLE DOOM

Explanation: 2 minutes after engaged, Loatheb casts his first Inevitable Doom. He continues to cast them every 30 seconds until the 5 minute 30 second mark. At this point, they are cast every 15 seconds. Inevitable Doom is an unavoidable debuff that does 2500 shadow damage after 10 seconds.

Solution: You can't mitigate the damage through resistances, you can't avoid it altogether, and you shouldn't expect heals because the healers are using their one heal per minute on the main tank. It is up to you to use a combination of Greater Shadow Protection potions, Healthstones, and Bandages to heal yourself after Inevitable Doom hits. The specifics of when to use your consumables is covered in the strategy section.

POISON AURA

Explanation: Every 12 seconds everyone within melee range of Loatheb takes about 400 nature damage over 12 seconds.

Solution: Judgement of Light is the key. Assign a Paladin to always keep Judgement of Light up on Loatheb and you can pretty much ignore the Poison Aura. You don't want to use your potion or bandage cooldowns to heal yourself because you need to save those cooldowns for the Inevitable Doom. And you can't expect heals because the healers are using their one heal per minute on the main tank. I suppose you could drink a Nature Resistance potion before the fight starts, but you should find that keeping Judgement of Light up on Loatheb is the easiest way to handle the Poison Aura.

SELF DECURSE

Explanation: Every 30 seconds Loatheb removes all curses from himself.

Solution: There is nothing you can do about it, reapply the curses and keep going.

SUMMON SPORE/FUNGAL BLOOM

Explanation: Every 12 seconds a Spore spawns. When this Spore is killed, it effects the 5 closest people with a debuff called Fungal Bloom. This debuff causes the player to produce zero threat and increases their critical hit chance by 50%.

Solution: You have to get the Fungal Bloom debuff. You need the huge DPS increase that it provides to kill Loatheb. The general plan is to send one group at a time to go kill a Spore and get Fungal Bloom. After one group gets it, they go back to what they were doing and the next group moves in. By rotating like this through every group the entire raid should always have Fungal Bloom. There are several nuances related to this ability, such as how to control where the Spore spawns and common pitfalls related to this ability, so please study the strategy section carefully!

PREPARATION

The groups are setup based around the Spores. Each group kills a Spore and gets the Fungal Bloom debuff for the extra DPS. Stack all of your DPS into groups 1-5 so your DPS groups are the first ones to get Fungal Bloom.

Groups 6-8 contain all of the healers and the main tank group (who should probably have a Warlock for Blood Pact).

In addition to the Spore related preparation, a healing rotation needs to be figured out. Healers can only heal every 60 seconds so you want to divide 60 by the total number of healers (typically 14-16) to figure out the gap between healers. Remember to deduct the 2.5 second cast time from each gap. It is advisable to use a mod to time the heals and control the rotation, but having one person in charge of telling people when to heal is also feasible.

STRATEGY

Make sure everyone gets into the room; the gate closes when Loatheb is engaged. Get a bunch of HoTs on the main tank and charge in. The tank should get agro fairly easily and start moving Loatheb into position.

Loatheb's position is important. Based on where he is in the room, the Spores are spawned in a specific location. You want to tank him on the north east corner of the platform in the middle of the room. This causes the Spores to spawn in the south west corner of the room. Conversely, if you tank him on the south east corner of the middle platform, the Spores spawn in the north west corner of the room. Either of these two positions is ideal.

A few seconds after he is engaged everyone is afflicted by Corrupted Mind. This is the queue for the healing rotation to begin. The first healer casts their big heal and about 2 seconds later the next healer is up. This rotation is very important to do accurately throughout the entire fight. The main tank must get consistent heals or they drop like a rock. If you can make it through one full healing rotation with everyone casting their heals at the correct time, it is fairly easy to simply heal the moment you can. No need to pay attention to a rotation once you know that you definitely want to cast your heal the moment you are able to. Pay attention to when it is your turn to heal initially and then pay attention to when you can heal again.

The first Spore spawns in the designated corner about 10 seconds into the fight. Group 1 should be waiting for it and ready to kill it quickly. They only have about 1,000 hit points so they die near instantly. After Group 1 kills their Spore and gets Fungal Bloom, they move out of the Spore spawn area and Group 2 moves in. Communication between groups is very important when rotating through the Spores, and keeping the Fungal Bloom debuff on most of the raid at all times is essential for the DPS boost.

One final thing to say about Spores, a healer needs to prioritize their heal over getting the Fungal Bloom debuff. While the 50% critical strike rating is great for big heals, it is much more important that you time your heal correctly. Always ignore the Spore if your heal is going to come up during the time you are supposed to go get Fungal Bloom.

For the first 2 minutes of the fight this is all you have to worry about. Keep your healing rotation consistently correct; don't let your main tank get very low. Make sure everyone is on top of their Spore spawn and keeping Fungal Bloom on themselves constantly.

At the 2 minute mark the first Inevitable Doom strikes. 10 seconds after it hits, everyone takes 2500 shadow damage. The Greater Shadow Resistance potion you drank before engaging absorbs the majority of the damage. Immediately after you take the damage, drink a new Greater Shadow Resistance potion in preparation for the next Inevitable Doom in 30 seconds.

Nothing has changed from the first 2 minutes. Everyone still needs to maintain their healing rotation and continue to get the Fungal Bloom debuff from the Spores. You just have to deal with Inevitable Doom in addition. The fight comes down to continuing what you did for the first 2 minutes and knowing the order that you use your consumables in.

As stated, the first Inevitable Doom is absorbed by the Greater Shadow Resistance potion you drank before the fight began. After that is eaten up by the first Inevitable Doom, drink a new Greater Shadow Resistance potion.

The second Inevitable Doom is applied 2 minutes 30 seconds into the fight. After the damage hits, you don't need to do anything. It is absorbed by the second Greater Shadow Resistance potion you drank.

The third Inevitable Doom hits at 3 minutes into the fight. Everyone has to bandage themselves after taking the damage.

The fourth Inevitable Doom hits 30 seconds later at the 3:30 mark. Use a Healthstone after taking the damage.

The fifth Inevitable Doom comes at the 4 minute mark. By this time your potion cooldown is over and you can drink a third Greater Shadow Resistance potion. Additionally, you need to use a bandage to heal yourself back to near-full hit points.

The sixth Inevitable Doom at the 4:30 mark comes and goes. Your Greater Shadow Resistance potion absorbs it. You don't do anything.

The seventh Inevitable Doom comes 30 seconds later at the 5 minute mark. At this point, bandage yourself back to full.

Now you are at the part of the fight where Inevitable Doom is cast every 15 seconds. You should have enough life to take one or two more Inevitable Dooms without using any more consumables, but you really need to kill Loatheb within the next 15-30 seconds or you're on your way to a wipe.

Loatheb is a fight based on correctly executing the healing rotation, the Spore spawn rotation, using your consumables correctly, and putting out enough DPS that he dies within about 5 minutes 30 seconds. As long as everyone does their job without any mistakes, he dies!

ABOMINATION WING

The Abomination Wing is the only wing with four bosses. Two of the fights are fairly easy, and two of the fights are quite challenging. The first boss—Patchwerk—is definitely one of the most infamous bosses in the game. Grobbulus has a reputation for being quite the pushover but if you aren't careful, he can cause some problems. Gluth is a very unique fight that involves dozens of zombie spawns. And Thaddius is an unforgiving fight that requires precise execution by the entire raid.

ABOMINATION WING MINIONS

BILE RETCHER	UNDEAD
EMBALMING SLIME	UNDEAD
LIVING MONSTROSITY	UNDEAD
MAD SCIENTIST	UNDEAD
NECROPOLIS ACOLYTE	HUMANOID
PATCHWORK GOLEM	UNDEAD
SLUDGE BELCHER	UNDEAD
STITCHED SPEWER	UNDEAD
SURGICAL ASSISTANT	UNDEAD

PATCHWERK

"No more play?" Patchwerk is one of the most discussed bosses in all of World of Warcraft. The fight is fairly simple as far as abilities go but the healers really need to be at the top of their game to handle the massive amounts of damage being done to the tanks.

LOOT

Band of Reanimation: Finger, +22 AGI, Equip: Increases attack power by 46

Cloak of Suturing: Back, 72 Armor, +12 SPI, +12 INT, Equip: Increases healing done by spells and effects by up to 48, Equip: Restores 5 mana per 5 sec

Desecrated Pauldrons: Classes: Rogue Warrior

Desecrated Shoulderpads: Classes: Warlock Mage Priest

Desecrated Spaulders: Classes: Shaman Druid Hunter Paladin

Severance: Axe Two-Hand, 235-354 Damage, Speed 3.60, 81.8 damage per second, +18 STA, +43 STR, Equip: Increases your critical strike rating by 28

The Plague Bearer: Shield, 3570 Armor, 78 Block, +21 STA, +15 Frost Resistance, Equip: Increases defense rating by 14

Wand of Fates: Wand, 119-222 Shadow Damage, Speed 1.50, 113.7 damage per second, +7 INT, +7 STA, Equip: Increases damage and healing done by magical spells and effects by up to 12, Equip: Increases your spell hit rating by 8

ABILITIES

HP	3997200		Damage	8319-8923
Abilities	**Hateful Strike**: An instant attack that strikes the target with the most health between the second and the fifth highest value on his threat list for 19975 to 27025 Physical damage.			
	Slime Bolt: Only used if players take too long to finish the encounter. Shoots poison at an enemy, inflicting 3238 to 3762 Nature damage, then 2375 to 2625 additional damage every 3 sec. for 6 sec.			
	Enrage: At 5% health, Patchwerk uses his Enrage ability. This increases his physical damage by 25% and his attack speed by 40%.			

BERSERK

Explanation: 7 minutes after engaging, Patchwerk goes Berserk and start doing significantly more damage. Just incase you manage to survive this new Berserk Patchwerk, 30 seconds later (at the 7:30 mark), he simply kills everyone with some AoE Slime Bolts.

Solution: You can't prevent the Berserk. It is a timer on the fight. You must have the DPS to kill him within 7 minutes or you are going to die.

ENRAGE

Explanation: At 5% life, Patchwerk enrages and does about 30% more damage.

Solution: Your main tank probably wants to use Shield Wall. It is possible to keep all the tanks alive, but just to be safe be loose with those big cooldowns to get through the last 5%.

HATEFUL STRIKE

Explanation: When Patchwerk is engaged, he creates a list of 3 people that he is going to hit with Hateful Strike. These 3 people are the 3 closest people to him, not including the main tank. He uses Hateful Strike every 0.8-1.5 seconds on the person who has the highest current hit points out of these 3 people. Hateful Strike does about 6,000-10,000 damage on a tank. If someone pulls agro off the main tank, or if of the tanks die, the Hateful Strike list is recreated based on agro position.

Solution: Hateful Strike is really the only part of the fight that you have to handle. The entire strategy section discusses in detail how Hateful Strike works and how to handle it. In summary, heal those tanks!

PREPARATION

There are a total of 4 tanks so make sure all of them are in the best possible tanking groups. Get them Devotion Aura and a Warlock for Blood Pact.

The Hateful Strike tanks should focus hit points, AC, dodge, and parry. Hateful Strike can not crush or crit, so defense is useless for them. The main tank should use their normal tanking gear because they take standard melee hits from Patchwerk.

The healing has to be setup very specifically. The main tank needs 3 healers, the first offtank needs 2 healers, the second offtank needs 2 healers, and the third offtank needs 2 healers. The third offtank is only used as a buffer to give the healers time to top off the first two offtanks. Make sure every healer knows who they are supposed to be healing.

Finally, make sure you maximize your DPS. Put Hunters and Warriors with Rogues for Trueshot Aura and Battle Shout. Put the Shadow Priests with Mages. Give as many melee DPS Windfury Totems as possible. Patchwerk is a DPS heavy fight and you want to squeeze out every bit from your raid through the group makeup.

STRATEGY

Get everyone except for the 4 tanks a good 30 yards away from Patchwerk. You only want the 4 tanks anywhere close to him when the fight starts. Wait until he paths close to the raid and pull him by having the main tank shoot him.

Move him back across the slime and wait for the first Hateful Strike. At this point, Patchwerk should be attacking the main tank, the Hateful Strike list is built with the 3 offtanks on it, and the first Hateful Strike is going to hit the offtank with the highest current hit points.

The first Hateful Strike hits the first offtank. About 1 second later, the second Hateful Strike hits the next offtank with the highest current life. If your healers are exceptionally fast at healing the offtanks to full, there is a chance that Hateful Strike is going to hit the same person twice in a row. But more likely than not, it is going to hit a second offtank.

After a few seconds of making sure the Hateful Strikes are hitting the proper people and letting the main tank build some threat, the raid begins to open up DPS and start getting him down. Patchwerk is not a very agro sensitive fight, but it is still possible to pull agro and ruin the careful balance of Hateful Strikes that needs to be maintained throughout the fight.

This is essentially how the fight goes from start to finish. The main tank holds agro, and the offtanks get hit by Hateful Strike every second or so, based on who has the highest current life, and the healers keep all 4 tanks topped off.

The hardest part of the fight is healing the offtanks fast enough. The main tank is taking significant damage, but it is fairly typical boss damage and shouldn't be too challenging for the 4 healers on the main tank to handle. It's those offtanks taking the Hateful Strike hits that are hard to heal, so this healing discussion involves them.

The healers on the first offtank have the easiest job. If their tank is at full life, you know that Hateful Strike is coming their way in the very near future. Always try to time your heals so that they land the moment Hateful Strike hits. Every healer must be constantly casting their heals, canceling their poorly timed heals, and watching for dodges, parries, and misses on their tank that would cause their heal to be an overheal.

It is advisable to have most of the offtank healers using big, long heals. But it is important for at least one of the 5 healers to be using fast heals. A lot of people swear by downranking heals to not use as much mana, but I always found it best to cancel your heals efficiently and do as little overhealing as possible while still topping off the tank very quickly.

The healers on the second offtank have a harder job guessing when their tank is about to take a Hateful Strike, but otherwise have essentially the same job.

And 2 healers on the last offtank won't have to heal their tank very often. Their tank only takes damage when both of the first two offtanks are not topped off. Hopefully the healing is on the ball and the first two offtanks get topped off very quickly, reducing the chance that the third offtank takes many Hateful Strikes. But it happens and the healers assigned to the third offtank have the important job of keeping the "buffer tank" topped off and ready to take that occasional Hateful Strike.

When you are first starting to learn Patchwerk it is likely that your tanks die very quickly. All it takes is practice. Your healers probably haven't had to do healing like this before and they need to learn how to proactively heal Hateful Strike instead of reacting to it when it hits.

Once you have confidence in your healing, use some DPS potions and take him down. At about 17%, have the first offtank use Shield Wall and Last Stand. This makes it so that they are the only tank who is taking Hateful Strike for the duration of the Shield Wall. Once their Shield Wall is down, the second offtank does the same thing, and then the third. It can be very helpful to essentially negate Hateful Strike for the last 17% or so with well timed Shield Walls.

At 5% he enrages and does about 30% more damage. Your main tank should use Shield Wall or they might die near instantly. Thankfully, once you've gotten this far it isn't too big of a deal to get that last 5% down and have a dead Patchwerk. Thank your healers and get ready to move on.

GROBBULUS

Grobbulus is arguably the easiest fight in all of Naxxramas. Grobbulus is simple and only requires one person at a time to run away from the raid as Grobbulus is kited around the room slowly.

LOOT

Desecrated Pauldrons: Classes: Rogue Warrior

Desecrated Shoulderpads: Classes: Warlock Mage Priest

Desecrated Spaulders: Classes: Shaman Druid Hunter Paladin

Glacial Mantle: Cloth Shoulder, 108 Armor, +18 STA, Equip: Increases damage and healing done by magical spells and effects by up to 16

Icy Scale Spaulders: Mail Shoulder, 448 Armor, +25 STA, +33 Frost Resistance

Midnight Haze: Dagger Main Hand, 40-108 Damage, Speed 1.80, 41.1 damage per second, +20 STA, +12 INT, Equip: Increases damage and healing done by magical spells and effects by up to 85

The End of Dreams: Mace Main Hand, 44-120 Damage, Speed 1.90, 43.2 damage per second, +13 INT, +13 STA, Equip: Increases damage and healing done by magical spells and effects by up to 95, Equip: Increases attack power by 305 in Cat, Bear, Dire Bear, and Moonkin forms only, Equip: Restores 5 mana per 5 sec

Toxin Injector: Gun, 82-153 Damage, Speed 2.00, 58.8 damage per second, +10 STA, Equip: Increases attack power by 28

ABILITIES

HP	2165150	Damage	4393-5824
Abilities	**Slime Spray**: Sprays all targets in front of Grobbulus for 3200 to 4800 Nature damage.		
	Poison Cloud: Lasts 1.25 minutes. The poison cloud deals 1110 to 1290 Nature damage every 1 sec.		
	Mutating Injection: The target creates a Poison Cloud after 10 sec. This also deals 4500 Nature damage to the target after 10 sec. Creates the Poison Cloud immediately if the debuff is removed with Cleanse or a similar spell.		
	Slime Stream: Inflicts 4500 Nature damage over 3 sec.		
	Summon Fallout Slime: Summons a Fallout Slime from the player effected by Slime Stream.		
	Mutagen Explosion: Inflicts 2380 to 3220 Physical damage to all enemies in a targeted area.		

MUTATING INJECTION

Explanation: Throughout the fight Grobbulus casts Mutating Injection on random people. It is a curable disease. If it is cleansed, everyone within 30 yards takes about 4,500 damage. If it is not cleansed, only the target who has Mutating Injection takes the 4,500 damage. After either of these possibilities, a Poison Cloud spawns under the player that does a couple thousand damage per tick and slowly expands before finally disappearing.

Solution: Don't cleanse Mutating Injection. It's much better to only have 1 person take the damage. In addition, the players who get Mutating Injection should run away from the raid, but not in an area where Grobbulus is being kited to. Mutating Injection is discussed in more detail in the strategy section, but overall you just don't want to cleanse it and don't want to spawn Poison Clouds in bad areas.

POISON CLOUD

Explanation: Grobbulus spawns Poison Clouds under him that slowly grow to be fairly big and do a couple thousand damage per second to any player who is inside of one. The Poison Clouds that Grobbulus spawns under him are identical to the ones that players spawn after being afflicted by Mutating Injection.

Solution: The main tank should slowly move Grobbulus around the room as the clouds are spawned, avoiding them and keeping ahead of them as they grow.

SLIME SPRAY

Explanation: Every 30 seconds or so Grobbulus sprays the area in front of him with slime, doing around 4,000 damage and spawning a Fallout Slime for every person it hits. The Fallout Slime has an AoE nature damage aura and hits fairly hard.

Solution: No one but the main tank should be in front of Grobbulus. This insures that only one Fallout Slime is spawned. Get the Fallout Slime tanked and kill it quickly before returning focus to Grobbulus. You need to keep the Fallout Slimes under control.

PREPARATION

There isn't anything special you have to do to prepare for Grobbulus. Give the main tank the usual group and spread out the healing.

Designate one or two tanks to pickup Fallout Slimes as they spawn. Make sure the DPS knows that killing Fallout Slimes is top priority when one is alive.

It is helpful to assign one or two healers to exclusively heal the players who get hit by Mutating Injection.

STRATEGY

Wait until Grobbulus is walking back up the stairs; this is the ideal time to pull him. The main tank should get agro and move him to the middle of the far wall.

The main tank slowly kites Grobbulus along the far wall as he spawns Poison Clouds below him. Don't go too fast, but don't go too slow either and take unnecessary damage from the Poison Clouds.

Anyone who gets Mutating Injection should run to an area that is both not where any of the raid group is, and not anywhere that Grobbulus is going to be kited to in the near future. During the first moments of the fight the best place to go for Mutating Injection is simply up the stairs.

DPS starts taking Grobbulus down. Watch for the Slime Sprays that spawn Fallout Slimes. The tank designated to pickup the Fallout Slime needs to get agro while everyone else refocuses their attention on getting the slime down quickly. After the slime is dead continue doing damage to Grobbulus.

People continue to get Mutating Injection and they should continue to "blow up" in an area that isn't going to hurt anyone or be in anyone's way.

That's pretty much all there is to the fight. Kite Grobbulus around the room to avoid Poison Clouds, kill the Fallout Slimes as they spawn, and pay attention to the Mutating Injections.

There are some things that can go wrong. Most commonly, someone doesn't notice they have Mutating Injection and spawn a Poison Cloud in the middle of the raid. This can be dealt with by moving everyone and dodging the cloud, but it is obviously preferred if everyone is simply paying attention and runs away when they get Mutating Injection. Another thing that can go wrong is Slime Spray hits someone other than the main tank. You really don't want to deal with more than one Fallout Slime at a time, but you can probably handle a few of them if something bad happens.

Overall the fight is fairly easy and you should get Grobbulus down within a few tries at the most!

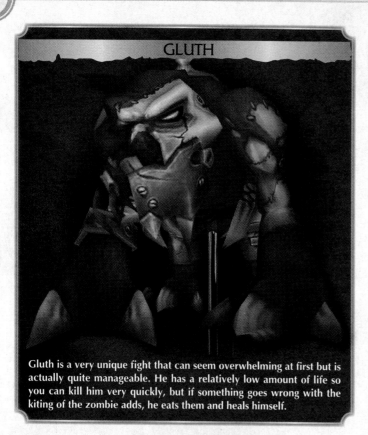

GLUTH

Gluth is a very unique fight that can seem overwhelming at first but is actually quite manageable. He has a relatively low amount of life so you can kill him very quickly, but if something goes wrong with the kiting of the zombie adds, he eats them and heals himself.

LOOT

Claymore of Unholy Might: Sword Two-Hand, 235-354 Damage, Speed 3.60, 81.8 damage per second, +20 STA, Equip: Increases attack power by 98

Death's Bargain: Shield, 3570 Armor, 78 Block, +12 STA, +12 INT, Equip: Increases your spell critical strike rating by 14, Equip: Increases healing done by spells and effects by up to 29, Equip: Restores 4 mana per 5 sec

Desecrated Belt: Classes: Warlock Mage Priest

Desecrated Bindings: Classes: Warlock Mage Priest

Desecrated Boots: Classes: Shaman Druid Hunter Paladin

Desecrated Bracers: Classes: Rogue Warrior

Desecrated Girdle: Classes: Shaman Druid Hunter Paladin

Desecrated Pauldrons: Classes: Rogue Warrior

Desecrated Sabatons: Classes: Rogue Warrior

Desecrated Sandals: Classes: Warlock Mage Priest

Desecrated Shoulderpads: Classes: Warlock Mage Priest

Desecrated Spaulders: Classes: Shaman Druid Hunter Paladin

Desecrated Waistguard: Classes: Rogue Warrior

Desecrated Wristguards: Classes: Shaman Druid Hunter Paladin

Digested Hand of Power: Held In Hand, +14 INT, +10 STA, Equip: Restores 10 mana per 5 sec

Gluth's Missing Collar: Neck, +24 STA, Equip: Increases your block rating by 14, Equip: Increases the block value of your shield by 15

Rime Covered Mantle: Cloth Shoulder, 108 Armor, +12 INT, +12 STA, Equip: Increases damage and healing done by magical spells and effects by up to 39, Equip: Increases your spell critical strike rating by 14

ABILITIES

HP	1665500	**Damage**	3954-5241
Abilities	**Frenzy:** Increases attack speed by 100% and damage by 50% for 8 sec.		
	Decimate: Reduces all nearby zombie chow and players to 5% health.		
	Summon Zombie Chow: Periodically summons Zombie Chow to feed Gluth.		
	Toxic Gas: Deals 219 to 281 Nature damage periodically.		
	Terrifying Roar: Flee in fear for 5 sec.		
	Infected Wound: Increases the Physical damage taken by 100 for 60 sec.		
	Zombie Chow Search: Gluth finds and kills a Zombie Chow, restoring 83275 of his health.		

DECIMATE

Explanation: Every 100-120 seconds Gluth casts Decimate. This brings everyone in the room to 5% life, including the zombies.

Solution: You can't prevent Decimate but it is a key part of the fight since it damages the zombies as well as your raiders. Decimate gets discussed in detail in the strategy section, but basically you want to heal everyone (tanks first) and kill all the zombies that are now at 5% life before Gluth can eat any of them.

DEVOUR ZOMBIE

Explanation: If a zombie gets too close to Gluth, he eats it and heals for about 5% of his total life.

Solution: Don't ever let zombies get too close to Gluth! You can't really afford to let him eat any because of the timed Enrage.

ENRAGE

Explanation: Moments after the third Decimate, or about 6 minutes into the fight, Gluth Enrages and kills the main tanks very quickly.

Solution: You have to kill Gluth before he Enrages.

FEAR

Explanation: Similar to Nefarian and all of the other bosses that Fear, every 20 seconds or so Gluth Fears everyone within about 25 yards.

Solution: You can't avoid the Fear but you can use it to your advantage. Since the tanks have to switch off because of the Mortal Wound, you can use the Fear to switch the tanking. Have the tank you want to get agro immune to Fear via Fear Ward or Berserker Rage, and let the current tank be feared. This should allow smooth transitions between tanks.

FRENZY

Explanation: Every 10 seconds or so Gluth Frenzies, causing him to gain increased damage and attack speed.

Solution: A Hunter Tranquilizing Shot rotation is necessary to keep Frenzy under control. Gluth should never be Frenzied for longer than a second or two.

MORTAL WOUND

Explanation: As Gluth deals damage to his current target, the Mortal Wound debuff is applied. Mortal Wound reduces healing effects by 10% per stack and can stack up to 10 times.

Solution: Two main tanks are needed for Gluth. Once Mortal Wound has stacked to 4 or 5 on one tank, the next tank needs to get agro and take over while the first tank waits for Mortal Wound to wear off. Using the Fear to switch tanks is the easiest way to accomplish this.

ZOMBIE SPAWN

Explanation: Zombies are spawned on top of the 3 grates in the room (referred to as the left grate, middle grate, and right grate when looking at the door) every 10 seconds. These zombies have a ton of life and hit fairly hard. Additionally, whenever they strike a player, a stackable debuff called Infected Wound is applied. This causes the player to take an extra 100 melee damage per stack.

Solution: Kite, kite, and more kiting! At least 3 people are assigned to kiting zombies; one per grate. They are also assigned a couple healers each to keep them alive. Until the Decimate hits, the goal is to kite the zombies around without taking much damage from them while keeping them under control. After Decimate hits, the zombies are at 5% life and agro on Gluth. They must be killed by the entire raid very quickly, before they can get to Gluth to be Devoured.

PREPARATION

Since there are two main tanks, make sure both of them have solid groups. Assign most of the healers to take care of whoever is currently the main tank. If you have Fear Ward, setup a Fear Ward rotation. Finally, designate at least 2 or 3 healers to top off each main tank after a Decimate. It is very important that the main tanks are quickly healed after Decimate.

After the tanking has been setup, it's time to think about the kiting. There are several ways to approach the kiting, but what consistently worked for us was assigning one Warrior to each spawn point, one or two healers per Warrior, and Hunters laying Frost Traps on the spawn points as often as they can. Assign each Warrior their spawn point and make sure they have some healing. The Hunters should figure out which grate they are going to focus traps on.

Once the tanking and kiting is arranged, you're ready to charge in.

STRATEGY

The first thing you notice is a long pipe that does a couple hundred damage per tick while inside of it. You have to run down this pipe every time you begin the fight. Having Priests and Druids put a HoT on everyone in their group mitigates most of the damage that the pipe does.

Charge down the pipe and drop into Gluth's room. Make sure the first main tank lands first and gets initial agro from Gluth. The tank drags Gluth straight back towards the door in his room. Against the door on the far wall is the ideal spot to tank him; as far away from the zombie spawn points as possible.

Before Gluth is in position the first Fear is cast. Either the first tank has Fear Ward and you can ignore this, or the offtank has Berserker Rage up and agro is switched to them. In either case, continue moving Gluth back towards the door on the far wall.

Frenzy is happening constantly throughout the fight. The Hunters should have their Tranquilizing Shot rotation setup and be communicating with each other. Keep those Tranqs coming and make sure Gluth is not Frenzied for more than a second or two, if that.

The first wave of zombies are spawned. The Warriors assigned to picking up the zombie adds should get agro with Hamstring and kite them in a circle using Frost Traps, Piercing Howl, and Earthbind Totems to assist them. They need to time their kiting loop so that they reach the spawn point just as another zombie spawns. The zombies are Undead and can be Shackled by a Priest, so using this to hold a zombie in place near its spawn point as a Warrior gets over there to pick it up can be very helpful.

Occasionally a zombie gets missed and probably head towards the main tank healers. A Hunter needs to pull it out of the healers and bring it towards a kiting Warrior. Don't let many zombies leak through; you really want to pick all of them up in a nice, big, slowed mass.

At this point Gluth is being tanked next to the door at the far wall. The main tanks are using Fear to bounce agro between each other, letting Mortal Wound reset. The Hunters are keeping Tranquilizing Shot up. The kiting Warriors are picking up zombies and dragging them around the room, far away from Gluth. And the DPS is working on Gluth.

About 105 seconds into the fight the first Decimate hits. Shortly before this happens, the kiting Warriors need to bring all of their zombies towards the back of the room; as far away from Gluth as possible. This allows extra time to kill them before they get to Gluth. Immediately after the Decimate hits the two main tanks require heals. Gluth continues to attack and it is entirely possible one of your tanks is going to die unless they are topped off quickly.

All of the zombies just took a ton of damage from Gluth so they are agro on him. The entire raid should focus on finishing off the zombies before they get to Gluth. You can not allow any zombies to reach Gluth and be Devoured by him. Thankfully they only have about 6,000 life left and are easy to kill with AoE damage.

Once all of the zombies are dead, you essentially go back to what you were doing. The main tanks should continue to bounce agro between them, the Hunters should continue to keep Tranquilizing Shot up, and the kiting Warriors should continue to keep the newly spawned zombies under control. The next Decimate is going to hit in about 105 seconds and it is handled the same way as the first one.

After the third Decimate, or about 6 minutes into the fight, Gluth Enrages and kills your main tanks. You have to kill him before this happens.

Keep everything about the fight under control, make it through 2 Decimates and you'll get Gluth down. Like I said, his hit points are relatively low so you can really do a lot of damage to him quickly.

THADDIUS

Thaddius is a very fun fight. It requires near perfect execution by every member of the raid or you are in for a world of pain. The charges he places on the raid can increase damage output by up to 200%, so if you like big numbers, this fight is for you.

Thaddius is divided into two very distinct phases. For the first part of the fight, you are dealing with the two mini bosses—Stalagg and Feugen. After you have defeated both of them, the second phase begins and you engage Thaddius himself.

LOOT

Desecrated Circlet: Classes: Warlock Mage Priest

Desecrated Headpiece: Classes: Shaman Druid Hunter Paladin

Desecrated Helmet: Classes: Rogue Warrior

Eye of Diminution: Trinket, Equip: Increases your spell critical strike rating by 28, Use: Reduces the threat you generate by ${35-35ax(0,$PL-60)}% for 20 seconds

Leggings of Polarity: Cloth Legs, 128 Armor, +20 STA, +14 INT, Equip: Increases damage and healing done by magical spells and effects by up to 44, Equip: Increases your spell critical strike rating by 28

Plated Abomination Ribcage: Plate Chest, 1087 Armor, +45 STR, +25 STA, Equip: Increases your critical strike rating by 14, Equip: Increases your hit rating by 10

Spire of Twilight: Staff Two-Hand, 140-250 Damage, Speed 3.20, 60.9 damage per second, +30 STA, +38 INT, Equip: Restores 10 mana per 5 sec, Equip: Increases healing done by spells and effects by up to 178

The Castigator: Mace One-Hand, 119-221 Damage, Speed 2.60, 65.4 damage per second, +9 STA, Equip: Increases your critical strike rating by 14, Equip: Increases your hit rating by 10, Equip: Increases attack power by 16

ABILITIES

HP	6662000	Damage	5491-7280
Abilities	**Polarity Shift**: Assigns each player within 100 yards a Positive or Negative Charge. **Positive Charge**: Damage done increased by nearby positively charged allies. Deals 2000 damage to nearby allies that are not positively charged every 5 sec. **Negative Charge**: Damage done increased by nearby negatively charged allies. Deals 2000 damage to nearby allies that are not negatively charged every 5 sec.		
	Ball Lightning: 100 yard range, Deals 7000 to 9000 Nature damage. Thaddius only uses this ability when no targets are in melee range.		
	Chain Lightning: Spell affects up to 15 targets, inflicting greater Nature damage to each successive target. Deals 1850 to 2150 Nature damage to the first target.		

PHASE 1 ABILITIES

LIGHTNING RODS

Explanation: Both of the mini bosses are standing near lightning rods that channel electricity into them. If you move either boss too far away from their rod, the electricity link breaks and the lightning rod begins to deal tens of thousands of damage to the raid at random.

Solution: Never bring either boss too far away from their lightning rod. That's all there is to it.

MANA BURN (FEUGEN'S ABILITY)

Explanation: Feugen mana burns everyone within about 30 yards.

Solution: Melee DPS are the primary damage dealers on Feugen, so none of the mana-using DPS classes have to worry about the Mana Burn. There are still healers on Feugen's side, but they can stay at maximum range to avoid getting hit.

WAR STOMP

Explanation: Both of the mini bosses have a War Stomp ability that does around 1,500 damage and stuns everyone within melee range.

Solution: Simply put, you have to deal with it. Heal anyone who gets hit by it and stay out of melee range whenever possible.

POWER SURGE (STALAGG'S ABILITY)

Explanation: Stalagg randomly gets a buff called Power Surge. This increases his melee damage very significantly. It lasts 10 seconds.

Solution: All heals on Stalagg's tank! You want to spam heals on the tank while Power Surge is up or there is the chance they are going to get killed near instantly. It's a ton of damage, do not underestimate it.

TOSS

Explanation: Every 20 seconds each boss tosses their current target (hopefully the person tanking them) to the opposite platform. Threat lists are swapped so the tank should continue to have agro when they land on the new platform.

Solution: Agro is very touchy during this fight because of the Toss. The tank who is tossed gets initial agro when they land, but it is still harder than usual to maintain after that. You can't avoid the Toss so it's just a matter of having your healers switch to the new tank and having everyone be extra mindful of their agro.

PHASE 2 ABILITIES

BALL LIGHTNING

Explanation: If no one is within melee range, Thaddius starts shooting Ball Lightning at players. They do around 8,000 damage.

Solution: Always have someone within melee range. You should never see a Ball Lightning.

CHAIN LIGHTNING

Explanation: Every few seconds Thaddius casts Chain Lightning. It is resistible (nature based attack) and can hit for anywhere from 500 to 2,500 damage.

Solution: A tiny bit of nature resistance gear can go a long way, but do not sacrifice much DPS at all for it. Additionally, having a Greater Nature Resistance potion on hand for emergencies can save your life once or twice during the fight. Overall, healers simply have to deal with the damage and keep everyone topped off.

ENRAGE

Explanation: At the 5 minute mark Thaddius Enrages and kills everyone.

Solution: Kill him within 5 minutes!

POLARITY SHIFT

Explanation: Every 30 seconds Thaddius gives everyone in the raid a random charge—positive or negative. If two (or more) players of opposite charges are within about 8 yards of each other, they do 2,000 damage to each other every couple seconds. If two (or more) players of similar chargers are within about 8 yards of each other, they increase each other's damage dealt by 10%.

Solution: Polarity Shift is the bread and butter of Thaddius. This is discussed in great detail in the strategy section. But if you just have to know, designate one side of Thaddius as the positive side, one side as the negative side, and keep everyone of the appropriate charge on their side.

PREPARATION

Put all of the ranged DPS dealers in odd numbered groups and all of the melee DPS in even numbered groups. Healing needs to be spread out as evenly as possible.

The odd groups are assigned to handling Stalagg on the left platform. The even groups are headed towards Feugen on the right platform.

Stalagg only needs 1 tank, but it is helpful to have an offtank on Feugen since the agro is fairly sensitive. You don't want a melee DPS getting instantly killed during the first phase of the fight.

The healing is spread out very evenly so the tanks on each side shouldn't be very difficult to handle.

The main reason healing is spread out is for phase 2. During phase 2, every group needs a designated healer to keep them topped off after Chain Lightning damage. Anyone not healing the group is focused on keeping the main tank alive.

You should have your tanks assigned for Stalagg and Feugen. The DPS should know which platform they are headed to. The healers know if they are healing the tank or the group during phase 2. And you're ready to go.

PHASE 1 STRATEGY

The odds are at the bottom of the left platform, the evens are at the bottom of the right platform. Engage both Stalagg and Feugen at the same time by running up the ramp and onto their platforms.

Stalagg is tanked in the middle of the platform by one Warrior. The ranged DPS attacking him can really be anywhere they feel like; just don't be in range of War Stomp. The healers don't expect much of a challenge until Stalagg gains Power Surge. While Power Surge is up, all healers need to continually cast heals on the tank. Keep the tank alive and Stalagg slowly goes down.

Feugen is also tanked in the middle of his platform. It is helpful to have a second tank building threat on the off chance that someone pulls agro during a Toss. It is better for the offtank to take a swing or two than have a squishier player get killed by Feugen. All of the healers need to make their way to max healing range to avoid the Mana Burn and focus on keeping the tank alive as well as topping off the melee DPS who are hit by War Stomp.

The Tosses happen every 20 seconds and they really aren't that big of a deal. It's the healers' job to pickup their new healing target and continue keeping them alive. Beyond this change of target by the healers, the Toss doesn't alter anything else.

DPS both mini bosses down evenly. You have to kill them within about 10 seconds of each other or the one that is alive resurrects the one that is dead and you have to essentially start over. It is advisable to stop DPS at about 10% to make sure they die at the same time.

Once both Stalagg and Feugen have been defeated, everyone jumps from the raised platform down to the lower platform that Thaddius is on. You can't just walk off; you have to actually jump and it is possible to miss the lower platform. Don't miss the jump onto the lower platform!

Phase 2 begins.

PHASE 2 STRATEGY

As you are looking at Thaddius from the entry of the room, designate the left side of him as the negative side, and the right side of him as the positive side. Every single player needs to know which side is negative and which side is positive.

After killing Stalagg and Feugen, everyone hops down to Thaddius' platform and goes to the positive side. Stand together in a nice pile about 10 yards away from his feet.

The main tank stands right in front of Thaddius and picks up agro the moment he becomes attackable.

Everyone assigned to heal the main tank needs to start right away. They take a significant amount of damage and should never get very low. Anyone not healing the main tank has to keep an eye on their group and top off people as they get hit by Chain Lightning.

At this point everyone needs to be on the positive side about 10 yards away from Thaddius' feet, he should be tanked and the tank is getting lots of heals, groups are being topped off by the healer assigned to their group after Chain Lightning damage, and DPS is beginning.

30 seconds into the fight Thaddius casts the first Polarity Shift. His hands start shooting lightning; it is really obvious when Polarity Shift is coming. Everyone needs to be ready for the Polarity Shift.

All players who are afflicted by the negative charge are to run directly through Thaddius to the negative side. The positively charged players are already in the proper place so they don't need to do anything. I can't stress this enough, move instantly without hesitation and get to the negative side as quickly as possible the moment you see your charge go negative. Do not run around Thaddius; he doesn't do any AoE abilities so there is no danger running directly through him. Move fast or you are guaranteed to die.

Hopefully at this point you have 20 players on the negative side with negative charges and 20 players on the positive side with positive charges. Stay grouped together on the appropriate side so that the 190% damage increase buff is applied; you need that extra damage to kill him before the 5 minute Enrage.

30 seconds after the first Polarity Shift, the second one happens. Thaddius' hands start shooting electricity again and everyone must watch for their charge to change. Sometimes your charge won't change and you don't need to move at all. Most of the time your charge changes and you need to run directly through Thaddius to the opposite side—where you should be.

This is pretty much how the entire fight goes. Keep the tank alive, keep the groups topped off after Chain Lightning damage, and stay on top of those Polarity Shifts. You can not afford to have anyone die because they messed up on a Polarity Shift or they didn't get heals after a Chain Lightning. Everyone needs to stay alive.

Keep Those Tanks Moving

The main tank is moving to their proper side with Polarity Shift just like everybody else. It is also helpful for the main tank to Taunt after every Polarity Shift to ensure that Thaddius remains on him during the movement.

The major cause of wipes is people messing up on Polarity Shift. Pay very close attention to your debuffs when Polarity Shift is coming and start moving the instant you know you have to.

Sometimes Thaddius moves a little bit; he isn't a stationary boss. This is okay; adjust your position so that everyone is about 10 yards away from his feet at all times.

It takes some practice but soon enough your raid acts like a well oiled Polarity Shifting machine. Everyone needs to be at the top of their game and not mess up the shifts or fail to do their job. A perfect execution of the plan leads to a dead Thaddius without much trouble.

DEATH KNIGHT WING

The first fight in the Death Knight Wing is fairly easy, but this is quite misleading as the next two fights are arguably the hardest in Naxxramas. Instructor Razuvious must be tanked by adds that Priests Mind Control. Gothik the Harvester spawns wave after wave of adds before finally showing himself. And The Four Horsemen are an extremely complicated masterpiece of planning and execution.

DEATH KNIGHT WING MINIONS

BONY CONSTRUCT	UNDEAD
DARK TOUCHED WARRIOR	UNDEAD
DOOM TOUCHED WARRIOR	HUMANOID
DEATH LORD	UNDEAD
DEATHCHILL SERVANT	UNDEAD
DEATHKNIGHT	UNDEAD
DEATHKNIGHT CAPTAIN	UNDEAD
DEATHKNIGHT CAVALIER	UNDEAD
DEATHKNIGHT UNDERSTUDY	HUMANOID
DEATHKNIGHT VINDICATOR	UNDEAD
NECRO KNIGHT	UNDEAD

DEATH KNIGHT WING MINIONS

NECRO KNIGHT GUARDIAN	UNDEAD
NECRO STALKER	BEAST
RISEN DEATHKNIGHT	UNDEAD
SHADE OF NAXXRAMAS	UNDEAD
SKELETAL SMITH	UNDEAD
SKELETAL STEED	UNDEAD
SPIRIT OF NAXXRAMAS	UNDEAD
STONESKIN GARGOYLE	UNDEAD
UNHOLY AXE	UNDEAD
UNHOLY STAFF	UNDEAD
UNHOLY SWORDS	UNDEAD
VENOM STALKER	BEAST

INSTRUCTOR RAZUVIOUS

Priests get to learn how to tank! Overall, Instructor Razuvious is not that hard of a fight. But bad things can happen and it may take your Priests a couple runs to master their new task of tanking.

ABILITIES

HP	1998600	Damage	17299-22933
Abilities	**Unbalancing Strike**: Inflicts 350% weapon damage and decreases defense skill by 100 for 6 sec.		
	Disrupting Shout: Burns 4050 to 4950 mana. This deals damage equal to the amount of mana it burns.		

TRIUMPHANT SHOUT

Explanation: Every 25 seconds Instructor Razuvious hits everyone within LoS with Triumphant Shout. This burns up to 4,000 mana and deals the same amount of damage.

Solution: Everyone with mana has to get out of LoS when Triumphant Shout is cast. It's a quick way to lose all your mana and possibly die.

UNBALANCING STRIKE

Explanation: A melee attack that does up to 50,000 damage.

Solution: You can not tank Instructor Razuvious in the normal sense; he has the tendency to instantly kill the usual tanks. You must tank him with the Deathknight Understudy adds by using Mind Control. They have Shield Wall on a 30 second cooldown and approximately 100,000 life.

PREPARATION

The first thing to do is assign 2 Priests to do the Mind Controls. Having an additional Priest as a backup can be helpful as well. These Priests alternate Mind Controls on the Deathknight Understudies and tank Razuvious throughout the fight. These Priests need to be wearing at least 30 spell hit rating worth of equipment. Mind Controls have a tendency to break early without some spell hit gear.

Since there are 4 Understudies, 4 offtanks are needed to keep them occupied when they aren't being Mind Controlled. Assign the offtanks and make sure they each have a healer.

LOOT

Desecrated Boots: Classes: Shaman Druid Hunter Paladin

Desecrated Sabatons: Classes: Rogue Warrior

Desecrated Sandals: Classes: Warlock Mage Priest

Girdle of the Mentor: Plate Waist, 612 Armor, +21 STR, +21 STA, +20 AGI, Equip: Increases your critical strike rating by 14, Equip: Increases your hit rating by 10

Iblis, Blade of the Fallen Seraph: Sword One-Hand, 70-131 Damage, Speed 1.60, 62.8 damage per second, Equip: Increases your critical strike rating by 14, Equip: Increases your hit rating by 10, Equip: Increases attack power by 26

Idol of Longevity: Idol, Equip: Gain up to 25 mana each time you cast Healing Touch

Signet of the Fallen Defender: Finger, 140 Armor, +24 STA, Equip: Increases your hit rating by 10

Veil of Eclipse: Back, 72 Armor, +10 INT, +10 STA, Equip: Increases damage and healing done by magical spells and effects by up to 28, Equip: Increases your spell penetration by 10

Wand of the Whispering Dead: Wand, 119-222 Shadow Damage, Speed 1.50, 113.7 damage per second, +10 INT, +9 SPI, Equip: Increases healing done by spells and effects by up to 22

STRATEGY

Have your 4 offtanking Warriors get their targets. The first Priest to Mind Control should stand up at the top of the ramp. Mind Soothe both of the close Understudies and begin the fight by Mind Controlling the close-left one.

The moment the Mind Control casts the fight begins. The Priest needs to use the Understudy's Taunt and Shield Wall right away. The offtanks need to pickup their Understudies and drag them to the top of the ramp.

Move Razuvious into position at the top corner of the ramp. The ideal position allows healers to have LoS to heal the tanking Understudy but not be within LoS of Razuvious himself.

At this point in the fight one Understudy is tanking Razuvious at the top of the ramp. The other Understudies are offtanked. And the next Priest to Mind Control is ready to relieve the first Priest. It is important that the next Mind Control happens quickly so the first Priest can get out of LoS of the Disrupting Shout that is about to happen.

After the second Priest has Razuvious tanked, the first Priest needs to get out of Razuvious' LoS so they don't take damage from Disrupting Shout.

Now it is just a matter of alternating Mind Controls. The next Priest up begins their cast when the current Priest has about 35 seconds left on their Mind Control. As soon as they get an Understudy Mind Controlled, they move into position, Taunt, and Shield Wall. The Priest being relieved cancels their Mind Control and waits about 20-25 seconds before bringing in the next Understudy. These 2 Priests rotate tanking with the Understudies like this throughout the entire fight.

One final note about Mind Controlling the Understudies, after Mind Control wears off they get a debuff called Mind Exhaustion that prevents them from being Mind Controlled again within 60 seconds. If the Priests smoothly transition their tanking without any early Mind Control breaks or mistakes, this shouldn't be a problem. But on occasion, the next Priest in line to Mind Control has to wait for Mind Exhaustion to wear off.

As this is happening, ranged DPS with mana are moving out of LoS every 25 seconds to avoid Disrupting Shout; nobody should die to it. The healers are mainly focused on making sure that none of the Understudies die while tanking Razuvious, but a couple healers are keeping an eye on the offtanks handling Understudies.

A successful Razuvious kill is almost entirely the responsibility of the Mind Controlling Priests. Give them a few tries to practice the positioning and the transitions, then take him down.

GOTHIK THE HARVESTER

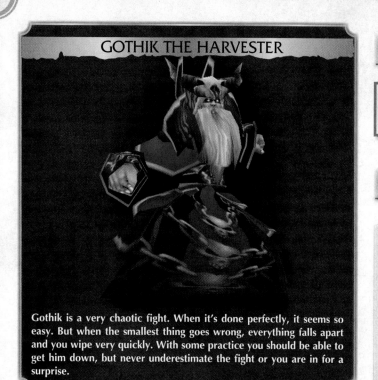

Gothik is a very chaotic fight. When it's done perfectly, it seems so easy. But when the smallest thing goes wrong, everything falls apart and you wipe very quickly. With some practice you should be able to get him down, but never underestimate the fight or you are in for a surprise.

LOOT

Boots of Displacement: Leather Feet, 190 Armor, +33 AGI, +21 STA, Equip: Increases your effective stealth level

Desecrated Boots: Classes: Shaman Druid Hunter Paladin

Desecrated Sabatons: Classes: Rogue Warrior

Desecrated Sandals: Classes: Warlock Mage Priest

Glacial Headdress: Cloth Head, 117 Armor, +20 STA, +21 INT, +40 Frost Resistance, Equip: Increases damage and healing done by magical spells and effects by up to 18

Polar Helmet: Leather Head, 224 Armor, +24 STA, +18 AGI, +44 Frost Resistance

Sadist's Collar: Neck, +24 STA, Equip: Increases your critical strike rating by 14, Equip: Increases attack power by 20

The Soul Harvester's Bindings: Cloth Wrist, 63 Armor, +14 STA, +11 INT, Equip: Increases your spell critical strike rating by 14, Equip: Increases damage and healing done by magical spells and effects by up to 21

ABILITIES

HP	399750	Damage	2811-3721
Abilities	**Harvest Soul:** Reduce enemy's health and mana by 10% for 2 min. Stacks.		
	Shadow Bolt: Inflicts 2070 to 2530 Shadow damage.		

PHASE 1 ABILITIES

UNRELENTING DEATHKNIGHT

Spawns 2 at a time from the side spawn points. Charges players, stunning them for 3 seconds. Can cast Shadow Mark on people within melee range; this deals about 1,000 damage and causes the Unrelenting Riders to hit you with Shadow Bolts while it is active.

UNRELENTING RIDER

Spawns 1 at a time from the middle spawn point. Has an AoE shadow damage aura. Shoots Shadow Bolts at anyone afflicted by Mark of Shadow.

UNRELENTING TRAINEE

Spawns 3 at a time, one from each spawn point. Humanoid, can be CC'ed. Not elite, low hit points. Can use a melee ability called Eagle Claw which deals damage to a player over 15 seconds. Additionally, can knockdown players while attacking them.

SPECTRAL DEATHKNIGHT

Has high life but can be stunned. Deals a lot of AoE damage through a Whirlwind attack and a Cleave. Also has a Mana Burn that hits nearby players. Finally, Sunders the armor of the player it is attacking.

SPECTRAL HORSE

Has the most hit points of any add. Can not be stunned or otherwise CC'ed. Has one special ability: a War Stomp that does minor damage and slows the movement speed of everyone within melee range.

SPECTRAL RIDER

Relatively low hit points. Shadow damage aura that pulses for 400 damage. Interruptible Life Drain ability that hits a player for a few hundred damage and restores life to the Rider.

SPECTRAL TRAINEE

Very low hit point ghost. Casts an arcane based AoE spell that hits for a few hundred damage.

PHASE 2 ABILITIES

HARVEST SOUL

Explanation: Randomly causes players to take 10% more shadow damage. This can stack and is not removable.

Solution: You can't really avoid Harvest Soul, you just have to kill Gothik quickly once he is on the ground so that it isn't allowed to stack very high.

SHADOW BOLT

Explanation: Hits players not in melee range for around 2,500 shadow damage.

Solution: Heal through it. By itself, Shadow Bolt is not a very big deal. It becomes a threat when it is hitting someone who has a few stacks of Harvest Soul on them.

PREPARATION

The raid is split in half; "live side" and "dead side." The live side is the left side of the room and they kill very predictable "Unrelenting" add spawns. Put 2 tanks, every Priest, and ranged DPS on the live side.

The dead side, on the right side of the room killing "Spectral" add spawns, kills adds that are sent to them by the live side. All of the melee DPS and any spare ranged DPS (preferably Hunters) are in charge of cleaning up the dead side. The dead side also needs at least 2 tanks.

Setup the groups knowing which classes are good for each side. Spread out the healing in the groups, but make sure all of the Priests are on the live side for Shackle Undead.

The live side's DPS is assigned very specifically. Evenly distribute all of the DPS onto all 3 platforms to kill the Unrelenting Trainees. Then split the DPS in half and assign each group a spawn point for the Unrelenting Deathknights. Since there is only 1 Unrelenting Rider at a time, and they are the most threatening target, nothing special is needed for them; all DPS focuses the Unrelenting Rider when one is up. All DPS on the live side should know which Unrelenting Trainee spawn point they are assigned to, which Unrelenting Deathknight spawn point they are assigned to, and that Unrelenting Riders must be killed by everyone as quickly as possible.

The dead side needs 2 assists. The first assist is in charge of killing Spectral Trainees. The Spectral Trainees are easy to kill and should drop very quickly. The second assist is in charge of choosing which non-Trainee mob to focus fire down. Dead side must kill things one at a time very quickly while keeping the Spectral Trainees under control.

STRATEGY

Make sure everyone is on their proper side before the fight begins. Once Gothik is engaged, the gate in the middle closes. You won't be able to get across again until very late in the fight.

Engage Gothik by hitting him with a random spell. He is immune to damage while on the balcony.

As soon as his speech is over, the adds on the live side start spawning. The first spawn is 3 Unrelenting Trainees. Kill them quickly; all 3 should die around the same time since all 3 are being attacked at once.

After the Unrelenting Trainees die on the live side, they respawn as Spectral Trainees on the dead side. This is how the spawns come to the dead side; they are sent over by the live side. Unrelenting Trainees are sent over as Spectral Trainees, Unrelenting Deathknights turn into Spectral Deathknights, and Unrelenting Riders spawn 2 mobs, Spectral Riders and Spectral Horses.

The live side is in control of how fast the dead side gets spawns. On one hand, the live side can't get overwhelmed by the spawns on their side; they have to kill things relatively quickly. But on the other hand, they can't kill too many things at once and send a ton of adds over to the dead side. The most common add to kill too quickly is the non-elite Unrelenting Trainees. Towards the end of the first phase, it is preferable to CC these instead of killing them.

The dead side kills whatever spawns. Spectral Trainees should die very quickly. The next priority target is the Spectral Riders and Horses, followed by the Spectral Deathknights. Do not allow any of the spawns to get near the healers; get them tanked and keep them tanked until they die. Practice quick assisting to take down targets one at a time as fast as you can. Greater Shadow Resist and Greater Arcane Resist potions are handy, but it is more of a DPS orientated encounter so using anything that maximizes DPS is preferred.

The live side has to manage their spawns in a very specific way. Let's go through every single spawn with advice on how to deal with it.

0:24 – 3 UNRELENTING TRAINEES
Kill all of the Trainees.
0:44 – 3 UNRELENTING TRAINEES
Kill all of the Trainees.
1:04 – 3 UNRELENTING TRAINEES
Kill all of the Trainees.
1:14 – 2 UNRELENTING DEATHKNIGHTS
Kill both of the Deathknights.
1:24 – 3 UNRELENTING TRAINEES
Kill all of the trainees.
1:39 – 2 UNRELENTING DEATHKNIGHTS
Kill both of the Deathknights.
1:44 – 3 UNRELENTING TRAINEES
Kill all of the Trainees.
2:04 – 3 UNRELENTING TRAINEES, 2 UNRELENTING DEATHKNIGHTS
Polymorph the Trainees and kill the Deathknights before the Trainees. Once both of the Deathknights are down, kill the remaining 3 Trainees.
2:14 – 1 UNRELENTING RIDER
Focus on and kill the Rider.
2:24 – 3 UNRELENTING TRAINEES
Polymorph all of the Trainees.
2:29 – 2 UNRELENTING DEATHKNIGHTS
Shackle both of the Deathknights.
2:44 – 3 UNRELENTING TRAINEES, 1 UNRELENTING RIDER
Polymorph or otherwise CC the Trainees, focus and kill the Rider. Try to kill a couple Trainees after the Rider is dead and before the next spawn, but leave the majority of them CC'ed.
2:54 – 2 UNRELENTING DEATHKNIGHTS
Shackle both of the Deathknights. There are now 4 Shackled Deathknights.
3:04 – 3 UNRELENTING TRAINEES
Kill at least 3 Trainees, but still leave some CC'ed; you don't want to overwhelm the dead side by sending too many Trainees over.
3:14 – 1 UNRELENTING RIDER
Focus on and kill the Rider.
3:19 – 2 UNRELENTING DEATHKNIGHTS
At this point you have a couple options. The easiest plan is to Shackle the next two Deathknights, that is, assuming you have at least 6 Priests. If you don't have Priests to spare, another option is to kill the Deathknights.
3:24 – 3 UNRELENTING TRAINEES
Kill the Trainees as quickly as you can. There is a 20 second gap before the next spawn so now is a good time to clean up any Trainees that are out of control. Always be careful not to send too many spawns over to the dead side, but don't let the live side get out of control.
3:44 – 3 UNRELENTING TRAINEES, 2 UNRELENTING DEATHKNIGHTS, 1 UNRELENTING RIDER
Focus the Rider first. Use a combination of CC (Frost Traps, Frost Nova, Shackle Undead, and Polymorph) to control the other spawns as best you can. As soon as the Rider is down, focus fire anything that is running around uncontrolled. You have 50 seconds to get your side under control.
4:34 – GOTHIK TELEPORTS INTO THE ROOM
Hopefully both sides are under control at this point. Gothik ports into the middle of the live side to be tanked and killed.

A combination of killing adds quickly and using CC abilities correctly is a win for the live side. It's a careful balance of not letting yourself be overwhelmed by spawns while not overwhelming the dead side with spawns by killing them too quickly.

The dead side has to kill their adds as fast as they can while keeping them under control. If anything makes it into the healers, the dead side is over. If DPS get killed by the various AoE attacks, you won't have the DPS to keep up. Practice picking targets and assisting to clean out the dead side quickly.

If you make it to the 4:34 mark without being in the process of wiping, you've probably got a Gothik kill on the way. He only has 399,750 hit points so he dies very quickly. The adds should be at a standstill with both sides under control before Gothik ports into the room. He ports to the center of the live side; have a tank waiting for him.

Get him tanked right as he shows up and focus all DPS on him. Don't forget about anything you have CC'ed! It would not be pretty if CC'ed mobs get loose.

After about 20 seconds on the live side, he ports over to the dead side. Tank him and continue to DPS. He ports back and forth every 20 seconds or so a few times before the gates open and everyone finishes him off.

The Gothik fight is very chaotic but proper execution of both sides should result in Gothik porting down to the floor with everything under control, followed by a quick kill of him.

THE FOUR HORSEMEN

The Four Horsemen is one of the most well designed encounters in the game. If you watched the fight without understanding the strategy, it would probably look like complete chaos. In actuality, every single step is carefully planned.

LOOT

Corrupted Ashbringer: Sword Two-Hand, 259-389 Damage, Speed: 3.60, 90.0 damage per second, -25 STA, Equip: Inflicts the will of the Ashbringer upon the wielder, Equip: Increases your critical strike rating by 28, Equip: Increases your hit rating by 10, Chance on hit: Steals 185 to 215 life from target enemy

Desecrated Breastplate: Classes: Warrior, Rogue

Desecrated Robe: Classes: Priest, Mage, Warlock

Desecrated Tunic: Classes: Paladin, Hunter, Shaman, Druid

Leggings of the Apocalypse: Leather Legs, 241 Armor, +15 STR, +31 AGI, +23 STA, Equip: Increases your critical strike rating by 28

Maul of the Redeemed Crusader: Mace Two-Hand, 244-367 Damage, Speed: 3.60, 84.9 damage per second, +29 STA, +24 INT, Equip: Restores 8 mana per 5 sec, Equip: Increases damage and healing done by magical spells and effects by up to 35

Seal of the Damned: Finger, +17 STA, Equip: Increases damage and healing done by magical spells and effects by up to 21, Equip: Increases your spell hit rating by 8, Equip: Increases your spell critical strike rating by 14

Soulstring: Bow, 123-229 Damage, Speed: 2.90, 60.7 damage per second, +6 STA, Equip: Increases your critical strike rating by 14, Equip: Increases attack power by 16

Warmth of Forgiveness: Trinket, Equip: Restores 10 mana per 5 sec, Use: Restores 500 mana

ABILITIES

THANE KORTH'AZZ

HP	599850	Damage	2745-3640
Abilities	**Mark of Korthazz:** Periodically damages all nearby targets and increases the damage they will take from future Marks of Korth'azz. Lasts 1.25 minutes.		
	Meteor: Deals 12825 to 14175 Fire damage evenly divided between all targets in an 8-yard area.		
	Shield Wall: Reduces all physical and magical damage taken by 75% for 20 sec.		

LADY BLAUMEUX

HP	499650	Damage	3844-5096
Abilities	**Mark of Blaumeux:** Periodically damages all nearby targets and increases the damage they will take from future Marks of Blaumeux. Lasts 1.25 minutes.		
	Shield Wall: Reduces all physical and magical damage taken by 75% for 20 sec.		
	Void Zone: Deals 900 to 1100 Shadow damage to enemies that stand within it.		

HIGHLORD MOGRAINE

HP	532960	Damage	2636-3494
Abilities	**Mark of Mograine:** Periodically damages all nearby targets and increases the damage they will take from future Marks of Mograinez. Lasts 1.25 minutes.		
	Shield Wall: Reduces all physical and magical damage taken by 75% for 20 sec.		
	Righteous Fire: Inflicts 2160 to 2640 Fire damage, plus an additional 600 Fire damage every 1 sec. for 8 sec.		

SIR ZELIEK

HP	499650	Damage	3844-5096
Abilities	**Mark of Zeliek:** Periodically damages all nearby targets and increases the damage they will take from future Marks of Zeliek. Lasts 1.25 minutes.		
	Shield Wall: Reduces all physical and magical damage taken by 75% for 20 sec.		
	Holy Wrath: Deals 495 to 605 Holy damage to the initial target, then jumps to nearby targets, dealing successively greater damage.		

HIGHLORD MOGRAINE

Ability: Righteous Fire, a weapon proc that hits for about 2,250 fire damage with an additional 4,800 damage over 8 seconds.

Counter: It's a weapon proc, Mograine can be disarmed, keep him disarmed as often as possible. Other than that, the healers have to heal through it. Mograine is probably the hardest of the Horsemen to heal.

LADY BLAMEUX

Ability: Void Zone, Every 12 seconds Blameux targets a random player within her Mark range and places a Void Zone under their feet. Standing in the Void Zone causes about 4,000 shadow damage per tick.

Counter: Get out of the Void Zone as quickly as possible. Usually you can make it out before it has a chance to do any damage, but at the worst you take one tick of damage. It is resistible shadow damage, so Shadow Protection from Priests is useful.

THANE KORTH'AZZ

Ability: Meteor, deals up to 15,000 fire damage divided by the number of players it hits.

Counter: Stay grouped up when at Thane. Think back to those Anubisath Defenders in Ahn'Qiraj. Make sure that Meteor hits as many people as possible and then heal up the damage. Using Greater Fire Resistance potions can help mitigate the damage.

SIR ZELIEK

Ability: Holy Wrath, targets a random player within 35 yards and hits them for about 500 damage. If there is another player within 5 yards, it jumps to them and the damage doubles. This continues until there aren't any players within 5 yards of the most recent target.

Counter: Only the tank should be within 35 yards of Zeliek at any time. As long as Holy Wrath is only hitting 1, maybe 2 people as the tanks are transitioning, it isn't a big deal.

ENRAGE

Explanation: After 100 Marks, the Horsemen Enrage. This causes them to cast their abilities very rapidly.

Solution: Kill them before 100 Marks!

MARK

Explanation: Every Horsemen casts a unique Mark (ie: Mark of Mograine) on everyone within 45-60 yards. Players afflicted by the Mark take extra damage from the next Mark. Being hit by a second Mark causes you to take 250 damage, a third is 1,000 damage, fourth is 3,000 damage, and the fifth is 5,000 damage. Sixth and up increment by 1,000 damage per application. This is shadow based damage but not resistible in any way.

Solution: Rotating around the Marks is the core part of the fight. Tanks, DPS, and healers each get a different rotation pattern. Tanks can take up to 8, maybe 9 Marks before they die. DPS want to take 3 Marks at a time. And Healers only take 2 Marks before heading to the next Horsemen.

SHIELD WALL

Explanation: Each of the Horsemen uses Shield Wall at 50% and 20% hit points. It lasts 20 seconds.

Solution: You can't prevent it. Wait it out.

SPIRITS

Explanation: After a Horsemen dies, their spirit remains in the location that they perished. The spirit continues to cast Marks but is immobile and doesn't use any special abilities.

Solution: They don't move but they can melee you if you get within melee range. Stay out of melee range and rotate with the Marks as usual.

PREPARATION

Positioning is very important. Mograine is tanked in the far left corner, Thane in the far right corner, Blameux in the close left corner, and Zeliek in the close right corner. The sides are referred to as "the far side" (with Mograine and Thane) and "the close side" (with Blameux and Zeliek).

Tanking, DPS, and healing are setup individually.

You need 8 tanks for the fight. Assign 4 tanks to both the far side and the close side. Figure out the order they are going to rotate in. For example on the far side, tank 1 starts on Mograine, tank 2 starts on Thane, tank 3 starts in the middle and is the first to rotate in, tank 4 starts in the middle and is the second to rotate in. Each side should have a 4 tank rotation setup.

Tanks on the far side need to use a fair amount of fire resistance gear since everything they are tanking deals heavy fire damage.

DPS is divided into 4 evenly distributed groups. Assign every DPS player to one of the four DPS groups. All of the DPS groups start out the fight in the middle of the room and begin their rotating (detailed in the strategy section) after the first Mark.

Healing is divided into 8 different groups. It's easiest to just use group numbers to designate the healing groups, so evenly distribute the healing throughout all 8 groups. The healing groups split up into all 4 corners. For example, at the beginning of the fight, the healers in group 1 and group 2 are in the far left corner, group 3 and group 4 healers are in the far right corner, group 5 and 6 healers are in the close left corner, and the last 2 groups are in the close right.

STRATEGY

Everyone should know what their job is before the pull is made. All of the tanks know where they start and when they rotate; all of the DPS know what DPS group they are in and where that groups starts; and all of the healers know which healing group they are in.

Everyone rotates in a different way after the initial pull.

The pull is straightforward; the first four tanks pickup their targets and move them into position as quickly as possible. Using a Hunter to peel the close side Horsemen is helpful. All of the tanks should be in position before the first Mark hits.

15 seconds into the fight: All four Horsemen are in position and being tanked. All of the DPS are sitting in the middle of the room. All of the healers are in their designated corners and healing the tanks. The first Mark is about to hit.

Tanking rotation:

20 seconds into the fight, at the first Mark, the first tank waiting in the middle of the room heads to Mograine or Blameux (depending on which side they are on) to relieve the current tank. Run in, Taunt, and hold the agro. The tank being relieved should stop attacking to allow the new tank to get agro as easily as possible. The newly relieved tank immediately takes off to the next Horsemen on their respective side to relieve the next tank. This relieved tank heads to the middle of the room as soon as they can. Once the fourth tank waiting in the middle sees a tank come in, they head out to relieve the person in front of them. This is how the rotation goes.

Far side example: Tank 1 is assigned to tanking Mograine in the far left corner at the start of the fight. Tank 2 is assigned to Thane in the far right corner at the start. Tanks 3 and 4 are waiting in the middle. 15 seconds into the fight Tank 1 has Mograine tanked and positioned correctly, Tank 2 has Thane tanked and positioned correctly, and Tanks 3 and 4 are in the middle waiting for the first Mark. The first Mark hits, Tank 3 heads to Tank 1 on Mograine to relieve them, as soon as Tank 3 has Mograine's agro, Tank 1 heads to Tank 2 on Thane to relieve them, as soon as Tank 1 has agro on Thane, Tank 3 heads to the middle. Finally, once Tank 4 sees Tank 2 coming to the middle, they head to Tank 3 on Mograine and relieve them. Continue rotating and relieving the tank in front of you.

The only real pitfall in the tanking rotation is leaving the middle before your original Mark resets. You have to wait in the middle of the room until your Mark is gone before going back to the first Horsemen to tank.

Taunt resists can be another problem, but with 4 tanks on each side there should be enough leeway to make it through one or two Taunt resists. Using the 4 piece Dreadnaught set bonus can help reduce the chances of this happening as well.

DPS rotation:

All of the DPS has been divided into 4 even groups and is waiting in the middle of the room when the first Mark is cast.

After the first Mark, DPS 1 begins to attack Mograine, DPS 2 begins to attack Thane, and the remaining DPS groups hold still. As soon as both of the first DPS groups have taken 3 Marks, they change places with DPS 3 and DPS 4. DPS 3 heads to Mograine and DPS 4 heads to Thane, while DPS 1 and 2 return to the middle.

At this point DPS 1 is afflicted by Mograine's Mark and waiting in the middle, DPS 2 is afflicted by Thane's Mark and is waiting in the middle, DPS 3 has just begun to attack Mograine, and DPS 4 has just begun to attack Thane.

After 3 more Marks, everybody rotates again, except it's a little different. DPS 3 and 4 head back to the middle. DPS 1 starts to attack Thane (since they do not have his Mark) and DPS 2 starts to attack Mograine. They do this for 3 Marks before returning to the middle.

That's how the DPS rotates. 3 Marks at a time, Horsemen 1, middle of the room, Horsemen 2, middle of the room, repeat.

Healing rotation:

The healers have the easiest rotation. At the start of the fight the healers from groups 1 and 2 are in the far left corner, group 3 and 4 healers in the far right, group 5 and 6 healers in the close left, and group 7 and 8 healers in the close right.

On the first Mark, all of the odd numbered healing groups rotate clockwise to the next Horsemen. The even numbered healing groups stay put until the second Mark.

As soon as the second Mark hits, all of the odd numbered healers have arrived in their new position. Now it is time for the even numbered healers to rotate clockwise to the next Horsemen.

That's all there is to it! Healers in odd numbered groups rotate on odd numbered Marks (1, 3, 5, etc); healers in even numbered groups rotate on even numbered Marks. If executed correctly, there is always be a few seconds of overlap at each corner before the next Mark hits. There should always be a healing group at every corner and no healer should ever be afflicted by more than 2 Marks.

Pay Attention

Healers who are at Zeliek and Blameux may notice that the tank doesn't take very much damage. Try to give the DPS groups in the middle of the room a few heals during any downtime!

THE FIGHT

As you can see, everyone has a very specific job. The fight comes down to everyone being able to do their job consistently correctly. Problems occur when someone makes a mistake. A healer might mess up their rotation and leave a tank with very little healing in the future. Or maybe a tank goes in from the middle too early and dies to the Mark. Little mistakes can turn into big problems as the fight goes on.

Once you have the rotation mastered, the fight is a matter of staying consistent. Mograine and Thane are slowly worked down to 0% before the DPS starts rotating to Blameux and, finally, Zeliek.

As soon as the first Horsemen dies—usually Mograine—the DPS that would normally rotate to him starts killing Blameux. The tanks that were tanking him stand in the middle ready to relieve the person on Thane. Once Thane dies, all of the DPS is rotating between Blameux and Zeliek (do not send melee DPS into Zeliek, ever!) and there are 4 tanks waiting in the middle as emergency replacements for anyone on the final Horsemen. The healers never really change anything about their rotation throughout the entire fight.

The fight becomes more forgiving of mistakes as more Horsemen die. You can afford to lose a tank or a healer or some DPS when there are only 2 Horsemen left, but it really shouldn't happen since the hardest Horsemen are dying first.

Keep everything under control until there is just one Horsemen left, and get him down. As soon as all 4 are dead, a chest spawns in the middle of the room that contains your well deserved loot. The order you kill the Horsemen in has no effect on what the loot is.

FROSTWYRM LAIR

You have reached the final wing of Naxxramas. Congratulations! Not many players get this far; you should be proud. Frostwyrm Lair has only two fights in it, but I hope you're prepared for a challenge.

SAPPHIRON

The giant, skeletal Dragon awaits you as you enter Frostwyrm Lair. At first you only see a big pile of bones. When you enter Sapphiron's room, the bones begin moving and form the dragon.

LOOT

Claw of the Frost Wyrm: Fist Weapon Off Hand, 75-140 Damage, Speed 1.50, 71.7 damage per second, +8 STA, Equip: Increases your critical strike rating by 14, Equip: Increases your hit rating by 10, Equip: Increases attack power by 22

Cloak of the Necropolis: Back, 77 Armor, +11 INT, +12 STA, Equip: Increases damage and healing done by magical spells and effects by up to 26, Equip: Increases your spell critical strike rating by 14, Equip: Increases your spell hit rating by 8

Eye of the Dead: Trinket, Equip: Increases healing done by spells and effects by up to 70, Use: Increases healing done by the next 5 spells by up to 450 for 30 seconds

Fortitude of the Scourge: Use: Permanently adds to a shoulder slot item increased Stamina by 16 and also grants 100 armor.

Glyph of Deflection: Trinket, Equip: Increases your block rating by 12, Equip: Increases the block value of your shield by 23, Use: Increases the block value of your shield by 235 for 20 seconds

Might of the Scourge: Use: Permanently adds to a shoulder slot item increased attack power by 26 and also increases your critical strike rating by 14

Power of the Scourge: Use: Permanently adds to a shoulder slot item increased damage and healing done by magical spells and effects up to 15 and also increases your spell critical strike rating by 14

Resilience of the Scourge: Use: Permanently adds to a shoulder slot item increased healing done by magical spells and effects up to 31 and also increases your mana regen by 5 mana per 5 sec

Sapphiron's Left Eye: Held In Hand, +12 STA, +8 INT, Equip: Increases damage and healing done by magical spells and effects by up to 26, Equip: Increases your spell critical strike rating by 14, Equip: Increases your spell hit rating by 8

Sapphiron's Right Eye: Held In Hand, +10 INT, +9 STA, Equip: Increases healing done by spells and effects by up to 62, Equip: Restores 4 mana per 5 sec

Shroud of Dominion: Back, 77 Armor, +11 STA, Equip: Increases your critical strike rating by 14, Equip: Increases attack power by 50

Slayer's Crest: Trinket, Equip: Increases attack power by 64, Use: Increases attack power by 260 for 20 seconds

The Face of Death: Shield, 3994 Armor, 87 Block, +21 STA, Equip: Increases your block rating by 12, Equip: Increases the block value of your shield by 21

The Restrained Essence of Sapphiron: Trinket, Equip: Increases damage and healing done by magical spells and effects by up to 40, Use: Increases damage and healing done by magical spells and effects by up to 130 for 20 seconds

ABILITIES

HP	3164450	Damage	6919-9173
Abilities	**Frost Breath:** Deals 75000 to 125000 Frost damage to all players within 200 yards. This has no effect on frozen players, and it is blocked by line of sight.		
	Life Drain: Drains 1750 to 2250 health and heals Sapphiron for 3500 to 4500 every 3 sec. for 12 sec.		
	Frost Aura: Deals 600 frost damage per second.		
	Blizzard: Summons a Blizzard, Up to two Blizzards can be active. Players struck are effected by "Chill". **Chill:** Deals 3063 to 3937 Frost damage every 2 sec. for 6 sec. Slows movement speed by 65% for 6 sec.		
	Icebolt: Deals 2625 to 3375 Frost damage and freezes the target in a block of ice for 20 sec. While encased in ice, the target cannot attack, move, or cast spells, but the target suffers no damage.		

BLIZZARD

Explanation: While Sapphiron is on the ground there are 2 large, slow moving Blizzards that make their way across the room. The Blizzard does around 3,500 damage per tick and slows movement speed significantly.

Solution: Dodge the Blizzard. You can't prevent it and you can't resist enough of it to live. Always be aware of where the Blizzard is and where it is going. It is similar to the sleep cloud used by the Emerald Dragons.

CLEAVE

Explanation: Sapphiron cleaves everyone in front of him regularly.

Solution: Only the main tank should be directly in front of Sapphiron.

ENRAGE

Explanation: After 15 minutes Sapphiron Enrages, causing the Frost Aura to do much more damage.

Solution: Sapphiron must be killed within 15 minutes.

FROST AURA

Explanation: Throughout the entire fight there is a Frost Aura that does anywhere from 0 to 600 damage per tick to everyone in the room.

Solution: This is where your frost resistance gear comes into play. The Frost Aura is resistible and you want to mitigate as much of the damage as possible through frost resistance. Even with as much frost resist as you can gather, players take a fair amount of damage from the Frost Aura and must be healed.

ICEBOLT

Explanation: While Sapphiron is in the air he shoots 5 Icebolts at 5 random players. The Icebolts do around 3,000 damage to the player and anyone within 10 yards of them. After being hit by an Icebolt, the player is turned into a block of ice that is immune to all damage, healing, and can not attack.

Solution: The Icebolts are essential to the fight because you must hide behind the ice blocks they create to avoid the Icebomb. Keep players above 3,500 life so that nobody dies to an Icebolt; problems can occur if your ice blocks die to the Icebolt. Since there is a 10 yard splash range, your raid has to stay spread out. Drinking Greater Frost Resistance potions while Sapphiron is in the air can help handle the damage that Icebolt does.

ICEBOMB

Explanation: When Sapphiron is in the air he emotes, "Sapphiron begins to take a deep breath…" About 5 seconds after this emote, a large ball of ice slams into the ground under Sapphiron and hits everyone in the room that is within LoS for at least 75,000 damage.

Solution: Every player in the room has to hide behind an ice block—one of the 5 ice blocks that are created by the Icebolt ability. If you are hiding behind an ice block, out of LoS, the Icebomb does not do any damage to you.

LIFE DRAIN

Explanation: Every 24 seconds Sapphiron casts Life Drain on a handful of random players. It is a removable curse that lasts 12 seconds and drains about 2,000 health per tick while restoring about 4,000 health to Sapphiron with each tick.

Solution: Decurse Life Drain as quickly as possible. You can't afford to let players die to it and you can't let Sapphiron heal himself.

PREPARATION

First and foremost everyone has to equip their frost resistance gear. You want to use the crafted gear obtained by having Exalted Argent Dawn faction. Everyone in the raid needs to be above 200 frost resist unbuffed. The only exception is the main tank; they wear their normal tanking gear.

When setting up the groups there are a few things to keep in mind. Every group needs to have someone who can remove curses. Every group needs a healer designated to heal the group. Any healer that is not on the group is on the main tank.

Make sure that everyone has a few Greater Frost Resistance potions, a Healthstone, and anything else that helps them stay alive as the fight goes on and healer mana runs low.

Spread out the DPS evenly and make sure the main tank has the usual Devotion Aura, Blood Pact group.

STRATEGY

The main tank charges into the room and immediately picks up Sapphiron. He is tanked in the middle of the room. It doesn't really matter which way he faces.

The rest of the raid is split up on each side of Sapphiron; odds on the left, evens on the right. They should quickly get into position, in range for DPS or healing, and near the decurser in their group.

Right away the Frost Aura begins doing damage. The healers designated to taking care of the group need to keep everyone alive.

Fairly soon the Blizzards show up. Keep an eye out for them and stay far away. You don't want to get caught in a Blizzard and waste healer mana unnecessarily, or worse, die to the Blizzard.

The first Life Drain hits. Decursers in each group must remove it as quickly as possible from everyone afflicted. Don't just decurse inside of your own group; try to help out anyone who gets hit by Life Drain on your side of the room. Quickly removing Life Drain is a key part of the fight.

At this point you have a feel for how it is when Sapphiron is on the ground. Heal the main tank, heal the groups, dodge the Blizzards, and get rid of those Life Drains. The strategy while he is on the ground does not change throughout the fight.

45 seconds into the fight Sapphiron takes flight. Everyone has to spread out in preparation for the Icebolts. The healers should make sure that everyone is above 3,500 hit points so that they don't die to an Icebolt.

The first Icebolt is cast and the first ice block is created. Everyone needs to take note of where each ice block is. Sometimes you have to travel quite a distance to get behind an ice block. This can be even more challenging if people are dying to Icebolts and the ice block is never created in the first place.

After 5 Icebolts there should be 5 ice blocks and everyone in the raid should be within 5 seconds of getting behind an ice block. You don't want to collapse behind the ice blocks too early; remember the Icebolt attack has a 10 yard splash radius and healer mana is already being tapped by the Frost Aura. It would be a problem if a dozen people were hiding behind an ice block and they were all hit by Icebolt. Don't completely collapse until the last Icebolt has been cast.

When Sapphiron emotes that he "begins to take a deep breath," the Icebomb has been cast. Everyone needs to be hiding behind an ice block or they are dead. After the Icebomb hits the ground, Sapphiron lands and you go back to the ground phase.

Assuming you made it through an Icebomb without anyone dying, you're well on your way to killing Sapphiron. Once you decide to use potions, surviving the 10 minutes or so needed to kill Sapphiron becomes less of a problem. The Frost Aura is completely manageable as long as everyone has some decent frost resistance gear. The key to the fight becomes getting through the air phase successfully without any deaths. He goes up into the air several times throughout the fight and you can't afford to lose a couple people each time; you won't have the DPS or healing or decursing to kill him towards the end.

Do some dry runs making sure you get through at least a couple Icebombs without any trouble, then use your potions and take him down.

KEL'THUZAD

The Lich King's top lieutenant. Kel'Thuzad is a very complicated fight that is separated into 2 phases. It takes some time to learn all of his abilities in both phases.

LOOT

Bonescythe Ring: Finger, +10 STA, +20 AGI, +20 STR, Classes: Rogue, Equip: Increases your hit rating by 10

Doomfinger: Wand, 146-271 Shadow Damage, Speed 1.50, 139.0 damage per second, Equip: Increases your spell critical strike rating by 14, Equip: Increases damage and healing done by magical spells and effects by up to 16

Frostfire Ring: Finger, +10 INT, +10 STA, Classes: Mage, Equip: Increases damage and healing done by magical spells and effects by up to 30, Equip: Increases your spell critical strike rating by 14

Gem of Trapped Innocents: Neck, +9 STA, +7 INT, Equip: Increases damage and healing done by magical spells and effects by up to 15, Equip: Increases your spell critical strike rating by 28

Gressil, Dawn of Ruin: Sword One-Hand, 138-257 Damage, Speed 2.70, 73.1 damage per second, +15 STA, Equip: Increases attack power by 40

Hammer of the Twisting Nether: Mace Main Hand, 36-120 Damage, Speed 1.90, 41.1 damage per second, +8 STA, +11 INT, Equip: Increases healing done by spells and effects by up to 238, Equip: Restores 8 mana per 5 sec

Kingsfall: Dagger One-Hand, 105-158 Damage, Speed 1.80, 73.1 damage per second, +16 AGI, Equip: Increases your critical strike rating by 14, Equip: Increases your hit rating by 10

Might of Menethil: Two-Hand Mace Two-Hand, 289-435 Damage, Speed 3.80, 95.3 damage per second, +46 STA, +20 STR, Equip: Increases your critical strike rating by 28

Nerubian Slavemaker: Crossbow, 151-281 Damage, Speed 3.20, 67.5 damage per second, Equip: Increases attack power by 24, Equip: Increases your critical strike rating by 14

Plagueheart Ring: Finger, +24 STA, Classes: Warlock, Equip: Increases damage and healing done by magical spells and effects by up to 29

Ring of Faith: Finger, +16 INT, +16 SPI, Classes: Priest, Equip: Increases healing done by spells and effects by up to 55

Ring of Redemption: Finger, +16 STA, +16 INT, Classes: Paladin, Equip: Increases healing done by spells and effects by up to 37, Equip: Restores 6 mana per 5 sec

Ring of the Cryptstalker: Finger, +20 AGI, Classes: Hunter, Equip: Restores 6 mana per 5 sec, Equip: Increases attack power by 40

Ring of the Dreadnaught: Finger, +27 STA, Classes: Warrior, Equip: Increases your dodge rating by 12, Equip: Increases defense rating by 15

Ring of the Dreamwalker: Finger, +16 STA, +16 INT, +16 SPI, Classes: Druid, Equip: Increases healing done by spells and effects by up to 37

Ring of the Earthshatterer: Finger, +16 STA, +16 INT, Classes: Shaman, Equip: Increases healing done by spells and effects by up to 37, Equip: Restores 6 mana per 5 sec

Shield of Condemnation: Shield, 3936 Armor, 90 Block, +10 STA, +10 INT, Equip: Restores 6 mana per 5 sec, Equip: Increases healing done by spells and effects by up to 59

Soulseeker: Staff Two-Hand, 142-265 Damage, Speed 3.20, 63.6 damage per second, +30 STA, +31 INT, Equip: Increases damage and healing done by magical spells and effects by up to 126, Equip: Increases your spell critical strike rating by 28, Equip: Increases your spell penetration by 25

Stormrage's Talisman of Seething: Neck, +12 STA, Equip: Increases your critical strike rating by 28, Equip: Increases attack power by 26

The Hungering Cold: Sword One-Hand, 140 Armor, 76-143 Damage, Speed 1.50, 73.0 damage per second, +14 STA, Equip: Increases sword skill rating by 14

The Phylactery of Kel'Thuzad

HP	3198000	Damage	6389-8458

Abilities

Frost Blast: Stuns the target and all nearby targets for 5 sec., decreasing their health by 25% per sec.

Shadow Fissure: Creates a glowing circle on the floor of Kel'Thuzad's chamber. After 5 sec., this fissure explodes, triggering a Void Blast.
Void Blast: Deals 62500 to 137500 Shadow damage to a target standing on top of Shadow Fissure.

Detonate Mana: After 5 sec., the target's mana is reduced by 50%, dealing damage to all nearby allies equal to the mana expended.

Frost Bolt: Inflicts 7438 to 9562 Frost damage and reduces movement speed by 65% for 4 sec.

Berserk: Physical damage dealt is increased by 500. Kel'Thuzad begins to periodically cast an area-of-effect Frost Bolt. See below – this is not the same as the other Frost Bolt he uses during the fight. **Frost Bolt**: Inflicts 2550 to 3450 Frost damage, reducing their movement speed by 50% for 4 sec.

Chains of Kel'Thuzad: Charms up to 5 targets, forcing them to serve Kel'Thuzad for 20 sec. Increases the target's damage by 200% and healing by 500%.

PHASE 1 ABILITIES

SOLDIER OF THE FROZEN WASTES

Low hit points, can be Shackled, relatively slow moving.

If it gets within melee range of its target, it casts Dark Blast which hits everyone in the area for around 2,000 damage and destroys the skeleton.

The skeletons should be Shackled and killed quickly. Every spawn point has a ranged DPS and a Priest assigned to it to handle the Soldiers that come.

SOUL WEAVER

High hit points, very slow.

If it gets within melee range of its target, it casts Wail of Souls which knocks everyone in front of it back and does around 4,500 damage.

The banshees must be focused fired one at a time by the Mages. They have to die very quickly and in the order that they attack.

UNSTOPPABLE ABOMINATION

Average hit points and movement speed.

Afflicts the person it is attacking with Mortal Wound. This reduces healing on the target by 10% with each application.

The melee DPS are in charge of taking down the abominations. The Mortal Wound really isn't a big deal since they should die very quickly. Get them tanked and DPS them down one at a time.

PHASE 2 ABILITIES

CHAINS OF KEL'THUZAD

Explanation: Mind Controls 4 random players. Threat list is cleared.

Solution: CC the Mind Controlled players and get Kel'Thuzad tanked again. Everyone has to be very careful with agro after a Mind Control until he is back on a tank.

FROST BLAST

Explanation: Randomly turns a few players and anyone near them into ice blocks. While in the ice block the player loses 20% of their health every second for 5 seconds.

Solution: Stay spread out so that as few people as possible are turned into ice blocks. The melee DPS are the most susceptible to this attack so they need to stay as spread out. Anyone who gets turned into an ice block needs at least 1 heal or they are going to die. The damage dealt to them is percentage based; one heal keeps them alive.

FROST BOLT – AOE

Explanation: Kel'Thuzad hits everyone in the room for around 3,000 damage.

Solution: You can't prevent it but it is resistible, both partially and entirely. A tiny bit of frost resistance gear and the occasional Greater Frost Resistance potion can help a lot. But players are hit by the AoE Frost Bolt and they simply need to be healed back up.

FROST BOLT – SINGLE TARGET

Explanation: 2.5 second cast time, hits the current target with a powerful Frost Bolt for up to 9,500 damage. This spell is interruptible.

Solution: You must interrupt the single target Frost Bolt. It has a fairly long cast time and is easy to catch. Failure to interrupt it can result in the death of a tank since it hits for so much damage.

GUARDIANS OF ICECROWN

Explanation: At 40% life, Kel'Thuzad summons 5 adds called Guardians of Icecrown. Up to 3 can be Shackled. If you try to Shackle more than 3, all of the Shackles are removed. Additionally, every time they change their agro target, their damage is increased by 15%.

Solution: Shackle the first 3 and keep them shackled. Don't shackle any more than 3! The last two can be tanked by a Warrior in DPS gear as long as they haven't been running around changing targets and getting their damage buffed. If the Warriors pick them up quickly, they can easily take the hits. Don't try to kill the Guardians; CC and offtank them.

MANA DETONATION

Explanation: Hits a random player with mana. After 5 seconds, the player blows up and loses half of their mana pool while dealing half of their mana pool worth of damage to all the players within 10 yards of them.

Solution: The player who gets Mana Detonation simply runs away from everyone nearby within 5 seconds. They lose half of their mana but hopefully they won't hurt anyone around them.

SHADOW FISSURE

Explanation: Randomly places Shadow Fissures on the ground under a player. These are black and purple glowing circles that instantly kill anyone on top of them.

Solution: There is a good 5 seconds before the Shadow Fissure opens and actually starts doing damage. Anyone who sees black and purple runes glowing under their feet needs to quickly move out of the way and let the Shadow Fissure open. It disappears shortly after.

PREPARATION

Assign a Priest and a ranged DPS class—preferably a Hunter or a Warlock—to each of the 7 cubbies that the phase 1 spawns are in. These Priest/DPS duos are in charge of killing any skeletons that come charging out of the cubby and into the raid.

Setup an assist for the Mages; they are in charge of taking down the banshees one at a time as quickly as they can.

Kel'Thuzad himself needs about 3 tanks because of the Mind Control. Assign the 3 tanks and give them the usual tanking groups. Additionally, these tanks are in charge of keeping the phase 1 abominations under control.

PHASE 1 STRATEGY

Everybody charges into the room at the same time. Head towards the circle in the middle; this is where you stay for all of the first phase. The Priest/DPS duos should find their assigned cubby and be ready to kill any approaching skeletons. The Mages are watching out for banshees and ready to kill them. The tanks and melee DPS are waiting for abominations to come.

You don't actually pull anything; you wait for things to come to you. If you try to pull a mob, it links with other nearby mobs resulting in a huge pull. Just sit in the middle of the room and be ready to do your job.

At the beginning of this phase, the mobs don't come very fast. A skeleton here, a banshee there, the occasional abomination, no big deal. This phase lasts 5 minutes and the rate at which the adds come to you speeds up. Towards the end of the phase, several of each type of add are agro.

Priests/DPS duos kill the skeletons that come from your cubby as quickly as possible. Since the spawns randomly agro, not all cubbies get the same amount. Try to help your neighboring cubby while still making sure that your's is under control. If you are standing there doing nothing for long periods of time, you're probably doing something wrong.

The Mages take out the banshees as quickly as they can. It is of the utmost importance that the banshees do not get out of control. You don't want to go into phase 2 with 5 banshees running around, you need to have almost all of them dead before the next phase begins.

Abominations aren't a very big deal. They run into the raid, they get tanked, they get killed by melee DPS. Keep them tanked and kill them quickly.

After 5 minutes of handling the spawns, everything that isn't already agro despawns and Kel'Thuzad engages. Phase 2 begins.

PHASE 2 STRATEGY

Clean up the adds from the first phase. There should be no skeletons or abominations alive, but there may be a couple banshees leftover. All of the ranged DPS can focus the banshees and get them down quickly.

The tanks run over to Kel'Thuzad and get ready to pick him up as soon as he becomes attackable. Once a tank has agro, let them keep agro until the Mind Control.

Nothing is predictable. All of Kel'Thuzad's abilities happen at random. It is up to the players to know how to counter every single one of his abilities.

The biggest threat is the Mind Control. DPS has a tendency to pull agro after a Mind Control, before Kel'Thuzad is back on a tank. You have to be very careful when a Mind Control happens. Let the tanks pick him up before you do anything! Another Mind Control related problem can occur if all of your tanks get hit by it. This happens rarely and there is no counter; you're in trouble. Try to kite Kel'Thuzad or maybe have a non-tanking Warrior use Shield Wall to hold him until the Mind Controls wear off. Finally, make sure the CC on the Mind Controlled players happens quickly and they stay CC'ed until it wears off. Players can do a lot of damage to the raid while Mind Controlled.

Another problem can be the Frost Blasts and ice blocks. Stay spread out so that the ice blocks do not affect more than 3 or 4 people at a time. It can be hard to get more than a couple heals off before the 5 seconds are up, and everyone who gets turned into an ice block needs to get at least one heal.

As long as the single target Frost Bolt is being interrupted consistently, it is not a very big deal.

The AoE Frost Bolts do a fair amount of damage, but since they are resistible they can be hit or miss. Most of the healing that isn't on the current tank should be focused on keeping everyone topped off so that they don't die to an AoE Frost Bolt.

Shadow Fissures are very easy to counter. Pay attention and move quickly when the runes appear beneath your feet.

At 40%, Kel'Thuzad spawns 5 Guardians of Icecrown. Shackle the first 3, but do not Shackle any more than 3 or all of the Shackles are removed. Get offtanks on the last 2 and don't let them change targets very often; if they change their agro target, their damage is increased by 15%. Warriors in DPS gear can easily tank a Guardian as long as they haven't had their damage increased more than once or twice. Don't try to kill the Guardians, focus on CC'ing and offtanking them. The Guardians should not be a huge threat as long as they don't get out of control.

The fight is chaotic since all of the abilities are random and there are many different attacks. It's a matter of knowing what the abilities are and how to counter them. With some practice, a lot of execution, and a little bit of luck, the Lich King is going to be very displeased in Kel'Thuzad for being defeated.

THE PHYLACTERY OF KEL'THUZAD

Much like Onyxia, Nefarian, and C'thun, Kel'Thuzad always drops an item that starts a quest called The Phylactery of Kel'Thuzad.

This item is used to start the quest The Fall of Kel'Thuzad which is turned in to Father Inigo Montoy at Light's Hope Chapel. You have the choice of two rewards:

Mark of the Champion (Physical): Trinket, Equip: Increases attack power by 150 when fighting Undead and Demons. It also allows the acquisition of Scourgestones on behalf of the Argent Dawn.

Mark of the Champion (Magic): Trinket, Equip: Increases damage done to Undead and Demons by magical spells and effects by up to 85. It also allows the acquisition of Scourgestones on behalf of the Argent Dawn.

ATIESH

Every boss in Naxxramas has a 36% chance to drop a Splinter of Atiesh. Atiesh is a very powerful staff originally owned by Medivh before being shattered at the destruction of Dalaran many years before.

Atiesh can be used by Druids, Mages, Priests, and Warlocks. Each class' version of the staff has slightly different stats.

Any player of these classes that collects 40 Splinters of Atiesh from the various Naxxramas bosses can combine the Splinters to form the Frame of Atiesh and begin the quest. The quest starts by sending you to speak with Anachronos outside of the Caverns of Time in Tanaris. He informs you that in order to complete Atiesh the Base and Head are needed.

The Base is a quest item that drops off of C'thun. Anyone who has the Atiesh quest can loot the Base and it always drops.

The Head is another quest item that drops off of Kel'Thuzad. Just like the Base, anyone with the quest can loot it and it is guaranteed to drop.

As soon as you have gathered the Base and the Head, return to Anachronos. At this point he provides you with a corrupted version of the staff. You must head to Stratholme to cleanse it.

Zone into Stratholme through the back gate. The rune where Atiesh, Hand of Sargeras is summoned is located in the courtyard through the left gate after entering the back door of Stratholme; it's near the fountain in the middle. Clear the area around the rune and use the quest item to summon the demon.

This demon is not a joke. He hits like a truck and has a pulsing AoE shadow damage aura. After a few moments of fighting him, his weapon can be disarmed. It is an extremely good sword that the melee DPS in your group should pick up and use against him.

With a few practice runs and maybe some consumables, Atiesh, Hand of Sargeras is slain and Atiesh is cleansed. Return to Anachronos to complete the quest and obtain the staff.

DRUID:

Atiesh, Greatstaff of the Guardian: Staff, 130-242 Damage, Speed: 2.90, 64.4 damage per second, +28 STA, +28 INT, +27 SPI, Equip: Restores 11 mana per 5 seconds to all party members within 30 yards, Equip: Increases healing done by spells and effects by up to 300, Equip: Increases attack power by 420 in Cat, Bear, Dire Bear, and Moonkin forms only, Use: Creates a portal, teleporting group members that use it to Karazhan.

MAGE:

Atiesh, Greatstaff of the Guardian: Staff, 130-242 Damage, Speed: 2.90, 64.4 damage per second, +31 STA, +32 INT, +24 SPI, Equip: Increases your spell hit rating by 15, Equip: Increases damage and healing done by magical spells and effects by up to 150, Equip: Increases the spell critical strike rating of all party members within 30 yards by 28, Use: Creates a portal, teleporting group members that use it to Karazhan.

PRIEST:

Atiesh, Greatstaff of the Guardian: Staff, 130-242 Damage, Speed: 2.90, 64.4 damage per second, +28 STA, +28 INT, +27 SPI, Equip: Increases healing done by magical spells and effects of all party members within 30 yards by up to 62, Equip: Increases your spell damage by up to 120 and your healing by up to 300, Use: Creates a portal, teleporting group members that use it to Karazhan.

WARLOCK:

Atiesh, Greatstaff of the Guardian: Staff, 130-242 Damage, Speed: 2.90, 64.4 damage per second, +30 STA, +29 INT, Equip: Increases your spell critical strike rating by 28, Equip: Increases damage and healing done by magical spells and effects by up to 150, Equip: Increases damage and healing done by magical spells and effects of all party members within 30 yards by up to 33, Use: Creates a portal, teleporting group members that use it to Karazhan.

ARMOR SETS

The Armorsmiths at Blizzard have been busy. Three new Raid sets have been crafted for each class. This section highlights each set completely and piece by piece. In addition to the statistics, this section allows you to see what they look like on.

ACQUISITION

Along with the armor comes a new system for armor drops. Bosses no longer drop random armor pieces, but token that can be turned in for an armor piece. With the new token system, it is easier to make a Raid run worth while, as up to three classes can trade a token in for the piece of armor it is affiliated towards. Specific armor token drop off certain bosses, but since up to three classes can use each token, almost always the gear benefits someone.

SET LIST

Each class has a list of armor sets designed to specifically enhance their roles and augment their abilities. Here is a list so that you'll have an idea what to look for in the tables that follow.

DRUID

| Tier 4 Raid Set | Malorne Harness/Malorne Raiment/ Malorne Regalia |
| Tier 5 Raid Set | Nordrassil Harness/Nordrassil Raiment/ Nordrassil Regalia |

HUNTER

Tier 4 Raid Set	Demon Stalker
Tier 5 Raid Set	Rift Stalker

MAGE

Tier 4 Raid Set	Aldor Regalia
Tier 5 Raid Set	Tirisfal Regalia

PALADIN

Tier 4 Raid Set	Justicar Raiment/Justicar Armor/ Justicar Battlegear
Tier 5 Raid Set	Crystalforge Raiment/Crystalforge Armor/Crystalforge Battlegear

PRIEST

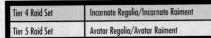

Tier 4 Raid Set	Incarnate Regalia/Incarnate Raiment
Tier 5 Raid Set	Avatar Regalia/Avatar Raiment

ROGUE

Tier 4 Raid Set	Netherblade
Tier 5 Raid Set	Deathmantle

SHAMAN

Tier 4 Raid Set	Cyclone Harness/Cyclone Raiment/ Cyclone Regalia
Tier 5 Raid Set	Cataclysm Harness/Cataclysm Raiment/ Cataclysm Regalia

WARLOCK

Tier 4 Raid Set	Voidheart Raiment
Tier 5 Raid Set	Corruptor Raiment

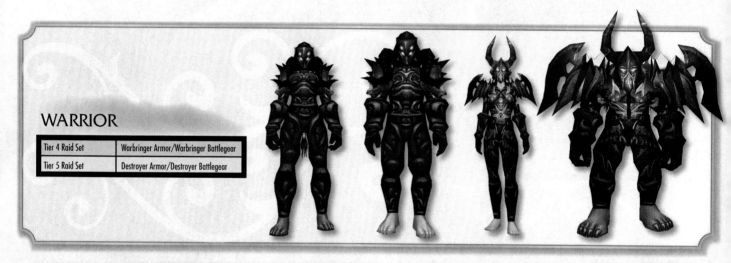

WARRIOR

Tier 4 Raid Set	Warbringer Armor/Warbringer Battlegear
Tier 5 Raid Set	Destroyer Armor/Destroyer Battlegear

MALORNE HARNESS

2 Pieces: Your melee attacks in Bear Form and Dire Bear Form have a chance to generate 10 additional Rage. Your melee attacks in Cat Form have a chance to generate 20 additional energy.

4 Pieces: Increases your armor by 1400 in Bear Form and Dire Bear Form. Increases your strength by 30 in Cat Form.

ITEM	ARM	AGI	INT	SPI	STA	STR
Stag-Helm of Malorne	490	33	19		30	41
Equip: Increases to hit rating by 12.						
Mantle of Malorne	410	27	9		25	33
Breastplate of Malorne	659	34	13		36	33
Gauntlets of Malorne	475		12		28	32
Equip: Increases critical strike rating by 24.						
Greaves of Malorne	640	32	26		39	42

MALORNE REGALIA

2 Pieces: Your harmful spells have a chance to restore up to 120 mana.

4 Pieces: Reduces the cooldown on your Innervate ability by 48 seconds.

ITEM	ARM	AGI	INT	SPI	STA	STR
Antlers of Malorne	308		29	22	28	
Equip: Increase spell critical strike rating by 24, Increases damage and healing effects done by magic spells and effects by 36.						
Pauldrons of Malorne	284		24	17	21	
Equip: Restores 5 mana per 5 seconds, Increases damage and healing effects done by magic spells and effects by 36.						
Chestpiece of Malorne	379		27	19	28	
Equip: Increases spell to hit rating by 19, Increases damage and healing effects done by magic spells and effects by 46.						
Gloves of Malorne	237		27	21	24	
Equip: Increase spell critical strike rating by 18, Increases damage and healing effects done by magic spells and effects by 33.						
Britches of Malorne	332		35	18	32	
Equip: Increase spell critical strike rating by 25, Restores 6 mana per 5 seconds, Increases damage and healing effects done by magic spells and effects by 44.						

MALORNE RAIMENT

2 Pieces: Your helpful spells have a chance to restore up to 120 mana.

4 Pieces: Reduces the cooldown on your Nature's Swiftness ability by 24 seconds.

ITEM	ARM	AGI	INT	SPI	STA	STR
Crown of Malorne	308		27	25	28	
Equip: Restores 10 mana per 5 seconds, Increases healing done by spells and effects by 68.						
Shoulderguards of Malorne	284		23	19	19	
Equip: Restores 5 mana per 5 seconds, Increases healing effects done by magic spells and effects by 68.						
Chestguard of Malorne	379		29	25	28	
Equip: Increases healing effects done by magic spells and effects by 88.						
Handguards of Malorne	237		25	24	22	
Equip: Restores 7 mana per 5 seconds, Increases healing effects done by magic spells and effects by 62.						
Legguards of Malorne	332		38	26	30	
Equip: Restores 5 mana per 5 seconds, Increases healing effects done by magic spells and effects by 68.						

NORDRASSIL HARNESS

2 Pieces: When you shift out of Bear Form, Dire Bear Form, or Cat Form, your next Regrowth spell takes 2 fewer seconds to cast.

4 Pieces: your Shred ability deals an additional 75 damage, and your Lacerate ability does an additional 15 per application.

ITEM	ARM	AGI	INT	SPI	STA	STR
Nordrassil Headdress	565	33	17		43	46
Nordrassil Feral-Mantle	468	34	11		28	35
Nordrassil Chestplate	727	30	17		43	46
Nordrassil Handgrips	514	27	18		40	35
Equip: Increases to hit rating by 14.						
Nordrassil Feral-Kilt	703	37	17		42	46
Equip: Increases to hit rating by 18.						

NORDRASSIL RAIMENT

2 Pieces: Increases the duration of your Regrowth spell by 6 seconds.

4 Pieces: Increases the final amount healed by your Lifebloom spell by 150.

ITEM	ARM	AGI	INT	SPI	STA	STR
Nordrassil Headguard	341		28	31	40	
Equip: Restores 8 mana per 5 seconds, Increases healing done by spells and effects by 103.						
Nordrassil Life-Mantle	314		27	16	26	
Equip: Restores 6 mana per 5 seconds, Increases healing done by spells and effects by 77.						
Nordrassil Chestguard	419		33	31	36	
Equip: Increases healing done by spells and effects by 103.						
Nordrassil Gloves	262		27	24	26	
Equip: Restores 9 mana per 5 seconds, Increases healing done by spells and effects by 77.						
Nordrassil Life-Kilt	367		36	27	37	
Equip: Restores 11 mana per 5 seconds, Increases healing done by spells and effects by 101.						

NORDRASSIL REGALIA

2 Pieces: When you shift out of Moonkin Form, your next Regrowth spell costs 450 less mana.

4 Pieces: Increases your Starfire damage against targets afflicted with Moonfire or Insect Swarm by 10%.

ITEM	ARM	AGI	INT	SPI	STA	STR
Nordrassil Headpiece	341		28	24	35	
Equip: Increases spell to hit rating by 10, Increases spell critical strike rating by 25, Increases damage and healing effects done by magic spells and effects by 54.						
Nordrassil Wrath-Mantle	314		27	16	26	
Equip: Increases spell to hit rating by 15, Increases damage and healing effects done by magic spells and effects by 41.						
Nordrassil Chestpiece	419		32	25	36	
Equip: Increases spell to hit rating by 19, Increases spell critical strike rating by 17, Increases damage and healing effects done by magic spells and effects by 54.						
Nordrassil Gauntlets	262		27	23	26	
Equip: Increases spell to hit rating by 15, Increases spell critical strike rating by 24, Increases damage and healing effects done by magic spells and effects by 41.						
Nordrassil Wrath-Kilt	367		36	26	37	
Equip: Increases spell to hit rating by 15, Increases spell critical strike rating by 26, Restores 7 mana per 5 seconds, Increases damage and healing effects done by magic spells and effects by 54.						

DEMON STALKER

2 Pieces: Reduces the chance you Feign Death ability will be resisted by 5%.

4 Pieces: Reduces the mana cost of you Multi-Shot ability by 10%.

ITEM	ARM	AGI	INT	SPI	STA	STR
Demon Stalker Greathelm	687	35	27		28	
Equip: Increases attack power by 66.						
Demon Stalker Shoulderguards	634		23		23	
Equip: Increases critical strike rating by 19, Increases attack power by 44, Restores 5 mana per 5 seconds.						
Demon Stalker Harness	846	26	35		24	
Equip: Increases attack power by 70, Restores 6 mana per 5 seconds.						
Demon Stalker Gauntlets	528	28	24		24	
Equip: Increases attack power by 58, Restores 6 mana per 5 seconds.						
Demon Stalker Greaves	740	40	30		30	
Equip: Increases to hit rating by 15, Increases attack power by 82.						

RIFT STALKER

2 Pieces: Your pet's attacks have a chance to heal you pet for 172 to 198.

4 Pieces: Your Steady Shot ability has a 5% increased critical strike chance.

ITEM	ARM	AGI	INT	SPI	STA	STR
Rift Stalker Helm	759	40	25		36	
Equip: Increases attack power by 82, Restores 10 mana per 5 seconds.						
Rift Stalker Mantle	700	26	24		26	
Equip: Increases to hit rating by 13, Increases attack power by 52.						
Rift Stalker Hauberk	934	40	19		40	
Equip: Increases to hit rating by 19, Increases attack power by 80, Restores 7 mana per 5 seconds.						
Rift Stalker Gauntlets	583	34	20		29	
Equip: Increases to hit rating by 19, Increases critical strike rating by 23, Increases attack power by 68.						
Rift Stalker Leggings	817	40	26		39	
Equip: Increases to hit rating by 18, Increases attack power by 92, Restores 7 mana per 5 seconds.						

ALDOR REGALIA

2 Pieces: Gives you a 100% chance to avoid interruption caused by damage while casting Fireball or Frostbolt.

4 Pieces: Reduces the cooldown on Presence of Mind by 24 seconds, on Blast Wave by 4 seconds, and on Ice Block by 40 seconds.

ITEM	ARM	AGI	INT	SPI	STA	STR
Collar of the Aldor	164		35	17	24	
Equip: Increases spell critical strike rating by 27, Increases damage and healing effects done by magic spells and effects by 41.						
Pauldrons of the Aldor	152		26	16	25	
Equip: Increases spell critical strike rating by 15, Increases damage and healing effects done by magic spells and effects by 27.						
Vestments of the Aldor	202		32	14	34	
Equip: Increases damage and healing effects done by magic spells and effects by 49.						
Gloves of the Aldor	126		22	19	19	
Equip: Increases spell to hit rating by 17, Increases spell critical strike rating by 19, Increases damage and healing effects done by magic spells and effects by 35.						
Legwraps of the Aldor	177		40	23	31	
Equip: Increases damage and healing effects done by magic spells and effects by 49.						

TIRISFAL REGALIA

2 Pieces: Increases the damage and mana cost of Arcane Blast by 20%.

4 Pieces: Your spell critical strikes grant you up to 70 spell damage for 6 seconds.

ITEM	ARM	AGI	INT	SPI	STA	STR
Crown of Tirisfal	181		36	24	30	
Equip: Increases spell critical strike rating by 24, Increases damage and healing effects done by magic spells and effects by 55.						
Mantle of Tirisfal	168		24	24	22	
Equip: Increases spell to hit rating by 11, Increases spell critical strike rating by 17, Increases damage and healing effects done by magic spells and effects by 40.						
Robes of Tirisfal	223		35	20	30	
Equip: Increases spell critical strike rating by 19, Increases damage and healing effects done by magic spells and effects by 55.						
Gloves of Tirisfal	140		27	18	26	
Equip: Increases spell critical strike rating by 27, Increases damage and healing effects done by magic spells and effects by 41.						
Legging of Tirisfal	195		36	26	37	
Equip: Increases spell to hit rating by 26, Increases spell critical strike rating by 17, Increases damage and healing effects done by magic spells and effects by 54.						

JUSTICAR RAIMENT

2 Pieces: Increases the amount healed by your Judgement of Light by 20.

4 Pieces: Reduces the cooldown of your Divine Favor ability by 15 seconds.

ITEM	ARM	AGI	INT	SPI	STA	STR
Justicar Diadem	1227		33		32	
Equip: Increases spell critical strike rating by 28, Restores 6 mana per 5 seconds, Increases healing done by spells and effects by 90.						
Justicar Pauldrons	1133		24		31	
Equip: Restores 5 mana per 5 seconds, Increases healing done by spells and effects by 68.						
Justicar Chestpiece	1510		35		28	
Equip: Increases spell critical strike rating by 17, Restores 6 mana per 5 seconds, Increases healing done by spells and effects by 90.						
Justicar Gloves	944		30		29	
Equip: Increases spell critical strike rating by 22, Increases healing done by spells and effects by 75.						
Justicar Leggings	1322		42		43	
Equip: Restores 11 mana per 5 seconds, Increases healing done by spells and effects by 88.						

JUSTICAR ARMOR

2 Pieces: Increases the damage dealt by your Seal of Righteousness, Seal of Vengeance, or Seal of Blood by 10%.

4 Pieces: Increases the damage dealt by your Holy Shield by 15%.

ITEM	ARM	AGI	INT	SPI	STA	STR
Justicar Faceguard	1227		24		43	
Equip: Improves defense rating by 29, Increases your dodge rating by 24, Increases damage and healing done by magical spells and effects by 27.						
Justicar Shoulderguards	1133		14		37	
Equip: Improves defense rating by 15, Increases your shield block rating by 17, Increases the block value of your shield by rating by 27, Increases damage and healing done by magical spells and effects by 26.						
Justicar Chestguard	1510		30		48	
Equip: Improves defense rating by 23, Increases your shield block rating by 23, Increases damage and healing done by magical spells and effects by 27.						
Justicar Handguards	944		24		34	
Equip: Improves defense rating by 23, Increases the block value of your shield by 35, Increases damage and healing done by magical spells and effects by 27.						
Justicar Legguards	1322		31		46	
Equip: Improves defense rating by 31, Increases your parry rating by 31, Increases damage and healing done by magical spells and effects by 36.						

JUSTICAR BATTLEGEAR

2 Pieces: Increases the damage bonus of your Judgement of the Crusader by 15%.

4 Pieces: Increases the damage dealt by your Judgement of Command by 10%.

ITEM	ARM	AGI	INT	SPI	STA	STR
Justicar Crown	1227	22	31		33	25
Equip: Increases damage and healing done by magical spells and effects by 36.						
Justicar Shoulderplates	1133	13	15		24	25
Equip: Increases hit rating by 16, Increases damage and healing done by magical spells and effects by 27.						
Justicar Breastplate	1510		33		24	29
Equip: Increases critical strike rating by 25, Increases damage and healing done by magical spells and effects by 30.						
Justicar Gauntlets	944		24		29	27
Equip: Increases critical strike rating by 24, Increases damage and healing done by magical spells and effects by 26.						
Justicar Greaves	1322	24	24		34	35
Equip: Restores 9 mana per 5 seconds, Increases damage and healing done by magical spells and effects by 41.						

CRYSTALFORGE RAIMENT

2 Pieces: Increases the armor granted by your Devotion Aura ability by 350.

4 Pieces: Reduces the casting time of your Holy Light spell by .25 seconds.

ITEM	ARM	AGI	INT	SPI	STA	STR
Crystalforge Greathelm	1355		28		37	
Equip: Increases spell critical strike rating by 24, Restores 10 mana per 5 seconds, Increases healing done by spells and effects by 103.						
Cyrstalforge Pauldrons	1251		26		34	
Equip: Increases spell critical strike rating by 16, Increases healing done by spells and effects by 77.						
Crystalforge Chestpiece	1668		36		30	
Equip: Increases spell critical strike rating by 31, Increases healing done by spells and effects by 103.						
Crystalforge Gloves	1042		25		31	
Equip: Increases spell critical strike rating by 24, Restores 9 mana per 5 seconds, Increases healing done by spells and effects by 77.						
Crystalforge Leggings	1459		36		37	
Equip: Increases spell critical strike rating by 32, Restores 10 mana per 5 seconds, Increases healing done by spells and effects by 101.						

CRYSTALFORGE ARMOR

2 Pieces: Increases the damage from your Retribution Aura by 15.

4 Pieces: Each time your use your Holy Shield ability you gain 100 block value against a single attack in the next 6 seconds.

ITEM	ARM	AGI	INT	SPI	STA	STR
Crystalforge Faceguard	1355		28		48	
Equip: Improves defense rating by 28, Increases your shield block rating by 19, Increases the block value of your shield by rating by 40, Increases damage and healing done by magical spells and effects by 36.						
Crystalforge Shoulderguards	1251		26		38	
Equip: Improves defense rating by 26, Increases your parry rating by 19, Increases damage and healing done by magical spells and effects by 22.						
Crystalforge Chestguard	1668		27		55	
Equip: Improves defense rating by 28, Increases the block value of your shield by rating by 51, Increases damage and healing done by magical spells and effects by 32.						
Crystalforge Handguards	1042		21		40	
Equip: Improves defense rating by 27, Increases your shield block rating by 22, Increases the block value of your shield by rating by 30, Increases damage and healing done by magical spells and effects by 29.						
Crystalforge Legguards	1459		27		54	
Equip: Improves defense rating by 35, Increases your shield block rating by 25, Increases the block value of your shield by rating by 35, Increases damage and healing done by magical spells and effects by 41.						

CRYSTALFORGE BATTLEGEAR

2 Pieces: reduces the cost of your Judgements by 35.

4 Pieces: Each time you cast a Judgement there is a chance it will heal all nearby party members for 244 to 256.

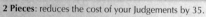

ITEM	ARM	AGI	INT	SPI	STA	STR
Crystalforge War-Helm	1355	24	23		46	33
Equip: Increases critical strike rating by 21, Increases damage and healing done by magical spells and effects by 47.						
Crystalforge Shoulderbraces	1251		15		34	30
Equip: Increases critical strike rating by 16, Increases damage and healing done by magical spells and effects by 35.						
Crystalforge Breastplate	1668		20		40	33
Equip: Improves hit rating by 23, Increases critical strike rating by 21, Increases damage and healing done by magical spells and effects by 47.						
Crystalforge Gauntlets	1042	25	23		35	30
Equip: Increases damage and healing done by magical spells and effects by 34.						
Crystalforge Greaves	1459	27	23		42	40
Equip: Improves to hit rating by 21, Increases critical strike rating by 22, Increases damage and healing done by magical spells and effects by 44.						

INCARNATE RAIMENT

2 Pieces: Your Prayer of Healing spell now also causes an additional 150 healing over 9 seconds.

4 Pieces: Each time you cast Flash Heal, your next Greater Heal cast within 15 seconds has its casting time reduced by .1, stacking up to 5 times.

PRIEST

ITEM	ARM	AGI	INT	SPI	STA	STR
Light-Collar of the Incarnate	164		34	25	28	
Equip: Restores 6 mana per 5 seconds, Increases healing done by spells and effects by 73.						
Light-Mantle of the Incarnate	152		30	22	19	
Equip: Increases healing done by spells and effects by 53.						
Robes of the Incarnate	202		32	20	30	
Equip: Increases healing done by spells and effects by 88.						
Handwraps of the Incarnate	126		26	18	28	
Equip: Restores 10 mana per 5 seconds, Increases healing done by spells and effects by 57.						
Trousers of the Incarnate	177		37	36	39	
Equip: Increases healing done by spells and effects by 88.						

INCARNATE REGALIA

2 Pieces: Your Shadowfiend now has 75 more stamina and lasts 3 seconds longer.

4 Pieces: Your Mind flay and Smite spells deal 5% more damage.

PRIEST

ITEM	ARM	AGI	INT	SPI	STA	STR
Soul-Collar of the Incarnate	164		35	24	28	
Equip: Improves spell hit rating by 16, Increases damage and healing done by magical spells and effects by 39.						
Soul-Mantle of the Incarnate	152		28	18	22	
Equip: Increases damage and healing done by magical spells and effects by 29.						
Shroud of the Incarnate	202		25	21	28	
Equip: Improves spell hit rating by 17, Increases damage and healing done by magical spells and effects by 46.						
Gloves of the Incarnate	126		26	21	28	
Equip: Improves spell critical strike rating by 24, Increases damage and healing done by magical spells and effects by 30.						
Leggings of the Incarnate	177		38	27	37	
Equip: Improves spell critical strike rating by 25, Increases damage and healing done by magical spells and effects by 43.						

AVATAR RAIMENT

2 Pieces: If your Greater Heal brings the target to full health you gain 100 mana.

4 Pieces: your Renew spell also increases all resistances by 15.

ITEM	ARM	AGI	INT	SPI	STA	STR
Cowl of the Avatar	181		28	31	40	
Equip: Restores 8 mana per 5 seconds, Increases healing done by spells and effects by 103.						
Mantle of the Avatar	168		26	20	26	
Equip: Improves spell critical strike rating by 16, Increases healing done by spells and effects by 77.						
Vestments of the Avatar	223		25	39	36	
Equip: Improves spell critical strike rating by 15, Increases healing done by spells and effects by 103.						
Gloves of the Avatar	140		27	29	26	
Equip: Restores 6 mana per 5 seconds, Increases healing done by spells and effects by 77.						
Breeches of the Avatar	195		36	27	37	
Equip: Restores 12 mana per 5 seconds, Increases healing done by spells and effects by 101.						

AVATAR REGALIA

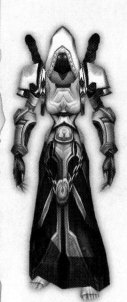

2 Pieces: Each time you cast an offensive spell, there is a chance you next spell will cost 150 lass mana.

4 Pieces: Each time your Shadow Word: Pain deals damage, it has a chance to grant your next spell cast within 15 seconds up to 100 damage and healing.

ITEM	ARM	AGI	INT	SPI	STA	STR
Hood of the Avatar	181		36	24	30	
Equip: Improves spell critical strike rating by 21, Improves spell hit rating by 24, Increases damage and healing done by magical spells and effects by 55.						
Wings of the Avatar	168		24	24	22	
Equip: Improves spell critical strike rating by 17, Improves spell hit rating by 15, Increases damage and healing done by magical spells and effects by 41.						
Shroud of the Avatar	223		35	20	30	
Equip: Improves spell critical strike rating by 23, Improves spell hit rating by 19, Increases damage and healing done by magical spells and effects by 55.						
Handguards of the Avatar	140		27	25	31	
Equip: Improves spell hit rating by 18, Increases damage and healing done by magical spells and effects by 41.						
Leggings of the Avatar	195		36	26	37	
Equip: Improves spell critical strike rating by 18, Improves spell hit rating by 25, Increases damage and healing done by magical spells and effects by 54.						

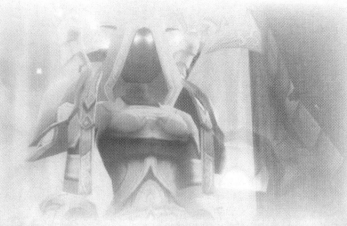

NETHERBLADE

2 Pieces: Increases the duration of your Slice and Dice ability by 3 seconds.

4 Pieces: Your finishing moves have a 15% chance of granting you a combo point.

ITEM	ARM	AGI	INT	SPI	STA	STR
Netherblade Facemask	308	28			39	
Equip: Improves to hit rating by 14, Improves critical strike rating by 29, Increases attack power by 78.						
Netherblade Shoulderpads	284	20			38	
Equip: Increases dodge rating by 10, Improves to hit rating by 13, Improves critical strike rating by 21, Increases attack power by 52.						
Netherblade Chestpiece	379	35			39	
Equip: Improves to hit rating by 11, Increases attack power by 74.						
Netherblade Gloves	237				34	
Equip: Improves to hit rating by 17, Improves critical strike rating by 25, Increases attack power by 72.						
Netherblade Breeches	332	43			40	
Equip: Improves to hit rating by 26, Increases attack power by 84.						

DEATHMANTLE

2 Pieces: Your Eviscerate and Envenom abilities cause 40 extra damage per combo point.

4 Pieces: Your attacks have a chance to make your next finishing move cost no energy.

ITEM	ARM	AGI	INT	SPI	STA	STR
Deathmantle Helm	341	39			48	
Equip: Improves critical strike rating by 25, Increases attack power by 78.						
Deathmantle Shoulderpads	314	34			37	
Equip: Increases dodge rating by 20, Improves critical strike rating by 13, Increases attack power by 54.						
Deathmantle Chestguard	419	33			57	
Equip: Improves to hit rating by 10, Improves critical strike rating by 17, Increases attack power by 94.						
Deathmantle Handguards	262	36			34	
Equip: Improves to hit rating by 24, Increases attack power by 70.						
Deathmantle Legguards	367	47			49	
Equip: Improves to hit rating by 15, Improves critical strike rating by 26, Increases attack power by 86.						

CYCLONE HARNESS

2 Pieces: Your Strength of Earth Totem ability grants an additional 12 strength.

4 Pieces: Your Stormstrike ability does and additional 30 damage per weapon.

ITEM	ARM	AGI	INT	SPI	STA	STR
Cyclone Helm	687	27	27		40	36
Cyclone Shouldplate	634	18	18		31	26
Equip: Increases to hit rating by 14.						
Cyclone Breastplate	846		23		31	33
Equip: Restores 8 mana per 5 seconds, Improves critical strike rating by 25.						
Cyclone Gauntlets	528	21	24		26	27
Equip: Restores 5 mana per 5 seconds, Improves hit rating by 19.						
Cyclone War-Kilt	740	35	24		52	35
Equip: Restores 10 mana per 5 seconds, Improves critical strike rating by 13.						

CYCLONE RAIMENT

2 Pieces: Your Mana Spring Totem ability grants an additional 3 mana every 2 seconds.

4 Pieces: Reduces the cooldown on your Nature's Swiftness ability by 24 seconds.

ITEM	ARM	AGI	INT	SPI	STA	STR
Cyclone Headdress	687		41		30	
Equip: Restores 8 mana per 5 seconds, Increases healing done by spells and effects by 75.						
Cyclone Shoulderpads	634		32		33	
Equip: Increases healing done by spells and effects by 68.						
Cyclone Hauberk	846		30		36	
Equip: Restores 10 mana per 5 seconds, Increases healing done by spells and effects by 68.						
Cyclone Gloves	528		28		28	
Equip: Restores 10 mana per 5 seconds, Increases healing done by spells and effects by 68.						
Cyclone Kilt	740		40		42	
Equip: Restores 11 mana per 5 seconds, Increases healing done by spells and effects by 95.						

CYCLONE REGALIA

2 Pieces: Your Wrath of Air Totem ability grants an additional 20 spell damage.

4 Pieces: Your offensive spell critical strikes have a chance to reduce the mana cost of your next spell by 270.

SHAMAN

ITEM	ARM	AGI	INT	SPI	STA	STR
Cyclone Faceguard	687		31		30	
Equip: Restores 8 mana per 5 seconds, Improves spell critical strike rating by 25, Increases damage and healing done by magic spells and effects by 39.						
Cyclone Shoulderguards	634		26		28	
Equip: Improves spell critical strike rating by 12, Increases damage and healing done by magic spells and effects by 36.						
Cyclone Chestguard	846		32		33	
Equip: Restores 8 mana per 5 seconds, Improves spell critical strike rating by 20, Increases damage and healing done by magic spells and effects by 39.						
Cyclone Handguards	528		29		26	
Equip: Restores 6 mana per 5 seconds, Improves spell hit rating by 19, Increases damage and healing done by magic spells and effects by 34.						
Cyclone Legguards	740		40		40	
Equip: Restores 8 mana per 5 seconds, Improves spell hit rating by 20, Increases damage and healing done by magic spells and effects by 49.						

CATACLYSM HARNESS

2 Pieces: Your melee attacks have a chance to reduce the cast time of your next Lesser Healing Wave by .1 second.

4 Pieces: You gain 5% additional haste from your Flurry ability.

SHAMAN

ITEM	ARM	AGI	INT	SPI	STA	STR
Cataclysm Helm	759	32	23		46	41
Equip: Improves hit rating by 21.						
Cataclysm Shoulderplates	700		21		37	30
Equip: Restores 6 mana per 5 seconds, Improves critical strike rating by 22.						
Cataclysm Chestplate	934	32	28		46	41
Equip: Improves hit rating by 19.						
Cataclysm Gauntlets	583	24	23		34	35
Equip: Increases hit rating by 24, Improves critical strike rating by 23.						
Cataclysm Legplates	817	32	31		31	41
Equip: Improves hit rating by 21.						

CATALYSM RAIMENT

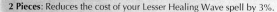

2 Pieces: Reduces the cost of your Lesser Healing Wave spell by 3%.

4 Pieces: Reduces the casting time of your Healing Wave spell by .2 seconds. In addition, your critical heals from Healing Wave, Lesser Healing Wave, and Chain Heal reduce the casting time of your next Healing Wave spell by .2 seconds.

ITEM	ARM	AGI	INT	SPI	STA	STR
Cataclysm Headguard	759		37		40	
Equip: Increases spell critical strike rating by 21, Increases healing done by spells and effects by 103.						
Cataclysm Shoulderguards	700		28		28	
Equip: Restores 8 mana per 5 seconds, Increases healing done by spells and effects by 79.						
Cataclysm Chestguard	934		33		36	
Equip: Restores 12 mana per 5 seconds, Improves spell critical strike rating by 24, Increases healing done by spells and effects by 90.						
Cataclysm Gloves	583		34		35	
Equip: Restores 6 mana per 5 seconds, Improves spell critical strike rating by 17, Increases healing done by spells and effects by 77.						
Cataclysm Legguards	817		47		48	
Equip: Restores 10 mana per 5 seconds, Increases healing done by spells and effects by 103.						

CATACLYSM REGALIA

SHAMAN

2 Pieces: Each time you cast an offensive spell, there is a chance your next Lesser Healing Wave will cost 380 less mana.

4 Pieces: Your Lightning Bolt critical strikes have a chance to grant you 120 mana.

ITEM	ARM	AGI	INT	SPI	STA	STR
Cataclysm Headpiece	759		28		35	
Equip: Restores 7 mana per 5 seconds, Improves spell critical strike rating by 26, Improves spell hit rating by 18, Increases damage and healing done by magic spells and effects by 54.						
Cataclysm Shoulderpads	700		19		26	
Equip: Restores 6 mana per 5 seconds, Improves spell critical strike rating by 24, Improves spell hit rating by 16, Increases damage and healing done by magic spells and effects by 41.						
Cataclysm Chestpiece	934		28		37	
Equip: Restores 10 mana per 5 seconds, Improves spell critical strike rating by 24, Improves spell hit rating by 10, Increases damage and healing done by magic spells and effects by 55.						
Cataclysm Handgrips	583		27		25	
Equip: Restores 7 mana per 5 seconds, Improves spell critical strike rating by 19, Improves spell hit rating by 19, Increases damage and healing done by magic spells and effects by 41.						
Cataclysm Leggings	817		46		48	
Equip: Improves spell critical strike rating by 24, Improves spell hit rating by 14, Increases damage and healing done by magic spells and effects by 54.						

VOIDHEART RAIMENT

2 Pieces: Your shadow damage spells have a chance to grant you 135 bonus shadow damage for 15 seconds and your fire damage spells have a chance to grant you 135 bonus fire damage for 15 seconds.

4 Pieces: Increases the duration of your Corruption and Immolate abilities by 3 seconds.

ITEM	ARM	AGI	INT	SPI	STA	STR
Voidheart Crown	164		36		39	
Equip: Improves spell critical strike rating by 19, Increases damage and healing done by magical spells by 40.
Voidheart Mantle	152		22		26	
Equip: Improves spell hit rating by 14, Increases damage and healing done by magical spells by 37.
Voidheart Robe	202		33		42	
Equip: Improves spell hit rating by 13, Increases damage and healing done by magical spells by 42.
Voidheart Gloves	126		28		34	
Equip: Improves spell critical strike rating by 22, Increases damage and healing done by magical spells by 35.
Voidheart Leggings	177		38		42	
Equip: Improves spell critical strike rating by 25, Improves spell hit rating by 17, Increases damage and healing done by magical spells by 49.

CORRUPTOR RAIMENT

2 Pieces: Healing spells heal your pet for 30% of the amount that they healed you.

4 Pieces: Your Shadowbolt spell hits increase the damage of Corruption by 3% and your Incinerate spell hits increase the damage of Immolate by 3%.

ITEM	ARM	AGI	INT	SPI	STA	STR
Hood of the Corruptor	181		33		57	
Equip: Improves spell critical strike rating by 31, Improves spell hit rating by 18, Increases damage and healing done by magical spells by 55.
Mantle of the Corruptor	168		24		37	
Equip: Improves spell critical strike rating by 21, Improves spell hit rating by 18, Increases damage and healing done by magical spells by 41.
Robe of the Corruptor	223		33		48	
Equip: Improves spell critical strike rating by 25, Improves spell hit rating by 23, Increases damage and healing done by magical spells by 55.
Gloves of the Corruptor	140		24		50	
Equip: Improves spell critical strike rating by 25, Improves spell hit rating by 11, Increases damage and healing done by magical spells by 42.
Leggings of the Corruptor	195		32		48	
Equip: Improves spell critical strike rating by 32, Improves spell hit rating by 24, Increases damage and healing done by magical spells by 55.

WARBRINGER ARMOR

2 Pieces: You have a chance each time you parry to gain Blade Turning, absorbing 200 damage for 15 seconds.

4 Pieces: Your Revenge ability causes your next damaging ability to do 10% more damage.

ITEM	ARM	AGI	INT	SPI	STA	STR
Warbringer Greathelm	1227	17			53	15
Equip: Improves defense rating by 24, Increases your shield block rating by 19, Increases the block value of your shield by rating by 39.						
Warbringer Shoulderguards	1133	15			38	14
Equip: Improves defense rating by 17, Increases your dodge rating by 26.						
Warbringer Chestguard	1510	17			48	16
Equip: Improves defense rating by 22, Increases your shield block rating by 23, Increases the block value of your shield by rating by 45.						
Warbringer Handguards	944	20			38	17
Equip: Improves defense rating by 23, Increases your parry rating by 29.						
Warbringer Legguards	1322	24			55	24
Equip: Improves defense rating by 33, Increases your dodge rating by 35.						

WARBRINGER BATTLEGEAR

2 Pieces: Your Whirlwind ability costs 5 less rage.

4 Pieces: You gain an additional 2 rage each time one of your attacks is parried or dodged.

ITEM	ARM	AGI	INT	SPI	STA	STR
Warbringer Battle-Helm	1227				45	45
Equip: Improves hit rating by 14, Improves critical strike rating by 24.						
Warbringer Shoulderpads	1133	22			33	32
Equip: Improves hit rating by 13.						
Warbringer Breastplate	1510				39	44
Equip: Improves critical strike rating by 26.						
Warbringer Gauntlets	944	23			33	34
Equip: Improves hit rating by 18.						
Warbringer Greaves	1322				54	51
Equip: Improves critical strike rating by 37.						

DESTROYER ARMOR

2 Pieces: Each time you use your Shield Block ability, you gain 100 block value against a single attack in the next 6 seconds.

4 Pieces: You have a chance each time you are hit to gain 200 haste rating for 10 seconds.

ITEM	ARM	AGI	INT	SPI	STA	STR
Destroyer Greathelm	1355	28			48	28
Equip: Improves defense rating by 30, Increases your dodge rating by 33.						
Destroyer Shoulderguards	1251	21			44	13
Equip: Improves defense rating by 29, Increases the block value of your shield by rating by 32.						
Destroyer Chestguard	1668	26			57	25
Equip: Improves defense rating by 27, Increases your dodge rating by 24, Improves hit rating by 24.						
Destroyer Handguards	1042	16			44	16
Equip: Improves defense rating by 25, Increases your shield block rating by 23, Increases the block value of your shield by rating by 44.						
Destroyer Legguards	1459	28			60	18
Equip: Improves defense rating by 39, Increases your shield block rating by 32, Increases the block value of your shield by rating by 33.						

DESTROYER BATTLEGEAR

2 Pieces: Your Overpower ability now grants you 100 attack power for 5 seconds.

4 Pieces: Your Bloodthirst and Mortal Strike abilities cost 5 less rage.

ITEM	ARM	AGI	INT	SPI	STA	STR
Destroyer Battle-Helm	1355				45	47
Equip: Improves hit rating by 21, Improves critical strike rating by 36.						
Destroyer Shoulderpads	1251				38	36
Equip: Improves hit rating by 18, Improves critical strike rating by 20.						
Destroyer Breastplate	1668				48	50
Equip: Improves hit rating by 15, Improves critical strike rating by 33.						
Destroyer Gauntlets	1042				46	44
Equip: Improves critical strike rating by 30.						
Destroyer Greaves	1459				57	52
Equip: Improves hit rating by 22, Improves critical strike rating by 32.						

Prepare To Baaaaa-ttle!

2 Polymorph

Ability — Arcane

Attach to target ally.

Attached ally can't attack or protect, loses all powers, and is a Sheep.

"Baaaaa."

AZEROTH 58/361   Art by: Vance Kovacs
©2006 UDC ©2006 Blizzard Entertainment, Inc.

World of WarCraft
TRADING CARD GAME

- Look for the latest booster set, Fires of Outland™, along with the Heroes of Outland™ and Through the Dark Portal™ starter sets.

- Each set contains new Loot™ cards to enhance your online character.

- Compete in tournaments for exclusive World of Warcraft® prizes!

Go to your local hobby store or visit
WWW.WOWTCG.COM

WORLD OF WARCRAFT
THE BURNING CRUSADE

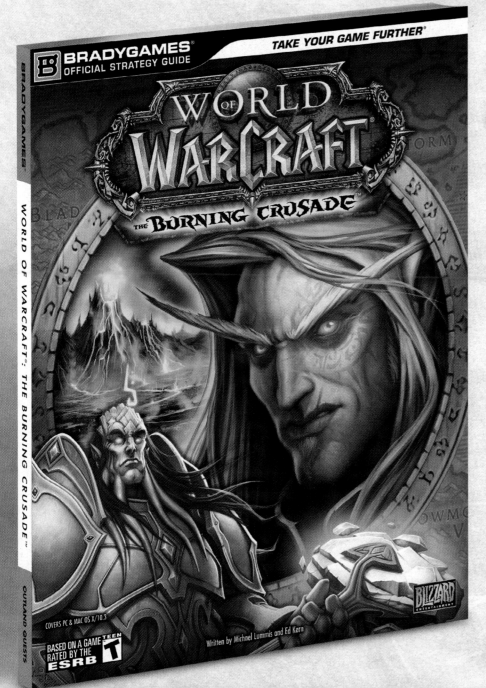

BRADYGAMES
OFFICIAL STRATEGY GUIDE

TAKE YOUR GAME FURTHER®

WORLD OF WARCRAFT
THE BURNING CRUSADE

COVERS PC & MAC OS X/10.3

BASED ON A GAME RATED BY THE ESRB — TEEN T

Written by Michael Lummis and Ed Kern

BLIZZARD ENTERTAINMENT

WORLD OF WARCRAFT: THE BURNING CRUSADE™

BRADYGAMES

Outland Quests

THE BURNING CRUSADE

NEW
- Races
- Maps
- PvP Combat

EXPANDED
- Weapons & Armor
- Quests
- Classes

UPDATED
- First Day
- Professions
- Factions

bradygames.com / wow

*For sale only at bradygames.com and its online affiliate partners.

BRADYGAMES

www.bradygames.com

BLIZZARD ENTERTAINMENT

www.worldofwarcraft.com

THE COMPANION TO THE #1 PC STRATEGY GUIDE IS HERE

Requires Zboard Gaming Keyboard. (Sold Separately)

OWNED.

ideazon.com/wow

DOMINATE

HALL OF HEROES

KAYAL

Michael Lummis
<Dovrani> Kirin Tor

Writing Credits: Shattered Halls, The Steamvault, Mana Tombs, Auchenai Crypts, Sethekk Halls, Shadow Labyrinth, Escape from Durnholde, Opening the Dark Portal, The Mechanar, The Botanica, The Arcatraz.

First, I would very much like to dedicate this book to Dr. Liviu Librescu, for heroism in a very real sense of the word. I dream of a world where we all shared such courage.

For my thanks, I stand by my gratitude from all previous World of Warcraft books. I owe each victory to my friends and helpers on the home front (steadfast Edwin Kern, the lovely Kathleen Pleet, Kurt "Grimclaw" Ricketts, and the unshakable Bret Preece, who joined us in this project). My hat is off, good fellows.

At Brady, I thank our inspired designers and my skilled editor, Brian Shotton, who has probably seen enough of my text now to be quite happily rid of me for a time!

To Blizzard, my gratitude strays from merely the profession to the personal for a moment; thank you for making a wonderful expansion. When someone works AND plays in the same world, it is very easy for something to grow stale over time. The Burning Crusade is quite the antithesis of that. The dungeons have been a joy to explore, defeat, and explain to others! /salute

PLAINSONG

Edwin Kern
<Dovrani> Kirin Tor

Writing Credits: Hellfire Ramparts, The Blood Furnace, The Slave Pens, The Underbog.

With a project as large as this one, it's hard to thank everyone involved quickly.

First, I'd like to thank all the folks at Blizzard for creating a game that I've been playing since release. I've played many characters across several servers and I'm still having a great time!

Second, this guide wouldn't look nearly as good as it does without the help from the other authors and the hard-working people at Brady Games. No one person can complete a project this massive. It takes a small army of authors, editors, designers, and guild-mates to make something like this possible at all…let alone making it this awesome.

Third, there are a lot of people across the nation and through World of Warcraft that have either helped me, grouped with me, or believed it me. I'd like to thank some of them here. Pamela "Mom" Mervis; Kathleen, Pam, Tonya, and Michelle at the Newport Safeway; Redxx who taught me how to be a hunter; Brent who helped show me how to be a tank; and David "Kernal" Kern. There are many others I've met through my travels on Azeroth and Outland. If you've grouped with Plainsong (Kirin Tor), Kanini (Elune), or Aldara (Undermine), thank you for making the game so enjoyable.

ISHILDA

Kathleen Pleet
<Dovrani> Kirin Tor

MOONCLOUD

Bret Preece
<Dovrani> Kirin Tor

CALAMITYJANE

Kurt Ricketts
<Dovrani> Kirin Tor

LOKNIK

<Buck-n-Uber> Dethroc

ADELHEID

Leigh Davis
Dethroc

RAGNROK

Drew K. Walker
<Twisted by Design>
Feathermoon

Writing Credits: Gruul's Lair

CYRDDIN

Jennifer Sims
<Buck-n-Uber> Dethroc

VANYA

Kenny Sims
<Buck-n-Uber> Dethroc

VOODSON

<Buck-n-Uber> Dethroc

<BUCK-N-UBER> DETHROC

DEATH&TAXES
ALLIANCE - KORGATH (PVP)

<DEATH & TAXES> KORGATH

BLOODSHOT

Andrei Ionescu
<Death & Taxes> Korgath

Writing Credits: Serpentshrine Cavern, the Eye, Battle of Mt. Hyjal, Black Temple

First and foremost I would like to thank the guild's past and present members who have made playing this great game into an extraordinary experience. To our raiding core, my gratitude, you have kept Death & Taxes at the forefront of the raid game for well over two years now. Without you, writing this would have been impossible.

To everyone who contributed to the guide, I am in your debt. Specifically, my thanks go out to Jalpesh "Luxx" Kachhadia for his help on every single aspect of my work and beyond, from strategies and screenshots to the management of the maniacal group of monkeys that is our raiding guild. To Xodexx and Ryuujin, thank you for your input on tanking issues, for healing advice the credits belong to Hagbard and Anujit. Finally, thanks to Wyndryder for his help with screenshots.

Many thanks to the fine people at BradyGames—particularly to Leigh Davis and Brian Shotton for their brave decision to entrust a newcomer with such a task—for their patience in putting up with me and for holding my hand when I needed it. I have been so impressed with your professionalism and hope I have the chance to work with you again in the future.

Finally, I would like to thank my amazing wife for her understanding when the game and the guide have kept me away from her. I love you so much. To me, you are perfect.

HOCKEN

Tyler Morgan
<Pacifist> Kel'Thuzad

Writing Credits: Naxxramas, Magtheridon's Lair, Kazzak, Doomwalker, Karazhan

I would like to thank everyone who has ever been a member of my guild: Pacifist. Playing the game for the content provided to us by Blizzard is one thing, but it's always been the great members of my guild and the players of Kel'Thuzad that have kept me playing these few years. I would also like to thank the editors and fellow writers at BradyGames for giving me the opportunity to do something I enjoy doing and making me proud of it. And another thank you to all of the players who have made level 1 characters on Kel'Thuzad, or posted on our guild forums, just to come say "hello" and "thanks." Its great knowing that the stuff we write is helping people enjoy and conquer the game. Finally, another big thanks to the folks who run WoWWiki, WoWHead, WoWGuru, and Allakhazam. The effort you put into creating and running your respective sites is greatly appreciated by everyone who uses them.

Come say hi on Kel'Thuzad or at our website: www.pacifistguild.org. I hope you enjoy the book! See you in Azeroth, Outlands, Northrend—where ever the game takes us!

PS: The secret numbers in the last Dungeon Companion spelled out: goons go home. The secret message for this book is: Jura va qbhog, gur orfg fgengrtl vf gb perngr n Uhagre gevnatyr.

<PACIFIST> KEL'THUZAD

HEWN

Brian Shotton
Friend of <Buck-n-Uber> Dethroc

Project Manager

Many moons have passed since we leapt from safety into the churning chaos of another Dungeon Companion. During the course of this book the World Dungeons and Raids have changed no less than three times. It is always chaos to chaos until suddenly apparently by accident order is achieved. I say apparently because I know how hard we have worked—Brent and I—to put the final product before you.

My partner on this quest, Brent Gann deserves all accolades for look, feel, and usefulness. He is a designer extraordinaire and an extremely hard worker. His eye for quality and his stubbornness to accept nothing less than what his vision demands proves his usefulness in every World of Warcraft project.

Areva Ragle has proved invaluable. Her ability to juggle many projects and still have ownership of the smallest task is truly a blessing. When I communicate something in "design barbaric" she understands and translates it onto the page. She is THE problem solver, a red flag waver, and a trusted co-worker. I would have no one else layout this book.

The authoring team was brilliant as usual. Michael Lummis, Ed Kern, and the rest of their team once again provided the majority of the content and were and always will be the backbone of every WoW project. However, two new players joined the team: Andrei Ionescu and Drew Walker. Both picked up the high end Raids and did outstanding jobs. Credit goes to them and their guilds—well done gents.

Once again Blizzard was wonderful to work with. The usual suspects, Brian Hsieh and Cory Jones, but a special thanks and congratulations go to Gina Williams on her first BradyGames title. You did a fine job on a book very thick with content. Also, though I never spoke with you or had any contact, the mysterious Arowe whose name appears on all my corrections, thanks.

My good friends Kenny Sims and Jennifer Sims, I have known you a long time. We have journeyed through Azeroth and Outland, slaying all manner of magical beasts. I look forward to our next adventure—I trust no one else with my online life.

My wife is so good. I have never met anyone so understanding of long hours, of late meetings, eleventh hour changes, and weekend work. I know she loves me, yet still feel undeserved. You make my job easier and my life truly wondrous. I love you.

DUNGEON COMPANION II

BRADYGAMES STAFF

Publisher
David Waybright

Editor-In-Chief
H. Leigh Davis

Creative Director
Robin Lasek

Licensing Manager
Mike Degler

CREDITS

Development Editor
Brian Shotton

Screenshot Editor
Michael Owen

Lead Designer
Brent Gann

Layout Designer
Areva

BRADYGAMES ACKNOWLEDGEMENTS

We would like to thank John Toebes and Christian Sumner for their efforts in retrieving alll the maps in this book; we hope you enjoy the art.

Lead Designer - Brent Gann

I would like to thank my wife Christine and daughter Gracen for all of their support and patience during this project. I love them very much.

BLIZZARD ACKNOWLEDGEMENTS

Creative Development Manager
Shawn Carnes

Director of Global Licensing and Business Development
Cory Hudson Jones

Producer
Gloria Soto

Licensing Manager
Gina Williams

Art Approvals
Joanna Cleland-Jolly

QA Approvals
Meghan Dawson, Drew Dobernecker, Joseph Magdalena, Andrew Rowe, Shawn Su, Rodney Tsing, Don Vu

Development Team Support
Luis Barriga, J. Allen Brack, Alexander Brazie, Tom Chilton, Jeff Kaplan, Jonathan LeCraft

Blizzard Special Thanks
Ben "But the minis…" Brode, Shane Cargilo, Tim Daniels, Mei Francis, Evelyn Fredericksen, Michael Gilmartin, Carlos Guerrero, John Hsieh, Chris Metzen, Justin Parker, Glenn Rane, Sean Wang